현직 교사 꼼샘이 알려주는

교원 임용 영어 수업실연

체크리스트
& 스크립트

발행일　초판 2025년 11월 15일
　　　　　개정판(1쇄) 2026년 1월 2일
발행인　조순자
편저자　고창훈
편집·표지디자인　서시영
발행처　인성재단(지식오름)

※ 낙장이나 파본은 교환해 드립니다.
※ 이 책의 무단 전제 또는 복제행위는 저작권법 제136조에 의거하여 처벌을 받게 됩니다.

정　가　38,000원　　　**ISBN**　979-11-7491-036-3

| 들어가며 |

합격선과 고작 0.33점밖에 차이가 나지 않은, 마치 벼랑 끝에 선 것과 같은 상황에서 스스로 가지고자 했던 마음가짐이 있습니다. '행운이 아님을 증명하자.'가 바로 그것이었죠.

합격이 간절했지만, 간절하기만 해서는 좋은 결과를 얻을 수가 없는 것이 시험이기 때문에, 불안할수록 차분해야만 했고 부정적인 생각이 들수록 긍정적인 부분을 찾아야만 했습니다.

'어떻게 해야 높은 점수를 받을 수 있을까?', '다른 사람들이 놓치고 있는 부분은 무엇일까?', '고득점 합격자들의 공통점은 무엇일까?' 정말 간절한 마음으로 수소문해 나가며 차곡차곡 만든 것이 지금부터 여러분께 보여드릴 이 책입니다.

이 책은 INPUT과 OUTPUT, 크게 두 부분으로 나뉘어 있습니다. INPUT에서는 수업 실연 고득점을 위한 71가지 체크리스트를 소개하고 하나씩 자세히 다룰 예정입니다. 곳곳에 예시 상황 T-talk를 추가하여 혹시나 영어에 자신이 없는 편이라도 쉽게 따라서 할 수 있도록 구성하였습니다. 이어서 OUTPUT에서는 수업 실연 예시 문항을 수록하였습니다. 기출 문제와 주제가 연계될 수 있도록 하였고, 다양한 문항 및 자료 요소를 두루 출제하여 실전적인 도움이 될 수 있도록 하였습니다. 이어서 예시 지도안과 스크립트, 실제 수업 실연 영상을 제공함으로써 가장 쉽고 직관적으로 T-talk를 연구하고 수업 실연에 대한 구체적인 그림이 머릿속에 그려질 수 있게끔 준비하였습니다.

그리고 이 책을 활용할 예비 교사 여러분이 모두 영어과인 만큼, 영어 심층 면접도 함께 준비할 수 있도록 '임용 심층 면접 다진고기'에 수록된 150여 개 답변에 대한 영어 번역도 함께 준비하였습니다. 너무 쉬운 표현이나 어휘보다는 면접에 맞는 중고급 수준으로 구성하여 매일 조금씩 나누어 공부하다 보면 면접에 최적화된 영어 구사 능력이 갖춰질 것으로 생각합니다.

'잘해야 한다.'라는 강박감이 얼마나 무섭고 고통스러운지 잘 알고 있습니다. 제가 겪었던 시행착오와 노하우를 바탕으로 여러분은 각자 마음의 짐을 약간은 덜어놓을 수 있었으면 좋겠습니다.

2022년, 첫 책이 출간되고 나서부터 정말 많은 관심과 사랑을 받았습니다. 모두 여러분 덕택입니다. 진심으로 감사합니다. 또한, 2차 시험 준비로 만나 지금까지 여전히 때로는 친구, 때로는 선배와 같은 인연을 이어나가고 있는 류진 선생님, 함께 교단에서 학생을 위해 힘쓰고 있는 이철 형님과 J에게 무한한 감사를 드립니다. 그리고 저의 교직 생활을 가까이서 함께 하며 다양한 영감을 불어넣어 주시는 선배, 후배, 동료 교사분들께도 감사의 말씀을 올립니다. 마지막으로 항상 든든한 모습으로 저를 응원하고 지켜주는 가족과 사랑하는 아내에게 헤아릴 수 없을 만큼 고마운 마음을 표합니다.

곰쌤 교실 : 공부법 이야기
고창훈

Special Thanks to

후배 수험생을 위하여 임용 2차 문항 복기에
참여해 주신 분들 모두에게
진심으로 감사의 마음을 전합니다.

김권택, 오종범, 박수민,
송현정, 최가람, 댕댕, 낌유

체스 합격자 한마디!

선배 합격자의 진심 어린 응원과 조언이 가득 담긴 메시지입니다!
공부하다가 지치거나 힘들 때, 방향이 잡히지 않을 때 한 번씩 읽어보세요.
우리 진짜 거의 다 왔습니다. 마지막 문턱입니다!
여러분도 합격자로서 당당히 메시지를 남길 수 있도록 조금만 더 힘을 내 봅시다!

2025년
전주(사립)합격자
(초수, 학교무경력)

안녕하세요! 저는 대학 졸업 후, 학교 경험 없이 자체 채용 사립학교에 최종 합격하게 되었습니다. 저는 총 네 곳의 학교에 응시했고, 서울 자사고 두 곳과 지방 자사고 두 곳에 응시했습니다. 당시에 무경력 초수는 절대 최종 합격까지 갈 수 없을 것이라는 얘기를 많이 들었기에, 이번에는 떨어지더라도 경험 삼아 응시해 보고자 하는 마음이 컸습니다. 저처럼 경험이 없는 초수분들도 꼭 최종합격 할 수 있다는 희망을 가지고 전형 치르시길 바라는 마음으로 합격 수기를 작성하게 되었습니다. 다만, 사립학교는 정말 학교 by 학교…. 준비하는 데에 학교 별 차이가 매우 크기 때문에 이 점을 참고해서 봐주시면 좋을 거 같습니다.

(1) 서류 : 자체채용 사립학교는 학교에서 따로 서류 양식을 제공합니다. 보통은 경력, 학교(초, 중, 고, 대), 학점과 기타 사항들을 이력서에 포함했던 거 같고 자기소개서 또한 학교마다 양식이 천차만별이었습니다. 자기소개서 작성은 항목별로 미리 칸을 나눠주는 학교도 있고, 아예 자유양식으로 쓰라는 학교도 있었습니다. 대부분 초수분들은 자소서에 담아낼 경험이 많지 않아 걱정이 많으실 텐데, 최대한 교사로서 자신의 강점이 무엇인지를 생각해 보시면 좋을 거 같습니다. 저는 뚜렷한 교직관, 전공과목 전문성(학과에서 공부한 것, 우수한 학점 등), 교수 경험(학원, 과외 경험) 등을 포함했고 최대한 명확하고 구체적으로 작성하려고 노력했습니다.

(2) 필기 : 자체 채용 사립 필기는 보통 임용고시(영교론, 영어학) 유형, 수능 유형, 기타 일반 영어형(특히 텝스 수준의 단어 문제 & 일영 독해유형), 논술형(교직 논술 및 영어 에세이 작성)이었습니다. 다만, 임고형 문제를 냈던 학교도 그닥 깊은 지식을 요구하지는 않았습니다. 영교론과 영어학 기본 지식을 묻는 유형이었고, 나머지는 대부분 지원자의 영어실력(특히 독해력)을 확인하기 위한 문제가 많았기 때문에, 자체 채용 사립을 준비하신다면 꼭 영어 실력을 키우기 위한 공부(ex. 수능 오답률 높은 문항 및 텝스, 토플 정도)를 하시는 게 좋을 거 같습니다.

(3) 실연 : 사립은 실연에 관해서도 너무나 정보가 없고 또 제각각이라 가장 어려운 거 같습니다. 저는 그래서 일단 뭐가 나올지 모르니 …. 교과서 지문/수능 지문/원서와 같이 다양한 지문으로 공립형/인강강사(강의식)형/한국어+영어 섞는 유형 등 그냥 나올 수 있는 모든 방법을 다 연습했습니다. 위탁 사립의 경우는 보통 교과서 지문을 주시는 경우가 많은 거 같은데, 자체 채용으로 시험 본 학교들은 수능 특강 영어 독해 연습 두 문제를 현장에서 풀고 독해 문제풀이식 수업 진행(어휘, 어법 꼭 포함할 것), 해외 원서 두 페이지 자유롭게 수업(모든 기자재 사용 가능), 공립형(자료와 디렉션 아주 세세하게 주어짐)으로 다양했습니다. 사실 모든 유형에 완벽하게 대비할 수 없으니, 어떤 지문이 주어지더라도 수업을 할 수 있는 틀을 만들어 두시는 게 가장 좋을 거 같습니다. 저는 도입(눈에 띄도록, 참신하게 주제로 유도함) → 어휘(멘티미터와 같은 에듀테크 활용) → 독해(전체 지문을 보고 마인드맵으로 흐름 파악 & 세부 내용 파악) → 확장 활동(세특 기재 가능한 참신한 활동)으로 설계했습니다. 실연을 설계하는 과정에서도 곰쌤 유튜브를 많이 참고했습니다. 지도안 작성을 요구하는 사립학교들이 많기 때문에, 지도안 작성 팁과 수업 실연 팁을 다룬 영상을 보며 초반에 수업 설계 연습할 때 많은 도움을 받았습니다. 또 사립은 영어/한국어 사용에 제한이 없는 경우가 많은데, 저는 영어로 진행했습니다. 제 강점은 영어 유창성이었기에 이걸 꼭 살리려고 했던 거 같아요. 다만, 한 학교에서는 "왜 문법을 영어로 설명 하셨냐?"라는 질문을 받기도 했습니다(최종 합격 했지만요). 정말 정답이 없는 부분이기 때문에 본인의 강점을 살려서 선택하시면 좋을 거 같습니다.

(4) 면접 : 무경력 초수가 가장 걱정하게 되는 부분인 거 같습니다. 또 사립 면접은 정말 학교마다 스타일이 많이 달라서, 대비하기도 어려운 거 같습니다. 그래서 일단, 사립학교 면접 기출(인터넷 카페와 유튜브 활용)을 모두 수집해서 약 150개 정도의 예상 질문을 모두 뽑았습니다. 하지만 문제를 뽑아도 학교 경험이 없다 보니 도대체 어떻게 답변해야 할지 모르겠는 경우가 많았습니다. 학교 현장에 관한 질문(문제 학생 지도, 교직 문화 등)은 현직 선생님들께서 알려주는 정보에 기반해서 구체적인 답변을 만들어내고자 노력했습니다. 저도 예상 질문에 답변을 작성하면서도 보통 너무 추상적이거나 이상적인 얘기만 하게 되는 경우가 많았어서, 곰쌤 유튜브 & 다진고기에 나오는 빈출 테마를 다룬 부분을 열심히 공부했던 거 같습니다. 저처럼 학교 경험이 없는 선생님들은 답변 작성하다가 막히는 부분을 다룬 챕터를 찾아가서 내용을 보충하시면서 답변을 구체화하시는 걸 추천해 드립니다.

마지막으로, 학교 경험이 없음에도 불구하고 곰쌤의 유튜브와 책을 통해 실제적이고 구체적인 정보를 많이 습득할 수 있었기 때문에, 실연과 면접에서 좋은 점수를 받을 수 있었던 거 같습니다. 특히 저처럼 초수로 사립학교(특히 자사고)를 준비하시는 선생님들은 준비에 많은 도움 얻으실 거라 확신합니다!

2025 부산(공립) 합격자 최O지 (7수, 1차 컷에서 뒤집기)

선생님들 안녕하세요 :) 2025학년도 중등 임용 평가원 지역 최종 합격자입니다. 저는 7수째에 합격한 꽤나 장수생입니다ㅎㅎ,, 장수가 되다 보니 올인은 생각하지 못하고 벌써 일 병행한 지도 4년 차 즈음 되어가는 중에 합격을 하게 되었습니다. 1차는 제가 합격 문을 닫고 들어가서 컷 점수였습니다,,, 게다가 업무에 이리저리 치여서 12월에는 2차 준비는커녕 사실 1차 합격에 대한 기대도 없이 열심히 일을 쳐내느라 바빴던 것 같아요. 1차 합격을 확인하자마자 가장 먼저 든 생각은 "큰일 났다" 였어요. 다른 분들보다 늦게 시작한 제게 잔뜩 밀려오는 불안감을 조금이나마 들어준 건 다진고기와 체스 책, 그리고 곰쌤 유튜브 영상들이었던 것 같아요. 밥 먹는 시간, 이동하는 시간, 공부에 지칠 때 끊임없이 답안을 만들어주신 영상, 실연 영상을 보고 들으려 노력했고 그러는 과정에서 곰쌤의 틀들이 자연스럽게 체득되었던 것 같아요. 그리고 연습문제들을 올려주시면 거기에 맞는 답안들도 생각해 보고 다른 선생님들의 아이디어들을 배우려고 코멘트 달아주신 것들을 열심히 살펴보고, 곰쌤이라면 어떻게 판서를 하실지, 수업을 어떻게 구성하실지 꼼꼼히 작성해 주신 지도안과 티처톡 내용을 꼼꼼히 살펴보고 시간 안에 디렉션을 모두 지키면서 학생들의 입장에서 이해하기 쉬운 수업을 구성하려 많이 고민해 봤던 것 같아요.

2차는 정답도 없고 시간은 짧다 보니 스스로에 대한 의심이 그 어느 때보다도 많이 들고 스트레스도 많이 받으실 것 같아요. 저도 2차를 다 보고 나오는 순간, 그리고 합격 결과를 확인하는 그 순간까지도 저의 부족함과 아쉬운 점에 대해서만 곱씹었어요. 저는 실연 과정에서 빠뜨린 디렉션도, 시간을 못 지킬 뻔해서 급하게 마무리한 디렉션도 있었습니다. 그럼에도 불구하고 제가 합격한 데에는 20분을 꽤 재미있게 하고 나왔다라고 느꼈던 부분이 면접관님들께 와닿지 않았을까 생각이 들더라고요. 그래서 2차는 "기세"라고 생각해 :) 간절히 준비하신 과정을 바탕으로 자신감 있게 즐기고 나오시면 면접관님들도 알아주실 거예요 ㅎㅎ

이 책을 보시는 모든 선생님 조금만 더 힘내시고 최종 합격하시길 진심으로 응원하겠습니다.

2025 서울(공립) 합격자 노진경 (초수, 수업실연만점)

곰쌤의 체스로 수업 실연을 준비하며.

초수로 바로 서울 임용시험에 도전하면서 많은 걱정이 있었습니다. 특히 서울은 2차 변별력이 높기로 유명해, 이렇게 경쟁이 치열한 지역에서 어떻게 단기간에 좋은 수업을 구성할 수 있을까 하는 고민이 컸습니다.

그러던 중 곰쌤의 체스를 접하게 되었고, 선생님께서 직접 제작하신 연습 문제를 풀어보며 스터디를 진행하고, 책에 QR코드로 제공되어있는 우수한 수업 영상을 연구하면서 좋은 수업이란 무엇인지 확실히 파악할 수 있었습니다. 덕분에 안정적인 점수로 합격할 수 있었습니다.

또한, 서울의 경우 지도안을 작성한 후 수업 실연을 해야 하기 때문에 지도안과 수업이 유기적으로 연결되는 것이 중요하다고 생각했습니다. 지도안 작성에 대한 부담이 컸지만, 곰쌤의 체계를 바탕으로 준비하면서 훨씬 수월하게 작성할 수 있었습니다. 특히 곰쌤의 활동 간 연계를 참고하여 수업 실연을 구성하니 더욱 높은 완성도를 갖출 수 있었고, 그 결과 좋은 성적을 거둘 수 있었습니다.

좋은 자료와 가이드를 제공해 주신 곰쌤께 진심으로 감사드립니다! 😄

2025
충북(공립) 합격자
오○은
(일병행3수,
최종컷 + 9.85)

　안녕하세요. 1차 시험 보느라 많이 힘들었을 텐데 잠시 충전의 시간을 갖고 2차 준비하시길 추천해요. 2차 준비를 시작하셨다면 1차 합격에 대한 걱정은 잠시 내려놓고 다진고기와 체스를 차분히 읽어보세요.

　2차 시험장 경험이 없는 수험생들이라면 2차 시험 유형, 주어지는 시간, 시험장 분위기, 답변 방법 등 내가 앞으로 준비해야 할 것들에 대한 아웃라인을 잡는 과정이 꼭 필요합니다. 전 다진고기와 체스를 읽으면서 틈틈이 곰쌤 유튜브를 시청했습니다. 곰쌤 유튜브를 시청하다 보면 자연스레 알고리즘이 2차 시험으로 이어지기 때문에 감을 잡을 수 있을 거예요.

　평가원 지역인지, 평가원이라면 비지도안인지 지도안인지 등을 살펴보며 각 지역에 맞게 면접과 수업 실연 준비를 해 나가시면 됩니다.

　저는 일병행중이라 스터디를 못 구했습니다. 곰쌤을 제 스터디원이라고 생각하고 제 답안과 곰쌤이 작성한 모범답안을 비교해 가며 저 만의 만점 답안을 만들어 보는 연습을 계속했습니다.

　[면접 연습 _ 다진고기]
　문제 구상(10분) - 답변 영상 촬영(10분) - 곰쌤 답안 확인 - 나만의 만점 답안 재작성 - 만점 답안 읽어보기 - 방금 읽어본 내용 보지 않고 다시 말하며 영상 촬영 순서로 매일 연습했습니다.

　[수업 실연 연습 _ 체스]
　수업 구상(20분) - 수업 실연 영상 촬영(20분) - 곰쌤 지도안으로 답변 확인 - 곰쌤 유튜브 영상 보며 내가 실연한 내용과 비교 - 수정할 부분 반영하여 수업 실연 영상 재촬영(20분) - 곰쌤 체크리스트 활용하여 재촬영 영상 최종 피드백 순서로 매일 연습했습니다.

　실전에서는 연습했던 실력이 발휘되지 않을 수 있습니다. 저는 면접 연습 때 1분 이내로 시간이 남았어요. 하지만 실제 시험장에서는 끝나고 타이머를 보니 4분이 넘게 남아 있었어요. 평소보다 말을 빠르게 했고, 구체화가 부족했던 거죠. 이후 다른 사람들의 복기를 찾아보니 한 문제는 방향성이 달라서 감점이 많이 될 것이라고 예상했어요. 결과적으로 면접은 2.62점 감점되었습니다.

　수업 실연도 늘 딱 맞춰서 끝났었는데 평가 날에는 끝나고 타이머를 보니 2분이 넘게 남아있었어요. Pair work를 Whole class로 진행했고, 학생들과의 상호작용 깊이가 연습 때보다 현저히 부족했습니다. 결과는 1.89점 감점이었습니다.

　생각보다 감점이 덜 된 이유는 자신감 때문이라고 생각합니다. 면접과 실연을 할 때 자신을 믿고 내가 옳다는 눈빛을 보여주세요. 시험장에서뿐만 아니라 2차를 준비하는 과정에서도 스스로에 대한 믿음이 가장 중요합니다. 합격을 확인하는 그 순간까지 화이팅입니다!

2025년 부산(공립) 합격자 김권택 (N수, 1차 +0.33에서 뒤집기)

다진고기와 체스로 뒤집기 성공, 기적은 있습니다!
임용 실연, 지도안, 면접은 정말 책에 쓰인 그대로 하셔야 합니다. 그냥 따라해서 동기화되어야 합니다! 그래야 성공합니다!

2025 부산(공립) 합격자 (N수, 지도안 소수점 감점)

N수생이자 최탈 3번의 경험을 갖고 있는 사람입니다. 선생님들, 하면 됩니다..!! 1년 올인하고 나머지 짧게는 6개월, 길게는 1년씩 거의 매년 일병행을 했습니다. 1차는 지식 싸움이지만, 2차는 경험 + 자신감 + 대담함 싸움 같습니다. 최탈하면 무너지는 자존감과 멘탈, 다신 일어나지 못할 것 같은 무기력함을 너무나도 잘 알고 있으므로 2차를 짜임새 있게 계획해서 준비하고, 최선을 다해 대비하고 싶었습니다. 이를 위해 곰쌤의 책과 유튜브를 적극 활용했습니다.

수업 실연에서 조별 활동에 ART 규칙을 활용했고, 이는 조별 활동에 너무나 적합했습니다. 인성 또한 가르치는 교사의 느낌이 전달돼서요! 그리고 기출 변형 중 19년도였던 거 같은데, change maker라는 단어가 저는 이번 수업 실연에서 사용하기 좋겠다고 생각해서 수업 연계를 그 표현으로 했고, 마지막 멘트를 Throughout today's class, you can make changes in our school by suggestion letter. You can make our school better! 이라고 하며 전체 수업을 아우르게끔 했습니다. 트렌드에 맞는 기출 변형 문제를 잘 만들어주신 덕분이라 생각합니다!

면접에서 생각을 잘 전달하기 위한 틀을 곰쌤 교실(유튜브 채널)에서 반복적으로 참고했고, 인풋 또한 조리 있게 말씀해 주셔서 이를 스터디에서 아이디어로 많이 활용했습니다. 특히, 이번 25년 면접에서 무기력한 아이를 위한 사제동행 프로그램과 마을 교육공동체에서 명언 및 사례 등을 활용했습니다. 감사합니다. 그리고 곰쌤 교실에서 알려주신 면접 틀을 제 어투로 바꿔 사용하니 조리 있게 말할 수 있었습니다. 덕분입니다! 감사합니다~

2차에서 가장 중요한 것은 누구 앞에서나 당당하게 수업하고, 자기 생각을 말할 수 있는 사람이란 것을 입증하는 것으로 생각하며 준비했습니다. 포인트는 당당하되, 거만하지 않게! 긴장하더라도, 할 말은 하고 주도적으로 면접장의 분위기를 이끌어가는 것! 이를 위해 당당한 말투와 알찬 아이디어, 귀에 쏙쏙 들어오는 면접 틀까지 도움 많이 받았습니다~ 초수이든, 저처럼 최탈의 고비를 겪으신 분들이든, 많은 분들이 곰쌤 교실 및 도서의 도움을 받아 합격하시길 바랍니다!

2025
서울(공립) 합격자
서○은
(초수합격)

먼저 1차 시험을 잘 헤쳐오신 선생님들 고생 많으셨습니다. 이제 조금만 더 힘내면 합격할 수 있습니다!

1차 시험이 끝나고 나면, 내가 써낸 답이 어떻게 채점될지 궁금하고 후회스러운 순간도 많이 떠오를 것입니다. 저 또한 일주일 내내 시험 생각이 머릿속에서 내내 떠나지 않았습니다. 하지만 2차 시험을 통과하기 위해 노력을 기울여 초수합격을 이룰 수 있었습니다.

실제로 저에게 도움이 되었던 2차 수업 실연 준비 팁 몇 가지를 소개하겠습니다.

1. 1차 복기를 하지 않는 것을 권장합니다. 복기를 하는 순간, 강사 카페, 임용생 커뮤니티를 찾아보게 되는데요. 보면서 내 답안의 부족한 점을 깨닫게 된다면, 12개월 동안 2차 준비에 집중이 안 됩니다.

2. 12월부터 수업 실연과 면접에 최선을 다하세요. 앞서 말씀드렸듯 12월은 사실 1차 시험 생각에 집중이 안 되는 달입니다. 하지만 1월 딱 한 달 준비한 사람과 12월까지 두 달간 준비한 사람의 실연 및 면접의 퀄리티는 분명히 다릅니다. 2차는 1차와 달리 준비 기간이 매우 짧기 때문에, 나의 태도, 수업 중의 습관 등은 실연과 면접에 그대로 드러나게 됩니다. 나쁜 자세나 습관을 1달 안에 알아채고 고치기 쉽지 않기 때문에, 조금이라도 연습 기간을 확보하는 것이 좋습니다.

3. 아웃풋을 연습할 때, 체스 교재의 다양한 팁을 바꾸어가며 연습해 보세요. 시험이 다가올수록 익숙해진 멘트만 하게 되고 실제 시험 당일에도 자신이 가장 많이 해봤던 멘트만 앵무새처럼 반복하게 됩니다. 그런데 수업 실연에서 새로운 패턴으로 수업할 것을 요구하면 굉장히 곤란해집니다. 따라서 연습 기간에 하나의 패턴만 연습할 것이 아니라, 체스 교재에 있는 여러 수업 방법을 계속해서 응용해 보세요. 예를 들어 단어 지도를 예문을 교사가 제공하는 경우, 지문 속 맥락에서 제공하는 경우, 학생들과 온라인 사전으로 예문을 찾는 경우, realia, picture 등등 다양한 경우를 나누어서 해보는 것입니다.

4. 연습 영상을 촬영하고 반드시 돌려보세요. 스터디 피드백이 반복될수록, 스터디원들은 제 수업에 익숙해져 잘 안 고쳐지는 비슷한 부분을 짚어주시는 경향이 있습니다. 또한 다들 영어 전공자라서 어른 수준의 문장을 구사하더라도 모두 이해하고 넘기는 경향이 있습니다. 그러나 수업의 주제를 끌어가는 것이나, 문장의 간결성, 인사할 때 꾸벅 먼저하고 관리 번호 말하는 습관 등등 남이 잘 알아채지 못하는 나의 습관이 분명히 있습니다. 연습 영상을 촬영하고 부끄럽더라도 반드시 영상을 돌려보면서 개선할 습관을 찾아보시길 바랍니다.

팁 전달을 마무리하며, 곰쌤께도 감사의 인사를 전하고 싶습니다. 체스 교재를 읽으며 물론 이것이 수업 실연 점수를 잘 받을 수 있도록 도와주는 교재이기도 하지만, 실제 수업을 성찰하는 데도 도움이 많이 된다고 생각합니다. 내 수업이 모든 학생을 다 고려하고 있는지 다시 한번 생각하게 하는 내용이었습니다. 감사합니다.

선생님들 동료 교사로 만나 뵙기를 기다리고 있겠습니다!

2025
서울(공립) 합격자
(N수 일병행, 컷
+0.33에서 뒤집기,
2차 초고득점)

곰쌤만 믿고 도전했습니다! (사립에서 공립 재임용)

학교에 근무하면서 공부할 시간이 거의 없었기에 1차 시험은 기대 없이 응시했습니다. 그런데 예상치 못하게 컷라인보다 0.33점 높은 점수로 합격했고, 순간 너무 행복했습니다. 하지만 기쁨도 잠시, 2차 시험을 준비해야 한다는 압박과 불안이 밀려왔습니다. 그래도 후회 없이 최선을 다해보자는 마음으로 곰쌤의 다진고기와 체스를 구매했습니다.

책을 읽으며 곰쌤도 저와 같은 상황을 겪었다는 걸 알게 되었고, 덕분에 마음을 다잡을 수 있었습니다. 그리고 열심히 노력한 결과, 2차에서 무려 96.53점이라는 높은 점수를 받을 수 있었습니다. 지금부터 제가 어떻게 공부했는지 공유해 보겠습니다.

1. 수업 시연

1월 2일부터 스터디를 구성해 체스 연습문제를 활용하며 서로의 수업 시연을 보고 피드백을 주고받았습니다. 저는 스터디원의 피드백뿐만 아니라, 합격한 친구들에게도 추가 피드백을 받았고, 특히 곰쌤이 유튜브에 올려주신 영상을 보며 부족한 점을 보완하려고 노력했습니다.

저는 곰쌤의 수업 흐름과 발상이 체계적이고 창의적이라고 생각하기 때문에 수험생 분들은 영상을 반복해서 보길 추천합니다. 수업 시연에서는 영어 실력도 중요하지만 교사가 자신감 있게 수업을 이끌어가는 모습이 더 중요하다고 생각합니다. 따라서 에너제틱한 수업을 연습하는 것이 좋습니다.

+ 지도안을 절대 간과하지 마세요! 1~2점 차이가 합격을 좌우할 수 있으므로, 스터디원들과 공유하며 비교 및 개선하는 것이 큰 도움이 됩니다.

2. 면접

2차 준비에서 가장 어려웠던 부분은 면접이었습니다. 면접에서는 단순한 영어 실력보다 면접용 틀과 적절한 표현을 활용하는 능력이 중요합니다. 즉, 영어 스피킹을 잘한다고 해서 면접을 잘 볼 수 있는 것은 아닙니다.

처음에는 답변 아이디어가 떠오르지 않고, 적절한 단어를 찾느라 머릿속이 하얘져 제대로 말하지 못했습니다. 그래서 3일 동안 체스에 나온 영어 예시 답변을 암기하고 복습했습니다. 이후에는 다진고기로 넘어가 곰쌤의 예시 답변도 같은 방식으로 익혔습니다. 처음엔 무모하고 시간이 오래 걸릴 것 같았지만, 일주일 정도 지나자 '구상의 차원' 단계까지 활용할 수 있게 되었고, 어떤 문제를 만나도 답변할 수 있는 수준이 되었습니다.

면접은 투자한 시간만큼 결과가 나오는 영역입니다. 또한, 정해진 답이 없기 때문에 다양한 시각에서 접근하면 공부한 아이디어를 활용해 충분히 답변할 수 있습니다. 결국, 면접에서는 내가 가진 아이디어를 얼마나 논리적으로 풀어내느냐가 핵심이며, 그런 점에서 곰쌤의 답변 틀은 최적의 방법이라고 생각합니다.

구상형 문제를 풀 때는 처음에는 긴 문장을 작성했지만, 이후에는 키워드만 적고 머릿속으로 답변의 흐름을 정리하는 연습을 했습니다. 덕분에 실전에서도 긴장했지만 끝까지 답변을 이어나갈 수 있었습니다.

충분한 암기와 연습이 있다면 누구나 해낼 수 있습니다!

3. 합격 후 느낀 점

사립 정교사로 일하고 있었지만, 1차를 합격한 후 공립에 꼭 가고 싶다는 마음이 간절해졌습니다. 불안한 마음에 남들과 비교하기도 하고, 시중에 나온 2차 관련 책을 모두 사야 하나 고민도 많았습니다.

하지만 지금 돌이켜보면 곰쌤 책만으로도 충분했습니다. 이 책들을 메인으로 공부하면서, 최근 이슈나 트렌드를 간략하게 정리하면 문제없습니다.

곰쌤 덕분에 정말 큰 도움을 받았고, 진심으로 감사드립니다. 앞으로도 곰쌤이 더 잘되시길 바랍니다. 선한 영향력, 정말 감사합니다! 😊

contents:

1장 INPUT : 체크리스트

1. CLASSROOM MANAGEMENT

가. L-centered Facilitation

1) Scaffolding — 26
2) T's Space — 28
3) Comprehension Check Questions — 30
4) Motivation — 33
5) Interaction — 35
6) Teacher Talk — 37
7) Grouping — 40
8) Circulation during Activities — 44
9) Mixed-level Treatment — 46

나. Presentation

1) Board — 49
2) Digital Devices — 51

다. Attitude

1) Verbal — 54
2) Nonverbal — 55

2. TEACHING ENGLISH

가. Receptive Skills

1) Vocabulary — 60
2) Reading — 68
3) Listening — 75

나. Productive Skills

1) Grammar — 80
2) Speaking — 85
3) Writing — 88

다. Evaluation

1) Design — 98
2) Giving Feedback — 101

라. Logical Development

1) Transition — 107
2) Balance — 111
3) Expansion — 113

3. 수업 실연 체크리스트

Check lists 1~71 — 120

contents:

2장 OUTPUT : 기출문제

1. 수업 실연 기출 문제
    가. 2025 기출문제   127
    나. 2024 기출문제   134
    다. 2023 기출문제   140
    라. 2022 기출문제   146
    마. 2021 기출문제   153
    바. 2020 기출문제   160
    사. 2019 기출문제   167
    아. 2018 기출문제   174
    자. 2017 기출문제   183

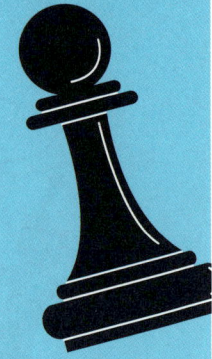

2. 예시답안 & 스크립트

　가. 2025 기출문제　　　　　　　　　　189
　나. 2024 기출문제　　　　　　　　　　204
　다. 2023 기출문제　　　　　　　　　　216
　라. 2022 기출문제　　　　　　　　　　230
　마. 2021 기출문제　　　　　　　　　　245
　바. 2020 기출문제　　　　　　　　　　260
　사. 2019 기출문제　　　　　　　　　　278
　아. 2018 기출문제　　　　　　　　　　292
　자. 2017 기출문제　　　　　　　　　　307

contents:

3장 OUTPUT : 실전연습

1. 수업 실연 연습 문제

가. 연습문제 1회 : 2024 기출 변형	322
나. 연습문제 2회 : 2023 기출 변형	328
다. 연습문제 3회 : 2022 기출 변형	335
라. 연습문제 4회 : 2021 기출 변형	341
마. 연습문제 5회 : 2020 기출 변형	347
바. 연습문제 6회 : 2019 기출 변형	354
사. 연습문제 7회 : 2018 기출 변형	360
아. 연습문제 8회 : 2017 기출 변형	366

2. 예시답안 & 스크립트

가. 연습문제 1회 : 2024 기출 변형	372
나. 연습문제 2회 : 2023 기출 변형	384
다. 연습문제 3회 : 2022 기출 변형	398
라. 연습문제 4회 : 2021 기출 변형	412
마. 연습문제 5회 : 2020 기출 변형	426
바. 연습문제 6회 : 2019 기출 변형	439
사. 연습문제 7회 : 2018 기출 변형	452
아. 연습문제 8회 : 2017 기출 변형	463

3. 수업 실연 Q&A

Q&A 1~10	474

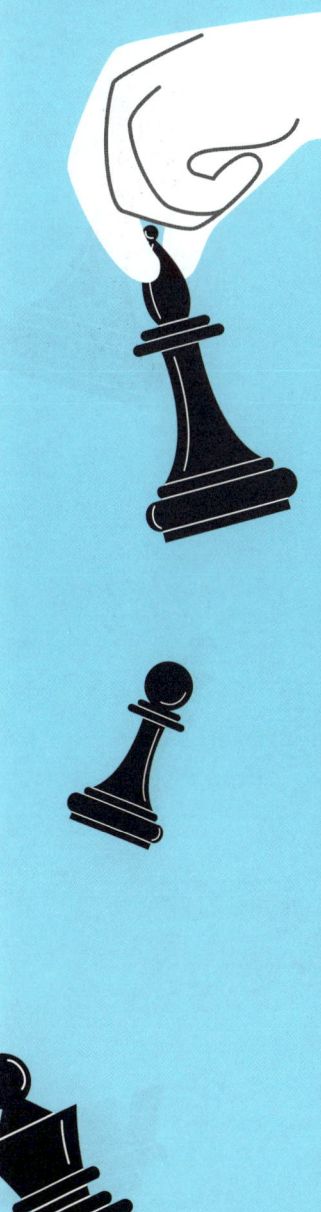

4장 영어과 심층면접 부록

1. 구상형 1번 번역 문항

    가. 기출 문제 번역 문항   488
    나. 실전 연습 문제 번역 문항   491

2. 번역 문항 예시 답변

    가. 기출 문제 번역 문항 예시 답변   496
    나. 실전 연습 문제 번역 문항 예시 답변   511

3. 주제별 아이디어 및 예시 답변

TOPIC 1	Preventing School Violence	524
TOPIC 2	Addressing School Violence	527
TOPIC 3	At-Risk Students	530
TOPIC 4	Teaching Morality	533
TOPIC 5	Self-management Competencies	536
TOPIC 6	Knowledge Information Processing Competencies	539
TOPIC 7	Creative Thinking Competencies	541
TOPIC 8	Aesthetic Sensitivity Competencies	544
TOPIC 9	Cooperative Communicative Competencies	546
TOPIC 10	Community Competencies	548
TOPIC 11	Providing Career Guidance	551
TOPIC 12	Basic Academic Skills Improvement	553
TOPIC 13	Health & Ecological Transformation Education	556
TOPIC 14	Multicultural Students	559
TOPIC 15	Motivating Students	561
TOPIC 16	Inclusive Classroom	566
TOPIC 17	Students in Need	568
TOPIC 18	Relationship with Parents	570
TOPIC 19	Relationship with other Teachers	573
TOPIC 20	Relationship with Students	577
TOPIC 21	Homeroom Management	582
TOPIC 22	Expertise on Teaching	586
TOPIC 23	Expertise on Assessment	591
TOPIC 24	Educational Perspective	596

곰쌤 영어과 수업 실연 체크리스트

1. CLASSROOM MANAGEMENT
    가. L-centered Facilitation
    나. Presentation
    다. Attitude

2. TEACHING ENGLISH
    가. Receptive Skills
    나. Productive Skills
    다. Evaluation
    라. Logical Development

3. 수업 실연 체크리스트
    Check list 1~71

1 INPUT : 체크리스트

CLASSROOM MANAGEMENT

수업 실연 체크리스트는 'CLASSROOM MANAGEMENT'와 'TEACHING ENGLISH' 두 파트로 나뉩니다. 이 중 이번 파트는 'CLASSROOM MANAGEMENT', 즉 교실 관리 부분으로, 수업 실연을 할 때 교사의 전체적인 교실 장악력을 의미합니다. 여기서 '교실 장악력'이란, 단순히 교사가 주는 인상을 이야기하는 것이 아니라 학생 중심 수업을 실현하기 위한 다양한 수업 기술 및 전략이 포함됩니다.

가 L-centered Facilitation

교사의 교실 관리 부분에서 가장 중요한 것은 바로 학생 중심 수업을 실현하는 것입니다. 학생 중심 수업이란, 교사 중심 수업과 대비하여 학생이 주도하는 교실 환경을 의미합니다. 교사의 가르침이 중심이 아니라 학생의 배움이 중심이 되는 것이죠. 이러한 교실 환경을 실현하기 위해서는 교사는 단순한 지식 전달자의 역할이 아니라, 촉진자 역할을 수행해야 합니다. 여기서 '촉진'이라는 단어는 '주입'과 반대되는 뜻으로, 교사가 일방적으로 지식을 알려주는 것이 아니라 학생의 배움이 활발히 일어날 수 있도록 도움을 주는 것이죠. 이렇게 교사로서 촉진자 역할을 수행하면서 학습자 중심 수업을 수업 실연에 보여주기 위해서는 다음과 같은 요소별 체크리스트를 고려해야 합니다.

(1) Scaffolding

학생 중심 수업을 보여주기 위해서는 학생의 잠재적 발달 영역을 고려한 수업이 설계되어야 합니다. 이를 가장 잘 나타낼 수 있는 부분이 바로 Scaffolding이죠. 이와 관련한 두 가지 체크리스트 살펴보도록 하겠습니다.

Check point #1.
♟ 교사가 적절한 Scaffolding을 제공하였는가?

첫 번째 체크리스트는 교사의 Scaffolding 제공 여부입니다. 여기에서는 두 가지 부분을 핵심적으로 고려해야 합니다.

1. 학생이 도움이 필요할 때 교사가 적극적으로 개입하였는가?
2. 그 학생이 도움을 받고 스스로 문제를 해결할 수 있는가?

수업 실연에서 이와 같은 상황을 가장 잘 가정할 수 있는 파트는 Reading입니다. 교사가 Reading Text에 등장하는 단어에 대한 Word list를 미리 준비해놓고 도움이 필요한 학생에게 다가가 제공한다는 상황 설정이 적합하죠.

<예시 상황 T-talk>
T : ① (Scaffolding-in) Oh, Dongwoo! Do you need any help? I see. The reading text is too difficult.

⇩

② (Scaffolding) Ok then, look at this. What do you see? Yes, this is the word list!

⇩

③ (Scaffolding-out) With this word list, can you do this by yourself? Great!

위와 같이 Scaffolding-in - Scaffoldng - Scaffolding-out 3단계로 교사와 학생의 상호작용을 가정하면 완벽한 Scaffolding 제공이 됩니다. 1단계 Scaffolding-in에서는 도움이 필요한지, 어떤 것이 어려운지 파악합니다. 그리고 2단계에서 학생에게 맞는 Scaffolding을 제공합니다. 마지막으로 3단계에서는 학생에게 이 Scaffolding으로 혼자 진행할 수 있는지 물어보고 교사의 개입을 마무리합니다.

Check point #2.
♟ Peer scaffolding이 일어났는가?

Scaffolding은 교사뿐만 아니라 교실 내에서 친구 사이에서도 일어날 수 있습니다. 이와 같은 Peer scaffolding을 수업 실연 상황에서 보여주면 다음과 같은 두 가지 효과를 의도할 수 있습니다.

1. **학습자 중심 수업 강화** : 학생들이 서로서로 알려주고 배우는 모습을 통해서 학습자 배움 중심환경을 교사가 운영하고 있다는 인상을 줄 수 있습니다.

2. **High Level 학습자에 대한 추가 과제 부여** : 학습자마다 활동 완료 속도가 다르므로 수준이 높은 학습자는 과제를 빨리 끝낼 수밖에 없습니다. (실제 교실에서도 이러한 상황이 항상 발생합니다) 이러할 경우, 'Student teacher'와 같은 역할을 부여하여 Peer scaffolding이 일어나는 상황을 교사가 자신의 수업에서 설계하여, 적극적으로 유도할 수 있습니다.

> <예시 상황 T-talk>
> T : Oh, Sumin! Have you already finished this activity? ⋯ Then, why don't you help your partner Minsu. Minsu just said he needed a help. Is it okay? ⋯ That would be so great. Like this, friends can be a better teacher!

위와 같이 활동을 빨리 끝낸 Sumin에게 자신의 짝꿍 Minsu를 도와주라는 상황을 가정함으로써 Peer scaffolding이 수업에서 일어나고 있음을 보여줄 수 있습니다. 그리고 마지막 'Friends can be a better teacher!'이라는 멘트로 Peer scaffolding을 확실히 보여주었죠.

> **Tip**
> 짝꿍은 이렇게 이름을 반대로 부르면 고민할 필요가 없어 편합니다. Sumin-Minsu 이렇게요.:)

(2) T's Space

교사가 교실 공간을 어떻게 활용하는가, 교사의 동선은 어떠한지에 대한 부분입니다.

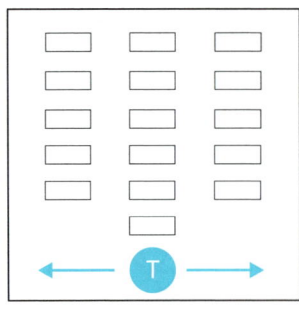
Teacher-centered

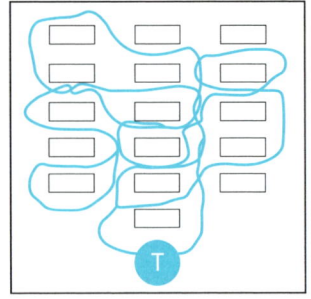
Learner-centered

위 그림을 보면 한 번에 이해할 수 있을 겁니다. 왼쪽의 교사 중심 수업에서 교사의 위치는 칠판 앞에만 한정된 것을 볼 수 있습니다. 그러나 오른쪽의 학생 중심 수업에서는 교사의 위치가

정해져 있지 않고 교실 전체를 돌아다니며 학생과 훨씬 가까이 위치한 것을 확인할 수 있죠. 이처럼, 학생 중심 수업이 진행된다는 것을 수업 실연에 보여주기 위해서는 여러분의 동선도 칠판 앞에서 있어서는 안 됩니다. 교실 전체를 무대로 활용할 줄 알아야 하죠!

Check point #3.
교사의 교실 사용 범위가 넓은가?

만약 여러분이 위의 왼쪽 그림과 같이 교탁 뒤에만 위치한다면 전체 교실의 10%밖에 활용하지 못하고 있는 겁니다. Group 활동뿐만 아니라 개별활동 지도를 할 시에도 최대한 넓은 공간을 활용하도록 합시다!

> **Tip**
> 채점관의 관점에서 교사가 칠판과 교탁 사이에서만 위치하는 것보다는 교실 전체를 활용할 줄 아는 수업 실연을 보았을 때 훨씬 더 자신감이 있어 보이고 능숙해 보입니다.

Check point #4.
교사의 위치가 학생과 가까운가?

제4의 벽이라고 들어보셨나요?

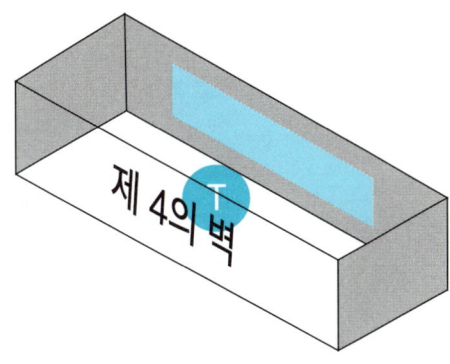

제4의 벽은 본래 연극 용어로, 무대 위와 관객석을 구분하는 경계를 일컫는 말입니다. 교실 환경도 마찬가지죠. 칠판 앞이 무대라면, 학생과 교사 사이에는 제4의 벽이 존재합니다. 우리는

이 벽을 무너뜨리고 나와야 합니다.

실제로 연극에서도 '제4의 벽이 무너졌다'라는 표현이 있습니다. 무대 위의 배우가 관객과 대화를 시도하고 상호 작용하는 모습을 의미하는 것입니다. 수업에서도 정확히 똑같은 모습이 일어나야 합니다. 교사로서 제4의 벽을 무너뜨리고 학생에게 다가가야 하는 것이죠.

제4의 벽이 지켜지는 순간 학생은 교사의 수업(연극)을 바라보는 관객이 될 뿐입니다. 그러나 교사가 제4의 벽을 허물면 그 순간 학생은 수업(연극) 자체의 일부가 되어 비로소 주도권을 가지게 되고 학생 중심 수업을 실현할 수 있습니다.

위 사진은 실제 제 교실의 책상 배치입니다. 이렇게 아예 책상 배치를 바꾸어서 제4의 벽이 존재하지 않도록 했죠. 이렇게 하면 모든 학생이 앞에서 두 번째 줄에 앉게 되는 효과가 있어 상호작용 효과를 극대화할 수 있었습니다.

> **Tip**
>
> 수업 실연에서 학생에게 Screen을 보라고 할 때 학생과 마주 본 상태에서 'Look at this screen.'이라고 지시하는 것이 아니라, 학생에게 다가가 학생 옆에서 'Look at the screen!'이라고 하며 제스쳐를 취해주는 것도 좋습니다. 교사가 제4의 벽을 허물고 학생의 자리에 가서 함께 스크린을 보는 것이죠! 별것 아닌 것 같아도 인상이 굉장히 다르게 느껴집니다.

(3) Comprehension Check Questions

학생들의 이해를 점검하는 것은 학습자 중심 수업에서 가장 중요한 부분입니다. 배움의 주체는 바로 학생이기 때문이죠. 그러니 교사로서 학생의 이해 수준이 현재 어느 정도 되는지 지속적으로 파악하고 이에 대한 이해를 바탕으로 다음 활동을 진행하여야 합니다. 여기서 가장 많이 실수하는 부분이 있습니다. 바로 수업의 템포가 학생에게 맞춰지지 않는다는 것입니다. '이거 했으니까 이제 이거 할 차례야'가 아니라 '이거 이해됐지? 그러면 이거 할 준비가 됐니? OK! 우리 이

거 해보자!'가 되어야 합니다. 체크리스트를 통해서 자세히 알아보도록 합시다!

Check point #5.
간단하고 명확한 CCQ가 제공되었는가?

교사의 CCQ는 최대한 쉽고 명확해야 합니다. 학생이 들었을 때 무엇을 물어보는지 단번에 대답할 수 있는 정도의 수준이 좋습니다. 지나치게 추상적인 질문보다는 Detail information을 물어보는 짧은 퀴즈 형식을 이용하는 것이 가장 확실합니다.

> <예시 상황 T-talk>
> T1 : Do you understand this reading text? (X)
> T2 : In this reading text, what are they celebrating? Yes Jongmin! They are celebrating Christmas! (O)
> T3 : What kind of future jobs did you see in this text? Thank you, Minjong! There were Drone pilot and Weather controller! (O)

위 예시 상황에서 T1의 CCQ는 질문 내용이 명확하지 않습니다. '이해'라는 개념 자체가 학생에게는 잘 와닿지 않기 때문이죠. 이해 확인 질문의 목적은 말 그대로 학생의 이해를 확인하기 위해서 하는 것입니다. 그런데 학생에게 직접 '이해했니?'라고 물어보는 것은 지나치게 일차원적인 이해 확인 질문일뿐더러 실제 교실 상황에서도 이러한 질문으로는 학생의 이해 정도를 파악하는 것은 불가능합니다. (학생들이 그냥 무의식적으로 '네~'하고 반응하거든요) 따라서, 질문을 T2와 T3의 발언과 같이 매우 구체적으로 해주는 것이 중요합니다! (TIP. 여기서 학생 이름까지 불러주면 활발한 상호작용이 일어나고 있다는 인상까지 줄 수 있습니다) 이처럼 교사의 질문이 구체적일수록 학생의 답변은 간결해질 수 있으며 CCQ는 이렇게 구체적인 질문과 간결한 답변으로 이루어져야 합니다.

Check point #6.
이해확인 작업이 주기적으로 일어나는가?

이러한 CCQ는 일회성이 아니라 수업 중 수시로 주기적으로 일어나야 합니다. 교사가 수업을 진행할 때 학생의 이해 정도를 파악하지 않으면 순식간에 교사 주도 수업의 인상이 남게 됩니다. 따라서 수업 실연을 연습할 때 CCQ를 습관화하는 것이 중요합니다. 이렇게 CCQ를 습관화하기 위해서는 다음과 같은 3가지를 기억하는 것이 좋습니다.

1. 교사의 활동 Direction 다음에는 반드시 CCQ!

> <예시 상황 T-talk>
> T : We are going to read this text and find the main idea. Dongwoo, What are we going to do?

위와 같이 Main Activity에 대한 설명 직후에는 반드시 CCQ를 진행하여 학생의 이해도를 점검하는 것이 필요합니다. 이는 수업 실연뿐만 아니라 실제 교실 환경에서도 반드시 이루어져야 하는 작업이기도 합니다. 왜냐하면 학생 중 활동 내용을 잘 숙지하지 못한 채로 참여하는 수가 은근히 많기 때문입니다. (그러면 그 학생은 교사가 의도한 활동을 제대로 수행하지 못하겠죠?!)

2. 학생의 발표(답변) 다음에도 CCQ!

> <예시 상황 T-talk>
> T : (Heewon 발표 후) Did you hear what Heewon just said? That's right, Wonhee! She said (Heewon 발표 내용).

위와 같이 학생의 발표 직후에는 그냥 넘어가는 것보다는 CCQ를 통한 상호작용을 보여주는 것이 좋은 방법입니다. 이렇게 하면 학생의 발표를 모두가 경청하고 있다는 교실 분위기를 연출할 수 있고 교사 역시도 친구가 발표할 때 경청하는 태도의 중요성을 인지하고 있다는 인상을 보여줄 수 있습니다.

3. 무의미한 Filler보다는 CCQ!

> <예시 상황 T-talk>
> T1 : Uhm... Okay... You know... So, we've just finished this reading text. (X)
> T2 : Alright, Jihwan! We've just finished WHAT? Yes! The reading text! (O)

T1과 같이 다음 T-talk을 고민할 때 무의미한 Filler를 사용하는 것보다 T2처럼 CCQ를 활용하면 영어 사용이 더 안정적이고 능숙해 보일 뿐만 아니라 학생과의 상호작용이 일어나고 있다는 것까지 보여줄 수 있습니다!

> **Tip**
>
> 혹시.... '복명복창'이라는 단어를 아시나요...? 상급자가 내린 명령을 하급자가 되풀이하는 군대 용어입니다. 예를 들면, 상급자가 '좌향좌'라고 하면 하급자가 '좌향좌'라고 되풀이하며 명령을 수행하는 것이죠. 이렇게 하면 상급자는 명령이 잘 전달되었다는 확인을 받을 수가 있고, 하급자는 상급자의 명령을 미처 듣지 못하였을 때 동료 하급자의 복명복창을 통해서 명령을 다시 되새길 수 있습니다.
>
> 교실 환경도 마찬가지입니다. 군대와 같은 수직적인 분위기는 아니지만 CCQ는 복명복창과 방식과 원리, 목적이 유사합니다. 교사가 학생에게 제시한 활동 내용 및 안내가 정확하게 전달되었는지 확인하는 과정이 필수적이고, 이러한 과정을 통해서 미처 집중하지 못했던 다른 학생들까지 주의 집중하게 하는 효과가 있죠.

(4) Motivation

학습자 중심 수업의 핵심은 학습자가 스스로 배움 활동을 주도해 나가는 것입니다. 그러므로 교사는 학습자가 스스로 내적 동기 부여를 느낄 수 있도록 적절하게 수업을 설계하고 진행할 수 있어야 합니다. 현실적으로는 '흥미/재미 요소'에 의존하여 학생의 동기를 자극하는 것이 대부분이지만 수업 실연 상황에서는 '재미있는 교사'보다는 '교육학적 지식이 풍부한 교사'라는 인상을 남기는 것이 유리하기 때문에 단순히 '재미'보다는 '해당 활동의 필요성과 효과'에 대해서 주기적으로 언급하며 학생의 학습 동기를 자극하는 모습을 보여주는 것이 좋습니다.

Check point #7.
♟ 해당 활동 전 필요성에 대하여 언급하였는가?

항상 새로운 활동을 시작하기 전에 해당 활동의 필요성에 대하여 언급할 필요가 있습니다. 그냥 활동을 소개하는 것 보다 '이 활동은 이래서 필요해'라고 이야기하는 것이 학생에게 더 동기 부여가 되겠죠!

> <예시 상황 T-talk>
>
> T1 : Before we read, what should we do? Yes Hyunjung, we should check vocabularies! Why? Yes! To understand better!
>
> T2 : We've just finished making posters. Don't you want to see your friend's poster? If so, why don't we have 'Presentation time'?

위와 같이 단순히 '단어 배우자', '발표하자'하는 것 보다 단어를 배우는 것에 관한 필요성과 발표 시간을 갖는 이유에 대해서 언급하면 훨씬 더 학생의 동기를 부여하는 수업 설계가 이루어졌다고 할 수 있습니다.

Check point #8.
해당 활동 후 효과에 대하여 언급하였는가?

활동이 끝나고 나서도 그 효과에 대해서 언급하면 학생의 동기가 부여됩니다.

<예시 상황 T-talk>
T1 : We've just finished WHAT? Yes Dawon, vocabularies! So, are you ready to read the text?
T2 : Okay, our presentation time has been over! So, were you able to see different ideas from your friends?

이렇게 단어 활동이 끝난 후, '읽기 활동에 대한 준비가 됐니?'라고 물어볼 수 있습니다. 마찬가지로 발표 활동이 끝난 후 '발표를 통해 다른 친구들의 생각을 들어볼 수 있었니?'라고 물어볼 수 있죠. 이처럼 각 활동이 끝나고 난 후 직전 활동의 효과에 대해 언급한다면 학생의 학습 동기가 강화됩니다.

> **Tip**
> 종종 'I think we are ready to ~'라는 표현을 사용하며 이전 활동과 다음 활동을 연결하는 경우가 많습니다. 그러나 이러한 표현은 교사가 임의로 학생의 준비도를 파악하는 뉘앙스의 표현이므로 삼가는 게 좋습니다. 학생 중심 수업에서는 학생이 스스로 자신이 준비되었는지를 판단해야 하므로 'Are you ready to ~?'라고 직접 물어보는 것이 좋습니다!

Check point #9.
활동마다 학생의 동기가 반복해서 부여되는가?

위와 같은 동기 부여가 활동마다 반복해서 이루어져야 합니다. 영어 수업 실연의 큰 틀은 'Schema activation → Receptive Skills → Productive Skills → Evaluation'으로 이루어집니다. 그리고 단계마다 활동이 있죠. 이 활동 간 연계를 보여줄 수 있는 것이 바로 '활동 전 필요성'과 '활동 후 효과'입니다. 이 두 가지 동기 부여 전략을 반복적으로 활용하는 것이 핵심입니다.

(5) Interaction

Interaction은 학생과의 상호작용을 의미합니다. 학생 중심 수업에서는 당연하게도 학생과의 끊임없는 상호작용이 중요한데, 혼자 1인 연극을 펼쳐야 하는 수업 실연 상황에서는 참 난감하기 그지없습니다. 학생이 없는 상황에서 학생과 상호작용이 활발히 일어나는 교실 환경을 어떻게 보여줄 수 있을까요? 체크리스트를 하나씩 살펴보도록 합시다.

Check point #10.
학생의 이름이 자주 불리는가?

가장 간단한 방법은 학생의 이름을 자주 불러주는 것입니다. 평소에 좋아하는 그룹이나 예능 프로에 나오는 연예인의 이름을 5~6개 정도 기억해 둡시다. 그리고 수업 실연할 때 반복해서 사용해 주는 것입니다.

> **Tip**
>
> 초반부에는 학생 이름을 불러주는 것을 의도하더라도 수업 실연 중후반으로 갈수록 학생 이름이 불리지 않는 경우가 많이 있습니다. 이럴 때를 대비하여 미리 'Okay', 'Thank you'와 같이 자주 쓰는 표현 직후에 학생 이름을 불러주는 것을 습관으로 하면 좋습니다. 'Okay! Suhyun', 'Thank you! Hyunsu!' 이렇게요. :)

Check point #11.
교사가 학생에게 질문을 자주 하는가?

학생 중심 수업에서 학생은 끊임없이 교사로부터 질문을 받게 됩니다. 바로 CCQ 때문이죠. 따라서 이 부분은 'Check point #6'와 맥락이 같습니다. 그러나 여기서 강조하는 부분은 '수업 실연 상황에서의 학생과의 상호작용'입니다. 실제 교실에서는 학생들이 앉아 있어서 자연스럽게 질문과 대답 형태의 대화가 오가지만 수업 실연에서는 그렇지 않습니다. 의도적으로 상호작용을 고려하지 않으면 자칫 교사 혼자서 수업 내용을 줄줄 읊는 상황이 발생합니다. 이러한 상황을 막기 위해서 수업 실연 상황에서만큼은 '질문을 의도적으로 자주 해야겠다'라는 생각을 지니고 있어야 합니다.

> **Tip**
>
> 수업 실연 상황에서 허공에 대고 질문을 하는 것이 뻘쭘할 수 있습니다. 그러나 이 방법이 상호작용을 보여주는 가장 확실한 방법입니다! 왜냐하면 아무도 없는데 질문을 한다면 당연히 '누군가가 있음을 가정하는구나'라고 받아들여지기 때문입니다. (마치 상황극처럼요) 그러나 질문을 하지 않고 계속 수업 내용을 이어 나간다면 학생이 배제된 교사 중심 수업의 느낌이 들 수밖에 없습니다.

Check point #12.

♟ 교사의 질문에 대답하는 주체가 학생인가?

이렇게 교사가 질문을 하면 당연히 대답하는 주체는 학생이어야 합니다. 이 부분은 실제 교실 환경이었다면 아주 자연스럽게 진행되겠지만, 그 누구도 없이 홀로 진행해야 하는 수업 실연 상황에서는 자주 벌어지는 실수입니다. 바로 교사의 질문에 교사가 자문자답하는 경우죠.

> <예시 상황 T-talk>
>
> T1 : Why was Paul so busy? That was because of his history homework! (X)
>
> T2 : Paul was so busy because of WHAT? Yes, Sohye! History homework! (O)

위 두 예시는 같은 상황이지만 교사의 T-talk 방식에 따라 학생과의 상호작용이 일어나고 있는지 그렇지 않은지 확실하게 차이가 납니다. T1은 자문자답의 방식이고 T2는 학생의 이름이 불리면서 대화가 이루어진 상황이죠.

> **Tip**
>
> 위의 T2 예시에서 두 가지 부분을 주목할 수 있습니다. 첫 번째는 의문문의 형태입니다. T1보다 T2와 같은 의문문(Wh-in-situ)을 구성할 때 교사는 문장을 구성하기 더 쉽고 학생은 질문에 무엇인지 더 직관적으로 이해할 수 있습니다. 두 번째는 학생의 이름입니다. 첫 번째는 학생의 이름이 불리지 않았지만, 두 번째는 학생의 이름을 직접적으로 언급함으로써 자문자답이 아님을 확실하게 보여줄 수 있었습니다.
>
> 위와 같이 수업 실연 상황에서는 교사가 질문하면 그에 대한 답은 어찌 됐든 교사의 입을 통해 말할 수밖에 없습니다. 이럴 경우, 다른 사람이 있음을 가정하는 형태의 의문문과 학생 이름이 등장하면 '자문자답'이 아닌 '학생의 답변을 옮긴 대답'이 되죠!

(6) Teacher Talk

Teacher Talk는 교사의 교실 영어 사용에 관한 것으로, 단순히 '교사의 유창한 영어 실력'을 의미하는 것이 아닙니다. 부담 갖지 마세요! 영어 수업 실연에서 '영어를 잘하는 것'은 '원어민과 같은 영어'가 아니라 '학생이 알아들을 정도로 쉬운 영어'를 구사하는 능력입니다. 이와 관련한 체크리스트를 살펴봅시다!

Check point #13.

학생 수준에 맞는 어휘 및 문장 구조를 사용했는가?

가장 많이 실수하는 것 중 하나입니다. 전공 영어 공부를 너무 오래 하다 보니 막상 내가 구사하는 영어가 알고 보니 학생들이 알아듣기에는 너무 어려웠던 경우가 많습니다. 학생 수준에 맞지 않는 단어나, 지나치게 복잡한 문장 구조를 사용하고 있었던 것이죠.

> <예시 상황 T-talk>
> T1 : We need some interaction here. Can you tell me what kind of future jobs we can expect? (X)
> T2 : Let's talk about this. What kind of future jobs do we know? Anyone?

T1과 T2를 비교하면 훨씬 더 언어 표현이 쉬워졌다는 것을 느낄 수 있습니다. T1의 'interaction', 'expect'와 같은 어휘뿐만 아니라 what으로 시작하는 의문사절이 tell의 목적어 역할을 하고 있어 문장 구조가 어렵습니다. 이를 T2와 같이 수정할 수 있습니다. 'We need some interaction' 대신에 'Let's talk about this.'로 훨씬 더 자연스럽고 알아듣기 쉬운 표현을 사용하였고, 'expect'에 해당하는 단어로 'know'를 사용하였습니다. 'Can you tell me'에 해당하는 부분도 'Anyone?'을 통해 학생과 대화를 시도하는 상황인 것을 표현하였죠.

Tip

어려운 어휘와 문장 구조를 사용하는 것을 경계해야 합니다. 최대한 쉬운 언어와 표현, 간단한 문장 구조를 사용하는 것이 수업 실연을 하는 사람으로서도 유리할 뿐만 아니라 채점관으로서도 '학생이 저 수업을 잘 따라갈 수 있겠다.'라는 인상이 듭니다!

Check point #14.

♟ 학생 수준에 맞는 속도로 구사하였는가?

영어 구사도 평소보다 훨씬 더 느리게 말해야 합니다. 종종 우리는 빨리 말할수록 유창하다는 인식이 있어 말을 빠르게 하려는 경향이 있습니다. 그리고 일부러 알아듣지 못하게 하려고(?) 빠르게 T-talk를 해버리는 때도 있죠. 우리는 지금 '채점관을 위한 영어'가 아니라 '학생을 위한 영어'를 한다는 사실을 잊지 말아야 합니다. 영어를 잘할 필요도 없고, 잘하는 것처럼 보일 필요도 없습니다. 학생들이 알아들을 수 있는 정도의 수준과 속도를 유지하면 됩니다.

> **Tip**
>
> 어느 속도로 구사해야 적당한지 감을 잡기 어려우시다면 제 유튜브 채널에 올라와 있는 영상을 참고 하시기를 바랍니다!
> 실제로 수업 실연을 진행한 속도 그대로 촬영하였습니다.

Check point #15.

♟ 교사의 활동 지시가 간결하고 명확한가?

이 부분은 영어교육론뿐만 아니라 TESOL에서도 매우 강조하고 있는 사항입니다. 교사의 활동 지시는 되도록 아주 간결하고 명확해야 합니다.

<예시 상황 T-talk>

T1 : We are going to discuss in groups, make a safety poster including 3 safety tips for 20 minutes and after that, you should present your poster in front of the class for 20 minutes, OK? (X)

T2 : For now, we are going to discuss in groups about making a safety poster. 5 minutes! Go!

(T's Circulation)

Okay, time's up! Next, we are going to make a poster. You should include 3 safety tips. How many? Thank you, Hyunjung! Three tips for 15 minutes. Go!

(T's Circulation)

Alright, are you guys finished with the posters? Great! Don't you want to see your friends posters? Perfect! Then, let's begin our presentation!

T1과 T2를 비교하면 T1이 훨씬 짧아 보이지만 내용상 그렇지 않습니다. 교사의 발화 한 번에 1) Group discussion, 2) Making a poster, 3) Presentation에 대한 활동 지시가 한 번에 들어있기 때문입니다. 이러한 형태의 활동 지시는 학생에게 잘 전달되지 않으므로 T2와 같이 활동 단계마다 지시 사항을 나눠주는 것이 좋습니다. 지금 당장 해야 할 것에 대한 지시 사항만 전달하는 것이죠!

> **Tip**
>
> 이렇게 지시 사항을 나누어서 전달하면 중간에 Circulation 시간이 확보되기 때문에 더 다양한 체크리스트 요소를 수업 실연에서 보여줄 수 있습니다!

Check point #16.
교사의 질문이 구체적인가?

학교 다닐 때 선생님이 질문하시고 아무도 대답하지 않는 상황이 벌어지는 일, 많이 겪어보셨죠? 이렇게 Teacher Talk를 진행할 때 한마디로 '갑분싸' 상황이 만들어져서는 안 됩니다. 학생이 대답할 수 있을 만한 질문을 제시해야 하고 이를 통해서 적절한 학생의 반응을 유도할 수 있어야 하죠.

> **<예시 상황 T-talk>**
>
> T1 : What is friendship? (X)
>
> T2 : Sumin, who is your best friend? Oh, Minsu? Then, we can say 'Sumin and Minsu have a friendship.'

위 상황은 'friendship'에 대해서 가르쳐주려고 하는 교사의 T-talk입니다. 그러나 T1과 같이 '우정이 뭐니?'라고 학생에게 물어보면 당연히 무엇이라고 말해야 할지 모르겠죠. 질문이 너무 광범위하고 주제도 추상적이기 때문입니다. 반면에 T2는 학생에게 가장 친한 친구가 누구인지 물어봄으로써 대화를 유도하고 있습니다. 그리고 그 대답을 통해서 friendship이 어떤 것인지 파악하도록 하고 있죠. 이처럼, 학생에게 질문을 할 때 교사의 질문이 학생으로서 즉각적으로 대답하기에 너무 광범위하거나 추상적인 주제는 아닌지 고려하면서 T-talk를 구사해야 합니다.

Check point #17.
배운 내용이 T-talk로 활용되었는가?

오늘 수업에서 배운 핵심 표현이나 문법이 T-talk를 통해서 직접 나타나면 그것만큼 더할 나위는 없겠죠! 학생으로서는 영어에 대한 노출 대부분이 교사에게서 오는 것이므로 교사가 직접 T-talk로서 오늘 배운 핵심 표현을 자연스럽게 구사한다면 아주 좋은 수업 실연이 될 것입니다!

> <예시 상황 T-talk>
> T : ('If I were you'가 핵심 표현일 때) Wow, Dongwoo, you've already finished with the writing using 'If I were you'! That is perfect! Then, why don't you help your partner? IF I WERE HIM, I would feel very grateful!

위와 같이 'if I were you'가 해당 수업 실연의 핵심 표현이라고 가정한다면 쓰기 활동에서 교사의 circulation 부분에 위와 같은 T-talk를 구사할 수 있습니다. 'IF I WERE HIM'이라는 부분에 강세를 두어 채점관에게 센스있는 모습을 어필할 수도 있죠! 물론 학생으로서도 해당 표현에 대한 인풋이 추가되니 좋은 학습 경험이 될 거라는 사실은 두말할 필요도 없고 말이죠!

(7) Grouping

학생 중심 수업에서 모둠 활동이 빠질 수가 없습니다! 학생끼리 서로 의견을 주고받으면서 Peer Scaffolding이 일어나기도 하고 교과 지식 외에도 협력과 의사 교환을 통한 인성적 발달도 꾀할 수 있기 때문입니다. 그래서인지 거의 매년 수업 실연에서 모둠 활동이 출제되고 있죠. 여기서는 모둠 활동을 수업 실연에서 보여줄 때 유의해야 할 체크리스트에 대해서 알아보겠습니다.

Check point #18.
전체 학생 숫자와 일치하는가?

너무 당연한 거 아니냐고요? 맞습니다! 그런데 당연할수록 간과하기 쉽습니다. 사실 제가 이 부분을 실수했죠. 하하…. 전체 학생 수가 30명인데 제가 그만 4인 1조를 만들어 버린 것입니다… 이 이후로 제가 수업 실연 피드백을 진행할 때 항상 학생 수에 맞는 그룹이 이루어졌는지 확인합니다. 그런데 저와 비슷한 실수를 하시는 분이 생각보다 꽤 있다는 것을 금방 알 수 있었습니다. 아마도 실제 교실 상황이었다면 남는 학생이 눈에 보이니까 무언가 잘못되었다는 것을 바로 알아차렸을 테지만 수업 실연 상황에서는 교실 환경을 머릿속에서 상상하는 상태로 진행해야 하니 이런 실수가 많은 것 같습니다. 여러분은 꼭 그룹을 구성할 때 남는 학생은 없는지 한 번 더 생각하는 습관을 지니시길 바랍니다.

> **Tip**
>
> 저의 실수 뒷이야기를 조금 더 말씀드리자면 저는 지도안을 쓸 때 학생 수를 잘못 계산하여 그룹을 구성하였고, 이후 구상실에서 제가 쓴 지도안을 보고 경악했습니다. 숫자가 잘못된 것을 거기서 알았거든요. 그래서 급하게 5인 1조로 수정하였고 수업 실연도 그렇게 진행하였습니다. 결과는 수업 실연 점수는 43.17/45, 지도안 점수는 13.27/15였습니다. 큰 폭의 감점은 아니지만 감점 이유는 아마도 그룹 숫자를 잘못 계산한 점(지도안), 지도안과 수업이 일치하지 않은 점(수업 실연)이 아닌가 생각합니다. 그래도 수업 실연에서 5인 1조로 바꾸었기 때문에 그 이상의 감점은 막은 게 아닌가 생각합니다. 30명인데 4인 1조로 그대로 진행했으면 '어라 2명은?'이라는 의문이 자연스레 들기 때문입니다.

Check point #19.

해당 활동에 적절한 인원을 배치하였는가?

활동마다 너무 많은 인원이 배치되어서도, 너무 적은 인원이 배치되어서도 안 됩니다. 교사로서 해당 활동에 필요한 인원수를 파악할 수 있는 능력도 필요하죠. 그러나 수업 실연을 준비하는 수험생으로서는 현장 경력이 없는 경우가 대다수이기 때문에 이러한 감각을 키우는 게 어려울 수 있습니다. 이럴 경우를 대비하여 한 가지 기준을 제시하자면, 오늘 배운 내용을 토대로 무언가 만들어 내는 Main Activity의 경우 3~5인, 그 외 Build-up Activity나 Evaluation의 경우는 Pair work가 적당합니다.

> <예시 상황 T-talk>
>
> T : This is a group work. So we are going to do this in groups. Alright! Jongmin, Minjong, Suhyun and Hyunsu, you guys are in Group 1. (손짓으로) Group 2, Group 3 (생략) and Group 6. (24명일 경우)

위와 같이 그룹을 만들 때 의도적으로 첫 번째 그룹은 이름을 다 불러주려고 노력했습니다. 또한, T-talk 대신 제스쳐를 적극적으로 사용하여 그룹을 만들고 있다는 것을 보여주었고 두세 개쯤 반복한 뒤 바로 마지막 그룹을 호명함으로써 시간을 절약하였습니다.

> **Tip**
>
> 그룹 활동은 수업 실연에서 한 번만 보여주는 것이 적당합니다. 그 외에는 특별한 지시 사항이 없는 한 개별활동이나 Pair work로 간단하게 보여주는 것도 시간을 절약하는 방법입니다. 너무 욕심을 내어서 모든 활동을 그룹 활동으로 하는 실수를 범하지 않도록 합시다!

Check point #20.

♟ 개인별 역할 부여가 이루어졌는가?

그룹 활동에서 가장 중요한 부분입니다! 그룹 활동을 기획할 때 교사로서 고려해야 할 점은 무임승차하는 학생이 없도록 하는 것입니다. 이를 위해서는 학생의 개별 책무성을 강화 해주어야 하죠. 실제 교실 환경에서는 간단하게 설문지를 통해 Peer Evaluation을 진행할 수 있지만, 수업 실연에서는 더욱 시스템적으로 잘 짜인 그룹 활동을 보여주는 게 좋습니다. 이를 위해서 '개인별 역할 부여'가 중요하죠! 그래서 반드시 수업 실연 상황에서 그룹을 짤 때, 구성원 모두에게 각자 1인 1역이 부여되었는지 확인하는 게 중요합니다. 아래는 제가 자주 사용한 역할 리스트입니다. 여러분도 나름의 기본 세팅을 만들어 놓고 활동마다 조금씩 변형하는 방식으로 진행하는 것이 효율적일 것입니다!

역할 명	역할	역할 명	역할
Leader	그룹장	Blogger	팀 과제 업로드
Writer	글 쓰기	Presenter	발표자
Word master	어휘 검색	Grammar checker	문법 확인

'Leader'는 말 그대로 팀 전체 구성원을 조율하는 역할입니다. 팀에서 어려움이나 갈등이 생기면 먼저 그룹장을 중심으로 자체적으로 해결하고, 그 후에 교사에게 도움을 청합니다. 'Writer'는 쓰기 과제가 있을 때, 문장을 쓰는 역할입니다. 물론 여러 학생이 동시에 글을 써도 되지만, 실제 교실 환경에서는 한 명이 맡아서 쓰는 것이 효율적이고, 글씨도 일정하므로 Writer를 지정하는 것을 선호합니다. 'Word master'는 작문할 때 필요한 어휘를 찾아주는 역할입니다. (때로는 재미있게 부르기 위해서 'Dictionary'라는 역할 명을 주기도 합니다) 요즘에는 학생이 모두 자신의 태블릿 PC가 있음을 가정하기 때문에, Word master 역할을 부여할 때 'You can bring your Tablet PC.'라고 안내해 주어도 좋습니다. 'Blogger'는 최종 팀 과제 완성물을 인터넷 커뮤니티에 올려주는 역할입니다. Google Classroom이 있다고 가정한 후 Blogger가 도맡아서

취합하여 최종 과제물을 제출하도록 하는 것이죠. 이렇게 하면 블랜디드 수업을 진행하고 있다는 인상을 남길 수 있습니다. (Google Classroom에서 다른 팀의 과제를 보고 댓글을 남기도록 안내해도 더 좋겠죠?!) 'Presenter'는 말 그대로 발표자입니다. 발표 활동이 있을 때 Presenter를 지정할 수 있습니다. 그러나 Presenter까지 지정하기에 인원수가 너무 많다 싶으면 Leader에게 Presenter의 역할을 부여할 수 있습니다. 'Grammar checker'는 문법을 확인해 주는 학생입니다. 이 학생도 Word master와 마찬가지로 태블릿 PC가 있다고 가정하고 'Grammarly' 등 문법 확인 소프트웨어 및 웹사이트를 사용하라고 안내합니다. 그러면 디지털 기기를 활용한 훨씬 더 최첨단(?)의 수업 실연 모습을 연출할 수 있습니다. 당연히 고득점은 덤이고요!

> **Tip**
>
> 쓰기 과제의 성격에 따라 위와 같이 거창한(?) 역할을 부여하지 않아도 될 때가 있습니다. 예를 들어, 한 그룹당 Safety tip을 3개 써야 하는 과제일 경우, 3인 1조를 구성하여 한 학생당 한 개의 Safety tip을 쓰라고 안내할 수 있습니다. 이럴 때는 칠판에 '1S=1S'처럼 개인별 역할 부여가 이루어졌음을 남겨주는 것도 좋은 수업 실연 전략입니다.

<예시 상황 T-talk>

<판서 내용>

Leader	
Writer	Blogger
Word master	Presenter

T : (위 판서를 보며 손가락을 짚으며) Students sitting here, raise your hand! You guys will be the Leaders. So you are leading the group, okay? And students sitting here, raise your hand! Okay, you guys will be the Writers. And students (손가락으로 짚으며) here? You will be the Word masters. So you can use your tablet PCs if your group needs to find some vocabularies. And here? Okay you guys are the Bloggers. Don't forget to upload your writings on Google Classroom. And lastly students here? Yes, you guys are the Presenters. So, make sure you need to prepare for the presentation, alright? Okay, Dongwoo! What's your job in your group? That's right, Blogger! So, are you ready? 15 minutes. Go!

위와 같이 역할 부여를 진행할 때 교사가 판서를 통해 자리마다 역할을 배정하면 아주 효율적입니다. 손가락으로 '여기에 앉은 학생들 손들어 보세요.'라고 말하며 '여러분의 역할은 이것입니다.'라고 알려주는 것이죠. 이때 Leader와 Writer, Presenter는 그 자체로 역할이 연상되므로 부연 설명을 굳이 덧붙이지 않아도 되지만 Blogger와 Word master는 Google Classroom과 Tablet PC를 사용하는 부분이므로 반드시 설명을 덧붙여주었습니다. 제 수업 실연의 차별점이 될 수 있다고 생각하였기 때문입니다. 그리고 위와 같이 마지막에 학생 한 명을 호명하여 CCQ를 진행하였죠. (저는 Blogger라는 역할을 필살기로 밀었기 때문에 CCQ로 지목된 학생을 Blogger라고 다시 상기시켜줌으로써 채점관에게 더 기억에 남는 수업 실연이 되려고 노력했습니다.)

(8) Circulation during Activities

교사의 활동 지시 후 순회 지도에 관한 부분입니다. 학생 중심 수업에서 절대로 빼놓을 수 없는 부분이죠! 왜냐하면, 교사의 순회 지도를 통해 개별적 피드백이나 칭찬을 통한 동기 부여, 도움이 필요한 학생에게 Scaffolding을 제공하는 등 학생 중심 수업에서 강조하는 다양한 요소를 보여줄 수 있기 때문입니다. 제가 순회 지도 부분을 고득점 필살 전략으로 활용한 만큼 꼭 이 부분을 어떻게 하면 수업 실연 장면에서 잘 드러낼 수 있는지 고민해보시길 바랍니다.

Check point #21.
Circulation이 적절한 활동을 잘 선택하였는가?

물론 실제 교실 환경에서는 교사가 학생들에게 활동 시간을 부여하면 자연스럽게 순회 지도가 이루어집니다. 그러나 수업 실연 상황에서는 제한시간이 있으므로 여러분이 스스로 판단하여 교사의 순회 지도가 적합한 활동을 잘 골라서 보여주어야 합니다. 제가 어떤 활동에서 순환 활동을 보여줄 것인지 결정한 기준은 다음과 같습니다.

1. Scaffolding을 보여줄 수 있는 활동
교사의 설명을 이해하는 정도는 학생마다 차이가 있을 수밖에 없으므로 학생 중심 수업에서 순회 지도의 목적은 개별화 학습에 있다고 해도 과언이 아닐 것입니다. 따라서, 교사는 활동 시간 내에 도움이 필요한 학생을 발견하고 적절히 개입할 수 있어야 합니다.

2. Mixed-Level Treatment를 보여줄 수 있는 활동
위 Scaffolding과 맥락을 같이합니다. 보통 Scaffolding이라고 함은 Low-level 학생을 위한 교사의 교육적 개입으로 이해하지만, 포괄적인 개념으로는 High-level 학생을 위한 추가 과제를 부여하는 것도 의미할 수 있습니다. 실제 교실 환경에서는 학생의 수준 차이가 크기 때문에 Low-level 학생과 High-level 학생의 과제 완성 속도가 극명하게 차이납니다. 따라서 교사의 순회 지도를 통해서 Low-level 학생뿐만 아니라 High-level 학생에게도 적절한 교사의 개입(추가 과제)을 보여주는 것이 아주 좋은 수업 실연 고득점 전략이 됩니다.

3. 그룹 활동

과제물을 만들어야 하는 그룹 활동의 경우 교사가 돌아다니며 진행 상황을 확인하는 과정이 필요합니다. 여기서도 마찬가지로 High-level group은 과제를 빨리 완성하였을 것이므로 적절한 긍정적 피드백을 제공해준 뒤 추가 과제를 부여하는 것이 좋습니다. 또한, Discussion과 같은 Speaking Activity의 경우 Turn-taking이 그룹 내에서 자체적으로 이루어지지 못하는 경우가 많으므로 교사의 적절한 개입을 보여주는 것이 좋습니다.

4. 활동 시간이 10분 이상일 경우

활동 시간이 길면 길수록 채점관도 교사의 순회 지도를 기대할 확률이 높습니다. 특히, 10분 이상 시간을 부여하였는데 아무것도 보여주지 않고 'Okay, time's up!'이라고 하면 자연스럽게 '그 시간 동안 교사는 무엇을 한 걸까?' 의문이 남을 수밖에 없죠. 그러므로 활동 시간을 조금 넉넉히 부여했다 싶으면 반드시 순회 지도에서 무엇을 보여줄지 미리 함께 고민하는 것이 구상 단계에서 필요합니다.

Check point #22.

♟ Circulation의 동선이 다양한가?

Circulation은 수업 실연 중 2번 이상 등장할 수 있습니다. 저의 경우 순회 지도를 통해서 1) Teacher Scaffolding 2) Peer Scaffolding 3) Positive Feedback 4) Low-level Treatment 5) High-level Treatment 이 다섯 가지를 모두 보여주는 것을 목표로 삼았기 때문에 반드시 순회 지도는 2번 이상 실시하였습니다. 이때, 동선을 의도적으로 다양화하는 것이 중요합니다. 수업 실연 상황에서는 웬만한 강심장이 아니고서야 극도로 긴장할 수밖에 없으므로 칠판 앞에서만 이리저리 움직이는 모습이 많이 나옵니다. 그래서 순회 지도를 해야 하는 상황에서도 한 곳으로만 계속 가는 모습이 종종 보이곤 하죠. 그렇지만 20년 가까이 학생들을 가르쳐온 채점관으로서는 여러분의 수업 실연에 학생들이 듣고 있는 모습을 상상하곤 하는데, 이러한 동선이 생각보다

신경 쓰일 수밖에 없습니다. 따라서 저는 의도적으로 교실 공간을 최대한 넓게 활용하여 순회 지도의 동선을 다양화하려고 노력하였습니다.

> **Tip**
>
> 너무 디테일(?)한 이야기일 수도 있지만 저는 의도적으로 Circulation을 칠판에서 가까운 쪽에서 하지 않고 최대한 먼 뒤쪽에서 보여주려고 했습니다. 채점관과 가까워지는 것이 부담스럽긴 하지만 실제 교실에서는 보통 맨 앞자리에 앉는 학생들보다는 맨 뒤에 앉는 학생들에게 교사의 개입이 많이 필요한 경우가 많기 때문입니다.

(9) Mixed-level Treatment

말 그대로 실제 교실 환경에서는 아주 당연하게도 다양한 수준의 학생들이 섞여 있습니다. 그리고 이와 같은 사실을 수업 실연 문제에서도 'Mixed-level'이라고 명시하고 있죠. 하지만 우리는 이러한 교실 환경이 너무나도 당연하기 때문에, 쉽게 간과하곤 합니다. 그러나 수업 실연은 하나의 엄연한 시험입니다. 그러므로 우리는 'Mixed-level이라고 쓰여있다'라는 사실을 '이 부분을 채점하겠다'라는 의미로서 받아들여야 하는 거죠! 따라서 저는 수업 실연에서 확실한 고득점을 받기 위해서 '나는 내 수업에서 Mixed-level을 의식하고 있다!'라는 것을 아주 확실하게 보여주려고 노력하였습니다.

Check point #23.
♟ Low-level에게 적절한 도움이 제공되었는가?

낮은 수준의 학생에게 적합한 도움이 제공되어야 하고, 이는 교사의 수업 준비 단계에서부터 고려되어야 합니다. 읽기 활동 중 어휘력이 부족한 학생을 위해서 Word list를 준비해두거나, 말하기 활동에서 Expression list, 쓰기 활동에서 Sample sentences나 Resource를 제공하는 것이 대표적인 예시입니다. 이때 'Check point #1'에서 다루었던 Scaffolding 3단계를 보여주면 좋겠죠!

> <예시 상황 T-talk>
> T : Oh, Group 3, do you need any help? Okay, so you are having difficulty with finding environmental problems. Then, why don't you use those newspapers and magazines I brought for you? With those things can you guys do this by yourselves? Perfect!

위의 예시처럼 Mixed-level Treatment는 그룹 활동에서도 예외가 아닙니다. 활동 진행에 어려움을 겪고 있는 그룹이 있다고 가정한 뒤, 도움이 필요한지, 어떤 어려움을 겪고 있는지 물어봅니다. (Scaffolding-in) 그다음 교사가 미리 준비한 Scaffolding을 제공합니다. 간혹 쓰기 주제 중, 학생 혼자서 떠올리기 까다로운 주제일 경우 저는 관련 주제를 담은 신문 기사나 잡지를 종종 제공하곤 했습니다. (Scaffolding) 그 후 교사가 제시한 Scaffolding 자료들을 보여주며 학생들이 혼자 할 수 있는지 물어봅니다. 그리고 혼자 할 수 있겠다는 대답을 듣고 칭찬 및 격려와 함께 개입을 종료합니다. (Scaffolding-out)

Check point #24.
High-level에게 적절한 과제가 추가되었는가?

사실 실제 교실 환경에서는 Low-level Treatment가 핵심이며 교사로서도 더 많은 고민과 노력이 요구됩니다. 그러나 수업 실연 상황에서는 High-level Treatment가 고득점의 열쇠입니다. 왜냐하면, Low-level Treatment는 누구나 떠올릴 수 있는 비교적 쉽고 당연한 요소지만 High-level Treatment는 대부분 간과하기 때문입니다. 따라서 시험에 합격하기 위해 수업 실연을 준비하는 우리로서는 Low-level Treatment뿐만 아니라 High-level Treatment까지 고려한 모습을 보여주어야 합니다.

<예시 상황 T-talk>
T : Oh, Jihwan, have you already finished? What a quick writer! Then, why don't you write another sentence about giving advice? You know the more advice we have, the better!

위와 같이 과제를 빨리 끝낸 학생이 있다고 가정한 뒤 추가 과제를 제시하는 것입니다. 저는 듣기와 읽기 같은 Receptive Skills는 추가 과제로 Student Teacher와 같은 Peer scaffolding을 보여주었고, 쓰기나 말하기와 같은 Productive Skills는 High-level을 위한 추가 과제로 해당 내용을 더 쓰거나 말해보는 과제를 제시하였습니다. 왜냐하면, Receptive Skills는 말 그대로 학생의 이해가 우선이므로 동료의 이해를 돕는 것이 더 중요하고, Productive Skills는 언어 사용이 우선이므로 해당 표현을 최대한 더 많이 활용할 기회를 제공하는 것이 중요하기 때문입니다.

Check point #25.

 교사의 긍정적 피드백이 함께 제시되었는가?

위와 같이 Low-level이든 High-level이든 교사의 개입이 이루어질 때는 반드시 교사의 긍정적 피드백이 함께 제공되어야 합니다.

> <예시 상황 T-talk>
> T1 : I'm so impressed by your effort!
> T2 : Keep up the great work!
> T3 : You don't have to hurry.
> T4 : Let's go step by step.
> -----
> T5 : What a quick writer!
> T6 : Wow, have you already finished?
> T7 : Why don't you write more about it?
> T8 : You know more practice makes better English!

T1~T4는 Low-level을 위한 긍정적 피드백의 예시입니다. 이처럼 Low-level일 경우에는 교사의 Scaffolding 제공 후 학생을 격려해주는 표현이 많이 사용됩니다. 주로 '혼자 힘으로 해내는 것이 의미가 있다.', '서두르지 말고 본인의 속도에 맞게 해도 된다.'라는 메시지가 적당합니다.

한편, T5~T8은 High-level을 위한 T-talk이며, 주로 학생의 수행 능력에 대한 교사의 감탄 표현과 함께 추가 과제를 제안합니다. 그리고 High-level 학생에게는 단순히 과제 완료에 대한 동기 부여에 그치지 않고 본질적인 영어 실력 향상을 근거로 하여 추가 과제를 수행해볼 것을 설득합니다.

Tip

무턱대고 빨리 끝난 학생에게 추가 과제를 시켜버리면 빨리 끝낸 것이 벌(?)인 것처럼 되어 버립니다. 그렇다고 빨리 끝내서 놀고 있는 학생에게 아무것도 안 할 수는 없는 노릇이죠. 따라서 High-level Treatment를 제공할 때는 반드시 폭풍 칭찬과 함께 추가 과제가 절대 Disadvantage가 아니라는 사실을 각인시켜주고, 오히려 영어 실력 향상에 도움이 된다는 방향으로 설득하여 진행해야 합니다.

Presentation

　　CLASSROOM MANAGEMENT의 두 번째 장은 Presentation입니다. 교사의 수업 내용 전달 방식에 관한 부분이죠. 여기에서는 판서와 전자기기 활용이 포함됩니다. 이전에는 교사용 컴퓨터나 빔프로젝터가 끝이었지만, 코로나를 기점으로 하여 모든 학생에게 전자기기가 보급되었고 이러한 현실 상황에 맞게 수업 실연에서도 학생용 Tablet PC가 교실 환경에 등장하는 추세입니다. 따라서 이번 장에서는 교사가 어떻게 이러한 기자재 등을 활용하여 수업 내용을 전달하는지 묻는 체크리스트에 관한 것입니다. 하나씩 살펴보도록 하죠!

(1) Board

　　수업 실연에서 판서가 빠질 수 없습니다. 실제 교실 환경에서 판서의 목적은 학생의 이해를 돕는 것이지만, 수업 실연에서는 위와 같은 목적 외에도 한 가지 더 있습니다. 바로 '내가 지시 사항을 수행했다는 증거를 남기는 것'이죠. 현실적으로 같은 내용의 수업 실연을 10번 이상 보고 있는 채점관으로서 100% 같은 집중력으로 모든 수험생의 수업 실연을 이해하고 따라가는 것은 불가능에 가깝습니다. 그러므로 종종 집중력이 흐려지는 부분이 생길 수밖에 없기 마련이고 이럴 때는 판서 내용을 보고서 '이 지시 사항이 잘 수행되고 있구나.'라는 인상을 받습니다. 이처럼, 수업 실연이 완벽한 시험이 될 수는 없지만 어떻게든 합격해야 하는 우리로서는 이러한 사소한 부분까지도 놓쳐서는 안 될 것입니다.

Check point #26.
판서의 내용이 명확한가?

　　당연히 판서의 내용은 한눈에 들어오기 쉽고 명확해야 합니다. 그렇게 하기 위해서는 짜임새 있게 구성된 판서를 연습하는 것이 중요하죠. 'Check point #9'에서 짧게 언급하였듯 영어 수업 실연의 큰 틀은 'Schema activation → Receptive Skills → Productive Skills → Evaluation'으로 이루어집니다. 따라서 판서도 이에 맞게 네 부분으로 나누어 왼쪽부터 각각의 단계에 맞는 활동에 대한 판서 내용을 이어나가는 것이 중요합니다.

<판서 예시>			
<Let's Talk>	<Let's Read>	<Let's Write>	<Check! Check!>
• Schema activation	• Main idea	• Sample writing	• Checklist
• Mind map	• Detail information	• Requirements	• Peer evaluation
• …	• …	• Grouping	• …

위와 같이 칠판을 네 부분으로 나누고 각각의 활동에 맞는 내용을 아래에 써주는 것입니다. <Let's Talk> 부분은 오늘 배울 내용에 대한 간단한 Schema activation 활동입니다. 대표적으로는 Pair work의 형태로 해당 주제에 관해 대화를 나눠보게 하고, 어떤 이야기를 나누었는지 학생과 상호작용 하면서 마인드맵으로 표현해주는 것입니다. <Let's Read>는 가장 일반적인 부분으로, Main idea와 Detail information을 찾게 합니다. Detail information은 교사가 Short quiz를 제공하여서 CCQ를 진행할 수도 있습니다. <Let's Write>는 주제에 따라서 <Making Safety Tips>나 <Save the Earth>와 같은 보다 실제적인 제목을 설정하는 것도 개성 있는 수업 실연을 하기 위한 좋은 전략입니다. 여기에서는 Sample Writing을 제공하고 글에서 반드시 포함되어야 할 Requirements를 제공합니다. 그리고 이 활동은 Main Activity이므로 그룹 활동이 될 확률이 높습니다. 따라서 개인별 역할 부여와 같은 Grouping에 관한 내용도 여기에 판서합니다. 마지막으로 <Check! Check!>는 Evaluation 부분입니다. 학생에게 Rubric이나 Checklist를 제공하는 방식이 가장 일반적입니다. 여기에서는 교수 내용과 평가의 일치가 이루어져야 하므로 <Let's Write> 부분의 Requirements와 <Check! Check!>의 Checklist의 요소가 서로 일치한다는 것을 화살표로 표현해주는 것이 좋습니다.

> **Tip**
>
> 악필이라고 너무 고민하지 않으셔도 됩니다. 대부분 판서가 어색하므로 수험생들 간 별로 차이가 나지 않습니다. 그러나 글자가 너무 작은 경우, 글을 쓰면 점점 위로 올라가거나 아래로 내려가는 습관이 있다면 연습을 꾸준히 해보시기 바랍니다. 연습만이 해결해줍니다!

Check point #27.

2가지 이상의 색상을 사용하였는가?

수업 실연 시험장마다 다르겠지만 저는 최소 2가지 이상의 색깔을 사용하려고 노력했습니다. 특히 Writing requirements나 Grouping은 중요한 부분이라고 판단하여 색깔을 다르게 표시했고 교수 내용과 평가가 일치됨을 강조하기 위하여 <Let's Write>에서 언급한 Requirements와 <Check! Check!>의 Checklist를 파란색 화살표로 연결하였습니다.

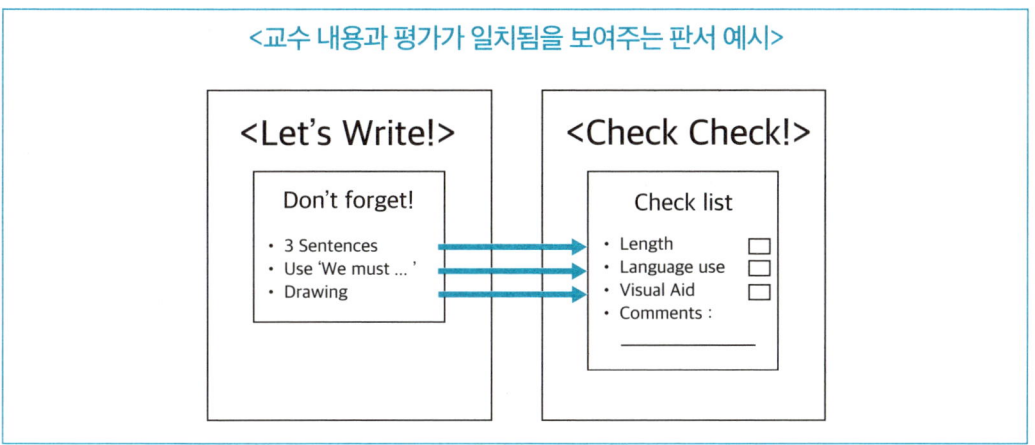

> **Tip**
>
> 왼손으로 판서를 할 경우, 판서를 할 때 학생과 등을 지게 됩니다. 치명적이라고 할 수는 없겠으나 실제로 왼손잡이 수험생의 수업 실연을 보면 학생과의 상호작용이 줄어든 것 같은 인상이 들 때가 있습니다. 그러므로 본인이 만약 왼손잡이라면 의도적으로 학생의 이름을 더 많이 불러주고 더 자주 다가가는 연습을 함으로써 교실 내 상호작용이 활발히 이루어지고 있다는 인상을 남길 수 있도록 하는 것이 좋습니다.

(2) Digital Devices

앞서 'Mixed-level Treatment'에서 이렇게 표현한 부분이 있습니다.

> ... 이와 같은 사실을 수업 실연 문제에서도 'Mixed-level'이라고 명시하고 있죠. 하지만 우리는 이러한 교실 환경이 너무나도 당연하기 때문에, 쉽게 간과하곤 합니다. 그러나 수업 실연은 하나의 엄연한 시험입니다. 그러므로 우리는 'Mixed-level이라고 쓰여있다'라는 사실을 '이 부분을 채점하겠다'라는 의미로서 받아들여야 하는 거죠! ...

이처럼, 수업 실연 문제에서 Classroom Settings에 명시된 모든 부분은 채점 요소가 될 수 있습니다. Digital Devices도 같은 맥락이죠. 이와 관련한 체크리스트 확인해보도록 합시다!

Check point #28.
스크린 화면을 사용하였는가?

보통 교실에는 빔프로젝터가 있다고 가정합니다. 따라서 이 부분을 수업 실연에서 보여주면 당연히 더 현실적인 수업이 되겠죠? 실제 교실에서는 거의 100% 빔프로젝터를 활용하여 수업을 진행하지만, 수업 실연 상황에서는 판서에 신경을 쓰다 보니 빔프로젝터 사용을 종종 잊는 경우가 있습니다. 따라서 구상 단계에서 어떤 부분을 빔프로젝터로 학생들에게 제시할 것인지 정해놓는 것이 좋습니다. 저는 수업 실연에서 다음과 같은 부분이 등장하면 스크린을 활용하였습니다.

1. Reading : Detail information에 대한 Comprehension Check Question 문항

위와 같은 첫 번째 경우는 주로 Reading에서 Detail information에 대한 CCQ를 진행할 때 Short Quiz 문항입니다. 여기서 중요한 것은 Detail information에 대하여 'CCQ를 진행하였다는 것'이지 'Short Quiz 문제 자체'가 아닙니다. 따라서 Short Quiz 문항을 칠판에 쓰고 있으면 시간이 아주 많이 소비되겠죠? 따라서 이러한 부분은 학생들에게 스크린에 두 문제가 나와 있다고 가정하고 수업을 진행하였습니다. 판서에는 'Q1, Q2'와 같이 간략하게 'Detail information에 대한 CCQ를 진행하였다'라는 흔적을 남겨두었고요.

<예시 상황 T-talk>

T : Look at the screen! What do you see? Yes, Minjong, there are two questions. Can you read the first one? Perfect!

<판서 예시>

<Let's Read>
- Main idea : ~~~
- Detail

| Q1 | √ |
| Q2 | √ |

2. Writing : Sample writing

두 번째 경우는 Sample writing을 제시할 때입니다. Sample writing도 역시 내용 자체가 중요한 것이 아니라 '제공하였다는 사실'과 '그 속에서 등장하는 요소들'이 중요합니다. 따라서 Sample writing을 제시할 때에도 학생들과 함께 스크린을 보며 수업을 진행하고 있는 상황을 가정하였습니다.

<예시 상황 T-talk>

T : Jongmin back there, do you see the screen? What do you see? Yes, it is a sample writing! Can you read the first sentence for us? Thank you, Jongmin! Like this, you should write the reason why we should protect the Earth in the first sentence. Okay? And next, we should …

<판서 예시>

<Save the Earth>
- Don't forget
  - Reason
  - What we can do
  - …

위와 같이 맨 뒤에 앉아 있는 학생에게 화면이 보이는지 묻고 상호작용을 통해 Sample writing이 제시되고 있다는 사실을 전달한 다음, Sample writing에서 드러나는 요소를 함께 파악하며 'Don't forget'의 형태로 Writing Requirements를 제시할 수 있습니다.

Tip

'Check point #4'에서 언급하였듯이, 아래 왼쪽 그림의 교사와 같이 칠판 앞에 있는 것보다 오른쪽 그림의 교사와 같이 학생의 시선에서 함께 Screen을 바라보면 더욱 노련(?)하고 학생 중심 수업의 인상을 줄 수 있습니다.

<교사의 위치 예시>

Check point #29.
교실에 제공된 기자재를 모두 활용하였는가?

Classroom Settings에 언급된 모든 기자재를 활용하는 것이 좋습니다. 요즘에는 학생이 개인 Tablet PC를 가지고 있다고 가정하므로 디지털 기기 활용 장면도 구상 단계에서 고민해 보시길 바랍니다.

> **Tip**
>
> 저는 아래와 같은 상황에서 Tablet PC를 활용하였습니다.
>
> 1. 생소한 주제
>   미래 직업이나 환경 문제 등 학생으로서 생소할 수 있는 주제는 Tablet PC를 이용하여 검색해 보도록 하였습니다.
>
> 2. Goggle Classroom 연계
>   오프라인 수업을 온라인 플랫폼과 연계하면 블랜디드 수업이 됩니다. Goggle Classroom에 영상을 업로드하고 이를 참고하여 활동을 진행하거나 활동 후 학생 성과물을 게시하여 공유하도록 하고 댓글을 남길 수 있게끔 수업을 운영할 수 있습니다.
>
> 3. 그룹 활동 중 어휘, 문법 검색
>   쓰기 수업에서 어휘를 검색하거나 문법성을 확인할 수 있도록 Tablet PC를 활용할 수 있습니다. Online dictionary나 Grammarly를 활용한 쓰기 수업도 진행해 보세요!

 Attitude

Attitude는 교사의 수업 실연 태도에 관한 부분입니다. 스터디에서 수업 실연 피드백을 주고 받다 보면 내용 중 거의 대부분이 Attitude에 해당하는 경우가 많죠. 그러나 그 내용이 단순히 '전체적인 인상'에 그치는 경우가 많습니다. 따라서 여기서는 조금 더 구체적으로 언어적 요소와 비언어적 요소로 나누어 살펴보고자 합니다.

(1) Verbal

교사의 T-talk와 관련한 부분입니다. 그러나 'Check point #13'~'Check point #17'이 학생의 관점에서 바라본 T-talk이었다면 여기에서는 교사의 영어 구사 자체에 관한 내용입니다.

Check point #30.
♟ 영어 구사가 안정적인가?

말 그대로 영어 교사를 선발하는 시험에서 영어 구사가 불안하다면 수업 실연 자체의 완성도가 크게 부족해 보일 수밖에 없습니다. 원어민처럼 유창하고 편안하게 영어를 구사할 실력까지는 요구되지 않지만 듣는 사람이 불편한 느낌이 들지 않을 정도의 수준은 필요합니다.

그러나, 너무 겁부터 먹을 필요는 없습니다! 20분 동안 영어로 혼자 떠들어야 하는 수업 실연이 처음에는 막막해 보이지만, 기출 문제를 보다 보면 'Schema activation → Receptive Skills → Productive Skills → Evaluation'이라는 큰 틀이 존재하는 것을 금세 깨달을 수 있을 겁니다. 따라서 각 단계에 맞는 활동과 이에 대한 T-talk 시나리오를 미리 준비해놓고 반복 연습 하는 것이 중요합니다.

Check point #31.
♟ 문법적으로 옳은 문장을 구사하는가?

학생에게는 교사의 T-talk가 유의미한 인풋 역할을 하기도 합니다. 따라서 교사는 비문을 최대한 지양하고 문법적으로 옳은 문장을 제공하여야 하죠. 가벼운 실수는 크게 개의치 않지만 'Check point #17'처럼 배운 내용을 T-talk로 활용할 때는 꼭 신경 써서 학생에게 유의미한 인풋을 제공할 수 있도록 해야 합니다!

> **Tip**
>
> 실수를 해서 T-talk를 수정해야 할 때가 있습니다. 이럴 때는 가볍게 'Sorry, my mistake' 또는 'Excuse me' 정도로 양해를 구하고 정정하면 됩니다. 그러나 중요한 것은 이와 같은 양해를 채점관에게 구하는 것이 아니라 교실에 있는 학생에게 양해를 구하는 모습으로 보여주는 것이 좋습니다.

(2) Nonverbal

교실 분위기는 교사가 내비치는 분위기에 따라 달라집니다. 성격이 차분한 선생님이 수업하실 때는 교실 분위기도 차분해지고 에너지가 넘치는 선생님의 수업 시간에는 분위기가 활발할 수밖에 없는 것처럼요. 몇 시간 동안 가만히 앉아서 같은 수업을 들어야 하는 채점관의 관점에서 생각해보면 단조로운 수업보다는 활발한 수업이 기억에 남을 것입니다. 그렇지만 '활발한 수업'이라는 것은 자신에게 어울리지 않는 자아를 꺼내어 스스로 어색함을 무릅써야 한다는 의미가 아니라, '학생과의 활발한 상호작용'을 통한 '몰입도가 높은 수업'을 의미합니다. 이러한 부분은 개인의 성향과 관련 없이 연습으로 완성할 수 있는 영역입니다. 하나씩 살펴보도록 하죠!

Check point #32.
♟ 목소리가 명확한가?

우연히 아나운서분이 대화하는 것을 보게 되었는데 새삼 깜짝 놀란 것이 있습니다. 바로 대화할 때와 뉴스 대본을 읽을 때가 완전 달랐던 것입니다! 그분은 대화 상황과 내용을 전달하는 상황을 정확하게 구분하여 전달력을 높일 수 있는 기술이 있으신 것이었죠. 사적인 상황과 공적인 상황에 맞게 자신의 전달력을 조절할 수 있었던 것입니다.

물론 수업 실연을 준비하는 우리가 마치 뉴스 진행자처럼 내용을 완벽하게 전달하는 것은 불가능합니다. 그러나 교사도 엄연히 교실 안에서는 학생에게 정보를 전달하는 역할을 가진다는 점에서 '교실 내 아나운서'라고 할 수 있습니다. 따라서 수업에서 교사의 목소리는 명확해야 하며 전달력이 높아야 합니다. 문장 끝을 흐리면서 말을 마무리하지 않거나 너무 목소리가 불안정하여 듣는 이에게 불안감을 주어서는 안 되겠죠. 100% 완벽할 필요는 없습니다. 다만, 단순히 '대화'를 한다기보다는 내용을 '전달'한다는 태도를 가볍게 떠올리며 수업 실연을 연습해 보기를 바랍니다.

> **Tip**
> 아나운서에 비유하다 보니 사투리에 대한 고민이 생기는 일도 있습니다. 짧은 시간 안에 고쳐지는 것도 아니고, 고칠 필요도 없으며, 채점에도 무관할 것으로 생각합니다. 사투리로 스트레스받을 시간에 수업 내용적인 측면을 고민해 보는 것을 추천합니다!

Check point #33.
♟ 톤이 다양한가?

수업 실연에서 말의 높낮이를 적절하게 조절할 줄 알면 훨씬 더 역동적인 분위기를 만들 수 있습니다. 이 외에도, 목소리를 작게 했다가 강조하는 부분에서 크게 말하거나, 잠깐의 공백을 주고 말을 이어 나가는 것도 하나의 방법이 될 수 있습니다. 여기서 핵심은, 교사의 발화가 너무 단조로우면 학생이 쉽게 지루함을 느낄 수 있다는 것입니다. (여기서 학생이란, 채점관을 의미하는 것이겠죠!) 따라서 T-talk 자체에서 다양한 변화를 주어 수업이 지나치게 단조로워지지 않도록 조절하는 연습도 필요합니다.

> **Tip**
>
> 모든 수업 실연 문제에는 해당 수업에서 가르쳐야 하는 핵심 문법이나 표현 또는 전체 내용을 포괄하는 주제나 2022 개정 교육과정에서 강조하는 역량이 포함되어 있습니다. 이러한 부분이 등장할 때마다 교사의 톤을 다양화해서 강조하는 효과를 주면 수업의 전달력이 훨씬 높아집니다. 게다가, 채점관에게는 능숙한 교사의 느낌을 줄 수 있을 뿐만 아니라, '문제에서 의도하는 부분을 정확하게 짚어내었다.'라는 인상까지 줄 수가 있죠!

Check point #34.
♟ 적절한 제스처가 사용되었는가?

긴장하게 되면 몸이 굳어버려서 입만 살아서 움직이는(?) 수업 실연이 나타나게 됩니다. 이보다 더 어색할 수는 없겠죠! 과하지는 않되 자연스러운 손짓과 몸짓으로 수업을 진행하는 연습을 해봅시다.

> **Tip**
>
> 수업 실연하는 모습을 영상으로 촬영해서 스스로 살펴보는 시간을 가지는 것이 중요합니다! 막상 할 때는 전혀 눈치채고 있지 못하다가 영상을 통해서 내 몸이 생각보다 굳어있거나, 제스처가 다소 과하다는 것을 제삼자의 관점에서 바라볼 수 있기 때문입니다.

Check point #35.
 Eye-Contact가 끊임없이 이루어지는가?

아무도 없는 교실이지만 Eye-Contact가 끊임없이 이루어지는 모습을 보여주어야 합니다. 왜냐하면 우리는 '학습자 중심 수업'을 진행하고 있는 교사이기 때문입니다. 학습자 중심 수업에서 교사는 끊임없이 학생의 배움 정도를 관찰하고 적절한 피드백을 제공하는 촉진자 역할을 해야 합니다. 그렇게 하기 위해서는 교사의 시선이 칠판에만 머무는 것이 아니라 학생 한 명 한 명을 바라봐야 하는 것이죠.

> **Tip**
>
> 채점관과 눈을 마주치지 않아도 됩니다. 왜냐하면 심층 면접에서는 채점관이 경청하는 역할이었다면, 수업 실연에서의 채점관은 관찰자 역할이기 때문입니다. 따라서 마치 채점관이 없는 것처럼 생각하고 수업을 진행해도 괜찮습니다. 다만, 수업 실연 교실에 마치 실제 학생이 있는 것처럼 느껴지게끔 사실적인 시선 처리가 필요합니다.

Check point #36.
 자신감 있는 태도가 유지되는가?

임용 시험에 합격하면 약 4주 뒤 즉시 현장에 투입됩니다. 그러니 채점관으로서는 '즉시 수업을 맡겨도 걱정 없을 사람'을 뽑고 싶어 할 수밖에 없죠. 다양한 채점 요소들이 있지만 그중에서 '전반적인 인상'을 채점하고자 한다면 자신감이 가장 중요할 것입니다. 왜냐하면 학생 앞에서 자신감이 없는 교사는 우물 앞에 내버려 둔 아이처럼 너무 불안하거든요. 따라서 자신의 전문성을 믿고 자신감 있게 학생들 앞에서 당당한 모습으로 수업을 진행하는 것이 중요합니다.

> **Tip**
>
> 없던 자신감이 갑자기 생기지는 않습니다. 그렇지만 '자신감이 가득 찬 연기'를 할 필요는 있습니다. 'Power pose'라고 불리는 자세를 수업 실연 태도에 녹아낼 수 있도록 연습해 보길 바랍니다. 속으로는 자신감이 없어 벌벌 떨더라도 큰 목소리와 곧은 자세, 여유로운 제스처가 바라보는 사람에게는 자신감이 충만해 보이는 느낌을 들게 합니다.
>
>

TEACHING ENGLISH

두 번째 파트 'TEACHING ENGLISH'는 영어교육론에 관한 부분입니다. 2015개정교육과정까지는 영어과 교과 교육과정으로 '읽기', '듣기', '쓰기', '말하기'의 네 영역을 제시하였으나, 2022개정교육과정에서는 위 네 영역이 '듣기', '읽기', '보기'를 포함하는 '이해(reception) 영역'과 '말하기', '쓰기', '제시하기'를 포함하는 '표현(production) 영역'으로 수정 개편되었습니다. 그리고 수업 실연에서도 이에 맞게 해당 영역의 요소를 가르치는 것이 핵심적으로 등장합니다. 따라서 이번 파트에서는 각각의 영역을 요구하는 문항이 출제되었을 경우 어떤 부분을 중점적으로 고민해야 하는지, 수업 진행은 어떻게 하면 좋을지, 평가는 어떻게 진행하여야 하며, 활동 사이 논리적 연계성은 어떻게 보여주어야 하는지를 알아보도록 하겠습니다.

> **Tip**
>
> 사실상 이 부분부터가 고득점의 핵심 전략이라고 할 수 있습니다. 왜냐하면 대부분 수업 실연 스터디를 보면 '수업에 대한 전반적인 인상'에 관한 피드백만 오갈 뿐 '수업 전문성'에 대하여서는 피드백이 빈약한 경우가 많기 때문입니다. 즉, 반쪽짜리 수업 실연만 준비하고 있는 것이죠! 한편, 이런 모습을 보면 '무엇 하러 그렇게 열심히 1차 시험 때 이론 공부를 열심히 했을까'하는 아쉬움이 남기도 합니다. 이론은 결국 적용하기 위해서 배우는 것이니까요. 따라서 우리는 이제부터 1차 시험을 준비하는 과정에서 열심히 쌓아 올린 이론적인 지식을 바탕으로 2차 시험부터는 실제 상황에 적용하는 연습이 필요합니다. 그리고 이러한 세부적인 기술들은 엄연히 인풋 과정이 필요한 것이기 때문에 미리 익혀두지 않으면 수업 실연에서 나타날 수가 없습니다. 따라서 무작정 수업 실연을 연습하기 전에, 차분한 마음으로 수업 실연에 관한 인풋을 쌓는 시간을 가지셨으면 좋겠습니다. 이 책을 읽고 계시는 모든 분이 꼭 지금부터 알려드릴 다양한 전략들을 자기 것으로 만들어 고득점으로 합격하시기를 바랍니다.

가 Receptive Skills

일반적으로 Receptive Skills는 영어과 교육과정에서 '읽기', '듣기', '보기'를 의미하지만, 수업 실연 체크리스트에서는 'Teaching Vocabulary'도 포함합니다. 따라서 이번 장에서는

'Vocabulary'와 'Reading', 'Listening' 영역이 출제되었을 때 각각 어느 부분을 중점적으로 고민해야 하는지, 그리고 어떻게 하면 수업 실연에서 고득점을 받을 수 있을지 살펴보도록 하겠습니다.

(1) Vocabulary

수업 실연에서 Receptive Skills에 관한 내용이 출제될 때 종종 어휘 학습을 요구하는 경우가 있습니다. 수업 실연 초반부에 등장하는 만큼 가장 명확하고 확실하게 보여주어서 기선 제압을 해야 합니다!

Check point #27.
단어 선택 과정에서 학생 의견이 고려되었는가?

보통은 해당 단어에 밑줄이 쳐져 있지만, 그렇지 않을 때도 있습니다. 이러한 경우는 교사에게 단어 선택 기회가 주어진 것으로, 설명을 완벽하게 잘할 수 있는 좋은 단어를 고를 수 있어야 합니다. 밑줄이 이미 그어져 있더라도 어휘 지도에서는 학생과 상호작용하며 학습자 중심 수업 분위기를 만드는 것이 가장 중요합니다. 이를 위한 간편한 방법은 바로 단어를 선택하는 기회를 학생에게 넘기는 것입니다!

<예시 상황 T-talk>

(Target word : 'stained')

T : ① Alright! We've just finished the 'Quick Search' activity. Did you find any difficult words?

⇩

② Oh, Jihwan! Can you share the difficult word you found?

⇩

③ Did everyone hear what Jihwan said? Yes, thank you, Dongwoo! He said the word 'stained'.

⇩

④ Is there anyone who knows the meaning of the word 'stained'? No one? Alright, then let's start the 'Guessing Game'!

---

①과같이 제일 처음 교사가 'Quick Search' 활동을 진행했다고 가정하고 어려운 단어가 있었는지 학생에게 물어봅니다. 그 후, ②에서처럼, 한 학생이 손을 들었다고 가정하고 그 학생의 이

름을 불러주면서 자신이 찾은 단어를 공유하도록 합니다. 여기까지만 진행하고 바로 교사가 어휘 학습 지도를 진행하여도 되지만, 시간적 여유가 있다면 다음과 같이 조금 더 학생과의 상호작용을 만들 수 있습니다. ③에서 해당 학생이 어렵다고 느낀 단어를 다른 학생의 발화를 통해서 교실 전체에 공유합니다. 그 후 ④에서 'Guessing Game'을 언급하며 교사의 단어 설명이 이어집니다. 위와 같은 단계로 단어 선택 과정에서 학생의 의견을 고려한 수업 실연을 보여줄 수 있습니다.

Tip

위의 ④에서 주목할 만한 다른 부분은, 교사가 반 전체에게 'stained'의 단어 뜻을 아는 학생이 있는지 알아보는 과정이 있다는 것입니다. 이 과정은 두 가지 의미를 지닙니다. 첫 번째로는 교사가 'Peer scaffolding'을 먼저 시도하였다는 것입니다. 학습자 중심 수업에서는 교사의 직접적인 내용 전달을 최소화하고 학생의 배움이 활발히 일어날 수 있도록 촉진해야 하므로 교사가 먼저 단어 뜻을 알려주기 전에 다른 학생을 통해서 해당 내용을 배울 수 있도록 기회를 제공하는 것이 적절합니다. 두 번째로는 해당 단어 설명이 교실 전체를 대상으로 하는 것이 적절한지, 개별 지도가 적절한지 파악하는 과정이 있다는 것입니다. 만약 'Stained'라는 단어를 모르는 학생이 혼자라면 굳이 교실 전체를 대상으로 하지 않고 그 학생에게만 개별적으로 알려주는 것이 더 학습자 중심 수업에 가깝겠죠!

Check point #38.

2개 이상의 교수법을 사용하였는가?

2개 이상의 단어를 가르쳐야 하는 경우, 두 단어 모두 같은 교수법으로 가르치는 것보다 여러 방식의 교수법을 사용할 수 있다는 것을 보여주는 것이 중요합니다. 왜냐하면 여러 개의 단어가 제시된 상황에서 모두 똑같은 방식으로 지도하는 것보다 다양한 교수법을 활용할 수 있는 모습을 보여주는 게 당연히 더 실력이 뛰어난 교사라는 인상을 줄 수밖에 없기 때문입니다. 따라서 이번 'Check point #38'에서는 수업 실연 상황에서 보여주기에 적합한 어휘 지도 방법을 아래와 같이 소개합니다.

1. Context clues

Context clues는 문맥을 활용하는 어휘 지도 전략입니다. 예문을 제공하는 방법도 있으나 수업 실연 상황에서는 판서에 시간을 많이 쓸 수 없고, 예문을 사용하면 교사 중심 수업 및 지루한 인상을 줄 수 있으므로 되도록 학생과 대화 상황을 가정하여 진행합니다.

<예시 상황 T-talk>

(Target word : 'vividly')

T : ① Hyunjung, what was the lunch menu today?

⇩

② Yes, it was cream spaghetti. So you are remembering today's lunch menu very 'vividly'.

⇩

③ So, can you guess the meaning of 'vividly'?

⇩

④ Wow, that was right Hyunjung! Did everyone hear what Hyunjung just said? She said 'remember vividly' means 'remember clearly'!

⇩

⑤ Then, Hyunjung, can you make a sentence with the word 'vividly'?

⇩

⑥ Great! Now I can see that you just 'vividly' understood the word.

'vividly'를 Context clue를 이용하여 가르치기 위해 ①에서 학생과 대화 상황을 가정합니다. 그 후, ②에서 점심 메뉴를 잘 기억하고 있다는 상황을 Context clue로 제공하며 'vividly'가 직접 사용된 문장을 T-talk로 제시합니다. 이후 ③에서 해당 단어의 의미를 유추할 수 있는지 질문합니다. ④와 같이 학생이 유추를 성공적으로 해내었다고 가정하고 반 전체 학생에게 'vividly'는 'clearly'와 의미가 비슷함을 알려줍니다. 이때 주의해야 할 점은 'vividly = clearly'가 교사가 알려준 것이 아니라 학생이 유추를 통해 알게 된 점이라는 부분을 드러내야 한다는 것입니다. 그 후 ⑤에서 학생에게 직접 문장을 만들어 보도록 함으로써 CCQ를 진행합니다. 마지막으로 ⑥에서 교사가 직접 대화 상황에서 Target word('vividly')를 사용하여 재치 있게 마무리합니다.

Tip

Context clues는 위와 같이 시간이 오래 걸리는 어휘 지도 전략이기 때문에 수업 실연 상황에서는 되도록 선택하지 않았습니다. 어휘 지도는 짧고 굵게, 그렇지만 임팩트 있고 확실하게 지나가는 게 가장 중요하거든요! 한편, Context clues는 수업 실연 지시 사항에 처음부터 명시되어 출제되는 경우가 많습니다. 따라서 이 부분을 꼭 익혀두시고, 어휘 지도는 5분 이내로 짧게 끝내는 것을 목표로 연습하는 것이 바람직합니다.

2. Visual Aids

두 번째 방법 Visual Aids는 말 그대로 시각 자료를 활용하는 것입니다. 교사가 사진을 준비할 수도 있고 그림을 그릴 수도 있죠. 사진을 준비한다면 스크린을 활용한 어휘 지도를 진행할 수 있으나, 그림을 그린다면 최대한 간단하게 판서해야 합니다.

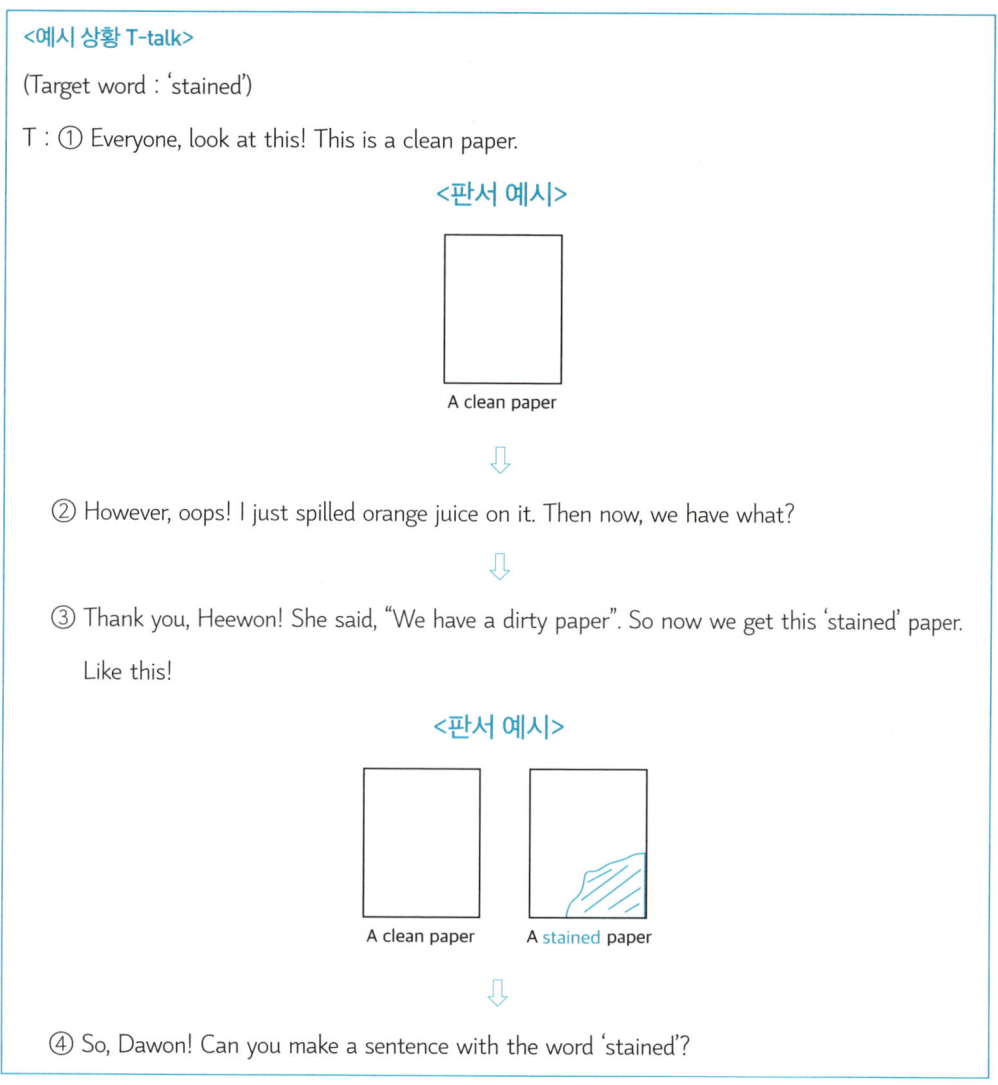

'stained'라는 단어는 그림으로 표현하기 가장 적절합니다. ①에서 깔끔한 종이를 그리며 'a clean paper'라고 언급합니다. 그리고 이어지는 ②에서 교사가 오렌지 주스를 엎질렀다는 상황을 가정하며 학생과 상호작용을 진행합니다. 여기서 이왕이면 약간의 연기(?)를 곁들여서 몰입감 있게 수업을 진행하여도 좋겠죠! 그 후 ③에서 자연스럽게 학생으로부터 'dirty'라는 단어를 유도하며 오늘의 Target word인 'stained'를 언급합니다. 그림 역시 다른 색깔을 이용하면 훨씬 더 인상적인 어휘 지도 수업 실연을 보여줄 수 있습니다. 그 후 ④의 T-talk처럼 CCQ를 진행하며 마무리합니다.

> **Tip**
>
> 제가 가장 자주 사용했던 방법입니다. 그림을 통해 설명하면 가장 직관적이고 인상적인 수업 실연이 되기 때문입니다. 말로 설명할 필요가 없으므로 교사로서는 T-talk의 부담이 덜할 뿐만 아니라 학생으로서는 훨씬 더 이해가 빠릅니다.

3. Word analysis

Word analysis는 접두사나 접미사에 주목하여 단어의 의미를 연상하게끔 유도하는 어휘 지도 전략입니다. 실제 학교 현장에서 가장 많이 쓰이고 있는 방법이죠!

<예시 상황 T-talk>

(Target word : 'unbelievable')

T : ① The word 'unbelievable' is made up of two parts. Can you guess?

② Great! Suhyun! The two parts are 'un' and 'believable'. 'Un' means 'Can't'. So, if 'believable' means 'we can believe.', can you guess the meaning of 'unbelievable'?

③ Amazing, Jongmin! It means 'we can't believe.'

⇩

④ Alright! So, can you make a sentence with the word 'unbelievable'?

접두사 'un'은 Word analysis를 사용하기에 가장 간편합니다. 위 ①에서 교사가 먼저 'unbelievable'이라는 단어가 두 부분으로 나뉜다는 사실을 알려주고 그 두 부분이 어떤 것인지 유추하게 합니다. ②에서 학생이 성공적으로 두 부분을 유추했다는 것을 가정하고 'un'이 'can't'라고 알려줍니다. 곧이어 만약 'believable'이라는 단어가 'we can believe.'의 의미라면 'unbelievable'은 어떤 의미가 될지 물어봅니다. 그 후 ③에서 학생이 해당 단어의 의미를 성공적으로 유추했다고 가정하며 상호작용을 이어갑니다. 마지막으로 ④에서 학생에게 해당 단어를 포함한 문장을 만들어 보라고 권유하며 CCQ를 진행합니다.

4. Word relations

Word relations는 Target word와 함께 동의어나 반의어, 상위어나 하위어 관계에 있는 단어를 언급함으로써 목표 단어의 의미를 유추할 수 있게끔 하는 어휘 지도 방법입니다. 여기서 주의해야 할 점은 교사가 제시하는 단어의 수준이 Target word보다 훨씬 더 쉬워야 한다는 것입니다. 따라서 해당 단어가 100% 완벽한 동의어 관계일 필요는 없습니다. 교실에 있는 학생 수준에 맞는 단어를 제시하여야 하므로 70% 정도만 의미가 통하더라도 수업 실연에서는 큰 문제가 없습니다.

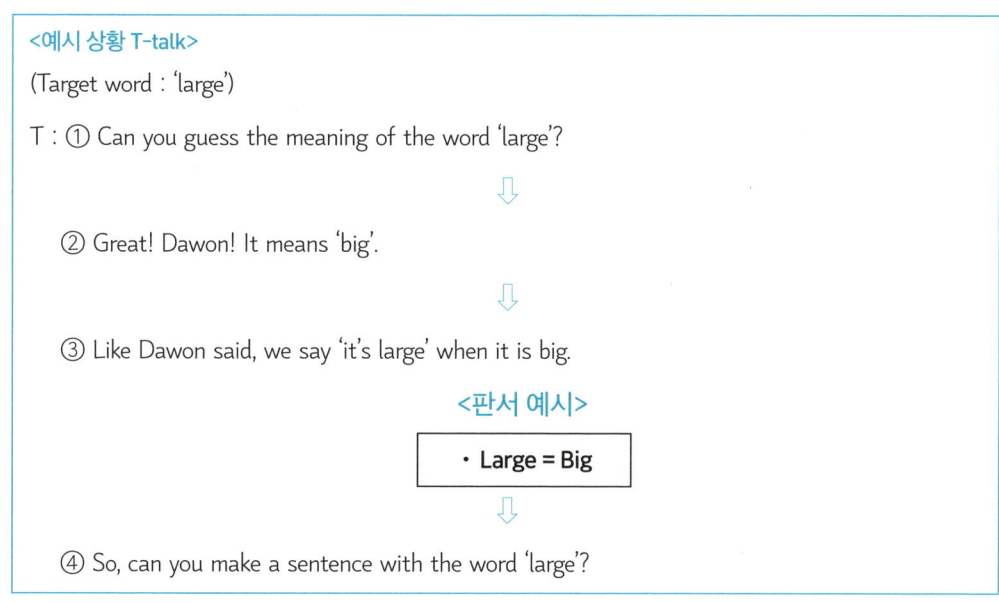

<예시 상황 T-talk>
(Target word : 'large')
T : ① Can you guess the meaning of the word 'large'?

② Great! Dawon! It means 'big'.

③ Like Dawon said, we say 'it's large' when it is big.

<판서 예시>
· Large = Big

④ So, can you make a sentence with the word 'large'?

위의 ①에서 교사가 Target word를 소개합니다. 그 후 ②에서 High-level student가 있다고 가정한 후 해당 학생이 동의어 'big'을 언급합니다. 그 후 ③에서 교사가 전체 학생을 대상으로 다시 한번 해당 단어의 의미를 알려주면서 간략하게 판서합니다. 마지막으로 ④에서 CCQ를 진행하며 마무리합니다.

한편, 아래와 같이 상위어/하위어를 이용하는 것도 좋은 방법이 될 수 있습니다.

<예시 상황 T-talk>

(Target word : 'Fruit')

T : ① Can you guess the meaning of the word 'Fruit'?

⇩

② Let me give you a hint. Apples, bananas and grapes are examples of 'fruit'.

<판서 예시>

- Fruit
  - apples, bananas
    grapes, ...

⇩

③ Then, if you understand its meaning, is there anyone who can tell me one example of 'fruit'?

⇩

④ Thank you, Suhyun! 'Melon' is another example of 'fruit'.

<판서 예시>

- Fruit
  - apples, bananas
    grapes, **melons**

위 ①에서 먼저 목표 단어 'fruit'를 소개한 다음 ②에서 힌트를 제공합니다. 여기서 힌트는 모든 학생이 쉽게 알아챌 수 있는 단어를 제시하여야 합니다. 그리고 이와 동시에 판서를 통해 상위어와 하위어의 관계를 나타냅니다. 그 후 ③에서 학생과의 상호작용 및 CCQ를 진행합니다. 위의 예시와 같이 상위어/하위어일 경우 학생에게 또 다른 예시를 들어보게 함으로써 간단명료하게 이해점검 확인을 할 수 있습니다. 마지막으로 ④에서 'Fruit'의 또 다른 예시를 학생이 성공적으로 제시하였다고 가정하고 다른 색깔로 판서합니다. 위와 같은 과정을 통해서 학생이 'Fruit'는 '과일'을 의미한다는 것을 정확하게 이해하였음을 보여줄 수 있습니다.

> **Tip**
>
> Word relations는 시간을 가장 절약할 수 있는 어휘 지도 방법입니다. 따라서 수업 실연의 전체 분량을 고려할 때 어휘 지도에 시간을 많이 할당할 수 없는 경우라면 동의어나 반의어를 사용하는 것을 고려 해야 합니다.

5. Realia

Realia는 실제 사물을 이용한 어휘 학습 방법입니다. 대표적으로는 책상을 가리키며 'desk'라고 하거나 물병을 보여주며 'water bottle'이라고 설명하는 것이죠. 그러나 수업 실연에서는 조금 더 인상적인 진행을 위해 사물을 직접적으로 나타내는 단어 말고도 얼마든지 교실 내 물건을 이용하여 목표 단어를 설명할 수 있습니다.

<예시 상황 T-talk>

(Target word : 'drop')

T : ① Can you guess the meaning of the word 'drop'?

⇩

② Okay, let me give you a hint. Look at me! I am holding a pen.

⇩

③ (쥐고 있던 펜을 놓으며) Oh, I 'dropped' the pen!

⇩

④ Now do you get the meaning of 'drop'? Then, show me you 'drop' something!

⇩

⑤ Great! Hyunjung just dropped her eraser!

먼저 ①에서 목표 단어에 대해 알고 있는 학생이 있는지 물어봅니다. 그리고 ②에서 힌트를 준다고 하며 자연스럽게 학생들의 Guessing을 유도합니다. 이때 펜을 들고 있는 모습이 상상되도록 제스처를 취해줍니다. 곧이어 ③에서 쥐고 있던 펜을 떨어뜨리며 'drop'을 설명합니다. 그리고 ④에서 학생의 이해 정도를 점검하기 위해 CCQ를 한 뒤, ⑤를 통해서 학생이 'drop'의 의미를 이해하였음을 보여줍니다.

Tip

Realia는 실제 교실에서도 많이 사용하는 방법입니다. 왜냐하면 실제 물건을 이용할 때 순간적인 수업 몰입도가 증가하기 때문입니다. 따라서 수업 실연에서도 적절한 제스처와 함께 Realia를 활용한 단어 지도를 진행하면 아주 인상적인 모습을 보여줄 수 있습니다!

Check point #39.

 학생이 Guessing을 성공했는가?

위 예시 상황에서 공통점을 알아차렸을 수 있었을 것입니다. 바로 교사가 정답을 이야기하는 것이 아니라, 학생이 해당 단어의 의미를 이야기한다는 것입니다! 이렇게 학습자 중심 수업에서는 학습자가 스스로 배울 내용을 알아차릴 수 있도록 교사가 환경을 제공해야 합니다. 이러한 관점을 어휘 지도에 접목하면 교사가 'A는 B라는 뜻이야.'라고 직접적으로 언급하는 것이 아니라, 'A의 뜻을 한번 맞춰볼까?'라고 시작하면서 다양한 힌트를 제공하고 학생이 직접 그 의미(B)를 유추하게끔 해보는 것이죠. 따라서 수업 실연 상황에서도 목표 단어에 대한 의미를 설명할 때 'Check point #38'에 등장한 사례와 같이 학생의 이름을 불러주면서 학생이 유추에 성공하였음을 보여주는 것이 중요합니다!

> <예시 상황 T-talk>
> T : Thank you Dongwoo! Did you hear what Dongwoo just said? He said A means B!

Tip

어휘 지도에 너무 많은 시간을 쓰지 않도록 주의해야 합니다. 요즘에는 출제 빈도가 낮아졌지만, 어휘 지도가 등장한다고 하더라도 5분 이내로 짧고 굵게 보여주고 넘어가는 연습 하여야 합니다. 초반부에 등장한다고 너무 긴장한 탓에 시간이 지체되기 시작하면 전체적인 수업 실연 밸런스가 무너지게 됩니다. 어휘 지도는 이어서 나올 Main activity를 준비하는 과정일 뿐이므로, 시간 배분 연습도 함께하는 것이 중요합니다!

(2) Reading

Reading은 수업 실연에서 매번 출제되는 영역입니다. 게다가 초반 50%를 차지하는 Main activity로 등장하곤 하죠. 따라서 이 부분은 반드시 충분한 연습을 통해서 자신감을 쌓아두는 것이 중요합니다.

Check point #40.

 Reading Strategy가 사용되었는가?

Reading에는 다양한 전략이 있지만, 수업 실연에서는 Skimming과 Scanning만 알아도 충분합니다.

1. Skimming

Skimming은 전체적으로 글을 빠르게 훑어보고 전반적인 주제를 파악하는 데 사용되는 읽기 전략입니다. 수업 실연에서는 Main idea를 찾는 활동에서 언급하기 적합합니다.

> <예시 상황 T-talk>
>
> T : ① So far, we just learned those difficult words. Then, are you ready to jump into the text?
>
> ⇩
>
> ② Great! So from now on, we are going to read the text for the main idea.
>
> ⇩
>
> ③ To find the main idea, do we have to read quickly or slowly?
>
> ⇩
>
> ④ Yes, Heewon! Quickly! I'll give you 1 minute. Go!

먼저 ①에서 어휘 학습이 끝났다는 것을 전제하고 이제 읽기 준비가 되었는지 학생에게 물어봅니다. ('Check point #8'에서 이미 살펴본 부분이죠!) 그다음 ②에서 지금부터 읽기 활동이 시작됨을 알리고, Main idea를 찾을 예정임을 안내합니다. ③부터 읽기 전략에 대한 언급이 시작됩니다. 이미 학생들과 읽기 수업을 여러 번 해보았다는 것을 가정하며 'Skimming' 전략을 암시하는 질문을 합니다. 여기서 'Skimming'이라는 단어는 전문용어이기 때문에 되도록 학생 수준에서 알기 쉬운 방식으로 풀어서 설명합니다. 그 후 ④에서 학생의 이름을 부르며 'Skimming' 전략을 이해하고 있음을 보여주고 1분 이내의 짧은 시간을 준 후 읽기 활동을 시작합니다.

2. Scanning

Scanning은 Skimming과 달리 이름이나 날짜 등과 같은 세부 내용에 관한 정보를 찾기 위해 사용하는 읽기 전략입니다. 수업 실연에서는 Main idea를 함께 찾는 과정에서 대략적인 위치가 어디 있는지 학생들이 이미 파악했다고 가정하고, Detailed information을 찾을 때 사용합니다.

<예시 상황 T-talk>

T : ① Okay so, the main idea was 'What makes a great leader.' Then, are you ready to read more about it?

⇩

② Awesome! So, everyone! Look at the screen there. Jihwan at the back, do you see the screen? ⋯ Alright! What do you see on the screen? ⋯ Yes, there is a question! ⋯ Can you read it for us, Jihwan? ⋯ Thank you! It was 'What was the three characteristics of a great leader?' ⋯ Great!

⇩

③ So we are going to read the text again, to find the answer. Are you ready?

⇩

④ Great. To find the answer, do you have to read everything closely? ⋯ No. Just read closely what you need.

⇩

⑤ Alright, Dongwoo! What do we have to do? ⋯ Yes, we need to find the three characteristics of a great leader. I will give you 2 minutes. Go!

위 ①에서 함께 Main idea를 찾았으니, 글을 더 자세히 읽을 준비가 되었는지 물어봅니다. 이렇게 항상 이전 활동의 의미를 되새기면서 다음 활동으로 넘어가야 동기 부여와 활동 간 연계성이 드러나기 때문에 T-talk로 강조하는 게 중요합니다! 그 후 ②에서 교사가 스크린을 통해 질문을 보여줍니다. (여기서 'Check point #4'에서 언급하였던 TIP을 활용해도 좋겠죠!) 맨 뒤 학생의 이름을 불러주며 스크린에 무엇이 보이는지, 그리고 그 질문은 무엇인지 읽어보게 함으로써 수업 실연을 진행합니다. ③에서 글을 읽는 목적이 질문에 답을 하기 위함임을 되새기고 ④에서 'Scanning' 전략을 언급합니다. 여기서도 마찬가지로 학생의 눈높이에 맞도록 최대한 간단하고 이해하기 쉽게 설명합니다. 마지막으로 ⑤에서 학생 이름을 부르고 우리가 글을 다시 읽는 목적을 상기시키며 CCQ를 진행합니다.

Check point #41.

Title에 대한 언급을 하였는가?

Reading text에서 제목은 글의 전체적인 내용을 집약적으로 드러내는 아주 중요한 요소이자 글쓰기의 기본입니다. 그러나 대부분 제목을 마치 당연한 것으로 여겨 아무런 언급을 하지 않고 지나치곤 합니다. 따라서 우리는 이러한 부분에 대한 경각심을 가질 필요가 있습니다!

읽기 수업에서 Title에 대해서 언급하면 훨씬 더 Main idea를 파악하기가 쉽고, 만약 문제에 Title이 제공되지 않았다면 Main idea를 파악하는 활동 후 간략하게 제목을 만들어 보는 활동으로 연계하여도 인상적인 수업 실연이 됩니다.

<예시 상황 T-talk>

Title이 있는 상황

T1 : (Main idea를 찾은 후) Dawon! Can you read the title for us? … Thank you! Like this, we can see that the title has close relationship with the main idea.

Title이 없는 상황

T2 : Do you see the title? … No. Then, why don't we make a title? … To make a title, what do we have to know first? … Thank you, Dawon! Dawon said we need to find the main idea!

위 예시 상황에서 T1은 Title이 있는 상황이고 T2는 Title이 없는 상황입니다. Title이 있는 경우에는 Main idea를 찾은 후 제목을 언급하며 서로 관련성이 깊음을 보여줄 수 있습니다. 이 때 Main idea 자체를 제목과 비슷하게 설정하면 더 좋겠죠! 한편, Title이 없을 때는 T2와 같이 제목을 함께 만들어 보자는 제안으로 Main idea를 찾는 활동과 연계할 수 있습니다.

위 T1과 T2의 사례에서 확인할 수 있는 것처럼. Main idea와 Title의 연계성을 강조하면 훨씬 더 짜임새 있고 전문적인 Reading 수업의 모습을 보여줄 수 있습니다!

Tip

Keyword와 Title을 연결할 수도 있습니다. 학생에게 빠르게 글을 읽어보게 한 다음 반복해서 등장하는 단어를 말해보게 하는 활동을 통해 키워드를 찾고, 이를 Main idea 찾는 데 활용할 수 있습니다. 더 나아가 이를 Title과 연결하여 설명할 수도 있죠! 여기서 찾은 Keyword가 Title에 포함되어 있도록 설계하면 더 논리적 연계성이 튼튼한 수업 실연이 됩니다.

Check point #42.
♟ Mixed-level을 고려하였는가?

읽기 수업은 첫 번째 Main Activity로 채점관이 가장 관심 있게 지켜보는 부분 중 하나입니다. 따라서 여기에서 적절하게 Circulation을 진행하며 Mixed-level을 고려하고 있다는 점을 효과적으로 보여주어야 합니다. ('Check point #23~#25'를 참고하세요!)

1. Low-level

읽기 지도에서 Low-level을 고려하는 가장 간단한 방법은 Word list를 제공하는 것입니다.

> <예시 상황 T-talk>
>
> T : ① Oh, Suhyun, do you have any problem?
>
> ⇩
>
> ② Okay, there are so many difficult words.
>
> ⇩
>
> ③ Then, why don't you look at the backside of this worksheet. … What do you see? … Yes, there is a 'Word list'!
>
> ⇩
>
> ④ With this word list, can you read by yourself? … Awesome! You are doing great!

Circulation 도중 ①에서처럼 어려움을 겪는 학생이 있다고 가정합니다. 그 후 ②에서 해당 학생이 겪고 있는 어려움에 대하여 파악합니다. 곧이어 ③에서 학습지 뒷면에 Word list가 있음을 알려주며 Scaffolding을 진행합니다. ('Check point #1'을 참고하세요!) 마지막으로 ④에서 Word list가 있다면 스스로 할 수 있는지 묻고, 격려와 함께 Low-level treatment를 마무리합니다.

2. High-level

Mixed-level이므로 Low-level뿐만 아니라 High-level 학생도 고려해야 합니다. 그러나 읽기 지도에서 High-level 학생에게 추가 읽기 과제를 부여하는 게 수업 실연에서 조금 과장되는 것 같아 마땅한 방법을 떠올리기 쉽지 않습니다. 이럴 때 가장 무난한 것이 바로 Peer scaffolding입니다.

> <예시 상황 T-talk>
>
> T : ① Oh, Hyunsu, have you already finished answering those questions?
>
> ⇩
>
> ② Wow! You are such a quick reader!
>
> ⇩
>
> ③ Then, why don't you help your partner, Suhyun? … Suhyun said she needed some help.
>
> ⇩
>
> ④ Awesome! Like this, friends can be a better teacher!

'Check point #2'와 유사한 예시입니다! Finding detailed information 활동 상황을 가정한 뒤, 교사의 Circulation중 ①에서 나타나는 바와 같이 High-level 학생이 주어진 과제를 일찍 끝냈다고 가정합니다. 그리고 ②와 같이 칭찬을 해줍니다. 이처럼 추가 과제를 제시하기 전에는 반드시 해당 학생에게 교사의 긍정적인 피드백을 함께 제공해주어야 합니다. 왜냐하면 '이것 끝냈으니, 이거 해!'라고 하는 것은 빨리 끝낸 것이 불이익이 되는 상황이 되어 버리기 때문입니다. 그 후 ③에서 자신의 파트너를 도와주는 것을 제안합니다. 여기서 짝꿍이 이미 도움을 요청했던 상황이라는 것을 전제해야 하므로 'Suhyun said she needed some help'라는 T-talk도 추가하였습니다. 마지막으로 ④에서 'Friends can be a better teacher!'이라는 T-talk로 Peer scaffolding을 강조합니다.

이렇게 위 ①~④까지 진행하면 High-level 학생도 고려하고, Peer scaffolding도 제공하는 일거양득의 수업 실연을 진행할 수 있습니다!

Check point #43.

♟ Comprehension Check가 이루어졌는가?

읽기 수업에서 Comprehension Check은 너무 중요합니다. 첫 번째 Main activity일 뿐 아니라, 해당 수업 실연의 전반적인 Topic이므로 이후 Productive Skills 영역과 연계되기 때문입니다. 따라서 본문 내용에 대한 이해가 잘 이루어졌는지 CCQ를 진행하고 가는 것이 중요하죠!

다만 여기서 CCQ를 어렵게 생각할 필요가 전혀 없습니다. 바로 'Finding detailed information' 활동이 CCQ에 해당하기 때문입니다! 보통은 수업 실연 지시 사항에 '세부 정보를 찾는 활동을 진행하라'는 지시 사항이 주어지기 마련이지만, 최근에는 이와 같은 지시 사항이 출제되지 않는 경향이 우세합니다.

만약 과거 흐름과 같이 '세부 정보를 찾는 활동을 진행하라'는 지시 사항이 요구된다면, 'Check point #40'의 Scanning 예시 상황처럼 실시하면 CCQ에 관한 부분도 함께 해결됩니다.

한편, 요즘 수업 실연과 같이 세부 정보를 찾으라는 지시 사항이 없는 경우에는 시간 관계상 아래 예시대로 학생과의 상호작용을 통해 아주 간단하게 CCQ를 진행하였음만 보여주고 다음 활동으로 넘어가는 것이 적절합니다.

<예시 상황 T-talk>
T : ① Okay, we just read about the leadership.

⇩

② Is there anyone who can tell us about three characteristics of a great leader?

⇩

③ Wow, what a loud voice! Yes it was 'Vision', 'Honesty' and 'Empathy'.

⇩

④ Alright! So far, we read about the leadership and the characteristics of a great leader. Then, are you ready to move on to the next part?

위 ①에서 교사가 리더십에 관한 글을 읽었음을 상기해줍니다. 그리고 ②에서 곧바로 학생과의 상호작용을 통해 Detailed information에 대한 정보를 물어봅니다. 그 후 ③에서 학생 1명의 이름을 부르는 것 대신 'What a loud voice!'라는 T-talk로 교실 전체가 해당 내용에 대해서 대답하였음을 보여줍니다. 마지막으로 ④에서 읽기 내용을 다시 한번 정리하고 다음 부분으로 넘어갈 준비가 되었는지 물어봅니다.

이렇게 세부 정보를 찾는 활동이 지시 사항으로 등장하지 않을 때는 위 ①~④ 단계로 T-talk를 간략하게 구성함으로써 Reading에 대한 CCQ를 진행하였음을 보여줄 수 있습니다.

(3) Listening

Receptive skills에는 Reading과 Listening이 있지만 사실상 수업 실연에서는 Reading만 출제되고 있습니다. 물론 앞으로도 그럴 가능성이 커 보이지만 방심해서는 안 되겠죠!

Check point #44.
Listening Strategy가 사용되었는가?

듣기 영역 역시도 Listening Strategy를 가르치는 것이 중요합니다. 왜냐하면, 학습자 중심 수업에서 교사는 Director가 아니라 Facilitator 역할을 해야 하기 때문입니다. 즉 물고기를 잡아다 주어서는 안 되고, 물고기를 잡는 방법을 알려 줘야 한다는 것이죠! 따라서 학습자의 주도적인 지식 습득을 위해서는 해당 영역에 대한 직접적인 지식 주입이 아니라, 스스로 지식을 습득할 수 있도록 하는 적절한 전략 지도가 반드시 이루어져야 합니다.

다만 수업 실연 상황에서 듣기 전략을 보여주는 것은 실제 수업 상황보다 더 어려움이 많을 수밖에 없습니다. 게다가, 수업 실연에서 Listening이 출제된다면 그 자체로 아주 화제가 될 만한 변화이므로 실험적인 문제가 출제되기는 어려우리라 생각합니다. 따라서 현실적이고 현명하게 Listening 영역을 준비하는 데에는 Note-taking 전략을 소개하는 것만으로도 수업 실연에서는 충분하다고 생각합니다.

'Note-taking'

<예시 상황 T-talk>

T : ① So far, we just checked those difficult words. Then, are you ready for Today's listening?

⇩

② Great! So from now on, we are going to listen to the dialogue and we need to find what they are talking about. Sounds good?

⇩

③ Okay then, before we start, while listening, what should we do?

⇩

④ Yes, Hyunjung! We need to take notes! Make sure you write down the repeated words, okay? Are you ready? Let's begin!

먼저 ①에서 단어 지도가 이루어졌다고 가정하고 오늘 듣기 수업을 할 준비가 되었는지 학생에게 물어봅니다. 그 후 ②에서 듣기 유형(Dialogue, Monologue, Lecture 등)에 관한 언급 후, 목표(Objective)를 알려줍니다. 여기서는 가장 무난한 'Dialogue'와 '대화의 주제'를 찾는 것을 듣기 활동 목표로 설정하였습니다. 이어지는 ③에서 듣기 전략에 대하여 언급할 것임을 알려주고 ④에서 학생과의 상호작용을 통해 Note-taking 전략을 소개합니다. 또한, '대화의 주제'를 파악하는 것이 목표이므로 반복되는 단어를 들어보게끔 안내합니다.

> **Tip**
>
> 위 ①~④를 보면 T-talk의 흐름이 읽기 수업과 비슷하다는 것을 알아차릴 수 있으실 겁니다. 이처럼 Listening도 결국 Reading text를 눈으로 읽는 것임이 아니라, 귀로 듣는 것임을 이해하고 같은 방식으로 접근하여 수업 실연 준비의 효율성을 높이시길 바랍니다!

Check point #45.
Input을 반복하여 제시하였는가?

듣기 지도에서는 인풋을 여러 번 반복하여 제시하는 것이 중요합니다. 간혹 시험 상황처럼 '한 번만 들려주어야 되는 것 아닌가?' 생각할 수 있습니다. 그러나, Listening은 엄연한 Receptive Skills이므로 학생이 해당 내용을 이해하기 위해서는 반복 청취가 중요함을 잊어서는 안 됩니다!

> <예시 상황 T-talk>
> T : ① (1회 듣기가 끝난 후) How much did you hear? Like 40% or 50%? Don't worry. I'll give you another chance. Let's listen to the dialogue again. Ready? Go!
>
>
>
> ② Okay, we just listened to the same dialogue twice. Then can you answer the question? Which items did the girl have to buy?

위 예시 상황과 같이 ①에서 1회 듣기가 끝난 후 교사는 학생의 이해 정도를 물어보고, 걱정하지 말라는 말과 함께 자신감을 심어주며 한 번 더 들려줍니다. 그리고 ②에서 같은 담화문을 두 번 들려주었다는 것을 강조하며, 듣기 전에 언급한 목표(위 예시에서는 Listening for detailed information)을 달성하였는지 확인합니다.

> **Tip**
>
> 가능성이 희박하겠지만 만약 Listening이 출제된다면 기존 Reading의 형식에서 많이 벗어나기는 힘들 것으로 감히 예상합니다. 즉, 'Listening for Main idea' → 'Listening for detailed information'으로 진행될 확률이 높다는 것이죠. 따라서 Reading과 마찬가지로 제일 처음에 Note-taking 전략을 소개하며 Main idea를 찾게 하고, 스크린을 통해 Detailed information을 요구하는 Question을 교사가 소개한 뒤, Listening for detailed information 활동을 진행하는 순서를 연습하는 것이 현명하리라 생각합니다. 그리고 실제 학생 수준에서는 생각보다 한 번에 세부 정보를 듣고 이해하는 것이 어려우므로 'Check point #45'와 같이 Listening for detailed information 단계에서 교사가 여러 번 들려주는 모습을 보여준다면 더 능숙한 수업 실연이 될 것입니다!

Check point #46.

♟ Mixed-level을 고려하였는가?

Reading과 마찬가지로 Listening도 Mixed-level을 고려한 모습을 보여주어야 합니다. 실제 교실 환경에서는 학생들의 수준이 읽기보다 듣기에서 훨씬 더 많이 벌어지는 경향이 있으므로 수업 실연 상황에서도 Mixed-level treatment가 예외가 될 수는 없습니다!

1. Low-level

듣기 수업에서는 Low-level 학생에게 Script와 Word list를 제공하는 것이 가장 직접적인 도움이 될 수 있습니다.

<예시 상황 T-talk>

T : ① Oh, Dongwoo, do you have any problem?

② Oh I see. The conversation is too fast to follow.

③ Then, why don't you look at the backside of this worksheet. … What do you see? … Yes, there is a 'Listening script' and 'Word list'!

④ With this script and word list, can you do it by yourself, this time? … Awesome! You are doing great!

전체적으로 Reading과 유사한 상황으로 진행됩니다. 첫 번째 Listening이 종료되고 두 번째 Listening을 시작하기 전, ①에서 학생이 어려움을 겪고 있다고 가정하고 도움이 필요한지 묻습니다. 그리고 ②에서 해당 학생의 어려움을 파악하고, 이어지는 ③에서 'Listening script'와 'Word list'를 언급하며 교사가 적절한 Scaffolding을 제공하고 있음을 보여줍니다. 마지막으로 ④에서 위와 같은 도움이 있으면 스스로 할 수 있는지 묻고 학생을 격려해준 뒤 교사의 Scaffolding을 마무리합니다.

2. High-level

듣기 수업에서 High-level 학생들을 고려하는 방법은 여러 가지가 있습니다. 조금 더 Detailed information을 요구하는 추가 질문(Extended questions)을 제공할 수도 있고, 핵심 문장에 대한 빈칸 학습지를 제공하고 Dictation을 해볼 수도 있죠. 그러나 이러한 추가 과제는 Productive skills 영역에서 충분히 보여줄 수 있으므로 Listening에서는 Reading과 마찬가지로 Peer scaffolding으로 High-level treatment가 진행됨을 보여주는 것이 가장 효율적이라고 생각합니다.

> <예시 상황 T-talk>
>
> T : ① Oh, Dongwoo, have you already finished answering the question?
>
> ⇩
>
> ② Wow! You are such a great listener!
>
> ⇩
>
> ③ Then, why don't you help your partner, Wonhee, this time? … Wonhee said she needed some help. You can help her by sharing your notes.
>
> ⇩
>
> ④ Awesome! Like this, friends can be a better teacher!

먼저 ①에서 High-level 학생이 주어진 과제를 일찍 끝냈다고 가정하고, ②에서 칭찬을 해줍니다. 그리고 ③에서 이번 듣기에서는 자신의 파트너를 도와줄 것을 제안합니다. 여기서도 마찬가지로 'Wonhee'가 도움이 필요하다는 상황을 전제하였고, 듣기 상황임을 고려하여 'by sharing your notes'라는 현실적인 Peer scaffolding 방법도 제시하였습니다. 마지막으로 ④에서 Reading과 같이 'Friends can be a better teacher!'이라는 T-talk로 Peer scaffolding을 강조하며 마무리합니다.

> **Tip**
>
> Listening 상황에서는 Circulation을 하며 학생과 대화하는 것이 불가능합니다. 교사가 한 학생과 대화를 하면, 다른 학생의 듣기에 방해될 수밖에 없기 때문입니다. 이러한 상황 설정의 제약으로 출제 확률이 더 희박하다고 생각하긴 하지만, Mixed-level treatment는 반드시 Circulation 상황에서만 이루어지는 것이 아닙니다. 'Check point #45'와 같이 Listening에서는 2회 이상 input 제공을 전제하기 때문에 첫 번째 듣기가 끝난 후 Low-level 학생을 빠르게 파악하여 간단하게 대화를 나눈 후, 두 번째 듣기를 시작할 수 있죠. 마찬가지로 High-level 학생은 첫 번째 듣기에서 이미 문제에 대한 답을 다 찾았으면 두 번째 듣기에 대한 동기가 사라지므로 이를 위한 적절한 Treatment로 Peer scaffolding을 보여주는 게 필요합니다. 따라서 Listening에서의 Mixed-level treatment는 전체적으로 Reading과 유사하되, Reading이 Circulation 도중에 진행되는 것이라면 Listening은 First listening과 Second listening 사이에 진행되는 것이라고 정리할 수 있습니다.
>
>

Check point #47.

♟ Comprehension Check가 이루어졌는가?

Listening이 단순히 Schema activation이 아니라 Reading을 대체하여 Main activity의 분량을 차지하며 출제된다면 듣기 내용에 대한 Comprehension Check도 당연히 이루어져야 합니다. 해당 주제가 앞으로의 수업 실연 활동을 관통하는 내용이 될 것이기 때문입니다.

Reading과 마찬가지로 Listening에서도 수업 실연 지시 사항에 '세부 정보를 찾기 위한 듣기(Listening for detailed information)'가 명확하게 드러나있다면 해당 활동을 진행하는 것으로 CCQ를 해결할 수 있습니다.

그러나 만약 이러한 지시 사항이 요구되지 않았다면 아래와 같이 간단한 학생과의 interaction으로 CCQ를 진행하고 넘어가는 것이 바람직합니다.

> <예시 상황 T-talk>
>
> T : ① Okay, we just listened to the dialogue about saving the Earth.
>
> ⇩
>
> ② Is there anyone who can tell us what we should do for the Earth?
>
> ⇩
>
> ③ Wow, what a loud voice! Yes it was 'Reduce', 'Reuse' and 'Recycle'.
>
> ⇩
>
> ④ Alright! So far, we listened to the students' conversation about 3R for saving the Earth. Then, are you ready to move on to the next part?

위 ①에서 교사가 'Saving the Earth'에 관한 대화를 들었다고 언급합니다. 그 후 ②에서 학생과의 상호작용을 가정하며 해당 듣기에 대한 Detailed information을 물어봅니다. 마찬가지로 Reading에서 살펴본 바와 같이 ③에서 'What a loud voice!'라는 표현으로 교실 전체가 해당 내용에 대하여 이해하였음을 보여줍니다. 마지막으로 ④에서 듣기 내용을 다시 한번 정리하고 다음 부분으로 넘어갈 준비가 되었는지 물어봅니다.

Productive skills

수업 실연에서 Receptive Skills가 전반전이라면 Productive skills는 후반전입니다. 전반부에 소개된 주제를 바탕으로 후반부에는 'Speaking'이나 'Writing' 활동을 진행하며 배운 내용을 직접 활용해보는 수업이 진행됩니다. Receptive Skills에서 'Reading', 'Listening'과 더불어 'Vocabulary'가 포함되었듯이, Productive skills에서는 'Speaking', 'Writing'과 더불어 'Grammar'도 포함됩니다.

(1) Grammar

'문법'이라고 하면 두려움부터 생기는 경우가 많습니다. 왜냐하면, 학창 시절에 배운 문법을 떠올리면 복잡하고, 어렵고, 지루한 것으로 생각하기 마련이기 때문입니다. 그러나 현재 영어 교과서에는 우리가 겪은 것만큼 문법 자체에 대한 설명이 많지 않습니다. 문법은 철저히 '의사소통을 위한 보조도구'로서 문법 규칙 자체에 대한 학습이 아니라 의미 전달을 정확하게 할 수 있게끔 해주기 위한 영역 중 하나로 필요한 부분만 최대한 핵심적이고 간략하게 소개되어 있습니다.

따라서, 수업 실연에서도 문법을 바라보는 태도를 위와 같이 유지하는 것이 중요합니다. 대부분 수업 실연은 우리가 직접 겪은 수업을 반영하는 경우가 많아서, 종종 문법 영역이 출제되면 지나치게 강의식 문법 수업으로 넘어 가버리는 상황을 많이 보아왔습니다. 그럴 때면 영어 교과서를 한번 직접 살펴보세요! 생각보다 문법에 관한 설명이 많지 않은 것을 확인할 수 있으실 겁니다. :)

Check point #48.
Discovery learning이 일어났는가?

오늘 배울 내용에 해당하는 문법 규칙을 소개하는 방법은 두 가지가 있습니다. 첫 번째는 교사가 직접 학생에게 소개(Present)하는 방식이고, 두 번째는 학생이 발견(Discover)하는 방식이죠. 실제 교실 상황에서는 첫 번째가 90% 이상일 것으로 생각되지만, 수업 실연에서는 두 번째 방법을 보여주는 것이 좋습니다. 왜냐하면, 우리는 '이상적인 수업 상황'을 보여주어야 하니까요.

수업 실연에서 Discovery learning을 보여줄 수 있는 가장 쉬운 방법은 교사가 문법 규칙을 직접 제시하지 않고 학생에게 반복되는 형태(form)를 찾아보라고 하는 것입니다.

> <예시 상황 T-talk>
> T1 : Today, we are going to learn 'will be -ing'. … We use 'will be -ing' when we want to express … (X)
> T2 : In the reading text, there is an expression that is used repeatedly. Can you find it? … Thank you, Dawon! Then, can you guess the meaning of 'will be -ing'? Let's talk about it. … Yes! It means …
> (O)

T1은 해당 수업 차시에서 배울 내용인 'will be -ing'를 직접 소개(Deductive)하고 있으며, 그 표현의 사용법에 대해서도 교사가 설명을 이어 나가고 있습니다. 반면에 T2는 읽기 수업과 연계하여 본문에 반복적으로 등장하는 표현이 있다고 언급(Inductive)하며 그것이 무엇인지 학생에게 묻고 있습니다. 그리고 학생과의 상호작용을 통해 'will be -ing'를 언제 사용하는지 guessing

을 유도하고 있죠. 이처럼 문법 규칙에 대해 Contextual analysis를 하게끔 유도하는 것이 Discovery learning의 한 가지 예시입니다.

> **Tip**
>
> 모든 단원에는 핵심 문법이 있으며, 해당 핵심 문법은 읽기 본문에 최소 2회 이상 반복되어 등장합니다. 따라서 읽기 본문을 활용하여 문법 형태에 대한 발견 학습이 일어나게끔 수업을 진행하는 것은 논리적으로 연결성이 뛰어나다고 할 수 있습니다.

Check point #49.

♟ 지난 시간과 연계되는가?

문법 개념은 수직적 연계성이 드러나는 나선형 구조(Spiral learning)입니다. 따라서 오늘 배우는 문법 규칙을 이해하기 위해서는 어떤 문법 규칙을 먼저 알아야 하는지 파악하고, 이를 지난 시간과 연계하여 설명을 이어 나가는 것이 중요합니다.

<예시 상황 T-talk>

T : ① Last time, we learned 'will'. When do we use 'will'? … Thank you, Suhyun! We use 'will' when we want to talk about the future.

⇩

② Then, how about 'be -ing'? … Yes, Heewon, We already know that we use 'be -ing' when something is ongoing.

⇩

③ Therefore, 'will be -ing' means what? Can you guess when we use it?

⇩

④ Perfect, Dongwoo! We use 'will be -ing' when something will be ongoing in the future!

⇩

⑤ Then, can you make a sentence with 'will be -ing'? … Awesome. Dongwoo just said 'I will be studying tomorrow morning.'

위 ①에서 교사가 지난 시간 'will'을 배웠다고 언급하고 학생과 상호작용을 통해 'will'의 의미를 되새깁니다. 마찬가지로 ②에서 'be -ing'도 학생과 상호작용하며 이미 알고 있는 내용임을 언급합니다. 이처럼 수업 실연에서는 자신의 필요에 맞게 얼마든지 상황을 가정할 수 있습니다. 따라서, 문법 수업에서 선행 지식으로 생각되는 내용은 '이전 시간에 배운 것임'을 전제하고 수업을 진행하면 훨씬 더 원활하고 수업 연계성도 도드라집니다. 이후 ③에서 앞선 내용을 바탕으로 학생에게 'will be -ing'의 의미를 유추해 볼 것을 제안합니다. ④에서 성공적으로 한 학생이 'will be -ing'의 뜻을 유추했다고 가정하고 학생의 발화를 통해 'when something will be ongoing in the future.'라는 개념을 끌어냅니다. 마지막으로 ⑤에서 배운 내용에 대한 CCQ를 진행하며, 학생이 'will be -ing'를 사용하여 문장을 스스로 만들어 내었음을 보여주고, 이 결과를 교실 전체에 공유하면서 마무리합니다.

Check point #50.

 Form에 대한 Noticing/Awareness가 일어났는가?

수업 실연에서 문법은 '어렵고 따분한 규칙'이 아니라 '원활한 의사소통'을 위한 보조도구입니다. 따라서 문법 수업은 '규칙'이 중심에 놓이는 것이 아니라, '의미'가 중심에 놓여야 합니다. 즉, 문법에 대한 모든 교사의 설명이 '이런 의미일 때는 이런 문법을 사용해' 또는 '이렇게 내용을 전달하고 싶을 때는 이런 형태를 써야 해'와 같이 흘러가죠.

그러나 아무리 의미 중심 문법 수업이라고 할지라도 언어 형태에 대한 알아차림은 일어나야 합니다. 그리고 이러한 알아차림을 가장 잘 표현할 수 있는 상황이 바로 교사의 피드백입니다.

<예시 상황 T-talk>

T : ① You guys all did a great job. However, I found that many of you made this kind of mistake.

<판서 예시>

- will be -ing
  - I will be play basketball next week

⇩

② Is this sentence correct? … No. We need to change something. … Can someone fix this sentence for us?

⇩

③ Perfect, Jihwan! We need to use 'playing', instead of 'play'.

<판서 예시>

- will be -ing
  - I will be ~~play~~ playing basketball next week

⇩

④ Don't forget this because we are going to use this expression in an upcoming writing activity today!

먼저, ①에서처럼 교사가 Positive feedback을 먼저 제공하는 것이 중요합니다. 왜냐하면 문법 교정 활동은 자칫 학생의 자신감을 많이 떨어뜨릴 위험이 있기 때문입니다. 그 후, 틀린 문장을 <판서 예시>와 같이 칠판에 적고, 실수한 학생이 가령 1명이라도 그 학생의 이름을 언급하지 않고 'many of you'라는 표현으로 해당 실수를 하는 학생이 많이 있음을 넌지시 표현합니다. 이어지는 ②에서 자연스러운 학생과의 상호작용을 통해 해당 문장의 문법성을 판단합니다. 그리고 교사가 직접 바로 답을 알려주지 않고, 'Can someone fix this sentence for us?'라는 표현으로 학생 참여 및 Peer scaffolding을 유도합니다. ③에서 한 학생이 올바르게 문장을 수정하였다고 가정하고, 교사가 다른 색깔로 판서하며 Form에 대한 Feedback을 진행합니다. 그리고 마지막 ④에서 방금 알려준 문법 규칙을 이어지는 쓰기 활동에서 사용할 것임을 예고하고 잊지 말 것을 다시 한번 강조합니다.

> **Tip**
>
> 틀린 예문을 어떻게 만들 것인지는 자유입니다. 그러나 여기서만큼은 '의미'가 아니라 'Form'에 집중하고 있다는 모습을 확실히 보여줄 수 있는 예시가 좋습니다!

(2) Speaking

수업 실연에서 Speaking 활동은 영화로 따지면 주연급 조연인 셈입니다. Speaking 영역 자체가 Main activity의 규모로 등장하지는 않지만, 종종 수업 실연 극 초반부 Schema activation 단계에서 Brainstorming으로 전체적인 주제에 관한 대화를 나누거나, 수업 실연 중반부 Pre-writing 활동으로서 글쓰기 주제에 대한 Discussion으로 등장하기 때문입니다.

Check point #51.
♟ Key expression을 제공하였는가?

Speaking 영역은 언제까지나 조연으로 등장하기 때문에 수업 실연에서 많은 시간을 할애하여 보여주기가 어렵습니다. 그러나 현실적으로 학생에게 가장 도움이 되면서 교사가 speaking 활동을 원활히 이끌 수 있도록 해주는 것은 해당 말하기 활동에서 사용할 재료를 직접 제공하는 것입니다. 즉, Key expression을 알려주는 것이죠!

> <예시 상황 T-talk>
>
> T : ① We all have worries and friends are great advisors. Then, why don't we talk about our worries and get some ideas from our friends? … Do you like it? … Perfect!
>
>
>
> ② Then Jongmin, what do you see on the first handout? … Yes, there are some useful expressions about giving advice.
>
>
>
> ③ So, with those expressions, let's talk with your partner about your worries and advice! I'll give you 2 minutes. Go!

수업 실연 극 초반부 Schema activation 단계에서 Brainstorming과 관련된 부분입니다. ① 과같이 교사가 오늘의 수업 주제를 언급하고, 학생들에게 서로 이야기해 볼 것을 제안합니다. 그러나 곧장 바로 Speaking activity로 넘어가지 않고, ②와 같이 한 학생과 상호작용하며 교사가 해당 주제에 대한 Key expression을 나누어주었다고 가정합니다. 그리고 ③에서 자신이 가지고 있는 Key expression을 바탕으로 짝과 대화해 보도록 합니다.

> **Tip**
>
> 수업 실연에서는 무턱대고 '짝과 이야기를 해봅시다'라는 T-talk를 많이 사용하지만, 실제 교실에서는 학생들이 Speaking에 대한 두려움이 매우 크기 때문에, 적절한 가이드 없이는 Speaking 활동 자체가 진행되지 않습니다. 이러한 관점에서 Key expression은 Speaking 영역을 Reading 영역으로 어느 정도 바꾸어주는 효과가 있으므로, 학생의 심리적 부담을 크게 줄여주고 적극적으로 활동에 참여할 의지가 생기게끔 동기를 부여하는 중요한 요소가 됩니다.

Check point #52.
Active participation이 강조되었는가?

Check point #53.
Respect friends가 강조되었는가?

Check point #54.
Turn-taking이 강조되었는가?

'Check point #52~54'는 Speaking 활동 중 Discussion과 관련이 깊습니다. 주로 Pre-writing 단계에서 자주 등장하죠. Discussion을 진행할 때 가장 중요한 세 요소를 꼽으라면 무임승차를 방지하는 'Active participation'과 나와 다른 의견을 수용할 줄 아는 태도인 'Respect friends', 그리고 친구의 말을 경청할 줄 아는 'Turn-taking'일 것입니다. 이 세 가지의 앞 글자를 따서 'ART rule'이라고 부르죠!

<예시 상황 T-talk>
T : ① Are you ready to have a discussion about friendship? … Great!

⇩

② However, whenever we have a discussion, which rule is important?

③ Yes, Dongwoo! The ART rule!

⇩

④ What's A? … Yes, Hyunjung, it is 'Active participation'. … What's R? … Thank you, Heewon, it is 'Respect friends', … What's T? … Perfect, Jihwan, it is 'Take turns'!

위 ①에서 교사가 우정에 관한 논의가 준비 되어있는지 물어보면서 대화가 시작됩니다. 그러나 곧바로 Discussion을 진행하지 않고, ②와 같이 Discussion rule에 대하여 학생에게 물어봅니다. 이처럼 교사가 직접 내용을 제시하지 않고 학생에게 물어보는 모습은 '해당 교사가 평소 수업 시간에 일정한 규칙을 미리 설정하고 수업을 안정적으로 진행하고 있다'라는 전문성을 보여줄 좋은 전략입니다. 그리고 ③에서 학생 한 명이 ART rule을 언급함으로써 '서로 간 지켜야 할 약속이 있는 교실'과 같은 모습이 만들어지죠. 여기서 'ART rule'은 채점관에게도 생소한 개념일 것이기 때문에 모두 이목이 쏠릴 것입니다. 이때 ④와 같이 학생과의 상호작용을 가정하며 하나씩 풀어서 설명해주는 것으로 Discussion rule을 전달합니다.

이러한 ART rule은 Discussion을 진행한 후 교사의 Circulation에서 다시 한번 강조할 수 있습니다.

<예시 상황 T-talk>
T : ① (첫 번째 그룹에게) Wow, everyone is participating very actively! You guys are doing so great! Keep up the great work!

⇩

② (두 번째 그룹에게) Uhm… Do you guys remember the 'T' rule'? … Yes! It was 'Take turns'! So make sure each one of you has a chance to talk.

교사의 Circulation 상황에서 ①과같이 첫 번째 그룹에게 'A rule'을 잘 지키고 있다고 칭찬합니다. 그 후 ②에서 두 번째 그룹에게 'T rule'을 상기시키며 모든 학생이 발언 기회를 가질 수 있도록 격려합니다. 위 ①~②와 같이 Circulation 상황에서의 'ART rule' 피드백을 통해 수업 실연에서 더욱 전문적인 Discussion 진행 능력을 보여줄 수 있습니다!

(3) Writing

Writing은 거의 매번 빠지지 않고 수업 실연에 출제되고 있는 단골 영역입니다. 수업 실연 후반 50%를 차지하는 부분이자 수업 목표와 직결되어 채점관도 가장 눈여겨보는 영역이 바로 Writing이기도 합니다. 과장을 살짝 보태자면, 지금까지의 모든 활동은 Writing을 위한 Build-up activity였으며, Writing이 바로 수업 실연의 화룡점정이 되어야 합니다. 사실상 수업 실연의 주인공이죠!

 Check point #55.

 Pre-writing 과정이 드러나는가?

하나의 완성된 글을 아무런 준비 없이 맨땅에 헤딩하듯 처음부터 만드는 것은 어려울 수 밖에 없습니다. 따라서 수업 실연에는 본격적인 글쓰기 활동 전에 Pre-writing이 지시 사항으로 종종 등장하며 앞서 살펴본 Speaking 영역을 빌려 Brainstorming, outlining, researching, organizing의 형태가 대표적으로 등장합니다.

그러나 위와 같은 활동이 Writing과 연계된 활동이라는 사실을 놓치는 경우가 많고 설령 Pre-writing 활동임을 알고 있다 할지라도 어떻게 연계성을 보여주어야 하는지 고민하는 경우가 많습니다. 이럴 때는 아래와 같은 글쓰기 피라미드를 떠올리는 것이 필요합니다.

< 글쓰기 피라미드 >

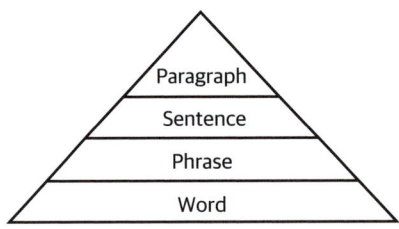

위와 같이 글은 Word - Phrase - Sentence - Paragraph의 순서로 단계(복잡성)가 높아집니다. 따라서, 최종 목표가 Paragraph라면 Pre-writing 단계에서 Sentence-level까지만 요구하고, 최종 목표가 Sentence면 Pre-writing 단계에서 Phrase나 Word 단계까지만 요구하는 것이 글쓰기의 연계성을 드러낼 수 있는 좋은 방법입니다.

<예시 상황 T-talk>

T : ① Before we start the discussion, what do you see on the third handout?

⇩

② Yes, Suhyun! There is a writing outline! So, during the discussion you should complete this outline form.

⇩

③ Don't worry because you don't have to write in a full sentence. Just complete the outline with keywords or phrases. Alright?

⇩

④ Ok, Dongwoo! Then, what should we do now? Yes, discuss and complete this outline. I'll give you 10 minutes. Go!

①에서 세 번째 Handout(수업 자료)을 보라고 하며 학생들에게 무엇이 있는지 물어봅니다. 이처럼, 교사의 수업 자료에 그림이나 표가 있을 때는 학생과 상호작용 상황을 가정하여 대화를 통해 수업 자료의 내용을 스스로 살펴보게끔 하는 것이 좋습니다. ②에서 해당 수업 자료에 Writing outline이 있음을 알려주고 Discussion을 진행하면서 해당 Outline을 완성하도록 안내합니다. 그러나 이어지는 ③에서 'full sentence'가 아니라 'word'나 'phrase'도 괜찮다고 알려줍니다. 이를 통해서 현재 진행하고자 하는 활동이 향후 본격적인 Writing 활동을 위한 Build up 활동임을 확실하게 보여줄 수 있습니다. 바로 여기서 Pre-writing 과정이 드러나는 것이죠! 이후 마지막 ④에서 학생 이름을 부른 후 CCQ를 진행하고 활동을 시작합니다.

Tip

Pre-writing이 끝난 후, 'Now, are you ready to write an essay?'와 같은 방식으로 연계성을 드러낼 수도 있습니다. 또한 'Based on the outline we just made, we are going to write an essay.'와 같은 T-talk도 활용할 수 있죠! 따라서, 수업 실연에 Pre-writing이 등장한다면 Worksheet를 함께 제공할 확률이 높으므로 여기서는 꼭 Word – Phrase – Sentence – Paragraph 단계를 살려 구조적으로 연계성 있는 Writing 수업을 디자인 하시길 바랍니다!

Check point #56.

Sample writing이 제시되었는가?

Writing에서 가장 중요한 것은, 바로 Sample writing을 학생들에게 보여주는 것입니다. 본격적인 쓰기 활동 전 Sample writing을 제시하면 학생이 앞으로 할 활동에 대하여 직관적으로 쉽게 이해할 수 있을 뿐만 아니라, '나도 할 수 있겠다'라는 자신감이 생기게 됩니다. 또한, 교사도 학생과 함께 Sample writing을 하나씩 살펴보면서 Writing의 조건을 간편하게 제시할 수 있는 등 활용도가 아주 높습니다.

<예시 상황 T-talk>

T : ① Alright, so far, we had a group discussion about friendship and made an outline. Then, are you ready to start writing about friendship? … Awesome!

⇩

② However, before we start writing, everyone look at the screen!

⇩

③ Hyunjung at the back, do you see the screen? … What do you see on the screen? … Yes, there is a writing!

⇩

④ This is an actual student's writing from the last year. Today, you will write exactly like this one. Sounds good? … Great!

⇩

⑤ Then, let's check some points in this writing. Hyunjung, can you read the first sentence? … Thank you, Hyunjung, like this sample writing, you should include …

①에서 '우정'에 관한 그룹 논의와 Outline 쓰기까지 마쳤으니 이제 쓰기 활동으로 들어갈 준비가 되었는지 학생들에게 물어봅니다. 학생이 준비되었음을 확인한 후, ②와 같이 학생에게 스크린을 보라고 안내합니다. ③에서처럼 맨 뒤에 앉은 학생도 화면이 잘 보이는지 확인하고 자연스럽게 대화를 이어 나가며 교사가 'Sample writing'을 준비하였음을 보여줍니다. ④에서 해당 Sample writing은 작년에 실제 학생이 완성한 작품이라는 점을 언급합니다. 이를 통해서 학생들은 자신도 충분히 해낼 수 있다는 자신감을 얻게 됩니다. 그리고 이어지는 ⑤에서 몇 가지 부분

을 짚고 넘어가자고 교사가 제안합니다. 여기서 교사가 짚는 부분은 'Writing requirements'에 해당합니다. 이처럼 본격적으로 Writing 활동을 시작하기 직전 Sample writing을 제시하면 학생들에게 Writing에 대한 설명과 동기 부여, Requirements에 대한 안내까지 순조롭게 이어 나갈 수 있습니다!

Check point #57.
Writing의 조건이 제시되었는가?

수업 실연에서 Free writing이 등장하는 경우는 거의 없습니다. 만약 있다면, Main activity가 아니라 Brainstorming에 가까울 것이겠죠. 따라서 Main activity로서 Writing 영역을 대비하기 위해서는 Writing requirements에 대한 준비가 꼭 필요합니다.

Writing requirements의 영역은 크게 세 가지로 나뉩니다. 첫 번째는 내용(Content)입니다. 주제 문장과 근거가 있는지, 또는 미래 직업이 소재라면, 해당하는 미래 직업과 그 직업의 특성 등 다양한 내용적 요소를 Writing requirements에 제시해야 합니다. 두 번째는 길이(Length)입니다. 일정한 문장 또는 단락 이상 글을 쓰라고 안내할 필요가 있으며, 그룹 활동일 경우에는 'Check point #20'에서 살펴본 것처럼, 개인별 역할 부여가 Role로 되지 않았다면 '1학생당 N문장 쓰기'와 같이 간단하게 분량에 대해 역할 부여를 할 수 있습니다. 마지막 세 번째는 언어 활용(Language focus)입니다. 여기에서는 해당 차시에 배운 Vocabulary나 Grammar, Key expression을 직접 활용해보도록 합니다. 만약 문법이 출제되었다면 꼭! 글쓰기 단계에서 해당 문법을 활용할 수 있게끔 Writing requirement를 구성해보세요. 처음부터 끝까지 아주 짜임새 있게 수업이 이어진 인상을 보여줄 수 있습니다.

<예시 상황 T-talk>

T : ① Let's check some points in this sample writing. Jihwan, can you read the first sentence? ⋯ Great! Like this, you should introduce a historical leader in the first sentence.

⇩

② And then, can you read the second sentence, Heewon? ⋯ Thank you! In the second sentence, you should write the reason why he or she is your role model.

⇩

③ Like this we have several writing requirements. You need a name of the leader and three reasons why he or she is your role model.

<판서 예시>

- **Don't forget!**
  - Leader, 3 Reasons

⇩

④ Second, your writing should be at least 4 sentences. Since we have four people in a group, one student should write at least one sentence. Sounds great? ⋯ Awesome!

<판서 예시>

- **Don't forget!**
  - Leader, 3 Reasons
  - 4 Sentences or more
    (1S=1S)

⇩

⑤ Lastly, we learned something new today. Do you remember? Yes, Jongmin! We learned 'It must have been ...'! So, your writing should include this key expression, okay?

<판서 예시>

- **Don't forget!**
  - Leader, 3 Reasons
  - 4 Sentences or more
    (1S=1S)
  - 'It must have been...'

①과 같이 Sample writing을 학생과 함께 확인하면서 Writing requirements를 안내합니다. 이를 통해서 교사는 예시와 함께 더 알기쉽고 명확하게 요구 조건을 전달할 수 있고, 학생은 Sample writing이 단순히 아무런 조건 없이 자유롭게 쓰여진 글이 아니라 약속된 요소(실제 교실 환경에서는 채점 기준)가 있다는 것을 깨닫게 됩니다. 이어서 ②에서는 다른 학생과 상호작용하며 두 번째 Writing requirements에 대하여 안내합니다. 그리고 ③에서 본격적으로 'Don't forget'이라는 판서를 통해 글쓰기 조건을 제시합니다. 앞서 이야기했던 내용 조건(Content)을 정리해주며, ④~⑤에서 길이(Length)와 언어 활용(Language focus) 조건을 이어서 제시합니다. ④에서는 4문장 이상의 길이 조건을 제시하면서 '1S=1S'라는 판서로 모둠 내 역할 배분까지 고려하였음을 보여주었고, ⑤에서는 오늘 배운 핵심 표현이 무엇인지 물어보면서 자연스럽게 'It must have been' 표현을 글쓰기 조건으로 안내합니다. 이렇게 Writing requirements에 대한 판서까지 모두 마치면 글쓰기 안내가 마무리 됩니다.

Check point #58.
♟ Authentic purpose가 제시되었는가?

Authentic purpose란, 말 그대로 글쓰기의 목적이 수업 자체가 아니라 실제 현실을 바탕으로 둔다는 것입니다. 예를 들면, 편지를 쓰는 활동이 수업 시간에 포함되었다면, 단순히 오늘 배운 어휘와 표현을 활용해서 편지의 형식으로 써보는 연습을 하는 것에 그치지 않고, 실제로 우체국에 가서 편지를 부치는 것이죠. 이렇게 교실 속 활동이 교실 밖 현실과 연결될 때 학생은 해당 활동에 관심과 흥미가 커집니다. 또한, 「2022 개정 교육과정」에서도 교실에서 배운 내용이 교실 밖 실제 상황에 적용될 수 있도록 '역량'을 길러내는 것을 중시하니, Authentic purpose를 제시하는 것은 이러한 관점과 일맥상통하기도 합니다. 따라서 저는 Writing 수업을 진행할 때 항상 Authentic purpose를 제시하였으며 이러한 부분이 1차에서 소수점 합격이라는 불리한 상황을 뒤집고 2차 고득점으로 최종 합격한 핵심 전략이 되었다고 생각합니다.

<예시 상황 T-talk>

T : ① So far, we've brainstormed about good things and bad things of our city. Then, are you ready to be 'Change makers?' … Awesome.

⇩

② Before we start, let's go to the writing worksheet. Can you read the title of the writing worksheet, Hyunjung? … Yes, it says 'Busan will be much better, if …', right?

⇩

③ So, we are going to write a suggestion to make Busan a better city. But guys! The best suggestion will be actually sent to the city hall so that you can be the actual 'Change makers' for Busan. Are you excited? … Perfect!

⇩

④ Great! Then, Heewon, what are we going to do now? Yes, we are going to write the suggestion to make Busan a better city. Don't forget these requirements. I'll give you 20 minutes. Go!

①에서 지금까지 우리 도시에 대하여 좋은 점과 나쁜 점을 브레인스토밍하며 Group discussion을 진행하였다고 가정하였습니다. 그리고 "Then, are you ready to be Change makers?"라는 표현으로 해당 활동이 'Change makers'가 되기 위한 Build up이었음을 알려주며 다음 활동에 대한 동기를 강화하고 수업 흐름의 논리적 연결성을 보여줍니다. ②에서는 나누어준 Writing worksheet을 보여주며 글쓰기 과제에 대하여 본격적으로 학생과 함께 살펴봅니다. 그리고 이어지는 ③에서 Authentic purpose가 제시됩니다. 지금부터 할 글쓰기가 단순히 교실 내에서만 머무는 것이 아니라, 가장 잘 쓴 결과물은 실제 시청에 학생 건의서를 보낸다는 부분을 언급합니다. 이를 통해서 학생들은 글쓰기 과제에 대하여 실제적 목표를 가지게 되어 동기가 한층 더 강화되고, 교사는 자신의 수업이 단순히 영어 글쓰기 역량 향상에 그치지 않고 민주 시민 역량까지 기를 수 있는 수업을 설계할 수 있게 됩니다. 그리고 마지막으로 ④에서 현재 우리는 'Suggestion'을 쓸 것이며, 이를 위한 'Writing requirements'를 다시 한번 강조하며 CCQ를 진행합니다. 이처럼 본격적인 활동 시작 전 교사의 안내 사항 T-talk가 너무 길어지면 정작 무엇을 해야 하는지 학생이 혼란스러워할 수 있습니다. 따라서 활동을 시작하기 직전 마지막 T-talk에는 다시 CCQ를 해줌으로써 수업 활동에 대한 길을 잃지 않도록 해주는 것이 중요합니다.

Check point #59.

Mixed-level을 고려하였는가?

글쓰기 영역은 후반부 50%를 차지하는 수업 실연의 주인공이고 해당 수업 목표와 직결되는 활동이기 때문에 반드시 학생(모둠) 수준을 고려한 Mixed-level treatment가 이루어져야 합니다. 따라서, 여기서도 마찬가지로 교사가 활동 시작 안내 후 Circulation을 진행하며 개별적으로 학생(모둠) 수준에 맞는 Scaffolding 및 추가 과제가 제시되어야 하죠! ('Check point #23~#25'를 참고하세요!)

1. Low-level

1-1. Writing Guide

Low-level을 위한 가장 간단한 Scaffolding은 바로 Writing guide를 제공하는 것입니다.

> <예시 상황 T-talk>
> T : ① Oh, Group 1, do you need any help?
>
> ⇩
>
> ② I see. You guys have no idea how to start a sentence.
>
> ⇩
>
> ③ Then, why don't you use this 'Writing guide'. … What do you see? … Yes, there are some examples of 'sentence starters' and 'structure frames!'
>
> ⇩
>
> ④ With this 'Writing guide', can you do this by yourselves? … Awesome! You guys are on the right track!

먼저 Circulation 도중 ①에서처럼 도움이 필요한 모둠이 있다고 가정합니다. 그 후 ②에서 해당 모둠이 겪고 있는 어려움에 대하여 파악합니다. 그리고 ③에서 교사가 미리 준비한 'Writing guide'를 제공하며 Scaffolding을 진행합니다. 이어서 마지막으로 ④에서 'Writing guide'가 있다면 스스로 할 수 있는지 묻고, 격려와 함께 Low-level treatment를 마무리합니다. 여기서도 'Check point #1'과 같이 'Scaffolding 3단계'를 T-talk로 나타내었죠!

> **Tip**
>
> 만약 위 T-talk를 보고 Reading에서 공부한 것이 떠오른다면 현재 수업 실연 Input이 아주 잘 쌓이고 있는 것입니다. 수업 실연에서는 이처럼 매번 반복 등장하는 상황이 있으므로 이에 대해서는 T-talk를 최대한 비슷하게 구성하여 시험 준비의 효율성을 높이는 것이 중요합니다!

1-2. Providing resources

위에서 살펴본 것처럼 'Writing guide' 제공이 가장 정석이고 무난한 방법이지만, 고득점이 필요하다면 다음과 같이 'Providing resources'도 아주 인상적이고 훌륭한 Scaffolding이 됩니다!

<예시 상황 T-talk>

T : ① Oh, Group 2, do you need any help?

⇩

② Okay. Coming up with some new ideas is difficult. I understand.

⇩

③ Then, why don't you check these magazines, news articles and essays that I brought for you? You can get various ideas about protecting environment from there.

⇩

④ With these resources, can you do this by yourselves? ··· Fantastic! I'm just so impressed!

전체적인 흐름은 비슷합니다. ①에서 먼저 도움이 필요한 모둠이 있다고 가정하고, ②에서 어떤 도움이 필요한지 파악합니다. 여기에서는 새로운 아이디어를 떠올리는 부분이 해당 모둠이 겪고 있는 어려움입니다. 이처럼 실제 교실 환경에서는 주제가 다소 생소하거나 전문적일 경우에는 활동 자체에 어려움을 겪는 학생들이 많이 있습니다. 이어서 ③에서 교사의 Scaffolding이 제공됩니다. 미리 관련 주제를 다룬 잡지와 신문 기사, 에세이를 준비해왔다고 가정하고 학생들에게 보여주면서 직접 해당 자료를 찾아보며 글쓰기에 대한 아이디어를 찾도록 해보는 것입니다. 그리고 마찬가지로 ④에서 교사가 제공한 Scaffolding으로 스스로 활동을 이어 나갈 수 있는지 물어보면서 긍정적 피드백을 제공한 뒤, Scaffolding-out으로 마무리합니다.

2. High-level

High-level treatment의 정석은 추가 과제 제시입니다. Productive skill의 향상을 위해서는 많이 사용하는 것이 핵심이기 때문에, 교실 환경에서도 최대한 많은 글쓰기 기회가 제공되어야 하며, 특히 High-level 학생에게는 해당 학생의 수준보다 한 단계 높은 과제(i+1)를 제공한다는 관점으로 접근하는 것이 좋습니다.

<예시 상황 T-talk>

T : ① Oh, Group 3, have you already finished writing all five safety tips?

⇩

② Wow! You're such quick writers!

⇩

③ Then, why don't you make two more safety tips? … You know it's never too much to be safe.

⇩

④ Awesome! You guys are making the world much safer.

---

①에서 High-level 그룹이 주어진 과제를 빨리 끝냈다고 가정합니다. 그리고 ②에서 교사의 칭찬이 뒤따라 제공됩니다. 'Check point #42'에서 살펴본 바와 같이, 항상 추가 과제를 제시하기 전에는 교사의 긍정적 피드백을 함께 제공해야 합니다! 그 후 ③에서 교사가 추가 과제로 두 가지 Safety tip을 더 쓸 것을 제시합니다. 그리고 '안전은 아무리 강조해도 지나치지 않다.'라는 T-talk로 학생들의 추가 과제에 대한 정당성을 부여합니다. 마지막으로 ④에서 'You guys are making the world much safer.'라는 T-talk로 학생들이 스스로 뿌듯함을 느끼며 활동에 참여할 수 있도록 동기 부여를 하며 마무리합니다.

> **Tip**
>
> 이렇게 항상 추가 과제를 제시할 때는 학생 눈치(?)를 많이 봐야 합니다. 자칫 잘못하면 빨리 끝낸 것이 손해라는 인상을 줄 수 있기 때문입니다. 따라서 추가 과제가 언급되기 전에 활동을 잘 끝냈다는 사실을 강조하며 칭찬을 2배, 3배로 더 많이 해준 뒤 비로소 과제가 제시되어야 합니다. 그리고 해당 과제를 수행하는 것에 대한 정당성을 부여하고 자긍심을 자극하여 자발적 참여 및 과제 수행에 대한 설득력을 높인다면 더 완벽한 T-talk가 되겠죠!

🔲 Evaluation

학습자 중심 수업에서 '평가'란 수업 행위를 마무리하고 학생의 성적을 산출하는 것이 아니라, 수업 과정의 일부로서 학생의 이해도를 파악하고 개선 방향을 찾을 수 있도록 도움을 주는 행위입니다. 따라서, 수업 실연에서도 '평가' 부분이 출제된다면 이러한 부분을 확실하게 강조하며 진행하는 것이 고득점을 받을 수 있는 좋은 전략입니다.

(1) Design

Design은 평가를 어떻게 설계할 것인지에 관한 부분입니다. 수업의 '결과'가 아니라 '과정'으로서의 평가를 진행하기 위해서는 평가 자체가 처음부터 이러한 목적에 맞게 설계되는 것이 중요하죠!

Check point #60.
♟ 평가 내용이 교수 내용과 일치하는가?

현장에서 끊임없이 강조되는 '교수평기 일체화'는 '교육과정', '수업', '평가', '기록'을 하나의 연속선상에 놓고 교육활동을 진행하는 것을 의미합니다. 즉, 학기 초 교사가 전체적인 계획을 수립(교육과정)하고, 이를 바탕으로 수업을 진행(수업)합니다. 그리고 수업 시간에 다룬 내용을 바탕으로 평가를 시행(평가)하고, 평가 활동의 전 과정에서 해당 학생의 참여도뿐만 아니라 학습 내용의 이해 정도, 적용 능력, 결과물의 완성도 등을 종합적으로 판단하여 학교생활기록부에 내용을 입력(기록)합니다. 이 모든 과정이 '하나의 교육활동'으로 유기적으로 통합되어야 한다는 관점이죠!

그러나 수업 실연 상황에서는 위와 같이 '교육과정 - 수업 - 평가 - 기록' 모든 단계의 일체화를 보여줄 필요는 없습니다. 왜냐하면 수업 실연에서 요구하는 부분은 아래와 같이 '수업'과 '평가' 단계이기 때문입니다. 물론 수업하기 전 전체적인 커리큘럼을 짜는 것과, 수업 후 기록하는 것까지 임용 시험에 포함되면 조금 더 완성된 '교수평기 일체화'를 보여줄 수 있겠지만, 아직은 그렇지 않다는 것이 현실입니다.

<교수평가 일체화>

실제 교육 현장

교육과정 — 수업 — 평가 — 기록

임용 2차 수업 실연

따라서, 수업 실연에서는 '교수평가 일체화'의 관점에서 '수업'과 '평가'가 유기적으로 연결되어 있다는 것을 보여주는 데 집중해야 합니다. 가장 간단한 방법은 바로 'Writing requirements'와 'Evaluation'의 항목을 연결 지어 보여주는 것입니다!

<예시 상황 T-talk>

T : ① So far, we've just finished writing about historical leaders. Then, don't you guys want to read the other groups' writings? ⋯ Awesome! ⋯ Then, why don't we begin the <Check! Check!> time, now?

⇩

② Let me give you the checklist. Take one and pass them to the back.

⇩

③ Alright, Jongmin! What do you see on the checklist? ⋯ Yes, it says 'Contents'. Can you read the meaning of 'Contents'? ⋯ Thank you! It means the writing should include the 'Leader' and '3 Reasons'. ⋯ What's the next one, Dawon? ⋯ Yes, it is 'Length'. What's the meaning of it? ⋯ Perfect! So, your friends' writings must be longer than 4 sentences. ⋯ Finally, what's the last one, Dongwoo? ⋯ Yes, it is 'Language'. What does it mean? ⋯ Yes, you should check if the writing has the expression 'It must have been…', alright?

<판서 예시>

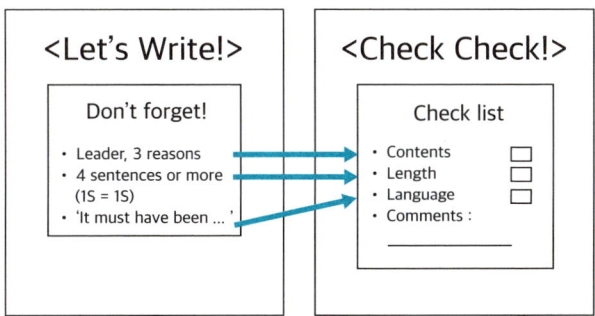

④ So from now on, with this checklist, we are going to read our friends' writings.

⑤ What are we going to do now, Suhyun, again? Yes, read your friends' writings and complete the checklist. I'll give you 10 minutes. Go!

먼저 ①에서 지금까지 글쓰기 활동을 마무리하였고, 다른 모둠의 글을 보고 싶지 않은지 교사가 제안하며 자연스럽게 <Check! Check!> 활동으로 넘어갑니다. 그리고 ②에서 교사가 Checklist를 나누어준다는 상황을 가정하고 ③에서 본격적으로 교사와 학생이 상호작용하며 Checklist 내용에 대해 살펴봅니다. 먼저 'Content'를 언급하며 교사가 판서로 'Content'를 적고, 그 의미가 무엇인지 학생에게 물어본 뒤, 'Leader'와 '3 Reasons'라는 대답을 확인하면서 강조 색 분필을 사용하여 <판서 예시>와 같이 연결합니다. 그 후, 이어서 같은 방법으로 'Length'는 기존 'Writing requirements'에서 판서하였던 '4 sentences or more' 부분과 연결하고, Language는 'It must have been...'과 연결합니다. 이와 같은 방식을 활용하면 판서의 분량을 줄여 시간을 절약할 수 있을 뿐 아니라, 'Writing requirements'에서 언급되었던 내용이 'Checklist'에서 다시 언급되는 모습을 보여줌으로써 'Writing' 수업과 <Check! Check!> 평가 활동이 유기적으로 연결됨을 직관적으로 나타낼 수 있습니다. 이후 ④에서 교사의 'Peer feedback' 활동에 관한 안내가 이어지고 ⑤에서 CCQ를 진행한 후, 활동이 시작됩니다.

Check point #61.
평가의 기준이 명확한가?

물론 학생 중심 수업에서 과정 중심 평가는 중간고사나 기말고사처럼 평가가 냉정하게 이루어지지는 않습니다. 그러나 아무리 '평가를 위한 평가'가 아니라 '배움을 위한 평가'라고 할지라도 평가의 기준을 명확하게 설정하는 것은 중요합니다. 왜냐하면 평가의 객관도가 확보되어야 진정한 평가 활동이라고 할 수 있으며, 정확한 기준을 '요구 수준'으로서 제시하여야 학생의 목표 달성 동기를 강화하여 배움을 촉진할 수 있기 때문입니다.

만약 객관도가 확보되지 않아 채점자마다 점수가 들쭉날쭉하다면, 그것은 '평가'가 아니라 개인의 '의견'에 가까울 것이며, 정확한 기준이 제시되지 않는다면, 학생으로서도 얼마나 해야 하는지 목표 설정이 어려워 동기가 감소할 수 있습니다. 따라서, 항상 평가 활동을 진행할 때는 여러 명이 실시해도 비슷한 결과를 보일 수 있을 만큼 '명확한 기준'을 제시하여야 합니다.

특히나 'Check point #60'에서처럼 Peer evaluation을 실시할 때는 더욱 명확한 기준을 제시하는 것이 중요합니다. 왜냐하면 학생이 직접 평가자가 되어 주어진 기준에 맞게 결과물을 정확하게 판단하는 연습이 활동의 목표이기 때문입니다. 따라서 위에서 살펴본 것처럼 'Content'는 'Leader'와 '3 reasons', 'Length'는 '4문장 이상', 'Language'는 'it must have been 사용하기'와 같이 구체적인 기준을 함께 소개하는 것이 중요합니다.

> **Tip**
>
> 그러나 아무리 과정 중심 평가라고 할지라도 천편일률적인 결과가 나온다면 전통적 평가 방식과 비교하여 과연 어떤 의미가 있는지 의문을 가질 수 있습니다. 이와 같은 한계를 극복하기 위하여 저는 항상 'Checklist'에 'Comment' 작성란도 함께 제공하여 학생의 의견을 자유롭게 나눌 수 있도록 평가를 설계하였습니다.

(2) Giving Feedback

학생 중심 수업에서 피드백은 떼려야 뗄 수가 없는 존재입니다. 왜냐하면 '배움을 위한 평가'는 단순히 평가 결과를 수집하는 것에 그치는 것이 아니라, 해당 결과에 대해 교사가 적절하게 교육적 반응을 해줌으로써 앞으로 더 발전할 수 있도록 격려하는 단계까지 포함되기 때문입니다. 따라서 수업 실연에서도 이와 같은 부분이 종종 강조되어 출제되는 경향이 있습니다.

Positive feedback이 구체적인가?

EBS 다큐 '학교란 무엇인가'에서 '칭찬의 역효과'에 대해 설명하는 에피소드가 있습니다. 칭찬이라면 마냥 좋을 것 같지만, 사실 그렇지 않죠. 단순히 결과만 칭찬한다면 학생들은 성공 경험을 얻기 위해 쉬운 과제를 선택하는 경향이 있지만, 과정을 구체적으로 칭찬한다면 학생들은 조금 더 어려운 도전적 과제를 선택하는 경향이 있습니다.

따라서, 교사로서도 학생들에게 긍정적 피드백을 제공할 때, 단순히 결과 지향적으로만 칭찬하는 것이 아니라 학생의 참여 의지, 과제 수행을 위한 노력, 협동하는 자세 등을 구체적으로 언급하면서 과정 중심적으로 Positive feedback을 제공해야 합니다.

> <예시 상황 T-talk>
> T1 : Wow, fantastic! (X)
> T2 : Wow, you guys are working together so actively. Fantastic! (O)
> T3 : Wow, everyone is participating in the discussion. Awesome! (O)

위 예시에서 T1은 단순한 칭찬이지만, T2와 T3는 정확하게 칭찬의 이유를 언급하면서 긍정적 피드백이 제공되고 있습니다. 이처럼, 교사가 Positive feedback을 제공할 때는, 흔히 말하는 '영혼 없는 칭찬'이 가장 역효과를 불러일으킵니다. 실제 교실 현장에서도 학생들은 아주 재빠르게 교사의 진심을 알아채곤 하죠. 따라서, 항상 긍정적 피드백을 제공할 때는 반드시 '이유 + 긍정적 반응'으로 T-talk를 구성하시길 바랍니다.

Tip

교사로서 어느 부분을 칭찬할지 선정하는 것도 중요합니다. 가령, '100점'을 칭찬한다고 하면 다음부터 학생은 '100점을 맞아야 칭찬을 받을 수 있구나'라고 생각하게 됩니다. 이렇게 되면 점점 어려운 과제에 도전하지 않고 자신이 맞출 수 있는 쉬운 과제만 찾아서 선택하게 됩니다. 게다가 하나라도 틀리면 실망하는 완벽주의의 오류에 빠지기 쉽죠. 그러나 '노력하는 과정'을 칭찬한다면 해당 학생은 노력 자체에 성취감을 느끼게 됩니다. 따라서 '별 노력이 필요 없는' 쉬운 문제보다는 '노력의 가치가 있는' 도전적 과제를 선택할 확률이 높아지게 되죠.

따라서 수업 실연에서는 교사가 어느 부분에 주목하여 긍정적 피드백을 제공할지 신중하게 선택해야 합니다. 대표적으로 출제되는 상황을 정리하면 아래와 같습니다.

1. 교사의 Scaffolding을 제공받는 상황 → 스스로 과제를 수행할 의지가 있음에 주목하며 칭찬
2. Peer Scaffolding을 제공한 상황 → 친구를 도와주는 배려심에 주목하여 칭찬
3. 활발히 모둠 활동에 참여하는 상황 → 모두가 활동 과정에 열정적인 태도를 보이고 있음에 주목하며 칭찬
4. 과제를 빨리 끝낸 상황 → 영어 실력 자체에 주목하여 칭찬 (이후 추가 과제 제시)

Check point #63.

 **Negative feedback 3요소가 지켜졌는가?**

실제 수업 실연에서 Negative feedback이 출제되는 경우는 문법 영역을 제외하고는 흔하지

않습니다. 그러나 만약 출제된다면 어떻게 제공하는 것이 좋은지 고민하게 만드는 부분이기도 합니다. 왜냐하면 자칫 Negative feedback이 잘못 제공되었다가는 영어에 대한 학생의 자신감 및 흥미를 하락시키는 역효과를 낳기 때문입니다.

따라서 교사는 Negative feedback을 제공할 때 아래와 같은 세 가지 요소를 지키는 것이 중요합니다.

1. 간결함

아무리 Negative feedback이 효율적인 학습을 촉진하는 데 꼭 필요한 것이라고 하지만, 학습자가 틀렸음을 지적하는 것이기 때문에 최대한 짧고 간결하게 끝나야 합니다. 왜냐하면 아무리 옳은 말이라도 Negative feedback이 지나치게 길어지면 부정적인 감정이 쌓이게 되어 교사의 조언이 마치 잔소리(?)처럼 느껴지기 때문입니다.

> <예시 상황 T-talk>
> T1 : Turn-taking is very important in the discussion because we need as many ideas as possible and everyone has different thoughts. So, I want you to give your group members chances to share their ideas. (X)
> T2 : What was the 'T rule'? ⋯ Yes! Just make sure everyone takes turns! (O)

T1과 T2 모두 Group discussion 중 'Taking turns'에 관한 Negative feedback을 제공하고 있습니다. T1는 Turn-talking이 중요한 이유를 풍부하게 설명하며 모둠 내 모든 구성원이 돌아가면서 발언권을 갖도록 독려하고 있습니다. 한편, T2는 'T rule'를 짧게 언급하며 'Just make sure everyone takes turns!'라는 표현으로 'Turn-taking'을 상기시킵니다. 만약 T1처럼 Feedback의 길이가 다소 길면, 학생에게 야단을 치는 것처럼 보일 수 있으므로, T2처럼 짧고 간결하게 중요한 부분만 되짚으며 Negative feedback을 마무리 짓는 것이 더 효과적입니다.

2. 명확함

Negative feedback을 통해서 Error correction을 할 때는 문법 개념을 설명하는 표현을 최대한 지양하고, 무엇이 옳은 형태인지 명확하게 제시하는 것이 좋습니다.

> <예시 상황 T-talk>
> T1 : We need to use the present perfect form, instead of the past form. (X)
> T2 : We need to use 'gone', instead of 'went'. (O)

T1은 'present perfect form'과 'past form'과 같은 문법 용어를 사용하고 있습니다. 반면 T2는 곧바로 'went' 대신에 'gone'을 사용하라고 안내하고 있죠. 학생으로서는 'present perfect form = gone', 'past form = went'를 떠올리는 부분 자체가 어렵기 때문에 T1보다 T2와 같은 Negative feedback이 더 직관적이고 이해하기 쉽습니다.

> **Tip**
>
> 실제 교과서에서도 문법적인 개념을 지칭하는 전문용어는 거의 등장하지 않습니다. 따라서, 문법 '규칙'에 의한 '정문/비문 판단력'보다는, 어떤 문법 '형태'가 어떤 '의미'를 전달하는지에 초점을 맞춰서 수업을 구성해야 합니다.

3. 익명성

Negative feedback을 제공할 때는 한 학생의 틀린 표현을 지적하는 방향이 아니라, '자주 하는 실수'의 형태로 '교실 전체'를 대상으로 언급하는 것이 바람직합니다.

> <예시 상황 T-talk>
>
> T1 : Jihwan made this mistake. In this case, we can fix the sentence … (X)
>
> T2 : Everyone look at this! I found that many of you made this kind of mistake. (O)

T1을 읽는 순간 아찔한 기분이 들었다면 아주 바람직한 반응입니다! 이렇게 학생의 이름을 콕 집어 말하면서 실수했다고 하면 다음부터 그 학생은 점점 영어에 대한 마음이 닫혀 여러분의 수업을 듣지 않을 것입니다. 한편, T2는 'Many of you'라는 표현으로 실수한 학생의 익명성이 지켜지고 있습니다. 그리고 설령 해당 실수를 한 학생이 단 한 명이더라도 선의의 거짓말을 통해 '실수를 한 게 나 혼자만이 아니구나'라는 기분이 들게 해주는 것이죠. 이처럼 영어 과목은 학습자의 자신감을 북돋우며 Affective filter를 고려하는 것이 아주 중요하므로 Negative feedback을 제공할 때는 익명성을 보장하여 학습자의 정서를 보호해야 합니다. ('Check point #50'의 예시 상황을 참고하세요!)

Check point #64.

♟ 학생이 Feedback에 참여하는가?

전통적으로 '평가'는 교사의 고유한 권한으로만 여겨졌습니다. 그러나 학생 중심 수업에서는 평가의 주체 역시 학생이 될 수 있습니다. 따라서, 수업 중 다양한 Feedback 상황에 대하여 학생이 직접 서로 생각을 나누고 참여하는 모습을 보여주는 것이 더욱 효과적으로 '배움을 위한 평가' 활동을 나타내는 좋은 고득점 전략입니다.

<예시 상황 T-talk>

T : ① Everyone! Please pay attention. I found that many of you made this kind of mistake.

<판서 예시>

- It must have ...
  - He must have went
    to the hospital.

② Is this sentence correct? … No, it isn't. … Then, can someone fix this sentence for us?

③ Awesome, Heewon! Did everyone hear what Heewon said? She said we need to use 'gone', instead of 'went'.

<판서 예시>

- It must have ...
  - He must have ~~went~~ **gone**
    to the hospital.

---

①에서 교사가 학생들의 주의를 집중시키며 많은 학생이 이와 같은 실수를 하였다며 예시 문장을 판서합니다. 그리고 ②에서 교사가 학생들과 상호작용하며 해당 문장의 문법성을 판단해 보도록 합니다. 틀린 문장이라는 대답을 들은 뒤, 교사가 직접 수정하면서 Feedback을 제공하지 않고 'Can someone fix this sentence for us?'라는 T-talk로 학생들이 Feedback 상황에 참여할 수 있도록 독려합니다. 그 후 ③에서 한 학생이 성공적으로 해당 문장을 바르게 고쳤다고 가정하고, 교실 전체에 그 학생의 답변을 공유합니다.

Check point #65.

 Revise에 대한 언급이 있는가?

평가의 목적이 '배움'이라면 피드백을 제공한 후 학생이 다시금 주어진 피드백을 바탕으로 자신의 결과물을 수정할 기회를 가지는 것이 마땅합니다. 따라서 수업 실연 상황에서도 평가 활동이 이루어진 후 자신이 받은 피드백을 바탕으로 스스로 2차 점검하며 개선해보도록 언급하는 것이 필요합니다.

> <예시 상황 T-talk>
> T : ① Okay, time's up! Please return the writing and the checklist to your friends. … Did everyone get your writings and checklists? … Perfect!
>
>
>
> ② Then, why don't we upgrade our writing because now we have useful advice from our friends?
>
>
>
> ③ Awesome! Use the checklist and revise your writing. I'll give you 5 minutes. Go!

①에서 <Check! Check!> 활동이 끝난 후 학생들에게 다른 모둠의 Writing을 Checklist와 함께 다시 돌려주라고 이야기합니다. 그 후 ②에서 친구들로부터 유용한 조언을 얻었으니, 우리의 글을 업그레이드해보자며 Revising 활동을 제안합니다. 마지막으로 ③에서 Checklist를 활용하여 글을 수정하자는 안내와 함께 활동 시작을 알립니다.

한편, Revising 활동을 Google classroom과 연계하여 온-오프라인 블랜디드 형식으로 진행하면 아주 인상적인 수업 실연이 됩니다.

> <예시 상황 T-talk>
> T : ① Okay, time's up! Please return the writing and the checklist to your friends.
>
>
>
> ② Make sure you upload your revised writing on Google classroom after you check the advice from your friends. Alright?

위 ①~②와 같이 Peer feedback 제공이 끝난 후 Google classroom에 수정된 글을 게시하라고 안내하며 수업을 마무리할 수 있습니다. 이와 같은 방식은 교실에서 Revising 활동을 진행하는 것보다 T-talk가 짧아 시간이 절약될 뿐만 아니라 오프라인 수업이 온라인으로 연결되는 블랜디드 수업의 모습을 보여줄 수도 있죠!

Logical Development

Logical Development는 전체적인 수업 흐름에 관한 부분입니다. 활동이 하나하나 개별적이지 않고 서로 유기적으로 연결되어 있는지, 전체적인 분량상 균형이 적절한지, 그리고 최종적으로 해당 수업을 통해서 학생이 어떤 역량을 함양할 수 있을지를 살펴보는 영역이죠.

(1) Transition

Transition은 활동과 활동 사이의 전환입니다. 모든 활동은 서로 유기적으로 연결되어 있으므로 수업 실연에서 각 활동 간 논리적 연계성을 보여주는 것이 중요할 수밖에 없죠.

Check point #66.
 활동간 연계가 자연스러운가?

전체적인 건물 구조를 알고 있어야 이 기둥이 왜 필요한지 설명할 수 있는 것처럼, 각 활동이 왜 제시되었는지, 그 이유를 파악하기 위해서는 수업 실연의 전체적인 흐름을 미리 알고 있는 것이 중요합니다.

<수업 실연의 흐름>
Schema activation ⇨ Receptive Skills ⇨ Productive Skills ⇨ Evaluation

수업 실연의 큰 틀은 위와 같으며 각 흐름에 맞게 수업 목표를 달성하기 위한 활동들이 나열되어 있습니다. 즉, 이유 없이 등장하는 활동은 없다는 것이죠! 따라서 수업 실연 문제지를 받으면, 주어진 활동들에 대하여 각 활동이 왜 제시되었는지, 그 목적부터 고민해야 합니다.

단계	예시 활동	목적
Schema activation	• 짝과 대화 나누기 • 마인드맵	• 오늘 수업 주제에 대한 관심과 흥미 유발
⇩	⇩	⇩
Receptive Skills	• 읽고 이해하기	• 해당 주제 관련 지식 습득
⇩	⇩	⇩
Productive skills	• 글쓰기 • 영어를 활용한 결과물 만들기	• 배운 내용을 실생활에 적용 • 영어 활용 및 핵심 표현 연습
⇩	⇩	⇩
Evaluation	• 체크리스트 평가 • 발표 • 교사/동료 피드백	• 자신의 결과물을 공유 • 평가 활동에 참여하며 메타인지 향상

위 표는 수업 실연 흐름에 맞게 단계별 예시 활동 및 목적을 정리한 것입니다. 위 내용을 바탕으로 수업 활동간 연계를 자연스럽게 하기 위해서는 단계별 활동 목적을 떠올리며 다음 활동을 고려하였을 때 이번 활동은 무엇이 목적이었는지 떠올리는 연습을 할 필요가 있습니다.

1. Schema activation → Receptive Skills

수업 실연마다 수업 전체를 아우르는 주제가 있습니다. '환경 보호', '미래 직업', '청소년 리더십', '우정' 등 교과서에 등장하는 다양한 소재가 해당 수업 실연의 주제로서 출제될 수 있죠. 따라서 위 단계에서는 해당 주제에 대한 학생의 관심 및 흥미를 불러일으키는 활동이 제시됩니다. 그리고 그 활동 이후에는 대표적인 Receptive skill 영역인 Reading이 진행되죠. 따라서 이러한 부분을 T-talk로 잘 드러내는 것이 중요합니다.

<예시 상황 T-talk>

T : ① Today, we are going to talk about 'Friendship'. ··· What is friend? Tell me one word when you think of 'friend'.

<판서 예시>

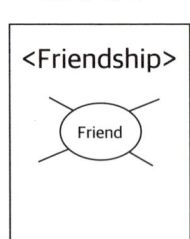

② Alright! So far, we've talked about 'friendship'. Then, are you ready to learn more about 'friendship'? … Perfect!

①에서 교사는 오늘의 수업 주제인 '우정'에 대하여 언급하며, '친구'를 떠올리면 생각나는 한 단어를 이야기해보라고 합니다. <판서 예시>와 같이 전체 교실을 대상으로 마인드맵 활동을 진행함으로써 해당 주제에 관한 관심과 흥미를 유발합니다. 이후 ②에서 지금까지 우정에 관한 이야기를 나누었다는 것을 언급하며 '우정'에 대해 더 알고 싶지 않냐는 질문으로 자연스럽게 Reading 활동으로 넘어갑니다.

2. Receptive Skills → Productive skills

여기서는 학생이 해당 주제에 대하여 새로운 지식을 얻고 난 후, 이를 직접 활용해보는 것에 초점을 둔 T-talk를 보여주어야 합니다. 배운 영어적 지식을 활용할 수도 있고 해당 주제를 실생활과 연결 지어 적용해볼 수도 있죠.

<예시 상황 T-talk>
T : ① We've just read the beautiful story of two old friends. What was important for keeping the friendship? … Yes, it was 'Trust'.

② However, would it be all? We know that there are many other important things to keep the friendship, right? … Then, why don't we write about our own idea of 'friendship'? Are you guys ready? … Awesome!

①에서 Reading 활동이 끝난 후 간단하게 CCQ를 진행하고 있습니다. 두 친구의 우정 이야기를 다시 되짚으며 Text에서 등장한 가장 중요한 요소가 'Trust'였음을 언급하고 있죠. 이를 바탕으로 ②에서 자연스럽게 'would it be all?'이라는 표현으로 'Trust' 이외에 또 무엇이 중요할지 생각해보도록 합니다. 그리고 이것에 대하여 써보자는 T-talk로 Receptive skill에서 Productive skill로 논리적 연계성을 보여주고 있죠!

3. Productive skills → Evaluation

이 단계에서는 학생의 글쓰기 활동이 끝나고 평가로 넘어가는 부분입니다. 따라서 교실 내에서 결과물을 공유하고 Checklist 및 Peer feedback 부분에 초점을 둔 T-talk를 구성하는 것이 중요합니다.

> <예시 상황 T-talk>
>
> T : ① So far, we've just finished writing about the important things to keep the friendship.
>
> ⇩
>
> ② However, I was so excited that every group has different ideas. So, don't you guys want to know your friend's idea? … Great! Then, presenters, are you ready? … Perfect! Let's begin the <Show time>!

①에서 Writing 활동이 끝났음을 언급하며 친구 관계를 유지하기 위해 중요한 부분을 각자 생각해보았음을 가정합니다. 이후 ②에서 교사가 모든 그룹의 생각이 다양했다는 사실을 언급하며, 다른 친구의 생각이 궁금하지 않은지 물어봅니다. 그리고 'Presenters, are you ready?'라는 T-talk로 발표자들에게 준비되었는지 물어본 후, 자연스럽게 Productive skills 활동에서 Evaluation 활동으로 넘어갑니다.

Check point #67.

General to Personalization 전개가 나타나는가?

'1:1 맞춤형 수업'이 예시로서 종종 등장하는 'Personalization'의 의미는 '개별화'입니다. 즉, 학생 개개인의 스타일, 능력 수준, 관심사 등을 고려한 수업 방식을 의미하죠.

그러나 여기서 'Personalization'의 의미는 수업 실연에서 활동 전개의 방향성을 의미합니다. 즉, 활동이 일반적(General)인 주제에서 학생 개인의 경험에 초점을 맞춘(Personalized) 방향으로 진행되어야 한다는 의미죠.

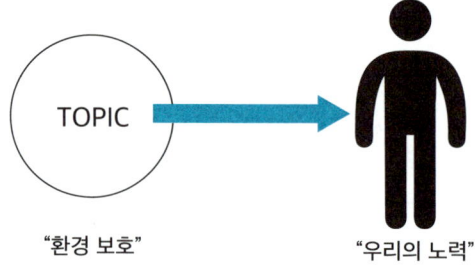

예를 들면 위 그림과 같이 읽기 영역에서 Topic으로 '환경 보호'가 제시되고, Writing에서 '환경 보호를 위한 우리의 노력'이 글쓰기 과제로 제시되는 것입니다. '일반적인 주제'에서 '나'와 관련짓는 방향으로 나아가는 것이죠.

따라서, 수업 실연에서 논리적 연계성을 강화하기 위해서는 이처럼 'General to Personalization'으로 전개되는 활동의 흐름을 T-talk로 드러낼 필요가 있습니다.

> <예시 상황 T-talk>
> T1 : So far, we've read about 'Endangered animals'. Then, what can WE do for them?
> T2 : We've just finished reading about 'Great leaders'. Then, what kind of leader do YOU want to be?
> T3 : In the reading text, there were so many problems on Earth. Then, how can WE solve these problems?
> T4 : The reading text was about the friendship between two scientists. Then, why don't we bring this into OUR lives? Do you have your own story?

위 T1~T4는 모두 'General'한 주제에서 'Personalized'한 활동으로 진행되는 모습을 보여주는 T-talk의 좋은 예시입니다. 위의 대문자로 표시된 부분에 강세를 주어 T-talk를 구성한다면 'Gerneral to Personalization'의 흐름을 훨씬 더 효과적으로 강조할 수 있을 것입니다!

(2) Balance

Balance는 말 그대로 '균형'이라는 의미입니다. 수업에서 전체적인 균형이 잡혀있지 않으면 학습에도 효과적이지 않을 뿐만 아니라, 수업 전개 자체에 미숙한 인상을 드러내게 됩니다. 따라서 수업 실연을 연습할 때는 '균형'에 대하여 고민하는 자세가 필요하며, 여기서는 조금 더 구체적으로 '내용적 균형'과 '시간적 균형'으로 나누어 살펴보도록 하겠습니다.

 Check point #68.

Main activity와 Build-up activity가 구분되는가?

Main activity와 Build-up activity를 구분해야 한다는 것은 내용적 균형에 초점을 맞춘 부분입니다. 'Check point #66'에서 살펴본 것처럼, 모든 활동은 각각 독립된 것이 아니라 서로 유기적으로 연결되어 이전, 이후 활동과 깊은 연관성을 가지고 있습니다. 따라서 해당 활동이 'Main activity'인지, 'Build-up activity'인지 정확하게 판단하고 전체적인 수업을 구상하는 연습이 필요합니다!

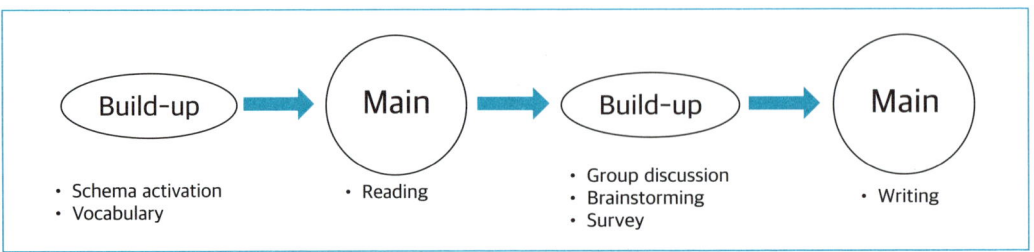

위 그림은 내용적 균형의 관점에서 수업 실연의 패턴을 나타낸 것입니다. 수업 실연에서는 두 개의 Main activity가 등장하며, 이를 위한 두 개의 Build-up activity가 함께 나타납니다. 첫 번째 Main activity는 Receptive skill의 대표 격인 Reading이며, 이를 위한 Build-up activity로 Reading topic에 대한 Schema activation과 Reading text에 등장하는 Vocabulary learning이 있습니다. 두 번째 Main activity는 Productive skill인 Writing이며 이를 위한 Build-up activity로 조별 Discussion이나 Brainstorming, 또는 Survey가 있습니다.

물론, 활동의 구체적인 지시 사항은 해마다 달라질 가능성이 있겠지만 지금까지의 경향을 살펴보면 Receptive skill과 Productive skill에서 각각 한 가지씩 Main activity가 구성되고, 이를 위한 Build-up activity가 함께 등장한다는 패턴을 파악할 수 있습니다. 따라서, 수업 실연 문제지를 받았을 때 각각의 지시 사항을 살펴보며 위 패턴에서 어떤 활동에 관한 지시 사항인지 하나씩 대입해보며 내용적 균형을 맞추는 연습을 진행해야 합니다.

Check point #69.
활동간 적절한 시간적 균형이 이루어졌는가?

책으로 공부하다 보면 자연스레 인풋이 많이 쌓이게 됩니다. 이렇게 인풋을 많이 쌓은 상태에서 수업 실연 연습을 꾸준히 지속하다 보면, 어느샌가 욕심이 생겨 보여주고 싶은 부분이 너무 많아지게 됩니다. 결국, 활동 하나하나에 쏟는 시간이 많아지고 제한시간을 초과하게 되죠. 따라서, 수업 실연을 연습할 때는 항상 제한시간을 두고 '시간적 균형'에 대해서도 고민하는 태도가 필요합니다.

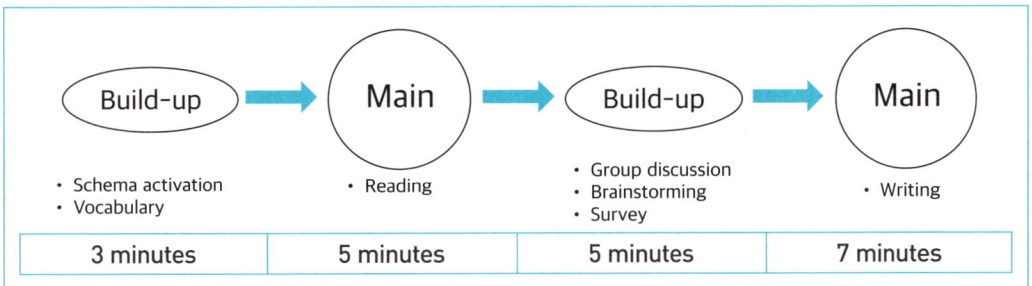

'Check point #68'에서 다룬 내용적 균형에 따라 시간적 배분을 하자면 위 그림과 같습니다. 수업 실연 도입부터 첫 번째 'Main activity'까지는 3분 정도를 할당하고, 이후 Reading 활동은 5분을 배정합니다. 그 후 Writing 활동에 들어가기 전 'Build-up activity'는 Grouping 등 시간이 더 필요할 확률이 높으므로 첫 번째 'Build-up activity'보다 조금 더 많은 시간인 5분을 할당하였고 이후 남은 7분 동안 Evaluation과 Writing을 포함한 두 번째 'Main activity'를 마무리합니다.

물론 항상 시간을 정확하게 지킬 순 없지만, 위와 같이 단계마다 대략적인 시간을 미리 할당해놓고 연습하는 것이 '시간적 균형'에 맞는 수업 실연을 준비하는 좋은 전략입니다.

> **Tip**
>
> 제한시간이 15분인 지역은 '3분-5분-5분-7분' 대신 '2분-4분-4분-5분'으로 시간을 배분하여 연습하시길 추천합니다. T-talk를 10~20% 정도 빠르게 진행하고, Circulation을 축소하거나 생략하는 방식으로 시간을 단축할 수 있습니다.

(3) Expansion

Expansion은 수업 내용의 확장을 의미합니다. 여기서 '확장'이란, 교실 안에서 배운 내용이 교실 밖, 즉, 학생의 삶에 어떤 교육적 영향을 줄 수 있는지와 관련됩니다. 이와 관련만 마지막 두 가지 체크리스트 살펴보도록 합시다!

Check point #70.

수업에서 배운 내용이 교실 밖 활동과 이어지는가?

논리적 연계성의 범위는 수업이 끝나면서 마무리되는 것이 아니라 수업 시간이 끝난 이후도 포함됩니다. 예를 들면, '환경 보호'에 관련된 단원을 읽고 '환경 보호를 위해 우리가 할 수 있는 노력'에 관한 글을 썼다면, 이를 바탕으로 '환경 보호를 실천하는 행동'으로 이어져야 한다는 것이죠! 이렇게 '교실 안'에서 배운 내용이 '교실 밖'까지 이어질 수 있을 때 비로소 '교실 속에서 배운 지식'이 '교실 밖 실천'으로 확장되었다고 할 수 있을 것입니다.

<예시 상황 T-talk>

T : ① Today, we read about future jobs and wrote about our own future.

② Then, do you remember where we are going to go next week? … Yes, Dongwoo! We are going to go to the 'Future Jobs Exhibition'!

③ So, based on what we learned today, let's make our future plans next week!

수업이 모두 끝난 후 Wrap-up 상황에서의 T-talk입니다. ①에서 오늘 미래 직업에 대하여 글을 읽었고, 자신의 미래에 대하여 글을 썼다고 정리합니다. 그 후 ②에서 다음 주에 어디를 방문하기로 했는지 학생과의 상호작용을 통해 물어보고 'Future jobs exhibition'이라는 대답을 유도합니다. 마지막으로 이어지는 ③에서 '오늘 배운 내용을 바탕으로 다음 주에 우리의 미래 계획을 만들어 보자'라는 내용의 T-talk로 수업에서 배운 내용을 교실 밖 활동과 자연스럽게 이어지도록 하며 해당 수업 차시를 마무리합니다.

Tip

실제 응시 지역의 랜드 마크를 넣어서 T-talk를 구성하면 더 인상적인 수업 마무리를 만들 수 있습니다. 저는 위 'Future Job Exhibition'이 BEXCO에서 열린다고 언급하며 '다음 주 현장 체험 학습 때 오늘 배운 내용을 참고해보자'라며 수업을 마무리하였습니다.

Check point #71.
현행 교육 과정에서 강조하는 인성요소/역량이 언급되었는가?

우리나라를 이끌어갈 인재를 양성하기 위하여 교육부에서는 '교육과정'을 제시하며, 이는 총론과 각론으로 구성되어 있습니다. 총론이 우리가 앞으로 나아가야 할 이상적 목표를 제시하고 있다면, 각론은 교과에서 어떤 방법으로 해당 목표를 실현할 것인지 구체적인 방안을 그리고 있습니다. 총론이 숲이라면, 각론은 나무인 셈이죠.

따라서 모든 교과서는 위 교육과정에 따라 제작되며, 실제 현장에서도 국가 수준 교육과정을 지역 수준 – 학교 수준 – 교사 수준으로 재구성하며 '교실 수업'의 형태로 학습자에게 교육적 경험이 제공됩니다.

이를 교사 선발의 관점에서 바라본다면, 수업 실연 시험은 '국가 수준'의 교육적 목표가 반영되어 만들어진 문항을 '교사 수준'에서 어떻게 해석하고 실현할 것인지 그 능력을 측정하고자 하는 시험입니다. 즉, 같은 지시 사항과 수업 자료가 제시되더라도 교사가 이를 어떤 교육적 목표를 지니고, 어떻게 해석하여 어떤 교육 활동으로 풀어내느냐에 따라 천차만별로 수업의 형태는 달라질 수밖에 없죠.

따라서, 시험을 준비하기 위해서는 수업 실연 문항 역시 이러한 '교육과정'의 큰 틀 아래에서 제작될 수밖에 없다는 사실을 기억해야 하며, 더 나아가 고득점을 받기 위해서는 현행 교육과정이 추구하는 이상향이 무엇인지 정확하게 파악하고 이를 수업에 반영할 줄 알아야 합니다.

2022 개정 교육과정의 내용 중 수업 실연의 관점에서 살펴볼 만한 주제는 '추구하는 인간상과 핵심 역량'이며 이를 정리하면 아래와 같습니다.

인간상	자기주도적인 사람	전인적 성장을 바탕으로 자아정체성을 확립하고 자신의 진로와 삶을 스스로 개척하는 사람
	창의적인 사람	폭넓은 기초 능력을 바탕으로 진취적 발상과 도전을 통해 새로운 가치를 창출하는 사람
	교양 있는 사람	문화적 소양과 다원적 가치에 대한 이해를 바탕으로 인류 문화를 향유하고 발전시키는 사람
	더불어 사는 사람	공동체 의식을 바탕으로 다양성을 이해하고 서로 존중하며 세계와 소통하는 민주시민으로서 배려와 나눔, 협력을 실천하는 사람
핵심 역량	자기관리 역량	자아정체성과 자신감을 가지고 자신의 삶과 진로를 스스로 설계하며 이에 필요한 기초 능력과 자질을 갖추어 자기주도적으로 살아갈 수 있는 능력
	지식정보처리 역량	문제를 합리적으로 해결하기 위하여 다양한 영역의 지식과 정보를 깊이 있게 이해하고 비판적으로 탐구하며 활용할 수 있는 능력
	창의적 사고 역량	폭넓은 기초 지식을 바탕으로 다양한 전문 분야의 지식, 기술, 경험을 융합적으로 활용하여 새로운 것을 창출하는 능력
	심미적 감성 역량	인간에 대한 공감적 이해와 문화적 감수성을 바탕으로 삶의 의미와 가치를 성찰하고 향유하는 능력
	협력적 소통 역량	다른 사람의 관점을 존중하고 경청하는 가운데 자신의 생각과 감정을 효과적으로 표현하며 상호협력적인 관계에서 공동의 목적을 구현하는 능력
	공동체 역량	지역·국가·세계 공동체의 구성원에게 요구되는 개방적 포용적 가치와 태도로 지속 가능한 인류 공동체 발전에 적극적이고 책임감 있게 참여하는 능력

위와 같이 2022 개정 교육과정에서 추구하는 인간상으로는 '자기주도적인 사람', '창의적인 사람', '교양 있는 사람', '더불어 사는 사람'으로 총 4가지를 제시하고 있으며, 핵심 역량으로는 '자기관리 역량', '지식정보처리 역량', '창의적 사고 역량', '심미적 감성 역량', '협력적 소통 역량', '공동체 역량'으로 총 6가지입니다.

2015 개정 교육과정	2022 개정 교육과정
전인적 성장을 바탕으로 자아정체성을 확립하고 자신의 진로와 삶을 개척하는 자주적인 사람	전인적 성장을 바탕으로 자아정체성을 확립하고 자신의 진로와 삶을 스스로 개척하는 자기주도적인 사람
다양한 상황에서 자신의 생각과 감정을 효과적으로 표현하고 다른 사람의 의견을 경청하며 존중하는 의사소통 역량	다른 사람의 관점을 존중하고 경청하는 가운데 자신의 생각과 감정을 효과적으로 표현하며 상호협력적인 관계에서 공동의 목적을 구현하는 협력적 소통 역량

위 표는 2015 개정 교육과정에서 2022 개정 교육과정으로 넘어오면서 개선된 부분을 요약한 것입니다. 먼저, '자주적인 사람'에서 '자기주도적인 사람'으로 문구가 바뀌고, '스스로'라는 단어가 추가된 것으로 보아, 이번 교육과정에서는 학생이 스스로 자신의 삶에 대해 책임감을 지니고 자율적인 판단을 내릴 수 있는 모습을 강조하는 것을 알 수 있습니다. 또한, '의사소통 역량'이었던 것이 '협력적 소통 역량'으로 바뀌었고, '다른 사람의 관점을 존중하고 경청', '상호협력적인 관계에서 공동의 목적을 구현'이라는 표현이 추가된 것으로 보아, '협력'의 가치를 더욱 강조하고 있다는 느낌을 받을 수 있습니다.

위 개선 사항을 종합하였을 때 2022 개정 교육과정에서 더욱 강조하고자 하는 키워드는 '자기주도성'과 '협력'임을 알 수 있습니다.

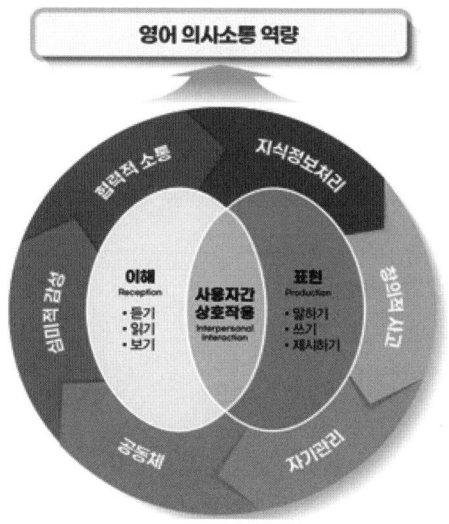

출처: 2022 개정 교육과정 영어과 각론

이와 관련하여 영어과에서는 '이해'와 '표현' 영역을 기반으로 총론이 제시하는 6가지 핵심 역량을 두루 계발하여 최종적으로 '영어 의사소통 역량'을 함양할 수 있도록 하는 것을 목표로 삼고 있습니다.

따라서, 수업 실연을 진행할 때는 위 역량 중 어떤 역량이 해당 차시 및 활동에서 주로 다루어지는지 유심히 살펴볼 필요가 있으며, 중학교에서 고등학교까지 영어과 교육과정의 역량별 키워드를 정리하면 다음과 같습니다.

역량	키워드
협력적 소통	• 참여 목적과 상황에 맞는 소통 • 다양한 견해를 수용하고 갈등을 조정
지식정보처리	• 목적에 맞게 검색, 수집, 이해, 분석, 평가, 활용 • 정보 윤리를 준수하며 활용 • 매체 활용 발표
창의적 사고	• 다양한 분야의 지식, 기술, 경험을 융합적으로 활용 • 비판적 사고, 창의적 표현 • 인문학적 상상력
자기관리	• 다양한 학습 전략 사용 • 영어 학습에 대한 지속적인 관심과 흥미 및 동기부여 • 스스로 학습 수행 및 평가(성찰) • 실수를 두려워하지 않고 자신감을 바탕으로 발표
공동체	• 지역, 국가, 세계 공동체의 구성원 • 문화 정체성 및 타문화 고유성, 타문화 가치 이해 • 공감, 배려, 관용 및 포용적 태도 • 공동체 문제 해결 • 의사 결정 과정에 적극적으로 참여
심미적 감성	• 인간에 대한 공감적 이해 및 감수성 • 삶의 의미와 가치를 발견하고 향유 • 인문학적 소양

이뿐만 아니라, 지금까지 출제된 수업 실연 주제 및 활동 역시 당시 교육과정에서 추구하는 핵심 역량과 밀접한 관련이 있었습니다.

출제연도	주제	핵심 활동	관련 핵심 역량
2025	Universal Design	제안서 쓰기	협력적 소통, 공동체, 지식정보처리
2024	Wisdom	대본 만들기	심미적 감성, 창의적 사고
2023	Comfort Zone	미래 목표 설정하기	자기관리
2022	Enemy pie	이야기 만들기	협력적 소통, 공동체, 창의적 사고
2021	Lunch menu	제안서 작성하기	공동체, 지식정보처리
2020	Future jobs	희망 직업 소개하기	자기관리, 지식정보처리
2019	Recycle	제안서 작성하기	공동체, 지식정보처리
2018	Safety tips	안전 수칙 만들기	자기관리, 공동체
2017	Creative writing	이야기 만들기	심미적 감성, 창의적 사고

이처럼 앞으로의 영어과 수업 실연 역시 현행 교육과정을 바탕으로 출제가 이루어질 것이므로, 이를 염두에 두고 자신의 수업에서 어떤 핵심 역량을 강조할 것인지 생각하며 수업 실연을 연습할 필요가 있습니다.

> <예시 상황 T-talk>
>
> T : ① It's time to wrap up the class. What was the main topic of today's class?
>
>
>
> ② Thank you, Heewon! It was the 'Comfort Zone'. So, based on what we've learned today, I want you to become a person who knows better about yourself, setting your own future goals to go forward!

위 ①~②는 '자기관리 역량'을 강조하고 있는 T-talk의 예시입니다. ①에서 수업을 마무리할 시간임을 언급하며 오늘 수업의 주제가 무엇인지 학생들에게 묻고 있습니다. 그 후 ②에서 핵심 주제는 'Comfort Zone'이었음을 상기시키고 'I want you to become a person who knows better about yourself, setting your own future goals to go forward!'라는 표현으로 '자기관리 역량'을 함양한 '자기주도적인 사람'이 되기를 희망한다는 점을 강조합니다. 이를 통해서 단순히 수업 내용에만 집중하는 교사가 아니라, 해당 교육과정에서 추구하는 인간상과 핵심 역량을 고려한 수업을 설계하고 진행할 수 있는 교사임을 보여줄 수 있습니다.

수업실연 체크리스트!

스터디 상황에 맞게 활용할 수 있도록 수정이 가능한 엑셀 파일을 제공합니다.
(비밀번호: Chess)

영역	항목	분류	#	Check lists	Points (O-△-X)	Comments
CLASSROOM MANAGEMENT	L-centered Facilitation	Scaffolding	1	교사가 적절한 Scaffolding을 제공하였는가?		
			2	Peer scaffolding이 일어났는가?		
		T's space	3	교사의 교실 사용 범위가 넓은가?		
			4	교사의 위치가 학생과 가까운가?		
		Comprehension Check Question	5	간단하고 명확한 CCQ가 제공되었는가?		
			6	이해확인 작업이 주기적으로 일어나는가?		
		Motivation	7	해당 활동 전 필요성에 대하여 언급하였는가?		
			8	해당 활동 후 효과에 대하여 언급하였는가?		
			9	활동마다 학생의 동기가 반복해서 부여되는가?		
		Interaction	10	학생의 이름이 자주 불리는가?		
			11	교사가 학생에게 질문을 자주 하는가?		
			12	교사의 질문에 대답하는 주체가 학생인가?		
		Teacher Talk	13	학생 수준에 맞는 어휘 및 문장 구조를 사용했는가?		
			14	학생 수준에 맞는 속도로 구사하였는가?		
			15	교사의 활동 지시가 간결하고 명확한가?		
			16	교사의 질문이 구체적인가?		
			17	배운 내용이 T-talk로 활용되었는가?		

CLASSROOM MANAGEMENT		Grouping	18	전체 학생 숫자와 일치하는가?		
			19	해당 활동에 적절한 인원을 배치하였는가?		
			20	개인별 역할 부여가 이루어졌는가?		
		Circulation during Activities	21	Circulation이 적절한 활동을 잘 선택하였는가?		
			22	Circulation의 동선이 다양한가?		
		Mixed-level Treatment	23	Low-level에게 적절한 도움이 제공되었는가?		
			24	High-level에게 적절한 과제가 추가되었는가?		
			25	교사의 긍정적 피드백이 함께 제시되었는가?		
	Presentation	Board	26	판서의 내용이 명확한가?		
			27	2가지 이상의 색상을 사용하였는가?		
		Digital Devices	28	스크린 화면을 사용하였는가?		
			29	교실에 제공된 기자재를 모두 활용하였는가?		
	Attitude	Verbal	30	영어 구사가 안정적인가?		
			31	문법적으로 옳은 문장을 구사하는가?		
		Nonverbal	32	목소리가 명확한가?		
			33	톤이 다양한가?		
			34	적절한 제스처가 사용되었는가?		
			35	Eye-Contact가 끊임없이 이루어지는가?		
			36	자신감 있는 태도가 유지되는가?		

영역	항목	분류	#	Check lists	Points (○-△-X)	Comments
TEACHING ENGLISH	Comprehensive skills	Vocabulary	37	단어 선택 과정에서 학생 의견이 고려되었는가?		
			38	2개 이상의 교수법을 사용하였는가?		
			39	학생이 Guessing을 성공했는가?		
		Reading	40	Reading Strategy가 사용되었는가?		
			41	Title에 대한 언급을 하였는가?		
			42	Mixed-level을 고려하였는가?		
			43	Comprehension Check가 이루어졌는가?		
		Liestening	44	Listening Strategy가 사용되었는가?		
			45	Input을 반복하여 제시하였는가?		
			46	Mixed-level을 고려하였는가?		
			47	Comprehension Check가 이루어졌는가?		
	Productive skills	Grammar	48	Discovery learning이 일어났는가?		
			49	지난 시간과 연계되는가?		
			50	Form에 대한 Noticing/Awareness가 일어났는가?		
		Speaking	51	Key expression을 제공하였는가?		
			52	Active participation이 강조되었는가?		
			53	Respect friends가 강조되었는가?		
			54	Turn-taking이 강조되었는가?		

TEACHING ENGLISH		Writing	55	Pre-writing 과정이 드러나는가?	
			56	Sample writing이 제시되었는가?	
			57	Writing의 조건이 제시되었는가?	
			58	Authentic purpose가 제시되었는가?	
			59	Mixed-level을 고려하였는가?	
	Evaluation	Design	60	평가 내용이 교수 내용과 일치하는가?	
			61	평가의 기준이 명확한가?	
		Giving Feedback	62	Positive feedback이 구체적인가?	
			63	Negative feedback 3요소가 지켜졌는가?	
			64	학생이 Feedback에 참여하는가?	
			65	Revise에 대한 언급이 있는가?	
	Logical Development	Transition	66	활동간 연계가 자연스러운가?	
			67	Gerneral to Personalization 전개가 나타나는가?	
		Balance	68	Main activity와 Build-up activity가 구분되는가?	
			69	활동간 적절한 시간적 균형이 이루어졌는가?	
		Expansion	70	수업에서 배운 내용이 교실 밖 활동과 이어지는가?	
			71	현행 교육 과정에서 강조하는 인성요소/역량이 언급되었는가?	

곰쌤 영어과 수업 실연 체크리스트

1. 수업 실연 기출 문제

   가~자. 기출문제 (2025~2017)

     1) 문제

     2) 지도안

2. 예시답안 & 스크립트

   가~자. 기출문제 (2025~2017)

     1) 판서 노트 및 예시 영상

     2) 지도안 예시

     3) 스크립트

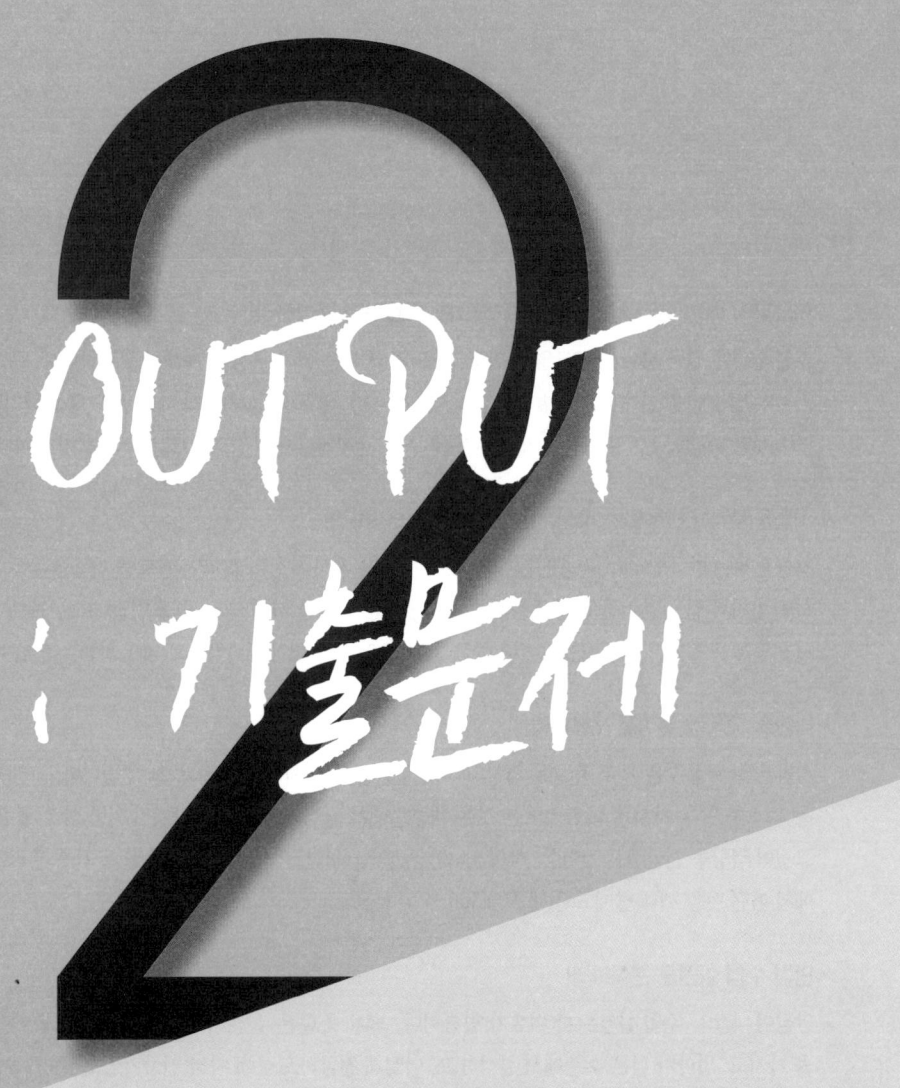

Chapter 01

수업 실연 기출 문제

📌 기출문제 연습 TIP

※ 지금까지 배운 수업 실연 Check Point를 떠올리며 구상하라!

수업 실연은 결국 하나의 발표일 뿐이고, 발표의 70%는 이미 구상 단계에서 결정됩니다. 즉, 얼마나 완성도 있는 수업 실연을 설계하는지가 고득점의 핵심입니다. 발표를 능숙하게 하는 것도 중요하지만, 그것은 고작 30%에만 해당될 뿐, 결국 점수의 대부분은 구상 단계에서 이미 결정된다는 사실을 잊지 마세요!

※ 기출문제에서 반복되는 지시 사항이 있는지 파악하라!

기출문제는 반복됩니다. 처음에는 모든 것이 새로운 지시 사항이겠지만, 연도를 거듭할수록, 기존에 출제된 지시 사항이 수업 실연 기출의 절반 정도를 차지한다는 사실을 깨달을 수 있을 것입니다. 기출문제 연습을 하시면서 이렇게 반복되는 지시 사항을 정리하고, 자기만의 수업 실연 시나리오로 자동화하는 연습이 꼭 필요합니다!

※ 나만의 고득점 무기를 포함하라!

시험 당일 채점관은 모두 똑같은 형식의 수업 실연을 수십 차례 연속으로 보게 됩니다. 그래서 나만의 특색있는 요소를 한두 가지 정도 반영하는 것은 채점관에게 긍정적인 인상을 남기기 위한 아주 좋은 전략이 됩니다. 그것이 역량을 언급하는 것이든, ART rule이든, T-talk이든, 상황별로 유용한 무기를 준비한 다음 구상 단계에서 어떤 것을 꺼내 쓸지 고민해 보세요!

※ 만점 수업 실연을 분석하라!

만점이 나오는 수업 실연은 다 이유가 있습니다. 모두 똑같은 수업 자료를 제공받더라도 이것을 어떤 통찰력을 가지고, 얼마나 깊은 수준에서 분석하고, 어떻게 전달하느냐에 따라 천차만별로 달라지기 때문입니다. 네이버 카페에 제가 직접 시범을 보인 만점 수업 실연 영상이 모두 준비되어 있으니, 기출문제 연습 후 꼭 모범 영상을 확인하시고 분석 하시기 바랍니다!

<곰쌤 시범 영상 확인하기>

가 2025 기출문제

Classroom settings

- Class time : 100 minutes
- Students : 24 High school 1st Graders
- Level : Mixed
- Aids : Digital whiteboard, Laptop, Online dictionary, Tablet PCs, PPT slides etc

Lesson information

- Unit title : Design for Everyone
- Objectives

    ✓ Students will be able to guess what the following text will be about.
    ✓ Students will be able to understand the text based on the Graphic Organizer.
    ✓ Students will be able to complete suggestion writing following the criteria.

지시사항

- 응시자 작성 내용 1 (Pre-reading)

    ✓ <자료 1>의 제목으로 글의 소재를 유추하는 활동을 진행할 것
    ✓ <자료 1>의 그림을 활용하여 유니버설 디자인의 특징을 추측하는 짝 활동을 진행할 것

- 응시자 작성 내용 2 (Reading)

    ✓ <자료 1>의 밑줄 친 단어 중 하나를 가르칠 것
    ✓ <자료 1>의 네모 친 표현의 형태를 가르칠 것
    ✓ <자료 2>의 도식 조직자를 완성하여 내용을 정리할 것

- 응시자 작성 내용 3 (Pre-writing)

    ✓ 학교의 유니버설 디자인 현황에 대해 모둠 토의를 실시할 것
    ✓ 모둠 활동을 통해 <자료 3>을 완성할 것

- 응시자 작성 내용 4 (Writing)

    ✓ <자료 3>을 바탕으로 <자료 4>를 완성할 것
    ✓ <자료 4>의 평가 기준을 활용하여 동료 평가를 실시할 것
    ✓ 제안하는 글에 관한 교사의 피드백을 제공할 것

(1) 문제
<자료 1>

<DESIGNING INCLUSIVE ENVIRONMENTS>

Universal Design refers to the design of products, environments, and systems that are usable by all people, regardless of age, ability, or background. It aims to remove barriers and make adaptation for everyone, fostering inclusion and equity in everyday life.

One of the primary features of Universal Design is equality. It is to avoid segregating users based on their abilities or needs. This means creating environments that allow everyone to participate equally. For example, automatic sliding door systems accommodate people with mobility challenges because they eliminate the need to physically open doors. In addition, low-floor buses provide easy access for wheelchair users, elderly passengers, and parents with strollers, by ensuring mobility for all groups.

Another important feature of Universal Design is flexibility. It is the ability to accommodate a wide range of individual preferences and requirements. For instance, adjustable desks and chairs in schools allow students of different heights and physical abilities to work comfortably by benefiting individuals with diverse physical needs. Furthermore, captioned videos support the needs of individuals with hearing impairments. This feature in videos emphasizes the importance of making content accessible to a wider audience, ensuring inclusivity for diverse users.

<자료 2>

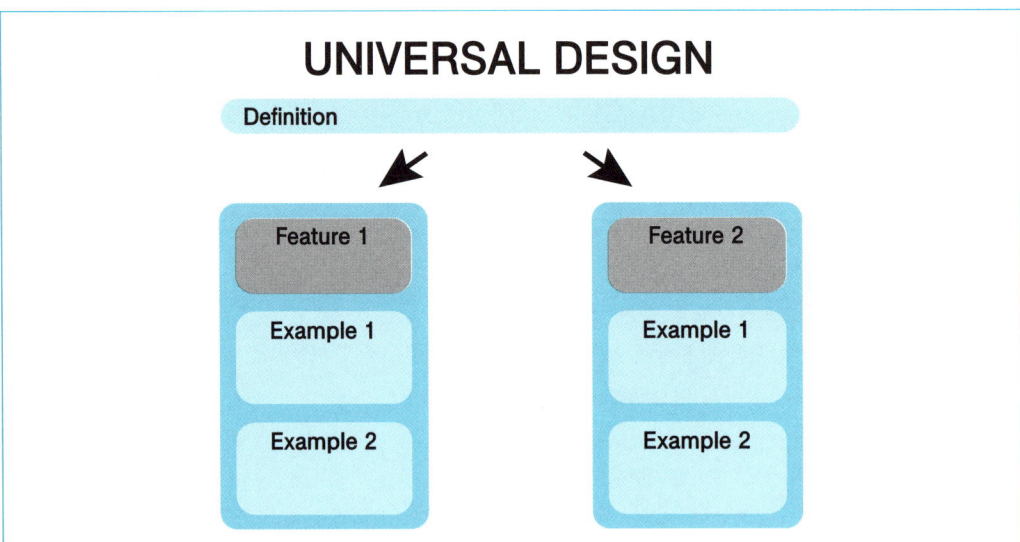

<자료 3>

Group number		Student names	
What we found	How we want to change		What we expect

<자료 4>

< Let's Write a Suggestion for School! >

We found that _____
_____
_____, (Problem)
which makes it hard for them to enjoy school life. This does not accommodate everyone's needs.

To solve this problem, we want to change _____
_____
_____, (Solution)
using Universal Design. This change will make the school more comfortable.

In the future, we expect _____
_____
_____. (Expectation)
This will create a better school for everyone.

<Peer Assessment Criteria>		<Check!>	
1. Organization	Is this writing well-organized and logical?	Yes ☐	No ☐
2. Creativity	Is this solution creative and original?	Yes ☐	No ☐
3. Language Use	Are the sentences and the words grammatical and appropriate?	Yes ☐	No ☐

(2) 지도안

단원명	Design for Everyone				시간	100 mins
대상	• Students : 24 High school 1st Graders • Level : Mixed					
수업 목표	✓ Students will be able to guess what the following text will be about. ✓ Students will be able to understand the text based on the Graphic Organizer. ✓ Students will be able to complete suggestion writing following the criteria.					
교수·학습 교구	Digital whiteboard, Laptop, Online dictionary, Tablet PCs, PPT slides etc					
핵심역량	자기 관리	지식정보처리	창의적 사고	심미적 감성	협력적 소통	공동체
		✓			✓	✓

<교수 학습 지도안>

단계	교수·학습 활동	유의점 및 활용 교구
도입 (5분)	*인사, 출석 확인, 교실 내 안전 점검 *학습 주제, 수업 준비 상태 확인	
전개1 (15분)	응시자 작성 내용 1 (Pre-reading) ✓ <자료 1>의 제목으로 글의 소재를 유추하는 활동을 진행할 것	PPT slides '자료 1'
	✓ <자료 1>의 그림을 활용하여 유니버설 디자인의 특징을 추측하는 짝 활동을 진행할 것	PPT slides '자료 1'

	응시자 작성 내용 2 (Reading)	
	✓ <자료 1>의 밑줄 친 단어 중 하나를 가르칠 것	
		Online dictionary '자료 1'
전개2 (20분)	✓ <자료 1>의 네모 친 표현의 형태를 가르칠 것	
		'자료 1'
	✓ <자료 2>의 도식 조직자를 완성하여 내용을 정리할 것	
		'자료 2'

전개3 (25분)	**응시자 작성 내용 3 (Pre-writing)**	
	✓ 학교의 유니버셜 디자인 현황에 대해 모둠 토의를 실시할 것	PPT slides
	✓ 모둠 활동을 통해 <자료 3>을 완성할 것	'자료 3'
전개4 (30분)	**응시자 작성 내용 4 (Writing)**	
	✓ <자료 3>을 바탕으로 <자료 4>를 완성할 것	'자료 3' '자료 4'

전개4 (30분)	✓ <자료 4>의 평가 기준을 활용하여 동료 평가를 실시할 것	'자료 4'
	✓ 제안하는 글에 관한 교사의 피드백을 제공할 것	
마무리 (5분)	*활동 마무리, 다음 차시 안내 *주변 정리 지도, 인사	

2024 기출문제

Classroom settings

- Class time : 100 minutes
- Students : 24 High school 1st Graders
- Level : Mixed
- Aids : Digital whiteboard, Laptop, Online dictionary, Tablet PCs etc

Lesson information

- Unit title : Spread Wisdom
- Objectives
  ✓ Students will be able to write a skit related to the proverb.
  ✓ Students will be able to use correct pronunciation of their writings.

지시사항

• 응시자 작성 내용 1
  ✓ <자료 1>과 <자료 2>의 밑줄 친 표현이나 어휘 중 1개를 선택하여 맥락을 활용하여 가르칠 것
  ✓ <자료 1>의 속담 중 하나에 해당하는 상황을 교사 임의로 제시하고 학생들에게 알아맞혀 보도록 할 것
  ✓ <자료 2>를 읽고 주제를 파악하게 할 것

• 응시자 작성 내용 2
  ✓ 모둠을 구성하여 <자료 3>의 Topic, Characters, Setting을 정하도록 할 것
  ✓ <자료 3>의 Scene 대본을 작성하도록 할 것
  ✓ <자료 4>를 활용하여 각 그룹의 글쓰기를 자기 평가하도록 할 것

• 응시자 작성 내용 3
  ✓ <자료 3>의 대본을 활용하여 읽기 연습을 할 것
  ✓ 학생들의 발음, 강세, 억양 등에 대하여 피드백을 제공할 것

(1) 문제

<자료 1>

> **< Let's learn some popular proverbs of other countries! >**
>
> - English : A smooth sea never makes a skilled sailor.
> - Norwegian : Experience is the best teacher, but the tuition is high.
> - Latin : Still waters run deep.
> - African : A tree is known by its fruit.
> - German : Fear makes the wolf bigger than it is.
> - Jewish : Great oaks from little acorns grow.

<자료 2>

> **Topic**
> A smooth sea never makes a skilled sailor.
>
> **Characters**
> Jessica, Paul, Eric
>
> **Settings**
> A busy schedule of high school students
>
> **Scene #1**
> Paul : *(Looks exhausted)* It is really busy doing all the homework. I have to take a math test, write a science report and study for the history quiz. I don't have enough time to do all of them.
> Jessica and Eric : You are right. It is too busy to be a high school student.
>
> **Scene #2**
> Eric : <u>What a relief!</u> The challenging week was just finally over!
> Jessica : Yes, it was really busy but we made it.
> Paul : I agree. Although it was really hard, I think it was a great experience. The storm made us stronger!

<자료 3>

< Let's make a SKIT! >

Topic : _____

Characters : _____

Settings : _____

Scene #1 : _____
Character 1 : _____
Character 2 : _____

○ ○ ○

Scene #2 : _____
Character 1 : _____
Character 2 : _____

○ ○ ○

<자료 4>

< Self Check! >

#	Check list	Scale		
1	Do I have all the requirements?	1	2	3
2	Is my writing well-organized?	1	2	3
3	Is my writing clear and accurate?	1	2	3

(2) 지도안

단원명	Spread Wisdom				시간	100 mins
대상	• Students : 24 High school 1st Graders • Level : Mixed					
수업 목표	✓ Students will be able to write a skit related to the proverb. ✓ Students will be able to use correct pronunciation of their writings.					
교수·학습 교구	Digital whiteboard, Laptop, Online dictionary, Tablet PCs etc					
핵심역량	자기 관리	지식정보처리	창의적 사고	심미적 감성	협력적 소통	공동체
		✓	✓		✓	

< 교수 학습 지도안 >

단계	교수·학습 활동	유의점 및 활용 교구
도입 (5분)	*인사, 출석 확인, 교실 내 안전 점검 *학습 주제, 수업 준비 상태 확인	
전개1 (25분)	응시자 작성 내용 1 ✓ <자료 1>과 <자료 2>의 밑줄 친 표현이나 어휘 중 1개를 선택하여 맥락을 활용하여 가르칠 것 ------------------------------------ ------------------------------------ ------------------------------------ ------------------------------------ ------------------------------------ ------------------------------------ ✓ <자료 1>의 속담 중 하나에 해당하는 상황을 교사 임의로 제시하고 학생들에게 알아맞혀 보도록 할 것 ------------------------------------ ------------------------------------ ------------------------------------ ------------------------------------ ------------------------------------ ------------------------------------ ------------------------------------	'자료 1' '자료 2' '자료 1'

전개1 (25분)	✓ <자료 2>를 읽고 주제를 파악하게 할 것	'자료 2'

전개2 (35분)	응시자 작성 내용 2	
	✓ 모둠을 구성하여 <자료 3>의 Topic, Characters, Settings을 정하도록 할 것	'자료 3'
	✓ <자료 3>의 Scene 대본을 작성하도록 할 것	'자료 3'

	✓ <자료 4>를 활용하여 각 그룹의 글쓰기를 자기 평가하도록 할 것	
		'자료 4'
전개3 (30분)	응시자 작성 내용 3	
	✓ <자료 3>의 대본을 활용하여 읽기 연습을 할 것	
		'자료 3'
	✓ 학생들의 발음, 강세, 억양 등에 대하여 피드백을 제공할 것	
마무리 (5분)	*활동 마무리, 다음 차시 안내 *주변 정리 지도, 인사	

2023 기출문제

Classroom settings

- Class time : 90 minutes
- Students : 26 Middle school 3rd Graders
- Level : Mixed
- Aids : Digital whiteboard, Laptop, Online dictionary, Tablet PCs, PPT slides etc

Lesson information

- Unit title : Beyond Your Comfort Zone
- Objectives
  ✓ Students will be able to infer the meaning of the title using a quote.
  ✓ Students will be able to describe the four zones and connect them to their own experiences.
  ✓ Students will be able to write about their goal beyond the comfort zone based on their personal experience.

지시사항

- 응시자 작성 내용 1 (Reading)
  ✓ <자료 1>에 인용된 명언을 활용하여 제목의 의미를 추론할 것
  ✓ 'Comfort Zone'을 벗어나야 하는 이유에 관해 언급할 것

- 응시자 작성 내용 2 (Pre-writing)
  ✓ <자료 2>의 4가지 영역(Zone)에 관해 설명하고 학생의 경험을 나누도록 유도할 것
  ✓ 예문을 통해 <자료 2>의 밑줄 친 어휘 표현 3개를 가르칠 것
  ✓ 각 영역(Zone)에 해당하는 어휘 표현을 연결하며 <자료 2>를 완성하도록 할 것

- 응시자 작성 내용 3 (Writing)
  ✓ 교사의 예시를 제공하여 <자료 3>에 제시된 표를 완성하도록 할 것
  ✓ 완성된 표를 바탕으로 짝과 함께 이야기를 나누고 개별적으로 <자료 3>을 완성할 것
  ✓ 글쓰기에 사용된 언어 표현에 관해 교사의 피드백을 제공할 것

(1) 문제

<자료 1>

<Beyond Your Comfort Zone>

"The greatest danger for most of us is not that our aim is too high and we miss it, but that it is too low and we reach it."

Michelangelo Buonarroli

    There are four different zones that people experience when they try new things. First, the Comfort Zone is where we feel safe and do things we're used to. Everything feels easy and familiar here. Next is the Fear Zone. This is where we feel nervous or unsure about ourselves. We might worry about failing or what others will think. It takes courage to leave the comfort zone and step into the fear zone. If we keep going, we reach the Learning Zone. In this zone, we try new things, solve problems, and learn new skills. It may be hard, but we start to grow. Finally, there is the Growth Zone. Here, we set bigger goals and become more confident. We change in a good way and improve ourselves.

    I had an experience like this. I was in the school choir and enjoyed singing with my friends. But I was too shy to sing alone. Singing a solo sounded scary to me. One day, I decided to challenge myself and try out for a solo part in the school musical. I was really nervous, but I gave it a try. To my surprise, I got the part! I was so proud of myself. I felt more confident, and I also became a better singer through practice. Leaving my comfort zone helped me grow.

<자료 2>

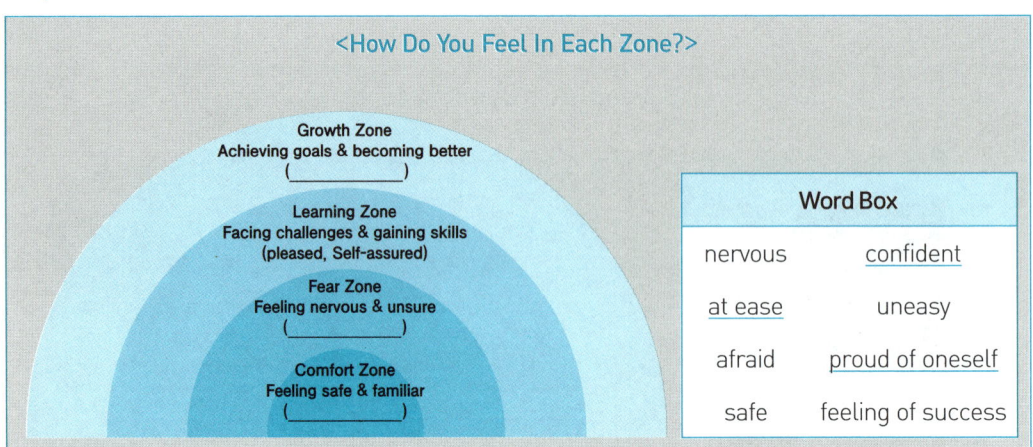

<자료 3>

<My plan to go beyond the 'Comfort Zone'>

My 'Comfort Zone'	
New goal	
Reasons for the goal	
Expected difficulties	
Planned actions	

Let me introduce my plan to go beyond my comfort zone. First, my comfort zone is _____. My new goal is _____. I set this goal because _____ _____. Of course, I can expect some difficulties along the way. They are _____ _____. To achieve my goal, I am planning to _____.

(2) 지도안

단원명	Beyond Your Comfort Zone			시간	90 mins	
대상	• Students : 26 Middle school 3rd Graders • Level : Mixed					
수업 목표	✓ Students will be able to infer the meaning of the title using a quote. ✓ Students will be able to describe the four zones and connect them to their own experiences. ✓ Students will be able to write about their goal beyond the comfort zone based on their personal experience.					
교수·학습 교구	Digital whiteboard, Laptop, Online dictionary, Tablet PCs, PPT slides etc					
핵심역량	자기 관리	지식정보처리	창의적 사고	심미적 감성	협력적 소통	공동체
	✓	✓			✓	

<교수 학습 지도안>

단계	교수·학습 활동	유의점 및 활용 교구
도입 (5분)	*인사, 출석 확인, 교실 내 안전 점검 *학습 주제, 수업 준비 상태 확인	
전개1 (20분)	응시자 작성 내용 1 (Reading) ✓ <자료 1>에 인용된 명언을 활용하여 제목의 의미를 추론할 것 ✓ 'Comfort Zone'을 벗어나야 하는 이유에 관해 언급할 것 	'자료 1'

	응시자 작성 내용 2 (Pre-writing)	
	✓ <자료 2>의 4가지 영역(Zone)에 관해 설명하고 학생의 경험을 나누도록 유도할 것	'자료 2'
전개2 (30분)		
	✓ 예문을 통해 <자료 2>의 밑줄 친 어휘 표현 3개를 가르칠 것	'자료 2'
	✓ 각 영역(Zone)에 해당하는 어휘 표현을 연결하며 <자료 2>를 완성하도록 할 것	'자료 2'

	응시자 작성 내용 3 (Writing)	
	✓ 교사의 예시를 제공하여 <자료 3>에 제시된 표를 완성하도록 할 것	PPT slides '자료 3'
전개3 (30분)	✓ 완성된 표를 바탕으로 짝과 함께 이야기를 나누고 개별적으로 <자료 3>을 완성할 것	'자료 3'
	✓ 글쓰기에 사용된 언어 표현에 관해 교사의 피드백을 제공할 것	
마무리 (5분)	*활동 마무리, 다음 차시 안내 *주변 정리 지도, 인사	

라 2022 기출문제

〖 Classroom settings 〗

- Class time : 90 minutes
- Students : 26 Middle school 3rd Graders
- Level : Mixed
- Aids : Digital whiteboard, Laptop, PPT slides etc

〖 Lesson information 〗

- Unit title : Enemy Pie
- Objectives
  - ✓ Students will be able to predict the story using the title and context.
  - ✓ Students will be able to find the details of the text using a graphic organizer.
  - ✓ Students will be able to create a group story with a plot twist.

〖 지시사항 〗

- 응시자 작성 내용 1
  - ✓ <자료 1>의 제목으로 이야기의 내용을 추측하는 활동을 진행할 것
  - ✓ 주제에 관해 짝과 경험을 나누는 활동을 진행할 것
  - ✓ 맥락을 통해 <자료 1>의 밑줄 친 단어 중 하나의 의미를 추측하도록 할 것

- 응시자 작성 내용 2
  - ✓ <자료 1>의 주제를 찾는 활동을 진행할 것
  - ✓ 그래픽 오거나이저를 제시하여 <자료 1>의 세부 정보를 찾는 활동을 진행할 것

- 응시자 작성 내용 3
  - ✓ 모둠 활동을 위한 개인별 역할을 부여할 것
  - ✓ 모둠 활동을 통해 플롯 트위스트가 포함된 <자료 3>을 완성할 것
    (교사는 <자료 2>를 참고할 것)

- 응시자 작성 내용 4
  - ✓ 채점 루브릭을 제시하여 <자료 3> 발표에 대한 동료 평가를 진행할 것
  - ✓ 갈등을 해결한 자기 경험을 짝과 함께 나눠보도록 할 것
  - ✓ 영어 사용에 관한 교사의 피드백을 제공할 것

(1) 문제

<자료 1>

<Enemy Pie>

It was all good until Jeremy Ross moved into the neighborhood, right next to my best friend Stanley. I did not like Jeremy Ross. He laughed at me when he struck me out in a baseball game. He had a party on his trampoline, and I wasn't even invited. But my best friend Stanley was.

Jeremy Ross was the one and only person on my enemy list. I never even had an enemy list until he moved into the neighborhood. But as soon as he came along, I needed one. I hung it up in my tree house, where Jeremy Ross was not allowed to go.

Dad understood stuff like enemies. He told me that when he was my age, he had enemies, too. But he knew of a way to get rid of them. I asked him to tell me how. "Tell you how? I'll show you how!" he said. He pulled a really old recipe book off the kitchen shelf. Inside, there was a worn-out scrap of paper with faded writing. Dad held it up and looked at it. "Enemy Pie," he said, satisfied.

You may be wondering what exactly is in Enemy Pie. I was wondering, too. But Dad said the recipe was so secret, he couldn't even tell me. I decided it must be magic. I begged him to tell me something - anything. "I will tell you this," he said. "Enemy Pie is the fastest known way to get rid of enemies."

Now, of course, this got my mind working. What kinds of things - disgusting things - would I put into a pie for an enemy? I brought him earthworms and rocks, but he didn't think he'd need those.

...

As for Enemy Pie, I still don't know how to make it. I still wonder if enemies really do hate it or if their hair falls out or their breath turns bad. But I don't know if I'll ever get an answer, because I just lost my best enemy.

<Key Concept>
A plot twist is a literary technique that introduces a unexpected and surprising change in the plot in a work of fiction.

<자료 2>

*NOTE FOR TEACHERS : This summary is ONLY for teachers. Students are not provided with the following summary.

> **Summary of Enemy Pie:**
>
> In Enemy Pie by Derek Munson, a young boy is excited for summer until he meets Jeremy Ross, a new kid in the neighborhood, who quickly becomes his "enemy." Upset, the boy turns to his dad, who suggests making an "Enemy Pie" to get rid of enemies. However, there's a catch : the boy must spend the entire day with Jeremy Ross before the pie will work. Reluctantly, the boy spends time with Jeremy, and to his surprise, they have a great time playing games and riding bikes. By the end of the day, the boy realizes that Jeremy Ross isn't an enemy after all—they've become friends. He finally understands that "Enemy Pie" wasn't about revenge ; it was a clever way to show that spending time together can change how we see others.

<자료 3>

Group Number : ____

Now, of course, this got my mind working. What kinds of things - disgusting things - would I put into a pie for an enemy? I brought him earthworms and rocks, but he didn't think he'd need those.

(Write your group's story here)

As for Enemy Pie, I still don't know how to make it. I still wonder if enemies really do hate it or if their hair falls out or their breath turns bad. But I don't know if I'll ever get an answer, because I just lost my best enemy.

(2) 지도안

단원명	Enemy Pie				시간	90 mins
대상	• Students : 26 Middle school 3rd Graders • Level : Mixed					
수업 목표	✓ Students will be able to predict the story using the title and context. ✓ Students will be able to find the details of the text using a graphic organizer. ✓ Students will be able to create a group story with a plot twist.					
교수·학습 교구	Digital whiteboard, Laptop, PPT slides etc					
핵심역량	자기 관리	지식정보처리	창의적 사고	심미적 감성	협력적 소통	공동체
			✓		✓	✓

<교수 학습 지도안>

단계	교수·학습 활동	유의점 및 활용 교구
도입 (5분)	*인사, 출석 확인, 교실 내 안전 점검 *학습 주제, 수업 준비 상태 확인	
전개1 (15분)	<center>응시자 작성 내용 1</center> ✓ <자료 1>의 제목으로 이야기의 내용을 추측하는 활동을 진행할 것 ✓ 주제에 관해 짝과 경험을 나누는 활동을 진행할 것 	'자료 1'

전개1 (15분)	✓ 맥락을 통해 <자료 1>의 밑줄 친 단어 중 하나의 의미를 추측하도록 할 것	'자료 1'
전개2 (20분)	응시자 작성 내용 2 ✓ <자료 1>의 주제를 찾는 활동을 진행할 것	'자료 1'
	✓ 그래픽 오거나이저를 제시하여 <자료 1>의 세부 정보를 찾는 활동을 진행할 것	PPT slides '자료 1'

전개3 (20분)	**응시자 작성 내용 3**		
	√ 모둠 활동을 위한 개인별 역할을 부여할 것		
	√ 모둠 활동을 통해 플롯 트위스트가 포함된 <자료 3>을 완성할 것		'자료 3' *교사는 '자료 2'를 참고할 것
전개4 (25분)	**응시자 작성 내용 4**		
	√ 채점 루브릭을 제시하여 <자료 3> 발표에 대한 동료 평가를 진행할 것		PPT slides '자료 3'

전개4 (25분)	✓ 갈등을 해결한 자기 경험을 짝과 함께 나눠보도록 할 것
	✓ 영어 사용에 관한 교사의 피드백을 제공할 것
마무리 (5분)	*활동 마무리, 다음 차시 안내 *주변 정리 지도, 인사

2021 기출문제

Classroom settings

- Class time : 100 minutes
- Students : 30 High school 1st Graders
- Level : Mixed
- Aids : Digital whiteboard, Laptop, PPT slides etc

Lesson information

- Unit title : Healthy Food, Happy Life!
- Objectives
    - ✓ Students will be able to find the main idea and details from the text.
    - ✓ Students will be able to create a healthy menu through the discussion.
    - ✓ Students will be able to write a suggestion letter for a healthy menu.

지시사항

- 응시자 작성 내용 1
    - ✓ 학생의 동기 부여를 위한 교사의 질문을 제시할 것
    - ✓ <자료 1>을 활용하여 짝과 함께 말하기 활동을 진행할 것
    - ✓ 짝 활동 결과에 관한 학생과 교사의 상호작용을 포함할 것

- 응시자 작성 내용 2
    - ✓ <자료 2>의 주제를 찾는 활동을 진행할 것
    - ✓ <자료 2>의 세부 정보에 관한 이해점검 확인을 실시할 것
    - ✓ 밑줄 친 세 단어 중 하나를 가르칠 것

- 응시자 작성 내용 3
    - ✓ 모둠 토의를 통해 <자료 3>을 완성할 것
    - ✓ 학생 참여를 유도하며 촉진자 역할을 수행할 것
    - ✓ 모둠 토의에 관한 교사의 피드백을 제공할 것

- 응시자 작성 내용 4
    - ✓ <자료 4>를 활용하여 개별 글쓰기 활동을 진행할 것
    - ✓ 글쓰기 평가 기준을 제시하고 설명할 것
    - ✓ 글에 관한 동료 평가를 실시할 것

(1) 문제
<자료 1>

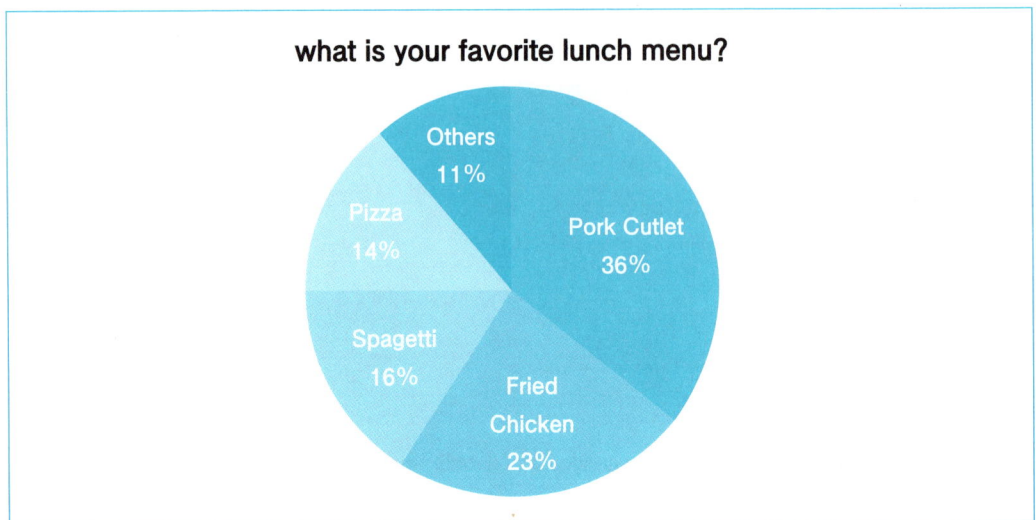

<자료 2>

Teenagers are growing up, so a healthy and balanced diet is really important for their growth and development. It's also good to know what each food does for your body. Different healthy foods have different key functions. First, foods like salmon, nuts, and pumpkin seeds can help <u>boost</u> your brainpower. They can make your brain sharper and help prevent short-term memory loss. Second, protein-rich foods such as chicken, beans, and eggs help you grow physically, like getting taller and stronger. Third, beans, green leafy vegetables, and bananas have <u>abundant</u> nutrients that are important for making your bones strong. Finally, kimchi and sweet potatoes can help reduce stress, <u>elevating</u> your mood and making you feel happier. Eating a variety of these foods can help you grow up healthy!

<자료 3>

#	Dish name	Main ingredients	Reasons why it is healthy
1			
2			

<자료 4>

My Suggestion for Healthy Menu

Name: _____

_____
_____
_____
_____
_____
_____
_____

(2) 지도안

단원명	Healthy Food, Happy Life!				시간	100 mins
대상	• Students : 30 High school 1st Graders • Level : Mixed					
수업 목표	✓ Students will be able to find the main idea and details from the text. ✓ Students will be able to create a healthy menu through the discussion. ✓ Students will be able to write a suggestion letter for a healthy menu.					
교수·학습 교구	Digital whiteboard, Laptop, PPT slides etc					
핵심역량	자기 관리	지식정보처리	창의적 사고	심미적 감성	협력적 소통	공동체
	✓	✓			✓	

<교수 학습 지도안>

단계	교수·학습 활동	유의점 및 활용 교구
도입 (5분)	*인사, 출석 확인, 교실 내 안전 점검 *학습 주제, 수업 준비 상태 확인	
전개1 (15분)	**응시자 작성 내용 1** ✓ 학생의 동기 부여를 위한 교사의 질문을 제시할 것 ──────────────────── ──────────────────── ──────────────────── ──────────────────── ──────────────────── ──────────────────── ──────────────────── ✓ <자료 1>을 활용하여 짝과 함께 말하기 활동을 진행할 것 ──────────────────── ──────────────────── ──────────────────── ──────────────────── ──────────────────── ──────────────────── ────────────────────	PPT slides '자료 1'

	✓ 짝 활동 결과에 관한 학생과 교사의 상호작용을 포함할 것	
	응시자 작성 내용 2	
	✓ <자료 2>의 주제를 찾는 활동을 진행할 것	
전개2 (20분)		'자료 2'
	✓ <자료 2>의 세부 정보에 관한 이해점검 확인을 실시할 것	
		'자료 2'

전개2 (20분)	✓ 밑줄 친 세 단어 중 하나를 가르칠 것	
전개3 (25분)	응시자 작성 내용 3	
	✓ 모둠 토의를 통해 <자료 3>을 완성할 것	'자료 3'
	✓ 학생 참여를 유도하며 촉진자 역할을 수행할 것	

	✓ 모둠 토의에 관한 교사의 피드백을 제공할 것	
	응시자 작성 내용 4	
	✓ <자료 4>를 활용하여 개별 글쓰기 활동을 진행할 것	'자료 4'
전개4 (30분)	✓ 글쓰기 평가 기준을 제시하고 설명할 것	PPT slides '자료 4'
	✓ 글에 관한 동료 평가를 실시할 것	
마무리 (5분)	*활동 마무리, 다음 차시 안내 *주변 정리 지도, 인사	

바 2020 기출문제

Classroom settings

- Class time : 100 minutes
- Students : 30 High school 1st Graders
- Level : Mixed
- Aids : Digital whiteboard, Laptop, PPT slides etc

Lesson information

- Unit title : Search for Future Jobs
- Objectives

  ✓ Students will be able to find the main idea and details from the text.
  ✓ Students will be able to understand the correct usage of 'will be -ing'.
  ✓ Students will be able to write a paragraph about the future job.

지시사항

- **응시자 작성 내용 1**
  ✓ 스크린을 활용하여 수업 주제에 관한 디지털 미디어 자료를 제시할 것
  ✓ 학생의 동기 부여를 위한 교사의 질문을 제시할 것
  ✓ <자료 1>을 활용하여 미래 직업에 관해 생각을 나누는 짝 활동을 진행할 것

- **응시자 작성 내용 2**
  ✓ <자료 2>의 주제를 찾는 활동을 진행할 것
  ✓ <자료 2>의 세부 정보에 관한 이해점검 확인을 실시할 것
  ✓ 밑줄 친 표현 'will be -ing'를 가르칠 것

- **응시자 작성 내용 3**
  ✓ 모둠 활동을 통해 <자료 3>을 완성할 것
  ✓ 모둠 활동 중 교실을 순회하며 촉진자 역할을 수행할 것
  ✓ 학생 발표에 관한 교사의 피드백을 제공할 것

- **응시자 작성 내용 4**
  ✓ <자료 4>에 제시된 글쓰기 조건을 강조하며 글을 완성하도록 할 것
  ✓ 동료 평가를 위한 기준을 제시하고 각각을 설명할 것
  ✓ 글쓰기 결과에 대하여 짝 활동을 진행할 것

(1) 문제

<자료 1>

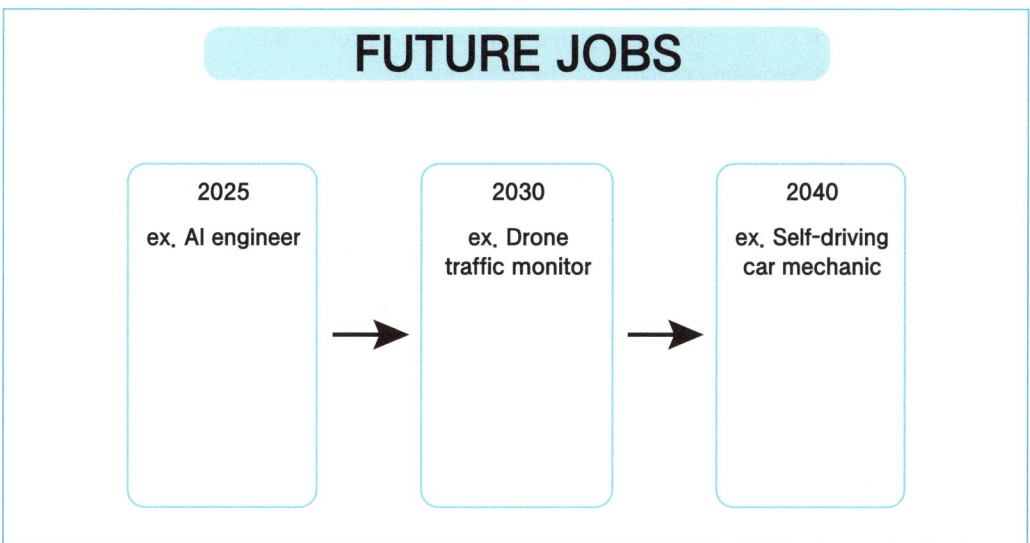

<자료 2>

   We do not know what jobs will exist in the future. A report says that most jobs from 2020 will disappear, and many people will be working in different fields. Some experts say that most kids in kindergarten today will do jobs that do not exist because their future jobs have not been created yet. Some jobs we have now will still exist in the future, but they will change, just like everything else. Many new jobs will come from the development of science and technology, especially artificial intelligence. In the near future, people will be pursuing careers such as drone traffic monitors, who watch and control drone movements, and self-driving car mechanics, who fix self-driving cars. There will be many more new jobs like these.

<자료 3>

<Group Project Worksheet>

1. Discuss with your group members and decide your group's future job.
2. Fill in the blanks below and practice for the presentation.

Career Guide : Our Future

- Drone traffic monitor
  - Job description : _____
  - Required skill : _____

- Self-driving car mechanic
  - Job description : _____
  - Required skill : _____

- Weather modification specialist
  - Job description : _____
  - Required skill : _____

- *(Your group's future job)*
  - Job description : _____
  - Required skill : _____

<자료 4>

<My Future Job>

* **Writing Requirements**
  - Your future job and the reason why you chose it
  - Job description and its required skills
  - 'Will be -ing'
  - More than 5 sentences

_____
_____
_____
_____
_____
_____

(2) 지도안

단원명	Search for Future Jobs				시간	100 mins	
대상	• Students : 30 High school 1st Graders • Level : Mixed						
수업 목표	✓ Students will be able to find the main idea and details from the text. ✓ Students will be able to understand the correct usage of 'will be -ing'. ✓ Students will be able to write a paragraph about the future job.						
교수·학습 교구	Digital whiteboard, Laptop, PPT slides etc						
핵심역량	자기 관리	지식정보처리	창의적 사고	심미적 감성	협력적 소통		공동체
	✓	✓			✓		

<교수 학습 지도안>

단계	교수·학습 활동	유의점 및 활용 교구
도입 (5분)	*인사, 출석 확인, 교실 내 안전 점검 *학습 주제, 수업 준비 상태 확인	
전개1 (15분)	응시자 작성 내용 1 ✓ 스크린을 활용하여 수업 주제에 관한 디지털 미디어 자료를 제시할 것 ✓ 학생의 동기 부여를 위한 교사의 질문을 제시할 것	PPT slides

전개1 (15분)	✓ <자료 1>을 활용하여 미래 직업에 관해 생각을 나누는 짝 활동을 진행할 것	'자료 1'
전개2 (20분)	응시자 작성 내용 2	
	✓ <자료 2>의 주제를 찾는 활동을 진행할 것	'자료 2'
	✓ <자료 2>의 세부 정보에 관한 이해점검 확인을 실시할 것	PPT slides '자료 2'

전개2 (20분)	✓ 밑줄 친 표현 'will be -ing'를 가르칠 것	'자료 2'
전개3 (25분)	응시자 작성 내용 3	'자료 3'
	✓ 모둠 활동을 통해 <자료 3>을 완성할 것	
	✓ 모둠 활동 중 교실을 순회하며 촉진자 역할을 수행할 것	

전개3 (25분)	✓ 학생 발표에 관한 교사의 피드백을 제공할 것		
전개4 (30분)	응시자 작성 내용 4		
	✓ <자료 4>에 제시된 글쓰기 조건을 강조하여 글을 완성하도록 할 것		'자료 4'
	✓ 동료 평가를 위한 기준을 제시하고 각각을 설명할 것		'자료 4'
	✓ 글쓰기 결과에 대하여 짝 활동을 진행할 것		
마무리 (5분)	*활동 마무리, 다음 차시 안내 *주변 정리 지도, 인사		

2019 기출문제

Classroom settings

- Class time : 90 minutes
- Students : 24 Middle school 3rd Graders
- Level : Mixed
- Aids : Digital whiteboard, Laptop, PPT slides etc

Lesson information

- Unit title : Small Actions for the Blue Planet
- Objectives
  ✓ Students will be able to find the main idea and details from the text.
  ✓ Students will be able to answer the questions about their personal experiences.
  ✓ Students will be able to write a suggestion for recycling.

지시사항

- 응시자 작성 내용 1
  ✓ <자료 1>의 소재에 관하여 배경지식 활성화를 위한 활동을 진행할 것
  ✓ <자료 1>의 밑줄 친 단어 중 하나를 가르칠 것
  ✓ <자료 1>을 읽고 주제를 찾도록 할 것

- 응시자 작성 내용 2
  ✓ <자료 1>의 세부 내용을 찾는 활동을 진행하고 학생 이해도를 점검할 것
  ✓ <자료 2>를 활용한 짝 활동을 진행할 것

- 응시자 작성 내용 3
  ✓ <자료 3>을 활용하여 설문조사를 위한 짝 활동을 진행할 것
  ✓ 활동 중 교실을 순회하며 촉진자 역할을 수행할 것
  ✓ 내용이나 형식 측면에서 학생 오류에 관한 교사의 피드백을 제공할 것

- 응시자 작성 내용 4
  ✓ <자료 4>를 위한 교사의 예시를 제공할 것
  ✓ 모둠 활동을 통해 <자료 4>를 완성할 것

(1) 문제

<자료 1>

<LET'S RECYCLE PROPERLY!>

Hello everyone! My name is Jiho, and I am the president of the school eco-club, Green Avengers. I'm here because recycling in our school is not done properly. So, I will tell you how to recycle better.

First, many students throw drink containers into the recycling bin without rinsing them. After finishing your drink, rinse the container before recycling it.

Second, we often forget to <u>remove</u> labels from plastic bottles. Before recycling, take off the labels.

Third, <u>stained</u> paper cannot be recycled. For example, pizza boxes should not go into the recycling bin, but many students put them there. Instead, throw them in the garbage can.

Fourth, do not put garbage into the recycling bin. If <u>recyclable</u> items are mixed with trash, they cannot be recycled.

In conclusion, if we recycle properly, our school will be more eco-friendly. I strongly believe that small actions can make a big difference. Thank you for listening.

<자료 2>

<Talk with your friend!>

#	Problem in our school	Suggestions for better school
1		
2		
3		
4		

<자료 3>

<How often do you recycle properly?>

Questions	Never	Rarely	Sometimes	Always
1. How often do you rinse your containers before throwing away?				ex. |||||
2. How often do you remove labels from bottles before recycling them?				
3. How often do you throw stained papers in the garbage bin?				
4. How often do you put recyclable items into the recycling bin?				
5. (Your question)				

<자료 4>

<Our Suggestions for Better School>

Group number	
Student names	

Hello everyone! We are group number _____. We are here because we want to tell you the survey result. The most serious problem in our school about recycling is that _____
_____.

So, we want to tell you our suggestions for better school. We should _____
_____
_____.

(2) 지도안

단원명	Small Actions for the Blue Planet				시간	90 mins
대상	• Students : 24 Middle school 3rd Graders • Level : Mixed					
수업 목표	✓ Students will be able to find the main idea and details from the text. ✓ Students will be able to answer the questions about their personal experiences. ✓ Students will be able to write a suggestion for recycling.					
교수·학습 교구	Digital whiteboard, Laptop, PPT slides etc					
핵심역량	자기 관리	지식정보처리	창의적 사고	심미적 감성	협력적 소통	공동체
		✓			✓	✓

<교수 학습 지도안>

단계	교수·학습 활동	유의점 및 활용 교구
도입 (5분)	*인사, 출석 확인, 교실 내 안전 점검 *학습 주제, 수업 준비 상태 확인	
전개1 (15분)	응시자 작성 내용 1 ✓ <자료 1>의 소재에 관하여 배경지식 활성화를 위한 활동을 진행할 것 ------------------------------------	PPT slides '자료 1'
	✓ <자료 1>의 밑줄 친 단어 중 하나를 가르칠 것 ------------------------------------	'자료 1'

	✓ <자료 1>을 읽고 주제를 찾도록 할 것	
		'자료 1'
	응시자 작성 내용 2	
	✓ <자료 1>의 세부 내용을 찾는 활동을 진행하고 학생 이해도를 점검할 것	
전개2 (20분)		PPT slides '자료 1'
	✓ <자료 2>를 활용한 짝 활동을 진행할 것	
		'자료 2'

	응시자 작성 내용 3	
	✓ <자료 3>을 활용하여 설문 조를 위한 짝 활동을 진행할 것	
		'자료 3'
전개3 (20분)	✓ 활동 중 교실을 순회하며 촉진자 역할을 수행할 것	
	✓ 내용이나 형식 측면에서 학생 오류에 관한 교사의 피드백을 제공할 것	

	응시자 작성 내용 4	
전개4 (25분)	✓ <자료 4>를 위한 교사의 예시를 제공할 것	PPT slides '자료 4'
	✓ 모둠 활동을 통해 <자료 4>를 완성할 것	'자료 4'
마무리 (5분)	*활동 마무리, 다음 차시 안내 *주변 정리 지도, 인사	

마 2018 기출문제

📘 Classroom settings

- Class time : 100 minutes
- Students : 30 High school 1st Graders
- Level : Mixed
- Aids : Digital whiteboard, Laptop, PPT slides etc

📘 Lesson information

- Unit title : Ready for Natural Disasters!
- Objectives
    - ✓ Students will be able to find details from the reading text.
    - ✓ Students will be able to describe the pictures about the safety tips.
    - ✓ Students will be able to create a safety manual for earthquake.

📘 지시사항

- 응시자 작성 내용 1 (Pre-reading)
    - ✓ <자료 1>의 내용과 글의 구조를 파악하도록 할 것
    - ✓ 학생 수준을 고려하여 <자료 1>의 밑줄 친 세 단어를 가르칠 것
    - ✓ 맥락을 활용하여 단어 학습에 대한 이해도를 점검할 것

- 응시자 작성 내용 2 (Reading)
    - ✓ 세부 정보를 찾기 위한 읽기 활동을 진행할 것
    - ✓ 세부 정보 이해도에 대한 교사의 피드백을 제공할 것
    - ✓ 지진 상황 행동 요령이 왜 중요한지 생각해 볼 수 있도록 격려할 것

- 응시자 작성 내용 3 (Speaking)
    - ✓ <자료 2>의 그림을 묘사하는 모둠 활동을 진행할 것
    - ✓ 그림을 묘사하는 것에 관한 교사의 예시를 제공할 것
    - ✓ 내용과 형식을 기준으로 활동에 대한 교사의 피드백을 제공할 것

- 응시자 작성 내용 4 (Writing)
    - ✓ 모둠 활동을 통해 <자료 3>을 완성할 것
    - ✓ 활동 중 모둠을 순회하며 촉진자 역할을 수행할 것
    - ✓ <자료 3>에 대한 평가 활동을 진행할 것

(1) 문제
<자료 1>

<SAFETY COMES FIRST!>

We don't know when an earthquake will happen, but when it does, it can be dangerous. That's why we need to know how to get ready before it happens and what to do when it does.

How to get ready before it happens
1. Fix or store things that might fall and cause harm.
2. Learn where the fire extinguishers are located.
3. Be aware of where to evacuate.
4. Know how to turn off the gas, electricity, and water.
5. Practice earthquake safety drills regularly.

What to do when it happens
- Indoors : Drop to the ground, take cover, and hold on.

- Inside : Stay away from windows, glass, and heavy items.
- Outside : Go to an open area away from buildings.
- Moving vehicle : Pull over, stop, and wait until the shaking ends.

<자료 2>

<자료 3>

<6 TIPS DURING AN EARTHQUAKE>	
<Your tip>	<Your tip>
(Drawing)	(Drawing)
<Your tip>	<Your tip>
(Drawing)	(Drawing)
<Your tip>	<Your tip>
(Drawing)	(Drawing)

(2) 지도안

단원명	Ready for Natural Disasters!		시간	90 mins
대상	• Students : 30 High school 1st Graders • Level : Mixed			
수업 목표	✓ Students will be able to find details from the reading text. ✓ Students will be able to describe the pictures about the safety tips. ✓ Students will be able to create a safety manual for earthquake.			
교수·학습 교구	Digital whiteboard, Laptop, PPT slides etc			
핵심역량	자기 관리	지식정보처리	창의적 사고	심미적 감성	협력적 소통	공동체
	✓	✓			✓	

<교수 학습 지도안>

단계	교수·학습 활동	유의점 및 활용 교구
도입 (5분)	*인사, 출석 확인, 교실 내 안전 점검 *학습 주제, 수업 준비 상태 확인	
전개1 (15분)	응시자 작성 내용 1 (Pre-reading)	
	✓ <자료 1>의 내용과 글의 구조를 파악하도록 할 것	'자료 1'
	✓ 학생 수준을 고려하여 <자료 1>의 밑줄 친 세 단어를 가르칠 것	
		'자료 1'

	✓ 맥락을 활용하여 단어 학습에 대한 이해도를 점검할 것	
전개1 (15분)		
전개2 (20분)	응시자 작성 내용 2 (Reading)	
	✓ 세부 정보를 찾기 위한 읽기 활동을 진행할 것	'자료 1'
	✓ 세부 정보 이해도에 대한 교사의 피드백을 제공할 것	'자료 1'

전개2 (20분)	✓ 지진 상황 행동 요령이 왜 중요한지 생각해 볼 수 있도록 격려할 것	

전개3 (25분)	응시자 작성 내용 3 (Speaking)	
	✓ <자료 2>의 그림을 묘사하는 모둠 활동을 진행할 것	'자료 2'
	✓ 그림을 묘사하는 것에 관한 교사의 예시를 제공할 것	PPT slides '자료 2'

전개3 (25분)	✓ 내용과 형식을 기준으로 활동에 대한 교사의 피드백을 제공할 것	
전개4 (30분)	응시자 작성 내용 4 (Writing)	
	✓ 모둠 활동을 통해 <자료 3>을 완성할 것	'자료 3'
	✓ 활동 중 모둠을 순회하며 촉진자 역할을 수행할 것	

	✓ <자료 3>에 대한 평가 활동을 진행할 것	
전개4 (30분)		'자료 3'
마무리 (5분)	*활동 마무리, 다음 차시 안내 *주변 정리 지도, 인사	

2017 기출문제

Classroom settings

- Class time : 90 minutes
- Students : 30 Middle school 3rd Graders
- Level : Mixed
- Aids : Digital whiteboard, Laptop, PPT slides etc

Lesson information

- Unit title : Stories Behind Pictures
- Objectives
  - ✓ Students will be able to understand the story based on 5Ws1H questions.
  - ✓ Students will be able to write the story ending based on the context.
  - ✓ Students will be able to create their own stories based on the picture.

지시사항

- 응시자 작성 내용 1
  - ✓ <자료 1>의 밑줄 친 세 단어를 가르칠 것
  - ✓ 5W1H 질문을 활용하여 <자료 1>의 세부 정보를 찾기 위한 읽기 활동을 진행할 것

- 응시자 작성 내용 2
  - ✓ 이야기의 결말을 창작하며 <자료 1>의 빈칸을 완성할 것
  - ✓ 내용과 언어 사용을 기준으로 완성된 빈칸에 대하여 교사의 피드백을 제공할 것

- 응시자 작성 내용 3
  - ✓ <자료 2>를 활용하여 <자료 3>을 위한 교사의 예시를 제공할 것
  - ✓ 모둠 활동을 통해 <자료 3>을 완성할 것

- 응시자 작성 내용 4
  - ✓ <자료 3>에 관한 동료 평가를 진행할 것
  - ✓ 동료 평가를 바탕으로 글쓰기 퇴고 활동을 진행할 것

(1) 문제
<자료 1>

<THOMAS AND THE GORILLAS>

On a hot summer day in Chicago, the Anderson family decided to visit the zoo near the town, called Brookfield Zoo. Mrs. Jane and Mr. Anderson had two young children : three−year−old Thomas and six−month−old Sally. Thomas was especially excited because he loved watching the animals, particularly the gorillas.

As soon as the Anderson family arrived, they headed straight to the gorilla exhibit. There were six adult gorillas and a three−month−old baby gorilla. Instead of being in cages, they lived in a large, peaceful field. Unlike traditional zoos, Brookfield Zoo had an animal−friendly system called a 'moat,' which was a safe area dug into the ground. The moat filled with water was covered by the fence so that the visitors couldn't fall in and gorillas couldn't escape.

While the family was watching the gorillas, baby Sally began to cry. Mrs. Jane handed her to Mr. Anderson and started searching her bag for a bottle of juice. In just those few moments, Thomas was climbing up the fence.

_____
_____
_____
_____

<자료 2>

	5W1H	KEY WORDS
1	who	
2	what	
3	when	
4	where	
5	how	
6	why	

_____
_____
_____
_____

<자료 3>

	5W1H	KEY WORDS
1	who	
2	what	
3	when	
4	where	
5	how	
6	why	

_____
_____
_____
_____

(2) 지도안

단원명	Stories Behind Pictures				시간	90 mins
대상	• Students : 30 Middle school 3rd Graders • Level : Mixed					
수업 목표	✓ Students will be able to understand the story based on 5Ws1H questions. ✓ Students will be able to write the story ending based on the context. ✓ Students will be able to create their own stories based on the picture.					
교수·학습 교구	Digital whiteboard, Laptop, PPT slides etc					
핵심역량	자기 관리	지식정보처리	창의적 사고	심미적 감성	협력적 소통	공동체
		✓	✓		✓	

<교수 학습 지도안>

단계	교수·학습 활동	유의점 및 활용 교구
도입 (5분)	*인사, 출석 확인, 교실 내 안전 점검 *학습 주제, 수업 준비 상태 확인	
전개1 (15분)	응시자 작성 내용 1 ✓ <자료 1>의 밑줄 친 세 단어를 가르칠 것 ------ ✓ 5W1H 질문을 활용하여 <자료 1>의 세부 정보를 찾기 위한 읽기 활동을 진행할 것 ------	'자료 1' PPT slides '자료 1'

	응시자 작성 내용 2	
전개2 (20분)	✓ 이야기의 결말을 창작하며 <자료 1>의 빈칸을 완성할 것	'자료 1'
	✓ 내용과 언어 사용을 기준으로 완성된 빈칸에 대하여 교사의 피드백을 제공할 것	
전개3 (30분)	응시자 작성 내용 3 ✓ <자료 2>를 활용하여 <자료 3>을 위한 교사의 예시를 제공할 것 | | 5W1H | KEY WORDS | | 1 | who | | | 2 | what | | | 3 | when | | | 4 | where | | | 5 | how | | | 6 | why | |	PPT slides '자료 2'

		✓ 모둠 활동을 통해 <자료 3>을 완성할 것	
전개3 (30분)			'자료 3'
전개4 (20분)		응시자 작성 내용 4	
		✓ <자료 3>에 관한 동료 평가를 진행할 것	
			'자료 3'
		✓ 동료 평가를 바탕으로 글쓰기 퇴고 활동을 진행할 것	
마무리 (5분)	*활동 마무리, 다음 차시 안내 *주변 정리 지도, 인사		

Chapter 02

예시답안 & 스크립트

가 2025 기출문제

(1) 판서 노트 및 예시 영상

수업실연 예시
2025 기출 변형
동영상 바로가기

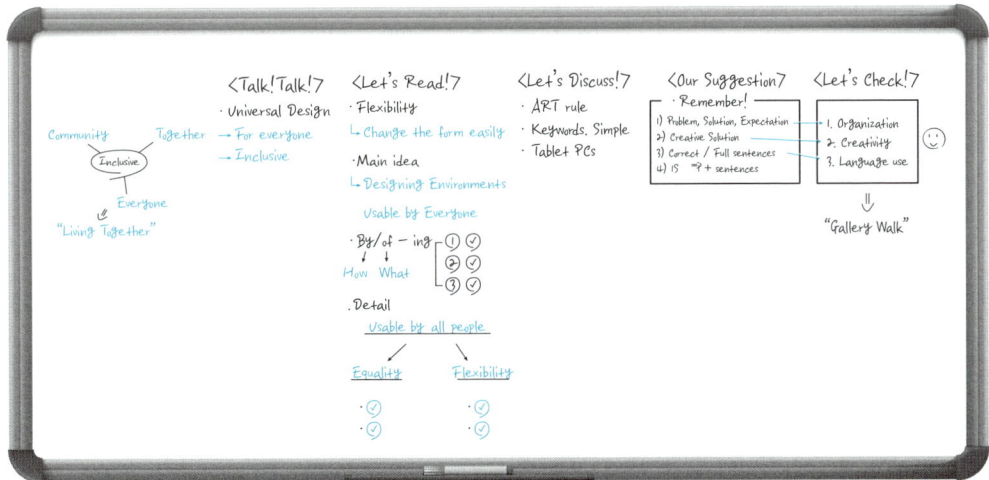

(2) 지도안 예시

단원명	Design for Everyone		시간	100 mins
대상	• Students : 24 High school 1st Graders • Level : Mixed			
수업 목표	✓ Students will be able to guess what the following text will be about. ✓ Students will be able to understand the text based on the Graphic Organizer. ✓ Students will be able to complete suggestion writing following the criteria.			
교수·학습 교구	Digital whiteboard, Laptop, Online dictionary, Tablet PCs, PPT slides etc			
핵심역량	자기 관리	지식정보처리	창의적 사고	심미적 감성	협력적 소통	공동체
		✓			✓	✓

<교수 학습 지도안>

단계	교수·학습 활동	유의점 및 활용교구
도입 (5분)	*인사, 출석 확인, 교실 내 안전 점검 *학습 주제, 수업 준비 상태 확인	

전개1
(15분)
	<center>응시자 작성 내용 1 (Pre-reading)</center>
	<center>✓ <자료 1>의 제목으로 글의 소재를 유추하는 활동을 진행할 것</center>
	●Guessing from the title
	• [전체] 교실 전체 상호작용을 통해 <자료 1>의 'Inclusive'의 의미를 떠올리면 연상되는 단어가 무엇인지 묻는다.
	  • (예상 답변) : Together, Everyone, Community
	• 교사는 학생의 답변을 마인드맵으로 정리한다.
	
	<center><마인드맵 예시>
	'Inclusive'</center>
	
	• 마인드맵을 바탕으로 글의 소재를 유추해 보도록 한다.
	  • (예상 답변) : Living together
		PPT slides '자료 1'

	<center>✓ <자료 1>의 그림을 활용하여 유니버설 디자인의 특징을 추측하는 짝 활동을 진행할 것</center> ● Talk! Talk! • <자료 1>의 그림에 주목하게 한다. • [짝, 5분] 짝을 지은 후, <자료 1>의 그림에 대하여 유니버설 디자인의 특징에 관한 생각을 나눠보도록 한다. • 교사는 다양한 정답이 나올 수 있음을 강조하며 자유롭게 의견을 나누는 분위기를 형성한다.	PPT slides '자료 1'

	<예시 발화> 교사 : In this 'Talk! Talk!' activity, all ideas are welcome. There's no right answer. Just feel free to talk!	
	● Transition • [전체] 짝과 함께 나눈 내용을 공유하며 글을 읽을 준비가 되었는지 확인한다.	
전개2 (20분)	응시자 작성 내용 2 (Reading)	
	√ <자료 1>의 밑줄 친 단어 중 하나를 가르칠 것	

	● Teaching Vocabularies using realia
	• [전체] <자료 1>의 단어를 간략히 살펴보게 한 후, 어려운 단어가 있는지 묻는다.
	  • 예시 : 'flexibility'
	• 일반 줄과 고무줄을 학생들에게 제공하며 양옆으로 늘려보라고 안내한다.
	<예시 발화>
	교사 : This is a normal rope. Can you stretch it out to each side? ... No! That's because it doesn't have flexibility. Now, try this rubber band. Feels different, right? This is flexibility.
	• Realia를 통해 학생들이 'flexibility'의 의미를 유추하도록 한다.
	  • (예상 답변) : Change the form easily
	• 'Flexibility'를 활용한 문장을 만들어 보게 함으로써 이해 확인 점검을 실시한다.
		Online
		dictionary
		'자료 1'

	√ <자료 1>의 네모 친 표현의 형태를 가르칠 것	

	● Main idea
	• [개별, 3분] <자료 1>의 Main idea를 파악하게 한다.
	• Skimming 전략을 지도하여 글의 주제를 파악하도록 한다.
	  • 빠른 속도로 글을 훑어보며 반복되는 단어를 확인하도록 한다.
	• [전체] 학생과의 상호작용을 통해 글의 주제를 교실 전체에 공유하고 판서한다.
	  • Main idea : Designing environments usable by everyone
	● Noticing the Target Form
	• [전체] 글을 읽는 도중, 반복되어 나타나는 형태를 알아차린 학생이 있는지 확인한다.
	• 학생과 함께 글에 사용된 Target form을 찾아보며 표시한다.
	• 'By'와 'Of'를 언제 사용하는지 학생들과 대화를 통해 지난 내용을 상기한다.
	<예시 발화>
	교사 : When do we use 'by' and 'of'? Do you remember? ... Yes! We use them when we want to express something about 'How' and 'What'!
	• 상기한 내용을 바탕으로 아래 질문을 통해 'By/Of + ing' 형태를 지도한다.
	  1) Low-floor buses provide easy access BY HOW?
	    → BY ENSURING mobility for all groups
		'자료 1'

	2) Adjustable desks allow all students to work comfortably BY HOW? → BY BENEFITING individuals with diverse needs 3) Captioned videos emphasizes the importance OF WHAT? → OF MAKING content accessible to everyone • 'By/Of + ing'를 활용한 문장을 만들어 보게 함으로써 학생의 이해를 확인한다.	

전개2
(20분)
	✓ <자료 2>의 도식 조직자를 완성하여 내용을 정리할 것
	● Transition
	• [전체] 지금까지 파악한 글의 내용을 바탕으로 세부 내용을 찾을 준비가 되었는지 확인한다.
	● Detail information
	• <자료 2>의 도식 조직자를 학생들에게 제공하고 구조를 함께 확인한다.
	• [개별, 10분] Scanning 전략을 지도하여 질문에 대한 답을 찾도록 한다.
	• 글 전체가 아니라 필요한 부분만 선별하여 읽도록 한다.
	• 아래 지도 사항에 따라 순회 지도를 실시한다.
	
	    <순회 지도 사항>
	    • 참여를 북돋우며 활동 중 어려움을 겪고 있는 학생을 파악한다.
	    • High-level : 활동 참여에 대한 긍정적 피드백을 제공하고, Student teacher 역할을 부여하여 다른 학생을 도울 수 있도록 한다.
	    • Low-level : Peer-scaffolding을 유도하며 동료 학습자로부터 도움을 받도록 한다.
	
	• [전체] 학생과의 상호작용을 통해 답변을 함께 확인하고 정리한다.
		'자료 2'

전개3 (25분)	응시자 작성 내용 3 (Pre-writing) ✓ 학교의 유니버설 디자인 현황에 대해 모둠 토의를 실시할 것 ● Group discussion • 4인 1조로 6개의 모둠을 구성한다. • ART rule을 안내하고 이에 대한 규칙을 상기한다. < ART rule > A : Active participation, R : Respect others, T : Take turns • 모둠 토의 중, 학생들이 ART rule을 잘 지키는지 순회 지도를 실시한다. ✓ 모둠 활동을 통해 <자료 3>을 완성할 것 ● Pre-writing activity • [모둠, 15분] 모둠 토의를 통해 <자료 3>을 완성하도록 한다. • 추후 글쓰기 활동을 고려하여 <자료 3>은 단어나 구처럼 단순한 구조로 작성할 수 있음을 안내한다. • 관련된 정보를 찾기 위해 개인별 Tablet PC를 사용할 수 있음을 안내한다. • 아래 지도 사항에 따라 순회 지도를 실시한다.	PPT slides '자료 3'

	<순회 지도 사항> • 참여를 북돋우며 활동 중 어려움을 겪고 있는 학생을 파악한다. • High-level : 긍정적 피드백을 제공하고 더 많은 제안 사항을 작성할 수 있도록 추가 과제를 부여한다. • Low-level : ART rule 강조, School news paper 제공	
전개4 (30분)	**응시자 작성 내용 4 (Writing)** ✓ <자료 3>을 바탕으로 <자료 4>를 완성할 것 ● Sample writing • [전체] 화면을 통해 <자료 4>를 위한 교사의 예시를 학생들에게 보여준다. • 학생들과의 상호작용을 통해 <자료 4>에 대한 글쓰기 조건을 제시한다. <글쓰기 조건> 1. Organization : Problem, Solution, Expectation 2. Creativity : Creative solution 3. Language use : Correct sentences 4. Role : 1 Student → 1+ Sentence ● Our Suggestion • [모둠, 20분] <자료 3>의 모둠 토의 결과를 바탕으로 조건에 따라 <자료 4>의 제안하는 글을 완성하도록 안내한다. • Authentic purpose : 우수 작품은 교장선생님께 제안 편지를 발송할 예정이라는 점을 강조하며 실제적 동기부여를 실시한다. • 글쓰기 활동 중 아래 사항에 따라 순회 지도를 실시한다. <순회 지도 사항> • 참여를 북돋우며 활동 중 어려움을 겪고 있는 학생을 파악한다. • Low-level : <자료 3>의 모둠 토의가 글쓰기 활동을 위한 Build-up activity임을 언급하며 이를 활용할 수 있도록 안내한다. • High-level : 활동 결과에 대해 칭찬한 후, 다른 제안을 추가로 작성할 수 있도록 격려한다.	'자료 3' '자료 4'
	✓ <자료 4>의 평가 기준을 활용하여 동료 평가를 실시할 것 ● Checking Evaluation Criteria • <자료 4> 아래의 평가 기준을 함께 확인하고 판서한다. • 평가 기준이 글쓰기 활동 전 안내된 <글쓰기 조건>과 연결됨을 보여주며 교수 내용과 평가가 일치함을 강조한다. ● Gallery Walk • [전체] 교실 벽면에 학생들의 글을 전시할 수 있도록 한다. • [전체, 10분] 교실 안을 자유롭게 둘러보며 다른 모둠의 글을 평가할 수 있도록 한다.	'자료 4'

	✓ 제안하는 글에 관한 교사의 피드백을 제공할 것 ● Giving feedback • [전체] 논리적이고 독창적이며, 문법적으로 잘 작성된 글을 모둠원과 함께 완성하였다는 점을 강조하며 긍정적 피드백을 제공한다. <예시 발화> 교사 : When I was walking around, I found that every group member was participating very actively. Not only that, your suggestions were very logical and creative with the grammatically correct sentences. … Awesome! Let's give ourselves a big hand!	
마무리 (5분)	*활동 마무리, 다음 차시 안내 *주변 정리 지도, 인사	

(3) 스크립트

> 응시자 작성 내용 1 (Pre-reading)

✓ 〈자료 1〉의 제목으로 글의 소재를 유추하는 활동을 진행할 것

Okay, students.

So far we've talked about the unit title and the lesson objectives. Then, are you guys ready to begin today's class? Awesome. So let me give you this worksheet. Take one and pass them to the back. Take one and pass them to the back. 현우, at the back! Did you get the… Perfect.

So, what do you see on the first worksheet? Yes, there is a reading text, right? So, can you read the title out loud? Perfect. So the title is – 'Designing Inclusive Environments', right? So let's begin today's class with the keyword 'inclusive'. Okay?

So, the keyword: 'inclusive'. So, which words can you come up with when you think of the word 'inclusive'? Any ideas? Yes, 희원! Yes, "together" is a good word. So, 'together'. And what else? Yes, 호영! Yes, "everyone" is a good word as well. So, 'everyone'. Everyone. And what else? Yes, 지환! Oh, yes! You can think of the word "community". So, 'community'. Community is a good word for inclusive.

So, like this, with the keyword from the title, can you guess today's topic? Yes, 다원! Oh, did everyone hear what 다원 just said? He said today's topic will be 'living together'. That's a great guess, 다원! So today, we are going to learn about living together. Okay? Awesome!

✓ 〈자료 1〉의 그림을 활용하여 유니버설 디자인의 특징을 추측하는 짝 활동을 진행할 것

So, everyone! We just guessed today's topic from the title. Then, are you guys ready to talk more about living together? Perfect. So it's time for talk. So, 'Talk! Talk!'. Everyone, let's go back to the first worksheet. What else can you see?

Yes, 현정! Yes, you can see the picture, right? That is the picture of the universal design. So from now on, we are going to talk about it. Okay? So we are going to talk about universal design – its characteristics. Okay?

So we are going to do this with your partners. So, 수현, 현수 – you two! You two. And lastly, you two. Does everyone have their own partners? Perfect. So, with your partners, we are going to talk about the characteristics of universal design – what it is or why we need it. Okay?

However, in this 'Talk! Talk!' activity, it is very important to remember what? Yes, 지환! Yes, all ideas are welcome. So, keep in mind that there is no right answer. Just feel free to talk. All right? I'm going to give you 5 minutes. Talk with your partners. Go!

One minute left, students. Okay, time's up. So, let's share your ideas together.

So, what are the characteristics of universal design? Any ideas? Yes, 호영 and 영호. Yes, it is designed for everyone. That's a great idea. So the first characteristic is 'For everyone'. That's a great answer. And what else?

Yes, 재우 and 우재! Oh yes, 'Inclusive' is another characteristic. So the second one is 'Inclusive'. Universal design is inclusive design. Perfect!

응시자 작성 내용 2 (Reading)

✓ 〈자료 1〉의 밑줄 친 단어 중 하나를 가르칠 것

So class, we just finished talking about the universal design. Then, are you guys ready to learn more about the universal design? Awesome! So it's time for reading. So let's read!

However, before we actually read the text, what do we have to learn first? Yes, 지환! Yes, we need to learn some difficult words, right?

So everyone, let's quickly look at the words in the first worksheet and find some difficult words. Are there any difficult words? Just say the word out loud. Okay. So I can hear the word 'flexibility' from many of you guys. So today's word is 'flexibility'.

So everyone, I just brought a real object. What can you see? Yes, 민수! Yes, this is just a normal rope. Then I will give it to you. 민수, can you stretch the rope to each side? No, you can't, right? That's because it doesn't have flexibility.

However, everyone! What's in my hand? Yes, 현수! Yes, this is the rubber band, right? So 민수, why don't you try this one? Can you stretch the rubber band to each side? Yes, you can, right? That means you just felt the flexibility from the rubber band.

Then with these two different experiences, can you guess the meaning of the word 'flexibility'? Yes, 나현! Oh, did everyone hear what 나현 just said? She said flexibility means change the form easily. That's a great guessing, 나현. So, flexibility means change the form easily.

Then class! Can you guys make a sentence with the word flexibility? Yes, 다원! Oh, your glasses have good flexibility, so they don't break easily. That's a perfect sentence.

✓ 〈자료 1〉의 네모 친 표현의 형태를 가르칠 것

So far, we just learned this difficult word.

Then, are you guys ready to read the text? Perfect. Then everyone, whenever we read the text, what do we have to find first? Yes, 수현! Yes, we need to find the main idea first, right?

So we are going to find the main idea. However, to find the main idea, do we have to read quickly or slowly? Yes, 우재! Yes, we need to read quickly. So you don't have to understand every single word. Just read quickly and find the main idea. I'm going to give you 3 minutes. Find the main idea. Go!

1 minute left, students. Okay, time's up.

So let's check the main idea together. What was the main idea? Any volunteers? Yes, 현정! Oh, designing environments usable by everyone. That's perfect. So, the main idea is designing environments… what? Yes, 희원. Yes, usable by everyone. That's a great main idea, 현정!

So we just read the text to find the main idea. However, while you were reading, is there anyone who could find an expression that is used repeatedly? Yes, 희원! Oh, did everyone hear what 희원 just said? She said the expression - 'by/of ~ing' is used repeatedly.

So, from now on, we are going to talk about this: 'by/of ~ing'. So everyone! Let's go back to the reading text again and underline these key expressions. So, 상민! Did you find all of them? So, how many were there? Yes, there are three of them. Then, let's talk about this. So class, we already learned when to use by. Do you guys remember? Yes, 수민. Yes, we use 'by' when we want to talk about 'how', right? And how about 'of'? When do we use 'of'? Yes, 영호! Yes, we learned that - we use 'of' when we want to say something about 'what'. Right?

Then everyone, let's look at the screen. 재우, at the back! Can you see the screen? Perfect. So, what do you see on the screen? Yes, there are three questions, right? So can you read the first one? Yes, it says, "Lower floor buses provide easy access by how?" Then, can you guys answer to this question? Yes, 호영. Yes, "by ensuring mobilities for all groups". That's a great answer. So we just answered for the number one. And finally, the last one. Can you read the last question, 수현? Yes, it says, "Captioned videos emphasize the importance of what?" So can anyone answer to this question? Yes, 은수! Yes. "Of making content accessible to everyone", right? So ... "of making content accessible to everyone". That's a great answer, 은수. So like this, we just learned when to use 'by/of ~ing'. Then, can you guys make a sentence with this key expression? Yes, 지환! Oh yes, "I got great scores by studying hard." That's a great sentence.

✓ 〈자료 2〉의 도식 조직자를 완성하여 내용을 정리할 것

So far, everyone! We just read the text for the main idea and we just learned today's key expression. Then, are you guys ready to read the text a little bit more closely? Perfect. So, it's time to read for the details. All right? So everyone, let's look at the second worksheet. What do you see? Yes, 현우! Yes, there is a graphic organizer, right? So let's see how it is organized. So what can you see in the first part? Yes, it says there's a definition. And below the definition, what can you see? Yes, 현정! Yes, there are two features, right? And for each feature, what else can you see? Yes, 종민! Yes, there are two examples, right? So your graphic organizer looks like this.

So from now on, we are going to read the text again to find the answers to this graphic organizer. However, to find these specific answers, do we have to read everything, or can we just read the necessary part? Yes, 민재! Yes, we don't need to read everything, right?

So I'm going to give you 10 minutes. Read the text again to find the answer to this graphic organizer. All right? 10 minutes. Go!

Oh, 수민, you already finished? Wow, what a quick reader! Then why don't you help your friend 민수? I heard 민수 needs some help. Can you guys do that? Awesome. So like this, friends can be a better teacher. 1 minute left, students. Does anyone need more time? Okay, time's up.

So let's check the answers all together. So what is the definition of universal design? Any volunteers? Yes, 영호! Oh yes, "usable by all people". That's a great definition. So, "usable by all people". And the next part, the features. What's the first one? Any volunteers? Yes, 재우! Yes, it was "equality". So the first one was "equality". "Equality". And what's the second one? Yes, 나영! Yes, it says "flexibility", right? So the second one was "flexibility". Then, what was the first example for "equality"? Yes, 현정! Yes, it was automatic sliding door, right? And the last one, what was the second one for 'flexibility'? Yes, 은우! Yes, it was captioned videos, right? So like this, we just found the details with the graphic organizer.

응시자 작성 내용 3 (Pre-writing)

✓ **학교의 유니버설 디자인 현황에 대해 모둠 토의를 실시할 것**

So far, we just read about the universal design. Then, how about our school? Don't you want to talk about it? Awesome. So, let's discuss. It's time for the discussion. So everyone, we are going to do this in groups. 수현, 현수, 민종, 종민 - you four! You four! And finally, the last group, group 6 - you four! So, is everyone in a group? Perfect.

So everyone, in the group discussion, what is the rule number one? Yes, 희원! Yes, the ART rule, right? So don't forget about the ART rule. So let me quickly remind you of this rule. So what was A? Yes, 민종! Yes, it was Active participation. And what was R? Yes, 영호! Yes, it is Respect others. And what was T? Yes, 현수! Yes, T was Take turns. So keep in mind that - this is our rule number one in the discussion. All right?

✓ 모둠 활동을 통해 〈자료 3〉을 완성할 것

Then everyone, let's look at the third worksheet. What do you see? Yes, 민재! Yes, it is the group discussion worksheet, right? So from now on, I'm going to give you 15 minutes. 15 minutes to discuss with your group members to complete this third worksheet. All right? However, because this is just a discussion, it is important to write in what? Yes, 수현! Yes, it is important to be simple, with keywords. That means you don't have to write in what? Yes, 영호! Yes, you don't have to write in full sentences, because discussion should come first. All right? So, you can write in keywords and just be simple. Okay?

And remember that - you can also use your tablet PCs to find information for the discussion. So, you can use your tablet PCs. I'm going to give you 15 minutes. Discuss with your group members. Complete the third worksheet. Go!

Oh, 종민, I can see you're actively participating, but what was the T rule? Yes, Take turns. So make sure that everyone has a chance to talk. All right? And group 4, do you need any help? Oh, you couldn't find any problems for the suggestion? Then why don't you look at this school newspaper? I just brought for you guys. So with this school newspaper, can you do this group work by yourselves? Awesome. So if you need any more help, just feel free to call me. All right?

And group 5, you already finished? Wow, what brilliant students! Then why don't you write more suggestions? Because the more suggestions you will give, the better our school will be. Can you guys do that? Awesome! Keep up the good work. 1 minute left, students. Does any group need more time? Okay, time's up.

응시자 작성 내용 4 (Writing)

✓ 〈자료 3〉을 바탕으로 〈자료 4〉를 완성할 것

So, we just finished the group discussion about our school's universal design. Then, are you guys ready to write your own suggestion? Awesome. So it's time to write our suggestion. Everyone, let's look at the screen here. 민수, at the back! Do you see the screen? Awesome. So, what do you see on the screen? Yes, there is a sample writing, right? So like this, there are several things you should remember. So, remember these things when you write your suggestion. Okay?

So, what can you find in the sample writing? Any ideas? Yes, 현정! Oh, yes. In the sample writing, there's 'Problem', 'Solution' and 'Expectation', right? So, like this, your writing should have 'Problem', 'Solution' - and what was the last one? Yes, 현재! Yes, 'Expectation'. Okay? So that your writing can be logical.

And what else can you find? Yes 수현! Yes, the sample writing has very creative solution, right? So like this, your solution should be creative. Okay? Creative solution. And what else can you find? Yes, 정은! Oh yes, it is written in full sentences. So remember that - based on the simple keywords from the third worksheet, you should write correct and full sentences this time. Okay?

And lastly, how many members in your group? Yes, there are four students, right? So, keep in mind that - one student should write at least one or more sentences so that everyone has a role in the group. So remember these things when you write your group's suggestion. However, before we start, let me tell you this. The best group's writing will be actually sent to the principal's office to make our school a better place. How does it sound? Are you guys excited? Awesome.

So, I'm going to give you 20 minutes. 20 minutes to do what, 희원? Yes! To write your group suggestion. All right? 20 minutes. Go!

Oh, group 1. Do you need any help? Oh, you don't know how to start? Then why don't you go back to the third worksheet? Because that's a build-up activity for this one. Can you guys do that? Awesome. So if you need any more help, just don't hesitate to raise your hand. All right? Perfect! I love your effort.

And group 6, you're already finished? Wow, what quick writers! Then why don't you write another group suggestion? Because you already know that the possibility of universal design is endless. Can you do it? Awesome. So keep up the good work. 1 minute left, students. Does any group need more time? Okay, time's up.

✓ **〈자료 4〉의 평가 기준을 활용하여 동료 평가를 실시할 것**

All right. So, we just finished writing our group suggestion. Then, don't you want to see your friend's suggestion? Awesome. So, it's time for check. So, let's check. Let me give you this Peer Assessment Card. So, take one and pass them to the back. 상민, at the back! Did you get the Peer Assessment Card? Perfect.

So, what do you see in the first one? Yes, it says Organization, right? So the first one is the organization — organization of the writing. So what does this mean? Yes, 현수! Yes! As you can see in the fourth worksheet as well, this means if the writing is logical. So make sure that your friend's writing has this: 'Problem', 'Solution', and 'Expectation'. And what is the second one? Yes, 상우! Yes, it says 'Creativity', right? So the second one was creativity. And what does this mean? Yes, 재우! Yes! This means if the writing has creative solution. All right? And what's the last one? Yes, 현정! Yes, it says 'Language Use', right? So the last one was 'Language Use'. And what is 'Language Use'? Yes, 우현! Yes! This means if the writing has correct and full sentences, as you can also see in the fourth worksheet.

So with this Peer Evaluation Card, we are going to do a Gallery Walk. How does it sound? Exciting? Awesome! So, from now on, we are going to do the gallery walk. Group 1, put your writing on this wall. Group 2, over there. And finally, last group, group 6! Put your writing over here.

So students, I'm going to give you 10 minutes. 10 minutes to walk around the classroom, read your friend's writing, and give your Peer Assessment Card. All right? So everyone, stand up! Walk around the classroom! Go! 1 minute left, students. Okay, time's up. Please go back to your seats.

✓ **제안하는 글에 관한 교사의 피드백을 제공할 것**

Okay, so we just finished the gallery walk. However, when I was walking around the classroom together, I could find that all of the writings were very logical, with a creative solution. And not only that, you all successfully used correct and full sentences in your group suggestion. So, I want to give this big smile on this one. I'm so proud of you guys.

You deserve a big hand. Let's give ourselves a big hand. Awesome.

So before we wrap up, let's quickly go over today's class. So what was today's topic? Yes, 나영! Yes, it was 'inclusive'. So we read about what? Yes, 호영. Yes, we read about universal design. And we did what? Yes, 수영! Yes, we did discussion. And we wrote about what? Yes, we wrote our own suggestions. So, with today's class, I want you to become a person who can take care of your own communities to live together. Can you guys do that? Awesome. So that's all for today, and have a great weekend!

2024 기출문제

(1) 판서 노트 및 예시 영상

수업실연 예시
2024 기출 변형
동영상 바로가기

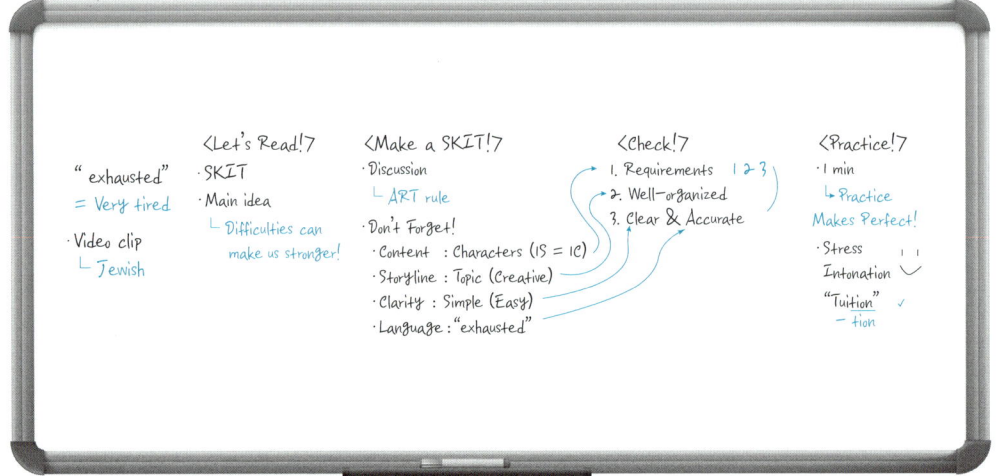

(2) 지도안 예시

단원명	Spread Wisdom				시간	100 mins
대상	• Students : 24 High school 1st Graders • Level : Mixed					
수업 목표	✓ Students will be able to write a skit related to the proverb. ✓ Students will be able to use correct pronunciation of their writings.					
교수·학습 교구	Digital whiteboard, Laptop, Online dictionary, Tablet PCs etc					
핵심역량	자기 관리	지식정보처리	창의적 사고	심미적 감성	협력적 소통	공동체
		✓	✓		✓	

<교수 학습 지도안>

단계	교수·학습 활동	유의점 및 활용 교구
도입 (5분)	*인사, 출석 확인, 교실 내 안전 점검 *학습 주제, 수업 준비 상태 확인	
전개1 (25분)	**응시자 작성 내용 1** ✓ <자료 1>과 <자료 2>의 밑줄 친 표현이나 어휘 중 1개를 선택하여 맥락을 활용하여 가르칠 것 ● Teaching Vocabulary • [전체] <자료 1>, <자료 2>를 학생에게 나누어주고 생소한 어휘를 파악하도록 한다. • 해당 의미를 추론할 수 있도록 주변 어휘의 의미를 통해 예시를 제공한다. <예시 발화> 교사 : Who knows the meaning of 'exhausted'? … Let me give you a hint. Let's look at the word around the target word 'exhausted'. What do you see? 학생 : Homework, math test, science report, history quiz … 교사 : Yes! How would you feel if you have to do all of them? 학생 : I would be very tired. 교사 : That's correct! 'Exhausted' means 'tired'. • 의미를 성공적으로 추론한 후, 해당 어휘에 대한 예문을 말해보게 함으로써 이해 확인 점검을 실시한다. ✓ <자료 1>의 속담 중 하나에 해당하는 상황을 교사 임의로 제시하고 학생들에게 알아맞혀 보도록 할 것 ● Guessing from the video • [전체] Screen을 활용하여 학생에게 Video clip을 보여준다.	'자료 1' '자료 2' '자료 1'

	< Video clip > 줄거리 : 스티브 잡스의 아주 사소한 발명품이 대기업을 창립의 시초가 된 이야기	'자료 1'
• 영상 줄거리를 학생과 함께 되짚으며 <자료 1>의 Jewish 속담에 관한 이야기임을 유추할 수 있도록 한다.		
<div align="center">✓ <자료 2>를 읽고 주제를 파악하게 할 것</div>		

● Main idea
• <자료 2>의 구성 요소에 주목하며 Skit 장르에 대해 소개한다.
• [개별, 2분] Skimming 전략을 사용하여 <자료 2>의 Main idea를 파악하게 한다.
  • 빠른 속도로 글을 훑어보며 이야기의 흐름을 살펴보도록 한다.
• 아래 지도 사항에 따라 순회 지도를 실시한다.
 < 순회 지도 사항 >
• 참여를 북돋우며 활동에 어려움을 겪는 학생을 찾는다.
• Low-level : <자료 2> 뒤편의 <Vocabulary list>를 제시한다.
• [전체] 학생과의 상호작용을 통해 글의 주제를 교실 전체에 공유하고 판서한다.
  • Main idea : Difficulties can make us stronger.
• [전체] 글의 Topic과 Main idea의 관련성에 다시 한번 주목하게 한다.
		'자료 2'

<div align="center">응시자 작성 내용 2</div>		
<div align="center">✓ 모둠을 구성하여 <자료 3>의 Topic, Characters, Settings을 정하도록 할 것</div>		
• <자료 3>을 소개하고 4인 1조로, 6개의 모둠을 구성한다. • Topic, Characters, Setting을 정하기 위해 토의를 실시한다. • [모둠, 10분] 모두 각자 의견을 제시할 수 있도록 하고, 아래 ART rule을 지키도록 독려한다. < ART rule > A : Active participation, R : Respect others, T : Take turns • 토의 중 아래 지도 사항에 따라 순회 지도를 실시한다. < 순회 지도 사항 > • 참여를 북돋우며 활동 중 어려움을 겪고 있는 모둠을 파악한다. • Low-level : ART rule 재강조, <자료 1>의 Proverb를 참고하도록 격려한다.		'자료 3'
<div align="center">✓ <자료 3>의 Scene 대본을 작성하도록 할 것</div>		
● Let's make a SKIT! • 학생들에게 Tablet PC를 꺼내어 Online classroom에 접속하게 한다. • 교사의 예시를 화면으로 보여주며 아래 글쓰기 조건을 제시한다.		

<글쓰기 조건>

1. Content : Characters (1S = 1C)
2. Storyline : Topic (Creative)
3. Clarity : Simple (Easy)
4. Language : 'exhausted'

- [개별, 20분] 위 조건에 따라 문서 공유 기능을 활용하여 <자료 4>를 완성하도록 한다.
- Authentic purpose : 완성 작품을 토대로 Short-form videos를 만들 것이라고 언급한다.

<예시 발화>

교사 : I'm telling you that this is going to be a huge project. We are going to make short-form videos based on your skits for the school's social media. Isn't it awesome?

- 아래 지도 사항에 따라 순회 지도를 실시한다.

<순회 지도 사항>

- 참여를 북돋우며 활동 중 어려움을 겪고 있는 학생을 파악한다.
- Low level : AI Story builder 앱을 소개하여 활용할 수 있도록 한다.
- High level : 긍정적 피드백을 제공한 뒤, 세 번째 장면도 만들도록 한다.

'자료 3'

✓ <자료 4>를 활용하여 각 그룹의 글쓰기를 자기 평가하도록 할 것

● Self Check

- <자료 4>를 제공하고 각각의 문항에 대한 설명과 Scale에 대한 구분을 상호작용을 통해 알아본다.
  - 평가 기준이 글쓰기 조건과 연결됨을 강조한다.

<글쓰기 조건>	<평가 기준>
1. Content	1. Requirement
2. Storyline	2. Well-organized
3. Clarity, 4. Language	3. Clear and accurate

- <Self Check>의 기준이 이전 활동의 <글쓰기 조건>과 연결됨을 보여주며 교수 내용과 평가가 일치함을 강조한다.
- [모둠, 5분] 조별로 상의하며 <자료 4>를 작성하도록 한다.

'자료 4'

응시자 작성 내용 3

✓ <자료 3>의 대본을 활용하여 읽기 연습을 할 것

● Preparing for presentation

- [모둠, 15분] <자료 3>에서 자신이 맡은 Character의 대사를 반복적으로 읽고 암기할 수 있도록 한다.

'자료 3'

	• Short-form video 제작을 위해 연극 제한 시간은 1분임을 강조하며 반복 읽기에 집중할 수 있도록 격려한다. <예시 발화> 교사 : Practice makes perfect! The more you practice, the faster your speaking will be! • 아래 지도 사항에 따라 순회 지도를 실시한다. <순회 지도 사항> • 참여를 북돋우며 활동 중 어려움을 겪고 있는 학생을 파악한다. • Low level : Online dictionary의 발음 읽기 기능을 활용하도록 한다. ✓ 학생들의 발음, 강세, 억양 등에 대하여 피드백을 제공할 것 ● Giving feedback • [전체, 5분] 강세와 억양에 대해서 긍정적 피드백을 제공하고, 발음 부분에서 자주 하는 실수를 언급하며 부정적 피드백을 제공한다. 　• (예시) 'tuition'에서 '-tion' 발음 지도	'자료 3'
마무리 (5분)	*활동 마무리, 다음 차시 안내 *주변 정리 지도, 인사	

(3) 스크립트

응시자 작성 내용 1

✓ 〈자료 1〉과 〈자료 2〉의 밑줄 친 표현이나 어휘 중 1개를 선택하여 맥락을 활용하여 가르칠 것

Okay, students! So far, we've talked about the unit titles and the lesson objectives. Then, are you ready to start today's English class? Perfect! Let me give you this first and second handouts. Take one and pass them to the back. 수현, at the back, did you get the handouts? What do you see on the first handout? Yes, 동우! Yes, there are many proverbs, right? How about the second handout? What do you see, 종민? Yes, there is a reading text, right?

From now on, I'm going to give you 30 seconds, 30 seconds to quickly go over those English words and find any difficult ones. So, 민수, what are we going to do? Yes, we are going to quickly go over the English words in the first and second handouts to find the difficult English words, all right? 30 seconds—go! Okay, time's up. Tell me some difficult words that you found. Okay, I can hear the word "exhausted" from many of you guys. Does anyone know the meaning of the word "exhausted"? Okay then, let me give you a hint. So today's word is 'Exhausted'. Just look at the words around the target word "exhausted." What do you see? Yes, 현우! He had a math test. Yes, 재우! He had a science report. Yes, 종민! He had a history quiz, right? So, how would you feel when you have to prepare for all those three things at the same time? Yes, 민수! You must be very tired. So, the word "exhausted" means what? Yes, 희원! It means "Very tired". Then, can you get the meaning of the word "exhausted"? Perfect! Then 수민! Can you make a sentence with this word, "exhausted"? That's a great sentence! Awesome!

✓ 〈자료 1〉의 속담 중 하나에 해당하는 상황을 교사 임의로 제시하고 학생들에게 알아맞혀 보도록 할 것

All right, we just finished checking the difficult word. Then, are you ready to move on to the next part? Perfect! Everyone, let's look at the first handout. What do you see, 다

원? Yes, there are proverbs from many other countries, right? From now on, I'm going to show a short video clip, and this video clip is about one of those proverbs. Okay? I want you to guess which one is related to this video clip. All right? So, 동우! What are we going to do? Yes, we are going to watch a short video clip and we are going to guess which one is related to this video clip. All right? Okay, everyone! Let's look at the screen here! 지환, at the back, do you see the screen? Okay! So, let's watch the video clip.

We just finished watching the video clip. Let's talk about it together. So ... Let's talk about the video clip! Who was in the video? Yes, 희원! Yes, it was Steve Jobs, right? In the very beginning, Steve Jobs made what? Yes, 다원! Yes, he made a digital device, right? However, was it big? Yes, 현정! No, it was very simple and very small, right? However, many years later, it became what? Yes, 수현! Yes, it became a very huge global company, right? So, Steve Jobs started very small, but after putting in a lot of effort into it, he became what? Yes, he became the CEO of a huge global company. Then, can you guess which proverb is related to this video clip? Yes, 상우! Oh, did everyone here what 상우 just said? He said the Jewish proverb, "Great oaks from little acorns grow," is related to this video clip. Do you agree? Perfect!

✓ 〈자료 2〉를 읽고 주제를 파악하게 할 것

All right! So, we just finished learning the difficult words and the famous proverbs from many different countries. Then, are you ready to read the text? Perfect! So... It's time to read! Let's read! Everyone, let's look at the second handout. What do you see? Yes, 민재! Yes, there is a reading text, right? However, do you feel familiar with this kind of reading text? No, right? So, 다원! What do you see in the reading text? Yes, there are 'Characters', 'Settings' ... Yes, 민재! Yes, 'Topic'! So, this kind of reading text, we call ... Yes, 'Skit'! So, from now on, we are going to read this skit. Are you excited? Awesome! So, from now on, I'm going to give you two minutes, two minutes to find the main idea, okay? So, you are going to find the main idea. However, to find the main idea, do we have to read quickly or slowly? Yes, 수민! Yes, we have to read quickly, right? So, you don't have to understand every single word. Just read quickly and find the main idea. I'm going to give you two minutes. Two minutes—go!

Oh, 동우! Do you need any help? Oh, the words are so difficult! Then, why don't you look at the back of the worksheet? What do you see? Yes, there is a vocabulary list, right? So, with this vocabulary list, can you find the main idea by yourself? Perfect! I love your effort! Keep up the good work! One minute left, students! Does anyone need more time? Okay, time's up! Let's check the main idea together.

Is there any volunteer? Yes, 지환, at the back. Oh, did everyone hear what 지환 just said? He said the main idea of this reading text is "Difficulties..." "Difficulties...", what? Yes, "Difficulties can make us ..." "Make us" how? Yes, "Make us stronger". He said the main idea of this skit is "Difficulties can make us stronger." Do you agree? Perfect! However, everyone! Let's look at the top of the second handout. What do you see? Yes, 종민! Yes, there is a topic, right? It says, "A smooth sea never makes a skilled sailor.", right? Like this, the main idea has a very close relationship to the topic. Okay?

응시자 작성 내용 2

✓ 모둠을 구성하여 〈자료 3〉의 Topic, Characters, Setting을 정하도록 할 것

All right! So far, we just finished reading the skit, and this was related to ...? Yes, 수현! Yes, this was related to an English proverb, right? However, is this the only proverb that we have? No, right? Then, why don't we make another skit with another proverb? Sounds great? Perfect! So, let's make a skit! Everyone, let's look at the third handout. We are going to do this in groups. 수현, 현수, 종민, 민종, you four! You four! And finally the last group, you four! Is everyone in their group? Perfect! With your group members, we are going to make a skit.

However, before we make the skit, what do we have to decide first? Yes, 지환! Yes, we have to decide the 'Topic', 'Characters' ... and 'Setting', right? From now on, we are going to have a discussion to decide those three things, all right? So 동우! What are we going to do? Yes, we are going to have a short discussion. However, whenever we have this kind of discussion, which rule do we have to follow? Yes, 민서! Yes, we need to follow the ART rules, right? What was 'A'? Yes, 현정! Yes, it was "Active participation." What was 'R'? Yes, 종민! Yes, it was "Respect others." So, make sure you respect your friends ideas. All right? What was the last part, 'T'? Yes, 다원! Yes, that means "Take turns." Make sure everyone gets a chance to talk. Okay?

I'm going to give you 10 minutes, 10 minutes to decide what? Yes, 현정! Yes, decide those three things, 'Topic', 'Characters', and 'Settings'. All right? Ten minutes—go! Oh, 수현! I like your active participation! However, what was the "T" rule? Yes, "Take turns," right? Make sure everyone is talking. Okay? Perfect! One minute left, students! Does any group need more time? Okay, time's up.

✓ 〈자료 3〉의 Scene 대본을 작성하도록 할 것

So, we just decided on the 'Topic', 'Characters', and 'Settings', right? Then, are you ready to create your own skit? Great!

So, everyone! Let's open up your tablet PCs and come to the online classroom. So, 종민! Are you in the online classroom? Perfect! What do you see there? Yes, there is a sample writing, right? So like the sample writing, there are several things you should remember. So ... I'll say, "Don't forget!" Like the sample writing, your skit must include those contents, okay? 'Content'! 'Content' means ...? Yes, 수현! Yes, that means characters. How many characters in total? Yes, 종민! Four characters! And how many people are in our group? Yes, 현정! Yes, four students, right? So, one student should take one character, so that each one of you has a role. Okay? Awesome!

What else can you find in the sample writing? Yes, 다원! Yes, there is a storyline, right? So, like this sample writing, you should think about the storyline. All right? Especially, this storyline must be related to what? Yes, 동우! Yes, it should be related to the topic! Okay? Topic that you decided about the proverb, all right? And because we are going to make a story, it is important to be what? Yes, 현정! Yes, because we are going to make a storyline, it is very important to be creative. Okay? Make sure you're showing us your creativity in the skit. All right?

What else can you find in the sample writing? Is it long or short? Yes, 수민! Yes, the sample writing uses very simple sentences, right? So, the third part is 'Clarity', and this means …? Yes, 수현! It means 'Simple'! Remember that it's not just a reading text; it's a conversation between the characters. So, make sure your sentence is simple and … Yes, 동우! It should be easy to understand. Okay? For the last one, I want you to think about the 'Language'. Do you remember today's word? Yes, 민재! Yes, it was "Exhausted," right? Make sure you use today's vocabulary, "Exhausted." All right?

I'm going to give you 20 minutes, 20 minutes to work with your group members to make a skit, all right? However, everyone! Attention, please! I want to tell you that this is going to be a huge project. That means we are going to make a short-form video with this skit. How does that sound? Exciting? The best short-form video will be uploaded to our school's social media. Sounds great? Awesome! So, I'm going to give you 20 minutes, 20 minutes to do what, 희원? Yes, we are going to make a skit. All right? Don't forget these things! I'm going to give you 20 minutes! 20 minutes—go!

Oh, group two, do you need any help? Oh, it's very difficult to make a story? I understand; it is very hard to be creative. Then, why don't you use the AI Story Builder? It's in your tablet PC. That will help you to make a creative story! So, with this AI Story Builder, can you do this by yourself? Perfect! Keep up the good work! Oh, group five! Are you guys already finished? Wow, what quick and creative writers! Then, why don't you make another scene? Because the more situations we have, the better we can understand about the proverb. How does that sound? Can you do that? Perfect! I love your effort! One minute left, students! Does any group need more time? Okay, time's up!

✓ 〈자료 4〉를 활용하여 각 그룹의 글쓰기를 자기 평가하도록 할 것

All right! So, I can see that every group just finished making their own skits.

So everyone! Whenever we finish writing, what do we do? Yes, 현정! Yes, we need to check our writing, right? So… Let's do the 'Check Time'! So, everyone! Let's look at the fourth handout! So 지환, at the back! What do you see on the fourth handout? Yes, there is a self-checklist, right? How many questions in there? Yes, 다원! Yes, there are three questions. Can you read the first one? The first question was, "Do I have all the requirements?" So... the first one was 'Requirements'. What does that mean, Can anyone tell us about the 'Requirements'? Yes, 현수! Yes, it is about the content, right? So make sure your skit has the 'Characters', as well as the 'Topic', and 'Settings'. Okay?

What was the second question? Yes, 종민! Yes, the second question was, "Is my writing well-organized?" So... the second one is about 'Well-organized'. What does it mean by "Well-organized"? Yes, 동우! Yes, that means ... like we just said, it's about the storyline, okay? If your writing is related to the topic, that means your writing is well-organized. All right? What was the last one? Yes, 호영! Yes, it says, "Is my writing clear and accurate?" Right? So... the last one was 'Clear & Accurate'. What does that mean? Yes, 현우! Yes, it means the writing is simple. And ...? Yes, 종민! The writing has the word "Exhausted." Okay?

So, how many points can you give for each question? Yes, three! Right? So, if your group's writing is 'Very Great', you should give three. If your writing is just 'Great', you give two points. And finally, if your writing is just 'So-So', you can give just one point, okay? Okay, so! I'm going to give you five minutes! Five minutes to quickly read your skit again and complete those self-checklist. Okay? I'm going to give you five minutes, five minutes to do what, 다원? Yes, talk with your group members and give points based on the self-checklist. All right? Five minutes—go!

응시자 작성 내용 3

✓ 〈자료 3〉의 대본을 활용하여 읽기 연습을 할 것

All right! So we just finished checking our skits based on those three questions. Then, are you ready for the short-form video? Perfect! However, before we actually do an acting, what do we have to do? Yes, 다원! Yes, we need to practice, right? So, it's 'Practice Time'! Let's practice. So everyone! You all have your characters, right? From now on, I'm going to give you 15 minutes, 15 minutes to practice again and again and memorize your lines, all right? However, because we're going to make a short-form video, how much time do we have for each group? Yes, 민정! Each group has one minute. Okay? But don't worry!

Because we all know the famous proverb about this situation. What was it? Oh, yes, 희원! Did everyone hear what 희원 just said? She said, "Practice ...", what? Yes, "Practice Makes ...", what? Yes, thank you, 현정! "Practice Makes Perfect!" Okay?

So, don't worry, because the more you practice, the better your speaking will be. All right? I'm going to give you 15 minutes. 15 minutes to do what? Yes, 수민! Yes, practice your lines, okay? Make sure each group has one minute! Practice until all of your group members take less than one minute, okay? I'm going to give you 15 minutes! 15 minutes—go! Oh, 호영! Do you need any help? Oh, you don't know how to pronounce this word? Then why don't you open your tablet PC and go to the online dictionary? Can you see the small speaker button beside the word? Great! Can you click it? That's how you can learn the pronunciation of the word. All right? With this online dictionary, can you practice by yourself? Perfect! Keep up the good work! One minute left, students! Does any group need more time? Okay, time's up!

✓ 학생들의 발음, 강세, 억양 등에 대하여 피드백을 제공할 것

Okay students! We just finished practicing for the acting, right? I want to tell you that everyone has great stress and intonation when practicing! So, about your stress and intonation, I would say you guys were perfect! Let's give a big hand! Great job! However, when I was walking around, I heard that many of you made a mistake when pronouncing this word. Many of you said, "tui-TION" Is that the correct sound? No, right? How should we pronounce this word? Yes, 다원! Yes, we should pronounce it "tuition," instead of 'tui-TION', right? Repeat after me—"tuition." Perfect!

So, remember that if you have this kind of "T-I-O-N", at the end of the word, it doesn't sound "TION" It sounds "SHON." So, this word is "tuition." Okay? So remember this part, when you see this kind of words, okay? All right! We just finished practicing for the real acting. Then are you ready to make a short-form video? Perfect! So let's begin the real show!

다 2023 기출문제

(1) 판서 노트 및 예시 영상

수업실연 예시
2023 기출 변형
동영상 바로가기

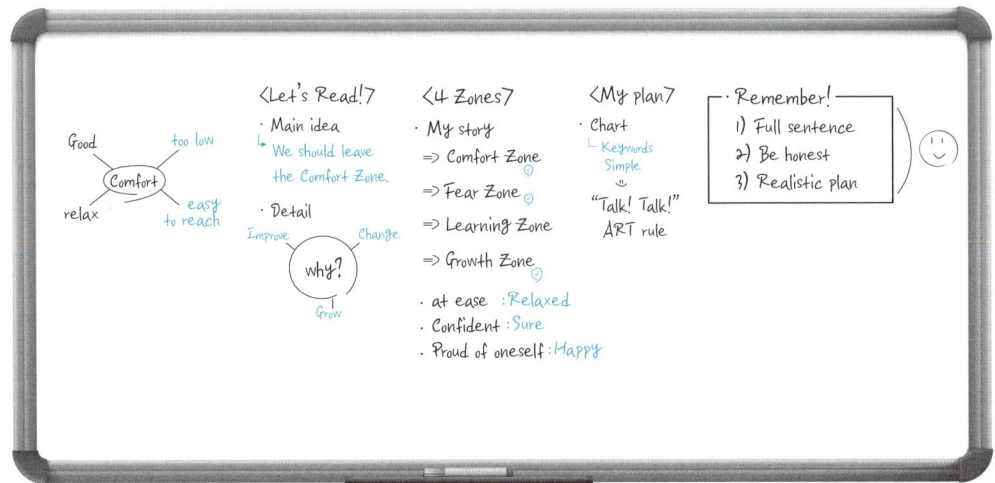

(2) 지도안 예시

단원명	Beyond Your Comfort Zone			시간	90 mins	
대상	• Students : 26 Middle school 3rd Graders • Level : Mixed					
수업 목표	✓ Students will be able to infer the meaning of the title using a quote. ✓ Students will be able to describe the four zones and connect them to their own experiences. ✓ Students will be able to write about their goal beyond the comfort zone based on their personal experience.					
교수·학습 교구	Digital whiteboard, Laptop, Online dictionary, Tablet PCs, PPT slides etc					
핵심역량	자기 관리	지식정보처리	창의적 사고	심미적 감성	협력적 소통	공동체
	✓	✓			✓	

<교수 학습 지도안>

단계	교수·학습 활동	유의점 및 활용 교구
도입 (5분)	*인사, 출석 확인, 교실 내 안전 점검 *학습 주제, 수업 준비 상태 확인	
전개1 (20분)	<center>응시자 작성 내용 1 (Reading)</center> <center>✓ <자료 1>에 인용된 명언을 활용하여 제목의 의미를 추론할 것</center> ●Guessing • [전체] 학생들에게 'Comfort'라는 단어가 주는 인상에 대해 말해보도록 한다. • 학생 예상 반응: Good, Relax, Calm 등 • <자료 1>의 명언을 함께 읽은 후, 해당 맥락을 바탕으로 'Comfort'와 관련된 단어가 무엇일지 다시 한번 생각해 보도록 유도한다. • 교사는 학생 상호작용 결과를 마인드맵으로 정리한다. Good — Comfort — Too low Relax — Comfort — Easy to reach • [전체] 마인드맵으로 판서한 추론 과정을 언급하며, 제목에 언급된 'Comfort Zone'은 처음의 예상과 달리 부정적인 의미였음을 다시 한번 정리한다. <예시 발화> 교사 : At first, we thought that 'Comfort Zone' was something good. However, after we read what Michelangelo had said, it was what? ... Yes, it was something we should get out!	'자료 1'

전개1
(20분)
	● Transition
	• [전체] 직전 활동에서 파악한 제목의 의미를 바탕으로, 글을 읽을 준비가 되었는지 확인한다.
	
	✓ 'Comfort Zone'을 벗어나야 하는 이유에 관해 언급할 것
	
	● Main idea
	• [개별, 2분] <자료 1>를 읽고 Main idea를 파악하게 한다.
	• Skimming 전략을 지도하여 글의 주제를 파악하도록 한다.
	  • 빠른 속도로 글을 훑어보며 반복되는 단어를 확인하도록 한다.
	• 아래 지도 사항에 따라 순회 지도를 실시한다.
	　<순회 지도 사항>
	　• 참여를 북돋우며 활동 중 어려움을 겪고 있는 학생을 파악한다.
	　• Low-level : <자료 1> 뒤편의 Vocabulary list를 참고하도록 한다.
	• [전체] 학생과의 상호작용을 통해 글의 주제를 교실 전체에 공유하고 판서한다.
	  • Main idea : We should leave the Comfort Zone!
	• [전체] 글의 주제와 제목과의 연관성을 강조한다.
	
	● Detail information
	• [전체] Screen을 통해 교사가 준비한 질문을 함께 확인한다.
	  • 질문 : Why should we leave our Comfort Zone?
	• [개별, 3분] Scanning 전략을 지도하여 질문에 대한 답을 찾도록 안내한다.
	  • 글 전체가 아니라 필요한 부분만 선별하여 읽도록 한다.
	• 아래 지도 사항에 따라 순회 지도를 실시한다.
	　<순회 지도 사항>
	　• 참여를 북돋우며 활동 중 어려움을 겪고 있는 학생을 파악한다.
	　• High-level : 활동 참여에 대한 긍정적 피드백을 제공하고, Student teacher 역할을 부여하여 다른 학생을 도울 수 있도록 한다.
	　• Low-level : 동료 학습자로부터 도움을 받을 수 있도록 Peer-scaffolding을 유도한다.
	• [전체] 학생과의 상호작용 결과를 마인드맵으로 정리한다.
	  • 예상 답변 : Improve, Change, Grow 등		

전개2 (30분)	응시자 작성 내용 2 (Pre-writing) ✓ <자료 2>의 4가지 영역(Zone)에 관해 설명하고 학생의 경험을 나누도록 유도할 것 ● Transition • [전체] Comfort Zone을 벗어나기 위해서는 4가지 영역에 대해 잘 알고 있어야 한다는 사실을 언급하며 <자료 2>를 소개한다. ● T's anecdote • [전체] 학생과 상호작용을 바탕으로 각 영역을 하나씩 언급하며 해당 영역에 관한 교사의 일화를 제시한다.	'자료 2'	

	• 교사의 일화와 비슷한 경험이 있는지 학생과 대화하며 나눈 내용을 판서한다. <예시 발화> 교사 : When I was your age, I used to be scared of speaking in front of people. So I avoid being in front of them. That was my 'Comfort Zone'. … Do you have an experience like this?	'자료 2'

전개2
(30분)
	✓ 예문을 통해 <자료 2>의 밑줄 친 어휘 표현 3개를 가르칠 것
	● Transition
	• [전체] <자료 2>의 빈칸에 주목하며, 이를 채우기 위해서는 Word Box의 단어를 먼저 알아야 함을 안내한다.
	● Teaching Vocabularies
	• [전체] 'at ease', 'confident', 'proud of oneself'의 뜻을 아는 학생이 있는지 물어본 후, 각각의 단어에 대한 예문을 Screen을 통해 제시한다.
	• 'at ease'
	  • (예문) He slept all day completely at ease, doing nothing.
	  • 학생과 상호작용을 통해 'confident'는 'Sure of yourself'와 비슷한 의미임을 추론할 수 있도록 한다.
	• 'confident'
	  • (예문) After practicing several times, she looked confident.
	  • 학생과 상호작용을 통해 'confident'는 'Sure of yourself'와 비슷한 의미임을 추론할 수 있도록 한다.
	• 'proud of oneself'
	  • (예문) He was proud of himself because he didn't make any mistakes.
	  • 학생과 상호작용을 통해 'proud of oneself'는 'Happy about yourself'와 비슷한 의미임을 추론할 수 있도록 한다.
		'자료 2'

	✓ 각 영역(Zone)에 해당하는 어휘 표현을 연결하며 <자료 2>를 완성하도록 할 것 ● Transition • [전체] 이해한 단어를 바탕으로 <자료 2>를 완성할 준비가 되었는지 확인한다. ● Word Match • [개별, 3분] Word Box에 있는 'Feeling word'를 각 영역에 연결하도록 안내한다. <예시 발화> 교사 : So from now on, we are going to match the feeling words to the right zone! • [전체] 학생과의 상호작용을 통해 활동 결과를 공유한다.	'자료 2'

	응시자 작성 내용 3 (Writing)	
	✓ 교사의 예시를 제공하여 <자료 3>에 제시된 표를 완성하도록 할 것	
	● Teacher's example • [전체] 화면을 통해 <자료 3>에 제시된 표 완성을 위한 교사의 예시를 보여준다. • 글쓰기를 위한 준비 활동이므로 단어나 구처럼 간단한 구조로 작성해도 된다는 사실을 안내한다. <예시 발화> 교사 : Since this is a buildup activity for the writing, you can write as simple as possible, with keywords!	PPT slides '자료 3'
	✓ 완성된 표를 바탕으로 짝과 함께 이야기를 나누고 개별적으로 <자료 3>을 완성할 것	
전개3 (30분)	● Talk! Talk! • [짝, 5분] 짝과 함께 <자료 3>의 표에 대한 서로의 생각을 나누도록 한다. • 아래 ART rule을 지키도록 독려한다. <ART rule> A : Active participation,　　R : Respect others,　　T : Take turns ● Beyond 'Comfort Zone' • [개별, 15분] <자료 3>의 표와 짝과 함께 나눈 대화를 바탕으로 전체 내용을 완성하도록 안내한다. 　• 아래 글쓰기 조건을 안내한다. <조건> 1. Make full sentences 2. Be honest 3. Realistic plan ● Giving authentic purpose • 자신의 글은 영어 수업 타임캡슐에 보관하여 졸업할 때 돌려줄 예정임을 안내한다. <예시 발화> 교사 : Your writings will be put into the English class time capsule and they will be returned when you graduate. ⋯ Does it sound great? Perfect! • 글쓰기 활동 중 아래 사항에 따라 순회 지도를 실시한다.	'자료 3'

	<순회 지도 사항> • 참여를 북돋우며 활동 중 어려움을 겪고 있는 학생을 파악한다. • Low-level : <자료 3>의 표가 글쓰기 활동을 위한 Outline임을 언급하며 이를 활용할 수 있도록 안내한다. • High-level : 활동 결과에 대해 칭찬한 후, Comfort Zone을 벗어날 다른 계획을 추가로 작성하도록 격려한다.	
	✓ 글쓰기에 사용된 언어 표현에 관해 교사의 피드백을 제공할 것	
	● **Giving feedback** • [전체] Full sentence, Be honest, Realistic plan을 모두 잘 지켰다는 점을 강조하며 긍정적 피드백을 제공한다. <예시 발화> 교사 : When I was walking around, I found that everyone wrote their plans very successfully. Not only you made full sentences but also your writings were very honest and realistic. ⋯ Awesome! Let's give ourselves a big hand!	
마무리 (5분)	*활동 마무리, 다음 차시 안내 *주변 정리 지도, 인사	

(3) 스크립트

> 응시자 작성 내용 1 (Reading)

✓ 〈자료 1〉에 인용된 명언을 활용하여 제목의 의미를 추론할 것

Okay, students. So far, we've talked about the unit title and the lesson objectives. Then, are you guys ready to begin today's class? Perfect. Then let me give you this worksheet. Take one and pass them to the back. Take one and pass them to the back. 상민, at the back! Did you get the worksheet? Awesome.

So, what can you see in the first worksheet? Yes, there's a reading text. So, can you read the title? Yes, it says 'Beyond Your Comfort Zone', right? So, let's talk about the title first. So, which word can you come up with when you think of the word "comfort"? So, let's talk about it. So, let's think about the word "comfort." Any ideas?

Yes, 수현? Yes, that's a great word. So, 수현 just said - she can think of the word "good." And what else? Yes, 동우! Yes, "Relax" is a great word. So, "relax" is a word when you think of the word "comfort." So, like this, we just came up with these two words: "good" and "relax."

Then, everyone! Let's look at the first worksheet again. Below the title, what can you see? Yes, 지환? Yes, there is a famous saying from Michelangelo, right? So, let's read it out loud together. Perfect. Then, everyone! Let's think about it again. After we read the famous saying from Michelangelo, which word do you have in mind when you see the word "comfort"? Yes, 희원! Yes, "too low" — that's a great word. So, "too low." And what else? Yes, 나현? Yes, "easy to reach," right? So, "too easy to reach" — that's a great word.

So, everyone! We first thought that - 'Comfort Zone' is something we can relax in or something good. However, after we read Michelangelo's famous saying, the 'Comfort Zone' is what? Yes, something we should get out, right? So, like this, we just guessed the meaning of the title from the famous saying.

Then, are you guys ready to read the text? Perfect. So, it's time to read. Let's read.

✓ **'Comfort Zone'을 벗어나야 하는 이유에 관해 언급할 것**

Everyone, when we read the text, we first have to find what? Yes, 동우! Yes! We need to find the main idea, right? So, from now on, we are going to find the main idea of this reading text. To find the main idea, do we have to read quickly or slowly? Yes, we need to read quickly, right? So, you don't have to understand every single word — just read quickly and find the main idea. I'm going to give you 2 minutes. Find the main idea. Go!

Oh, 현우! Do you need any help? Oh, the words are so difficult? Then, why don't you look at the back of the worksheet? What do you see? Yes, there is a vocabulary list, right? So, with this vocabulary list, can you find the main idea by yourself? Perfect. Keep up the good work. One minute left, students.

Okay, time's up. So, let's check the main idea together. So, what was the main idea? Any volunteers? Yes, 다원! Oh, did everyone hear what 다원 just said? He said the main idea of this reading text is "we should leave the comfort zone." The main idea was: we should leave — we should leave — where? Yes, 현정! we should leave the comfort zone. Comfort zone! Perfect. So, like this, we just found the main idea.

Then, everyone, let's look at the title again. What was the title? Yes, it was 'Beyond the Comfort Zone', right? So, remember that - the title and the main idea have a very close relationship to each other. All right?

So far, we just found the main idea. Then, are you guys ready to read the text a little bit more closely? Awesome. So, it's time to find some details. So, let's find some details. So, everyone, let's look at the screen. 정은, at the back! Do you see the screen? Perfect. So, what can you see on the screen? Yes, there is a question, right? So, can you read the question out loud? Perfect. So, the question was: why we should leave the comfort zone, right?

So, from now on, I'm going to give you 3 minutes — 3 minutes — to find the answer to the question: why we should leave the comfort zone. All right? So, we are going to read the text again to find why — why we should leave the comfort zone. All right?

However, to find the answer to this question, do we have to read everything? Or can we just read only the necessary part? Yes, 현정! Yes! You don't need to read everything.

I'm going to give you three minutes. Find the answer. Go!

Oh, 영수! You already finished? Wow, what a quick reader. Then why don't you help your friend 수영? I heard she needs some help. Can you guys do that? Perfect. Like this, friends can be a better teacher. Keep up the good work. One minute left, students.

Okay, time's up. So, let's check the answers together. So, why should we leave the comfort zone? Any ideas? Yes, 지환! Oh, Yes, "to improve ourselves." That's a great word. So, "to improve." And what else? Yes, 다윈! Yes, that's because it helps us grow, right? So, we should leave our comfort zone for our own growth. And what else? Yes, 현우! Oh, yes! That's because we should change ourselves. That's a great word. So, "we should change ourselves." Perfect!

응시자 작성 내용 2 (Pre-writing)

✓ 〈자료 2〉의 4가지 영역(Zone)에 관해 설명하고 학생의 경험을 나누도록 유도할 것

All right. So far, we just read the text twice — first for the main idea, and second for the detail. Then, don't you guys want to get out of the comfort zone? Yes, right? However, to get out of the comfort zone, we should learn what? Yes, 지환! Yes, we should first learn the four zones, right? So, let's talk about those zones — the four zones.

So, from here, I'm going to tell you my story. So, this is my story — so, teacher's story. When I was a middle school student like you, I always tried to avoid being in front of others because that was kind of comfortable. So, I was in which zone? Yes, 현정! Yes! That was my comfort zone. So, that was my comfort zone.

And three years later, I went to high school. And in one high school class, I had a chance to give a presentation. And at that time, I was very nervous and unsure. So, in which zone was I? Yes, 호영! Yes, I was in the fear zone, right? So, that was my fear zone. I felt fear being in front of others.

So, because I was so nervous, I practiced a lot. And thanks to the hard work, I could finish my presentation successfully. And at that time, I felt the sense of accomplishment.

I felt so great. So, this shows I was in which kind of zone? Yes, 민수! Yes, that was my learning zone — so, my learning zone.

And after that, as a teacher, I kept trying to develop myself — to be a better teacher — setting a new goal. So, which zone am I in now? Yes, 현수! Yes, the growth zone. So, the last zone was the growth zone. Perfect. So, like this, I just told you my story of these four zones.

Don't you guys have your own stories? Any volunteer? Oh, yes, 수영! Wow, that's a beautiful story. Did everyone hear what 수영 just said? Then, can anyone briefly summarize what 수영 just said? Let's talk about 수영's comfort zone first. Yes, 현우! Yes, she said she avoided studying math. So, that was her comfort zone — because studying math is difficult.

And what else? How about her fear zone? Yes, 수현! Yes, she said she felt nervous and unsure when she got the wrong answer, right? However, what about the learning zone? Can anyone tell us about 수영's learning zone? Yes, 호영! Yes, she studied hard and paid lots of attention to the math class, right? Then she felt what? Yes — in the learning zone, she felt the sense of accomplishment. She got the better score.

And then what? What can you tell us about 수영's growth zone? Yes, 영수! Yes, she said — she's no longer afraid of the wrong answers, and even she's trying to challenge the more difficult ones, right? So, like this, we just talked about our experience about the four zones.

Then, are you guys ready to get out of your own comfort zone? Awesome!

✓ 예문을 통해 〈자료 2〉의 밑줄 친 어휘 표현 3개를 가르칠 것

Then, everyone, let's look at the second worksheet. What do you see on the second worksheet? Yes, 지환! Yes, there are four zones that we just talked about. However, there is something strange. Can you tell us? Yes, 지민! Yes, there are blanks, right? So, to fill in those blanks, we should first learn what? Yes, we should learn vocabularies, right?

So, which words can you find difficult? Just say out the word. Okay, I can hear the word 'at ease'. And what else? Okay, 나현 — the word 'confident'. Yes, that's a difficult word

— 'confident'. And what else? Yes, 수민? Yes, the expression 'proud of oneself'. Yes, 'be proud of oneself' — that's a difficult expression.

Then class, does anyone know the meaning of those words? All right, then let me give you a hint. Everyone, look at the screen. 상민, at the back! Do you see the screen? All right. So, what can you see on the screen? Yes, there is an example sentence, right? So, can you read the first one? Yes, the first one was: He slept all day, completely at ease, doing nothing.

Then, with this sample sentence, can you guess the meaning of the word 'at ease'? Yes, 수현! Oh, did everyone hear what 수현 just said? She said the expression 'at ease' means 'relaxed'. That's a great guessing, 수현! So, 'at ease' means 'relaxed'. Perfect.

And the second one — 'confident'. So, 현우, at the back! Do you see the example sentence on the screen? Awesome. So, can you read it for us? Yes, it says: After practicing several times, she looked confident. Right? Then, can you guess the meaning of the word confident? Yes, 다원! Yes, that means 'be sure of yourself'. So, 'confident' means 'sure' — so, this means 'sure'.

And the last word — 'proud of oneself'. So, 재우! Can you read the last example sentence on the screen? Yes, it says: He was proud of himself because he didn't make any mistakes. Right? So, everyone, what would you feel when you didn't make any mistakes? Yes, 수민! Yes, you'd feel very happy, right? So, 'proud of oneself' means 'being happy about yourself'. All right?

✓ 각 영역(Zone)에 해당하는 어휘 표현을 연결하며 〈자료 2〉를 완성하도록 할 것

So far, we just learned these three difficult words. Then, are you guys ready to match the words to each zone? Perfect. So, I'm going to give you 3 minutes — 3 minutes to match those feeling words and complete the second worksheet. 3 minutes. Match the words. Go.

One minute left, students. Does anyone need more time? Okay, time's up. So, let's check the answers together. So, which words go to the comfort zone? Any volunteers? Yes, 호영! Yes — 'at ease' and 'safe'. So, we got the words for the comfort zone.

And the last one — how about the growth zone? Any volunteers? Yes, 상우! Yes —

'feeling of success'. And what else? Yes, 현정! Yes — 'proud of oneself'. And the last one? Yes, 수정! Yes — it was 'confident'. Perfect. So, we finally got the words for the growth zone.

응시자 작성 내용 3 (Writing)

✓ **교사의 예시를 제공하여 〈자료 3〉에 제시된 표를 완성하도록 할 것**

So, like this, we just finished matching the feeling words to each zone. Then, are you guys ready to make some plans to go beyond the comfort zone? Awesome. So, it's time to make a plan. So, it's time to make my plan.

All right. So, everyone! Let's look at the screen again. 희원, at the back! Do you see the screen? Perfect. So, what do you see on the screen? Yes, there is a teacher's example, right? So, like this teacher's example on the screen, we are going to complete the chart first. Okay? So, it's time to complete the chart on the third worksheet. All right?

However, everyone! Because this is just a buildup activity, you don't have to write in — what? Thank you, 민수! Yes, you don't have to write in full sentences — not yet, okay? So, you can just write with the keywords, making it as simple as you can. All right? So remember that — you can use the keywords and make it simple. Okay? So I'm going to give you 5 minutes. Complete the chart in the third worksheet. Go!

One minute left, students. Does anyone need more time? Okay, time's up.

✓ **완성된 표를 바탕으로 짝과 함께 이야기를 나누고 개별적으로 〈자료 3〉을 완성할 것**

All right, students. So, we just finished filling out the chart with my own experience.

Then, don't you want to share your experience with your friends? Awesome. So, let's begin the 'Talk! Talk! time' here. So, it's time for 'Talk! Talk!'. All right? So, we are going to do this with your partners.

So, 수현, 현수 - you two! 종민, 민종 - you two! You two! And lastly, you two. Does everyone have their own partners? Awesome. So, with your partners, I'm going to give you 5 minutes — 5 minutes to share your experience based on the chart. All right?

However, whenever we do this kind of 'Talk! Talk!' activity, which rule do we have to follow? Yes, 호영! Yes, we need to follow the ART rule, right? So, don't forget the ART rule when you do this 'Talk! Talk!' activity.

So, let's quickly remind of it. What was A? Yes, 동우! Yes — it was Active participation. And what was R? Yes, 현정! Yes — it was Respect others. So, make sure you respect your partner's experience. All right? And what was T? Yes, 희원! Yes, T means Take turns. Okay? So remember this ART rule.

I'm going to give you 5 minutes. 5 minutes, share your experience. Go! One minute left, students. Okay, time's up. So, we just shared our experience with our partners. Then, are you guys ready to write your plan to go beyond the comfort zone? Awesome.

Then, everyone! Let's look at the screen. 지환, at the back! Do you see the screen? Perfect. So, what do you see on the screen? Yes, there are some writing requirements, right? So, there are several things you should remember. So, don't forget this. You should remember.

So, what was the first thing? Can you read? Yes, 지현! Yes — it says 'Full sentence', right? So, the first thing was the full sentence. So, based on what you simply wrote in the chart, you should use full sentences here. Okay?

And second — what does it say? Yes, 은수! Yes — it says 'Be honest', right? So, because we are going to write your own experience, we are going to be honest. Okay? So the second one was 'Be honest'.

And what was the last one? Yes, 정은! Yes — it says 'Realistic plan', right? So, to go beyond the comfort zone, it is really important to set a realistic plan. All right? So, the third one was realistic — 'Realistic plan'. Okay? So remember these things when you write your own plans to go beyond your comfort zone.

Okay? So, everyone! Just before we start, let me tell you this — your writings from this activity will be put into the English Class Time Capsule, and they will be returned when you graduate. How does it sound? So exciting? Awesome!

So, I'm going to give you 15 minutes. Remember those three things. Make your plans to go beyond the comfort zone. Go.

Oh, 수민, do you need any help? Oh, you don't know how to write? Then why don't you go back to your chart about your experience — because that was kind of the buildup activity for this one. Can you do that? Awesome. So, if you need any more help, just don't hesitate to call me. All right? Awesome. Keep up the good work.

And 민재, you already finished? Wow, what a quick writer! Then, why don't you write about another comfort zone? Because the more comfort zones you can get out of, the better person you will be. Can you do that? Awesome. I love your effort.

One minute left, students. Does anyone need more time? Okay, time's up.

✓ 글쓰기에 사용된 언어 표현에 관해 교사의 피드백을 제공할 것

So, we just finished writing our own plans to go beyond our comfort zone. And there was one thing I want to tell you. When I was walking around the classroom, I could find that — all of you guys were using full sentences from the keywords. And I could also find that — everyone was very honest with the very realistic plan. So, I want to tell you this: Good job on this, everyone! You can be proud of yourself — like we just learned this word. So, I want to give you a big hand. Let's give ourselves a big hand! Awesome.

So, before we wrap up, let's quickly go over today's class. So, we first talked about what? Yes, 동우! Yes — we talked about the comfort zone. And we learned what? Yes, 현정! Yes — we learned about those four zones. And we wrote about what? Yes, 희원! Yes, we wrote about — "How can we go beyond our comfort zone?"

So, with today's class, I want you to become a person who is brave enough to break your comfort zone and get out of it to develop yourself. Can you guys do that? Awesome. So, that's it for us today. And have a great weekend!

라 2022 기출문제

(1) 판서 노트 및 예시 영상

수업실연 예시
2022 기출 변형
동영상 바로가기

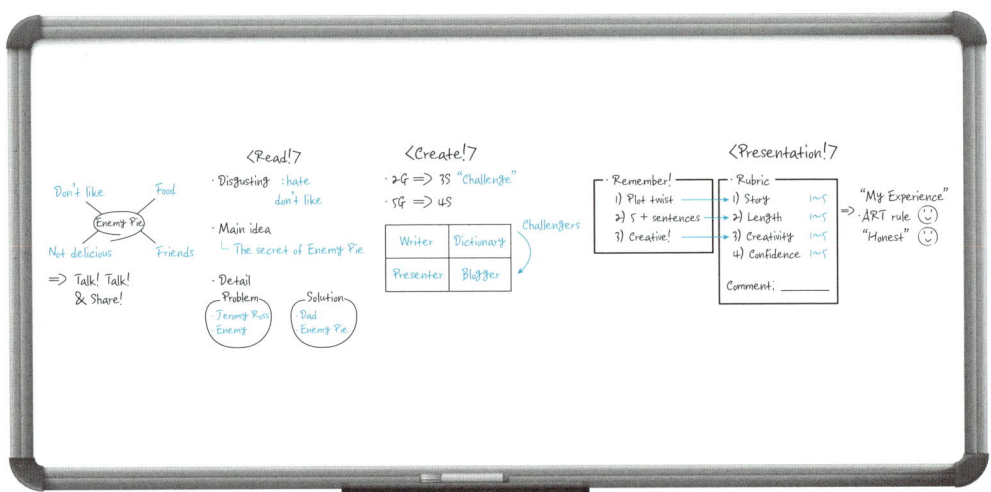

(2) 지도안 예시

단원명	Enemy Pie				시간	90 mins
대상	• Students : 26 Middle school 3rd Graders • Level : Mixed					
수업 목표	✓ Students will be able to predict the story using the title and context. ✓ Students will be able to find the details of the text using a graphic organizer. ✓ Students will be able to create a group story with a plot twist.					
교수·학습 교구	Digital whiteboard, Laptop, PPT slides etc					
핵심역량	자기 관리	지식정보처리	창의적 사고	심미적 감성	협력적 소통	공동체
			✓		✓	✓

<교수 학습 지도안>

단계	교수·학습 활동	유의점 및 활용 교구
도입 (5분)	*인사, 출석 확인, 교실 내 안전 점검 *학습 주제, 수업 준비 상태 확인	
전개1 (15분)	**응시자 작성 내용 1** ✓ <자료 1>의 제목으로 이야기의 내용을 추측하는 활동을 진행할 것 ● Guessing from the title • [전체] 교실 전체 상호작용을 통해 <자료 1>의 'Enemy'와 'Pie'의 뜻을 각각 묻는다. • 합쳐진 단어 'Enemy pie'의 뜻은 무엇일지 물어보고 이를 통해 이야기의 내용을 추측하도록 한다. • 교사는 학생의 답변을 마인드맵으로 정리한다. <마인드맵 예시> 'Ememy pie' • 정리한 내용을 바탕으로 이야기의 내용을 추측하도록 유도한다. ✓ 주제에 관해 짝과 경험을 나누는 활동을 진행할 것 ● Talk! Talk! • [짝, 5분] 마인드맵을 바탕으로 학교생활 중 'Enemy'에 관한 자신의 경험을 짝과 함께 이야기를 나눠보도록 한다. • 교사는 다양한 정답이 나올 수 있음을 강조하며 자유롭게 의견을 나누는 분위기를 형성한다.	'자료 1'

	<예시 발화> 교사 : In this 'Talk! Talk!' activity, all ideas are welcome. There's no right answer. Just feel free to talk!	
	√ 맥락을 통해 <자료 1>의 밑줄 친 단어 중 하나의 의미를 추측하도록 할 것	
	● Teaching Vocabularies using context • [전체] <자료 1>의 단어를 간략히 살펴보게 한 후, 처음 보는 단어가 있는지 묻는다. 　• 예시 : 'disgusting' • <자료 1>에서 'disgusting'과 맥락상 밀접한 관련이 있는 표현을 찾아보도록 한다. 　• 'earthworms'와 'rocks'라는 표현이 같은 맥락에 쓰였다는 사실에 주목하며, 음식에 만약 위와 같은 것이 들어가면 어떨지 묻는다. 　• 'disgusting = hate'라는 의미를 성공적으로 추론하게 한 후, 직접 문장을 만들어 보게 함으로써 이해 확인 점검을 실시한다.	'자료 1'
전개2 (20분)	응시자 작성 내용 2	
	√ <자료 1>의 주제를 찾는 활동을 진행할 것	
	● Main idea • [개별, 5분] <자료 1>를 읽고 Main idea를 파악하게 한다. • Skimming 전략을 지도하여 글의 주제를 파악하도록 한다. 　• 빠른 속도로 글을 훑어보며 전체적인 이야기 내용을 파악하도록 한다. • 아래 사항에 따라 순회 지도를 실시한다. 　<순회 지도 사항> 　• 참여를 북돋우며 활동 중 어려움을 겪고 있는 학생을 파악한다. 　• Low-level : <자료 1>에서 반복적으로 등장하는 단어를 중점적으로 찾아 읽어보도록 한다. • [전체] 학생과의 상호작용을 통해 글의 주제를 교실 전체에 공유하고 판서한다. 　• Main idea : The Secret of Enemy Pie • [전체] 글의 주제와 제목과의 연관성을 강조한다.	'자료 1'
	√ 그래픽 오거나이저를 제시하여 <자료 1>의 세부 정보를 찾는 활동을 진행할 것	
	● Graphic organizer • 아래 그래픽 오거나이저를 학생들에게 나누어주고, <자료 1>이 Problem과 Solution의 구조로 되어 있음을 안내한다. 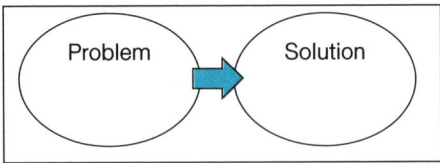	PPT slides '자료 1'

전개2 (20분)	• [개별, 10분] Scanning 전략을 지도하여 그래픽 오거나이저 속 빈칸에 들어갈 키워드를 찾도록 한다. 　• 글 전체가 아니라 필요한 부분만 선별하여 읽도록 한다. • 아래 지도 사항에 따라 순회 지도를 실시한다. 　　<순회 지도 사항> 　　• 참여를 북돋우며 활동 중 어려움을 겪고 있는 학생을 파악한다. 　　• High-level : 활동 참여에 대한 긍정적 피드백을 제공하고, Student teacher 역할을 부여하여 다른 학생을 도울 수 있도록 한다. 　　• Low-level : 동료 학습자로부터 도움을 받도록 Peer-scaffolding을 유도한다. • [전체] 학생과의 상호작용을 통해 답변을 공유하고 판서한다. 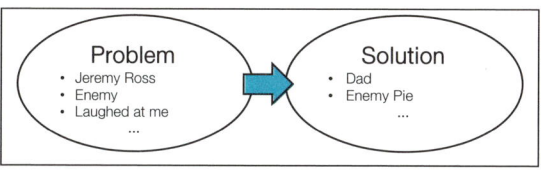 ● Transition 　• [전체] 중간에 생략된 부분과 <Key Concept>의 'Plot twist'를 언급하며 이야기를 창작할 준비가 되었는지 확인한다.
전개3 (20분)	**응시자 작성 내용 3** ✓ 모둠 활동을 위한 개인별 역할을 부여할 것 ● Grouping • 3명으로 구성된 조 2개, 4명으로 구성된 조 5개로 총 7개의 모둠을 구성한다. 　• 3인 1조로 구성된 조를 'Challenge group'으로 소개하고, 참여를 희망하는 학생을 모집한다. 　　<예시 발화> 　　교사 : Since we have 26 students, we are going to have 2 challenge groups. Each challenge group will have 3 students. Who wants to take on the challenge to improve your English? Any volunteers? • 앉은 자리에 따라 역할을 아래와 같이 부여한다. 　　<역할 부여> 	Writer	Dictionary	• Writer : 문장 작성 • Dictionary : Tablet PC로 단어 검색, 문법 확인 | 	Presenter	*Blogger	• Presenter : 발표 담당 • Blogger : Online Classroom에 게시 | 　　*Challenge group은 Dictionary가 Blogger의 역할을 겸하도록 한다.

전개3 (20분)	✓ 모둠 활동을 통해 플롯 트위스트가 포함된 <자료 3>을 완성할 것 ● Create a story • [전체] Screen을 활용하여 학생들에게 'Sample writing'을 제시한다. • 'Sample writing'을 함께 확인하며 아래 글쓰기 조건을 제시한다. 　<글쓰기 조건> 　1. Story ： Plot twist 　2. Length ： 5+ sentences 　3. Be creative! • Authentic purpose ： 우수 작품은 English class storybook으로 출판될 것임을 안내한다. • [모둠, 20분] 글쓰기 조건에 따라 <자료 3>를 완성하도록 한다. • 교사는 아래 지도 사항에 따라 순회 지도를 실시한다. 　<순회 지도 사항> 　• 참여를 북돋우며 활동 중 어려움을 겪고 있는 학생을 파악한다. 　• Low level ： 이야기 창작에 어려움이 있을 경우, <자료 3> 뒤편의 'Guide questions'를 활용하도록 안내한다. 　• High level ： 긍정적 피드백을 제공한 뒤, Plot twist는 무궁무진함을 언급하며 다른 버전의 이야기를 쓸 수 있도록 추가 과제를 제시한다.	'자료 3' *교사는 '자료 2'를 참고할 것
전개4 (25분)	응시자 작성 내용 4 ✓ 채점 루브릭을 제시하여 <자료 3> 발표에 대한 동료 평가를 진행할 것 ● Peer evaluation • 개인별로 평가 기준이 포함된 <Peer evaluation rubric>을 제공한다. • 평가 기준이 글쓰기 기준과 연결됨을 강조한다. 　<Peer evaluation rubric> 　　　　　　　　　　　Name ： _____ 　　　　Presenter/Group ： _____/_____ | 1. Story	Plot twist	1~5
2. Length	5+ sentences	1~5
3. Creativity	Creative	1~5
4. Confidence	Eye contact, Loud voice	1~5
Comment ：		| • 개인별로 평가 기준이 포함된 <Peer evaluation rubric>을 제공한다. ● Presentation • 각 모둠에서 Presenter 역할을 맡은 학생의 준비 상태를 확인한다. 　• (예시) Alright, time's up! Presenters, ae you ready? Great! Let's begin the presentations now!	PPT slides '자료 3'

전개4 (25분)	✓ 갈등을 해결한 자기 경험을 짝과 함께 나눠보도록 할 것	
	● Transition • [전체] 발표가 끝난 후, 이와 비슷한 경험이 있었는지 물어보며 말하기 활동에 대한 준비도를 확인한다. 　• (예시) We just finished watching our friends' presentations and there were a lot of stories. Don't you have a similar experience? ● My experience • [짝, 5분] 짝과 함께 이야기 속에 등장하는 주인공과 비슷한 경험(갈등을 해결한 경험)이 있었는지 대화를 나눠보도록 한다. • ART rule을 강조하며 말하기 활동을 실시한다. 　　　　　　　　　　< ART rule > 　A : Active participation,　　R : Respect others,　　T : Take turns	
	✓ 영어 사용에 관한 교사의 피드백을 제공할 것	
	● Giving feedback • [전체] ART rule을 잘 지키면서 대화를 한 것, 자신의 경험을 나눌 때 솔직했던 것을 언급하며 긍정적 피드백을 제공한다. 　　　　　　　　　　< 예시 발화 > 교사 : When I was walking around, I found that everyone was following the ART rule. Not only that, I was very impressed that you were very honest when you shared your experience with your friends. … Awesome! Let's give ourselves a big hand!	
마무리 (5분)	*활동 마무리, 다음 차시 안내 *주변 정리 지도, 인사	

(3) 스크립트

응시자 작성 내용 1

✓ 〈자료 1〉의 제목으로 이야기의 내용을 추측하는 활동을 진행할 것

Okay, students. So far, we've talked about the unit title and the lesson objectives. Then, are you guys ready to start today's class? Perfect. So, I'm going to give you this worksheet. Take one and pass them to the back. Take one and pass them to the back. 호영, at the back! Did you get the worksheet? Perfect.

So, what do you see on the first worksheet? Yes, there is a story. It was 'Enemy Pie'. So from now on, we are going to begin today's class with 'Guessing with the title'. So let's guess with the title 'Enemy Pie'. So everyone, what does it mean by "enemy"? Which words can you come up with when you think of the word "enemy"? Yes, 동우! Yes, 'Someone you don't like', right? So, 'Someone you don't like'. And what else? How about "pie"? What is pie? Yes, 현우! Yes, it is food, right? So pie is food. Then what is 'Enemy Pie'? What would this 'Enemy pie' taste like? Delicious or not delicious? Yes, 다원! Yes, you don't think it's delicious, right? So it will not be delicious.

So like this, we just talked about the title 'Enemy Pie'. Then, can you guess what this story will be with this title? Yes, 종민! Oh, did everyone hear what 종민 just said? He said, the 'Enemy pie' will be the story about giving something not delicious to the enemy. That's a great guessing, 종민!

All right. So far, we just guessed the story with the title. Then, are you guys ready to talk more about it? Perfect.

✓ 주제에 관해 짝과 경험을 나누는 활동을 진행할 것

Let me begin the 'Talk Talk' Time. So it's 'Talk Talk'. From now on, we are going to talk with your partners. So, 종민, 민종 - you two! 현정, 정현 - you two! You two! And lastly, you two. So, does everyone have their own partners? Perfect.

So, with your partners, we are going to talk about today's topic. Can anyone tell us what it is? Yes, 지환! Yes, it was the enemy. So we are going to talk about your enemy in your school life. All right? However, in this 'Talk Talk' activity, we should remember what? Yes, 다원! Yes, we should remember all ideas are welcome. So there is no right answer. Just feel free to talk. All right? I'm going to give you 5 minutes. Talk with your partners. Go.

One minute left, students. Okay, time's up. Then, let's share what you talked with your partners. So 'Let's share'. Do we have any volunteers? Yes, 현정 and 정현! Oh, that's a beautiful story. Thank you for sharing. All right, so like this, we just talked about our school experience about the enemies and shared in our class.

Then, are you guys ready to read another interesting story? Perfect. So let's begin the reading time. So let's read.

✓ 맥락을 통해 〈자료 1〉의 밑줄 친 단어 중 하나의 의미를 추측하도록 할 것

However, before reading, what do we have to do first? Yes, 현정! Yes, we need to learn some difficult words. So everyone, let's quickly check if there's a difficult word in the first worksheet. Did you guys find some difficult words? Just say the words out loud. Okay, I can hear the word "disgusting." So today's word is "disgusting." So today's word is "disgusting."

Does anyone know the meaning of the word "disgusting"? All right, then let me give you a hint. So let's look at the context of the word "disgusting." Which word can you find around the word "disgusting"? Yes, 동우! Yes, you can find 'the earthworms', right? And what else? Yes, 재우! Yes, 'the rocks', right? So let's imagine that someone gives you a sandwich, but inside there's an earthworm and rock. How would you feel, 다원? Would you like it? No way! You won't like it, right? That's because you think the sandwich is 'disgusting'.

Then, can you guess the meaning of the word "disgusting"? Yes, 호영! Oh, did everyone hear what 호영 just said? He said "disgusting" means something you don't like. So that means something you hate. That's a great guessing, 호영! So "disgusting" means something you hate or you don't like.

All right. So, do you understand the meaning of the word "disgusting"? Then, can you make a sentence with the word "disgusting"? Yes, 수현! Oh, "If you don't clean your room, it will be disgusting." That's a perfect sentence! So like this, we just learned this difficult word. Then, are you guys ready to read the text? Perfect!

> 응시자 작성 내용 2

✓ 〈자료 1〉의 주제를 찾는 활동을 진행할 것

So from now on, we are going to find the main idea from the text. All right. So from now on, it's time to find the main idea. However, to find the main idea, do we have to read quickly or slowly? Yes, 영호! Yes, we need to read quickly, right? So you don't have to understand every single word. Just read quickly and find the main idea. I'm going to give you 5 minutes. 5 minutes, go.

Oh, 수현! Do you need any help? Oh, you can't find the main idea? Then why don't you find the keyword that is used repeatedly? Because keywords can be a hint for the main idea. Can you do that? Perfect. I love your effort!

One minute left, students. Does anyone need more time? Okay, time's up. So let's check the main idea together. Can anyone share your main idea? Yes, 다원! Oh, did everyone hear what 다원 just said? He said the main idea of this reading text is "The secret of Enemy Pie." So the main idea is "The secret of Enemy Pie." The secret of Enemy Pie. Do you guys agree? Perfect.

Then everyone, we just found the main idea. Then, class! Let's look at the title again. What was it? Yes, it was 'Enemy Pie', right? So like this, remember that the main idea and the title have a very close relationship with each other. All right? Awesome!

✓ 그래픽 오거나이저를 제시하여 〈자료 1〉의 세부 정보를 찾는 활동을 진행할 것

So, because we just found the main idea, are you guys ready to read the text a little bit more closely? Perfect. Then everyone, let me give you this worksheet. Take one and pass them to the back. Take one and pass them to the back. 수연, at the back! Did you get the worksheet? Perfect.

So what do you see in the worksheet? Yes, there is a graphic organizer, right? So from now on, we are going to find some details with the graphic organizer. So let's find some detail. So, 다원! In the graphic organizer, which things can you find? Yes, it says "problem". And what else? Yes, 지환! Yes, it says "solution," right? So 'Problem and Solution'. So your graphic organizer looks like this, right?

Then everyone! So from now on, we are going to read the text again to find the keywords for this graphic organizer. All right? However, to find the keywords for this graphic organizer, do we have to read everything or can we just read only the necessary part? Yes! We can choose what we need to read, right? So from now I'm going to give you 10 minutes. 10 minutes to read the text again to find the keywords for this graphic organizer. Are you guys ready? So, 10 minutes. Find the keywords for the problem and solution. Go!

Oh, 현우! You already finished? Wow, what a quick reader! Then why don't you help your partner, 우헌? I heard 우헌 needs some help. Can you guys do that? Awesome! So like this, friends can be a better teacher! Keep up the good work. One minute left, students. Does anyone need more time? Okay, time's up.

So, let's check the answers together. What kind of keyword can you find for this problem? Yes, 현정! Yes, 'Jeremy Ross', right? So it was 'Jeremy Ross'. And why was 'Jeremy Ross' the problem? Yes, 희원! Yes, he laughed at me, right? So he became what? Yes, 재우! Yes, he became the enemy, right? So the enemy. So that was the problem.

And how about the solution? Can anyone share your idea for the solution? Yes, 동우! Oh, you wrote 'Dad' for the keyword! That's right. So to find the solution, the main character asked Dad for advice. And what else for the solution? Yes, 민종! Yes, the solution was 'Enemy Pie'. So Dad's solution was 'Enemy Pie'.

So like this, we just read the story twice — once for the main idea, and another for the detail. However, everyone! Let's look at the reading text again. There's something strange. Can you find it? Yes, 호영! Yes! Some part is missing. Then what else can you find below the reading text? Yes, 상우! Yes, it says "plot twist," right?

Then, with the plot twist, are you guys ready to create the story for the missing part? Awesome! So let's begin creating the story. So let's create.

> 응시자 작성 내용 3

✓ **모둠 활동을 위한 개인별 역할을 부여할 것**

From now on, we are going to create a story with your group members.

However, how many students in our class? Yes, there are 26 students. So we are going to make two groups — two groups of three students each — and five groups of four students. All right? So these two groups will be 'the challenge group' because there are fewer students here.

So, who wants to take on the challenge to improve your English? Any volunteers? Yes, 수현, 현수 and 종민! You three! And who else? 호영, 영호 and 재우 - you three! So, you guys are in the challenge group. All right? And for the rest of the students, let me make you a group. You four, you four! And finally, the last group — group five — you four. So, is everyone in a group? Perfect.

So, have a seat with your group members. All right! So, you guys are sitting like this, right? So let me give each of you guys a role. So, students sitting here, raise your hand. Okay, okay. So you guys are going to be the writers. And students here, raise your hand. All right, okay. So you guys are going to be the dictionaries.

And dictionaries, what do we have to do? Yes, 수현! Yes! If your group members need to find the word or check the grammar, that's your job. So remember that you can use your tablet PCs to find the online dictionary or grammar checker. All right?

And students here, raise your hand. Okay, okay. So you guys are going to be the presenters. So remember that we are going to have a presentation after we create a story. All right? And lastly, students here, raise your hand. So, you guys are going to be the bloggers. Okay?

However, for the challenge group, remember that - the dictionary should take the blogger's job too. All right? So this is for the challengers. Okay?

So bloggers, what do we have to do? Yes, 나영! Yes! We need to upload our final version of the story to the online classroom, right? All right, so like this, we just get our roles. Then, are you guys ready to create a story with your group members? Perfect.

✓ **모둠 활동을 통해 플롯 트위스트가 포함된 〈자료 3〉을 완성할 것**
(교사는 〈자료 2〉를 참고할 것)

Then everyone, let's look at the screen here. 상민 at the back! Can you see the screen? Perfect. So, what do you see on the screen? Yes, there is a sample writing. What can you find in the sample writing? Any ideas? Yes, 우영! Yes, there's a plot twist, right?

So like this, there are several things you should remember when you create a story. So remember this — when you create a story! Like 우영 just said, we should have the plot twist. All right? So the first thing was plot twist. So make sure your group writing has a plot twist. All right?

And what else can you find? How about the length of the story? Yes, 재우! Yes, right. So like 재우 just said, you should write at least five or more sentences. Okay? So the story should be long enough. And what else? How about the storyline? Yes, 건우! Yes, it is very creative, right? So remember that your story should be creative. Okay?

So remember these three things when you create a story. All right? So just before we start, let me tell you this — the best group's writing will be actually published in our English class storybook. How does it sound? Exciting? Awesome!

So I'm going to give you 20 minutes. 20 minutes to do what, 재우? Yes, we are going to write a story. And what's your role, 수현? Yes, you are going to be the blogger, right? So, 20 minutes - create a story. Go!

Oh, group four, do you need any help? Oh, you don't know how to create a story? Yes, it's very difficult to come up with new things. Then, why don't you look at the back of the worksheet? What do you see? Yes, there are several guide questions. I believe those questions will help you to think outside the box. So, with those guide questions, can you guys do this work by yourselves? Awesome! So if you need any more help, just feel free to raise your hand. All right? Perfect. Keep up the good work!

And challengers group, you already finished? Wow, what quick writers! Then, why don't you write another story with a different plot twist? Because you guys already know that - the possibility of plot twists is endless. Can you guys do that? Perfect. So I'm sure that - you guys will make fantastic stories. Keep up the good work! One minute left, students. Does any group need more time? Okay, time's up.

응시자 작성 내용 4

✓ 채점 루브릭을 제시하여 〈자료 3〉 발표에 대한 동료 평가를 진행할 것

Okay, so far, we just finished writing our group's story. Then, don't you want to know another group's story? Perfect! Let's begin the presentation time. So it's time for the presentation. However, whenever we have this kind of presentation, which one do we have to check first? Yes, 다원! Yes, we need to check the rubric, right?

So let me give you this peer evaluation rubric. Take one and pass them to the back. Take one and pass them to the back. So, 상민 at the back! Did you get the rubric? So what do you see in the first part? Yes, it says "the story," right? So in the rubric, there are several things you should check. So the first thing was 'The story'.

And about the story — what does this mean, "Story"? Yes, 지환! Yes, it means 'the plot twist', right? So based on how much you like the plot twist of your friend's writing, you can give one to five points. All right?

And what's the second part? Yes, 동우! Yes, it was 'Length', right? So the second part was the length. And what does that mean? Yes, it was five or more sentences. So you can give one point for each sentence. So if your friend's writing has more than five sentences, you can get five points.

And what else? Yes, 은영! Yes, it says 'Creativity', right? So the third part was creativity. So, what does that mean? Yes, that means if the writing is creative. If you think your friend's writing is creative, you can give one to five points.

And not only these things — because it is a presentation, we have what? Yes, 은정! Yes, it says 'Confidence', right? So the fourth part was the confidence. Because this is a presentation, the presenter should be confident to give a presentation. All right?

And what does that mean, the confidence? Yes, 지환! Yes, it means the eye contact and the loud voice. So based on how much you like the presentation, you can give one to five points to your friend's writing.

And lastly, what can you see? Yes, 희원! Yes, there is 'Comments', right? So make sure you give a comment for your friend's presentation. So, based on this peer evaluation rubric, we are going to check our friends' writing. So, presenters in each group, are you guys ready? Awesome. So the presentation begins now.

✓ 갈등을 해결한 자기 경험을 짝과 함께 나눠보도록 할 것

All right. So far we just finished watching our friend's presentations, and there were a lot of creative stories with plot twists. Then — don't you guys have similar experiences? Don't you want to share? Awesome. So let's begin to share my experience. So, based on the presentation, let's begin to share my experience. All right?

So from now on, I'm going to give you 5 minutes. 5 minutes to talk with your partners and share your experience similar to your friend's writing. However, whenever we do this kind of activity, which rule do we have to follow? Yes, 상민! Yes, we need to follow the ART rule, right?

So remember this ART rule. So what was 'A', 현우? Yes, it was Active participation. And what was 'R'? Yes, 우현! Yes, 'R' is Respecting others. So make sure you respect your partner's experience. And what is 'T'? Yes, 재우! Yes, 'T' was Take turns. So each student must have a chance to talk. All right? 5 minutes - share your experience. Go! One minute left, students. Okay, time's up.

✓ 영어 사용에 관한 교사의 피드백을 제공할 것

All right. So we just finished talking about our experience with our partners. However, when I was walking around the classroom, I was very impressed. Everyone was following the ART rule — good job on this, students!

And not only that — I could find that everyone was very honest when you shared your experience to your partners. So I was very impressed because all of you guys were very honest. I'm so proud of you guys for this one too. So, let's give ourselves a big hand! Good job, everyone!

So, just before we finish, let's go over today's class. So in the very beginning, we talked about what? Yes, we talked about the enemy. And we did what? Yes, 다원! Yes, we found the problem and the solution. And we did what? Yes, 영수! Yes, we created a story and we watched our friend's presentation.

So, with all these activities, let's go back to the first part — Enemy Pie. So now, can you guess the secret of the word Enemy Pie? Yes, 우영! Yes, it was to change enemies into what? Yes, 민재! Yes, 'Friends', right? So, Enemy Pie was about the friends. So with today's class, I want you to become a person who can get along with the people around you. Can you guys do that? Perfect. So that's all for today — and have a great weekend!

 2021 기출문제

(1) 판서 노트 및 예시 영상

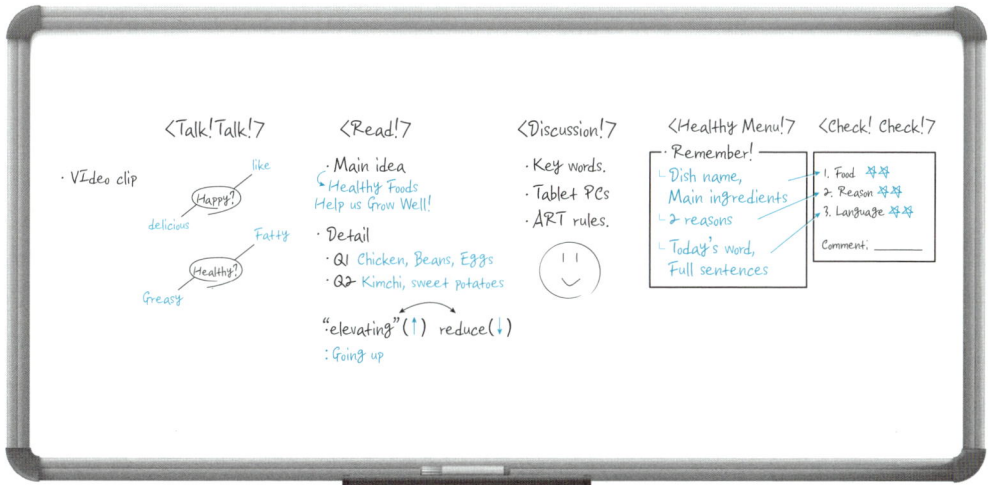

(2) 지도안 예시

단원명	Healthy Food, Happy Life!			시간	100 mins	
대상	• Students : 30 High school 1st Graders • Level : Mixed					
수업 목표	✓ Students will be able to find the main idea and details from the text. ✓ Students will be able to create a healthy menu through the discussion. ✓ Students will be able to write a suggestion letter for a healthy menu.					
교수·학습 교구	Digital whiteboard, Laptop, PPT slides etc					
핵심역량	자기 관리	지식정보처리	창의적 사고	심미적 감성	협력적 소통	공동체
	✓	✓			✓	

<교수 학습 지도안>

단계	교수·학습 활동	유의점 및 활용 교구
도입 (5분)	*인사, 출석 확인, 교실 내 안전 점검 *학습 주제, 수업 준비 상태 확인	
전개1 (15분)	**응시자 작성 내용 1 (Reading)** ✓ 학생의 동기 부여를 위한 교사의 질문을 제시할 것 ● Short Video Clip • [전체] 주제에 관한 학생의 관심을 불러일으키기 위해 유명 연예인의 먹방 영상을 보여준다. • 영상 내용에 관한 이야기를 나눈 뒤 Screen을 통해 아래 질문을 제시한다. <Screen> • Do they look happy? • Do they look healthy? • [전체] 학생과 상호작용을 통해 위 질문에 대한 답변을 나눈다. ● Transition • 영상을 보고 나눈 내용을 바탕으로 친구와 함께 더 이야기를 나누고 싶지 않은지 묻는 방식으로 자연스럽게 학습 참여 동기를 유발한다. ✓ <자료 1>을 활용하여 짝과 함께 말하기 활동을 진행할 것 ● Talk! Talk! • [짝, 5분] 학생들에게 <자료 1>을 나누어주고 짝과 함께 아래 질문에 대한 서로의 생각을 말해보도록 한다. • 질문 1. Are they happy menus? • 질문 2. Are they healthy menus? • 교사는 다양한 정답이 나올 수 있음을 강조하며 자유롭게 의견을 나누는 분위기를 형성한다.	PPT slides '자료 1'

<예시 발화>

교사 : In this 'Talk! Talk!' activity, all ideas are welcome. There's no right answer. Just feel free to talk!

전개1 (15분)	✓ 짝 활동 결과에 관한 학생과 교사의 상호작용을 포함할 것

● Mind mapping
- [전체] 학생과의 상호작용을 통해 짝 활동 결과를 교실 전체에 공유한다.
- 마인드맵을 통하여 짝 활동 결과에 대한 키워드를 판서한다.

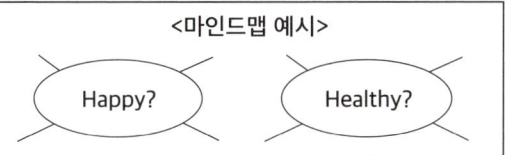

● Transition
- 완성된 마인드맵을 살펴보며 이번 차시 소재에 관한 흥미를 유발한다.
- 해당 소재에 관해 더 알아볼 준비가 되었는지 확인한다.

<예시 발화>

교사 : We learned that even though happy menus make us happy, they don't always make us healthy. Then, how can we be both 'happy' and 'healthy'? Don't you want to know about it?

응시자 작성 내용 2

✓ <자료 2>의 주제를 찾는 활동을 진행할 것

● Main idea
- [개별, 3분] <자료 2>를 학생에게 나누어주고 Main idea를 파악하게 한다.
- Skimming 전략을 지도하여 글의 주제를 파악하도록 한다.
  - 빠른 속도로 글을 훑어보며 반복되는 단어를 확인하도록 한다.
- 아래 사항에 따라 순회 지도를 실시한다.

<순회 지도 사항>
- 참여를 북돋우며 활동 중 어려움을 겪고 있는 학생을 파악한다.
- Low-level : 반복되는 단어를 찾는 것이 Main idea를 파악하는 데 도움이 된다는 사실을 안내한다.

- [전체] 학생과의 상호작용을 통해 글의 주제를 교실 전체에 공유하고 판서한다.
  - Main idea : Healthy foods help us grow well.
- [전체] 글의 제목이 없음을 강조하며, 글의 제목을 직접 지어보도록 제안한다.

<예시 발화>

교사 : Since we found the main idea, why don't we make the title? Do you have any good idea?
학생 : I think 'Let's eat healthy food!' is a great title.

전개2 (20분) — '자료 2'

전개2
(20분)
	✓ <자료 2>의 세부 정보에 관한 이해점검 확인을 실시할 것
	● Detail information
	• [개별, 5분] Screen을 통해 세부 정보를 찾기 위한 질문을 학생들에게 제시한다.
	  • 질문1. What foods help you grow taller?
	    • (정답: Chicken, beans, and eggs)
	  • 질문2. What foods help you reduce stress?
	    • (정답: Kimchi and sweet potatoes)
	• Scanning 전략을 지도하여 질문에 대한 답을 찾도록 한다.
	• 글 전체가 아니라 필요한 부분만 선별하여 읽도록 한다.
	• 아래 지도 사항에 따라 순회 지도를 실시한다.
	
	<순회 지도 사항>
	• 참여를 북돋우며 활동 중 어려움을 겪고 있는 학생을 파악한다.
	• High-level : 활동 참여에 대한 긍정적 피드백을 제공하고, Student teacher 역할을 부여하여 다른 학생을 도울 수 있도록 한다.
	• Low-level : Peer-scaffolding을 유도하며 동료 학습자로부터 도움을 받도록 한다.
	
	• [전체] 학생과의 상호작용을 통해 답변 공유하고 판서한다.
		'자료 2'

	✓ 밑줄 친 세 단어 중 하나를 가르칠 것
	● Teaching Vocabularies
	• [전체] 글을 읽는 동안 이해하기 어려웠던 단어가 있었는지 파악한 후 어휘 지도를 실시한다.
	• (예시) 'elevating' : Context clues & Word relations
	  • <자료 2>에서 'elevating'과 맥락상 밀접한 관련이 있는 표현을 찾아보도록 한다.
	  • 'reduce stress'와 'elevating your mood'라는 표현이 같은 맥락에 쓰였다는 사실에 주목하며, 'elevating'은 'reduce'의 반의어라는 것을 추론하도록 한다.
	  • 'reduce'는 'going down', 'elevating'은 'going up'임을 시각적으로 판서한다.
	  • 의미를 성공적으로 추론한 후, 직접 문장을 만들어 보게 함으로써 이해 확인 점검을 실시한다.	

전개3
(25분)
	응시자 작성 내용 3
	✓ 모둠 토의를 통해 <자료 3>을 완성할 것
	● Group discussion
	• [모둠, 20분] 3인 1조로 10개의 모둠을 구성한다.
	• 모둠 토의를 통해 <자료 3>을 완성하도록 한다.
	  • 추후 글쓰기 활동을 고려하여 <자료 3>은 단어나 구처럼 단순한 구조로 작성할 수 있음을 안내한다.
	  • 재료나 건강한 이유를 찾기 위해서 개인별 Tablet PC를 사용할 수 있음을 안내한다.
		'자료 3'

전개3 (25분)	• 모두 각자 의견을 제시할 수 있도록 하고, 아래 ART rule을 지키도록 독려한다. < ART rule > A : Active participation, R : Respect others, T : Take turns	
	✓ 학생 참여를 유도하며 촉진자 역할을 수행할 것	
	• 토의 중 아래 지도 사항에 따라 순회 지도를 실시한다. < 순회 지도 사항 > • 참여를 북돋우며 활동 중 어려움을 겪고 있는 학생을 파악한다. • Low-level : ART rule 재강조, 메뉴 개발에 어려움을 겪는 모둠에게는 'Recipe book'을 제공한다. • High-level : 활동 참여에 대한 긍정적 피드백을 제공하고 추가 메뉴를 개발할 수 있도록 한다.	
	✓ 모둠 토의에 관한 교사의 피드백을 제공할 것	
	● Giving feedback • [전체] 모둠 토의 활동 후 아래와 같이 토의 과정에 대한 긍정적 피드백을 제공한다. 　• (예시) ART rule을 잘 지켰다는 점, <자료 3>을 성실히 잘 완성했다는 점 등 < 예시 발화 > 교사 : I was so impressed that you were all participating very actively! Not only that, I could see that all of the dishes were very healthy! Awesome!	
전개4 (30분)	응시자 작성 내용 4	
	✓ <자료 4>를 활용하여 개별 글쓰기 활동을 진행할 것	
	● Healthy Menu • [개별, 15분] 모둠 토의 내용을 바탕으로 <자료 4>를 완성하도록 한다. 　• <자료 3>의 메뉴 이름, 재료, 건강한 이유를 참고하도록 한다. ● Giving authentic purpose • 우수 제안서는 학교 급식실에 보낼 기회가 주어진다는 점을 언급하며 학생의 동기를 부여한다. < 예시 발화 > 교사 : The best suggestion for healthy menu will be sent to our school cafeteria so that students can enjoy happy and health lives. … Does it sound great? Perfect!	'자료 4'
	✓ 글쓰기 평가 기준을 제시하고 설명할 것	
	● Sample writing • [전체] 화면을 통해 <자료 4>에 대한 교사의 예시를 학생들에게 보여준다. • 학생들과의 상호작용을 통해 <자료 4>에 대한 글쓰기 평가 기준을 제시한다.	PPT slides '자료 4'

전개4 (30분)	<예시 발화> 교사 : What do you see on the screen? … Yes, it is a teacher's example. Like this, there are several things you should remember when you write 'My Suggestion for Healthy Menu'. <글쓰기 평가 기준> 1. Food : Dish name, Main ingredients 2. Reason : 2 Reasons why it is healthy 3. Language : Today's word, Full sentence • 글쓰기 활동 중 아래 사항에 따라 순회 지도를 실시한다. <순회 지도 사항> • 참여를 북돋우며 활동 중 어려움을 겪고 있는 학생을 파악한다. • Low-level : <자료 3>이 <자료 4>의 준비 과정이었음을 언급하며 모둠 토의 활동 결과를 참고할 수 있도록 안내한다. • High-level : 활동 결과에 대해 칭찬한 후, 메뉴가 많을수록 우리 학교에 더 큰 도움이 됨을 강조하며 추가 메뉴를 작성하도록 격려한다. ✓ 글에 관한 동료 평가를 실시할 것 ● Peer evaluation • 학생들에게 평가 기준이 포함된 <Peer check card>를 제공한다. <Peer check card> | 1. Food	Dish name	☆
	Main ingredients	☆
2. Reason	2 Reasons	☆☆
3. Language	Today's word	☆
	Full sentence	☆
Total stars : ☆☆☆☆☆☆☆		
Comment :		| • <Peer check card>의 기준이 이전 활동의 <글쓰기 평가 기준>과 연결됨을 보여주며 교수 내용과 평가가 일치함을 강조한다. • [짝, 5분] 짝의 글을 읽어보며 <Peer check card>를 작성하도록 한다.	PPT slides '자료 4'
마무리 (5분)	*활동 마무리, 다음 차시 안내 *주변 정리 지도, 인사	

(3) 스크립트

>> 응시자 작성 내용 1

✓ 학생의 동기 부여를 위한 교사의 질문을 제시할 것

Okay, class.

So far, we talked about the unit title and the lesson objectives. Then, are you guys ready for today's class? Perfect! Then, everyone, let's look at the screen here. 상민, at the back! Do you see the screen? Perfect.

So, what do you see on the screen? Yes, there is a very famous mukbang video, right? So, from now on, we are going to watch this video clip, and then we are going to talk about it. So, we are going to watch this short video clip. All right? So, everyone, eyes on the screen. The video starts now.

Okay, so we just finished watching this video clip. Then, everyone, let's look at the screen again. Below the video clip, what do you see? Yes, 수현! Yes, there are two questions, right? So, can you read the first question? Yes, it was "Do they look happy?" right? And what about the second question? Can you read it for us? Yes, it was "Do they look healthy?" right?

And how do you think about this second question? Yes, 호영! Yes, they didn't look so healthy, right? So like this, we just began today's class with this famous mukbang video. Then, can you guess the topic for today's class? Yes, 현정! Yes, it is food! Then, are you guys ready to talk more about the food? Perfect!

✓ 〈자료 1〉을 활용하여 짝과 함께 말하기 활동을 진행할 것

So, everyone, let me give you this worksheet. Take one and pass them to the back. Take one and pass them to the back. 은수, at the back! Did you get the worksheet? Perfect. So, what do you see on the first worksheet? Yes, there are several lunch menus, right?

So, from now on, we are going to talk with your partners. So, 현수, 수현, you two! 종민, 민종, you two! You two! And lastly, you two. Does everyone have their own partners?

Perfect. So, with your partners, we are going to talk about those menus.

But before we start, I'll just show you these two questions. All right? So, everyone, let's look at the screen here. 지환, at the back! Do you see the screen? Perfect. So, can you read the first question? Yes, it says, "Are they happy menus?" Right? So, the first question is: Are they happy menus? And what about the second question? Yes, 다원! Yes, the second question was: Are they healthy menus? Right? So, we are going to talk about it: Are they healthy menus?

So, from now on, I'm going to give you five minutes. Five minutes to talk about these questions with the lunch menus in the first worksheet. All right? However, in this 'Talk! Talk!' activity, we should remember what? Yes, 종민! Yes, we should remember that all ideas are welcome. All right? So, there is no right answer. Just feel free to talk with your partners. Five minutes — talk with your partners. Go!

✓ 짝 활동 결과에 관한 학생과 교사의 상호작용을 포함할 것

Okay, time's up. So, let's share what you talked about with your partners. Any volunteers for the first question? Yes, 현수 and 수현! Oh, yes! They are happy menus because you like them, right? So, they are happy menus because you like them. And what else? Yes, 호영 and 영호! Yes, they are happy menus because they're delicious, right? So, this is delicious food.

And what else? Any volunteers for the second question? Yes, 동우 and 우현! Yes, they are not healthy menus because they are — yes — so fatty, right? It is so fatty food. And what else? Yes, they're not healthy food because they're so greasy, right? So, they are so greasy.

So like this, after we talked about it, we just learned that even though they are happy menus, they're not necessarily healthy menus. Right? Then, how can we be both happy and healthy? Don't you want to know about it? Then, are you ready to move on to the next part? Awesome!

응시자 작성 내용 2

✓ 〈자료 2〉의 주제를 찾는 활동을 진행할 것

Then, everyone! Let's look at the second worksheet. What do you see? Yes, 현정! Yes, there's a reading text, right? So, from now on, we are going to read the text about the food. All right? So, it's time to read. So, let's read!

However, when we read the text, which one do we have to find first? Yes, 동우! Yes, we need to find the main idea, right? So, from now on, we are going to find the main idea for this reading text. Okay? However, to find the main idea, do we have to read quickly or slowly? Yes 현정! Yes, we need to read quickly, right?

So you don't have to understand every single word. Just read quickly and find the main idea. I'm going to give you 3 minutes. 3 minutes — go! Oh, 민재! Do you need any help? Oh, you don't know how to find the main idea? Then, why don't you find the keyword that is used repeatedly? Because the keyword can be a hint for the main idea. Can you do that? Perfect! Keep up the good work. 1 minute left, students.

Okay, time's up! So, let's check the main idea together. So, what was the main idea? Is there any volunteer? Yes, 지환! Oh, did everyone hear what 지환 just said? He said the main idea is "Healthy foods help us grow well." So the main idea was: Healthy foods help us — yes, how? Yes, 현정! — grow well. So, the main idea of this reading text was: "Healthy foods help us grow well." Do you guys agree? Perfect!

However, everyone! Let's look at the reading text again. There is something strange. Can you find it? Yes, 다원! Yes, there's no title, right? So, because we just found this main idea, why don't we make a title for this reading text? Any ideas? Yes, 호영! Yes, "Let's Eat Healthy Food." That's a great title!

So, remember that the title and the main idea have very close relationship with each other. All right? Awesome!

✓ 〈자료 2〉의 세부 정보에 관한 이해점검 확인을 실시할 것

All right. So far, we just found this main idea. Then, are you guys ready to read the text a little bit more closely? Perfect! So it's time to find more details.

So, let's talk about the detail. Everyone, let's look at the screen. 상우, at the back! Do you see the screen? Yes, what do you see on the screen? Yes, there are two questions. Can you read the first question? Yes, 동우! It was, "What foods help you grow taller?" right? And what about the second question? Yes, 희원! Yes, it was, "What foods help you reduce stress?" right?

So, from now on, we are going to read the text again and find those answers to those two questions. All right? So, we are going to find the answers for these two questions. However, to find the answers for these two questions, do we have to read everything, or can we just read only the necessary part? Yes, 현우! Yes, we can read the necessary part, right?

So, I'm going to give you 5 minutes. 5 minutes to do what, 민종? Yes, read the text again and find the answer to those two questions on the screen. Okay? 5 minutes — go! Oh, 상민! You already finished? Wow, what a quick reader! Then, why don't you help your friend 민상? Because I heard 민상 needs some help. Can you do that? Awesome.

So like this, friends can be a better teacher. Keep up the good work! 1 minute left, students. Okay, time's up! So, let's check the answers together.

So, what was the answer for the first question: "What foods help you grow taller?" Any volunteer? Yes, 영호! Yes, chicken was the answer. So, the chicken. And what else? Yes, 수현! Yes, beans. And what else? Yes, 다원! Yes, the last one was eggs. So, chicken, beans, eggs — these foods are very helpful to grow taller.

And how about the second question: "What foods help you reduce stress?" Any volunteer? Yes 종민! Yes, it was kimchi, right? So the answer for the second question was kimchi. And what else? Yes, 동우! Yes, it was sweet potatoes, right? So it was sweet potatoes. So, those two foods will help you to reduce the stress.

✓ **밑줄 친 세 단어 중 하나를 가르칠 것**

So far, we just read the text twice — one for the main idea and another for the detail. However, while you were reading the text twice, were there any difficult words? Just say the word out loud. All right. So, I can hear the word "elevating." So, today's word is "elevating".

To guess the meaning of this word, let me give you a hint. So, everyone! Let's look at the words around the word "elevating." Which one can you find? Yes, 민수! Yes, you can find "reduce," right? So I will write "reduce" here. And then, what does the word "reduce" mean? Can anyone tell us? Yes, 민재! Yes, it means "going down," right? So this is "going down."

However, if I say "elevating" has an opposite meaning of this word, can you guess the meaning of the word "elevating"? Yes, 현정! Yes, it means "going up," right? So, "elevating" means "going up," which has exactly the opposite meaning of this "reduce." That was great guessing, 현정!

So, can anyone make a sentence with the word "elevating"? Yes, 호영! Oh, Yes! "Music is elevating my mood." That's a perfect sentence!

응시자 작성 내용 3

✓ **모둠 토의를 통해 〈자료 3〉을 완성할 것**

Okay, students. So we just read the text about the healthy foods. But do you really think that's all? No way, right? Because healthy food is endless! Then, are you guys ready to talk more about the healthy foods? Perfect!

So, it's time for the discussion. Time for the discussion! So, everyone! Let's look at the third handout. What do you see on the third handout? Yes 동우! Yes, it says, "Let's make our new healthy menu," right?

So, from now on, we are going to do this in groups. 종민, 민종, 현수, you three! You three! You three! And finally, the last group — group 10, you three. So, is everyone in the group? Perfect!

So, from now on, we are going to talk with your group members and create the healthy menus. All right? However, because this is just a discussion, you don't have to write in what? Yes 현우! Yes, you don't need to write a full sentence. Okay? So you can just use the keywords, because discussion is more important.

And secondly, make sure you can use your own tablet PCs to find the information of ingredients or the reasons why it is healthy. All right? So, you can use tablet PCs here. Tablet PCs.

And lastly, and most importantly, whenever we have this kind of discussion, which rule do we have to follow? Yes, 영수! Yes, we need to follow the ART rule, right? So, what was A? Yes, 현우! Yes, it was Active Participation. And what was R? Yes, 지환! Yes, it was Respect Others. So, make sure you respect your friends' ideas. All right? And what was T? Yes, 동현! Yes, it was Take Turns, right?

So remember this ART rule, when you discuss with your group members. All right? I'm going to give you 20 minutes. 20 minutes to do what, group 2? Yes, discuss with your group members to make healthy menus. All right? 20 minutes — go!

✓ 학생 참여를 유도하며 촉진자 역할을 수행할 것

Oh, group one! I can see 현수 is participating very actively. But what was the T rule? Do you remember? Yes, it was Take Turns. So make sure everyone gets the chance to talk. All right? Perfect.

And group three, do you need any help? Oh, it is too difficult to create the new menu? I understand. Then, why don't you use this recipe book I just brought for you guys? It has many different kinds of healthy menus. So, with this recipe book, can you guys do this work by yourselves? Awesome!

So, if you need any more help, just feel free to raise your hand. All right? Perfect. And group six, you already finished? Wow, what quick menu creators! Then, why don't you make another menu? Because there are tons of different options for these healthy menus. Can you guys do that? Perfect.

1 minute left, students. Does any group need more time? Okay, time's up.

✓ 모둠 토의에 관한 교사의 피드백을 제공할 것

Okay, so we just finished the group discussion. And I want to tell you this. So, when I was walking around the classroom, I could find that everyone is participating very well, talking about healthy menus. So, I want to give you guys this big smile. Good job, everyone! So, let's give ourselves a big hand. Perfect.

So, everyone! So far we just created two healthy menus with our group members. Then, are you guys ready to write an actual suggestion for the lunch menu? Awesome!

응시자 작성 내용 4

✓ 〈자료 4〉를 활용하여 개별 글쓰기 활동을 진행할 것

So, it's time to write a suggestion for the healthy menu. So, it's time to write about the healthy menu. However, this is going to be an individual work. So, everyone, let's go back to your seats. Awesome.

So, from now on, based on the discussion on the third worksheet, we are going to write a suggestion for the healthy menu. However, before we start, let me tell you this.

The best suggestion for the healthy menu will be actually sent to the school cafeteria, so that everyone in our school can enjoy your own healthy menu. And that will be very helpful to live happy and healthy lives. How does it sound? Doesn't it sound exciting? Perfect!

✓ 글쓰기 평가 기준을 제시하고 설명할 것

So, everyone! Let's look at the screen here. 영수, at the back! What do you see on the screen? Yes, there is a teacher's example, right? So, like this, there are several things you should remember when you write this suggestion. All right? So, there are several things you should remember.

So 현정, can you read the first part? Like this, your writing should have the dish name and the main ingredients. All right? So, the first thing you should remember is the dish name. And what was the second one? Yes 희원! Yes, it was the main ingredient. So, the second thing was main ingredient. So remember that your writing should have these two things: dish name and main ingredients.

And what else can you find in the teacher's example? Yes, 호영! Yes, there are reasons why it is healthy, right? So, like this, your writing should have two reasons why it is healthy. Okay? And what else? What else can you find in the sample writing? Yes, 다원! Yes, it has today's word, right? So make sure you include today's word, which is 'elevating'.

And what else? Yes 지환! Yes, all the sentences are written in what? Yes 수현! Yes, in full sentences, right? So remember that you should use full sentences here. Okay? So, based on what you wrote — the keywords in the discussion, at this time, you should use full sentences. All right? Perfect.

So, remember these things. I'm going to give you 15 minutes. 15 minutes to do what, 지환? Yes — write a suggestion for your own healthy menu. All right? 15 minutes — go!

Oh 수민, do you need any help? Oh, it's too difficult to write a suggestion? Then why don't you look at the third worksheet? Because the third worksheet is a buildup activity for this one. Yes! So with those discussion results, can you do this work by yourself? Perfect! Keep up the good work. And if you need any more help, just feel free to call me. All right? Awesome.

And 민수, you already finished? Wow, what a quick writer! Then why don't you write more healthy menus? Because the more suggestions you give, the healthier and happier our students will be. Can you do that? Awesome. I love your effort.

1 minute left, students. Does anyone need more time? Okay, time's up.

✓ 글에 관한 동료 평가를 실시할 것

Okay, so we just finished writing our healthy menus. Then, don't you want to know your friend's healthy menu? Awesome! So, let's begin this 'Check Check' Time. So, it's time for check!

Everyone, let me give you this peer check card. Take one and pass them to the back.

Take one and pass them to the back. 호영, at the back! Did you get the peer check card? Perfect.

So, what do you see in the first part? Yes, it says "Food," right? So the first thing was about the food. And can you tell us more detail, 지환? Yes, it says "the dish name and the main ingredients." So if your partner's writing has those dish name and main ingredients, you can give two stars for each of them. Okay? Perfect.

And what was the second one? Yes 동우! Yes, it says "the reason," right? So your writing should have the reasons. And how many reasons? Yes, 현우! Yes, it should have two reasons, right? So if your friend's writing has those two reasons, you can give two stars for this one. All right?

And what was the third one? Yes, 희원! Yes, it says "the language," right? So what is the language, by the way? Yes 현정! Yes, it says today's word and full sentences. So if your friend's writing has today's word and full sentences, you can give two stars for each one of them.

So how many stars can we give in total? Yes — six stars. And what was the last part? Yes 재우! Yes, it says "comments," right? So make sure you write a comment for your friend's writing. All right?

So, with this peer check card, we are going to check our partners' writing. So, 민종, 종민 you two! 수현, 현수, you two! You two! And lastly, you two. Does everyone have their own partners? Perfect.

So, I'm going to give you 5 minutes. 5 minutes to read your friend's writing and give stars and comments for your partners. All right? So, exchange your writings. 5 minutes — go!

Okay, time's up. So, we just finished checking our friend's writing. However, just before we wrap up, let's go over today's class.

In the very beginning, we saw a video clip about what? Yes, 현우! Yes, it was about the food, right? And then, we read about the healthy food. And we did what? Yes, we actually created the healthy menus for our school, right?

So, with today's class, I want you to become a person who can live happy and healthy lives. Can you guys do that? Awesome. So, that's it for us — and have a great weekend!

2020 기출문제

(1) 판서 노트 및 예시 영상

수업실연 예시
2020 기출 변형
동영상 바로가기

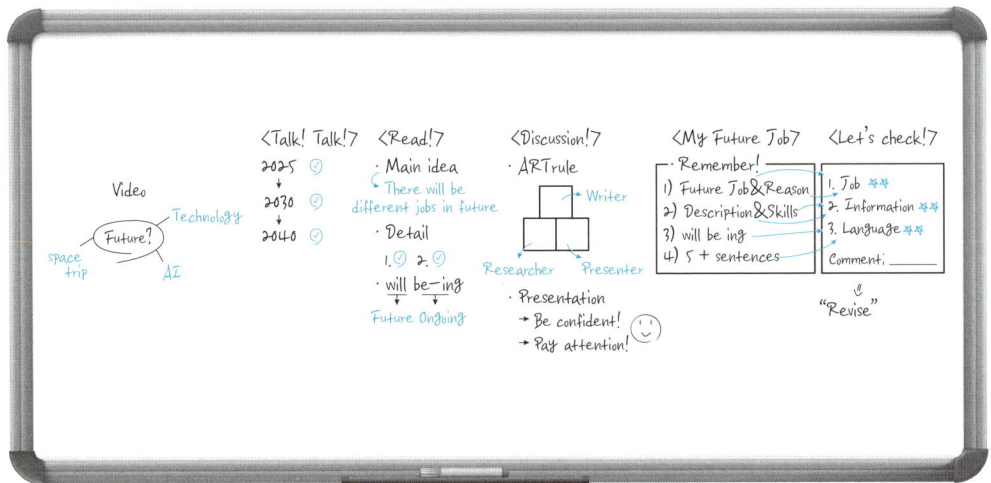

(2) 지도안 예시

단원명	Search for Future Jobs				시간	100 mins	
대상	• Students : 30 High school 1st Graders • Level : Mixed						
수업 목표	✓ Students will be able to find the main idea and details from the text. ✓ Students will be able to understand the correct usage of 'will be –ing'. ✓ Students will be able to write a paragraph about the future job.						
교수·학습 교구	Digital whiteboard, Laptop, PPT slides etc						
핵심역량	자기 관리	지식정보처리	창의적 사고	심미적 감성	협력적 소통		공동체
	✓	✓			✓		

<교수 학습 지도안>

단계	교수·학습 활동	유의점 및 활용 교구
도입 (5분)	*인사, 출석 확인, 교실 내 안전 점검 *학습 주제, 수업 준비 상태 확인	
전개1 (15분)	<center>응시자 작성 내용 1 (Reading)</center> ✓ 스크린을 활용하여 수업 주제에 관한 디지털 미디어 자료를 제시할 것 ● Schema activation • [전체] 로봇 택시, 드론 배달 등 미래 도시의 모습을 담은 영상을 시청한다. • 영상에서 어떤 내용이 있었는지 학생 상호작용을 바탕으로 정리한다. <예시 발화> 교사 : What did you find interesting in the video? 예상 답변 : Robot taxi, AI house keeper 등 ● Transition • 시청한 영상을 바탕으로 오늘의 수업 주제를 유추하도록 한다. ✓ 학생의 동기 부여를 위한 교사의 질문을 제시할 것 ● Our Future • [전체] 스크린을 활용하여 'What would happen in our future?'라는 질문을 제시하고 이에 대한 생각을 자유롭게 나눠보도록 유도한다. • 마인드맵을 통하여 학생 상호작용 결과를 정리한다. • (예시) : Technology, AI, Computer, Space <마인드맵 예시> 'Future?'	PPT slides

	● Transition • 학생들에게 <자료 1>을 나눠주며 마인드 맵에 정리한 내용을 바탕으로 미래 직업에 대해 짝과 함께 이야기를 더 나눠볼 준비가 되었는지 확인한다.	
	✓ <자료 1>을 활용하여 미래 직업에 관해 생각을 나누는 짝 활동을 진행할 것	
	● Talk! Talk! • [짝, 5분] 학생들에게 <자료 1>을 바탕으로 미래에는 어떤 직업이 등장할지 이야기를 나눠보도록 한다. • 교사는 다양한 정답이 나올 수 있음을 강조하며 자유롭게 의견을 나누는 분위기를 형성한다. <예시 발화> 교사 : In this 'Talk! Talk!' activity, all ideas are welcome. There's no right answer. Just feel free to talk! • 짝 활동 결과를 교실 전체에 공유하며 미래 직업에 대해 더 알아볼 준비가 되었는지 확인한다. • (예시) : Space shuttle developer, Planet constructor, Mars tour guide 등	'자료 1'
	응시자 작성 내용 2	
	✓ <자료 2>의 주제를 찾는 활동을 진행할 것	

전개2
(20분)
	● Main idea
	• [개별, 3분] <자료 2>를 읽고 Main idea를 파악하게 한다.
	• Skimming 전략을 지도하여 글의 주제를 파악하도록 한다.
	  • 빠른 속도로 글을 훑어보며 반복되는 단어를 확인하도록 한다.
	• 아래 지도 사항에 따라 순회 지도를 실시한다.
	<순회 지도 사항>
	• 참여를 북돋우며 활동 중 어려움을 겪고 있는 학생을 파악한다.
	• Low-level : <자료 2> 뒤편의 Vocabulary list를 참고하도록 한다.
	• [전체] 학생과의 상호작용을 통해 글의 주제를 교실 전체에 공유하고 판서한다.
	  • Main idea : There will be different jobs in future.
	• [전체] 글의 제목이 없음을 강조하며, 글의 제목을 직접 지어보도록 제안한다.
	<예시 발화>
	교사 : Since we found the main idea, why don't we make the title? Do you have any idea?
	학생 : I think 'Get ready for the future job!' is a great title.
		'자료 2'

	✓ <자료 2>의 세부 정보에 관한 이해점검 확인을 실시할 것	
	● Detail information • [개별, 5분] Screen을 통해 세부 정보를 찾기 위한 미션을 학생들에게 제시한다. 　1) MISSION : Find ALL future jobs from the text! • Scanning 전략을 지도하여 질문에 대한 답을 찾도록 한다. 　• 글 전체가 아니라 필요한 부분만 선별하여 읽도록 한다. • 아래 지도 사항에 따라 순회 지도를 실시한다. 　　<순회 지도 사항> 　　• 참여를 북돋우며 활동 중 어려움을 겪고 있는 학생을 파악한다. 　　• High-level : 활동 참여에 대한 긍정적 피드백을 제공하고, Student teacher 역할을 부여하여 다른 학생을 도울 수 있도록 한다. 　　• Low-level : 동료 학습자로부터 도움을 받도록 Peer-scaffolding을 유도한다.	PPT slides '자료 2'
전개2 (20분)	• [전체] 학생과의 상호작용을 통해 답변을 공유하고 판서한다.	
	✓ 밑줄 친 표현 'will be -ing'를 가르칠 것	
	● Noticing the Target Form • [전체] 글을 읽는 도중, 반복되어 나타나는 형태를 알아차린 학생이 있는지 확인한다. • 학생과 함께 글에 사용된 Target form을 찾아보며 표시한다. • 'will'과 'be -ing'를 언제 사용하는지 학생들과 대화를 통해 지난 내용을 상기한다. 　• (예시) : We use 'will' when something happens in the future. 　• (예시) : We use 'be -ing' when something is ongoing. • 상기한 내용을 바탕으로 'will be -ing'의 의미를 유추하도록 한다. 　　<예시 발화> 　교사 : We learned when we use 'will' and 'be -ing'. Then, can you guess when we use 'will be -ing'? ... Yes! We use it when something ongoing happens in the future. • 'will be -ing'를 활용한 문장을 만들어 보게 함으로써 학생의 이해를 확인한다.	'자료 2'
	응시자 작성 내용 3	
	✓ 모둠 활동을 통해 <자료 3>을 완성할 것	
전개3 (25분)	● Group discussion • 3인 1조로 10개의 모둠을 구성한다. • [모둠, 5분] 모둠원과 토의를 통해 'Career Guide'에 작성할 미래 직업을 선정하도록 한다.	'자료 3'

	• 모두 각자 의견을 제시할 수 있도록 하고, 아래 ART rule을 지키도록 독려한다. **\<ART rule\>** A : Active participation,　R : Respect others,　T : Take turns • 선정한 미래 직업을 바탕으로 'Career Guide'를 작성할 준비가 되었는지 확인한다. • 앉은 자리에 따라 역할을 아래와 같이 부여한다. **\<역할 부여\>** | Writer | • Writer : 문장 작성 | | Researcher | Presenter | • Researcher : Tablet PC로 정보 검색 • Presenter : 발표 담당 • [모둠, 15분] 주어진 역할에 따라 \<자료 3\>을 완성하도록 한다.	'자료 3'
전개3 (25분)	√ 모둠 활동 중 교실을 순회하며 촉진자 역할을 수행할 것 ● **Facilitation** • 교사는 아래 지도 사항에 따라 순회 지도를 실시한다. **\<순회 지도 사항\>** • 참여를 북돋우며 활동 중 어려움을 겪고 있는 학생을 파악한다. • Low level : 미래 직업에 대한 뉴스 기사, 잡지 등을 제공한다. • High level : 긍정적 피드백을 제공한 뒤, 미래 직업은 무궁무진함을 언급하며 다른 미래 직업에 관한 정보를 찾을 수 있도록 추가 과제를 제시한다. √ 학생 발표에 관한 교사의 피드백을 제공할 것 ● **Presentation** • 모둠별로 발표 준비가 되었는지 확인한다. • [전체] 발표 전, 발표자와 청중의 역할에 대해 상기한다. 　• 발표자 : Be confident, Don't be afraid of making mistakes 　• 청중 : Pay attention, Listen carefully, Make eye contact ● **Giving feedback** • [전체] 발표를 진행한 후, 발표자와 청중의 역할을 잘 지켰다는 점을 강조하며 긍정적 피드백을 제공한다. **\<예시 발화\>** 교사 : I was very impressed that all presenters were very confident. Not only that, I could find that everyone was listening very carefully. … Awesome! Let's give ourselves a big hand!	

전개4 (30분)	응시자 작성 내용 4	'자료 4'
	√ <자료 4>에 제시된 글쓰기 조건을 강조하여 글을 완성하도록 할 것	

● Sample writing
- 교사의 Sample writing을 제시하며 <자료 4>에 대한 학생 이해를 돕는다.
- <자료 4>의 글쓰기 조건이 Sample writing에 어떻게 나타났는지 함께 확인한다.

● My Future Job
- [개별, 15분] <자료 4>의 글쓰기 조건에 따라 글을 완성하도록 한다.
- Authentic purpose : 완성 작품은 English class time capsule에 보관되어 10년 뒤 열어볼 것이라고 안내하며 실질적 동기를 부여한다.

<예시 발화>
교사 : Your writings will be put into the English class time capsule and you can open it after 10 years. … Does it sound exciting? Perfect!

- 아래 지도 사항에 따라 순회 지도를 실시한다.

<순회 지도 사항>
- 참여를 북돋우며 활동 중 어려움을 겪고 있는 학생을 파악한다.
- Low level : <자료 4> 뒤편의 Writing guide와 outline을 참고하도록 한다.
- High level : 긍정적 피드백을 제공한 뒤, 직업의 다양성을 강조하며 다른 직업을 주제로 써보도록 추가 과제를 부여한다.

√ 동료 평가를 위한 기준을 제시하고 각각을 설명할 것

● Peer check card
- 학생들에게 평가 기준이 포함된 <Peer check card>를 제공한다.

<Peer check card>

1. Job	Name	☆
	Reason	☆
2. Information	Description	☆
	Required skills	☆
3. Language	'will be -ing'	☆
	5+ sentences	☆
Total stars : ☆☆☆☆☆☆		
Comment :		

- <Peer check card>의 기준이 <자료 4>의 Writing Requirements와 연결됨을 보여주며 교수 내용과 평가가 일치함을 강조한다.

전개4 (30분)	✓ 글쓰기 결과에 대하여 짝 활동을 진행할 것 ● Peer evaluation • [짝, 5분] 짝의 글을 읽어보며 <Peer check card>를 작성하도록 한다. ● Peer revision • [짝, 5분] 작성한 <Peer check card>를 함께 확인하며 서로의 글을 수정하도록 한다. • 더 나아진 자신의 글을 확인하며 동료 확인 활동의 효과를 깨닫도록 한다. <예시 발화> 교사 : Can you see that your writing became much better from your friend's advice? ... Like this, remember that you can also learn from your friends!	
마무리 (5분)	*활동 마무리, 다음 차시 안내 *주변 정리 지도, 인사	

(3) 스크립트

> 응시자 작성 내용 1

✓ 스크린을 활용하여 수업 주제에 관한 디지털 미디어 자료를 제시할 것

Okay, students. So far we've talked about the unit title and the lesson objectives. Then, are you guys ready to begin today's class? Perfect. Then everyone, let's look at the screen!

호영, at the back! Do you see the screen? Perfect. So, what do you see on the screen? Yes, there is a video clip. So from now on, we are going to watch this short video clip. All right? So let's watch a video. Okay? So everyone, eyes on the screen. The video begins now.

Okay. So we just finished watching this video clip. Then let's talk about it. What did you find interesting in the video? Yes, 수현! Yes, there was a robot taxi, right? And what else? Yes, 동우! Yes, you saw the AI housekeeper, right?

Then everyone! With this video clip, can you guess the topic of today's—Yes, 상우! Yes, it is 'The Future'. So today, we are going to learn about the future. Are you guys excited? Awesome!

✓ 학생의 동기 부여를 위한 교사의 질문을 제시할 것

Then everyone, let's watch the screen again. 수민, at the back! Do you see the screen? Perfect. So what do you see on the screen? Yes, there is a question, right? Can you guys read it out loud? So the question was, "What would happen in our future?" Right?

So from now on, we are going to talk about this question in our classroom. So what would happen in our future? So what do you think? Any volunteers?

Yes, 현우! He said in our future, the technology will be advanced. So in the future, we will have better technology. And what else? Yes, 상민! Yes, we will use AI. So we will use AI in the future. And what else? Yes, 종민! Oh yes, space trip can happen in our future. The space trip. The space trip. That's a great idea.

So far, we just talked about what our future will be like. Then are you guys ready to move on to the next part? Awesome. Then let me give you this worksheet. Take one and pass them to the back.

민수, at the back! Did you get the worksheet? So what do you see on the first worksheet? It says "The Future Jobs." So, based on what we talked in our classroom, are you guys ready to talk more about the future jobs with your partners? Awesome!

✓ 〈자료 1〉을 활용하여 미래 직업에 관해 생각을 나누는 짝 활동을 진행할 것

So let's begin 'the Talk Talk Time' here. So it's time for talk. We are going to do this with your partner. So, 현수, 수현—you two! You two. And lastly, you two. Does everyone have their own partners? Perfect.

So with your partners, I'm going to give you 5 minutes. 5 minutes to talk about the future jobs in 2025, 2030, and 2040. All right? However, because this is 'Talk Talk activity', it is very important to remember what?

Yes, 동우! Yes, keep in mind that all ideas are welcome. There's no right answer. Just feel free to talk. All right? Five minutes. Talk about the future job in the first worksheet. Go!

One minute left, students. Okay, time's up. So let's share your ideas together. So let's share our ideas for 2025, 2030, and 2040. So any volunteers for 2025?

Yes, 다원 and 원희! Yes, space shuttle developer. That's a great future job. And what else? Yes, 호영 and 영호! Oh, planet constructor! That's a great future job as well. And lastly, what else? Yes, 재우 and 우재! Oh, Mars tour guide. That's a very interesting job. So, 'Mars tour guide'.

응시자 작성 내용 2

✓ 〈자료 2〉의 주제를 찾는 활동을 진행할 것

Okay. So we just finished talking about our future jobs. Then, don't you guys want to learn more about the future jobs? Perfect. So it's time for reading. So let's read!

So whenever we have a reading text, we should first find what? Yes, 동우! Yes, we need to find the main idea, right? So from now on, we are going to find the main idea first.

So the main idea. However, to find the main idea, do we have to read quickly or slowly? Yes, 희원. Yes, we need to read quickly, right? So from now, I'm going to give you 3 minutes. 3 minutes to quickly read the text and find the main idea.

So you don't have to understand every single word. I'm going to give you 3 minutes. Find the main idea. Go!

Oh, 수민! Do you need any help? Oh, the words are so difficult? Then why don't you look at the back of the worksheet? What do you see? Yes, there is a vocabulary list, right? So with this vocabulary list, can you find the main idea by yourself? Awesome. Keep up the good work.

1 minute left, students. Does anyone need more time? Okay, time's up.

So let's check the main idea together. So what was the main idea? Yes, 지환! Oh, did everyone hear what 지환 just said? He said the main idea of this reading text is "There will be different jobs in our future." So the main idea of this reading text is "There will be different jobs." Different jobs when?

Yes, 희원. Yes, "in the future." So like this, we just found the main idea.

However, everyone! Let's look at the text again. There is something strange. Can you guys find it? Yes, 은수! Yes, there's no title, right? So why don't we make a title? Do you have any ideas?

Yes, 동우! Oh, that's great. He said, "Get Ready for the Future Job" will be the great title. Do you guys agree? Awesome. So like this, remember that main idea and the title have a very close relationship to each other. All right? Perfect.

✓ 〈자료 2〉의 세부 정보에 관한 이해점검 확인을 실시할 것

We just found the main idea and we just made a title. Then, are you guys ready to read the text a little bit more closely? Perfect. So let's find the detail. So this time, let's find the details.

So everyone, let's look at the screen. 재우, at the back! Do you see the screen? Perfect.

So what do you see on the screen? Yes, there is a reading mission. So can you read today's mission out loud?

Yes! It says, "Find all future jobs in the reading text." Right? So from now on, we are going to read the text a little bit more closely to complete today's reading mission. All right?

However, to find the details, do we have to read everything or can we just read only the necessary part? Yes, 희원! Yes, we don't need to read everything, right?

So, I'm going to give you 5 minutes. 5 minutes to complete the mission, which was to find the future jobs. 5 minutes. Go!

Oh, 현우! You already finished? Wow, what a quick reader! Then why don't you help your friend, 우현? Because I heard 우현 needs some help. Can you guys do that? Perfect. Like this, friends can be a better teacher.

1 minute left, students. Okay, time's up.

So let's check the answer together. So how many future jobs can you find in this reading text? Yes, 수현! Yes, there were two, right?

So what was the first one? Yes, 현우! Yes, it says "Drone Traffic Monitor." So the first one was Drone Traffic Monitor.

And what was the second one? Yes, 수현! Yes! It was "Self-driving Car Mechanic," right? So, Self-driving Car Mechanic. That was our two future jobs. Perfect.

✓ 밑줄 친 표현 'will be – ing'를 가르칠 것

So far, we just read the text twice. First for the main idea, and second for the detail. However, while you were reading the text twice, is there anyone who could find an expression that was used repeatedly?

Yes, 희원! Oh, did everyone hear what 희원 just said? She said the expression "will be ~ing" was used repeatedly. So today, we are going to talk about the expression "will be ~ing."

So everyone, let's go back to the reading text and find these "will be ~ing" expressions and underline them. 재우, did you find all of them? Perfect. So how many were there? Yes, there were two, right?

So I can see that everyone could find the expression in the reading text. Then let's talk about it together.

Everyone! We already learned when we use "will" in middle school. Do you guys remember? Yes, 현우! Yes! We use "will" when something is happening in the future. Right?

And when do we use "be ~ing"? Yes, 희원! Yes, we use "be ~ing" when something is ongoing, right?

Then can you guys guess when we use this "will be ~ing" expression? Yes, 우재! Oh, did everyone hear what 우재 just said? He said we can use "will be ~ing" when something ongoing happens in the future. Do you guys agree?

Then can you guys make a sentence with "will be ~ing"? Yes, 지환! "I will be enjoying vacation next month." That's a great sentence! Keep this expression in mind because we're going to use it later. All right?

응시자 작성 내용 3

✓ 모둠 활동을 통해 〈자료 3〉을 완성할 것

So far, we just finished reading about the future jobs. However, would that be all? No way, right? There will be more different jobs in our future, right?

Then why don't we discuss with our group members? Are you guys excited? So this is time for the discussion. We are going to do this in groups.

수현, 현수, and 민수—you three! You three. And lastly, group 10, you three. So is everyone in group? Perfect.

So everyone, let's look at the third worksheet. What does it say in question number one? Yes, 상현! Yes, we need to decide our group's future job.

So from now, I'm going to give you 5 minutes to talk with your group members to decide your group's future job.

However, whenever we do this kind of discussion, which rule do we have to follow? Yes, 현수! Yes, we need to follow the ART rule, right? So remember the ART rule.

So let's quickly remind ourselves of this ART rule. So what was A? Yes, 다원! Yes, it was Active participation. And what was R? Yes, 영호! Yes, it was Respect others. And lastly, what was T? Yes, 정은! Yes, T was Take turns, right?

So I'm going to give you 5 minutes. 5 minutes to do what, 희원? Yes, you need to discuss with your group members to decide your future job. Okay? 5 minutes. Go!

1 minute left, students. Does any group need more time? Okay, time's up.

So have you guys decided your group's future job? Then, are you guys ready to make the career guide for our group project? Perfect.

However, before we start this group project, let me give each of you a role. So you guys are sitting like this, right?

Students sitting here, raise your hand. Okay. Okay, so you guys are going to be the writer. All right? So you should write your career guide.

Students sitting here, raise your hand. Okay. So you guys are going to be the researcher. So researchers, what do you have to do?

Yes, 상우! Yes, you need to find the information about the job description and the required skills. So remember that the researchers can take your own tablet PCs and find the information for your group. All right?

And lastly, students sitting here, raise your hand. Okay. So you guys are going to be the presenters. So make sure that we are going to have a presentation for this group project.

So everyone, I'm going to give you 15 minutes. 15 minutes to do what, 재우? Yes! We are going to write the career guide. And what is your role, 은수? Yes, you are a researcher, okay?

15 minutes. Complete the third worksheet. Go!

✓ 모둠 활동 중 교실을 순회하며 촉진자 역할을 수행할 것

Oh, group 7! Do you need any help? Oh, you need more information about the future jobs? Then why don't you use this newspaper and magazines that I brought for you guys?

So with these news articles and magazines, can you do this job by yourselves? Perfect.

So if you need any more help, just don't hesitate to raise your hand. Okay?

And group 1! You already finished? Wow, what quick writers! Then why don't you find more future jobs? Because you already know that anything can happen in the future. Can you guys do that? Awesome. Keep up the good work.

1 minute left, students. Does any group need more time? Okay, time's up.

✓ 학생 발표에 관한 교사의 피드백을 제공할 것

So everyone, based on the group discussion, we just finished making the career guide. Then don't you want to see other groups' career guides? Perfect.

So let's begin the presentation. It's time for the presentation.

However, before we start the presentation, let me quickly remind you of our roles. So first, for the presenters, it is important to be what? Yes, 우현! Yes! It is very important for presenters to be confident.

So remember that—be confident, presenters! Don't be afraid of making mistakes. That's okay.

And the audience, we need to remember what? Yes, 상민! Yes, listen carefully. So we need to pay attention. Pay attention to the presentation. Listen carefully. Make eye contact. All right?

So presenters, are you guys ready? Okay, the presentation begins now.

Okay, students. So we just finished watching our friends' presentations. However, there was one thing I want to tell you. I was very impressed that all of the presenters were very confident.

Not only that, I could find that everyone was really listening carefully, paying attention to the presentation. So I want to give you this smile. I'm so proud of you guys. So let's give ourselves a big hand. Perfect.

> ## 응시자 작성 내용 4

✓ 〈자료 4〉에 제시된 글쓰기 조건을 강조하며 글을 완성하도록 할 것

So far, we just finished the group project. Then, are you guys ready to write your own future job? Perfect.

So it's time to write about My Future Job. This is going to be individual work, because everyone will have their own future job.

So everyone, let's look at the screen. 호영, at the back! Can you see the screen? Perfect. So what do you see on the screen? Yes, there is a sample writing, right?

So like this sample writing, you are going to write your own future job based on the writing requirements on the fourth worksheet. Okay?

So let's check one by one. So remember this when you write your own future job. All right?

So the first one, what can you see? Yes, it says future job and reason why you chose it, right? So you should remember that—the future job and what? Yes, the reason why you chose it, okay?

And what was the second one? Yes, 현수! Yes! So the second one was job description and what? Yes, its required skills, right?

And what was the third one? Yes, 우재! Yes, it was "will be ~ing", right? So today's expression "will be ~ing"—you should use it. Okay?

So remember that you should use "will be ~ing".

And what was the last one? Yes, 민종! Yes! It says you should write more than five sentences, right? So five or more sentences, as you can see in the sample writing as well. All right?

So remember these things when you write your own future job.

However, before we start, let me tell you this. Your writing will be put into the English class time capsule, and you can open it 10 years later. How does it sound? Exciting? Awesome!

So I'm going to give you 15 minutes. 15 minutes. Go!

Oh, 지환! Do you need any help? Oh, you don't know how to write? Then why don't you look at the back of the worksheet? What do you see? Yes, there's a writing guide and outline, right?

So with this writing guide and outline, can you write your own future job by yourself? Perfect. So if you need any more help, just feel free to call me. Awesome. I love your effort.

And 상민, you already finished? Wow, what a quick writer! Then why don't you write another writing with another future job? Because you know the possibility of future jobs is endless. Can you do that? Awesome. Keep up the good work.

1 minute left, students. Does anyone need more time? Okay, time's up.

✓ **동료 평가를 위한 기준을 제시하고 각각을 설명할 것**

Okay, so we just finished writing My Future Job. Then, don't you guys want to see your friend's future job? Awesome. So let's begin the Check Time. Let's check.

Let me give you this Peer Check Card. So take one and pass them to the back. 우현, at the back! Did you get the Peer Check Card?

So what do you see in the first part? Yes, it says Job, right? So the first part was about the job. For the Job part, how many stars can you give? Yes, you can give two stars, right?

And what is Job? What does that mean? Yes, 재우! Yes! That means the future job and the reason, right? So if your friend's writing has future job and reason, you can give two stars.

And what was the second one? Yes, 영호! Yes, it says Information, right? So the second one was Information. How many stars can you give for the information? Yes, you can give two stars, right?

And what is Information? What does that mean? Yes, 동우! Yes! It is job description and skills.

And what's next? Yes, 정은! Yes! It says Language, right? So the third part was Language. How many stars can you get for the language? Yes, 희원. Yes, you can give two stars.

And what should we check for the language? Yes, 동호! Yes, the language—you should check if your friend's writing has the key expression and if the writing is more than five sentences.

And lastly, as you can see, don't forget to write the comment for your friend's writing. Okay?

So with this Peer Check Card, are you guys ready to read your friend's writing? Awesome.

✓ 글쓰기 결과에 대하여 짝 활동을 진행할 것

So everyone, we are going to exchange your writing with your partners. 수현, 현수—you two! 종민, 민종—you two! And lastly, you two. Does everyone have their own partners? Perfect.

So exchange your writing with your partners. You finished? I'm going to give you 5 minutes. 5 minutes to read your friend's writing based on this Peer Check Card. Okay? 5 minutes. Go!

1 minute left, students. Okay, time's up. Then return your partner's writing with your Peer Check Card.

So now, you all have your writing with your friend's Peer Check Card, right? However, after the Check Time, what do we have to do?

Yes, 현우! Yes! We should change our writing, right? So from now on, it's time to revise.

Revise your writing based on your friend's Peer Check Card. Okay? I'm going to give you 5 minutes. Based on the Peer Check Card, revise your writings together. Ask questions to your partners and give advice for your friend's writing.

All right? 5 minutes. Revise together. Go!

1 minute left, students. Okay, time's up.

So we just finished revising our writings with our partners. Can you guys see that your writing became much better from your friend's advice? Perfect.

So like this, remember that you can also learn from your friends. All right?

So everyone, just before we wrap up, let's go over today's class. What was today's topic? Yes, 은수! Yes, it was the future.

So we read about what? Yes, 재우! We read about the future job, and we discussed with our group members about the future job.

And we wrote what? Yes, 우현! Yes! We wrote about our own future job.

So with today's class, I want you to become a person who can prepare for the future by yourselves. Can you guys do that? Awesome.

So that's it for us today, and have a great weekend!

2019 기출문제

(1) 판서 노트 및 예시 영상

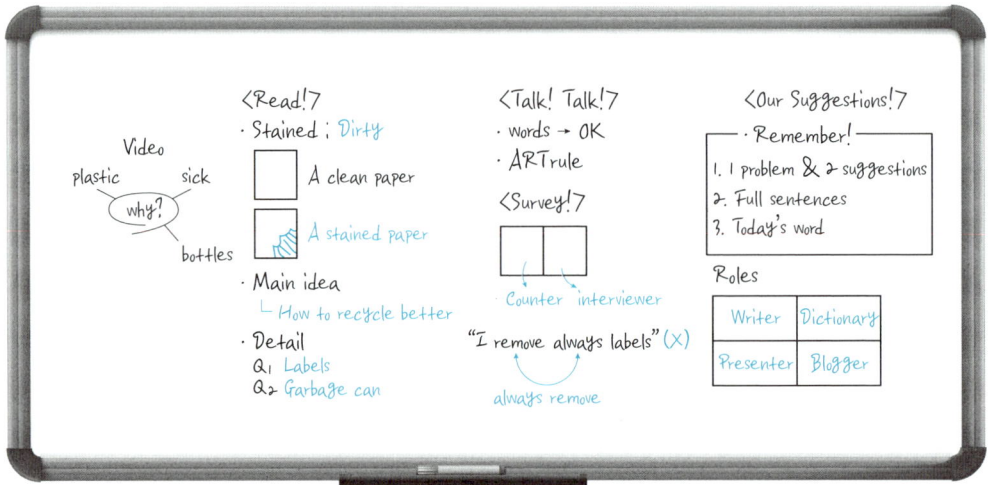

(2) 지도안 예시

단원명	Small Actions for the Blue Planet	시간	90 mins
대상	• Students : 24 Middle school 3rd Graders • Level : Mixed		
수업 목표	✓ Students will be able to find the main idea and details from the text. ✓ Students will be able to answer the questions about their personal experiences. ✓ Students will be able to write a suggestion for recycling.		
교수·학습 교구	Digital whiteboard, Laptop, PPT slides etc		

핵심역량	자기 관리	지식정보처리	창의적 사고	심미적 감성	협력적 소통	공동체
		✓			✓	✓

<교수 학습 지도안>

단계	교수·학습 활동	유의점 및 활용 교구
도입 (5분)	*인사, 출석 확인, 교실 내 안전 점검 *학습 주제, 수업 준비 상태 확인	
전개1 (15분)	**응시자 작성 내용 1** ✓ <자료 1>의 소재에 관하여 배경지식 활성화를 위한 활동을 진행할 것 ● Schema activation • [전체] 바다 환경 오염으로 고통받는 해양 생물 영상을 제시한다. • [전체, 3분] 영상에 관한 학생 상호작용 결과를 마인드맵을 활용하여 판서한다. <마인드맵 예시> (Why?) ● Transition • 완성된 마인드맵을 살펴보며 이번 차시 주제에 관한 관심을 유발한다.	PPT slides '자료 1'
	✓ <자료 1>의 밑줄 친 단어 중 하나를 가르칠 것 ● Teaching Vocabulary • [전체] <자료 1>을 학생에게 나누어주고 어려운 단어가 있는지 확인하게 한다. • 상호작용을 통해 어떤 단어를 어려워하는지 파악하고 해당 단어를 추론할 수 있도록 맥락을 제공한다.	'자료 1'

단계	내용	자료
	<예시 발화> 교사 : Does anyone know the meaning of 'stained'? … Okay. Let me give you a hint. 　　　　A clean paper　　　A stained paper • 의미를 성공적으로 추론한 후, 직접 문장을 만들어 보게 함으로써 이해 확인 점검을 실시한다.	'자료 1'
전개1 (15분)	✓ <자료 1>을 읽고 주제를 찾도록 할 것 ● Main idea • [개별, 3분] <자료 1>를 읽고 Main idea를 파악하게 한다. • Skimming 전략을 지도하여 글의 주제를 파악하도록 한다. 　• 빠른 속도로 글을 훑어보며 반복되는 단어를 확인하도록 한다. • 아래 지도 사항에 따라 순회 지도를 실시한다. 　<순회 지도 사항> 　• 참여를 북돋우며 활동 중 어려움을 겪고 있는 학생을 파악한다. 　• Low-level : <자료 1>에서 반복되는 단어를 중점적으로 찾아보도록 한다. • [전체] 학생과의 상호작용을 통해 글의 주제를 교실 전체에 공유하고 판서한다. 　• Main idea : How to recycle better • [전체] 글의 주제와 제목과의 연관성을 강조한다.	'자료 1'
전개2 (20분)	응시자 작성 내용 2 ✓ <자료 1>의 세부 내용을 찾는 활동을 진행하고 학생 이해도를 점검할 것 ● Detail information • [개별, 5분] Screen을 통해 세부 정보를 찾기 위한 질문을 학생들에게 제시한다. 　1) What should we take off before recycling a plastic bottle? 　2) Where should we throw away a dirty pizza box? • Scanning 전략을 지도하여 질문에 대한 답을 찾도록 한다. 　• 글 전체가 아니라 필요한 부분만 선별하여 읽도록 한다. • 아래 지도 사항에 따라 순회 지도를 실시한다. 　<순회 지도 사항> 　• 참여를 북돋우며 활동 중 어려움을 겪고 있는 학생을 파악한다. 　• High-level : 활동 참여에 대한 긍정적 피드백을 제공하고, Student teacher 역할을 부여하여 다른 학생을 도울 수 있도록 한다. 　• Low-level : 동료 학습자로부터 도움을 받도록 Peer-scaffolding을 유도한다.	PPT slides '자료 1'

전개2 (20분)	• [전체] 학생과의 상호작용을 통해 답변을 공유하고 판서한다.	
	√ <자료 2>를 활용한 짝 활동을 진행할 것	
	● Talk! Talk! • [짝, 10분] 짝과 함께 <자료 2> 완성을 위한 토의를 실시하도록 한다. • 추후 글쓰기 활동을 고려하여 단어나 구처럼 간단한 구조로 작성할 수 있도록 안내한다. • 아래 ART rule을 지키도록 독려한다. < ART rule > A : Active participation, R : Respect others, T : Take turns • 짝 활동 중 아래 지도 사항에 따라 순회 지도를 실시한다. <순회 지도 사항> • 참여를 북돋우며 활동 중 어려움을 겪고 있는 학생을 파악한다. • Low-level : ART rule 재강조, 문제점을 찾기 힘들어하는 짝에게 School news paper를 제공한다. • High-level : 활동 참여에 대한 긍정적 피드백을 제공하고 더 많은 문제점과 해결책을 찾아보도록 격려한다.	'자료 2'
전개3 (20분)	응시자 작성 내용 3	
	√ <자료 3>을 활용하여 설문 조사를 위한 짝 활동을 진행할 것	
	● Mingling activity • 2인 1조로 조를 편성하여 각 학생에게 Interviewer와 Counter의 역할을 부여한다. • Interviewer : 다른 학생에게 질문, Counter : 답변을 듣고 숫자 집계 • [짝, 10분] 짝과 함께 교실을 돌아다니며 설문 조사를 진행하도록 한다.	'자료 3'
	√ 활동 중 교실을 순회하며 촉진자 역할을 수행할 것	
	● Facilitation • 설문 조사 활동 중 아래 지도 사항에 따라 순회 지도를 실시한다. <순회 지도 사항> • 참여를 북돋우며 활동 중 어려움을 겪고 있는 학생을 파악한다. • Low-level : 응답자를 찾지 못한 짝은 교사가 적극적으로 개입하여 활동을 촉진한다. • High-level : 활동 결과에 대해 칭찬하고 <자료 3>의 5번 질문을 작성하여 추가 조사를 진행할 수 있도록 안내한다.	
	√ 내용이나 형식 측면에서 학생 오류에 관한 교사의 피드백을 제공할 것	

	● Giving feedback
	• [전체] 형식 측면에서 자주 하는 실수를 언급하며 교사의 피드백을 제공한다.
	  • (예시) I remove always labels. (X)
	  • 오류 수정 과정에서 학생 참여를 유도하며 Peer scaffolding이 일어날 수 있도록 한다.	

	• 실수한 학생이 특정되지 않도록 유의한다.		
전개4 (25분)	응시자 작성 내용 4		
	✓ <자료 4>를 위한 교사의 예시를 제공할 것		
	● Sample writing • [전체] 화면을 통해 <자료 4>를 위한 교사의 예시를 학생들에게 보여준다. • 학생들과의 상호작용을 통해 <자료 4>에 대한 글쓰기 조건을 제시한다. <예시 발화> 교사 : What do you see on the screen? … Yes, teacher's example! Like this, there are several things you should remember. <조건> 1. 1 Problem & 2 suggestions 2. Full sentences 3. Today's word	PPT slides '자료 4'	
	✓ 모둠 활동을 통해 <자료 4>를 완성할 것		
	● Grouping • 4인 1조로 6개의 모둠을 구성하고 구성원의 역할을 아래와 같이 부여한다. • 앉은 자리에 따라 역할을 아래와 같이 부여한다. <역할 부여> 	Writer	Dictionary
Presenter	Blogger | • Writer : 문장 작성 • Dictionary : Tablet PC로 단어 검색, 문법 확인 • Presenter : 발표 담당 • Blogger : Online Classroom에 게시 • Authentic purpose : 우수 작품은 교장선생님께 제안 편지를 발송할 예정이라는 점을 강조하며 실제적 동기부여를 실시한다. • [모둠, 15분] 글쓰기 조건에 따라 <자료 4>를 완성하도록 한다. • 교사는 아래 지도 사항에 따라 순회 지도를 실시한다. <순회 지도 사항> • 참여를 북돋우며 활동 중 어려움을 겪고 있는 학생을 파악한다. • Low level : <자료 2>와 <자료 3>이 <자료 4> 활동을 위한 준비 과정이었음을 강조하며 이를 활용할 수 있도록 안내한다. • High level : 긍정적 피드백을 제공한 뒤, 문제에 대한 제안을 하나 더 쓸 수 있도록 추가 과제를 제시한다.	'자료 4'	
마무리 (5분)	*활동 마무리, 다음 차시 안내 *주변 정리 지도, 인사		

(3) 스크립트

> 응시자 작성 내용 1

✓ 〈자료 1〉의 소재에 관하여 배경지식 활성화를 위한 활동을 진행할 것

　Okay, students. So far, we talked about the unit title and the lesson objectives. Then, are you guys ready for today's class? Awesome! Then, everyone, look at the screen here. 호영 at the back, can you see the screen? Great. So, what do you see on the screen? Yes, there is a video clip, right? So, from now on, we are going to start today's class with a video clip. So, let's watch a short video clip.

　Great. So, everyone, as I just told you, we are going to watch this short video clip, and then we are going to talk about it. All right? So, eyes on the screen. Let's watch this video clip.

　Okay, so we just finished watching this video clip. In the video clip, what did you see? Yes, 희원! Yes, you saw animals in the ocean, right? How did they look? Happy or unhappy? Yes, 다원! Yes, they didn't look so happy, right? So, why don't we talk about why they didn't look so happy? Do we have any volunteer? Yes, 지환! Yes, that was because they were sick, right? And what else? Yes, 현우! Yes, that was because they were uncomfortable because of the bottles, right? And what were those bottles made of? Yes, 종민! Yes, they were made of plastic, right? So, plastic here, plastic.

　So like this, we just watched this video clip and talked about what? Yes, 지환! Yes, why they looked unhappy in the ocean. Then, can you guess the topic of today's class? Yes, 동우! Oh, did everyone hear what 동우 just said? He said today's topic will be environment. Do you guys agree? Perfect! Then, are you ready to learn more about the environment?

✓ 〈자료 1〉의 밑줄 친 단어 중 하나를 가르칠 것

　Great! Then, everyone, let me give you this worksheet. Take one and pass them to the back. Take one and pass them to the back. 상우 at the back! Did you get the worksheet? Perfect.

　So, what do you see on the first worksheet? Yes, there is a reading text, right? So, from now on, we are going to read about the environment. So, let's read!

However, before we actually read the text, what do we have to learn first? Yes, 수민! Yes, we need to learn some difficult words, right? So, everyone, let's look at the first worksheet and check if there's any difficult words.

So, class! Were there any difficult words? Just say the words loudly! Oh, I can hear the word "stained" from many of you guys. So, "stained."

Then, does anyone know the meaning of the word "stained"? All right, then let me give you a hint. Everyone, look at here. So, let's say that I have a clean paper here — a clean paper. So this is a clean paper. However, let's say I have orange juice and spill it on it. If that happens, the paper would look like this. It would look like this. And we call this a stained paper here. Stained paper.

Then, can anyone guess the meaning of the word "stained"? Yes, 현우! Oh, did everyone hear what 현우 just said? He said "stained" means "dirty." So here, "stained" means "dirty." Then, 수현! Can you make a sentence with the word "stained"? Oh, you have stained shirts? That's a good sentence.

Okay, so I can see that everyone understands this word "stained." Then, are you guys ready to read the text?

✓ 〈자료 1〉을 읽고 주제를 찾도록 할 것

Perfect! All right. So, everyone, whenever we read the text, which one do we have to find first? Yes, 재우! Yes, we need to find the main idea first, right? So from now on, we are going to find the main idea. So, the main idea!

However, to find the main idea, do we have to read quickly or slowly? Yes, 상민! Yes, we need to read quickly, right? So you don't have to understand every single word. Just read quickly and find the main idea. I'm going to give you 3 minutes. 3 minutes—go!

Oh, 동우, do you need any help? Oh, you don't know how to find the main idea? Then, why don't you find the keyword that is used repeatedly? Because the keywords can be a hint for the main idea. Can you do that? Perfect! I love your effort!

1 minute left, students. Does anyone need more time? Okay, time's up.

So, let's check the main idea together. So what was the main idea? Any volunteer? Yes, 지환! Oh, did everyone hear what 지환 just said? He said the main idea is 'How to recycle better'. So the main idea was 'How to recycle better'. Do you guys agree? Awesome!

Then, everyone, we just found the main idea, which was 'How to recycle better'. But everyone, look at the title. 수현, can you read the title for us? Yes, it was "Let's Recycle Better," right? So like this, remember that title and the main idea have very close relationship with each other. All right?

응시자 작성 내용 2

✓ 〈자료 1〉의 세부 내용을 찾는 활동을 진행하고 학생 이해도를 점검할 것

Perfect! So we just found the main idea. Then, are you guys ready to read the text a little bit more closely? Perfect. So from now on, let's find some details. So let's find some detail about this reading text.

So everyone, look at the screen here. 현정, at the back! Do you see the screen? Perfect. So, what do you see on the screen? Yes, there are two questions, right? So, what's the first question? Can you read together? Yes, it was "What should we take off before recycling a plastic bottle?" right? And what about the second one? Can you read together? Yes, it was "Where should we throw away a dirty pizza box?" right?

So from now on, I'm going to give you five minutes. Five minutes to read the text again and find the answers for those two questions. All right?

However, to find the answers for these questions, do we have to read all of it, or can we just read only the necessary part? Yes, 다원! Yes, we can read the necessary part, right?

So I'm going to give you 5 minutes. 5 minutes to do what, 동우? Yes, we are going to find the answers for those two questions. All right? 5 minutes—find the answers. Go!

Oh, 수민, you already finished? Wow, what a quick reader! Then, why don't you help your friend 민수! I heard 민수 needs some help. Can you do that? Awesome. Like this, friends can be a better teacher. Keep up the good work!

1 minute left, students. Does anyone need more time? Okay, time's up.

So, let's check the answers all together. So, we had two questions, right? So, what was the answer for this first question? Can anyone share? Yes, 호영! Yes, it was "labels," right? So we should take off labels before we recycle the plastic bottles. So, the first one is "labels." Great job, 호영!

And what was the second one? Any volunteer? Yes, 현우! Yes, we should throw away the dirty pizza box to where? Yes, to the garbage can. Yes, it was not to the recycle bin, but it was a garbage can.

All right. So far, we just finished reading the text twice: one for the main idea and another for the detail.

However, this reading text was about Jiho's school. Then, how about our school? Don't you want to talk about it? Awesome!

✓ 〈자료 2〉를 활용한 짝 활동을 진행할 것

So, let's begin a 'Talk! Talk! Time' here. So it's time for talk. 'Talk! Talk!' here. So, everyone, look at the second worksheet. 현정, what can you see in the second worksheet? Yes, there is a problem and suggestion chart, right?

So from now on, we are going to talk with your partners. So, 종민, 민종, you two! 현정, 정현, you two! And you two!

Does everyone have their own partners? Perfect!

So, with your partners, we are going to talk about the problems and suggestions for our school. All right?

To complete this chart, you don't have to write in a full sentence. You can just write words — just words or phrases — that would be okay, because this is just speaking activity. All right? Perfect!

However, whenever we do this kind of 'Talk Talk activity', which rule do we have to follow? Yes, 호영! Yes, we need to follow the ART rule, right?

So, what was 'A'? Yes, 현우! Yes, it was 'Active Participation'.

And what was 'R'? Yes, 다원! Yes, it was 'Respect others', right? So, remember that you respect your partner's idea.

And what was 'T'? Yes, 수현! It was 'Take Turns', right?

So remember this ART rule when you talk with your partners. All right? Perfect.

So I'm going to give you 10 minutes. 10 minutes to do what, 종민 and 민종? Yes, talk with your partners and complete the second handout. All right? 10 minutes—go!

Oh, 수현 and 현수! Do you need any help? Oh, you don't know what's the problem of our school.

Then why don't you look at this school newspaper I just brought for you guys? With this school newspaper, can you find the problems and suggestions by yourselves? Perfect.

So if you need any more help, just feel free to call me. All right?

And 호영 and 영호, you already finished? Wow, what quick learners!

Then, why don't you write more suggestions for the problems? Because the more suggestions we have, the better our school will be.

Can you guys do that? Perfect!

1 minute left, students. Does any pair need more time?

Okay, time's up!

응시자 작성 내용 3

✓ 〈자료 3〉을 활용하여 설문조사를 위한 짝 활동을 진행할 것

So far, we just finished talking with our partners. Then, don't you want to know other pairs' ideas?

Perfect! Then, let's begin the class survey. So, it's survey time. Let's do the survey!

So, everyone, let's look at the third handout. What do you see? Yes, 희원 and 원희! Yes, you can see the survey worksheet, right?

So, from now on, we are going to walk around the classroom with your partner and ask questions, get the answers. All right? Perfect!

So, everyone, look at here. So, you guys are sitting like this, right?

So, students here, raise your hand! Okay. Okay. So you're going to be the interviewer. Okay? So you're going to ask questions to your friends. All right?

So, interviewer. And students sitting here, raise your hand! Okay. So, you're going to be the counter.

So, if your partner asks the question and your friend answers to the question, you count the number. All right? Perfect.

So, I'm going to give you 10 minutes. 10 minutes to do what, 재우 and 우재?

Yes, we are going to walk around the classroom, ask questions, do the survey.

And 호영, what's your role? Yes, you are going to be the counter. All right?

So, everybody stand up. Walk around the classroom. 10 minutes—go!

✓ **활동 중 교실을 순회하며 촉진자 역할을 수행할 것**

Oh, 현우 and 우현, do you need any help? Oh, you can't find another group to ask?

Then, why don't you go to 현수 and 수현 over there? I think they are in the same situation with you guys.

Can you do that? Perfect.

Oh, 종민 and 민종, you already finished? Wow, what brilliant students!

Then, what do you see in the fifth question? Yes, it says "Your question," right?

So why don't you make your own question and do the survey again?

Because the more questions you have, the better the survey result will be.

Can you guys do that? Perfect. Keep up the good work!

1 minute left, students. Does anyone need more time?

Okay, time's up. So, let's go back to your seats. Awesome.

✓ **내용이나 형식 측면에서 학생 오류에 관한 교사의 피드백을 제공할 것**

All right. So, we just finished the survey.

However, when I was walking around the classroom, I found that many of you guys used this sentence.

That was "I remove always labels." "I remove always labels." Is this a correct sentence? No, right?

So, how can we change this?

Yes, 종민! Oh, did everyone hear what 종민 just said?

He said we should say, "I always remove labels," instead of "I remove always labels."

So, it should be like this: "I always remove labels."

So, let's practice. Let's read this sentence again: "I always remove labels."

Perfect!

Other than this one, your survey was perfect. Let's give ourselves a big hand!

Great job, everyone!

응시자 작성 내용 4

✓ 〈자료 4〉를 위한 교사의 예시를 제공할 것

All right. So, we just finished the class survey.

Then, are you guys ready to write the actual suggestion for our school? Perfect!

So, let's write our suggestion — our suggestions for the school.

So, everyone, let's look at the screen here. 수민, at the back! Do you see the screen? Perfect.

So, what do you see on the screen? Yes, there's a teacher's example, right?

So, can you read the first part? Awesome.

So like this, there are several things you should remember when you write your own suggestions. So remember these things.

So, the first thing was like 수민 just read.

How many problems can you find in the sample writing? Yes, 동우! Yes, there's one problem, right?

So, your writing should have one problem.

And how many suggestions? Yes, 다원! Yes, there are two suggestions, right?

So, your writing should have one problem and two suggestions.

And second, what can you find in the teacher's example? Yes, 호영! Yes, the writing is written in full sentences, right?

So for the second part, you should write full sentences. Okay?

So, based on the keywords we wrote right here, you should make the full sentence over here. All right?

And lastly, we should include what? Yes, 희원! Yes, we should include 'Today's word' — Today's word, which was "stained."

All right? Perfect. So, remember these things when you write your own suggestions. All right?

✓ 모둠 활동을 통해 〈자료 4〉를 완성할 것

So, we are going to do this in groups. So, 종민, 민종, 수현, 현수 you four! You four!

And finally the last group, group six, you four!

Is everyone in the group? Perfect.

So, before we start, let me give you the roles. So, let's give some roles. All right?

So, you guys are sitting like this, right? Then, let me give each of you guys a role. All right?

So, first, students here, raise your hand. Okay. Okay, you guys are going to be 'The writer'. All right?

And students here, raise your hand. All right. Okay, you guys are going to be 'The dictionary'.

Dictionary. Dictionaries, what do we have to do? Yes, bring your own tablet PCs.

And if your group needs to find some difficult words or check the grammar, that's your job. All right? Perfect!

And students sitting here, raise your hand. Okay. And you guys are going to be 'The presenter'.

So, presenter here, make sure you prepare the presentation after the writing. Okay?

And lastly, students sitting here, raise your hand. All right. So, you guys are going to be 'The blogger'.

Blogger. So, bloggers, what do we have to do? Yes, 은수! Yes, we need to upload our final writing to the online classroom. Okay? Perfect.

Then, are you guys ready to write your own suggestions? Awesome!

Just before we start, let me tell you this: the best group suggestions will be actually sent to the principal's office.

How does this sound? Does it sound exciting? Awesome!

So, I'm going to give you 15 minutes. 15 minutes to do what? Group two?

Yes, we are going to write our suggestions for the better school.

And what is your role, 수현? Oh yes, you're a 'Blogger', right?

All right. I'm going to give you 15 minutes. 15 minutes—go!

Oh, group one, do you need any help? Oh, you don't know how to start writing?

Then, why don't you look at the second handout and the third handout? Because those were kind of buildup activity for this one.

With those second and third handouts, can you guys do this work by yourselves? Perfect.

And if you need any help, just feel free to raise your hand. All right? Awesome.

And group five, you finished already? Wow, what quick writers!

Then, why don't you write more suggestions? Because the more suggestions you provide, the better chance we have a better school.

How does it sound? Can you guys do that? Awesome. Keep up the good work!

1 minute left, students. Does any group need more time? Okay, time's up.

All right. So, everyone, we finished writing and we also watched our friends' presentation.

So, just before we wrap up, let's go over today's class.

So, today, we watched the video. And we read about what? Yes 현정! Yes, we read about how to recycle better.

And we talked about what? Yes, 호영! Yes, we talked about our school's problems and suggestions.

And then what? Yes 지환! Yes, we wrote our suggestions.

So, with today's class, I want you to become a person who can take care of your surrounding environments.

Can you guys do that? Awesome.

So, that's all for today. And have a great weekend!

마 2018 기출문제

(1) 판서 노트 및 예시 영상

수업실연 예시
2018 기출 변형

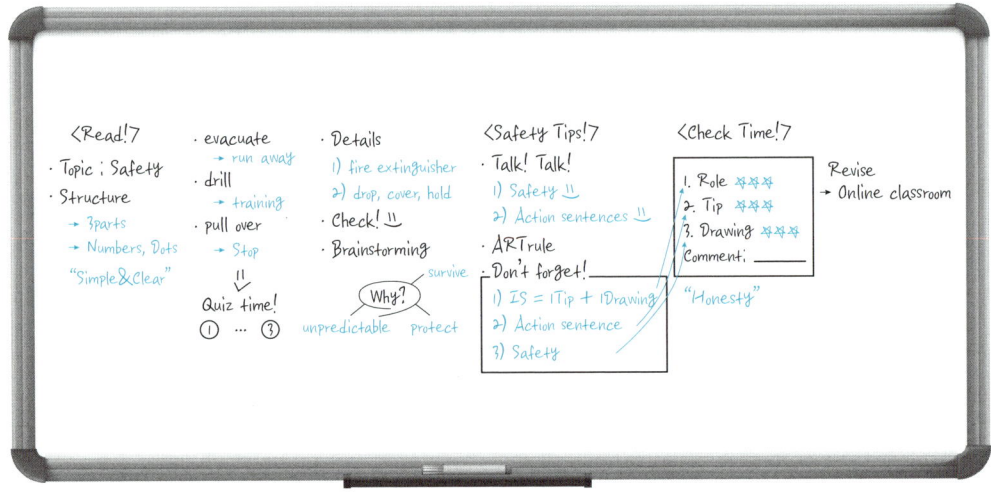

(2) 지도안 예시

단원명	Ready for Natural Disasters!				시간	100 mins
대상	• Students : 30 High school 1st Graders • Level : Mixed					
수업 목표	✓ Students will be able to find details from the reading text. ✓ Students will be able to describe the pictures about the safety tips. ✓ Students will be able to create a safety manual for earthquake.					
교수·학습 교구	Digital whiteboard, Laptop, PPT slides etc					
핵심역량	자기 관리	지식정보처리	창의적 사고	심미적 감성	협력적 소통	공동체
	✓	✓			✓	

<교수 학습 지도안>

단계	교수·학습 활동	유의점 및 활용 교구
도입 (5분)	*인사, 출석 확인, 교실 내 안전 점검 *학습 주제, 수업 준비 상태 확인	

전개1
(15분)
	응시자 작성 내용 1 (Pre-reading)
	✓ <자료 1>의 내용과 글의 구조를 파악하도록 할 것
	
	● **Topic**
	• [개별, 3분] <자료 1>를 학생에게 나누어주고 Topic를 파악하게 한다.
	• Skimming 전략을 지도하여 글의 소재를 파악하도록 한다.
	  • 빠른 속도로 글을 훑어보며 반복되는 단어를 확인하도록 한다.
	• 아래 지도 사항에 따라 순회 지도를 실시한다.
	
	<순회 지도 사항>
	• 참여를 북돋우며 활동 중 어려움을 겪고 있는 학생을 파악한다.
	• Low-level : Title이 Topic의 힌트가 될 수 있음을 언급한다.
	
	• [전체] 학생과의 상호작용을 통해 글의 주제를 교실 전체에 공유하고 판서한다.
	  • Topic : Safety
	
	● **Text structure**
	• [전체] 학생과 상호작용을 통하여 글의 구조적 특징에 대해 파악한다.
	  1) '서론-지진 피해 예방-지진 대피' 3단계로 이루어짐
	  2) Listing numbers과 bullet point로 짧고 간결하게 내용을 전달함
	
	<예시 발화>
	교사 : What characteristics did you find in the text?
	학생 : There are numbers and dots.
	교사 : Why do we use those listing numbers and bullet points?
	학생 : To make sentences short and clear!
		'자료 1'

	✓ 학생 수준을 고려하여 <자료 1>의 밑줄 친 세 단어를 가르칠 것	
전개1 (15분)	● Teaching Vocabularies • [전체] 'evacuate', 'drill', 'pull over'의 뜻을 아는 학생이 있는지 물어본 후, 각각의 단어에 대해 다음과 같은 방식으로 지도한다. 　• 'Mixed-level'임을 고려하여 High level 학생을 통한 'Peer scaffolding'을 적극적으로 활용한다. • 'evacuate': Word relation from interaction 　• 학생과 상호작용을 통해 'evacuate'와 같은 뜻을 지닌 'run away'를 소개하며 해당 단어의 의미를 파악하도록 한다. 　• (예시) When there's an earthquake, we need to do WHAT? Yes — we need to run away! That means we need to evacuate! • 'drill': Context clues from peer scaffolding 　• <자료 1>에서 'drill'과 밀접한 관련이 있는 단어를 찾아보도록 한다. 　• 'drill'이 'Practice', 'Regularly'와 함께 쓰였다는 부분을 주목하여 'drill'은 'training'과 비슷한 뜻을 가진 단어임을 파악하도록 한다. • 'pull over': Visual aid by video clip 　• 자동차 기어를 'Push'하는 것과 'Pull'하는 것에 따라 차가 움직이고 서는 영상을 보여주고 'pull over'는 'stop'과 같은 의미임을 파악하도록 한다.	'자료 1'
	✓ 맥락을 활용하여 단어 학습에 대한 이해도를 점검할 것	
	● Comprehension check • [전체] 두 개의 서로 다른 사진 세 쌍을 Screen으로 보여주며 'evacuate', 'drill', 'pull over'에 대한 학생 이해도를 점검한다. 　• 'evacuate': 급히 이동하는 모습(정답) vs 공부하고 있는 모습 　• 'drill': 여가를 즐기고 있는 장면 vs 무언가 연습하고 있는 장면(정답) 　• 'pull over': 움직이는 차 사진 vs 세워져 있는 차 사진(정답)	
	응시자 작성 내용 2 (Reading)	
	✓ 세부 정보를 찾기 위한 읽기 활동을 진행할 것	
전개2 (20분)	● Detail information • [개별, 5분] Screen을 통해 세부 정보를 찾기 위한 문제를 학생들에게 제시한다. 　<Screen> 　1) Before the earthquake happens, it is important to know the location of ＿＿＿＿＿＿. 　2) When the earthquake happens while you are indoors, ＿＿＿＿ to the ground, take ＿＿＿＿, and ＿＿＿＿ on. • Scanning 전략을 지도하여 질문에 대한 답을 찾도록 한다. 　• 글 전체가 아니라 필요한 부분만 선별하여 읽도록 한다. • 아래 지도 사항에 따라 순회 지도를 실시한다.	'자료 1'

	<순회 지도 사항> • 참여를 북돋우며 활동 중 어려움을 겪고 있는 학생을 파악한다. • High-level : 활동 참여에 대한 긍정적 피드백을 제공하고, Student teacher 역할을 부여하여 다른 학생을 도울 수 있도록 한다. • Low-level : 동료 학습자로부터 도움을 받도록 Peer-scaffolding 을 유도한다. • [전체] 학생과의 상호작용을 통해 답변 공유하고 판서한다. 　• (예시) fire extinguishers / drop, cover, hold	
전개2 (20분)	✓ 세부 정보 이해도에 대한 교사의 피드백을 제공할 것 ● **Comprehension check through 'Total Physical Response'** • [전체] 모두 눈을 감으라고 안내한 다음, 교실 내 소화기 위치를 손가락으로 짚어보라고 안내한다. • [전체] 눈을 뜨고, 자리에서 일어나라고 안내한 다음, 현재 지진이 발생한 상황이라고 가정하고 'Drop', 'Cover', 'Hold'에 맞춰 실제 행동으로 표현하도록 안내한다. ● **Giving feedback** • [전체] 학생 참여 및 이해도에 관한 긍정적 피드백을 제공한다. ✓ 지진 상황 행동 요령이 왜 중요한지 생각해 볼 수 있도록 격려할 것 ● **Brainstorming** • [짝, 5분] 짝과 함께 지진 상황 행동 요령이 왜 중요한지 생각을 나눠보도록 한다. 　• 교사는 다양한 정답이 나올 수 있음을 강조하며 자유롭게 의견을 나누는 분위기를 형성한다. • [전체] 교사는 학생들의 생각을 판서로 정리하며 교실 전체에 공유한다. <예시 발화> 교사 : Let's share what you talked. Anything is fine. There's no right answer. This is just brainstorming. 학생 : Survive, To protect our lives, It's unpredictable 등 ● **Transition** • 읽기 활동을 통해 알게 된 내용을 바탕으로 Safety Tip을 만들 준비가 되었는지 확인한다.	'자료 1'
전개3 (25분)	응시자 작성 내용 3 (Speaking) ✓ <자료 2>의 그림을 묘사하는 모둠 활동을 진행할 것 ● **Talk! Talk!** • Safety Tip을 만들기 위해서는 <자료 2>의 그림에 대한 이해가 필요하다는 점을 강조하며, 말하기 활동을 소개한다. • 6명씩 5개의 그룹을 형성하고, 그림을 통해 알 수 있는 사실에 관해 이야기를 나눠보도록 안내한다.	'자료 2'

전개3 (25분)	✓ 그림을 묘사하는 것에 관한 교사의 예시를 제공할 것 ● Demonstration • 활동을 시작하기 전, Screen을 통해 그림 묘사에 관한 교사의 예시를 제공한다. <Screen> (머리에 책을 올리고 대피하고 있는 학생들의 사진) • Run to the safe zone. • Protect your head. • 교사의 예시를 함께 확인하며 묘사 조건 두 가지를 제시한다. • 1) About 'Safety' 2) Use 'Action sentences' • [모둠, 15분] ART rule을 강조하며 말하기 활동을 실시한다. <ART rule> A : Active participation, R : Respect others, T : Take turns • 말하기 활동 중 아래 지도 사항에 따라 순회 지도를 실시한다. <순회 지도 사항> • 참여를 북돋우며 활동 중 어려움을 겪고 있는 학생을 파악한다. • Low-level : ART rule / 묘사 조건 재강조 • High-level : 활동 참여에 대한 긍정적 피드백을 제공하고 더 풍부한 내용을 묘사할 수 있도록 추가 과제를 부여한다.	PPT slides '자료 2'
	✓ 내용과 형식을 기준으로 활동에 대한 교사의 피드백을 제공할 것 ● Giving feedback • [전체] Content 부분은 '안전'에, Language use 부분에서는 '명령문을 잘 사용하였다'는 것을 언급하며 긍정적 피드백을 제공한다. <예시 발화> 교사 : When I was walking around and listening to your descriptions, I found that everyone was talking about safety with the action sentences. … Awesome! Let's give ourselves a big hand! ● Transition • 그림에 대한 이해를 바탕으로 'Safety Tip'을 만들 준비가 되었는지 확인한다.	
전개4 (30분)	응시자 작성 내용 4 (Writing) ✓ 모둠 활동을 통해 <자료 3>을 완성할 것 ● Safety Tip • [모둠, 20분] 아래 완성 조건에 따라 기존 모둠에서 <자료 3>을 완성하도록 안내한다. <완성 조건> • Role : 1 student = 1 Tip & 1 Drawing • Tip : Use action sentence. • Drawing : About safety	'자료 3'

● **Giving authentic purpose**
  • 우수 작품은 교내에 게재된다는 사실을 언급하며 학생의 동기를 부여한다.

  > <예시 발화>
  > 교사 : The best safety tip will be posted in our school so that students can protect themselves. … Does it sound great? Perfect!

✓ 활동 중 모둠을 순회하며 촉진자 역할을 수행할 것

● **Facilitation**
  • 쓰기 활동 중 아래 지도 사항에 따라 순회 지도를 실시한다.

  > <순회 지도 사항>
  > • 참여를 북돋우며 활동 중 어려움을 겪고 있는 학생을 파악한다.
  > • Low-level : <자료 2>가 <자료 3>의 준비 과정이었음을 언급하며 <자료 2>의 활동 결과를 참고할 수 있도록 안내한다.
  > • High-level : 활동 결과에 대한 칭찬과 재난 안전 교육의 중요성을 강조하며 추가 Tip과 drawing을 완성할 수 있도록 격려한다.

✓ <자료 3>에 대한 평가 활동을 진행할 것

● **Self evaluation**
  • 모둠별로 평가 기준이 포함된 <Self evaluation card>를 제공한다.
    • 평가 기준이 글쓰기 기준과 연결됨을 강조한다.

  <Self evaluation card>

  Group number : ____

1. Role	1 student = 1 Tip & 1 Drawing	☆☆☆
2. Tip	Use action sentence.	☆☆☆
3. Drawing	About safety	☆☆☆
Comment :		

  • [모둠, 5분] Self evaluation에서는 'Honesty'가 가장 중요하다는 것을 강조하며 자기 평가 활동을 실시한다.

● **Writing revision**
  • 자기 평가를 바탕으로 Safety tip을 수정한 뒤, Online classroom에 게시하도록 안내한다.
  • 다음 시간에 Best safety tip을 투표할 예정임을 공지한다.

'자료 3'

마무리 (5분)
*활동 마무리, 다음 차시 안내
*주변 정리 지도, 인사

(3) 스크립트

응시자 작성 내용 1 (Pre-reading)

✓ 〈자료 1〉의 내용과 글의 구조를 파악하도록 할 것

Okay, students. So far we've talked about the unit title and the lesson objectives. Then, are you guys ready to begin today's class? Perfect! So let me give you this worksheet. Take one and pass them to the back. Take one and pass them to the back. 호영, at the back! Did you get the worksheet? Great.

So what do you see on the first worksheet? Yes, there is a reading text, right? So from now on, we are going to begin the class with reading. So let's read! We are going to find the topic. So let's find the topic first. However, to find the topic, do we have to read the text quickly or slowly? Yes, 민수! Yes, we need to read the text quickly, right? So you don't have to understand every single word. Just read quickly and find the topic for the reading text. All right? I'm going to give you 3 minutes. 3 minutes, go!

Oh, 민재, do you need any help? Oh, you don't know how to find the topic? Then why don't you look at the title, because title can be a great hint for the topic. Can you do that? Perfect! Keep up the good work! Okay, time's up students! Were you guys able to find the topic? Great. So can you guys share? Oh, yes, 희원! Oh, did everyone hear what 희원 just said? She said the topic for this reading text is 'Safety'. Do you guys agree with that? Perfect.

Then everyone, let's look at the text again. This reading text seems to be a little bit different from what we have seen from the middle school. Can you guess what it is? Yes, 종민! Yes, the structure is different, right? So we are going to talk about the structure, the structure of this reading text. So let's talk about it together. Which things can you find about the structure of this reading text? Yes, 희원! Oh, yes! It has three parts, right? So it has three parts. And what else can you find? Yes, 지환! Yes, there are numbers and dots, right? So there are numbers and dots. So let's think about it. Why do we need this listing numbers and bullet points in this reading text? Yes, 나영! Oh, did everyone hear what 나

영 just said? She said, "We need this structure to make the text simple and clear." That's a great idea. So we need this structure to make the text simple and clear. Perfect!

✓ 학생 수준을 고려하여 〈자료 1〉의 밑줄 친 세 단어를 가르칠 것

So far we found the topic and we talk about the structure. Then are you guys ready to read the text? Awesome! However, before we read the text, what do we have to learn first? Yes, 다원! Yes, we need to learn some difficult words, right? So, were there any difficult words while you are reading the text? All right, I can hear the word "evacuate." So, our first word is 'evacuate'. All right. So let me give you a hint here. When there is an earthquake, we need to do what? Yes 종민! Yes, we need to run away, right? That means we need to 'evacuate'. Then, can you guess the meaning of the word 'evacuate'? Yes 수현! Yes, 'evacuate' means 'run away'. So, 'evacuate' is 'run away'. That's a great guessing! And is there another difficult word? Oh, I can hear the word 'drill' from many of you guys. So, the next word is 'drill'. So for this time, let's check the context. Which words can you find around the word 'drill'? Yes, 다원! Yes, you can find 'practice'. And what else? Yes 호영! Yes, 'regularly'. So we have two hints here: practice and regularly. So with these two hints, can you guess the meaning of the word 'drill'? Yes, 지환! Oh, did everyone hear what 지환 just said? He said practice regularly is 'training'. That's a great guess! So 'drill' means 'training' - 'to practice regularly'. And did you guys have another difficult word in this reading text? Oh, yes, 'pull over' is a difficult word. Yes, so 'pull over'. So for the word 'pull over', I just prepared the video clip. So everyone, let's watch this short video clip.

All right, so we just watched the video clip. In the video clip, the man was in the car and pushed the gear to the front. Then what happened? Yes, 희원! Yes, the car moved. And right after that, the man pulled the gear to his arm. Then what happened? Yes, 수민! Yes, the car stopped, right? So can you guess the meaning of the word 'pull over'? Yes, 재우! That's perfect. So 'pull over' means 'to stop the car'. Great!

✓ 맥락을 활용하여 단어 학습에 대한 이해도를 점검할 것

Okay, so we just learned these three difficult words. But before we start reading, we need to check how well you understand these words. So let's begin the quiz time. So it's quiz time! I just prepared the three quizzes. So let's see the first quiz. Everyone, look at the screen. 지환 at the back, can you see the screen? Great. So what do you see on the screen? Yes, there are two pictures, right? What can you see in the first picture? Yes 종민! Yes, people are moving fast, right? And what about the second picture? What can you see? Yes 동우! Yes, people are studying, right? Then which picture explains the word 'evacuate'? Yes 수현! Oh yes, the first picture, right? So we got the first quiz correct. Great job, everyone.

And the last one, the third quiz. So everyone, look at the screen again. 재우 at the back, do you see the screen? All right. So what can you see in the first picture? Yes, the car is moving, right? And how about the second picture? Yes, 현정! Yes, the car stopped, right? And then which one explains the word 'pull over'? Yes, 현우! Yes, the second one, right? Great! So we all got these three quizzes. So I can see everyone understood these three difficult words correctly. Then, are you guys ready to read the text a little bit more closely? Awesome!

응시자 작성 내용 2 (Reading)

✓ 세부 정보를 찾기 위한 읽기 활동을 진행할 것

So from now on, we are going to read the text for the details. So let's find some details. So everyone, let's look at the screen. 수민, what do you see on the screen? Yes, there are two sentences, right? However, there is something strange in the two sentences. Yes, 현우! Yes, that's because there are several blanks, right? So from now on, we are going to read the text again and find the answer for the blanks in the sentences. Okay? However, to find the answer, do we have to read everything or just the necessary part? Yes, 현정! Yes, we can read only the necessary part to find the answer, right? So from now on, I'm going to give you 5 minutes. 5 minutes to do what, 재우? Yes, we are going to find the answer for the blanks for those two sentences on the screen. Okay? I'm going to give you five minutes. 5 minutes, go!

Oh, 현수! You finished already? Wow, you're such a quick reader! Then why don't you help your friend 수현? I heard 수현 needs some help. Can you do that? Perfect! So like this, friends can be a better teacher! Keep up the good work! 1 minute left, students. Does anyone need more time? Okay, time's up! So let's check the answers together. So what was the answer for the first blank? Can you guys share? Thank you, 민수! Yes, it was 'fire extinguisher', right? So the first answer was 'fire extinguisher'. Did everyone get the answer? Perfect! And what was the second one? Yes, 현정! Yes, it was 'drop', 'cover', and 'hold', right? So the second one was 'drop', 'cover', and 'hold'. Did everyone get this answer? Perfect!

✓ 세부 정보 이해도에 대한 교사의 피드백을 제공할 것

Okay, so far, we just found those answers. But before we move on to the next part, let me quickly check how well you understand this part. So let's check. All right, everyone close your eyes and think about where the fire extinguisher is in our classroom. Can you point it with your fingers? Perfect! Open your eyes. I can see everyone knows where the fire extinguisher is in our classroom. Yes, it is right in the corner over there. And everyone, stand up. So let's imagine that there is an earthquake right now. What do we have to do? Yes 현우! Yes, we have to first drop to the ground, right? So everyone, let's practice. Drop to the ground! Perfect! And what's next? Yes, 수현! Yes, we have to take cover, right? So, cover your head right now! All right, I can see everyone is covering their heads with the desk. Perfect! Then, what's the last one? Yes, 희원! Yes, we have to hold on, right? So we need to hold on to the desk legs until the shake ends. Great! So everyone, stand up and go back to your seats. All right, so with this short practice, I could find that everyone is understanding the important points very well. So good job on this! You guys deserve a big hand. Let's give ourselves a big hand! Great!

✓ 지진 상황 행동 요령이 왜 중요한지 생각해 볼 수 있도록 격려할 것

So far, we read about what we have to do before the earthquake and during the earthquake. Then why is it so important? Don't you want to talk about it? Awesome! So let's have a brainstorming here. So it's time for the brainstorming. So before we share ideas with class, I'm going to give you 5 minutes to talk with your partner first. 수현, 현수, you two! 종민, 민종, you two! You two! And lastly, you two. So does everyone have their partners? Perfect! So with your partners, talk about why it is so important to know about these safety tips. All right? So talk about why it is so important to learn these safety tips. However, because this is a brainstorming, it is very important to keep in mind what? Yes, 호영! Yes, there is no right answer, right? So keep in mind that there is no right answer. Anything is fine because this is just a brainstorming. I'm going to give you 5 minutes. 5 minutes, go!

Okay, time's up. So let's share what you talked with your partner. Can anyone share? Yes, 현수! Oh yes, because we need to survive. That's a great answer. And what else? Yes, 호영 and 영호! Yes, that's because we need to protect ourselves. That's a great answer. And what else? Oh yes, 종민 and 민종! Yes, because the earthquake is unpredictable. Because it is unpredictable. That's a great answer. Okay! So far, we just finished brainstorming about why it is important to know about the safety tips. Then, are you guys ready to actually make safety tips? Perfect!

응시자 작성 내용 3 (Speaking)

✓ 〈자료 2〉의 그림을 묘사하는 모둠 활동을 진행할 것

Then everyone! From now on, let's make the safety tips. So let's make the safety tips! Everyone, let's look at the second handout. What do you see on the second handout? Yes, 수현! Yes, there are pictures, right? How many pictures can you see? Yes, 현우! Yes, there are six pictures, right? So to make a safety tip, it is first important to understand the pictures. So from now on, we are going to have some time for talking about the pictures. All right? Okay! Let's have a 'Talk Talk Time', first. Talk Talk! So we are going to do this in groups. 수현, 현수, 민종, 종민, 호영 and 영호, you six! You six! And finally the last group, group five, you six. Is everyone in the group? Perfect! So with your group members, we are going to talk about those pictures, okay?

✓ **그림을 묘사하는 것에 관한 교사의 예시를 제공할 것**

However, to describe the picture, let me give you an example. So everyone, look at the screen here. 지환 at the back, do you see the screen? Perfect. So what do you see on the screen? Yes, there is a picture, right? And in the picture, students are moving fast, covering their heads, right? So like this, there are several things you should remember when you describe the picture. Like 지환 just said, the first thing is about the safety. So your description must be about the safety. All right? And 동우! What else can you see below the picture? Yes, there are two sentences, right? And can you read the first one? Yes, it was 'Run to the safe zone'. And can you read the second one, 수현? Yes, it was 'Protect your head', right? So like this, when you describe the picture, you need to use those action sentences, okay? So the second part you need to remember is: Use action sentences. All right? So I'm going to give you 15 minutes. 15 minutes to talk with your group members and describe the pictures. However, whenever we do this kind of talk activities, which rule do we have to follow? Yes, 현수! Yes, we need to follow the ART rule, right? So remember the ART rule. So, what is A? Yes, 동우! Yes, it was 'Active participation'. And what was R? Yes, 다원! Yes, 'Respect others'. So make sure you respect your friends' ideas. All right? And the last part, what was T? Yes, 현우! Yes, it was 'Take turns', right? Okay, so remember the ART rule. I'm going to give you 15 minutes. 15 minutes to do what, 동우? Yes, describe the pictures. All right? 15 minutes. Go!

Oh, 다원! I can see you're participating very actively. Great job! However, what was the T rule? Do you remember? Yes, 'Take turns'. So, make sure everyone is talking. All right? And group three, I could hear that your description was perfect. But do you remember the second point? Yes, we should use the action sentences, right? So make sure you use those action sentences. Okay? Perfect. Oh, group five, you already finished? Wow, you guys are such active students! Then why don't you describe more about it? Because it's always better safe than sorry. Can you guys do that? Perfect. 1 minute left, students. Does any group need more time? Okay, time's up.

✓ **내용과 형식을 기준으로 활동에 대한 교사의 피드백을 제공할 것**

Okay, so we just finished this 'Talk! Talk!' activity, and there is something I want to tell you. When I was walking around and listening to your descriptions, I could find that everyone was talking about the safety. That was great! Not only that, I was very impressed that you were using these action sentences very well. I'm so proud of you. I want to give you a big hand! Great job, everyone! So, with this 'Talk! Talk!' activity, are you guys ready to make safety tips for your own? Perfect!

응시자 작성 내용 4 (Writing)

✓ **모둠 활동을 통해 〈자료 3〉을 완성할 것**

All right, everyone! Let's look at the third handout. What do you see, 현우! Yes, it says 'Six Tips During an Earthquake'. So from now on, we are going to make these safety tips in your groups. All right? However, there are several things you should remember when you make these safety tips. So I will say, "Don't forget!" here. So the first thing — how many students in your group? Yes, there are six students, right? So each member should have their role. So the first one is: one student should write one tip and one drawing. Okay? So each group member is going to take each part. And for the second part, we should use what kind of sentence? Yes 수현! Yes, we should use those action sentences. Okay? Action sentence! And this is because what? Yes, this is because we need to be simple and clear, because it's safety tips, right? And for the last one, the third one — for the drawing, it's going to be about what? Yes, 희원! Yes, it should be about the safety. Okay? So don't forget these three things when you make the safety tips for the earthquake. All right? Awesome!

However, just before we start, let me tell you this: the best safety tips will be posted in our school so that students can protect themselves during the earthquake. How does this sound? Exciting? Perfect! From now on, I'm going to give you 20 minutes. 20 minutes to make six tips for the earthquake. All right? Don't forget these three things. 20 minutes. Go!

✓ **활동 중 모둠을 순회하며 촉진자 역할을 수행할 것**

Oh, group two, do you need any help? Oh, you don't know what to begin with? Then why don't you look at the second worksheet, because the second worksheet was kind of a warm-up activity for this one. Was that helpful enough to finish this activity by yourselves? Keep up the good work! And if you need any more help, just feel free to call me! All right? And group four, you're already finished? Wow, what quick drawers and writers! Then why don't you write more tips and more drawings, because you can never emphasize safety too much. Can you guys do that? Perfect. 1 minute left, students. Does any group need more time? Okay, time's up.

✓ **〈자료 3〉에 대한 평가 활동을 진행할 것**

All right, we just finished making 'Six Tips During the Earthquake'. However, after we finished writing, what do we have to do? Yes, we need to check our writing, right? So it's time for checking. So let's have a check time. So everyone, let me give you this self-evaluation card. Take one and pass them to the back. Take one and pass them to the back. So, 수민 at the back! Did you get this self-evaluation card? Perfect! So what do you see on the first part? Yes, it says 'the Role', right? So, the first part was about the role. And what does it mean? Yes, 호영! Yes, it means your group members' role. So if your group members did one tip and one drawing, you can give three stars here. All right? And what's the second one? Yes, 다원! Yes, it says 'Tip', right? So, the second one was 'Tip'. And what does that mean? Yes 현우! For the tips, it should be written in action sentences, because it should be simple and clear. So for the second part, you can give three stars if it is perfect, and two stars if it is just good, and one star if it needs to improve. And for the third part, what do you see? Yes 동우! Yes, it says 'Drawing', right? So, the third part was 'Drawing'. And what does that mean? Yes, 재우! Yes, drawing means safety. So your drawing should be about the safety. So you can give three stars for the perfect, two stars just good, one star if it needs to improve. Okay? And lastly, what do you see? Yes, 호영! Yes, there's 'Comment', right? So make sure you can give a comment to yourselves. Okay? With this self-evaluation worksheet, we are going to check our writings. However, whenever we do this self-evaluation, what's the most important thing? Can anyone tell us? Yes, 종민! Yes, 'being honest' is very important. So make sure 'being honest'! Honesty is the most important thing when you do this activity. All right? So I'm going to give you 5 minutes. 5 minutes to check your group's writing on your own. 5 minutes. Go!

Okay, time's up. So we just finished checking our own writing. Then what do we have to do next? Yes, 은수! Yes, we need to revise our writing, right? So make sure you revise your writing based on the self-evaluation card. And upload — upload to where? Yes, 호영! Yes, to our online classroom. Okay? So that we can vote for the best safety tip. All right? Perfect.

So students, in today's class, we did what? Yes, 정은! Yes, we first read about the safety. And we did what? Yes, 재우! We made the safety tips for the earthquake, right? So through today's class, I want you to become a person who can protect yourselves during the natural disasters. Can you guys do that? Perfect. So that's all for today, and have a great weekend!

차 2017 기출문제

(1) 판서 노트 및 예시 영상

수업실연 예시
2017 기출변형
동영상 바로가기

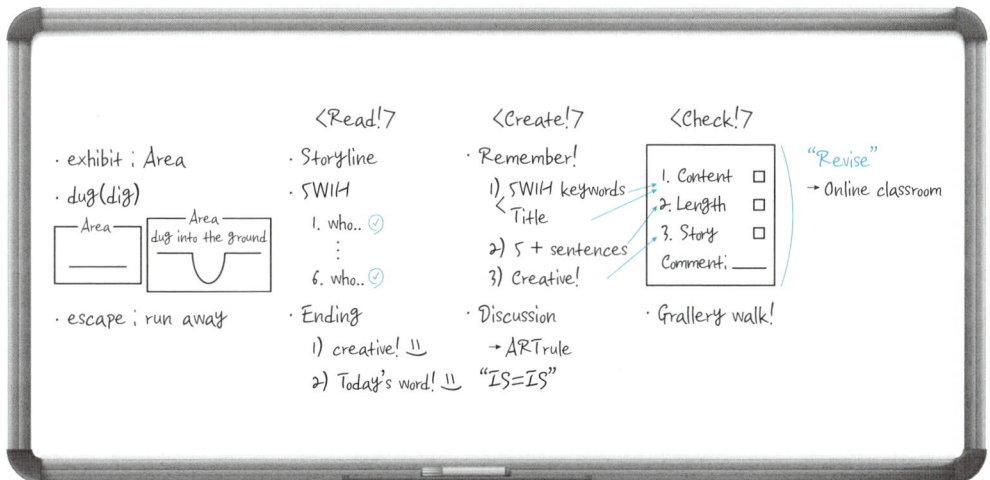

(2) 지도안 예시

단원명	Stories Behind Pictures				시간	90 mins
대상	• Students : 30 Middle school 3rd Graders • Level : Mixed					
수업 목표	✓ Students will be able to understand the story based on 5Ws1H questions. ✓ Students will be able to write the story ending based on the context. ✓ Students will be able to create their own stories based on the picture.					
교수·학습 교구	Digital whiteboard, Laptop, PPT slides etc					
핵심역량	자기 관리	지식정보처리	창의적 사고	심미적 감성	협력적 소통	공동체
		✓	✓		✓	

<교수 학습 지도안>

단계	교수·학습 활동	유의점 및 활용 교구
도입 (5분)	*인사, 출석 확인, 교실 내 안전 점검 *학습 주제, 수업 준비 상태 확인	

전개1
(15분)
	응시자 작성 내용 1
	✓ <자료 1>의 밑줄 친 세 단어를 가르칠 것
	
	● Teaching Vocabularies
	• [전체] 'exhibit', 'dug', 'escape'의 뜻을 아는 학생이 있는지 물어본 후, 각각의 단어에 대해 다음과 같은 방식으로 지도한다.
	• 'exhibit' : Guessing from the context clue
	  • 'Exhibit'이 'Gorilla'와 함께 쓰였다는 부분을 주목하여 'Tiger exhibit', 'Penguin exhibit'에서는 무엇을 볼 수 있을지 물어보며 자연스럽게 의미를 추론하도록 한다.
	• 'dug' : Visual Aids
	  • 원래 형태가 'dig (to make a hole)'을 파악하게 한다.
	  • 아래 그림을 칠판에 판서하며 'dug'의 의미를 유추할 수 있도록 지도한다.
	
	| Area | Area dug into the ground |
	|---|---|
	| ——— | ⌣ |
	
	• 'escape' : Word relation from interaction
	  • 학생과 상호작용을 통해 'escape'와 같은 뜻을 지닌 'run away'를 소개하며 'escape'의 의미를 파악하도록 한다.
	  • (예시) When there's a fire, we need to do WHAT? Yes — we need to run away! That means we need to escape!
		'자료 1'

	● Transition • 어휘 학습은 읽기를 위한 준비 과정이었음을 강조하며 다음 내용에 대한 학생 준비도를 파악한다.	
	✓ 5W1H 질문을 활용하여 <자료 1>의 세부 정보를 찾기 위한 읽기 활동을 진행할 것	
전개1 (15분)	● Story line • [개별, 2분] Skimming 전략을 사용하여 <자료 1>의 전체 이야기 흐름을 파악하도록 지도한다. • 아래 사항에 따라 순회 지도를 실시한다. <순회 지도 사항> • 참여를 북돋우며 활동에 어려움을 겪는 학생을 찾는다. • Low-level : <자료 1> 뒤편의 <Vocabulary list>를 제시한다. • [전체] 학생과의 상호작용으로 파악한 줄거리를 확인한다. ● Detail information • [전체] Screen을 통해 교사가 준비한 '5W1H' 질문을 함께 확인한다. <Screen> • WHO went to the zoo? • WHEN did they go to the zoo? • WHAT did Thomas like? • WHERE did they go first? • WHY was there a moat? • HOW did Thomas get into danger? • [개별, 10분] Scanning 전략을 지도하여 질문에 대한 답에 밑줄 치도록 안내한다. • 글 전체가 아니라 필요한 부분만 선별하여 읽도록 한다. • 아래 지도 사항에 따라 순회 지도를 실시한다. <순회 지도 사항> • 참여를 북돋우며 활동 중 어려움을 겪고 있는 학생을 파악한다. • High-level : 활동 참여에 대한 긍정적 피드백을 제공하고, Student teacher 역할을 부여하여 다른 학생을 도울 수 있도록 한다. • Low-level : 동료 학습자로부터 도움을 받을 수 있도록 Peer-scaffolding을 유도한다. • [전체] 학생과의 상호작용을 통해 파악한 내용을 확인한다.	PPT slides '자료 1'
	응시자 작성 내용 2	
	✓ 이야기의 결말을 창작하며 <자료 1>의 빈칸을 완성할 것	
전개2 (15분)	● Create the Ending • [전체] <자료 1>의 결말 부분이 없다는 것에 주목하게 한다. • 이야기의 결말을 만들기 위한 아래 두 가지 조건을 제시한다. • 1) Content : Creativity, 2) Language use : 1 Today's word	'자료 1'

전개2 (15분)	• [개별, 5분] 위 조건에 맞게 결말을 완성하도록 한다. • 아래 지도 사항에 따라 순회 지도를 실시한다. **<순회 지도 사항>** • 참여를 북돋우며 활동 중 어려움을 겪고 있는 학생을 파악한다. • High-level : 활동 참여에 대한 긍정적 피드백을 제공하고, 조금 더 풍부하게 내용을 추가 해보도록 격려한다. • Low-level : 'Guide questions'을 제공하여 다음에 무슨 일이 벌어질지 생각하는 데 도움을 받을 수 있도록 한다. ✓ 내용과 언어 사용을 기준으로 완성된 빈칸에 대하여 교사의 피드백을 제공할 것 ● Giving feedback • [전체] Content 부분은 창의성에, Language use 부분에서는 모두 오늘 배운 어휘를 잘 포함하였다는 것을 언급하며 긍정적 피드백을 제공한다. **<예시 발화>** 교사 : When I was walking around, I found that everyone finished the story very creatively. Not only that, I was also very impressed because everyone used 'Today's word' successfully! … Awesome! Let's give ourselves a big hand! ● Transition • 이야기의 결말을 성공적으로 완성하였으므로, 새롭게 이야기를 창작해 볼 준비가 되었는지 확인한다.	
전개3 (30분)	**응시자 작성 내용 3** ✓ <자료 2>를 활용하여 <자료 3>을 위한 교사의 예시를 제공할 것 ● Teacher's demonstration • 학생들에게 <자료 3>을 위한 교사의 'Sample writing'에 주목하도록 한다. • [전체] Screen을 활용하여 학생들에게 완성된 <자료 2>를 제시한다. ● Writing requirements • 교사의 예시를 함께 확인하며 <자료 3> 완성을 위한 글쓰기 조건을 제시한다. **<조건>** 1. Content : 5W1H Key words, Title 2. Length : 5+ sentences 3. Story : Creative	PPT slides '자료 2'

	5W1H	KEY WORDS
1	who	Fatner bear, Baby bear
2	what	Igloo
3	when	At night
4	where	Outside the igloo
5	how	Worried, Sad
6	why	Too big

Fatner Bear and the igloo

A baby bear and a big bear are outside at night, They are near an igloo.
The baby bear sits and looks at the igloo. The big bear stands and looks worried
They want to go inside the igloo, but the big bear is too big!

전개3 (30분)

√ 모둠 활동을 통해 <자료 3>을 완성할 것

● Group discussion
- [모둠, 5분] 5인 1조로, 6개의 모둠을 구성한다.
- 그룹 토의를 통해 <자료 3>에 대한 5W1H Keywords를 채워 넣도록 한다.
  - Keywords는 단어나 구처럼 단순한 구조로 작성할 수 있음을 안내한다.
- 모두 각자 의견을 제시할 수 있도록 하고, 아래 ART rule을 지키도록 독려한다.

  < ART rule >
  A : Active participation,   R : Respect others,   T : Take turns

- [전체] Keyword 작성이 마무리되었는지 확인하고 이를 바탕으로 이야기를 창작할 준비가 되었는지 점검한다.

● Creating short story
- [모둠, 15분] 한 학생당 한 문장 이상 쓰도록 개인별 역할을 안내하며 <자료 3>를 완성하도록 한다.
  - (판서) 1S = 1S (One student = One sentence)
- Authentic purpose : 우수 작품은 'Class storybook'에 게재된다는 사실을 언급하며 학생의 동기를 부여한다.

  < 예시 발화 >
  교사 : The best story will be posted in our class storybook so that everyone can enjoy your creative story. … Does it sound great? Perfect!

- 아래 지도 사항에 따라 순회 지도를 실시한다.

  < 순회 지도 사항 >
  - 참여를 북돋우며 활동 중 어려움을 겪고 있는 학생을 파악한다.
  - Low level : 수업용 Tablet PC를 제공하고 번역기 사용법을 안내한다.
  - High level : 긍정적 피드백을 제공한 뒤, 조금 더 자세히 써볼 수 있도록 추가 과제를 부여한다.

'자료 3'

전개4 (20분)	응시자 작성 내용 4	'자료 3'
	✓ <자료 3>에 관한 동료 평가를 진행할 것	
	● Peer evaluation • 개인별로 평가 기준이 포함된 <Check list card>를 6장씩 제공한다. • 평가 기준이 글쓰기 기준과 연결됨을 강조한다. | <Check list card>		
1. Content	5W1H Keywords	
	Title	
2. Length	5+ sentences	
3. Story	Creative	
Comment :		| ● Gallery walk • 교실 벽면에 각 모둠의 글을 전시할 수 있도록 한다. • <Check list card> 수거를 위한 상자를 글 아래에 두도록 안내한다. • [개별, 10분] 교실을 돌아다니며 <Check list card>를 작성한 후 상자에 넣도록 한다.	
	✓ 동료 평가를 바탕으로 글쓰기 퇴고 활동을 진행할 것	
	● Writing revision • 모둠별로 Writing과 <Check list card> 상자를 수거하도록 한다. • [개별, 5분] 친구들의 <Check list card>를 확인하며 모둠의 글을 수정한다. • 수정된 결과물을 Online Classroom에 올리도록 안내하며 활동을 마무리한다.	
마무리 (5분)	*활동 마무리, 다음 차시 안내 *주변 정리 지도, 인사	

(3) 스크립트

응시자 작성 내용 1

✓ 〈자료 1〉의 밑줄 친 세 단어를 가르칠 것

Okay, students. So far we talked about the unit title and the lesson objectives. Then, are you guys ready for today's class? Perfect. Then let me give you this worksheet. Take one and pass them to the back. Take one and pass them to the back. 수민, at the back! Did you get the worksheet? Great. So what do you see on the worksheet? Yes, there is a reading text, right? But before we read, what do we have to do first? Yes, 재우! Yes, we need to learn some vocabularies, right? So let's check some difficult words.

Our first word is 'exhibit'. Does anyone know the word 'exhibit'? Okay, then let me give you a hint. Let's check the context. So which word can you see around the word 'exhibit'? Yes, 현우! Yes, there's 'gorilla', right? So when you go to the 'gorilla exhibit', which animal do you think we can see? Yes, 호영! Yes, we can see gorillas, right? And what about 'penguin exhibit'? Yes, 동우! Yes, we can see penguins in 'penguin exhibit', right? And how about 'tiger exhibit'? Yes, 상우! Yes, we can see tigers in there. So can you guess the meaning of the word 'exhibit'? Oh, yes, 종민! Oh, did everyone hear what 종민 said? He said 'exhibit' is 'area'. So if you say 'gorilla exhibit', it's gorilla area.

Let's check the second word. The second word is 'dug'. And actually this word is originally 'dig'. Does anyone know the meaning of the word 'dig'? Yes, 수현! Oh, did everyone hear what 수현 just said? She said 'dig' means 'to make a hole'. That's perfect. So let me give you a hint here for the word 'dug'. This is the 'normal area'. If I say this is the 'normal area', 'area dug into the ground', If I say 'area dug into the ground', it would look like this. 'The area dug into the ground' would look like this. So did you guys get the meaning of the word 'dug'? Perfect!

And finally, the last word. What was the last word? Yes, 재우! Yes, it was 'escape'. Does anyone know the word 'escape'? All right, then let me give you a hint. What do we have to do if there's a fire? Yes, 지환! Yes, we need to 'run away', right? That means we need to 'escape'. So can you guess the meaning of the word 'escape'? Yes, 다원! Yes, it means 'run away'. Great! So far we just learned these three difficult words. Then, are you guys ready to read the text? Awesome!

✓ **5W1H 질문을 활용하여 〈자료 1〉의 세부 정보를 찾기 위한 읽기 활동을 진행할 것**

So it's time for reading. So let's read! Everyone, look at the first worksheet. What do you see on the first worksheet? Yes, 희원! Yes, there's a story, right? So from now on, I'm going to give you 2 minutes. 2 minutes to get the storyline. Okay? So we are going to find the storyline.

However, to find the storyline, do we have to read quickly or slowly? Yes, 상우! Yes, we need to read quickly. So you don't have to understand every single word. Just find the storyline. All right? I'm going to give you two minutes. 2 minutes, go!

Oh, 동우, do you need any help? Oh, the words are so difficult. Then why don't you look at the back of the worksheet? What do you see? Yes, there is a vocabulary list, right? So with this vocabulary list, can you find the storyline by yourself? Perfect! I love your effort! One minute left, students. Does anyone need more time? Okay, time's up. All right. So can anyone share your storyline? Okay, 현우! Wow, that was a great summary. So like this, we just read this story to get the storyline. Then, are you guys ready to read this story a little bit more closely? Perfect.

Then everyone, look at the screen here. 은수 at the back, can you see the screen? Perfect! So what do you see on the screen? Yes, there are questions, right? How many questions can you see, 다원? Yes, there are six questions. But each question has a keyword. Can you guys find it? Yes, 동우! Yes, 'Who' is a keyword. Yes, 종민! Yes, 'Where' is also a keyword. And what's the last one? Yes, 지환! Yes, 'How' is the keyword. So these keywords, we call what? Yes, 희원! Yes, we call these keywords '5W1H'. So from now on, we are going to read a little bit more closely to answer those 5W1H questions. Are you guys ready? Great! I'm going to give you 10 minutes. 10 minutes to read the story again and answer those 5W1H questions.

However, to answer those questions, do we have to read everything or just the necessary part? Yes, 재우! Yes, we can just read only the necessary part, right? So read the text again, find the answer, and underline it. All right? I'm going to give you 10 minutes. 10 minutes. Go! Oh, 현우, you already finished? Wow, what a quick reader! Then why don't you help your friend, 우현? I heard 우현 needs a help. Can you help him? Perfect. So like this, friends can be a better teacher. One minute left, students. Does anyone need more time? Okay, time's up.

So let's check the answers all together. So what was the first question? Yes, 희원! Yes, it was 'Who went to the zoo?', right? So what was the answer? Yes, 다원! Yes, it was 'The Anderson family'. So 'The Anderson family'. And what was the last one? 'How did Thomas get into the danger?', right? So what was the answer? Can you guys share? Yes, 종민! He got into danger because 'he was climbing up the fence'. Right? That was great answer.

응시자 작성 내용 2

✓ **이야기의 결말을 창작하며 〈자료 1〉의 빈칸을 완성할 것**

All right. So students, we just read this story twice, but there is something strange. Can you guys find it? Yes, 다원! Oh, did everyone hear what 다원 just said? He said there is no ending, right? So from now on, we are going to make the ending on our own. How does that sound? Exciting? Perfect! So it's time to write an ending. However, there are two things you need to remember to make an ending. The first thing is your story should be creative. So be creative. And for the second one, before we read, what did we learn? Yes, 호영! Yes, we learned those difficult words, right? So try to use these difficult words. Okay? So use today's word. All right? I'm going to give you five minutes. Five minutes to do what, 지환? Yes, we are going to write the ending for this story. Okay? Five minutes. Go!

Oh, 재우, you already finished? Wow, what a quick writer. Then why don't you write a little bit more about it? Because the more stories you have, the more the interesting your story will be. Can you do that? Great. Keep up the good work!

And 민수, do you need any help? Oh, you don't know what's going to be next? Yes, it's really difficult to think what would happen next. Then why don't you look at the back of the worksheet? What do you see? Yes, there are several 'Guide questions', right? So with those guide questions, can you make the ending for your own? Perfect! So if you need any more help, just feel free to raise your hand. All right? Great! One minute left, students. Does anyone need more time? Okay, time's up.

✓ 내용과 언어 사용을 기준으로 완성된 빈칸에 대하여 교사의 피드백을 제공할 것

All right. So we just finished writing the ending for this story, and there's something I want to tell you. When I was walking around, I found that everyone's writing was very creative. So you guys wrote very creative stories. And not only that, I could also find that everyone used today's word very successfully. So great job on this too! So you guys deserve a big hand. So let's give ourselves a big hand! Perfect!

So we just finished writing the ending. Then, are you guys ready to create your own story? Perfect. So it's time to create. So let's create!

응시자 작성 내용 3

✓ 〈자료 2〉를 활용하여 〈자료 3〉을 위한 교사의 예시를 제공할 것

So everyone, let's look at the screen here. 지환 at the back, can you see the screen? Okay. So what do you see on the screen? Yes, there is teacher's example, right? And what else can you see? Yes, 동우! Yes, there are 5W1H keywords, right?

So like this, we are going to create our own story. But there are several things you should remember. So remember these things. Remember!

So like 동우 just said, you should write the 5W1H keywords. So the first thing is 5W1H keywords. And what else can you see? Yes, 수현! Yes, there is a title. What was the title? Yes, 희원! It was 'Father Bear and the Igloo', right? So like this, your writing should have the title. That was the first thing.

And in the teacher's example, how many sentences can you find? Yes, 종민! Yes, there are five sentences, right? So like this teacher's example, your writing should have more than five sentences. Okay? Five or more sentences.

And finally, the last one. Last one you should remember is — let me give you a hint. To make a story, it is important to be what? Yes, 희원! Yes, 'Creative'! So the last one is

'Remember to be creative'. Okay? Perfect!

✓ 모둠 활동을 통해 〈자료 3〉을 완성할 것

Great! So we are going to create the story in groups. So 수현, 현수, 희원, 원희 and 종민, you five — you five. And finally, the last group — group six — you five. Is everyone in the group? Perfect.

So from now on, I'm going to give you five minutes — five minutes to have a short discussion. Okay? So, let's have a short discussion first. And this is going to be for what? Yes, 지환! Yes, we need to find the keywords for 5W1H questions, right?

So I'm going to give you five minutes — five minutes to discuss with your group members and write the keywords for 5W1H words. However, whenever we have this kind of discussion, which rule do we have to follow? Yes, 재우! Yes, we need to follow the ART rule, right?

So remember the ART rule. So what was A? Yes, 수현! Yes, it was 'Active participation'. And what was R? Yes, 희원! Yes, 'Respect others'. So make sure you respect your friends' ideas, all right? And what was T? Yes, 다원! Yes, T was 'Take turns', right?

So I'm going to give you five minutes — five minutes to write the keywords. So you don't have to make the full sentences. Just write the keywords or phrases. All right? Five minutes. Go!

Okay, time's up, students! So did you guys finish writing the keywords? Awesome! Then are you ready to create your stories? Great!

So I'm going to give you 15 minutes — 15 minutes to create your group's story. All right? However, everyone should have their role, right? So let me give you this role. So one student should write at least one sentence, okay? So one student should write at least one sentence.

Just for your notice before we start, I want to tell you that the best writing will be posted in our class storybook. How does it sound? Exciting? Awesome. So I'll give you 15 minutes — 15 minutes to do what, 동우? Yes, create the story, and remember these three things, all right? 15 minutes. Go!

Oh, group two, do you need any help? Oh, it's too difficult to write a story in English?

Then why don't you open up your tablet PC and use the translation app? Great! So with this translation app, can you guys do this by yourselves? Perfect! So if you need any more help, just feel free to call me. All right? Great!

And group five, did you guys already finish? Wow, that's great. You guys are such quick writers. Then why don't you write more details? Because the more details you have, the better your storyline will be. Can you do that? Great. Keep up the good work!

One minute left, students. Does any group need more time? Okay, time's up.

응시자 작성 내용 4

✓ 〈자료 3〉에 관한 동료 평가를 진행할 것

All right. So we just finished writing our group stories with friends. Then, don't you want to read your friends' stories? Great. So it's time for checking. So let's check.

So let me give you these checklist cards. Take six cards and pass them to the back. So take six cards and pass them to the back. How many cards did I say? Yes, you should take six cards. Okay?

So let's see what we have in the checklist card. 호영 at the back, did you get all these six checklist cards? Great. So what can you see in there? Yes, it says the 'Content', right? So the first one is 'Content'. And what's the 'Content'? Yes, 종민! Yes, it says the '5W1H keywords' and 'the title', right? So if your friend's writing has those '5W1H keywords' and 'the title', you should check here. Okay?

And what's the second one? Yes, 희원! Yes, it says 'Length', right? So the second one is 'Length'. And what is 'Length'? Yes, like 현우 just said, if your friend's writing has more than five sentences, you should check here. Okay?

And what was the third one? Yes, 지환! Yes, it says the 'Story', right? I just said the story should be what? Yes, 종민! The story should be creative, right? So if your friend's story is creative, you should check here.

And what can you see in the last part? Yes, 다원! Yes, there is 'Comment', right? So don't forget to write a comment for your friend's writing. All right?

So with these checklist cards, we are going to do the gallery walk. Okay? So let's prepare for the gallery walk. So it's time for the gallery walk.

So group one, put your writing on this wall. Group two, over there. And lastly, group six, over here. And did you guys notice that there are boxes for the checklist cards? Perfect.

So from now on, I'm going to give you 10 minutes — 10 minutes to walk around the classroom, read your friends' writing, and put your checklist cards in each box. Okay?

So 현우! What are we going to do? Yes, we are going to walk around the classroom and read our friends' writing. Okay? 10 minutes. Go!

✓ 동료 평가를 바탕으로 글쓰기 퇴고 활동을 진행할 것

Okay, time's up. So everyone, please go back to your seats.

Okay, so we just finished checking our friends' writing. Then what do we have to do next? Yes, 상우! Yes, we should revise our story, right? So we are going to revise — revise our story based on the checklist. Okay?

So students, bring your boxes to your group. So group one, did you get your box? And lastly, group six, do you have your box? All right! So from now on, I'm going to give you five minutes — 5 minutes to open up your boxes, read your friends' comments, and change your group writing. Okay? I'm going to give you 5 minutes — 5 minutes. Go!

Okay, time's up. Did you finish revising your stories? Perfect. Then, make sure you upload your final version of your story to the online classroom — the online classroom — so that we can vote for the best writing to the storybook. Okay?

All right! So in today's class, we did what? Yes, 수민! We read the story. And we made what? Yes, 호영, we made our own ending. And we also did what? Yes, 현우! Yes, we also created our own stories. So with today's class, I want you to become a more creative person in the future. Can you guys do that? Awesome! So that's all for today, and have a great day!

곰쌤 영어과 수업 실연 체크리스트

1. 수업 실연 연습 문제

가~아. 연습문제 1회~8회 기출변형(2024~2017)

1) 문제

2) 지도안

2. 예시답안 & 스크립트

가~아. 연습문제 1회~8회 기출변형(2024~2017)

1) 판서 노트 및 예시 영상

2) 지도안 예시

3) 스크립트

3. 수업 실연 Q&A

Q&A 1~10

3
OUTPUT : 실전연습

Chapter 01

수업 실연 연습 문제

가 연습문제 1회 : 2024 기출변형

Classroom settings

- Class time : 100 minutes
- Students : 24 High school 1st Graders
- Level : Mixed
- Aids : Digital whiteboard, Laptop, Online dictionary, Tablet PCs etc

Lesson information

- Unit title : Spread Wisdom
- Objectives
   - ✓ Students will be able to make comics related to the proverb.
   - ✓ Students will be able to act based on their comics.

지시사항

- 응시자 작성 내용 1
   - ✓ <자료 1>의 속담으로 짝 활동을 진행할 것
   - ✓ <자료 2>의 밑줄 친 표현을 맥락을 활용하여 지도하고 이해 확인 점검을 진행할 것
   - ✓ <자료 2>를 읽고 빈칸에 들어갈 속담 두 가지를 <자료 1>에서 찾아보게 할 것

- 응시자 작성 내용 2
   - ✓ 실제적 목적을 제시하여 <자료 3>에 대한 학생의 동기를 강화할 것
   - ✓ 모둠을 구성하고 <자료 3>을 완성하도록 할 것
   - ✓ <자료 3>의 내용으로 연극 발표 연습을 진행할 것

- 응시자 작성 내용 3
   - ✓ <자료 4>의 평가 기준을 3가지 제시할 것
   - ✓ 발표에 관한 학생의 소감을 듣고 피드백을 제공할 것

(1) 문제

<자료 1>

<Famous Korean Proverbs>
1. A journey of a thousand miles　　•　　　　•　a. after losing the cow.
2. There's no use to fix the barn　　•　　　　•　b. when lifted together.
3. When the upper stream is clear,　•　　　　•　c. begins with a single step.
4. Even a sheet of paper is lighter　•　　　　•　d. the lower stream will be clear too.

<자료 2>

Characters: Jessica, Paul, Eric
Scene #1: Three high school students are talking in the classroom.
Topic: _____

① I'm juggling a lot right now. I have to take a math test,
② write a science report and study for the history quiz.
③ I don't have enough time to do all of them!
④ You are right. It is too busy to be a high school student. I wish there were 48 hours in the day.
⑤ But we all have 24 hours.
⑥ That's right. Maybe we can help each other as well.
⑦ We can study together and get it all done. That sounds good! We'll split up the work and do it together.
⑧ Thanks, guys. That would help a lot. No problem! Let's start with the math.

I think I need to do step by step.

Related proverbs
① _____
② _____

그림 : 주휘정(@hwi_juu3)

<자료 3>

<Let's make Comics!>

Characters : _____

Scene #1 : _____

Cut #1	Cut #2
Cut #3	Cut #4

Korean Proverb : _____

<자료 4>

<Let's check!>

#	Criteria	Meanings	Points		
1			1	2	3
2			1	2	3
3			1	2	3

Comments :

(2) 지도안

단원명	Spread Wisdom				시간	100 mins
대상	• Students : 24 High school 1st Graders • Level : Mixed					
수업 목표	✓ Students will be able to make comics related to the proverb. ✓ Students will be able to act based on their comics.					
교수·학습 교구	Digital whiteboard, Laptop, Online dictionary, Tablet PCs etc					
핵심역량	자기 관리	지식정보처리	창의적 사고	심미적 감성	협력적 소통	공동체
			✓	✓	✓	✓

<교수 학습 지도안>

단계	교수·학습 활동	유의점
도입 (5분)	*인사, 출석 확인, 교실 내 안전 점검 *학습 주제, 수업 준비 상태 확인	
전개1 (30분)	응시자 작성 내용 1 ✓ <자료 1>의 속담으로 짝 활동을 진행할 것 ✓ <자료 2>의 밑줄 친 표현을 맥락을 활용하여 지도하고 이해 확인 점검을 진행할 것	

	✓ <자료 2>를 읽고 빈칸에 들어갈 속담 두 가지를 <자료 1>에서 찾아보게 할 것
전개2 (35분)	응시자 작성 내용 2
	✓ 실제적 목적을 제시하여 <자료 3>에 대한 학생의 동기를 강화할 것
	✓ 모둠을 구성하고 <자료 3>을 완성하도록 할 것

	✓ <자료 3>의 내용으로 연극 발표 연습을 진행할 것	
	응시자 작성 내용 3	
	✓ <자료 4>의 평가 기준을 3가지 제시할 것	
전개3 (25분)		
	✓ 발표에 관한 학생의 소감을 듣고 피드백을 제공할 것	
마무리 (5분)	*활동 마무리, 다음 차시 안내 *주변 정리 지도, 인사	

연습문제 2회 : 2023 기출 변형

Classroom settings

- Class time : 100 minutes
- Students : 24 High school 1st Graders
- Level : Mixed
- Aids : Digital whiteboard, Laptop, Online dictionary, Tablet PCs etc

Lesson information

- Unit title : Comfort Zone
- Objectives
    - ✓ Students will be able to understand how to get out of the 'Comfort Zone'.
    - ✓ Students will be able to write their plans about the future.

지시사항

- **응시자 작성 내용 1**
    - ✓ <자료 1>을 활용하여 사전지식 활성화 활동을 진행할 것
    - ✓ <자료 2>를 읽고 글의 주제를 파악하게 할 것
    - ✓ <자료 2>의 빈칸을 완성하고 학생 참여 활동을 진행할 것
    - ✓ 'It is difficult to …' 표현을 맥락을 통해 지도할 것

- **응시자 작성 내용 2**
    - ✓ <자료 3>을 활용하여 쓰기 전 활동을 진행할 것
    - ✓ <자료 4>에 대한 글쓰기 조건을 제시할 것
    - ✓ <자료 4>를 완성하고 긍정적 피드백과 부정적 피드백을 제공할 것

- **응시자 작성 내용 3**
    - ✓ <자료 4>에 대한 동료 평가를 실시할 것
    - ✓ 수업 주제와 관련한 학생의 역량을 언급할 것

(1) 문제

<자료 1>

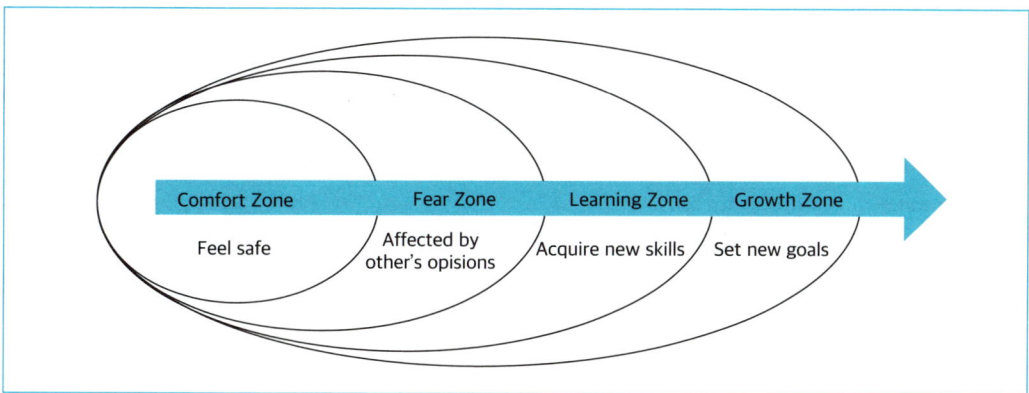

<자료 2>

<Change Yourself!>

It is difficult to get out of the 'Comfort Zone'. However, if you really want to go beyond your limit, you need to step out of your daily routine and change yourself. Of course, it is difficult to do this, but I'm sure you can do it! Here are 5 ways to get yourself out of the 'Comfort Zone'.

<5 ways to get yourself out of the 'Comfort Zone'>

1. Set Goals : If it is difficult to set goals, just slow down and try one by one.
2. Try New Things Often : Do things that feel a bit scary sometimes.
3. Do Things That Feel Strange : Try stuff that makes you uncomfortable.
4. Learn from Mistakes : When things go wrong, figure out what you can learn.
5. _____

<자료 3>

<Self Survey>

- Q1. What is your 'Comfort Zone'?
  A. _____
- Q2. What do you fear?
  A. _____
- Q3. What do you want to learn?
  A. _____
- Q4. What's your plan to achieve it?
  Step 1. _____, Step 2. _____, Step 3. _____

<자료 4>

Write about Yourself:
<My Plans to Grow>

I used to feel safe when ____*(about your comfort zone)*____ . I also felt scared when ____*(about your fear zone)*____ . However, I decided to change myself from today. I'm not going to stay in the safe zone and I don't want to feel fear from it anymore. Instead, I'm going to learn ____*(about your learning zone)*____ for myself. I know _____ , but I won't give up easily. My plans to achieve this are as follows. First, ___*(Step 1)*___ . Second, ___*(Step 2)*___ . Lastly, ___*(Step 3)*___ . By following these steps, I believe I can get into the Growth zone.

(2) 지도안

단원명	Comfort Zone				시간	100 mins
대상	• Students : 24 High school 1st Graders • Level : Mixed					
수업 목표	✓ Students will be able to understand how to get out of the 'Comfort Zone'. ✓ Students will be able to write their plans about the future.					
교수·학습 교구	Digital whiteboard, Laptop, Online dictionary, Tablet PCs etc					
핵심역량	자기 관리	지식정보처리	창의적 사고	심미적 감성	협력적 소통	공동체
	✓				✓	

<교수 학습 지도안>

단계	교수·학습 활동	유의점
도입 (5분)	*인사, 출석 확인, 교실 내 안전 점검 *학습 주제, 수업 준비 상태 확인	
전개1 (35분)	응시자 작성 내용 1 ✓ <자료 1>을 활용하여 사전지식 활성화 활동을 진행할 것 ✓ <자료 2>를 읽고 글의 주제를 파악하게 할 것	

✓ <자료 2>의 빈칸을 완성하고 학생 참여 활동을 진행할 것

✓ 'It is difficult to ...' 표현을 맥락을 통해 지도할 것

응시자 작성 내용 2

✓ <자료 3>을 활용하여 쓰기 전 활동을 진행할 것

전개2
(40분)

✓ <자료 4>에 대한 글쓰기 조건을 제시할 것

✓ <자료 4>를 완성하고 긍정적 피드백과 부정적 피드백을 제공할 것

응시자 작성 내용 3
✓ <자료 4>에 대한 동료 평가를 실시할 것

전개3
(15분)

	✓ 수업 주제와 관련한 학생의 역량을 언급할 것	
마무리 (5분)	*활동 마무리, 다음 차시 안내 *주변 정리 지도, 인사	

연습문제 3회 : 2022 기출 변형

Classroom settings

- Class time : 90 minutes
- Students : 24 Middle school 3rd Graders
- Level : Mixed
- Aids : Digital whiteboard, Laptop, Online dictionary, Tablet PCs, Stickers etc

Lesson information

- Unit title : Making relationships
- Objectives
  ✓ Students will be able to predict the story based on the context.
  ✓ Students will be able to write about making a great relationship with friends.

지시사항

- **응시자 작성 내용 1**
  ✓ <자료 1>을 활용하여 학생 참여를 유도하는 활동을 진행할 것
  ✓ <자료 2>의 밑줄 친 표현을 가르칠 것
  ✓ <자료 2>를 활용하여 이야기 추측하기 활동을 진행할 것

- **응시자 작성 내용 2**
  ✓ <자료 3>을 시청하고 모둠 토의를 진행할 것
  ✓ <자료 3>에 관한 모둠 토의 주제 2가지를 제시할 것
  ✓ 모둠 토의 활동에 관한 교사의 피드백을 제시할 것

- **응시자 작성 내용 3**
  ✓ 모둠 토의 내용을 바탕으로 <자료 4>를 완성하게 할 것
  ✓ <자료 4>에 관한 글쓰기 조건 3가지를 제시할 것
  ✓ <자료 4>의 결과물을 공유하는 활동을 진행할 것

(1) 문제

<자료 1>

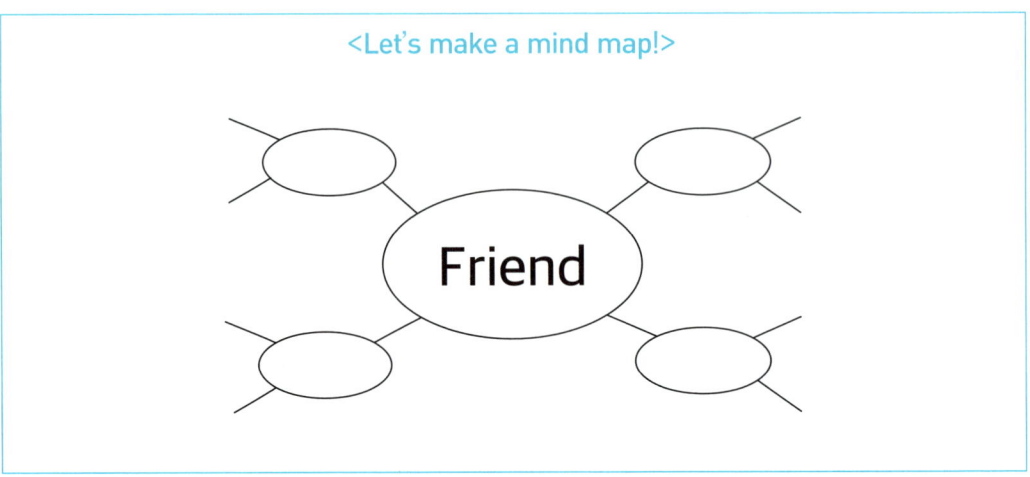

<자료 2>

The kitchen is bright and warm.
A father is looking at an old book. His son watches with interest.

SON (excited) Dad, how did you deal with enemies when you were a kid?
DAD (smiling) I'll show you. Watch closely.

The father takes out a worn-out book from the shelf.
He finds a page with a old recipe.

DAD (holding up the page) "Enemy Pie," it says.
SON (curious) What's in it?
DAD (smiling) It's a secret recipe.

The son begs for more information.

SON Please, just a hint?
DAD I'll tell you this much. Enemy Pie is the quickest way to make enemies disappear.

<자료 3>

*NOTE FOR TEACHERS : This summary is ONLY for teachers. Students are not provided with the following summary.

<Video clip of Benjamin Franklin and his rival>

Benjamin Franklin wanted to borrow a rare book from his rival, but instead of directly asking, he wrote a letter praising the book and expressing admiration for his rival's collection. His rival, flattered by the praise, gladly lent him the book, which helped to mend their relationship and eventually turned them into friends.

<자료 4>

<How to build a great relationship with friends>

To build a great relationship, I think ___(your idea)___ is very important. That is because _____.
Second, _____.
Lastly, _____.

<Sticker board>

How much did you like my writing? Give me your stickers!

(2) 지도안

단원명	Making relationships				시간	90 mins
대상	• Students : 24 Middle school 3rd Graders • Level : Mixed					
수업 목표	✓ Students will be able to predict the story based on the context. ✓ Students will be able to write about making a great relationship with friends.					
교수·학습 교구	Digital whiteboard, Laptop, Online dictionary, Tablet PCs, Stickers etc					
핵심역량	자기 관리	지식정보처리	창의적 사고	심미적 감성	협력적 소통	공동체
			✓		✓	✓

<교수 학습 지도안>

단계	교수·학습 활동	유의점
도입 (5분)	*인사, 출석 확인, 교실 내 안전 점검 *학습 주제, 수업 준비 상태 확인	
전개1 (20분)	응시자 작성 내용 1 ✓ <자료 1>을 활용하여 학생 참여를 유도하는 활동을 진행할 것 --- ✓ <자료 2>의 밑줄 친 표현을 가르칠 것 ---	

	✓ <자료 2>를 활용하여 이야기 추측하기 활동을 진행할 것	
전개2 (30분)	응시자 작성 내용 2	
	✓ <자료 3>을 시청하고 모둠 토의를 진행할 것	
	✓ <자료 3>에 관한 모둠 토의 주제 2가지를 제시할 것	

	✓ 모둠 토의 활동에 관한 교사의 피드백을 제시할 것	
	응시자 작성 내용 3	
전개3 (30분)	✓ 모둠 토의 내용을 바탕으로 <자료 4>를 완성하게 할 것 ✓ <자료 4>에 관한 글쓰기 조건 3가지를 제시할 것	
	✓ <자료 4>의 결과물을 공유하는 활동을 진행할 것	
마무리 (5분)	*활동 마무리, 다음 차시 안내 *주변 정리 지도, 인사	

라 연습문제 4회 : 2021 기출 변형

Classroom settings

- Class time : 90 minutes
- Students : 24 Middle school 3rd Graders
- Level : Mixed
- Aids : Digital whiteboard, Laptop, Online dictionary, Tablet PCs etc

Lesson information

- Unit title : Healthy Body, Healthy Mind
- Objectives
  - ✓ Students will be able to understand the negative effects of unhealthy foods.
  - ✓ Students will be able to create healthy food in groups.
  - ✓ Students will be able to introduce how to make healthy food to the class.

지시사항

- 응시자 작성 내용 1
  - ✓ <자료 1>의 메뉴를 비교하며 무엇을 더 좋아하는지 말해보도록 할 것
  - ✓ <자료 2>의 주제를 파악하고 제목 짓기 활동을 진행할 것

- 응시자 작성 내용 2
  - ✓ <자료 2>의 내용을 바탕으로 <자료 3>을 완성할 것
  - ✓ <자료 3> 활동 진행 시 학생 수준별 맞춤 지도를 실시할 것
  - ✓ <자료 2>의 'It ... that' 표현을 설명하고 학생의 이해를 확인할 것

- 응시자 작성 내용 3
  - ✓ <자료 4>의 활동 이해를 돕기 위한 교사의 예시를 제시할 것
  - ✓ <자료 4>를 완성하고 모둠 발표를 진행할 것

- 응시자 작성 내용 4
  - ✓ 모둠 발표에 관한 동료 평가 기준을 4가지 제시할 것
  - ✓ 발표 후 청중의 태도에 관한 피드백을 제공할 것

(1) 문제

<자료 1>

<Which menu do you like better?>	
Menu A	Menu B
• Tofu Bibimbap • Grilled Chicken Breast Salad • Steamed Broccoli • Fresh Fruit with Greek Yougurt	• Fried Chicken with French Fries • Bacon and Onion Rings • Macaroni and Cheese • Cookie and Cream Ice cream

<자료 2>

Fried foods, like French fries and fried chicken, are yummy and easy to find. But it is these kinds of oily foods that we should avoid! Eating them too much can't be good for teenagers. When teenagers eat lots of fried foods, they can gain too much weight. These foods also can hurt their heart, making them sick. In addition, eating fried food too much can cause stomachache and make it hard to digest food. Moreover, it is our brain that we should worry about. Eating these foods can make it harder for teenagers to do well in school. Some research shows that eating unhealthy food has a negative effect on students' test scores.

<자료 3>

<Why should we avoid eating fried food?>
1.
2.
3.
4.
5. *(Your idea)*

<자료 4>

	Food name : How to make it 1. 2. 3. 4. … The reason why we recommend this food : _____
(Draw your food here)	

(2) 지도안

단원명	Healthy Body, Healthy Mind				시간	90 mins
대상	• Students : 24 Middle school 3rd Graders • Level : Mixed					
수업 목표	✓ Students will be able to understand the negative effects of unhealthy foods. ✓ Students will be able to create healthy food in groups. ✓ Students will be able to introduce how to make healthy food to the class.					
교수·학습 교구	Digital whiteboard, Laptop, Online dictionary, Tablet PCs etc					
핵심역량	자기 관리	지식정보처리	창의적 사고	심미적 감성	협력적 소통	공동체
		✓	✓	✓	✓	

<교수 학습 지도안>

단계	교수·학습 활동	유의점
도입 (5분)	*인사, 출석 확인, 교실 내 안전 점검 *학습 주제, 수업 준비 상태 확인	
전개1 (25분)	응시자 작성 내용 1 ✓ <자료 1>의 메뉴를 비교하며 무엇을 더 좋아하는지 말해보도록 할 것 ✓ <자료 2>의 주제를 파악하고 제목 짓기 활동을 진행할 것	

	응시자 작성 내용 2
	✓ <자료 2>의 내용을 바탕으로 <자료 3>을 완성할 것
전개2 (15분)	✓ <자료 3> 활동 진행 시 학생 수준별 맞춤 지도를 실시할 것
	✓ <자료 2>의 'It ... that' 표현을 설명하고 학생의 이해를 확인할 것

전개3 (30분)	응시자 작성 내용 3
	✓ <자료 4>의 활동 이해를 돕기 위한 교사의 예시를 제시할 것
	✓ <자료 4>를 완성하고 모둠 발표를 진행할 것

전개4 (10분)	**응시자 작성 내용 4** ✓ 모둠 발표에 관한 동료 평가 기준을 4가지 제시할 것 ✓ 발표 후 청중의 태도에 관한 피드백을 제공할 것
마무리 (5분)	*활동 마무리, 다음 차시 안내 *주변 정리 지도, 인사

마 연습문제 5회 : 2020 기출 변형

Classroom settings

- Class time : 100 minutes
- Students : 24 High school 1st Graders
- Level : Mixed
- Aids : Digital whiteboard, Laptop, Online dictionary, Tablet PCs etc

Lesson information

- Unit title : Future Jobs
- Objectives
  ✓ Students will be able to use an appropriate strategy to find the main idea.
  ✓ Students will be able to share their ideas properly in the discussion.
  ✓ Students will be able to introduce their future jobs with their name cards.

지시사항

- 응시자 작성 내용 1
  ✓ <자료 1>에 제시된 미래 직업 분야 중 1개를 예시와 함께 설명할 것
  ✓ <자료 1>을 활용하여 희망 미래 직업 분야의 관심도를 표현하게 할 것

- 응시자 작성 내용 2
  ✓ <자료 2>의 제목을 활용하여 읽기 전 활동을 진행할 것
  ✓ <자료 2>의 주제를 읽기 전략을 사용하여 파악하도록 할 것
  ✓ <자료 2>를 활용하여 모둠 토의를 실시하고 그 결과를 공유할 것

- 응시자 작성 내용 3
  ✓ <자료 3>을 활용하여 말하기 활동을 진행할 것
  ✓ <자료 3>의 직업 중 1개를 선택하여 <자료 4>를 완성할 것

- 응시자 작성 내용 4
  ✓ 블랜디드 수업 환경을 활용하여 <자료 4>에 대한 동료 평가를 실시할 것
  ✓ 동료 평가 활동에 대한 교사의 긍정적 피드백을 제공할 것

(1) 문제

<자료 1>

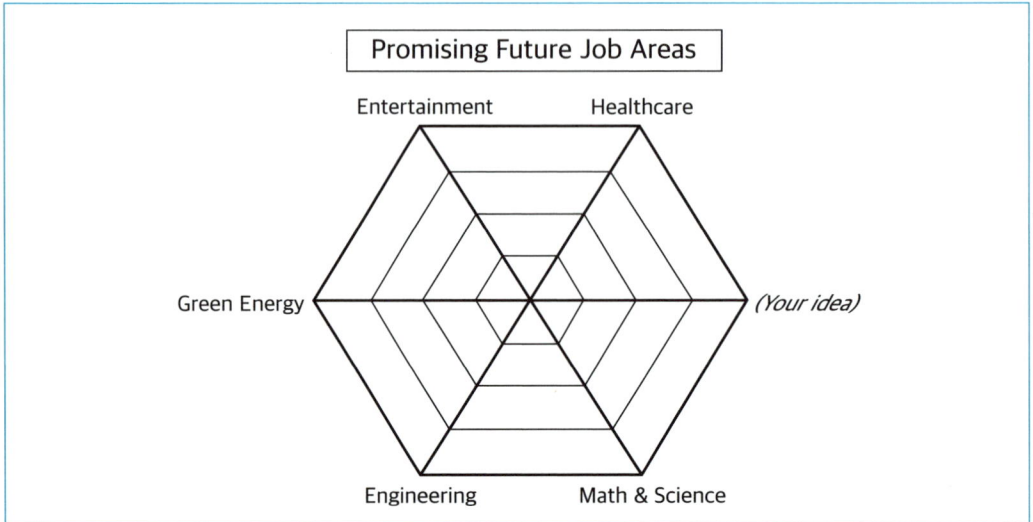

<자료 2>

<Where did Elevator Operators Go?>

As technology got better, elevators changed a lot. In the past, people called elevator operators helped us go up and down in buildings. They pressed buttons and made sure everything was safe. But now, elevators can do these things all by themselves! They have special buttons we can press to choose where we want to go. Because of this, we don't need elevator operators anymore. Technology helps us move in elevators more easily and safely without needing someone to do it for us.

Discussion question

Q. 'Technology replaces jobs', do you agree with this? Why or why not?
Q. What should we do to prepare for the future?

<자료 3>

<Promising Future Jobs>
My Job Area :
Job examples from your area
1. *(Your idea)*
2. *(Friend's idea)*
3. *(Friend's idea - optional)*
4. *(Friend's idea - optional)*

<자료 4>

(Note for teachers : This material is individually assigned to students in Online Classroom)

<My Future Name Card>

Directions : Make your future name card and give some explanations about it.

(Your Photo)	• **Personal info.** *(Your name)* *(Your job)* • **Contacts** *(Your Phone number)* *(Your E-mail)*

I'm interested in ___*(My Job Area)*___ . Therefore, I want to be a ___*(My Job)*___ . To explain this job, it is _____. There are two reasons why I think this is promising in the future. First, _____.
Second, _____.

(2) 지도안

단원명	Future Jobs				시간	100 mins
대상	• Students : 24 High school 1st Graders • Level : Mixed					
수업 목표	✓ Students will be able to use an appropriate strategy to find the main idea. ✓ Students will be able to share their ideas properly in the discussion. ✓ Students will be able to introduce their future jobs with their name cards.					
교수·학습 교구	Digital whiteboard, Laptop, Online dictionary, Tablet PCs etc					
핵심역량	자기 관리	지식정보처리	창의적 사고	심미적 감성	협력적 소통	공동체
	✓	✓			✓	

<교수 학습 지도안>

단계	교수·학습 활동	유의점
도입 (5분)	*인사, 출석 확인, 교실 내 안전 점검 *학습 주제, 수업 준비 상태 확인	
전개1 (15분)	응시자 작성 내용 1 ✓ <자료 1>에 제시된 미래 직업 분야 중 1개를 예시와 함께 설명할 것 ──────────────── ──────────────── ──────────────── ──────────────── ──────────────── ──────────────── ──────────────── ──────────────── ✓ <자료 1>을 활용하여 희망 미래 직업 분야의 관심도를 표현하게 할 것 ──────────────── ──────────────── ──────────────── ──────────────── ──────────────── ──────────────── ──────────────── ────────────────	

	응시자 작성 내용 2
전개2 (25분)	✓ <자료 2>의 제목을 활용하여 읽기 전 활동을 진행할 것
	✓ <자료 2>의 주제를 읽기 전략을 사용하여 파악하도록 할 것
	✓ <자료 2>를 활용하여 모둠 토의를 실시하고 그 결과를 공유할 것

전개3 (40분)	응시자 작성 내용 3
	✓ <자료 3>을 활용하여 말하기 활동을 진행할 것
	✓ <자료 3>의 직업 중 1개를 선택하여 <자료 4>를 완성할 것

전개4 (10분)	응시자 작성 내용 4
	✓ 블랜디드 수업 환경을 활용하여 <자료 4>에 대한 동료 평가를 실시할 것

	✓ 동료 평가 활동에 대한 교사의 긍정적 피드백을 제공할 것	
마무리 (5분)	*활동 마무리, 다음 차시 안내 *주변 정리 지도, 인사	

바 연습문제 6회 : 2019 기출 변형

📖 Classroom settings

- Class time : 90 minutes
- Students : 24 Middle school 3rd Graders
- Level : Mixed
- Aids : Digital whiteboard, Laptop, Online dictionary, Tablet PCs etc

📖 Lesson information

- Unit title : Change Makers
- Objectives
  ✓ Students will be able to find paragraph structure of the reading text.
  ✓ Students will be able to share their ideas properly in the discussion.
  ✓ Students will be able to write their suggestions for the better school.

📖 지시사항

- **응시자 작성 내용 1**
  ✓ <자료 1>에 제시된 사진을 보고 대화를 나누어보는 짝 활동을 진행할 것
  ✓ <자료 1>에 관한 대화 주제 1가지를 교사가 제시할 것

- **응시자 작성 내용 2**
  ✓ <자료 2>의 밑줄 친 단어를 맥락을 활용하여 지도할 것
  ✓ <자료 2>의 주제를 파악하도록 할 것
  ✓ <자료 2>의 글의 구조를 언급하며 세부 정보를 찾는 활동을 진행할 것

- **응시자 작성 내용 3**
  ✓ <자료 3>을 활용하여 모둠 토의를 진행할 것
  ✓ 토의 중 모둠을 순회하며 촉진자 역할을 수행할 것

- **응시자 작성 내용 4**
  ✓ 토의 내용을 바탕으로 <자료4>를 완성할 것
  ✓ 실제적 목표를 제시하여 활동 참여 동기 부여를 할 것

(1) 문제

<자료 1>

<자료 2>

Today, I want to talk about recycling PET bottles. It's essential to recycle them properly to help the environment.

Here's how: First, empty the bottles completely and make sure that nothing is left inside. Second, rinse the bottles quickly to prepare them for recycling. Finally, take a moment to remove any caps and labels from the PET bottles.

By recycling PET bottles correctly, we can all make a positive impact on our planet. Thank you for your attention, and let's work together to create a greener future.

<자료 3>

<자료 4>

<Our Suggestions For The Better School!>

Introduction

Today, we want to talk about _____
_____

Body

Here's how : _____
_____
_____
_____

Conclusion

_____
Thank you for your attention, and let's make our school better together!

(2) 지도안

단원명	Change Makers				시간	90 mins
대상	• Students : 24 Middle school 3rd Graders • Level : Mixed					
수업 목표	✓ Students will be able to find paragraph structure of the reading text. ✓ Students will be able to share their ideas properly in the discussion. ✓ Students will be able to write their suggestions for the better school.					
교수·학습 교구	Digital whiteboard, Laptop, Online dictionary, Tablet PCs etc					
핵심역량	자기 관리	지식정보처리	창의적 사고	심미적 감성	협력적 소통	공동체
		✓			✓	✓

<교수 학습 지도안>

단계	교수·학습 활동	유의점
도입 (5분)	*인사, 출석 확인, 교실 내 안전 점검 *학습 주제, 수업 준비 상태 확인	
전개1 (10분)	**응시자 작성 내용 1** ✓ <자료 1>에 제시된 사진을 보고 대화를 나누어보는 짝 활동을 진행할 것 ✓ <자료 1>에 관한 대화 주제 1가지를 교사가 제시할 것	
전개2 (15분)	**응시자 작성 내용 2** ✓ <자료 2>의 밑줄 친 단어를 맥락을 활용하여 지도할 것	

	✓ <자료 2>의 주제를 파악하도록 할 것	
	✓ <자료 2>의 글의 구조를 언급하며 세부 정보를 찾는 활동을 진행할 것	
전개3 (25분)	응시자 작성 내용 3	
	✓ <자료 3>을 활용하여 모둠 토의를 진행할 것	

	✓ 토의 중 모둠을 순회하며 촉진자 역할을 수행할 것	

전개4 (30분)	응시자 작성 내용 4	
	✓ 토의 내용을 바탕으로 <자료4>를 완성할 것	
	✓ 실제적 목표를 제시하여 활동 참여 동기 부여를 할 것	

마무리 (5분)	*활동 마무리, 다음 차시 안내 *주변 정리 지도, 인사	

연습문제 7회 : 2018 기출 변형

Classroom settings

- Class time : 90 minutes
- Students : 24 Middle school 3rd Graders
- Level : Mixed
- Aids : Digital whiteboard, Laptop, Online dictionary, Tablet PCs etc

Lesson information

- Unit title : Better Safe Than Sorry
- Objectives
  - ✓ Students will be able to understand how to use a fire extinguisher.
  - ✓ Students will be able to compare two different content delivery formats.
  - ✓ Students will be able to make fire safety posters with visual aids.

지시사항

- 응시자 작성 내용 1
  - ✓ <자료 1>의 밑줄 친 단어 중 1개를 선택하여 그 의미를 추론할 수 있도록 지도할 것
  - ✓ <자료 1>을 활용하여 수업 주제에 관한 관심과 흥미를 유도할 것

- 응시자 작성 내용 2
  - ✓ <자료 2>의 제목을 보고 글의 내용을 추론하도록 할 것
  - ✓ 읽기 전략을 사용하여 <자료 2>의 주제를 파악하도록 할 것
  - ✓ 글의 제목과 연관지어 <자료 2>의 세부 정보에 대한 이해 확인 질문을 제시할 것
  - ✓ 내용 전달 방법의 관점에서 <자료 3>의 내용을 비교하도록 할 것

- 응시자 작성 내용 3
  - ✓ 모둠을 구성하고 개인별 역할을 부여할 것
  - ✓ 조건 2개를 제시하여 <자료 4>를 완성하도록 할 것
  - ✓ 활동 결과에 대한 긍정적 피드백을 2가지 제공할 것

(1) 문제
<자료 1>

<True or False?>

1. It's okay to play with matches or lighters. (T/F)
2. If you smell smoke, you should find where it started from by yourself. (T/F)
3. You should have a fire escape plan and practice it. (T/F)
4. If there's smoke in the room, it's safer to crawl on the floor to escape. (T/F)
5. It's okay to use an elevator during a fire. (T/F)

<자료 2>

<Remember PASS!>

It's very important to know where the fire extinguisher is in your classroom. Do you know where it is? Awesome! Using a fire extinguisher is easy if you remember the word 'PASS'. First, you should pull the pin at the top of the extinguisher to unlock it. Next, you should aim the nozzle at the base of the fire, not at the flames, so you can put out the fire. Then, you should squeeze the handle to spray the fire-stopping stuff. Finally, you should sweep the nozzle from side to side to cover the area of the fire until it is out.

<자료 3>

1	2
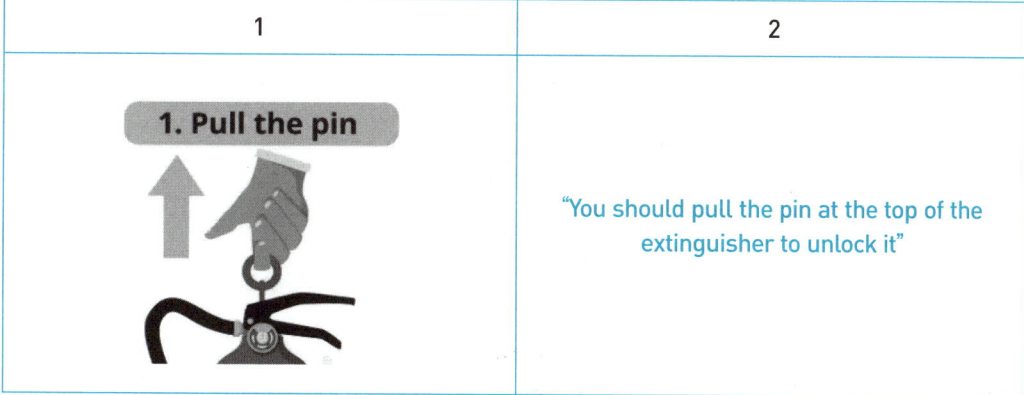	"You should pull the pin at the top of the extinguisher to unlock it"

<자료 4>

<Remember PASS!>	
① Pull the pin	② _____
	(Your drawing here)
③ _____	④ _____
(Your drawing here)	(Your drawing here)
Where is the fire extinguisher in my school? *(Optional)*	

(2) 지도안

단원명	Better Safe Than Sorry				시간	90 mins
대상	• Students : 24 Middle school 3rd Graders • Level : Mixed					
수업 목표	✓ Students will be able to understand how to use a fire extinguisher. ✓ Students will be able to compare two different content delivery formats. ✓ Students will be able to make fire safety posters with visual aids.					
교수·학습 교구	Digital whiteboard, Laptop, Online dictionary, Tablet PCs etc					
핵심역량	자기 관리	지식정보처리	창의적 사고	심미적 감성	협력적 소통	공동체
		✓			✓	✓

<교수 학습 지도안>

단계	교수·학습 활동	유의점
도입 (5분)	*인사, 출석 확인, 교실 내 안전 점검 *학습 주제, 수업 준비 상태 확인	
전개1 (20분)	**응시자 작성 내용 1** ✓ <자료 1>의 밑줄 친 단어 중 1개를 선택하여 그 의미를 추론할 수 있도록 지도할 것 ✓ <자료 1>을 활용하여 수업 주제에 관한 관심과 흥미를 유도할 것	

		응시자 작성 내용 2	
전개2 **(30분)**		✓ <자료 2>의 제목을 보고 글의 내용을 추론하도록 할 것	
		✓ 읽기 전략을 사용하여 <자료 2>의 주제를 파악하도록 할 것	
		✓ 글의 제목과 연관지어 <자료 2>의 세부 정보에 대한 이해 확인 질문을 제시할 것	
		✓ 내용 전달 방법의 관점에서 <자료 3>의 내용을 비교하도록 할 것	

	응시자 작성 내용 3	
	✓ 모둠을 구성하고 개인별 역할을 부여할 것	
전개3 (30분)		
	✓ 조건 2개를 제시하여 <자료 4>를 완성하도록 할 것	
	✓ 활동 결과에 대한 긍정적 피드백을 2가지 제공할 것	
마무리 (5분)	*활동 마무리, 다음 차시 안내 *주변 정리 지도, 인사	

아 연습문제 8회 : 2017 기출 변형

Classroom settings

- Class time : 90 minutes
- Students : 26 Middle school 2rd Graders
- Level : Mixed
- Aids : Digital whiteboard, Laptop, Online dictionary, Tablet PCs etc

Lesson information

- Unit title : Neighbor Hero
- Objectives
  - ✓ Students will be able to find detailed information based on 5W1H.
  - ✓ Students will be able to interview their friends based on 5W1H.
  - ✓ Students will be able to report the story based on their interviews.

지시사항

- 응시자 작성 내용 1
  - ✓ <자료 1>의 그림을 활용하여 짝 활동을 진행할 것
  - ✓ 짝 활동 결과를 교실 전체에 공유하며 학생과 상호작용 할 것

- 응시자 작성 내용 2
  - ✓ <자료 2>의 주제를 파악하도록 할 것
  - ✓ <자료 2>에서 세부 정보를 찾아 <자료 3>을 완성할 것
  - ✓ <자료 3> 활동 시 어려움을 겪는 학생에게 적절한 도움을 제공할 것

- 응시자 작성 내용 3
  - ✓ <자료 4> 활동을 위한 교사의 예시를 제공하고 인터뷰를 진행할 것
  - ✓ <자료 4>를 바탕으로 <자료 5>를 완성할 것
  - ✓ <자료 5>에 대한 발표 평가 기준 3가지를 제시하고 발표를 진행할 것

(1) 문제
<자료 1>

?

<자료 2>

<Teenager Saves Neighbor from Fire>

In the quiet neighborhood of Oakwood Heights, a teenager named Adam became a hero last night. At precisely 11:45 PM, as he was walking home from a friend's house, passing by Elm Street, he saw smoke coming from a neighbor's house and quickly acted. Adam broke a window and went inside to save the old person who couldn't get out. He helped them get to safety before the fire got worse. Adam's bravery happened late at night when everyone was sleeping because he cared about his neighbor and didn't want them to get hurt. Because of him, a big problem was stopped, and now everyone in the neighborhood is thankful and proud of him.

<자료 3>

<5W1H Questions>

#	5W1H	Questions	answer
1	who	Who became a hero last night?	
2	what	What did he do?	
3	when	When did he saw the smoke?	
4	where	Where was the smoke coming from?	
5	how	How did he help the old person?	
6	why	Why did he do such a brave job?	

<자료 4>

		<Friend Interview>	
#	5W1H	Questions	Your answer
1	who	Who is your interviewee?	
2	what	What did he/she do?	
3	when	When did he/she do it?	
4	where	Where did he/she do it?	
5	how	How did he/she do it?	
6	why	Why did he/she do it?	

<자료 5>

(Note for teachers : This material is individually assigned to students in Online Classroom)

Headline : _____

(photo here)

(2) 지도안

단원명	Neighbor Hero				시간	90 mins
대상	• Students : 26 Middle school 2rd Graders • Level : Mixed					
수업 목표	✓ Students will be able to find detailed information based on 5W1H. ✓ Students will be able to interview their friends based on 5W1H. ✓ Students will be able to report the story based on their interviews.					
교수·학습 교구	Digital whiteboard, Laptop, Online dictionary, Tablet PCs etc					
핵심역량	자기 관리	지식정보처리	창의적 사고	심미적 감성	협력적 소통	공동체
		✓			✓	

<교수 학습 지도안>

단계	교수·학습 활동	유의점
도입 (5분)	*인사, 출석 확인, 교실 내 안전 점검 *학습 주제, 수업 준비 상태 확인	
전개1 (15분)	응시자 작성 내용 1 ✓ <자료 1>의 그림을 활용하여 짝 활동을 진행할 것 ✓ 짝 활동 결과를 교실 전체에 공유하며 학생과 상호작용 할 것	

	응시자 작성 내용 2	
	✓ <자료 2>의 주제를 파악하도록 할 것	

전개2 (25분)

	응시자 작성 내용 2 (계속)	
	✓ <자료 2>에서 세부 정보를 찾아 <자료 3>을 완성할 것 ✓ <자료 3> 활동 시 어려움을 겪는 학생에게 적절한 도움을 제공할 것	

전개3 (40분)

	응시자 작성 내용 3	
	✓ <자료 4> 활동을 위한 교사의 예시를 제공하고 인터뷰를 진행할 것	

	✓ <자료 4>를 바탕으로 <자료 5>를 완성할 것	
	✓ <자료 5>에 대한 발표 평가 기준 3가지를 제시하고 발표를 진행할 것	
마무리 (5분)	*활동 마무리, 다음 차시 안내 *주변 정리 지도, 인사	

Chapter 02

예시답안 & 스크립트

가 연습문제 1회 : 2024 기출 변형

(1) 판서 노트 및 예시 영상

수업실연 예시
2024 기출 변형
동영상 바로가기

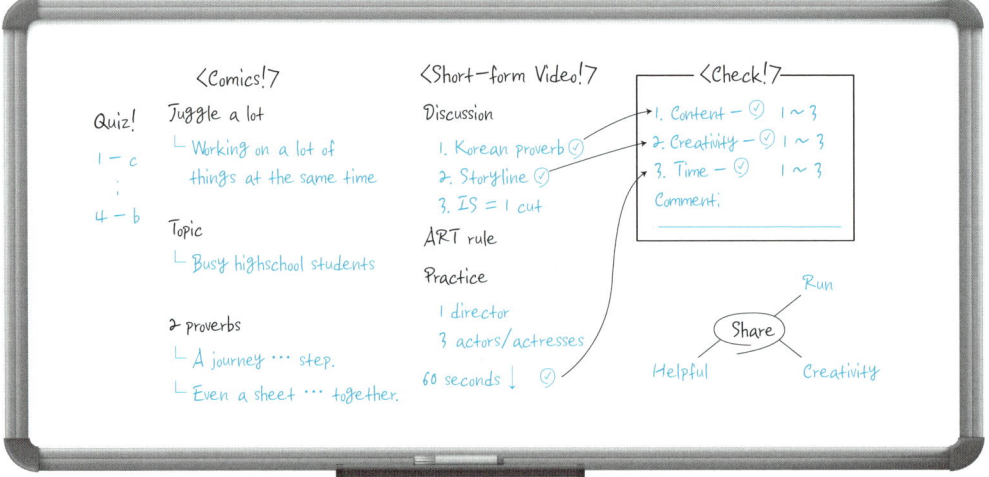

(2) 지도안 예시

단원명	Spread Wisdom				시간	100 mins
대상	• Students : 24 High school 1st Graders • Level : Mixed					
수업 목표	✓ Students will be able to make comics related to the proverb. ✓ Students will be able to act based on their comics.					
교수·학습 교구	Digital whiteboard, Laptop, Online dictionary, Tablet PCs etc					
핵심역량	자기 관리	지식정보처리	창의적 사고	심미적 감성	협력적 소통	공동체
			✓	✓	✓	✓

<교수 학습 지도안>

단계	교수·학습 활동	유의점
도입 (5분)	*인사, 출석 확인, 교실 내 안전 점검 *학습 주제, 수업 준비 상태 확인	
전개1 (30분)	응시자 작성 내용 1 ✓ <자료 1>의 속담으로 짝 활동을 진행할 것 ●Schema activation • [짝, 5분] 짝을 나누어 <자료 1>의 문제를 함께 풀어보게 한다. • [전체] 정답을 하나씩 맞춰보며 속담의 의미를 확인한다. ● Transition • <자료 1>을 바탕으로 오늘 차시 주제를 예상하도록 하며 <자료 2>를 소개한다. <예시 발화> 교사 : So far, we just finished the short quiz about the Korean proverbs. Then, are you ready to read the story about it? 학생 : Yes, teacher! 교사 : Great! Then, let's go to the second worksheet. ✓ <자료 2>의 밑줄 친 표현을 맥락을 활용하여 지도하고 이해 확인 점검을 진행할 것 ● Teaching Vocabulary • [전체] 밑줄 친 표현에 대해 주목하게 하고 그 의미를 추론할 수 있도록 맥락을 제공한다. <예시 발화> 교사 : Does anyone know the meaning of the underlined expression? … Okay. Let me give you a hint. Let's look at the drawing. How does Paul look? 학생 : I think Paul is working on a lot of things at the same time. 교사 : Like this, drawing can be a great hint for the meaning of the word. • 의미를 성공적으로 추론한 후, 직접 문장을 만들어 보게 함으로써 이해 확인 점검을 실시한다.	

	✓ <자료 2>를 읽고 빈칸에 들어갈 속담 두 가지를 <자료 1>에서 찾아보게 할 것

● **Story line**
- [개별, 3분] Skimming 전략을 사용하여 <자료 2>의 Topic을 파악하게 한다.
  - 빠른 속도로 글을 훑어보며 전체 이야기의 흐름을 알 수 있도록 안내한다.
- 아래 지도 사항에 따라 순회 지도를 실시한다.

> <순회 지도 사항>
> - 참여를 북돋우며 활동에 어려움을 겪는 학생을 찾는다.
> - Low-level : <자료 2> 뒤편의 <Vocabulary list>를 제시한다. 만화의 특성을 이용하여 인물의 행동이나 표정으로 단어의 의미를 유추할 수 있도록 안내한다.

- [전체] 학생과의 상호작용을 통해 Topic을 정리한다.
  - Topic : Busy high school students

전개1 (20분)

● **Find the proverbs**
- [개별, 5분] <자료 2>의 어떤 부분이 <자료 1>의 어떤 속담과 연결될지 찾도록 한다.
- Scanning 전략을 지도하여 질문에 대한 답을 찾도록 한다.
  - 글 전체가 아니라 필요한 부분만 선별하여 읽도록 한다.
- 아래 지도 사항에 따라 순회 지도를 실시한다.

> <순회 지도 사항>
> - 참여를 북돋우며 활동 중 어려움을 겪고 있는 학생을 파악한다.
> - High-level : 활동 참여에 대한 긍정적 피드백을 제공하고, Student teacher 역할을 부여하여 다른 학생을 도울 수 있도록 한다.
> - Low-level : 동료 학습자로부터 도움을 받을 수 있도록 Peer-scaffolding을 유도한다.

- [전체] 학생과의 상호작용을 통해 답변 공유하고 판서한다.
  - Paul "I need to do step by step" → A journey of a thousand miles begins with a single step
  - Jessica "We can help each other as well" → Even a sheet of paper is lighter when lifted together

	응시자 작성 내용 2
	✓ 실제적 목적을 제시하여 <자료 3>에 대한 학생의 동기를 강화할 것
	● **Transition** • <자료 2>의 내용을 바탕으로 <자료 3>을 소개한다. <예시 발화> 교사 : So far, we just finished reading comics using Korean proverbs. Then, why don't we make our own comics, using different proverbs? ● **Giving authentic purpose** • <자료 3>에 대한 참여 동기를 강화하기 위하여 완성 작품을 토대로 Short-form videos of Korean proverb를 만들 것이라고 언급한다. <예시 발화> 교사 : I'm telling you that this is going to be a huge project. Guess what? We are going to make short-form videos of Korean proverbs based on the comics, so that many foreign people can learn Korean easily. How does that sound? … Awesome!
전개2 (35분)	✓ 모둠을 구성하고 <자료 3>을 완성하도록 할 것
	● **Grouping** • 4인 1조를 구성하여 총 여섯 모둠을 만든다. • [모둠, 10분] 다음과 같은 안내 사항과 함께 그룹 논의를 진행한다. • 1) Korean proverb를 정할 것, 2) Storyline을 만들 것, 3) 각자 Cut #1~#4 중 하나를 맡을 것 • 아래 ART rule을 지키도록 독려한다. < ART rule > A : Active participation, R : Respect others, T : Take turns • [모둠, 20분] 위 1)~3) 내용이 모두 정해졌는지 그룹별로 확인하고 <자료 3>을 완성하도록 한다. • 교사는 아래 지도 사항에 따라 순회 지도를 실시한다. <순회 지도 사항> • 참여를 북돋우며 활동 중 어려움을 겪고 있는 학생을 파악한다. • Low level : 교사가 준비한 'Korean proverb dictionary'를 제공한다. • High level : 긍정적 피드백을 제공한 뒤, 남은 시간 동안 해당 속담으로 다른 Storyline을 만들어 볼 것을 제안한다.

	✓ <자료 3>의 내용으로 연극 발표 연습을 진행할 것	
	● Practice for acting • [모둠, 3분] 연극 발표 준비 과정으로 아래와 같이 역할을 상의하여 나눈다. 　• Director (1명), Actor/Actress (3명) 　• 각 역할은 그룹 내 토의로 정하도록 하고, 서로의 의견을 존중할 것을 강조한다. 　　• Director : Lead the group, record videos 　　• Actor/Actress : Perform based on the storyline • [모둠, 15분] 주어진 시간 동안 연극 발표 준비를 할 수 있도록 안내한다. 　• 60초 이내로 연극이 진행될 수 있도록 안내한다.	
전개3 (25분)	응시자 작성 내용 3	
	✓ <자료 4>의 평가 기준을 3가지 제시할 것	
	● Check list • 학생들에게 <자료 4>를 소개한다. • 상호작용을 통해 Check list를 완성한다. <예시 발화> 교사 : What are the important things in the presentation? 학생 : I think it should include the Korean proverb. 교사 : Right! So, the first part is 'Content', which means 'Korean proverb.' • 예시: <Peer evaluation> | 1. Content | Korean proverb | | | 2. Creativity | Storyline | | | 3. Time | 60 seconds | | Comments : _____ • <Peer evaluation>의 항목이 이전 활동 <글쓰기 조건> 및 <연극 조건>과 연결됨을 보여주며 교수 내용과 평가가 일치함을 강조한다. • 연극 발표를 진행하고 <Peer evaluation>을 작성하도록 한다.	
	✓ 발표에 관한 학생의 소감을 듣고 피드백을 제공할 것	
	● Giving feedback • [전체] 발표가 끝난 후 발표 내용에 대하여 학생과 상호작용하며 활동 참여에 관한 긍정적 피드백을 제공한다. <예시 발화> 교사 : Can anyone share your idea of the presentation? … Thank you everyone! However, I was so impressed that you were all very creative story writers, professional directors and passionate actors and actresses! Thank you again for the great performances!	
마무리 (5분)	*활동 마무리, 다음 차시 안내 *주변 정리 지도, 인사	

(3) 스크립트

> 응시자 작성 내용 1

✓ 〈자료 1〉의 속담으로 짝 활동을 진행할 것

Okay, students, so far we've talked about the unit title and the lesson objectives. Then, are you guys ready for the English class? Great! Then, let me give you this worksheet. So, take one and pass them to the back. Take one and pass them to the back. 수현 at the back, did you get the worksheet? Perfect! Then, what do you see on the worksheet? Yes, there are famous Korean proverbs, right? So from now on, with your partner... So, 수현, 현수 you two! 종민, 민종, you two! You two ... Does everyone have their partners? Then let's begin today's class with a short quiz. So it's 'Quiz time!'

So, from now on, I'm going to give you five minutes, five minutes to talk with your partner and match the famous Korean proverb. Okay? Five minutes, go! One minute left, students. Does anyone need more time? Okay, time's up. So let's check the answers together. What's the first one? "A journey of 1,000 miles..." What's next? Yes, 지원! "...begins with a single step." So the answer is C. And what was the last one? "Even a sheet of paper is lighter..." And what's next? Yes, 소민! Yes, "...when lifted together." So four and B. All right, so far we just finished answering those quizzes. Then, can you guys guess today's topic for this class? Yes, 동우! Yes, today we are going to learn about Korean proverbs. Are you guys excited? Perfect!

✓ 〈자료 2〉의 밑줄 친 표현을 맥락을 활용하여 지도하고 이해 확인 점검을 진행할 것

Then, everyone, let's look at the second worksheet.

What do you see on the second worksheet? Yes, 종민! Yes, there are comics, right? So from now on, we are going to read comics. So it's 'Comics time!' However, before we read, what do we have to do first? Yes, 민수! Yes, we need to learn some difficult words, right? So, everyone, let's quickly read the comics. There is an underlined sentence. Can you read? What a loud voice! Awesome! Yes, the underlined sentence was "I am juggling a lot." So before reading, we are going to learn this expression. So, "juggling a lot." Is there anyone who's familiar with this expression? All right, then let me give you a hint. Everyone, let's look at the drawing. How does Paul look? Does it look good or bad? Yes, 다원! Yes, he doesn't look so good, right? Then, let's look at the second cut. What kinds of subjects can you see on Paul's hands? Yes, 민수! Yes, there is science and … Yes, 현정! Yes, mathematics. Yes, 민재! Yes, there is history, right? So Paul is doing all of these subjects. Then, can you guess the meaning of "juggling a lot?" Yes, 은우! Oh, did everyone hear what 은우 just said? He said, "juggling a lot" means working on a lot of things at the same time. So "juggling a lot" means working on a lot of things, how? Yes, "at the same time!"

So … "at the same time." Then, 현우! Can you make a sentence with this expression? Yes, "Juggling a lot can be very stressful." That's a great sentence and that's true. So, like this, remember that in comics, drawings can be a great hint for the meanings of the words. Okay? Great!

✓ 〈자료 2〉를 읽고 빈칸에 들어갈 속담 두 가지를 〈자료 1〉에서 찾아보게 할 것

Okay, so far we just finished learning these difficult words. Then, are you guys ready for reading comics? Great! So, from now on, we are going to find the topic. However, to find the topic, do we have to read quickly or slowly? Yes, 재원! Yes, we need to read quickly, right? So you don't have to read every single word, just read quickly and find the topic. I'm going to give you three minutes. Three minutes, go! Oh, 은정, do you need any help? Oh, the words are so difficult? Then why don't you look at the back of the worksheet. What do you see? Yes, there is a vocabulary list. So with this vocabulary list, can you find the topic by yourself? Perfect, keep up the good work! One minute left, students. Okay, time's up. So let's check the topics together. So, what was the topic of these comics? Yes, 수현! Oh, did everyone hear what 수현 just said? She said the topic of these comics is … "Busy high school students", right? Great! So the topic of these comics was … "Busy high school students." All right, so we just found the topic like this. Then, are you guys ready to read comics a little bit more closely? Awesome!

Then, 민수! What do you see below the comics? Yes, there are "Related proverbs", right? So from now on, I'm going to give you five minutes, five minutes to read the comics again and find the two related proverbs from the first worksheet. Okay? However, to find this kind of specific information, do we have to read the text from the beginning to the end or just read the necessary part? Yes, 종민! Yes, we can read the necessary part, right? So, I'm going to give you five minutes, five minutes to read the text again and find two related proverbs from the first worksheet. All right? Five minutes, go! Oh, 현우, are you already finished? Oh, what a quick reader! Then why don't you help your partner, 우현? I heard 우현 needs some help. Can you do that? Perfect! So like this, friends can be a better teacher. One minute left, students. Okay, time's up. So let's check the answers together. What were the two proverbs, two proverbs related to these comics? What was the first one? Yes, 희원! "A journey of a thousand miles begins with a single step." So let me write here, "A journey of a thousand miles begins with a single step." And 희원, how did you find it? Oh, yes! Did everyone hear what 희원 just said? She said she could find this proverb because Paul said, "I need to do step by step." That's a great job, 희원! And what was the second one? Yes, 지환! "Even a sheet of paper is lighter when lifted together," right? So the second one was … "Even a sheet of paper is lighter when…", how? Yes, "when lifted together." So … "when lifted together" It was the second proverb. 지환, how did you find it? Yes, that was because Jessica just said, "We can help each other as well."

응시자 작성 내용 2

✓ 실제적 목적을 제시하여 〈자료 3〉에 대한 학생의 동기를 강화할 것

So far we just finished reading the comics twice: One for the topic and another for the proverb. Then, why don't we make our own comics with another proverb? Because there are so many proverbs in the Korean language. How does that sound? Are you guys excited? Perfect! So everyone, let's look at the third worksheet. What do you see? Yes, 현정! Yes, it says, "Let's make comics," right? However, everyone, look at here! I want to tell you that this is going to be a huge project because we are going to actually make a short-form video with these comics. Are you guys interested? Awesome! So let's make a short-form video. So … "Short-form video." So, like I just said, we are going to make a short-form video based on the third worksheet. Okay? This video will be actually sent to the international students, and these videos will be very helpful to students who want to learn Korean. All right? Great! Then, are you guys ready for making comics? Perfect!

✓ 모둠을 구성하고 〈자료 3〉을 완성하도록 할 것

So we are going to do this in groups. 수현, 현수, 종민, 민종, you four! You four … You four … And finally, the last group, you four! So, everyone is in the group? Okay! So from now on, with your group members, we are going to complete the third worksheet. However, before we start, there are several things we need to decide. To decide something, what do we need? Yes, 현수! Yes, we need a discussion, right? So, it's time for the discussion. "Discussion." So, everyone, let's look at the screen. 재우, over there, do you see the screen? All right, so what do you see on the screen? Yes, there are discussion topics, right? So can you read the first one? Yes, so like this, in the discussion, you need to decide the Korean proverb. Okay? So first one, you need to decide the Korean proverb. And what's the second one? Yes, 현우! Yes, like 현우 just said, to make comics, we need a storyline, right? So with your group members, you are going to decide the storyline. All right? So second, you need to decide the storyline. And for the last discussion topic, how many cuts can you see in the third worksheet? Yes, 지환! Yes, there are four cuts, right? So one student should take one cut. Okay? I want you to decide who will take which cut. Okay? However, whenever we have this kind of discussion, which rule do we have to follow? Yes, 희원! Yes, we need to follow the ART rule, right? Don't forget about the ART rule. So what was 'A'? Yes, 민재! Yes, 'A' was 'Active participation.' And what was 'R'? Yes, 동규! Yes, it was 'Respect others.' So make sure you're respecting your friends' ideas. All right? And what was 'T'? Yes, 유진! Yes, 'T' was 'Take turns', right? So make sure everyone gets a chance to talk. Okay?

I'm going to give you ten minutes, 10 minutes to do what, group two? Yes, discuss and decide these topics. Okay, ten minutes, go! Oh, group five, do you need any help? Oh, it is too hard to decide the Korean proverb? Then why don't you use this? What do you see? Yes, it's a Korean proverb dictionary. There are many kinds of Korean proverbs in this dictionary. So, would it be helpful for your group discussion? Awesome! So if you need any more help, just feel free to call me. All right? One minute left, students. Okay, time's up. So, are you guys finished with the discussion? All right, so group one! What is your proverb? Okay! And group three! Can you tell us the storyline briefly? Perfect! And group six! Did you guys decide who will take which one? All right, so like this, we just finished the discussion. Then, are you guys ready for the third worksheet? Perfect! So, from now on, I'm going to give you twenty minutes, twenty minutes to make the comics in the third worksheet. Okay? Great!

So, 상민! What are we going to do? Yes, we are going to make comics in the third worksheet. I'm going to give you twenty minutes. Twenty minutes, go! Oh, group four, are you already finished? Wow, what a quick writer and painter! Then why don't you make another storyline with another proverb? Because the more proverbs we have, the more helpful it will be to the international students. Can you guys do that? Awesome! One minute left, students. Does any group need more time? Okay, time's up!

✓ 〈자료 3〉의 내용으로 연극 발표 연습을 진행할 것

All right, so we just finished making the comics. Then, are you ready for the short-form video? Perfect! So, from now on, we are going to do some practice for acting. All right? So ... let's have a 'Practice.' However, to start the practice, we need to decide the roles, right? So, to make a video, what kind of roles do we need? Yes, 재원! Yes, we need a director. And what else? Yes, 희원! Yes, we need actors and actresses, right? Then, from now on, we are going to decide one director ... one director and three actors or actresses. Okay? So I'm going to give you three minutes, three minutes to talk with your group members and decide the roles. All right? Make sure you're respecting your friends. Three minutes, decide your roles. Go!

Okay, time's up! Have you guys decided the roles? So directors, raise your hand. All right, so what do you guys have to do? Yes, you need to record the video and lead the group. Okay? And actors and actresses, raise your hands. Okay, so what are you guys going to do? Yes, you guys need to perform based on the storyline. All right? So right before you start, let me tell you this. Because we are going to make a short video, there's a time limit. How long would it be? Yes, 동우! Yes, make sure your video is less than sixty seconds. Okay? So make sure your acting is shorter than sixty seconds. I'm going to give you fifteen minutes, fifteen minutes to prepare for the acting. All right? Fifteen minutes, go!

> 응시자 작성 내용 3

✓ 〈자료 4〉의 평가 기준을 3가지 제시할 것

One minute left, students. Does any group need more time for practice? Okay, time's up! However, before we enjoy our friends' acting, what do we have to do first? Yes, 상우! Yes, we need to make a checklist, right? So … it's 'Check time.' 'Let's check!'

So, everyone, let's look at the fourth worksheet. What do you see? Yes, 현우! Yes, there is a peer-checking worksheet, right? So from now on, we are going to make this checklist together. So, what are the important things when you check your friends' acting? Yes, group three! Oh, did everyone hear what group three just said? They said it should include the Korean proverb. So I would say that's the 'Content.' So for the first thing, you should check about the content. Like group three just said, for the content, you should check if your friends' acting is including the Korean proverb. Okay? And what else? Yes, group five! Yes, the storyline, right? So you guys need to see if your friends' storyline is creative. So I would say the Creativity.' 'Creativity.' So, in this creativity, you guys need to check if your friends' storyline is creative. Okay? And what's the last one? Yes, group two! Yes, the time limit. All right? So the last part would be the time, and it should be less than what? Yes, group four! Yes, less than sixty seconds. So make sure your friends' acting is less than sixty seconds. Okay? So with these three parts, you can give points, okay? And below this checklist, what do you see? Yes, 민수! Yes, there is 'Comment', right? So make sure you leave a comment for your friends' presentation. Okay?

With this checklist, are you guys ready for the performance? Great! So let's have our first actors and actresses to the front. And director, give a sign when you're ready.

✓ 발표에 관한 학생의 소감을 듣고 피드백을 제공할 것

All right! So we just finished checking our friends' presentation. Then, why don't we share how we felt about it? So, let's share about the presentation. Is there any volunteer? Yes, 민수! Oh, yes! You thought it would be very helpful to the international students who want to learn the Korean language. Yes! So 민수 thought ... it would be very helpful. And what else? Yes, 현우! Oh, it was very fun to watch your friends' acting. Yes, that's true. So ... 현우 thought it was very fun. Like you guys just said, I thought it was very fun and it was very helpful. However, this is the thing I want to give you a big hand: it is your creativity. I was very impressed about the storyline because all of the storylines were very creative. So I thought it was the creativity that made your storyline both helpful and fun. Great job, everyone! And let's give ourselves a big hand. Thank you again to the directors and passionate actors and actresses. That's it for us, and have a great day!

연습문제 2회 : 2023 기출 변형

(1) 판서 노트 및 예시 영상

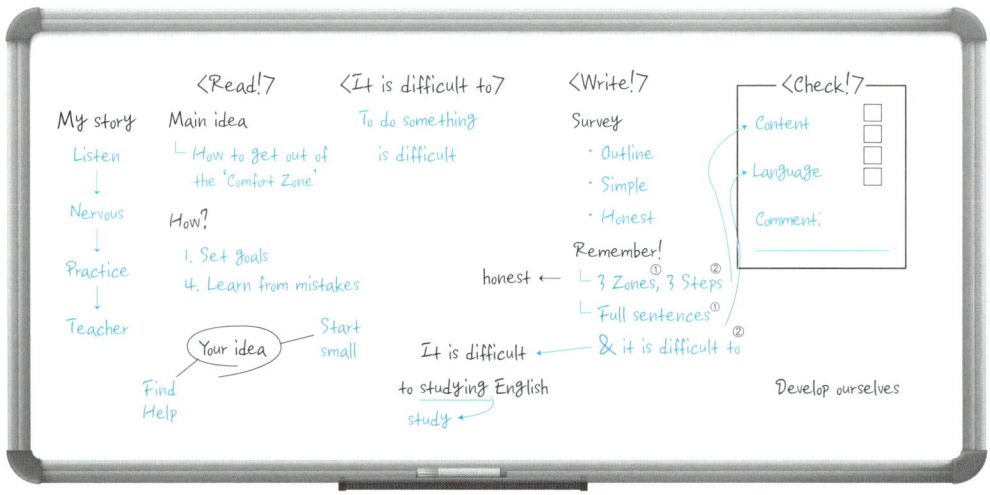

(2) 지도안 예시

단원명	Comfort Zone				시간	100 mins
대상	• Students : 24 High school 1st Graders • Level : Mixed					
수업 목표	✓ Students will be able to understand how to get out of the 'Comfort Zone'. ✓ Students will be able to write their plans about the future.					
교수·학습 교구	Digital whiteboard, Laptop, Online dictionary, Tablet PCs etc					
핵심역량	자기 관리	지식정보처리	창의적 사고	심미적 감성	협력적 소통	공동체
	✓				✓	

<교수 학습 지도안>

단계	교수·학습 활동	유의점
도입 (5분)	*인사, 출석 확인, 교실 내 안전 점검 *학습 주제, 수업 준비 상태 확인	
전개1 (35분)	**응시자 작성 내용 1** ✓ <자료 1>을 활용하여 사전지식 활성화 활동을 진행할 것 ● Teacher's anecdote • [전체] <자료 1>을 학생들에게 나누어주고 Comfort Zone에 관한 교사의 예시를 언급하며 학생과 상호작용을 진행한다. <예시 발화> 교사 : I used to be scared of talking in front of many people. So I avoid talking to others. I felt safe when I was doing that. That was my 'Comfort Zone'. … • 학생에게 이와 비슷한 경험이 있는지 질문하고 오늘 수업 주제를 소개한다. <예시 발화> 교사 : Do you guys have a similar experience to me? … Great! Today, we are going to learn about it. How does it sound? … Excited? Perfect! ✓ <자료 2>를 읽고 글의 주제를 파악하게 할 것 ● Find a topic • [개별, 3분] <자료 2>를 학생에게 나누어주고 글의 주제를 파악하게 한다. • Skimming 전략을 지도한다. • 빠른 속도로 글을 훑어보며 반복되는 단어를 확인하도록 한다. • 아래 지도 사항에 따라 순회 지도를 실시한다. <순회 지도 사항> • 참여를 북돋우며 활동 중 어려움을 겪고 있는 학생을 파악한다. • Low-level : <자료 2> 뒷면의 <Vocabulary list>를 제시한다.	

	• [전체] 학생과의 상호작용을 통해 글의 주제를 교실 전체에 공유하고 판서한다. 　• Main idea : How to get out of the 'Comfort Zone' • [전체] 글의 제목과 Main idea의 관련성에 다시 한번 주목하게 한다.
전개1 (35분)	✓ <자료 2>의 빈칸을 완성하고 학생 참여 활동을 진행할 것 ● Detail information • [개별, 5분] Screen을 통해 세부 정보를 찾기 위한 질문을 학생들에게 제시한다. 　• (예시) How can you get out of the 'Comfort Zone'? • Scanning 전략을 지도하여 질문에 대한 답을 찾도록 한다. 　• 글 전체가 아니라 필요한 부분만 선별하여 읽도록 한다. • 아래 지도 사항에 따라 순회 지도를 실시한다. 　<순회 지도 사항> 　• 참여를 북돋우며 활동 중 어려움을 겪고 있는 학생을 파악한다. 　• High-level : 활동 참여에 대한 긍정적 피드백을 제공하고, Student teacher 역할을 부여하여 다른 학생을 도울 수 있도록 한다. 　• Low-level : 동료 학습자로부터 도움을 받을 수 있도록 Peer-scaffolding을 유도한다. • [전체] 학생과의 상호작용을 통해 답변 공유하고 판서한다. 　• (예시) Set goals, Learn form mistakes 등 ● Brainstorming • [전체, 5분] 짝과 함께 의논하여 <자료 2>의 다섯 번째 빈칸을 완성하도록 한다. • 교사는 자유롭게 의견을 나누는 분위기를 형성하고 학생 답변을 칠판에 판서한다. • 다양한 정답이 나올 수 있음을 강조한다. 　<예시 발화> 　교사 : Let's share what you wrote. Anything is fine. There's no right answer. This is just brainstorming. 　학생 : Start small, Strong mindset, Find help, Plan future 등 ✓ 'It is difficult to …' 표현을 맥락을 통해 지도할 것 ● It is difficult to … • [전체] <자료 2>에서 반복적으로 등장하는 표현을 찾아보게 한다. • 학생들에게 아래와 같이 질문하며 'It is difficult to…'의 의미를 파악할 수 있도록 돕는다.

전개1 (35분)	**<예시 발화>** 교사 : If I say 'It is difficult to get out of the 'Comfort Zone', what's the difficult thing to me? 학생 : To get out of the 'Comfort Zone.' 교사 : Then, if I say 'It is difficult to set goals, what's the difficult thing to me? 학생 : To set goals. 교사 : That's right. So, 'It is difficult to do something' means 'To do something is difficult.' • 의미를 성공적으로 이해한 후, 직접 문장을 만들어 보게 함으로써 이해 확인 점검을 실시한다. **<예시 발화>** 교사 : Alright! We just learned the expression 'It is difficult to.' Then, can you make an example with this?
전개2 (40분)	**응시자 작성 내용 2** ✓ <자료 3>을 활용하여 쓰기 전 활동을 진행할 것 ● **Self survey** • [전체] Comfort Zone을 극복하는 방법을 토대로 자신에게 적용해볼 수 있도록 안내하며 <자료 2>와 <자료 3>의 연결성을 강조한다. **<예시 발화>** 교사 : So far, we've learned about the 'Comfort Zone.' Then, why don't we explore our own 'Comfort Zones'? • 학생들에게 <자료 3>을 제시하며, 이는 이후 <자료 4>를 위한 활동임을 강조하기 위해 아래와 같은 사항을 언급한다. **<예시 발화>** 교사 : This is just an outline for the next activity. So, don't worry too much about it. … You don't need to write full sentences. One or two words are fine. … Just make sure to be honest with your answers. • [개별, 10분] 1) 개요 작성 목적, 2) 간단한 표현 사용, 3) 솔직한 답변 - 위 3가지에 초점을 맞추어 <자료 3>를 완성할 수 있도록 안내한다. ✓ <자료 4>에 대한 글쓰기 조건을 제시할 것 ● **Transition** • 이전 활동이 해당 활동을 위한 준비였음을 언급하며 활동 간 연결성을 강조한다. **<예시 발화>** 교사 : We just finished answering to self survey. Then, are you ready to write about yourselves? … Awesome!

● Sample writing
- [전체] 화면을 통해 <자료 4>에 대한 교사의 예시를 학생들에게 보여준다.
- 학생들과의 상호작용을 통해 <자료 4>에 대한 글쓰기 조건을 제시한다.

<예시 발화>

교사 : Can you read the first sentence on the screen? … Thank you! Like this, you should write about your comfort zone in the first sentence. … How about the last one? … Thank you! Like this, you should include 3 steps to achieve it.

<조건>
1. Content : 3 Zones, 3 Steps
2. Language : Full sentence, 'it is difficult to …'

전개2
(40분)

✓ <자료 4>를 완성하고 긍정적 피드백과 부정적 피드백을 제공할 것

● My plans to growth
- Authentic purpose : 우수 작품은 교내 신문에 게시된다는 점을 강조하며 실제적 동기부여를 실시한다.
- [개별, 20분] <자료 3>의 설문지를 바탕으로 조건에 맞게 <자료 4>를 완성하도록 한다.
- 아래 지도 사항에 따라 순회 지도를 실시한다.

<순회 지도 사항>
- 참여를 북돋우며 활동 중 어려움을 겪고 있는 학생을 파악한다.
- Low-level : <자료 3>과 <자료 4>가 연결되어있음을 강조하며 해당 내용에 관련 내용을 작성할 수 있도록 Scaffolding을 제공한다.
- High-level : 활동 참여에 대한 긍정적 피드백을 제공하고, 목표를 달성하기 위한 계획을 더 써볼 수 있도록 추가 과제를 제시한다.

● Giving feedback
- [전체] Content 부분에서 성실도에 초점을 맞추어 긍정적 피드백을 제공하고, Language 부분에서 자주 하는 실수를 언급하며 부정적 피드백을 제공한다.
  - Content : 모든 내용을 성실하게 작성하였다는 점, 솔직함이 드러난다는 점 등
  - Language : I know it is difficult to studying(X) English. 등

전개3
(15분)
	응시자 작성 내용 3
	✓ <자료 4>에 대한 동료 평가를 실시할 것
	
	● Peer evaluation
	• [짝, 5분] 짝과 자신의 글을 바꾸어 읽고 아래 기준에 따라 평가해보도록 한다.
	• 아래 <Checklist>의 각 항목에 체크 표시를 하고, 의견을 작성하도록 안내한다.
	• 평가 기준이 글쓰기 기준과 연결됨을 강조한다.
	
	<Checklist>
	  1. Content 3 Zones
	         3 Steps
	  2. Language Full sentences
	         It is difficult to …
	  Comment : _____
	
	✓ 수업 주제와 관련한 학생의 역량을 언급할 것
	
	● Emphasizing competences
	• [전체] 학생과 상호작용을 통해 오늘 배운 내용을 되짚는다.
	• 자기 스스로 끊임없이 계발하는 태도의 중요성을 강조하며 자기 관리 역량을 언급한다.
	
	<예시 발화>
	교사 : Today, we learned about what?
	학생 : We learned how to get out of the 'Comfort Zone.'
	교사 : Yes! So, what kind of ability do you think will be important in the future?
	학생 : To develop ourselves!
	교사 : Exactly. I want you to grow into person who can step out of your 'Comfort Zone' and become the best version of yourself.

마무리 (5분)	*활동 마무리, 다음 차시 안내 *주변 정리 지도, 인사

(3) 스크립트

> 응시자 작성 내용 1

✓ 〈자료 1〉을 활용하여 사전지식 활성화 활동을 진행할 것

Okay, students. So far we've talked about the unit title and the lesson objectives. Then, are you guys ready for the English class? Great! So, let me give you this worksheet. Take one and pass them to the back. 상우 at the back, did you get the worksheet? Great. So, what do you see on the worksheet? Yes, there are four circles, right? Each circle has a name. What's the first one? Yes, 민수! Yes, it's Safe Zone. And what's the second? Yes, it's Fear Zone. And what else? Yes, it says Learning Zone. And what's the last one? Yes, 지환! Yes, it's the Zone of Growth. Then, are you guys familiar with these names?

All right, then let me give you my example. So, let me tell you my story. Is it interesting? Awesome! When I was in elementary school, I was a listener rather than a speaker. So, let me write here. I would just listen to others rather than talk to others. This is because I didn't like to be in front of others. I felt kind of safe in that way. So, this is the example of what? Yes, I was in the Safe Zone. However, one day in middle school, I was asked to be in front of the class and give a presentation. How did I feel? Yes, 재우! I felt nervous a lot. I was very nervous. That was because I was very scared of being laughed at by my classmates, and I was always trying to avoid being in front of others. So, this is the example of what? Yes, 희원! Yes, in the Fear Zone.

However, after this moment, I really wanted to change myself. I became tired of running away. So, I did what? Yes, 민재! I did lots of practice. Practice! There's a saying 'Practice makes perfect', right? So, I practiced a lot to be in front of others. All of this kind of work could be possible because I was in what kind of zone? Yes, 다원! Yes, I was in the Learning Zone. And now look at me here. Do I look scared of being in front of others? No, right? I finally became a teacher. So … The last part! I finally become a teacher. I'm no more scared of being in front of others. So, this is the example of what? Yes, 현우! Yes, it's the Growth Zone. So, like this, I just told you my story. Then, did you guys get the sense of those four zones? Perfect. Today we are going to learn about them. Are you guys excited? Awesome!

✓ 〈자료 2〉를 읽고 글의 주제를 파악하게 할 것

Then everyone, let's look at the second worksheet. What do you see on the second worksheet, 수민? Yes, there is a reading text, right? So, it's time for reading. Let's read! In this reading time, we are going to find the main idea first. However, to find the main idea, do we have to read quickly or slowly? Yes, 동희, we need to read quickly, right? So, you don't have to understand every single word. Just read quickly and find the main idea. All right? I'm going to give you 3 minutes. Three minutes, go! Oh, 동우, do you need any help? Oh, the words are so difficult? Why don't you look at the back of the worksheet? What do you see? Yes, there is a vocabulary list, right? So, with this vocabulary list, can you find the main idea by yourself? Perfect. Keep up the good work! One minute left, students. Okay, time's up. So, let's check the main idea together. What was the main idea? Is there any volunteer? Yes, 종민! Yes, the main idea was … 'How to …' how to do what? Yes, 다원! 'How to get out of… from where? Yes, 현정! Yes, 'How to get out of the Comfort Zone.' Right? So, the main idea was 'How to get out of the Comfort Zone.' Did you guys find it? Perfect.

Then everyone, we just found the main idea. However, let's look at the title. What's the title? Yes, 지환! Yes, it is "Change Yourself," right? So, how can we change ourselves? Yes, 현우! Yes, by getting out of the Comfort Zone. So, like this, remember that the main idea and the title have a very close relationship to each other. Okay? Great.

✓ 〈자료 2〉의 빈칸을 완성하고 학생 참여 활동을 진행할 것

Okay, so we just quickly read the text for the main idea. Are you guys ready to read the text a little more closely? Awesome! So, everyone, let's look at the screen here. 현수, at the back, can you see the screen? Great. So, what do you see on the screen? Yes, there is a question, right? So, can you guys read the question? What a loud voice! Great. So, the question was, 'How can you get out of the Comfort Zone', right? In the reading text, there are several ways for you to get out of the Comfort Zone. So, from now on, we are going to find them, okay? However, to find this kind of specific information, do we have to read from the beginning to the end, or just read only the necessary part? Yes, 현재! Yes, we can read the necessary part, okay? So, you don't have to read every single word. Just find the necessary part and answer to this question, okay? I'm going to give you five minutes. Five minutes, go!

Oh, 수현, you already finished? Wow, what a smart student! Then, why don't you help your partner, 현수? I heard 현수 needs some help. Can you do that? Perfect! So, like this, friends can be a better teacher. One minute left, students. Is there anyone who needs more time? Okay, time's up. Let's check the answers together. So, how can we get out of the Comfort Zone? What was the first one? Yes, 다원! Yes, we need to set goals, right? So, the first one is 'We need to set goals'. And what was the last one? Yes, 재우! Yes, we need to learn from mistakes, right? So, the last one was 'Learn from mistakes.' That's how we can get out of the Comfort Zone. So, like this, we just found the four ways to get out of the Comfort Zone. However, is there anything strange? Yes, we don't have the fifth one. So, from now on, we are going to talk with your partner. So, 현수, 수현, you two! 종민, 민종, you two! You two ... Everyone has their own partners? Perfect!

With your partners, we are going to talk about how to get out of the Comfort Zone. The fifth one is for your idea, okay? So, 동현, what are we going to do? Yes, we are going to talk with our partners and write down your ideas. I'm going to give you five minutes. Five minutes, go! One minute left, students. Does anyone need more time? Okay, time's up. Let's share your ideas together. So ... 'Your Idea'! This is just brainstorming. That means, there is no right answer! Just feel free to share your idea, all right? So, can anyone share your idea? Yes, 현우 and 우현! Oh, did everyone hear what 현우 and 우현 just said? They said we should start small to get out of the Comfort Zone. That's right! So, we should start small. That's a great idea. And what else? Yes, 동희 and 희동! Oh, that's a great idea as well. They said we can find some help. Yes, finding help is a great idea. So ... 'Find help'! That's a great idea!

✓ 'It is difficult to ...' 표현을 맥락을 통해 지도할 것

So far, we just finished reading the text twice: one for the main idea and another for the specific information. Is there anyone who could find an expression that is used repeatedly? Yes, 현정! Oh, did everyone hear what 현정 just said? She said the expression "It is difficult to" is used repeatedly in the reading text. So, everyone, let's quickly read the text again and find the expression. Yes, 재우, did you find it? Where is it? Yes, it's in the first sentence. Did everyone find it? Okay, underline it. And where is the second one? Yes, 은우! Yes, it's in the third line from the top, right? Did everyone find it? All right, underline it. And where's the last one? Yes, 정현! Everyone found it? All right, underline it. So, from now on, we are going to learn this key expression, which was? Yes, 종민! 'It is difficult to' So, we are going to learn this key expression: "It is difficult to."

Is there anyone who's familiar with this expression? All right, let me give you a hint. If I say, "It is difficult to get out of the Comfort Zone," what is the difficult thing to me? Yes, 지환! Yes, 'to get out of the Comfort Zone' is difficult. Then, if I say, "It is difficult to set goals," what is the difficult thing to me? Yes, 재우! Yes, 'to set goals' is the difficult thing to me, right?

Then, can you guys guess when we use this expression? Yes, 윤우! Oh, did everyone hear what 윤우 just said? He said we use this expression when we want to say 'To do something is difficult'.

So, this means ... 'To do something' is what? Yes, 현정! Yes, 'difficult!' So, we use this expression when we want to say 'To do something is difficult.' Then, 민재! Can you make a sentence with this expression? Yes, "It is difficult to learn from mistakes." That's a great sentence. So, remember this expression because we are going to use it in the upcoming writing. Okay? All right!

응시자 작성 내용 2

✓ 〈자료 3〉을 활용하여 쓰기 전 활동을 진행할 것

So far, we just finished reading about the Comfort Zone and learned the key expression. Then, don't you guys feel we need to change ourselves? Perfect! Are you ready to move on to the next part? Great.

Let's begin the 'Writing time.' So, it's time for 'Write!' So, everyone, let's look at the third worksheet. What do you see? Yes, 민수! Yes, there is a self-survey, right? From now on, we are going to do a survey of ourselves. Are you excited? Great.

It's time for the survey. However, you don't have to worry about this because this is just the preparation for the writing. You don't have to be perfect here; it's just an outline for the writing, okay? So, you don't have to worry about this because it's going to be an outline. That means you don't have to use the full sentence here. You can make it simple. So, you don't have to use the full sentences. You can use just keywords or phrases. That would be okay.

However, the last thing would be very important. Can you guess? What would be the most important thing in the self-survey? Yes, 다원! Yes, you need to be honest, okay? So, make sure you're being honest to yourself. All right? Great!

I'm going to give you 10 minutes, 10 minutes to complete the self-survey. Remember these three things. Ten minutes, go!

✓ 〈자료 4〉에 대한 글쓰기 조건을 제시할 것

One minute left, students. Does anyone need more time? Okay, time's up. We just finished the self-surveys which were going to be the outline. Then, are you guys ready for 'Write about Yourselves'? Perfect!

Everyone, let's look at the screen here. 준석 at the back, can you see the screen? Awesome! What do you see on the screen? Yes, there is a sample writing. Just quickly check the sample writing. What can you find? Yes, 현우! Yes, like this, when you write about yourself, there are several things you should remember.

So, remember these things when you write about yourselves. For the first thing, like the sample writing, how many zones can you find here? Yes, there are three zones, right? So, you should include 'About three zones'. And how many steps can you see? Yes, there are three steps, right? So, for the Growth Zone, you need the 'Three steps'. So, like this, you should include three zones and three steps.

And what else can you find? Yes, in the sample writing, there are all full sentences, right? So, you should use the full sentences. 'Full sentences!' When you did the self-survey, we just used keywords or phrases, right? However, in this writing, we are going to use full sentences.

And what else can you see? What was the key expression of today? Yes, 다원! Yes, it was "It is difficult to.", right? Make sure you're trying to use today's key expression, "It is difficult to", okay?

✓ 〈자료 4〉를 완성하고 긍정적 피드백과 부정적 피드백을 제공할 것

Before we start, everyone, look at here. I want to tell you that the best writing will be actually posted on the school newspaper. How does that sound? Are you guys excited? Great! From now on, I'm going to give you 20 minutes. 20 minutes to do what, 민수? Yes, we are going to write about ourselves, "My Plans to Grow", okay? Remember these things. Twenty minutes, go!

Oh, 수민, do you need any help? Oh, you don't know what to write? Then, why don't you use the self-survey? We just finished it together. Yes, it is the outline for this writing. With this self-survey, can you do this by yourself? Perfect! If you need any more help, just don't hesitate to raise your hand.

Oh, 나영, are you already finished? Wow, what a quick writer! Why don't you write more steps to achieve your goals, because the more steps you have, the better possibilities you get to achieve the goals? Can you do that? Perfect.

One minute left, students. Does anyone need more time? Okay, time's up. We just finished writing about "My Plans to Grow." and when I was walking around the classroom, there were two things I wanted to tell you.

The first thing is about the three zones and three steps. You guys all did a very great job! I'm so proud of this, because all of your writings were very honest. It was very honest. About your steps, about your zones. However, I also wanted to tell you about this. So, about this key expression, I could found many of you guys used this sentence. "It is difficult to studying English." So, when I was walking around, I could find many of you guys use this kind of sentence. Is this right sentence? No, it is not. Then, can you fix it? Yes, 지원! Oh did everyone hear what 지원 just said? She said we should change "studying" into what? Yes, we should use the word "study." Make sure you change this one, all right?

응시자 작성 내용 3

✓ **〈자료 4〉에 대한 동료 평가를 실시할 것**

Okay! So far, we just finished writing about our plans to grow. Now, don't you want to see your friends' writing? Perfect. Let's begin the check time. It's time for checking. However, whenever we do this kind of 'Check time', what was the thing that we need to see first? Yes, 재원! Yes, we have to see the checklist, right? So, I'm going to give you this checklist. Take one and pass them to the back. 민정, at the back, did you get the checklist? All right!

What do you see in the checklist? Yes, there are two parts, right? Can you read the first one? Yes, it says "Content.", right? So, the first one is 'The content.' And how many points are there in the content? Yes, there are two points, right? What are they? Yes, 은수! Yes, the first one is the three zones, and the second one is, yes, the three steps, right? Make sure you're checking this for the content, okay?

And what's the second part of the checklist? Yes, 유진! Yes, it says "Language", right? So, the second part is 'The language'. You should check about the language. And how many points are there? Yes, 동규! Yes, there are two points, right? So, what are they? Yes, the first one is full sentences, and what was the second one? Yes, it was the key expression, right?

Make sure your friend's writing includes these two things: The first one, the full sentences and the second one, "It is difficult to", which was the key expression of today.

And below the checklist, what can you see? Yes, there is 'The comment', right? Make sure you are leaving comments for your friend's writing, okay? All right, with this checklist, I'm going to give you five minutes, five minutes to check your partner's writing. So, give your writings to your partners. Did everyone finish changing it? I'm going to give you five minutes. Read your partner's writing and check it with this checklist. Five minutes, go!

✓ 수업 주제와 관련한 학생의 역량을 언급할 것

Okay, time's up. We just finished writing about ourselves and checking our friends' writing. Then, before we wrap up the class, let's go back to the unit title again. What was that? Yes, 수현! Yes, it was the 'Comfort Zone', right? It is very difficult to get out of the Comfort Zone. Still, we need to do that. Can you guess why? Yes, 다원! Yes, we need to prepare for the future, right?

To prepare for the future, we read about the Comfort Zone and we wrote about how to get out of it. So, like this, Can you guess what kinds of abilities will be needed in the future? Yes, 재원! Yes, 'To develop ourselves!' So, 'Develop ourselves!' Yes, exactly! I want you to become a person who can develop yourselves, get out of the Comfort Zone, and make the best version of yourselves. This ability was what I wanted you to learn in this class. So, that's it for us and have a great day!

연습문제 3회 : 2022 기출 변형

(1) 판서 노트 및 예시 영상

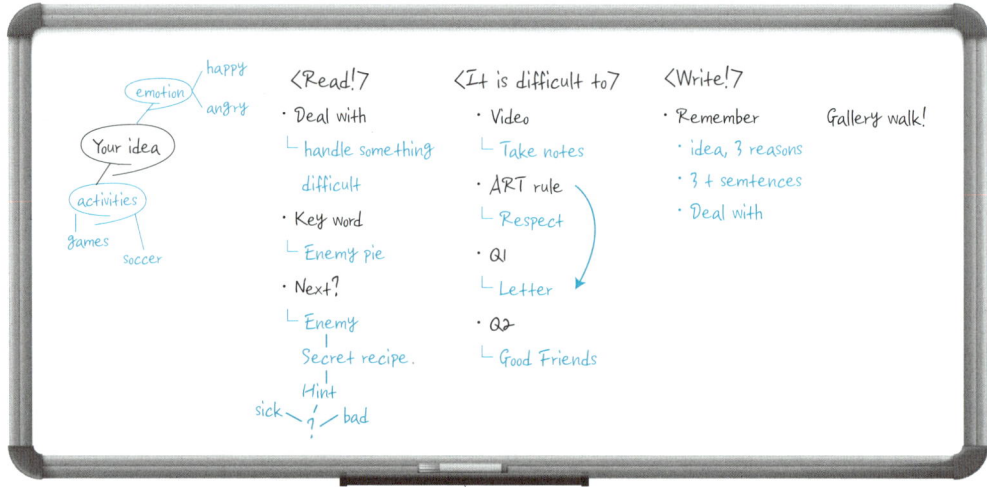

(2) 지도안 예시

단원명	Making relationships				시간	90 mins
대상	• Students : 24 Middle school 3rd Graders • Level : Mixed					
수업 목표	✓ Students will be able to predict the story based on the context. ✓ Students will be able to write about making a great relationship with friends.					
교수·학습 교구	Digital whiteboard, Laptop, Online dictionary, Tablet PCs, Stickers etc					
핵심역량	자기 관리	지식정보처리	창의적 사고	심미적 감성	협력적 소통	공동체
			✓		✓	✓

<교수 학습 지도안>

단계	교수·학습 활동	유의점
도입 (5분)	*인사, 출석 확인, 교실 내 안전 점검 *학습 주제, 수업 준비 상태 확인	
전개1 (20분)	**응시자 작성 내용 1** ✓ <자료 1>을 활용하여 학생 참여를 유도하는 활동을 진행할 것 ● Mind mapping • [전체] <자료 1>을 학생들에게 나누어주고 교실 전체를 대상으로 마인드맵 활동을 실시한다. • 학생의 대답을 바탕으로 교사는 적절한 곳에 판서하며 결과를 교실 전체에 공유한다. • (예시) Emotions - happy, angry 등, Activity - soccer, games 등 ● Transition • 완성된 마인드맵을 살펴보며 이번 차시에 대한 주제를 연상하도록 한다. ✓ <자료 2>의 밑줄 친 표현을 가르칠 것 ● Teaching Vocabulary • [전체] <자료 2>을 학생에게 소개하고 밑줄 친 표현에 대해 주목하게 한다. • 'deal with'의 뜻을 아는 학생들이 있는지 질문한다. • 해당 단어를 추론할 수 있도록 맥락을 제공한다. <예시 발화> 교사 : Let's check the sentence first. What do you mean by 'enemies'? … Yes, enemies are the people who don't like you. Then, are they easy to get along with or difficult? … Very hard, right? So, 'deal with' is 'to try to handle something difficult.' • 의미를 성공적으로 추론한 후, 직접 문장을 만들어 보게 함으로써 이해 확인 점검을 실시한다.	

● Transition
- 어휘 학습이 읽기 학습을 하기 위한 사전 준비 활동임을 언급하며 다음 활동과의 연결성을 강조한다.

<예시 발화>

교사 : Okay, we just learned this difficult expression. Then, are you ready for the reading?

✓ <자료 2>를 활용하여 이야기 추측하기 활동을 진행할 것

● Find a key word
- [개별, 3분] <자료 2>를 학생에게 소개하고 key word를 파악하게 한다.
- Skimming 전략을 지도하여 key word를 파악하도록 한다.
  - 빠른 속도로 글을 훑어보며 반복되는 단어를 확인하도록 한다.
- 아래 지도 사항에 따라 순회 지도를 실시한다.

<순회 지도 사항>

- 참여를 북돋우며 활동 중 어려움을 겪고 있는 학생을 파악한다.
- Low-level : 반복적으로 등장하는 단어를 찾을 수 있도록 한다.

- [전체] 학생과의 상호작용을 통해 글의 주제를 교실 전체에 공유하고 판서한다.
  - Key word : Enemy Pie

● What's next?
- [전체] Key word를 중심으로 Storyline을 정리하며 다음 내용을 추측할 수 있도록 한다.

<예시 발화>

교사 : We just found a key word. Then, let's check the storyline based on it. … In the beginning, the son was asking about what? … Dad was showing what? … What would happen next?

전개1 (20분)

응시자 작성 내용 2

✓ <자료 3>을 시청하고 모둠 토의를 진행할 것

● Transition
- 앞선 'Enemy pie'의 의미를 추측하기 위한 활동과 연계하여 라이벌과의 갈등을 해결한 Benjamin Franklin의 영상을 소개한다.

<예시 발화>

교사 : Alright. We just tried to make some guesses about the meaning of the 'Enemy pie'. Then, let me introduce this video clip. This will help you to deal with enemies.

● Watch a video clip
- [전체] 학생들에게 영상의 주제를 먼저 알려주고 세부 내용에 관하여 노트 필기를 할 수 있도록 안내한다.

전개2 (30분)

<예시 발화>

교사 : This is the story of Benjamin Franklin, who turned his rival into a friend. Let's see how he did it. … However, before we watch a video clip, what should we do?

학생 : We should take notes!

● Group discussion
- 학생들의 노트 필기 내용에 관한 긍정적인 피드백을 제공한 뒤, 해당 내용에 관하여 모둠 토의를 진행할 것이라고 안내한다.

✓ <자료 3>에 관한 모둠 토의 주제 2가지를 제시할 것

- 4인 1조로, 6개의 모둠을 구성한다.
- 화면을 통해 모둠 토의 주제 2가지를 제시한다.

<Screen>

1. How did Benjamin Franklin turn his rival into a friend?
2. What would 'the Enemy Pie' taste like, good or bad? and why?

- [모둠, 10분] 모두 각자 의견을 제시할 수 있도록 하고, 아래 ART rule을 지키도록 독려한다.

<ART rule>

A : Active participation, R : Respect others, T : Take turns

- 토의 중 아래 지도 사항에 따라 순회 지도를 실시한다.

<순회 지도 사항>

- 참여를 북돋우며 활동 중 어려움을 겪고 있는 학생을 파악한다.
- Low-level : ART rule 재강조, 토의에 어려움을 겪는 학생에게는 Benjamin Franklin과 Enemy Pie의 줄거리를 제공하여 촉진자 역할을 수행한다.
- High-level : 활동 참여에 대한 긍정적 피드백을 제공하고 아래 추가 질문에 대하여 토의할 수 있도록 안내한다.
  - (추가질문) What does it mean by 'make enemies disappear' in the DAD's last line?

✓ 모둠 토의 활동에 관한 교사의 피드백을 제시할 것

● Giving feedback
- [전체] 모둠 토의 활동 후 아래와 같이 토의 과정에 대한 긍정적 피드백을 제공한다.
  - (예시) ART rule을 잘 지켰다는 점, 토의 질문에 성실히 답했다는 점 등

<예시 발화>

교사 : I was so impressed that you were all participating very actively! Awesome!

	• 학생과 상호작용하며 모둠토의 결과를 교실 전체에 공유한다. **<예시 발화>** 교사 : Then, let's share what we talked about. … Oh, group 1 thought that 'the Enemy Pie' would taste good! Can you tell us why? • [전체] 상호작용 결과를 판서하며 토의 결과에 대한 긍정적 피드백을 제공한다.
전개3 (30분)	**응시자 작성 내용 3** √ 모둠 토의 내용을 바탕으로 <자료 4>를 완성하게 할 것 √ <자료 4>에 관한 글쓰기 조건 3가지를 제시할 것 ● **Transition** • 'Enemy Pie'가 '적을 친구로 만들기 위한 것'임을 다시 한번 요약하며 <자료 4>와 연결성을 강조한다. ● **How to build a great relationship with friends** • 교사의 예시를 화면으로 보여주며 <자료 4>에 대한 조건 3가지를 제시한다. **<조건>** 1. Content : 'Your idea', 3 reasons 2. Length : 3+ sentences 3. Language : Include 'deal with' • [개별, 15분] 위 조건에 따라 <자료 4>를 완성하도록 한다. • Authentic purpose : 우수 작품은 교내 신문에 실린다는 사실을 언급하며 학생의 동기를 부여한다. **<예시 발화>** 교사 : The best writing will be posted in our school newspaper so that everyone can learn from your great idea. … Does it sound great? Perfect! • 아래 지도 사항에 따라 순회 지도를 실시한다. **<순회 지도 사항>** • 참여를 북돋우며 활동 중 어려움을 겪고 있는 학생을 파악한다. • Low level : <자료 4> 뒷면의 '우정에 관한 명언'을 참고할 수 있도록 적절한 scaffolding을 제공한다. • High level : 긍정적 피드백을 제공한 뒤, 이유를 더 쓸 수 있도록 추가 과제를 제시한다.

	✓ <자료 4>의 결과물을 공유하는 활동을 진행할 것 ● Transition • 이전 활동이 해당 활동을 위한 준비였음을 언급하며 활동 간 연결성을 강조한다. <예시 발화> 교사 : We just finished writing our ideas of friendship. Then, don't you want to know about your friends' idea? … Awesome! Let's begin 'Gallery walk'! ● Gallery walk • [전체, 5분] 교실 벽면에 학생들의 글을 전시할 수 있도록 한다. • 학생들에게 스티커를 1개씩 나누어주고 교실 안을 자유롭게 둘러보며 가장 마음에 드는 글에 스티커를 붙일 수 있도록 한다. • 스티커를 줄 때, 앞서 언급한 글쓰기 조건을 모두 충족하는지 확인하도록 한다. <예시 발화> 교사 : Make sure you give a sticker to the writing that includes these things : 'Content', 'Length' and 'Language'
전개3 (30분)	
마무리 (5분)	*활동 마무리, 다음 차시 안내 *주변 정리 지도, 인사

(3) 스크립트

응시자 작성 내용 1

✓ 〈자료 1〉을 활용하여 학생 참여를 유도하는 활동을 진행할 것

Okay, students. So far we've talked about the unit titles and the lesson objectives. Then, are you guys ready for the English class? Great! Let me give you this worksheet. So take one and pass them to the back. Take one and pass them to the back. So, 지원, at the back, did you get the worksheet? Awesome.

So what do you see in the first worksheet? Yes, there is a mind map, right? So we are going to make a mind map all together. How does this sound? Sounds exciting? Great. So, 민수, what's the keyword of the mind map? Yes, it's 'Friend', right? So we are going to talk about a friend and make a mind map. What kinds of words do you have in mind when you think of a friend? Yes, 수현! Yes, 'Happy' is a great word. So 'Happy.' And what else? Yes, 희원! Oh, 'Angry?' Yes, sometimes friends can make us angry. Yes, 'Angry.' We have 'Happy' and 'Angry.' So these kinds of words we call what? Yes, 현우! Yes, we call them 'Emotions', right? So ... 'Emotions.' Friends can make us feel lots of emotions.

And what else? Yes, 호영! Yes, 'Games.' So you spend lots of time playing games, right? With your friends! And what else? Yes, 지환! Yes, playing soccer. You also play soccer with your friends. So these kinds of words we call what? Yes, 상우! Yes, so we call these kinds of words 'Activities', right? 'Activities!' So like this, we just finished making the mind map. Then can you guys guess today's topic? Yes, 다원! Yes, we are going to talk about friends. Are you guys excited? Great!

✓ 〈자료 2〉의 밑줄 친 표현을 가르칠 것

So everyone, let's look at the second worksheet. What do you see? Yes, 동우! Yes, there is a script, right? So from now on, we are going to read the script, okay? So let's read! However, before reading, what do we have to do? Yes, 재우! Yes, we should learn some difficult words, right? So everyone, let's look at the reading text. There is an underlined word. What is that? Yes, 수민! Yes, it's "deal with," right? So is there anyone who knows the meaning of the word "deal with"? All right, then let me give you a hint.

So the word "deal with." So everyone, let's look at the sentence. Can you read it for us? What a loud voice! Perfect. So the sentence was, "How did you deal with enemies when you were a kid?" Right? Then what does it mean by 'enemies?' Yes, 종민! Oh, did everyone hear what 종민 just said? He said enemies are the people who don't like you. Then let's think about this. Do you think it's easy or difficult to get along with enemies? Yes, 희원! Yes, it's very difficult to get along with enemies, right? So the expression "deal with" is trying to handle something difficult or something easy? Yes, 다원. Yes, something difficult, right? So "deal with" means … handle … something … easy or difficult? Yes, difficult! So 'Deal with' means 'handle something difficult.' So can you get the meaning of the word "deal with"? Perfect! Then 희원! Can you make a short sentence with this expression? Yes, "I don't like dealing with math problems." That's a great sentence. So far, we just learned this difficult word. Then are you guys ready for the reading? Perfect!

✓ 〈자료 2〉를 활용하여 이야기 추측하기 활동을 진행할 것

Okay, so everyone! From now on, we are going to read the text and find the keyword. Okay? However, to find the keyword, do we have to read quickly or slowly? Yes, 재원! We need to read quickly, right? You don't have to understand every single word. Just read quickly and find the keyword for this reading text. Okay? So I'm going to give you three minutes. Three minutes, Go!

Oh, 민재, do you need any help? Oh, it's too hard to find the keyword? Then why don't you find the word that is used repeatedly? Because keywords are used several times in the reading text. So can you find the keywords by yourself? Awesome! I love your effort! One minute left, students! Okay, time's up.

So let's check the keyword all together. So … 'Keyword!' So what was the keyword of this reading text? Yes, 다원! Oh, did everyone hear what 다원 just said? He said "Enemy Pie." "Enemy Pie" is the keyword of this reading text. And 다원! What made you think so? Yes, it is used repeatedly in the script, right? So like this, remember that keywords are used repeatedly. All right? Okay! So like this, we just found the keyword, which was "Enemy Pie." However, what is "Enemy Pie"? Do we know about it? Not yet, right? So let's talk about what would happen next. Sounds exciting? Great.

So let's talk about what would happen next. So to make a guess about what might happen next, what do we have to know first? Yes, 상민! Yes, we need to check the storyline, right? So from now on, let's talk about the storyline. Okay? So in the very beginning, the son was asking about what? You can check your reading text. Did you guys find it? So, 민재, what was the son asking about? Yes, it was how to deal with enemies, right? So in the very beginning, the son was asking about how to deal with enemies. And what happened next? Go back to your reading text and try to find it. Oh, 현수, did you find it? Okay, so what happened next? Yes, Dad talked about the "Enemy Pie," and it was a secret recipe, right? So it was a secret recipe. "Enemy Pie" was a secret recipe. And what happened next in the last part? Go back to your reading text again and find the information about it. Yes, 재우, did you find it? Yes, the son was asking for a hint, right? So the son wanted to get a hint about the secret recipe. Then let's talk about what would happen next. In the next part, what do you think will happen? Yes, 상우! Oh, yes, something bad will happen. Okay, that's a great guess. Something bad. And what else? Yes, 동규! Oh, the enemy will be sick after eating the "Enemy Pie." So the enemy will be sick. All right.

So we just read the script and we made a guess about what would happen next. Then don't you guys want to know what actually happened? Awesome! Then are you guys ready to move on to the next part? Great.

응시자 작성 내용 2

✓ 〈자료 3〉을 시청하고 모둠 토의를 진행할 것

So everyone, let's look at the screen here. So, 동우, at the back, can you see the screen? Great. So what do you see on the screen? Yes, there is a video clip. This is the story of Benjamin Franklin, who turned his rival into a friend. And this video is somehow related to "The Enemy Pie." So we are going to watch this video clip and have a discussion. Okay? Great.

So it's discussion time. Let's have a discussion. So everyone, before we watch this video clip, what do we have to do first? Yes! So whenever we watch a video clip, we should do what? Yes, we should take notes, right? So make sure you are taking notes when you're watching the video clip, okay? So get your pencils and papers and get ready for taking notes. Are you guys ready? Great. Then let's watch the video clip and let's see how Benjamin Franklin dealt with his enemies. Okay? All right. Let's watch the video.

Okay, we just finished watching the video clip. I can see many of you guys wrote down a lot of information. Then are you guys ready for the discussion? Awesome.

✓ 〈자료 3〉에 관한 모둠 토의 주제 2가지를 제시할 것

So we are going to have a discussion in groups. 현수, 수현, 민종, 종민, you four! You four ... You four ... And finally, the last group, you four. So everyone is in the group? Perfect.

Then let me give you the discussion topics. So everyone, look at the screen here. So group three at the back, can you see the screen? So what do you see on the screen? Yes, there are two questions, right? So what was the first question? Yes, it was, "How did Benjamin Franklin turn his rival into his friend?" Right? And what was the second one? Can you read the question for us, group five? Yes, it was, "What would the Enemy Pie taste like, good or bad, and why?" Right? So from now on, we are going to have a discussion with your group members.

However, whenever we have this kind of discussion, which rule do we have to follow? Yes, 현우! Yes, we have to follow the ART rule, right? So don't forget the ART rule. So what was A? Yes, 수현! Yes, it was 'Active participation', right? And what was R? Yes, 지환! Yes, it was 'Respect others.' So make sure you're respecting your friends' ideas. Okay? And what was T? Yes, 희원! Yes, it was 'Take turns,' right? So make sure everyone is talking. Okay? I'm going to give you 10 minutes. 10 minutes to have a discussion with those two topics on the screen. Okay? 10 minutes. Go!

Oh, group one, I can see 현수 is participating very actively. Great job. But what was the T rule? Yes, 'Take turns,' right? So make sure everyone gets a chance to talk. Okay?

And group three, do you need any help? Oh, the discussion topic is too difficult? Then why don't you use this? What do you see? Yes, there are summaries of Benjamin Franklin and the story "Enemy Pie." Can you guys get some hints from the summary? Great. Then can you do the discussion within the group? Awesome. I love your effort. So if you guys need any more help, just feel free to call me. All right?

And group six, are you guys already finished? Wow, what brilliant students. Then why don't you look at the back of the worksheet? What do you see? Yes, there is a bonus question, right? Can you read it? Yes, it's asking about the meaning of "make enemies disappear." Right? So why don't you talk about it because it's part of the story? Can you guys do that? Awesome.

One minute left, students. Does any group need more time? Okay, time's up.

✓ 모둠 토의 활동에 관한 교사의 피드백을 제시할 것

Okay, so we just finished the discussion with those two topics. And while I was looking around, this is the thing that I was so impressed about. And that was, I could see that everyone is respecting others. So everyone was respecting others. Great job! So like this, it is very important to respect others, even though you guys have different ideas. Because that's why we have discussions and that's the beauty of the discussion. Okay? Great! So you guys all did a great job and I'm so proud of you guys. So let's give ourselves a big hand. Perfect!

Then why don't we share our ideas? Sounds exciting? Great. So let's talk about the first question. So, question one: How did Benjamin Franklin turn his rival into a friend? Yes, group two. Yes, he sent a letter with the book, right? So yes, he sent a letter.

And how about question two? So do you think the Enemy Pie will be delicious? Yes, group six. Oh, you guys think it would be good? Can you tell us why? Oh, did everyone hear what group six just said? They said the Enemy Pie is to change the enemies into friends. That's a great idea, group six. So they said it will taste good because the Enemy Pie is to make friends. Awesome job, everyone!

So like this, remember if you follow the ART rule, you guys can get great ideas from the discussion. Okay?

응시자 작성 내용 3

✓ 모둠 토의 내용을 바탕으로 〈자료 4〉를 완성하게 할 것
✓ 〈자료 4〉에 관한 글쓰기 조건 3가지를 제시할 것

So we just finished the discussion. And what was the Enemy Pie? Was that a good thing or a bad thing? Yes, it was a good thing because it can help us to make a better relationship with friends, right? Then why don't we write about how to make a great relationship with our friends because there must be more ways to make friends. Are you guys excited? Perfect.

So it's time for writing. So it's writing time! Let's write! So everyone, look at the screen here. 지환, at the back, do you see the screen? What do you see on the screen? Yes, there is a sample writing, right? So can you read the first sentence? Thank you, 현우! So like this, there are several things you should remember when you're writing. Okay? So remember this! So like 현우 just said, you should include your idea. Your idea of how to build a great relationship.

So the first thing: You need 'Your idea.' And can you read the next sentence, 다원? Yes! Like this, you should include 'Reasons.' Reasons why your idea is helpful to build a great relationship. Okay? But how many reasons can you see? Yes, 희원! Yes, there are three reasons, right? So you should include three reasons.

And how about the length? How many sentences can you see in there? Yes, 호영! So like this, your writing should include more than three sentences. So make sure you guys have three or more sentences.

And the last part, what was the word that we learned at the beginning of the class? Yes, 민재! Yes, the word "deal with," right? So make sure you're using the word "deal with." Try to use this expression in your writing. Okay?

So before we start, everyone, look here. I want to tell you that the best writing will be posted on the school newspaper so that everyone can learn your idea. That would be very helpful to the freshman year students. How does that sound? Are you guys excited? Awesome!

So I'm going to give you 15 minutes. 15 minutes to do what, 동우? Yes, write about how to build a great relationship with your friends, all right? So make sure you're including these things. I'm going to give you 15 minutes. 15 minutes. Go!

Oh, 상우, do you need any help? Oh, you can't come up with some ideas? Then why don't you use this? What do you see? Yes, it's a list of famous words about friendship. So with this list, can you do this work by yourself? Awesome! Keep up the good work.

And 나영, are you already finished? Wow, what a quick writer! Then why don't you give another idea of how to make a great relationship with friends? Because the more ideas we have, the better we can make great relationships. Can you do that? Perfect.

One minute left, students. Does anyone need more time? Okay, time's up.

✓ 〈자료 4〉의 결과물을 공유하는 활동을 진행할 것

All right, so we just finished writing our own ideas of how to build a great relationship with our friends, right? Then don't you guys want to know about your friends' ideas? Awesome! So let's begin the gallery walk. So it's time for the gallery walk.

So students sitting here, you can put your writings on this left wall. And students sitting here, you can put your writings on this right wall. And students sitting in the middle, you can put your writings on the back of this classroom. Okay? So you guys finished putting your writings on the walls? Perfect!

Then let me give you these stickers. So take one and pass them to the back. Take one and pass them to the back. So everyone gets the stickers?

I'm going to give you five minutes. Five minutes to look around the classroom and give your sticker to the best writing. All right? However, how can we decide the best writing? Yes, 재우! Yes, we should think about these things, right?

So make sure your friends' writings include these things: idea, three reasons, and three or more sentences. And the last part, what was that? Yes, 현정! Yes, the expression "deal with." Okay? So remember these things and give your stickers to the best writing. Okay?

I'm going to give you five minutes to look around the classroom and let's see your friends' writings. Okay? I'm going to give you five minutes. Five minutes to do what, 지환? Yes, look around the classroom and give your stickers to the best writing. Okay? Five minutes. Go!

One minute left, students. Okay, time's up. So everyone, let's go back to your seats.

So before we wrap up the class, let's go back to the unit title again. What was that? Yes, 희원! Yes, it was making relationships, right? So about the relationship, we read about it, talked about it, and we wrote about it. Then do you guys feel a little bit more confident of yourselves about making relationships with friends? Awesome! That was just what I wanted for this class. So that's it for us and have a great day.

연습문제 4회 : 2021 기출 변형

(1) 판서 노트 및 예시 영상

수업실연 예시
2021 기출 변형

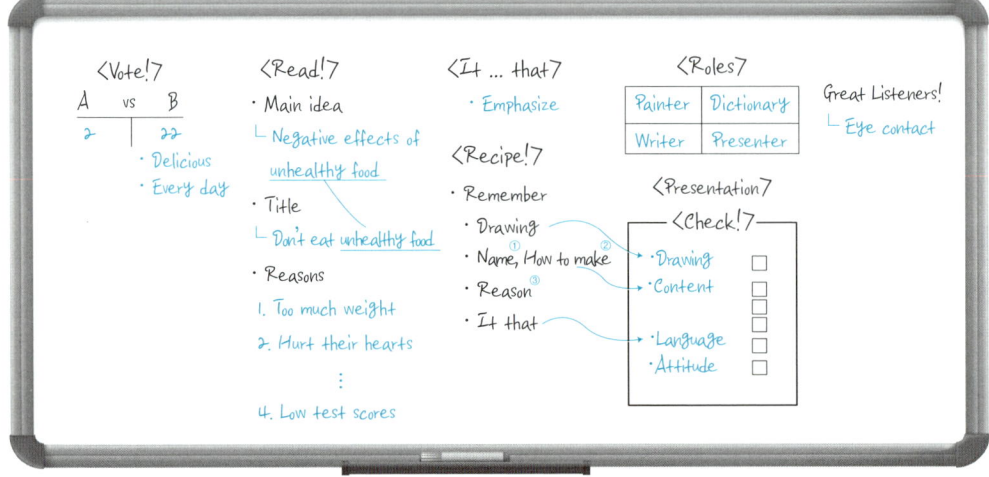

(2) 지도안 예시

단원명	Healthy Body, Healthy Mind				시간	90 mins
대상	• Students : 24 Middle school 3rd Graders • Level : Mixed					
수업 목표	✓ Students will be able to understand the negative effects of unhealthy foods. ✓ Students will be able to create healthy food in groups. ✓ Students will be able to introduce how to make healthy food to the class.					
교수·학습 교구	Digital whiteboard, Laptop, Online dictionary, Tablet PCs etc					
핵심역량	자기 관리	지식정보처리	창의적 사고	심미적 감성	협력적 소통	공동체
		✓	✓	✓	✓	

<교수 학습 지도안>

단계	교수·학습 활동	유의점
도입 (5분)	*인사, 출석 확인, 교실 내 안전 점검 *학습 주제, 수업 준비 상태 확인	
전개1 (25분)	응시자 작성 내용 1 ✓ <자료 1>의 메뉴를 비교하며 무엇을 더 좋아하는지 말해보도록 할 것 ● **Classroom voting** • [전체] <자료 1>을 학생에게 나누어준다. • 메뉴를 함께 살펴보며 학생들에게 어떤 것을 더 선호하는지 투표 활동을 진행한다. • 투표 결과를 바탕으로 그 이유에 대하여 짧게 말해보게 한다. <예시 발화> 교사 : Many students like Menu B over Menu A. Why do you prefer Menu B? • 학생의 의견을 정리하여 판서한다. ● **Transition** • <자료 1>을 바탕으로 오늘 차시 주제를 예상하도록 하며 <자료 2>를 소개한다. <예시 발화> 교사 : So far, we just talked about these two menus. Then, can you guess today's topic? 학생 : Food! ✓ <자료 2>의 주제를 파악하고 제목 짓기 활동을 진행할 것 ● **Main idea** • [개별, 3분] <자료 2>를 학생에게 나누어주고 Main idea를 파악하게 한다. • Skimming 전략을 지도하여 글의 주제를 파악하도록 한다. • 빠른 속도로 글을 훑어보며 반복되는 단어를 확인하도록 한다.	

전개1 (25분)	• 아래 지도 사항에 따라 순회 지도를 실시한다. ＜순회 지도 사항＞ • 참여를 북돋우며 활동 중 어려움을 겪고 있는 학생을 파악한다. • Low-level : ＜자료 2＞ 뒷면의 ＜Vocabulary list＞를 제시한다. • [전체] 학생과의 상호작용을 통해 글의 주제를 교실 전체에 공유하고 판서한다. 　• Main idea : Negative effects of unhealthy food • [전체] 글의 제목이 없음을 강조하며, 글의 제목을 직접 지어보도록 제안한다. ＜예시 발화＞ 교사 : Since we found the main idea, why don't we make the title? Do you have any good idea? 학생 : I think 'Don't eat unhealthy food!' is a great title.	
전개2 (15분)	**응시자 작성 내용 2** ✓ ＜자료 2＞의 내용을 바탕으로 ＜자료 3＞을 완성할 것 ● Detail information • [개별, 5분] ＜자료 3＞를 학생에게 보여주며 활동의 목표를 안내한다. • Scanning 전략을 지도하여 ＜자료 3＞을 완성하도록 한다. 　• 글 전체가 아니라 필요한 부분만 선별하여 읽도록 한다. ✓ ＜자료 3＞ 활동 진행 시 학생 수준별 맞춤 지도를 실시할 것 • 아래 지도 사항에 따라 순회 지도를 실시한다. ＜순회 지도 사항＞ • 참여를 북돋우며 활동 중 어려움을 겪고 있는 학생을 파악한다. • High-level : 활동 참여에 대한 긍정적 피드백을 제공하고, 'Your idea' 부분까지 작성할 수 있도록 추가 과제를 제시한다. 　• (예시 발화) 교사 : Wow, you are such a quick reader! Awesome! Then, why don't you write your idea here? You know there must be more reasons for it. • Low-level : Transition word에 대해 안내하며 학생이 스스로 답을 찾을 수 있도록 적절한 Scaffolding을 제공한다. 　• (예시 발화) 교사 : Do you remember the 'transition words' that we learned last time? … Great! Try finding those words. They will help you. • [전체] 학생과의 상호작용을 통해 ＜자료 3＞의 내용을 공유하고 판서한다. ✓ ＜자료 2＞의 'It ... that' 표현을 설명하고 학생의 이해를 확인할 것 ● It ... that • [전체] ＜자료 2＞에서 반복적으로 쓰인 표현을 찾아보게 하고 해당 문장을 밑줄친다.	

- 'It ... that' 표현을 언급하며 교사가 화면을 통해 제시하는 아래 문장과 비교한다.

<Screen>

1. We should worry about our brain.
2. It is our brain that we should worry about.

- 각 강조 대상이 되는 단어에 강세를 주어 읽음으로써 학생이 표현상의 차이점을 이해하도록 유도한다.
- 의미를 성공적으로 이해한 후, 직접 문장을 만들어 보게 함으로써 이해 확인 점검을 실시한다.

<예시 발화>

교사 : Alright! We just learned how to emphasize, using 'it that' expression. Then, can you make an example with this?

응시자 작성 내용 3

✓ <자료 4>의 활동 이해를 돕기 위한 교사의 예시를 제시할 것

● Write a healthy recipe!
- 4인 1조로 6개의 모둠을 구성한다.

● Sample writing
- [전체] 화면을 통해 <자료 4>에 대한 교사의 예시를 학생들에게 보여준다.
- 학생들과의 상호작용을 통해 <자료 4>에 대한 글쓰기 조건을 제시한다.

<예시 발화>

교사 : What do you see on the screen? … Yes, it is a drawing of 'Chicken breast salad'. Like this, you should draw your food on this worksheet.

<조건>

1. Drawing : Healthy food
2. Content : Name, How to make, Reason
3. Language : 'it ... that'

✓ <자료 4>를 완성하고 모둠 발표를 진행할 것

● Giving roles
- 구성원의 역할을 아래와 같이 부여한다.

<역할 부여>

Painter	Dictionary	• 좌석에 따라 역할 부여 • Painter : 그림 그리기 (실력 무관) • Dictionary : Tablet PC 지참, 단어 검색, 문법 확인
Writer	Presenter	• Writer : 문장 작성 • Presenter : 모둠 발표 담당자

전개3 (30분)	• Authentic purpose : 우수 작품은 실제 점심 급식 메뉴로 나온다는 점을 강조하며 실제적 동기부여를 실시한다. • [모둠, 15분] 글쓰기 조건에 따라 <자료 4>를 완성하도록 한다. • 교사는 아래 지도 사항에 따라 순회 지도를 실시한다. 　　　　　　　　　　<순회 지도 사항> 　• 참여를 북돋우며 활동 중 어려움을 겪고 있는 학생을 파악한다. 　• Low level : 교사가 준비한 'Recipe book'을 제공한다. 　• High level : 긍정적 피드백을 제공한 뒤, 다른 음식을 하나 더 쓸 수 있도록 추가 과제를 제시한다. ● Transition to presentation • <자료 4>를 완성한 후, 각 모둠에서 Presenter 역할을 맡은 학생의 준비 상태를 확인한다. 　　　　　　　　　　<예시 발화> 　교사 : Alright, time's up! Presenters, are you ready? Great! Let's begin the presentations now! • [전체] 발표 활동에 대해 교실 전체에 안내하고 동료 평가를 준비한다. 　　　　　　　　　　<예시 발화> 　교사 : Listeners, during the presentation, what do we need? 　학생 : Check list!
전개4 (10분)	응시자 작성 내용 4 ✓ 모둠 발표에 관한 동료 평가 기준을 4가지 제시할 것 ● Peer evaluation • 학생들에게 평가 기준이 포함된 <Check list>를 제공한다. 　• 평가 기준이 글쓰기 기준과 연결됨을 강조한다. 　　　　　　　　<Check list> | 1. Drawing	Healthy food
2. Content	Name
	How to make
	Reasons
3. Language	it ... that
4. Attitude	Confidence | • <Check list>의 기준이 이전 활동의 <글쓰기 기준>과 연결됨을 보여주며 교수 내용과 평가가 일치함을 강조한다. • 발표를 진행하고 <Check list>를 작성하도록 한다.

	✓ 발표 후 청중의 태도에 관한 피드백을 제공할 것	
	● Giving feedback • [전체] 발표가 끝난 후 발표 내용에 대하여 학생과 상호작용하며 동료 평가 태도에 관한 긍정적 피드백을 제공한다. <예시 발화> 교사 : I was so impressed that you were all great listeners! Especially you were making eye contact. Like this, it is important to make eye contact to show you're paying attention to the presentation. I'm so proud of you!	
마무리 (5분)	*활동 마무리, 다음 차시 안내 *주변 정리 지도, 인사	

(3) 스크립트

> 응시자 작성 내용 1

✓ 〈자료 1〉의 메뉴를 비교하며 무엇을 더 좋아하는지 말해보도록 할 것

Okay, students!

So far, we've talked about the unit titles and the lesson objectives. Then, are you guys ready for the English class? Perfect! So, I'm going to give you this worksheet. Take one and pass them to the back. Take one and pass them to the back. 종민, over there! Did you get the worksheet? Great!

So, what do you see on the first worksheet? Yes, there are two menus, right? Then I'm going to give you one minute, one minute to quickly go over the menus and decide which one you like better, okay? I'm going to give you one minute. One minute, go!

Okay, time's up, students. Did you guys decide the menu? Okay, then let's have a classroom vote here. Let's have a classroom vote. So, we have two menus, right? So, Menu A versus Menu B. Who prefers Menu A? Raise your hand. Only two students. Okay, so we have two students. And who prefers Menu B? Raise your hand. Oh, 22 students. Okay, 22 students. Then everyone, look at the results here. So, we can see that almost every student prefers Menu B to Menu A. Can you tell us why? Yes, 재우! Oh, did everyone hear what 재우 just said? He said he prefers Menu B because it is much more delicious. Yes, it is... delicious! Okay, and what else? Yes, 호영! Oh, because you eat it every day? Yes, Menu B is much more familiar! So, you eat it every day.

Okay, we just finished the classroom voting and quick survey. Then can you guys guess today's topic? Yes, 수현! Yes, today we are going to talk about food. How does this sound? Are you guys excited? Perfect!

✓ 〈자료 2〉의 주제를 파악하고 제목 짓기 활동을 진행할 것

Then everyone, are you ready to move on to the next part? Perfect!

So, 지환, what do you see on the second worksheet? Yes, there is a reading text, right? So, from now on we are going to read. It's reading time! In this reading time, we are going to first find the main idea. However, to find the main idea, do we have to read quickly or slowly? Yes, 희원! We need to read quickly, right? So, you don't have to understand every single word. Just read quickly and find the main idea. I'm going to give you three minutes. Three minutes, go.

Oh, 민재, do you need any help? Oh, the words are so difficult? Then why don't you look at the back of the worksheet? What do you see? Yes, there is a vocabulary list, right? So, with this vocabulary list, can you find the main idea by yourself? Perfect! Keep up the good work. One minute left, students. Okay, time's up. Then let's check the main idea together. Let's check the main idea.

So, what was the main idea for this reading text? Yes, 민수! Yes, it was the negative... Negative... What was that? Yes, negative effects of... What was that? Yes, 동우! Yes, negative effects of food, right? But what kind of food? Yes, unhealthy food. Negative effects of unhealthy food. So, the main idea was the negative effects of unhealthy food.

However, we just found the main idea like this, but in the reading text there is something strange. Can you guess what it is? Yes, 민수! Yes, did everyone hear what 민수 just said? He said there is no title, right? Then why don't we make a title for this reading text? Sounds great? Okay, let's make a title for this text. So, is there any suggestion? Yes, 현정! Oh, did everyone hear what 현정 just said? She said, "Don't eat..." What was that? Yes, "unhealthy food!" She said, "Don't eat unhealthy food!" She said this would be a great title. Do you guys agree?

So, like this, the main idea and the title have a very close relationship. Can you guys see that? Perfect!

> 응시자 작성 내용 2

✓ 〈자료 2〉의 내용을 바탕으로 〈자료 3〉을 완성할 것

So far we just found the main idea and made a title for this reading text. Then, are you guys ready to read the text a little bit more closely? Perfect!

Then everyone, look at the third worksheet. So, 수민, what do you see on the third worksheet? Yes, there is a question, right? Can you read the question for us? So, it was, "Why should we avoid eating fried food?" Right? From now on, I'm going to give you five minutes. Five minutes to read the text again and find the four reasons, four reasons why we should avoid eating fried food. Okay? However, to find these kinds of specific information, do we have to read the text from the beginning to the end or just read the necessary part? Yes, 다원! We should read only the necessary part, right? So, you don't have to read every single word. Just read the necessary part and find the four reasons why we should avoid eating fried foods. Okay?

Alright! So, 지환, what are we going to do? Yes, we are going to read again and complete the third worksheet, okay? I'm going to give you five minutes. Five minutes, go.

✓ 〈자료 3〉 활동 진행 시 학생 수준별 맞춤 지도를 실시할 것

Oh, 동우, do you need any help? Oh, you can't find where the answers are? Then do you remember the transition words we learned last time? Yes! So, in the reading text there are several transition words. They will help you to find the answers. Can you do that? Great! I love your effort. Oh, 다원, are you already finished? Wow, what a quick reader. Then why don't you write your idea about the reason why we should avoid fried foods? Because the more reasons we have, the better we can understand why we should avoid them. Can you do that? So, write your idea below the answer. Okay? Perfect! One minute left, students. Does anyone need more time? Okay, time's up. So, let's check the reasons together. Let's check the reasons.

So, we have four reasons, right? So, what was the first one? Why do we need to avoid the fried foods? Yes, 재원! We can get too much weight, right? So, the first one is... "Too much weight" Yes! And what was the second one? Yes, 동우! Yes, it can hurt our heart, right? "Hurt their hearts" And what was the last one? Yes, 수현! Yes, eating too much fried food can lead us to get low test scores. So, "Low test scores" Perfect!

✓ 〈자료 2〉의 'It ... that' 표현을 설명하고 학생의 이해를 확인할 것

So far we just read the text twice: One for the main idea and another for the four reasons. However, while you were reading, is there anyone who could find an expression that is used repeatedly? Yes, 호영! Wow, did everyone hear what 호영 just said? He said the expression "It ... that we should ..." is used repeatedly in the reading text. So everyone, let's go back to the reading text again and find the expression.

Oh, 현우, did you find the first one? Alright! Where is it? Yes, the second line from the top. Did everyone find it? Okay, underline it. And who found the second one? Yes 동희! Oh, the fourth line from the bottom. Did everyone find it? Okay, underline it. So, from now on, we are going to talk about the expression called "It ... that", okay? So everyone! Is there anyone who has heard about this expression? Okay, then let me give you a hint. Look at the screen here.

So, 상우, at the back! Can you see the screen? Yes, so what do you see on the screen? Yes, there are two sentences, right? So, can you read the first sentence, 민수? Yes, the first one is, "We should worry about our brain," right? However, can you read the second sentence, 희원? Yes, it says, "It is our brain that we should worry about." Then let me read those two sentences again. Just try to find the difference between those two sentences. Okay? So the first sentence was, "We should worry about our brain." However, I'm going to read the second sentence like this, "It is our brain that we should worry about." Then can you tell the difference between those two sentences? Which one sounds more dramatic? Yes, 종민? Yes, the second one. Then can you guys guess when we use this expression?

Yes, 지환! Wow, did everyone hear what 지환 just said? He said we use this expression when we want to emphasize. Yes, when we want to emphasize something, we can use this "it ... that" expression. Okay? Then can you guys make a sentence with this expression? Yes, 다원! Yes, "It is English class that I like the most." That's a great sentence. Awesome!

So, remember this expression because we are going to use it in the writing. Okay? Perfect!

> 응시자 작성 내용 3

✓ 〈자료 4〉의 활동 이해를 돕기 위한 교사의 예시를 제시할 것

Okay, so we just finished reading about the negative effects of unhealthy food and we learned today's key expression. Then, are you guys ready for the writing? Perfect! So, everyone, look at the fourth worksheet. What do you see on the fourth worksheet? Yes, 수현! Yes, there is a healthy recipe, right? So, from now on, we are going to make a recipe. So, it's "Recipe!" All right, so we are going to do this in groups. So, 현정, 정현, 수현, 현수, you four! You four ... You four ... And finally the last group, you four! Does everyone have their own group? Perfect.

So, with your group members, we are going to make a healthy recipe. Sounds great? Perfect! Then everyone, look at the screen here. So, 민수, over there, can you see the screen? What do you see on the screen? Yes, there is a teacher's example, right? What do you see in there? Yes, there is a drawing of healthy food, right?

So, like this, there are several things you should remember when you make a healthy recipe. Okay? All right, so you should remember this. So, like you guys just said, you first need the drawing. Okay, so drawing of the healthy food. You should need the drawing. And what else can you see in the teacher's example? Yes, 동우! Yes, so your food should have a name. And what else can you see? Yes, 민재! Yes, there is how to make it, right? So, you should include how to make How to make it. And what else? Yes, 희원! Yes, there is the reason why we are recommending this food, right? So, you should include the reason. The reason why you are recommending this. And lastly, do you guys remember today's key expression? Yes 호영! Yes, it was "it ... that," right? So, when you make a healthy recipe, try to use this expression: This "it ... that" expression to emphasize. All right? Perfect!

✓ 〈자료 4〉를 완성하고 모둠 발표를 진행할 것

Before we start, let me give each one of you guys a role. Okay? So let me give you a role. All right! So you guys are sitting like this, right? Okay, so students here, raise your hand! You guys are going to be 'the Painters.' So, what do you guys have to do? Yes, you are going to draw the healthy food. Okay? But you don't need to be perfect. Just try best of your job! Okay? And students here, raise your hand. All right, so you guys are going to be 'the Dictionaries.' So, Dictionaries, what do you have to do? Yes, 민수! If your group members need to find the words or check the grammar, that's your job. Okay? So, Dictionaries! You guys can bring your table PCs to find the words or check the grammar for your group members. Okay? All right. Then students sitting here, raise your hand. Yes, you guys are going to be 'the Writers.' So, you're going to write the sentences to complete the healthy recipe. Okay? Perfect! And lastly, students sitting here, raise your hand. Okay, so you guys are going to be 'the Presenters.' So, we are going to have a presentation after this. Make sure you're preparing for the upcoming presentation. Okay?

So, everyone, just before we start, look here. I'm going to tell you that the best recipe will be delivered to the school cafeteria and it will become a real lunch menu next week. How does that sound? Are you guys excited? Perfect! So, I'm going to give you 15 minutes. 15 minutes to do what, 다원? Yes, we are going to make a healthy recipe, right? So, remember these points. And 동우, what is your role in the group? Yes, you are a presenter, right? So, I'm going to give you 15 minutes. 15 minutes, go.

Oh, group one, do you guys need any help? Oh, it's too difficult to come up with a healthy food? Then, why don't you use this? What do you see? Yes, it's a recipe book from last year. You can find many examples of healthy foods. So, would it be helpful for coming up with some ideas? Perfect! Then can you guys do that by yourselves? Awesome! So, if you guys need any help, feel free to raise your hand. All right? Oh, group four, are you guys finished? Wow, what a quick writer and painter. Then why don't you make another food? Because, you know, there are many kinds of healthy food. The more we have, the healthier we'll become. Can you guys do that? Perfect! One minute left, students. Does any group need more time? Okay, time's up.

> 응시자 작성 내용 4

✓ 모둠 발표에 관한 동료 평가 기준을 4가지 제시할 것

So, we just finished making our own healthy food. Then presenters, are you guys ready? Okay, then let's have a presentation time.

It's time for the presentation. However, listeners, whenever we do this kind of presentation, what do we have to check first? Yes, 민재! We need to first check the checklist, right? So, let's have a checklist here. I'm going to give you this checklist. Take one and pass them to the back. Take one and pass them to the back. 민수 at the back, did you get the checklist? Okay, so how many parts can you see in the checklist? Yes, there are four parts, right? So, what's the first one, 종민? Yes, it is "Drawing', right? So, the first one is 'Drawing.' And what does that mean? Yes, 수민! Yes, it should be a drawing of the healthy food. So, it's from here. And what's the second part? Yes, 호영! Yes, it says 'the Content', right? So, you should check the content of the recipe. And how many points can you see in there? Yes, there are three points, right? So, what are they, 수현? Yes, there are 'the Name' and 'How to make it' and 'Reasons', right? So, these are from here. So, 'Name', 'How to make it', and 'the Reasons' These three things we should check for 'the Content.' And what was the third part? Yes, 재원! Yes, it says 'Language', right? So, the third part is 'Language.' And what does that mean? Yes, it means your writing should include the key expression. What was that? Yes, 종민! It was "it ...that" expression, right? So, you should include the "it ... that" expression. And the last part, what is the last part? Yes, 민수! Yes, it says 'the Attitude', right? So, the last part was 'the Attitude.' And what does that mean? Yes,희원! Yes, the presenters should be confident of your presentation. You don't need perfect pronunciation. Just make sure you're trying to be confident when using English, okay? So with this checklist, presenters, are you guys ready for the presentation? Perfect! So, let's have the first presentation to the front!

✓ 발표 후 청중의 태도에 관한 피드백을 제공할 것

Okay, so we just finished checking our presentation and there was one thing I was so impressed about. It was you guys are all great listeners. So, you guys are great listeners! This is because when I was looking around, I could see that all of you were making eye contact. So, I really liked your eye contact to the presentation because making eye contact means you are paying attention to the presentation. That's a great attitude for the listeners and that's why I'm so proud of you guys. So, let's give ourselves a big hand. Perfect!

마 연습문제 5회 : 2020 기출 변형

(1) 판서 노트 및 예시 영상

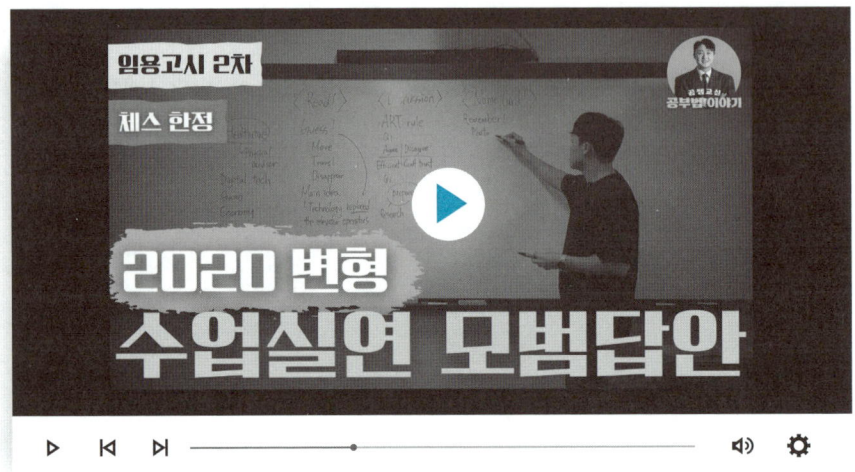

수업실연 예시
2020 기출 변형

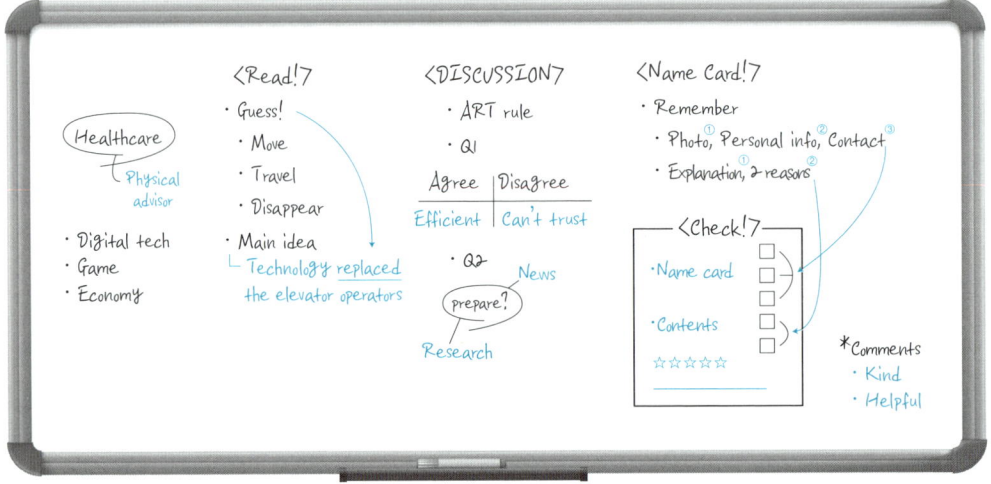

(2) 지도안 예시

단원명	Future Jobs				시간	100 mins
대상	• Students : 24 High school 1st Graders • Level : Mixed					
수업 목표	✓ Students will be able to use an appropriate strategy to find the main idea. ✓ Students will be able to share their ideas properly in the discussion. ✓ Students will be able to introduce their future jobs with their name cards.					
교수·학습 교구	Digital whiteboard, Laptop, Online dictionary, Tablet PCs etc					
핵심역량	자기 관리	지식정보처리	창의적 사고	심미적 감성	협력적 소통	공동체
	✓	✓			✓	

<교수 학습 지도안>

단계	교수·학습 활동	유의점
도입 (5분)	*인사, 출석 확인, 교실 내 안전 점검 *학습 주제, 수업 준비 상태 확인	
전개1 (15분)	**응시자 작성 내용 1** ✓ <자료 1>에 제시된 미래 직업 분야 중 1개를 예시와 함께 설명할 것 ● Teaching Vocabulary • [전체] <자료 1>을 학생에게 나누어주고 각 영역에 대해 주목하게 한다. • 학생들이 어려워하는 용어를 파악하고 해당 의미를 추론할 수 있도록 관련 분야 직업 예시를 제시한다. • 의미를 성공적으로 추론한 후, 해당 분야에 대한 다른 직업을 제시하도록 함으로써 이해 확인 점검을 실시한다. <예시 발화> 교사 : Which future job areas are you unfamiliar with? 학생 : What is 'Healthcare'? 교사 : It is about taking care of the health, especially for old people, such as physical advisors who give advice on what to eat or how to exercise. 학생 : Oh, now I understand! 교사 : Great. Then, can you give me another example of 'Healthcare'? 학생 : Physical therapist! ✓ <자료 1>을 활용하여 희망 미래 직업 분야의 관심도를 표현하게 할 것 ● Transition • 이전 활동이 해당 활동을 위한 준비였음을 언급하며 활동 간 연결성을 강조한다. <예시 발화> 교사 : Okay, now we all know the meanings of future job areas. Then, are you ready to know about yourselves?	

	● Schema activation • [짝, 5분] <자료 1>의 'Your idea' 부분을 짝과 함께 논의하여 채워보도록 한다. • [전체, 5분] Modeling : 교사의 예시를 학생들에게 보여주며 육각형에 자신의 관심도를 선으로 표시하게 한다. 　　<예시 발화> 　　교사 : As you can see here, check how much you are interested in each area and draw lines between them.
전개2 (25분)	**응시자 작성 내용 2** ✓ <자료 2>의 제목을 활용하여 읽기 전 활동을 진행할 것 ● Guessing • [전체] <자료 2>의 제목을 언급하고 무슨 뜻일지 질문하며 학생과 상호작용한다.. 　　<예시 발화> 　　교사 : Let's check the title first? What does it mean? Can you guess? 　　학생 : Disappear? Travel? Move? • 학생과의 상호작용(Guessing 활동)을 마인드맵으로 요약하여 판서한다. ✓ <자료 2>의 주제를 읽기 전략을 사용하여 파악하도록 할 것 ● Main idea • [개별, 2분] Skimming 전략을 사용하여 <자료 2>의 Main idea를 파악하게 한다. 　• 빠른 속도로 글을 훑어보며 반복되는 단어를 확인하도록 한다. • 아래 지도 사항에 따라 순회 지도를 실시한다. 　　<순회 지도 사항> 　　• 참여를 북돋우며 활동에 어려움을 겪는 학생을 찾는다. 　　• Low-level : <자료 2> 뒤편의 <Vocabulary list>를 제시한다. • [전체] 학생과의 상호작용을 통해 글의 주제를 교실 전체에 공유하고 판서한다. 　• Main idea : Technology replaced the elevator operators. • [전체] 글의 제목과 Main idea의 관련성에 다시 한번 주목하게 하며 앞서 실시한 Guessing 활동에 대한 답을 생각하게끔 한다. ✓ <자료 2>를 활용하여 모둠 토의를 실시하고 그 결과를 공유할 것 ● Group discussion • [모둠, 10분] 4인 1조로, 6개의 모둠을 구성한다. • 모두 각자 의견을 제시할 수 있도록 하고, 아래 ART rule을 지키도록 독려한다. 　　<ART rule> 　　A : Active participation,　　R : Respect others,　　T : Take turns • [전체] 학생과 상호작용하며 모둠토의 결과를 교실 전체에 공유하고 그 결과를 판서한다.

<판서 예시>

Q1	
Agree	Disagree
• Efficient	• Can't trust

Q2: How to prepare

응시자 작성 내용 3

✓ <자료 3>을 활용하여 말하기 활동을 진행할 것

전개3 (40분)

● **Transition**
- 이전 활동이 해당 활동을 위한 준비였음을 언급하며 활동 간 연결성을 강조한다.

<예시 발화>
교사 : Okay, now we realized that we need to prepare for the future. Then, don't you feel we should find more about the future jobs?

● **Mingling activity**
- [개별, 3분] <자료 3>에 자신의 관심 직업 영역과 예시 직업 1가지를 작성하도록 한다.
- [전체, 3분] 교실을 돌아다니며 같은 직업 분야를 선택한 학생을 찾도록 한다.
  - 그룹을 찾지 못하는 학생은 교사가 적극적으로 개입하여 그룹을 만들어 준다.
- [모둠, 2~4명, 10분] 해당 그룹 내에서 서로 질문을 주고받으며 <자료 3>을 완성하도록 한다.

<예시 발화>
교사 : You can make a group of 2, 3 or 4. It's up to you. Just make sure you guys have the same job area.

- 모두 <자료 3>을 완성했는지 확인하고 각자 자리로 돌아가게 한다.

✓ <자료 3>의 직업 중 1개를 선택하여 <자료 4>를 완성할 것

● **Transition**
- 이전 활동이 해당 활동을 위한 준비였음을 언급하며 활동 간 연결성을 강조한다.

<예시 발화>
교사 : So far, we just shared our ideas of promising future jobs and realized that there were more examples in our job areas. Then are you ready to decide which one would be the best for us?

● **My future name card**
- 학생에게 개인 Tablet PC를 꺼내어 Online Classroom에 접속하게 한다.
- Sample writing을 화면으로 보여주며 <자료 4>에 대한 글쓰기 기준을 제시한다.

전개3 (40분)	<글쓰기 기준> 1. Photo, Personal info., Contacts 2. Job explanation, 2 reasons • Authentic purpose : 우수 작품은 교실 게시판에 전시된다는 점을 강조하며 실제적 동기부여를 실시한다. • [개별, 20분] 자신이 작성한 <자료 3>을 바탕으로 <자료 4>를 완성하도록 한다. • 아래 지도 사항에 따라 순회 지도를 실시한다. <순회 지도 사항> • 참여를 북돋우며 활동 중 어려움을 겪고 있는 학생을 파악한다. • Low-level : 번역 프로그램이나 문법 확인 프로그램을 소개하며 적극적으로 활용할 수 있도록 격려한다. • High-level : 활동 참여에 대한 긍정적 피드백을 제공하고, 직업이 유망한 이유를 조금 더 써 볼 수 있도록 유도한다.	
전개4 (10분)	응시자 작성 내용 4 √ 블랜디드 수업 환경을 활용하여 <자료 4>에 대한 동료 평가를 실시할 것 ● Peer evaluation • Online classroom에서 다른 친구들의 Name card를 확인하게 한다. • 아래 <Check list>에 따라 별점을 0~5개까지 줄 수 있도록 한다. • 평가 기준이 글쓰기 기준과 연결됨을 강조한다. <Check list> | | | |---|---| | 1. Name card | Photo | | | Personal info. | | | Contacts | | 2. Contents | Job explanation | | | 2 reasons | Total : ☆☆☆☆☆ (0~5) Comments : _____ • [5분, 개별] 친구의 작품을 보고 별점과 Comment를 제공하도록 한다. √ 동료 평가 활동에 대한 교사의 긍정적 피드백을 제공할 것 ● Giving feedback • [전체] 교사의 온라인 동료 평가 관찰 결과를 바탕으로 긍정적 피드백을 제공한다. • (예시) 적극적으로 평가 활동에 참여했다는 점, 구체적인 칭찬 댓글이 달렸다는 점, 친절한 댓글을 작성하였다는 점, Job explanation이 정확하다는 점 등	
마무리 (5분)	*활동 마무리, 다음 차시 안내 *주변 정리 지도, 인사	

(3) 스크립트

> 응시자 작성 내용 1

✓ 〈자료 1〉에 제시된 미래 직업 분야 중 1개를 예시와 함께 설명할 것

Okay, students! So far we've talked about the unit title and the lesson objectives. Then, are you guys ready to start the English class? Great! So I'm going to give you this worksheet. Take one and pass it to the back. 현정, over there, did you get the worksheet? Great! What do you see on the worksheet? Yes, there are promising future job areas, right? Just quickly check those areas. Is there any unfamiliar word? Yes, 민수! Oh, the 'Healthcare' is quite unfamiliar with you. Is there anyone who knows well about the healthcare area?

Then let me give you an example of 'Healthcare.' So you guys are unfamiliar with this future job area, 'Healthcare.' Let me give you an example. Healthcare is about taking care of health, especially for old people. One example is a physical advisor. Physical advisors give some advice on how to exercise or what to eat to improve health. So, 민수, can you get the meaning of 'Healthcare'? Great! Then can you give us another example of 'Healthcare'? Oh, that's great! Did everyone hear what 민수 just said? He said, 'Physical therapist' is another great example of healthcare. That's a great example, 민수! Perfect!

✓ 〈자료 1〉을 활용하여 희망 미래 직업 분야의 관심도를 표현하게 할 것

So far, we just learned these unfamiliar future job areas. Then everyone, look at the first worksheet again. There's something strange. Can you guess? Yes, 현정! We have five future job areas, but one is missing, right? So from now on, with your partners—so 현정, 정현, you two! 수현, 현수, you two! You two! So everyone has their own partners? Great! With your partners, we are going to talk about future jobs and write down your own ideas, okay? So, 종민! What are we going to do? Yes, talk with your partner and write down your idea of future job areas, okay? I'm going to give you five minutes. Five minutes, go! One minute left, students. Okay, time's up.

So let's share your ideas together. Is there any volunteer? Yes, 지환! Oh, did everyone hear what 지환 just said? He said, 'Digital technology' is going to be a promising job area.

That's a great idea. So... 'Digital technology' will be a very promising future job area. And what else? Yes, 다원! Yes, 'Game' will be a very promising job area. And what else? Yes, 동우! Oh yes, 'Economy' will be a very promising job area. So, 'Economy'! Yes, that's a great idea, 동우! Okay, so we just finished our own ideas of future job areas.

Then everyone, look here. What do you see? Yes, it's a teacher's example, right? So like this, you are going to check how much you're interested in each area and draw lines between them. Can you guys do that? Great! I'm going to give you five minutes. Five minutes, go. One minute left, students. Does anyone need more time? Okay, time's up.

응시자 작성 내용 2

✓ 〈자료 2〉의 제목을 활용하여 읽기 전 활동을 진행할 것

So we just finished checking our own interests about the future job areas. So let's move on to the second worksheet. So 현정, what do you see on the second worksheet? Yes, there is a reading text, right? So from now on, it's going to be reading time. Let's read! So, 다원, can you read the title for us?

Yes, what was the title? "Where Did Elevator Operators Go?", right? The title is very interesting, isn't it? So before we read, let's make a guess with the title. So... Let's make a guess with the title! Let's talk about what the text might be about. There is no right answer. Feel free to share your ideas. Yes, 수현, they moved to another place. Yes, that's a great guessing! And what else? Yes, 종민! Oh, they are traveling. Yes, that's a great guessing. They can go on vacation. So 'traveling' is a great guessing. And what else? Yes, 희원! Oh, they disappeared all of a sudden. Yes, 'disappear' is a great guessing with the title.

So like this, we just made several guesses with the title. Someone said they moved to another place, someone said they are traveling, and someone said they just disappeared. Then, don't you want to know what actually happened? Are you ready to read? Great!

✓ 〈자료 2〉의 주제를 읽기 전략을 사용하여 파악하도록 할 것

So from now on, we are going to read the text and find the main idea. However, to find the main idea, do we have to read the text quickly or slowly? Yes, 수현, we need to read quickly, right? So you don't have to understand every single word. Just read quickly and find the main idea. I'm going to give you two minutes. Two minutes, go.

Oh, 상우, do you need any help? Oh, the words are so difficult. Then, why don't you look at the back of the worksheet? What do you see? Yes, there is a vocabulary list, right? So with this vocabulary list, can you do this work by yourself? Perfect! I love your effort! One minute left, students. Okay, time's up, students. So let's check the main idea all together. So what was the main idea of this reading text? Can anyone share your idea? Yes, 수현! Oh yes! So the main idea was technology... Technology did what? Yes, 종민, Technology replaced... Replaced who? Yes, 지환, replaced the elevator... What was that? Elevator, yes, that's right—operators. So the main idea was "Technology replaced the elevator operators", right?

Great! Then everyone, let's check the title again. The title was "Where Did the Elevator Operators Go?", right? So after we read, now we just realized the meaning of the title was what? Yes, it was "replaced". right?

✓ 〈자료 2〉를 활용하여 모둠 토의를 실시하고 그 결과를 공유할 것

Okay, so far we just read the text and found the main idea. Then, are you guys ready to talk about it? Great! Then, let's have a small discussion. It's discussion time! Let's have a small discussion here. So, 현수, what do you see below the text? Yes, there are two discussion questions, right? So from now on, we are going to have a small discussion with your group members.

So, 현수, 수현, 종민, 민종, you four! You four... You four... and last group, you four! Does everyone have their own group? Great! With your group members, share your ideas about those two discussion questions below the reading text, okay? However, whenever we have this kind of discussion, which rule do we have to follow? Yes, 지환, we have to follow the ART rule, right? The ART rule. So what was "A", 동우? Yes, "A" was "Active participation".

And what was "R", 희원? Yes, it was "Respect others." So make sure you're respecting your friends' ideas, okay? Then lastly, what was "T", 다원? Yes, "T" was "Take turns", right? So make sure everyone is talking.

Great? Then 현우, what are we going to do? Yes, we are going to have a small discussion with those two discussion questions, okay? I'm going to give you ten minutes. Ten minutes, go! Oh, group one, I can see 다원 is actively participating. However, what was the T rule? Yes, it was "Take turns", right? So make sure everyone is talking, great? Perfect! One minute left, students. Is there any group that needs more time? Okay, time's up. So everyone finished the discussion? Great!

So let's share what you talked about together. What was the first question? Yes, 희원! Yes, it was "Technology replaces jobs. Do you agree or disagree?", right? So the first question was, Technology replaces what? Yes, 종민, jobs! So do you agree or disagree? It was the first discussion question. So, is there any group who agrees with this idea? Yes, group two. Oh, did everyone hear what group two just said? They said technology will replace jobs because it is much more efficient. Yes, technology is much more efficient. However, is there any group who disagrees with this idea?

Yes, group five. Oh, did everyone hear what group five just said? They said technology will not replace jobs because we can't trust technology 100% yet. So, 'disagree' because we can't trust technology. That was a great idea, group five. So let's move on to the second question. What was the second question, 다원? Yes, it was, "What should we do to prepare for the future?" The second question was, "What should we do to prepare for the future?", right? So, "Prepare for the future" Okay! So, is there any volunteer to share your ideas? Yes, group one. Oh, that's right, we should read the newspapers. So we should check the news.

And what else? Yes, group four. Great, that's a great idea as well. So we should do some job research to prepare for the future. That was a great idea.

응시자 작성 내용 3

✓ 〈자료 3〉을 활용하여 말하기 활동을 진행할 것

 Okay, so far we just read about future jobs and we just finished the discussion about future jobs. Then don't you feel we should find out more about future jobs? Great! Then everyone, look at the third worksheet. What do you see, 동우? Yes, there is "Promising Future Jobs", right? So from now on, I'm going to give you three minutes, three minutes to write down your job area and one example job from that area, okay? So, 지환, what are we going to do? Yes, write down your job area and one example job from that area. I'm going to give you three minutes. Three minutes, go! One minute left, students. Okay, time's up.

 Everyone finished writing down your job areas? Great! So from now on, it's time to walk around and find someone who has the same interest with you, the same job area with you. Are you guys excited? Great! So I'm going to give you three minutes, three minutes to walk around the classroom and find someone who has the same job areas with you. You can make a group of two, three, or four. It doesn't matter. Just make sure you guys have the same interest, same job areas, okay? I'm going to give you three minutes. Three minutes, go.

 Oh, 지환, do you need any help? Oh, you can't find someone who has the same interest with you. Then what was your job area? Oh, mathematics? Then why don't you go talk with 민종 over there? I think he has the same interest with you. So, can you do that? Perfect!

 Okay, time's up. Does everyone have their own group? Great. So take the desk in front of you and have a seat there. So all you guys have the same job areas? Okay, this group is... Yes, engineering! And this group is... Yes, healthcare! Then from now on, I'm going to give you ten minutes, ten minutes to talk with your group members to share your job examples, okay? So, 수미, what are we going to do? Yes, we are going to share our job examples with your group members, okay? So I'm going to give you ten minutes. Ten minutes, go!

✓ 〈자료 3〉의 직업 중 1개를 선택하여 〈자료 4〉를 완성할 것

Okay, time's up. So far, with your group members, we just finished sharing our own job examples within the same job areas, right? Then are you ready to decide which one will be the best for us? Perfect! So it's time to make a name card. So, let's make the name card. Great! So everyone, open up your tablet PCs and come to the online classroom. So, 수현, over there, are you in the online classroom? Perfect!

So what do you see in there? Yes, there is a sample writing, right? Then in the sample writing, what do you see? Yes, there is a photo, right? So like this, there are several things you should remember when you make a name card, okay? So, remember these points when you make a name card. Remember this: the first one is, like 지환 just said, you should include the photo. Okay? And beside the photo, what do you see? Yes, 다원! Yes, there is 'Personal information', right? So like this, your name card should include personal information: Your name or your job.

And next, what can you see? Yes, 희원! Yes, there is 'Contacts', right? So, you should include the contacts: Your email or your phone number. And below the name card, what do you see? Yes, 재우! Yes, there is a job explanation. So you should include the job explanation. Job explanation. And what else? What else can you see in the sample writing? Yes, 현우! Yes, reasons, right. Reasons why the job is promising in the future. So you should include at least two reasons, two reasons why the job is promising in the future.

Okay, before we start, everyone, look here. I want to tell you that the best name card will be posted on the classroom bulletin board. How does that sound? Exciting? Perfect! So choose the best one from the third worksheet and complete the name card based on that. So, 수미, what are we going to do? Yes, we are going to choose the best one from the third worksheet and complete the name card, okay? Make sure you guys include these things. Okay, I'm going to give you 20 minutes. Twenty minutes, go.

Oh, 민재, do you need any help? Oh, you are having difficulties with writing some sentences? Then why don't you use a translation program or grammar checking program? You know, there are many things you can use in the online classroom. So with these programs, can you do this work by yourself? Great! Just make sure to feel free to call me if you need another help, okay? Good!

Oh, 민수, you already finished? Wow, what a quick writer. Then why don't you write more sentences about the reasons why your job is promising? Because the more reasons you have, the better you will understand about the future jobs. Can you do that? Perfect! One minute left, students. Does anyone need more time? Okay, time's up.

응시자 작성 내용 4

✓ 블렌디드 수업 환경을 활용하여 〈자료 4〉에 대한 동료 평가를 실시할 것

So we just finished making our own name cards. Then don't you guys want to see your friends' name cards? Perfect! Then let's begin the check time. So it's time for the check. Everyone, look at the right corner of the online classroom. What do you see, 현수? Yes, there is a checklist, right? Can you guys click it? Perfect.

So, 민수, how many parts can you see? Yes, there are two parts, right? So what was the first one? Yes, it is the name card. We should check the name card first. And how many points can you see in the name card? Yes, there are three points, right? So, there are three points. What are they? Yes, the first one is photo. And the second one is? Yes, 민수, it's personal information. And what was the last one? Yes, 수현, it was contacts. So, these three things will be the three points in the name card.

And what's the second part of the checklist? Yes, 다원! Yes, it is contents, right? So it's contents. So how many checkpoints in the contents? Yes, 수미, there are two points, right? So what are they? Yes, the first one is explanation. And what's the second one? Yes, 수현! Yes, it's two reasons, right? So when you check your friends' name cards, make sure you check these two points, okay?

So how many stars can you give in total? Yes, 지환, you can give five stars. So there are five stars that you can give. And below that, what can you see? Yes, 종민! You can leave comments, right? So make sure you leave comments to your friends' name cards, okay? So from now on, I'm going to give you five minutes. Five minutes to do what? Yes, 현수! We are going to check our friends' name cards and give stars, leave comments, okay? I'm going to give you five minutes. Scroll up and down and check your friends' name cards. Five minutes, go. One minute left, students. Does anyone need more time? Okay, time's up.

✓ **동료 평가 활동에 대한 교사의 긍정적 피드백을 제공할 것**

We just finished checking our friends' name cards. However, while I was looking around, there were two things I was so impressed: About your comments. Especially your comments... I was so impressed. The first one was you guys were very kind. You were leaving very kind comments to your friends' writing. So like this, make sure you're leaving very kind comments in the online classroom. Okay?

And second, your comments were very helpful. So, your comments were very kind and very helpful because I could see a lot of great advice that would improve your friends' name cards. So why don't we give a big hand for ourselves? Perfect! We just finished checking our friends' name cards. Then just before we wrap up the class, let's go back to the unit title again. What was the unit title? Yes, 지환. Yes, it was 'The Future Jobs', right?

So about future jobs, we read about it, and we talked about it, and we wrote about it. Then don't you feel you're a little bit confident of yourselves because you're better prepared for the future? Awesome! That was just what I wanted for this class. That's it for us, and have a great day!

연습문제 6회 : 2019 기출 변형

(1) 판서 노트 및 예시 영상

수업실연 예시
2019 기출 변형
동영상 바로가기

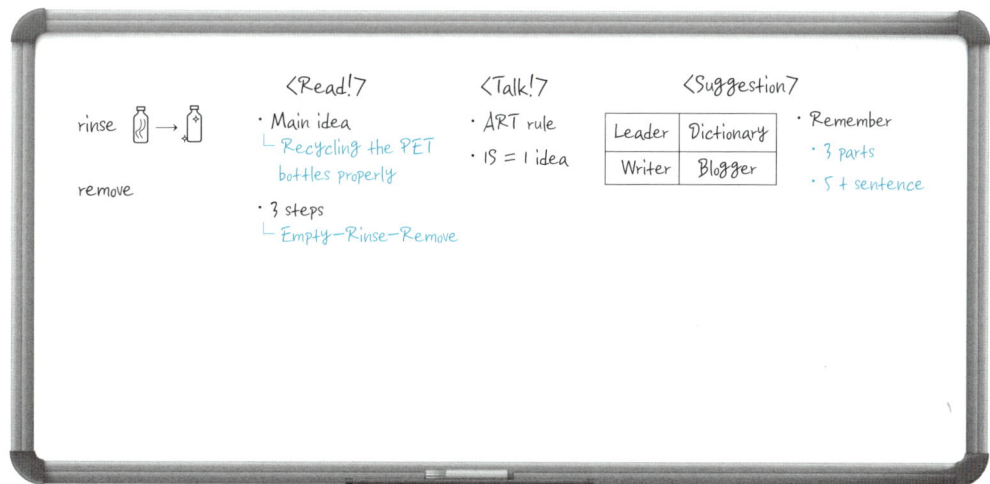

(2) 지도안 예시

단원명	Change Makers				시간	90 mins
대상	• Students : 24 Middle school 3rd Graders • Level : Mixed					
수업 목표	✓ Students will be able to find paragraph structure of the reading text. ✓ Students will be able to share their ideas properly in the discussion. ✓ Students will be able to write their suggestions for the better school.					
교수·학습 교구	Digital whiteboard, Laptop, Online dictionary, Tablet PCs etc					
핵심역량	자기 관리	지식정보처리	창의적 사고	심미적 감성	협력적 소통	공동체
		✓			✓	✓

<교수 학습 지도안>

단계	교수·학습 활동	유의점
도입 (5분)	*인사, 출석 확인, 교실 내 안전 점검 *학습 주제, 수업 준비 상태 확인	
전개1 (10분)	<center>응시자 작성 내용 1</center> ✓ <자료 1>에 제시된 사진을 보고 대화를 나누어보는 짝 활동을 진행할 것 ✓ <자료 1>에 관한 대화 주제 1가지를 교사가 제시할 것 ● **Small discussion** • [전체] <자료 1>을 학생에게 나누어준다. • 짝 토의를 실시하기 전, Screen을 활용하여 아래 질문을 제공한다. 　• (예시) What's the difference between the two pictures? • [짝, 5분] 짝을 나누어 주어진 주제로 이야기를 나눠보게 한다. ● **Transition** • <자료 1>의 토의 내용을 바탕으로 오늘 차시 주제를 예상하도록 하며 <자료 2>를 소개한다. <예시 발화> 교사 : What was the difference between the two pictures? 학생 : The bottles on the left are cleaner than the ones on the right. 교사 : Great! Then, which one do you like better for recycling? 학생 : The left ones. 교사 : Awesome! Then, don't you want to know more about how to recycle the bottles?	

	응시자 작성 내용 2

전개2
(15분)
	✓ <자료 2>의 밑줄 친 단어를 맥락을 활용하여 지도할 것
	
	● Teaching Vocabulary
	• [전체] <자료 2>을 학생에게 나누어주고 밑줄 친 단어에 대해 주목하게 한다.
	• 'rinse'와 'remove'의 뜻을 아는 학생들이 있는지 질문한다.
	• 해당 단어를 추론할 수 있도록 맥락을 제공한다.
	
	<예시 발화>
	교사 : This is a dirty bottle. However, when I 'rinse' it, now we have this clean bottle! Can you guess the meaning of 'rinse'?
	학생 : I think 'rinse' means 'wash'.
	
	• 의미를 성공적으로 추론한 후, 직접 문장을 만들어 보게 함으로써 이해 확인 점검을 실시한다.
	
	● Transition
	• 어휘 학습이 읽기 학습을 하기 위한 사전 준비 활동임을 언급하며 다음 활동과의 연결성을 강조한다.
	
	<예시 발화>
	교사 : Okay, we just learned some difficult words. Then, are you ready for the reading?
	
	✓ <자료 2>의 주제를 파악하도록 할 것
	
	● Main idea
	• [개별, 3분] <자료 2>를 학생에게 나누어주고 Main idea를 파악하게 한다.
	• Skimming 전략을 지도하여 글의 주제를 파악하도록 한다.
	  • 빠른 속도로 글을 훑어보며 반복되는 단어를 확인하도록 한다.
	• 아래 지도 사항에 따라 순회 지도를 실시한다.
	
	<순회 지도 사항>
	• 참여를 북돋우며 활동 중 어려움을 겪고 있는 학생을 파악한다.
	• Low-level : <자료 2> 뒤편의 <Vocabulary list>를 제시한다.
	
	• [전체] 학생과의 상호작용을 통해 글의 주제를 교실 전체에 공유하고 판서한다.
	  • Main idea : Recycling PET bottles properly
	• [전체] 글의 제목이 없음을 강조하며, 글의 제목을 직접 지어보도록 제안한다.
	
	<예시 발화>
	교사 : Since we found the main idea, why don't we make the title? Do you have any good idea?
	학생 : I think 'How to recycle PET bottles' is a great title.

✓ <자료 2>의 글의 구조를 언급하며 세부 정보를 찾는 활동을 진행할 것

● **Text structure**
- [전체] 학생과 상호작용을 통하여 글의 구조가 '서론', '본론', '결론'으로 이루어짐을 안내한다.

<예시 발화>

교사 : How many parts can you find in the reading text?
학생 : There are three parts!
교사 : Great! We call them 'introduction', 'body' and 'conclusion'.

● **Detail information**
- [개별, 5분] Screen을 통해 세부 정보를 찾기 위한 질문을 학생들에게 제시한다.
  - (예시) What are the 3 steps for recycling PET bottles?
- Scanning 전략을 지도하여 질문에 대한 답을 찾도록 한다.
  - 글 전체가 아니라 필요한 부분만 선별하여 읽도록 한다.
- 아래 지도 사항에 따라 순회 지도를 실시한다.

<순회 지도 사항>

- 참여를 북돋우며 활동 중 어려움을 겪고 있는 학생을 파악한다.
- High-level : 활동 참여에 대한 긍정적 피드백을 제공하고, Student teacher 역할을 부여하여 다른 학생을 도울 수 있도록 한다.
- Low-level : 동료 학습자로부터 도움을 받을 수 있도록 Peer-scaffolding을 유도한다.

- [전체] 학생과의 상호작용을 통해 답변 공유하고 판서한다.
  - 3 steps for recylcing PET bottles : Empty - Rinse - Remove

● **Transition**
- 학생과 상호작용을 통하여 글의 내용이 더 나은 미래를 만들기 위함임을 안내하고, 다음 활동과의 연관성을 강조한다.

<예시 발화>

교사 : So far, we just finished reading about recycling. However, why do we need to recycle?
학생 : For the better environment!
교사 : Perfect! Then, is there anything we can do for a better school? Why don't we talk about it?

전개2
(15분)

	응시자 작성 내용 3
	✓ <자료 3>을 활용하여 모둠 토의를 진행할 것

● **Group discussion**
- [모둠, 20분] 4인 1조로, 6개의 모둠을 구성한다.
- 한 학생당 한 개의 의견을 제시하여 <자료 3>을 완성하도록 한다.
- 아래 ART rule을 지킬 수 있도록 독려한다.

> **< ART rule >**
> A : Active participation, R : Respect others, T : Take turns

전개3 (25분)

✓ 토의 중 모둠을 순회하며 촉진자 역할을 수행할 것

- 토의 중 아래 지도 사항에 따라 순회 지도를 실시한다.

> **<순회 지도 사항>**
> - 참여를 북돋우며 활동 중 어려움을 겪고 있는 학생을 파악한다.
> - Low-level : ART rule 재강조, 토의에 어려움을 겪는 학생에게는 학생회 건의 사항을 참고할 수 있도록 한다.
> - High-level : 활동 참여에 대한 긍정적 피드백을 제공하고 추가 아이디어를 제시할 수 있도록 한다.

> **<예시 발화>**
> 교사 : If it is too difficult to come up with some idea, why don't you look at this paper I brought for you? What do you see?
> 학생 : There are suggestions from the student council.
> 교사 : That's right! With this suggestions, can you do this by yourselves?

	응시자 작성 내용 4
	✓ <토의 내용을 바탕으로 <자료4>를 완성할 것

● **For the better school**
- [모둠, 2분] <자료 3>에서 우리 학교에 가장 필요한 것 한 개를 선택하도록 한다.
- 이를 바탕으로 <자료 4>를 완성하기 위한 역할을 부여한다.

전개4 (30분)

<역할 부여>

Leader	Dictionary	• 좌석에 따라 역할 부여 • Leader : 팀 내 의견 조율, 갈등 해결 • Dictionary : Tablet PC 지참, 단어 검색, 문법 확인 • Writer : 문장 작성 • Presenter : 과제물 Online classroom에 게시
Writer	Blogger	

전개4 (30분)	• 교사의 Sample writing을 화면을 통해 제시하며 글쓰기 조건을 안내한다. **＜조건＞** 1. Complete the 3 parts 2. 5+ sentences ✓ 실제적 목표를 제시하여 활동 참여 동기 부여를 할 것 • Authentic purpose : 우수한 제안서는 실제로 교육청에 우편으로 전달된다는 사실을 언급하며 활동 참여 동기를 강화한다. **＜예시 발화＞** 교사 : The best writing will be delivered to the District Office of Education so that your suggestions can be actually realized! How does that sound? 학생 : Very excited! • [모둠, 20분] 학생에게 <자료 4>를 완성하도록 하며, 교사는 아래 지도 사항에 따라 순회 지도를 실시한다. **＜순회 지도 사항＞** • 참여를 북돋우며 활동 중 어려움을 겪고 있는 학생을 파악한다. • Low level : <자료 4> 뒤편의 <Expression list>를 제시한다. • High level : 긍정적 피드백을 제공한 뒤, 제안서를 하나 더 쓸 수 있도록 추가 과제를 부여한다.	
마무리 (5분)	*활동 마무리, 다음 차시 안내 *주변 정리 지도, 인사	

(3) 스크립트

> 응시자 작성 내용 1

✓ 〈자료 1〉에 제시된 사진을 보고 대화를 나누어보는 짝 활동을 진행할 것

✓ 〈자료 1〉에 관한 대화 주제 1가지를 교사가 제시할 것

Okay, students. So far, we've talked about the unit titles and the lesson objectives. Then, are you guys ready to start the English class? Great!

From now on, I'm going to give you this worksheet. Take one and pass them to the back. Take one and pass them to the back. 수미 at the back, did you get the worksheet? Great!

Then, what do you see on the worksheet? Yes, 종민, there are... How many pictures? Yes, there are two pictures. So, with those two pictures... Everyone, can you look at the screen there? 지환, at the back, can you see the screen? Okay!

What do you see on the screen? Great, there is a question, right? 지환, can you read the question for us? Yes, it says, "What's the difference between the two pictures?" Right?

So, from now on, with your partners, 수현, 현수, you two! 종민, 민종, you two! So, you two... Does everyone have their own partners? Great! With your partners, we're going to talk about the differences between those pictures.

동우, what are we going to do? Yes, we are going to talk about the differences between those pictures with your partners, okay? I'm going to give you five minutes. Five minutes, go!

One minute left, students. Is there anyone who needs more time? Okay, time's up. Let's share what you talked about with your partners.

So, 다원! Did you guys find any differences between those pictures? Did everyone hear what 다원 just said? He said the left one is cleaner than the right one. Why did you think so? Yes, because the left one doesn't have labels and caps, right? Then, which one do you like better for recycling? Yes, 희원! Yes, the left one! Right?

So, like this, today, we are going to learn about recycling. Are you ready to know more about recycling? Great!

응시자 작성 내용 2

✓ 〈자료 2〉의 밑줄 친 단어를 맥락을 활용하여 지도할 것

Everyone, look at the second worksheet. What do you see, 동우? Yes, there is a reading text, right? However, there are two underlined words. Can you read them for us?

Yes, 민수! Yes, the first one is 'rinse', right? Yes, 'rinse'! And what is the second one? Yes, 지환! Yes, it is 'remove', right? Is there anyone who knows the meaning of "rinse"? It is quite difficult, right? Then, let me give you a hint. This is a dirty bottle. However, if I rinse it, we are going to have this clean bottle. Then, can you guys guess the meaning of "rinse"?

Yes, 수현! Did everyone hear what 수현 just said? She said "rinse" means "wash." That was a great guessing, 수현! Then, let's talk about the second one, 'remove.' Is there anyone who can guess the meaning of the word 'remove'? Okay then, let me give you a hint. Everyone look at here! This is the cap. However, if I remove this, there is no cap here. Can you guess the meaning of the word 'remove'? Great, 종민! Then, can you remove the pencil from your desk? That's great!

So, I can see everyone just gets the meaning of 'rinse' and 'remove.' So far, we just learned two difficult words: "rinse" and "remove." Then, are you guys ready to read? Great!

✓ 〈자료 2〉의 주제를 파악하도록 할 것

Let's begin! The reading time! Let's read!

Because we are ready to read, we are going to find the main idea. However, to find the main idea, do we have to read quickly or slowly? Yes, 지환, we need to read quickly, right? You don't have to understand every single word. Just read quickly and find the main idea. I'm going to give you three minutes. Three minutes, go!

Oh, 민수, do you need any help? The words are so difficult? Then, why don't you look at the back of the worksheet? What do you see? Yes, 민수, there is a vocabulary list, right? With this vocabulary list, can you do this by yourself? Great, keep up the good work!

One minute left, students. Okay, time's up. Then, let's check the main idea together. What was the main idea of this reading text? Is there any volunteer? Yes, 종민! Did everyone hear what 종민 said? He said, the main idea is... Recycling... What's that? Yes, Recycling the PET bottles... Recycling the PET bottles, how? Yes, properly!

So, the main idea was Recycling the PET bottles properly. That's great, 종민! Like this, we just found the main idea. However, there is something strange in the reading text. Can you guess what it is? Yes, 지환! Did everyone hear what 지환 just said? He said, the reading text doesn't have a title. Then, why don't we make a title for it? Sounds great? Okay!

So, does anyone have suggestions for the title? Yes, 현정! Did everyone hear what 현정 just said? She said "How to Recycle the PET Bottles" can be a great title. Do you guys agree? Perfect!

✓ 〈자료 2〉의 글의 구조를 언급하며 세부 정보를 찾는 활동을 진행할 것

So far, we just made the title from the main idea. Then, are you guys ready to read a little more closely? Great! Everyone, look at the reading text again. How many parts can you see in the reading text? Yes, 수민! Yes, there are three parts. Each part had their own names. Do you guys remember? What was the name of the first part? Yes, 종민! Yes, we call it "Introduction." What was the name of the second part? Yes, 동우! Yes, it was "Body." And what was the last one? Yes, 희원, it was the "Conclusion."

Right? Then, everyone, look at the screen! 수현, at the back, can you see the screen? What do you see on the screen? Yes, there is a question, right? Can you read it for us? Yes, it is, "What are the three steps for recycling PET bottles?", right?

So from now on, we are going to read the text again to find what? Yes, to find the three steps... three steps for recycling PET bottles, okay? However, to find the specific information, do we have to read from the beginning to the end or do we have to read only the necessary part? Yes, 민재, we can read only the necessary part, right? You don't have to read every single word. Just find the three steps for recycling PET bottles, okay?

So, 수미, what are we going to do? Yes, we are going to read again and find the three steps to recycle the PET bottles, okay? I'm going to give you five minutes. Five minutes, go!

Oh, 수현, are you already finished? Wow, what a quick reader! Then, why don't you help your friend, 현수? I think she needs some help. That's great. So, like this, friends can be a better teacher!

One minute left, students. Is there anyone who needs more time? Okay, time's up. Let's check the answers together. What were 'the three steps' to recycle the PET bottles? Yes, 민수! Yes, it was "empty", right? We should first empty the bottle. What was the second one? Yes, 희원! Yes, it was… Yes, "rinse", right? The second step was "rinse." And what was the last one? Yes, 다원! Yes, we should "remove", right? So, these were the three steps to recycle the PET bottles properly.

However, why is it important for us to know about recycling properly? Yes, 지환! Yes! For the better environment, right? Then, is there anything we can do for the better school environment? Of course, right? Then, why don't we talk about making the better school environment? Are you guys excited? Great!

응시자 작성 내용 3

✓ 〈자료 3〉을 활용하여 모둠 토의를 진행할 것

Everyone, let's move on to the third worksheet. What do you see on the third worksheet? Yes, 다원! It says "For the Better School.", right? So, from now on, we are going to have a discussion with your group members. It's time to talk with your group members. So, it's time to talk! So, 현수, 수현, 종민, 민종, you four! You four… And, group six, you four! Is everyone in a group? Great.

So, with your group members, share your ideas for the better school. Okay? However, whenever we have this kind of discussion, which rule do we have to follow? Yes, 희원? Yes, we have to follow the ART rule, right? So, what was A, 동우? Yes, it was "Active participation." And what was R, 지환? Yes, it was "Respect others." So, make sure you're respecting your friends' ideas, okay? And what's the last one? Yes, 성현! Yes, it was take turns, right? So, make sure everyone is talking, okay? Great.

So, remember that one student should suggest at least one idea, okay? So, make sure each student gives their own idea. All right? So, 동우, what are we going to do? Yes, we are going to discuss and complete the third worksheet, okay? I'm going to give you 20 minutes. 20 minutes. Go!

✓ 토의 중 모둠을 순회하며 촉진자 역할을 수행할 것

Oh, group one, everyone is participating so actively. I'm so proud of you guys. Great, keep up the good work. And group three, do you guys need any help? Oh, it's too hard to come up with some ideas? Then why don't you look at this paper? What do you see? Yes, it's a suggestion from the student council, right? What kind of suggestion can you see? Yes, we should reduce the food leftovers, right? So, with these suggestions from the student council, can you do this work by yourselves? Great.

And group five, I can see 민수 is participating very well. However, what was the T rule? Yes, "Take turns", right? So, make sure everyone gets the chance to speak, okay? Great. Oh, group four, you already have all the four suggestions? Wow, what brilliant students. Then, why don't you make one more suggestion? Because the more suggestions we have, the better our school will be. Can you guys do that? Great.

One minute left, students. Is there any group that needs more time? Okay, time's up, students.

응시자 작성 내용 4

✓ 토의 내용을 바탕으로 〈자료4〉를 완성할 것

So, we just finished discussing how to make the better school, right? So, how many suggestions do you have, group one? Yes, four. And group two? Four. Oh, you guys have five suggestions? Great. So, like this, we have many suggestions, right?

So, from now on, I'm going to give you two minutes, two minutes to decide the most important one, the most necessary one for our school, okay? So, 수민, what are we going to do? Yes, 수민! We are going to choose the most necessary one, the most important one from your group's suggestions. Okay? I'm going to give you two minutes. Go.

Okay, time's up. So, every group chose their own group's idea? Okay, then are you guys ready to write a suggestion? Great. So, it's time to write a suggestion.

All right, it's time to write the suggestion letter. Okay! So we are going to do this in your groups, all right? So, you guys are sitting like this, right? Then let me give each of you a role. So, students sitting here, raise your hand. Okay, so you guys are going to be "the leaders", okay? So, what does a leader do? Yes, the leader should help the other group members, okay?

And students sitting here, raise your hand. So, you guys are going to be "the dictionary." So, what do they do? Yes, 다원! Yes, they search for the words and check the grammar, right? So, make sure you guys open up your tablet PCs and if your group members need to find some words or need to check the grammar, that's your job, okay?

Then students sitting here, raise your hand. Okay, so you guys are going to be "the writers." And lastly, students sitting here, raise your hand. Yes, you guys are going to be "the bloggers." And bloggers, what do you guys have to do? Yes, 희원! You guys need to upload your writing after the class, okay? On the Google Classroom! All right? Great! So, everyone has their roles, right?

Okay, then everyone look at the screen here. So, 지환, at the back, do you see the screen? Okay, what do you see on the screen? Yes, there is a sample writing, right? So, like this, there are several things you need to remember. So, remember these things when you write the suggestion, okay?

So, how many parts in the sample writing can you see, 다원? Yes, there are three parts, right? So, like this sample writing, your suggestion letters should have three parts, right? Three parts, which are? Yes, "introduction", 동우! And what's the next one? Yes, 희원, "the body." And what was the last one? Yes, 수현, "the conclusion."

So, your suggestion letters should have these three parts. And 현정, how many sentences can you see in the sample writing? Yes, there are five sentences, right? So, like this, your suggestion letters should have at least five or more sentences, okay? So, remember these two things: include three parts and more than five sentences, okay?

So, 민수, what are we going to do? Yes, we are going to write a suggestion letter. And 지환, what is your role in your group? Yes, you're a blogger, right? Then, are you guys ready? Great!

✓ **실제적 목표를 제시하여 활동 참여 동기 부여를 할 것**

Make sure that the best writing, the best suggestion letter will be actually sent to the Busan District Office of Education! Sounds exciting? Great. I'm going to give you 20 minutes. 20 minutes, go!

Oh, group two, do you guys need any help? Oh, you don't know how to start the sentences? Then why don't you look at the back of the worksheet? What do you see? Yes, there are expression lists, right? You can see many useful expressions to start sentences. Then, with this expression list, can you guys do this work by yourselves? Great!

And group four, are you guys already finished? Wow, what quick writers. Then, why don't you make another suggestion? Because there are many ways to make our school a better place. Can you guys do that? Perfect!

One minute left, students. Is there any group that needs more time? Okay, time's up. We just finished writing our group's suggestions for the better school, right? Then, let's see what kind of suggestions our friends have, and let's decide which one should be sent to the Busan District Office of Education to make it realized for our school.

 연습문제 7회 : 2018 기출 변형

(1) 판서 노트 및 예시 영상

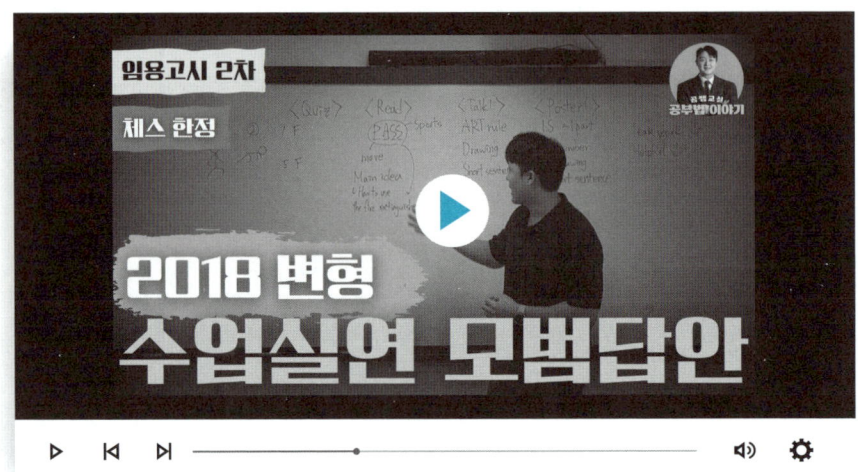

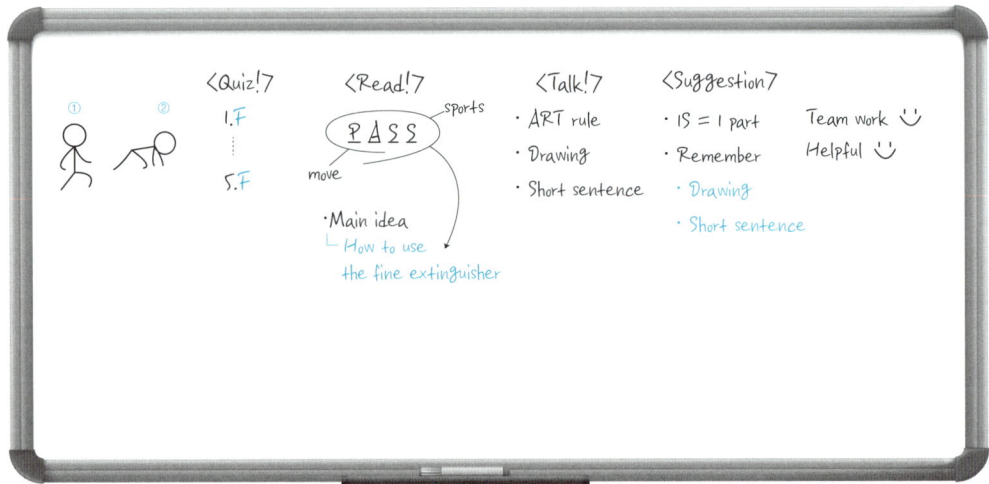

(2) 지도안 예시

단원명	Better Safe Than Sorry				시간	90 mins
대상	• Students : 24 Middle school 3rd Graders • Level : Mixed					
수업 목표	✓ Students will be able to understand how to use a fire extinguisher. ✓ Students will be able to compare two different content delivery formats. ✓ Students will be able to make fire safety posters with visual aids.					
교수·학습 교구	Digital whiteboard, Laptop, Online dictionary, Tablet PCs etc					
핵심역량	자기 관리	지식정보처리	창의적 사고	심미적 감성	협력적 소통	공동체
		✓			✓	✓

<교수 학습 지도안>

단계	교수·학습 활동	유의점
도입 (5분)	*인사, 출석 확인, 교실 내 안전 점검 *학습 주제, 수업 준비 상태 확인	
전개1 (20분)	응시자 작성 내용 1 ✓ <자료 1>의 밑줄 친 단어 중 1개를 선택하여 그 의미를 추론할 수 있도록 지도할 것 ● Teaching Vocabulary • [전체] <자료 1>을 학생에게 나누어주고 어려운 단어가 있는지 확인하게 한다. • 상호작용을 통해 어떤 단어를 어려워하는지 파악하고 해당 단어를 추론할 수 있도록 맥락을 제공한다. <예시 발화> 교사 : Does anyone know the meaning of 'crawl'? … Okay. Let me give you a hint. (1) (2) • 의미를 성공적으로 추론한 후, 직접 문장을 만들어 보게 함으로써 이해 확인 점검을 실시한다. ✓ <자료 1>을 활용하여 수업 주제에 관한 관심과 흥미를 유도할 것 ● Schema activation • [짝, 3분] 짝을 나누어 <자료 1>의 문제를 함께 풀어보게 한다. • [전체] 정답을 하나씩 맞춰보며 학생들의 생각을 공유한다.	

	● Transition • <자료 1>을 바탕으로 오늘 차시 주제를 예상하도록 하며 <자료 2>를 소개한다. <예시 발화> 교사 : So far, we just finished answering true or false questions about fire safety. However, there were many things we didn't know. Then, don't you feel we need to know more to protect ourselves?
전개2 (30분)	**응시자 작성 내용 2** ✓ <자료 2>의 제목을 보고 글의 내용을 추론하도록 할 것 ● Guessing • [전체] <자료 2>의 제목을 언급하고 무슨 뜻일지 질문하며 학생과 상호작용한다. <예시 발화> 교사 : Can you guess the meaning of title? 학생 : Pass the ball?, Sports?, Walk fast? • PASS가 대문자로 쓰인 사실에 주목하며 Scaffolding을 제공한다. ✓ 읽기 전략을 사용하여 <자료 2>의 주제를 파악하도록 할 것 ● Main idea • [개별, 3분] Skimming 전략을 사용하여 <자료 2>의 Main idea를 파악하게 한다. • 빠른 속도로 글을 훑어보며 반복되는 단어를 확인하도록 한다. • 아래 지도 사항에 따라 순회 지도를 실시한다. <순회 지도 사항> • 참여를 북돋우며 활동에 어려움을 겪는 학생을 찾는다. • Low-level : <자료 2> 뒤편의 <Vocabulary list>를 제시한다. • [전체] 학생과의 상호작용을 통해 글의 주제를 교실 전체에 공유하고 판서한다. • Main idea : How to use the fire extinguisher ✓ 글의 제목과 연관지어 <자료 2>의 세부 정보에 대한 이해 확인 질문을 제시할 것 ● Detail information • [전체] 글의 주제와 제목과의 연관성을 강조한다. • 글을 읽기 전 예상했던 것과 읽은 후 알게 된 점을 비교한다. <예시 발화> 교사 : Before reading, we thought PASS is about sports or moving something. However, now we know that PASS is about what? 학생 : How to use the fire extinguisher! 교사 : Right! Knowing how to use it is very important! Then, are you ready to read more closely? • [전체, 5분] 글을 한 번 더 읽고 PASS에 해당하는 부분을 밑줄을 치게 한다.

- Scanning을 활용하여 각 부분에 해당하는 문장이 어디에 있는지 찾게 한다.
- 학생과 상호작용을 통해 PASS는 각각 Pull, Aim, Squeeze, Sweep를 의미하는 것임을 언급한다.

✓ 내용 전달 방법의 관점에서 <자료 3>의 내용을 비교하도록 할 것

● **Visual Aids**
- 3인 1조로 여덟 개의 모둠을 구성한다.
- [모둠, 10분] <자료 3>을 제공하고 차이점을 모둠원과 함께 찾아보도록 한다.
- 아래 ART rule을 지키도록 독려한다.

> < ART rule >
> A : Active participation, R : Respect others, T : Take turns

- 아래 지도 사항에 따라 순회 지도를 실시한다.

> < 순회 지도 사항 >
> - 참여를 북돋우며 활동에 어려움을 겪는 학생을 찾는다.
> - Low-level : 어느 것이 더 내용을 파악하기 쉬운지 물어보고 그 이유를 생각해보게끔 한다.

● **Transition**
- 모둠 토의 결과를 교실 전체에 공유하고 Visual aid와 명령문(Short sentence)의 필요성에 대하여 언급한다.
- 소화기 사용법 4단계를 언급하며 <자료 4>를 소개한다.

응시자 작성 내용 3

✓ 모둠을 구성하고 개인별 역할을 부여할 것

● **Grouping**
- [모둠, 3분] 한 학생당 ②~④ 한 부분씩 담당하도록 안내하고, 각자 어느 부분을 맡을지 정하도록 한다.
- [전체] ②, ③, ④를 담당한 학생에게 각각 손을 들어보게 함으로써 개인별 역할 부여가 이루어졌음을 확인한다.

✓ 조건 2개를 제시하여 <자료 4>를 완성하도록 할 것

● **Remember PASS**
- ①을 예시로 들며 <자료 4>에 대한 조건 2가지를 제시한다.

> < 조건 >
> 1. Drawing
> 2. Use short sentences

- [모둠, 15분] 모둠원과 함께 협력하여 <자료 4>를 완성하도록 한다.
- Authentic purpose : 우수 작품은 교내에 게시된다는 사실을 언급하며 학생의 동기를 부여한다.

전개3 (30분)

전개3 (30분)	• 아래 지도 사항에 따라 순회 지도를 실시한다. <div style="border:1px solid"><순회 지도 사항> • 참여를 북돋우며 활동 중 어려움을 겪고 있는 학생을 파악한다. • Low level : Safety tip의 목적을 언급하며 앞서 언급한 두 조건을 강조한다. 해당 내용이 들어가야 하는 부분을 Reading text에서 발견할 수 있도록 Scaffolding을 제공한다. • High level : 긍정적 피드백을 제공한 뒤, 소화기의 위치를 그림으로 표현할 수 있도록 추가 과제를 제시한다.</div> ✓ 활동 결과에 대한 긍정적 피드백을 2가지 제공할 것 ● Giving feedback • [전체] 교사의 관찰 결과를 바탕으로 학생 결과물에 대한 긍정적 피드백을 제공한다. 　• (예시) 적극적으로 모둠 활동에 참여했다는 점, 한눈에 알아보기 쉽게 그림이 잘 그려졌다는 점, 글의 내용이 짧고 명확하게 잘 쓰였다는 점 등 • [전체] 오늘 배운 내용이 앞으로 어떤 도움이 될 수 있을지 질문한다. <div style="border:1px solid"><예시 발화> 교사 : Today, we learned about what? 학생 : We learned how to use fire extinguisher! 교사 : Awesome! Then can you protect our friends or ourselves from fire?</div>	
마무리 (5분)	*활동 마무리, 다음 차시 안내 *주변 정리 지도, 인사	

(3) 스크립트

> 응시자 작성 내용 1

✓ 〈자료 1〉의 밑줄 친 단어 중 1개를 선택하여 그 의미를 추론할 수 있도록 지도할 것

Okay, students! So far, we've talked about the unit title and the lesson objectives. Then, are you guys ready to start the English class? Great! So, I'm going to give you this worksheet. Take one and pass them to the back. Take one and pass them to the back. So, 동우 at the back, did you get the worksheet? Great! So, what do you see on the worksheet? Yes, there are true or false questions, right? From now on, I'm going to give you one minute to quickly check if there are any difficult words. Okay, one minute, go!

Okay, time's up, students! Were there any difficult words? Yes, 종민! Oh, the word "crawl" is a little bit difficult. Then, is there anyone who knows the meaning of the word "crawl"? Oh, I can see almost everyone finds it a little bit difficult. Then, let me give you a hint. I'm going to draw two people. So, one is like this and another is like this. So, one is walking, and another is crawling. Can you guess who is crawling? Yes, 수현, number two. So, this person is crawling. Did you get the meaning of the word "crawling"? Great! Then, 희원! Can you make a short sentence with the word "crawl"? Yes, did everyone hear what 희원 just said? She said, "The babies are good at crawling." That's a great sentence.

✓ 〈자료 1〉을 활용하여 수업 주제에 관한 관심과 흥미를 유도할 것

Okay, so we just finished checking the difficult word. Then, are you guys ready for those true or false questions? Good! So, from now on, we are going to answer those short quizzes. It's quiz time! Okay, so with your partners. So, 수현, 현수! You two. 종민, 민종! You two. So, does everyone have their own partners? Great! So, with your partners, we are going to answer those true or false questions. Just freely talk with your partner and answer those true or false quizzes, okay? I'm going to give you three minutes. Three minutes, go!

One minute left, students! Is there anyone who needs more time? Okay, time's up! Then, let's check the answers all together. So, what was the answer for number one? It's okay to play with matches or lighters. Is it true or false? Yes, 종민, it's false, right? So, does everyone think it's false? Great! And lastly, number five, it's okay to use an elevator during a fire. Is it true or false? Who thinks it's true? Okay, and who thinks it's false? I can see it's like 50-50. The answer is, it is false. Are you guys surprised?

So, like this, we just checked five true or false quizzes. However, there were many things that we didn't know about. Then, don't you feel we need to know more to protect ourselves? Then, are you guys ready to move on to the next part? Great!

응시자 작성 내용 2

✓ 〈자료 2〉의 제목을 보고 글의 내용을 추론하도록 할 것

Okay, everyone, let's move on to the second worksheet. It's reading time, so we are going to read about fire safety. Okay, then 종민! Can you read the title for us? Yes, what was the title? It was "Remember PASS," right? Then, why don't we guess the meaning of the word "PASS"? It says "PASS," right? So, what's the meaning of "PASS"? Can you guess?

Yes, 동우! Oh, it's about sports, right? Like passing the ball! So, it can be about sports. Yes, that's a great guess. And what else? Yes, 지환! Yes, "pass" is to move something to another place, right? So, he thinks it is related to some kind of movement. Move something to another place. That's a great guess. However, let me give you a hint here. Look at the title again. The word "PASS" is written in what kind of letters? Large 'P' - 'A' - 'S' - 'S' or small 'p' - 'a' - 's' -'s'? Yes, 현정! They are written in large letters. That means the reading text will be quite different from sports or moving something. Did you guys become curious? Then, are you ready to read? Awesome!

✓ 읽기 전략을 사용하여 〈자료 2〉의 주제를 파악하도록 할 것

So, from now on, we are going to read the text and find the main idea, okay? But to find the main idea, do you have to read quickly or slowly? Yes, 수현, we have to read quickly. You don't have to understand every single word. Just read quickly and find the main idea. I'm going to give you three minutes. Three minutes, go!

Oh, 민재, do you need any help? Oh, the words here are too difficult. Then, why don't you look at the back of the worksheet? What do you see? Yes, there is a vocabulary list, right? So, with this vocabulary list, can you find the main idea by yourself? Great! I love your effort. One minute left, students! Okay, time's up! So, let's check the main idea together. So, what was the main idea of this reading text? Mhm, oh yes, 다원! Oh, did everyone hear what 다원 just said? He said the main idea is... Yes, how to use what? Yes, how to use the fire... what was that? Yes, extinguisher. How to use the fire extinguisher. Great! That was the main idea.

✓ 글의 제목과 연관지어 〈자료 2〉의 세부 정보에 대한 이해 확인 질문을 제시할 것

So, like this, we just found the main idea. Then, let's go back to the title again. Before reading, we thought "PASS" means sports or move. However, after reading, "PASS" means what? How to use the fire extinguisher, right? Knowing how to use a fire extinguisher is very important. Then, are you guys ready to move on to the next part? Great! So, from now on, I'm going to give you five minutes, five minutes to find the word for P-A-S-S. Find the word for those four letters and underline it, okay? However, to find those kinds of information, do you have to read the word from the beginning to the end? No, 민수, right? We can just find the necessary part and read it. You don't have to read every single word. So, 동우, what are we going to do? Yes, read again and find the word for 'P' - 'A' - 'S' - 'S', okay? I'm going to give you five minutes. Five minutes, go!

Oh, 수현, you already finished? Wow, you are such a quick reader. Then, why don't you help your partner, 현수? I think she needs some help. Great! So, like this, friends can be better teachers. Keep up the good work. One minute left, students! Is there anyone who needs more time? Okay, time's up! So, let's check the answers all together. So, what was "P" here? Yes, it was "pull," right? And what was "A"? Yes, it was "aim." Thank you, 희원. And what was the "S"? Yes, we should "squeeze," right? Thank you, 지환. And what was the last "S"? Yes, 종민! It was "sweep." Did everyone underline those words in the reading text? Awesome!

So, so far, we just read the text about how to use the fire extinguisher, and it was "PASS." However, during a fire, would there be enough time to read those sentences? No, right? Then, why don't we express the same meaning differently? Sounds great, 지환? Okay! Then, are you guys ready to move on to the next part? Perfect!

✓ 내용 전달 방법의 관점에서 〈자료 3〉의 내용을 비교하도록 할 것

So, everyone, let's move on to the third worksheet. So, 수민, what do you see on the third worksheet? What do you see on the left? Yes, there is a picture, right? However, what do you see on the right, 다원? Yes, there is a sentence, right? So, from now on, we are going to have a small discussion, okay? So, it's talk time!

So, with your group members. So, 지환, 동우, 희원! You three. And 수현, 현수, 종민! You three. You three. You three. ... So, everyone is in the group? Perfect! So, with your group members, we are going to talk about the differences in the third worksheet. Got it? Great! However, whenever we do this kind of discussion, which rule do we have to follow? Yes, 민수? We have to follow the ART, the ART rule, right? So, what was "A"? Yes, it was active participation. And what is "R"? 수현! Yes, it was respect. So, make sure you're respecting your group members' ideas, okay? And lastly, what is "T"? Yes, 다원? Yes, it is taking turns, right? So, make sure everyone is talking, okay?

So, I'm going to give you 10 minutes, 10 minutes to find what? Yes, 수정! To find the difference between the right one and the left one. Ten minutes, go! Oh, group one, do you need any help? Oh, you're having difficulty finding the differences? Then, let's think like this. During a fire, which one could be more helpful? Then, let's talk within your group members about why the left one is more helpful. Can you do this by yourself? Okay! Wow, group three! Everyone is participating very actively! Great! Make sure you guys also take turns, okay?

Okay, time's up, students! So, let's share your group's ideas. So, what's the difference between the right one and the left one? Mhm, yes, group two. Did everyone hear what group two just said? Yes, group two said there is a drawing, right? So, the left one has a drawing. And what else? Yes, group one. Mhm, did everyone hear what group one just said? Yes, the sentence in the left one is shorter than the right one, right? So, the left one uses the short sentences. It's using the short sentences, right?

Like this, the right one and left one have the same meaning. However, which one is more useful? Yes, group four, the left one is more useful during a fire. Why? Yes, 종민? Yes, because the left one has a drawing and it's using a short sentence. Then, why don't we change the reading text we just read before into a drawing? Does that sound exciting? Great! So, let's check the next worksheet.

응시자 작성 내용 3

✓ **모둠을 구성하고 개인별 역할을 부여할 것**

So, group three, what do you see on the fourth worksheet? Yes, there is a poster, right? So, we are going to make a poster. Sounds great? All right, so it's time to make a poster. So, how many members do you have? Yes, three members. And how many parts in the poster? Yes, three parts, right? So, one student should take one part, okay? One student takes one part, okay? So, I'm going to give you three minutes, three minutes to decide who will take which part. Three minutes, go!

Okay, time's up, students! So, everyone has their own part? Students for the second part, raise your hand. Okay, and third part, raise your hand. Great! And finally, the last one, the fourth part, raise your hand. Okay! So, I can see that everyone has their own part. Then, are you guys ready to begin? All right!

✓ **조건 2개를 제시하여 〈자료 4〉를 완성하도록 할 것**

However, before we jump right into the poster, let's check this one. So, everyone look at the first part. What do you see? Yes, there is a drawing, right? So, make sure your poster should have a drawing, right? So, when you're making the poster, remember this. So, your poster should have what? Yes, 종민, it should have a drawing, okay? To understand better. And what else? Yes, 민수! Like the first part, make sure that your part is using what kind of sentence? A long sentence or a short sentence? Yes, a short sentence, right? So, make sure your sentence is short. Short sentences. So, this kind of sentence is more helpful during a fire, okay?

Then, are you guys ready to make the poster? Great! We are going to pick the best poster and it will be actually posted in our school. Sounds great? Awesome! I'm going to give you 15 minutes to make what? Yes, 지환, to make the poster. And remember those two things, okay? I'm going to give you 15 minutes. Fifteen minutes, go!

Oh, 재민, do you need any help? Mhm, oh, you don't know what to draw for the third part? Then, why don't you go back to the reading text we just read before? Yes, it is exactly related to the poster. Then, can you do this by yourself? Awesome! So, if you need any help, just feel free to call me, all right? Okay! Oh 지환! I can see that your drawing is perfect, but your sentence can be a little bit shorter. Why don't you make it shorter? Just look at the example part, the first part. Yes, can you do this by yourself? Great! Oh, group four, are you guys finished? Wow, what quick writers and drawers! Then, what do you see below the poster? Yes, it says, "Where is the fire extinguisher," right? Why don't you guys complete that part? Because knowing where the fire extinguisher is very important. Can you guys do that? Great! Keep up the good work.

One minute left, students! Is there anyone who needs more time? Okay, time's up!

✓ 활동 결과에 대한 긍정적 피드백을 2가지 제공할 것

All right, so we just finished making the poster. And there were two things that I was so impressed about. So, the first one is your teamwork. I can see everyone was participating very actively and everyone was really into their parts. That was great teamwork! Great job! And second, your posters were very helpful. This is because all of your posters have these two parts. What was that? Yes, 동우, it was a drawing. And what was the second one? Yes, 지환, it was short sentences, right? So, I can see that everyone has very helpful posters. I love your teamwork, and also, your posters were perfect during emergencies. Great job! Why don't we give a big hand for ourselves?

Great! So, before we finish, let's go back to the unit title. What was it? Yes, 희원! It was "Better Safe Than Sorry." So, we learned about what? Yes, how to use the fire extinguisher. And we made what? Yes, 민주, we made posters on how to use the fire extinguisher, which has four steps. What were they? Yes, 민수? Yes, it was "PASS," right? P-A-S-S. Awesome! Then, do you feel that you can protect yourselves during fire emergencies? Great! That's just what I wanted for this classroom. Okay, that was it for us. Have a great time!

연습문제 8회 : 2017 기출 변형

(1) 판서 노트 및 예시 영상

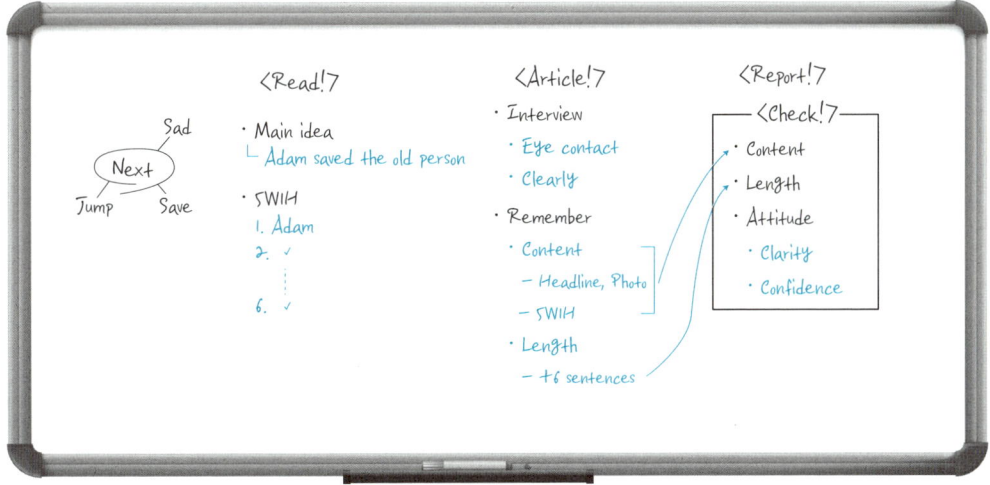

(2) 지도안 예시

단원명	Neighbor Hero				시간	90 mins
대상	• Students : 26 Middle school 2rd Graders • Level : Mixed					
수업 목표	✓ Students will be able to find detailed information based on 5W1H. ✓ Students will be able to interview their friends based on 5W1H. ✓ Students will be able to report the story based on their interviews.					
교수·학습 교구	Digital whiteboard, Laptop, Online dictionary, Tablet PCs etc					
핵심역량	자기 관리	지식정보처리	창의적 사고	심미적 감성	협력적 소통	공동체
		✓			✓	

<교수 학습 지도안>

단계	교수·학습 활동	유의점
도입 (5분)	*인사, 출석 확인, 교실 내 안전 점검 *학습 주제, 수업 준비 상태 확인	
전개1 (15분)	**응시자 작성 내용 1** ✓ <자료 1>의 그림을 활용하여 짝 활동을 진행할 것 ● Schema activation • [전체] <자료 1>을 학생에게 나누어주고 그림에 대하여 이야기를 나눈다. • [짝, 3분] 짝을 나누어 마지막 부분에 어떤 그림이 올지 이야기를 나누게 한다. ✓ 짝 활동 결과를 교실 전체에 공유하며 학생과 상호작용 할 것 ● Mind mapping • [전체] 학생과의 상호작용을 통해 짝 활동 결과를 교실 전체에 공유한다. • 마인드맵을 통하여 짝 활동 결과에 대한 키워드를 판서한다. <마인드맵 예시> Next? ● Transition • 완성된 마인드맵을 살펴보며 이번 차시 주제에 관한 흥미를 유발한다.	

	응시자 작성 내용 2	
	√ <자료 2>의 주제를 파악하도록 할 것	

● **Main idea**
- [개별, 3분] <자료 2>를 학생에게 나누어주고 Main idea를 파악하게 한다.
- Skimming 전략을 지도하여 글의 주제를 파악하도록 한다.
  - 빠른 속도로 글을 훑어보며 반복되는 단어를 확인하도록 한다.
- 아래 지도 사항에 따라 순회 지도를 실시한다.

  < 순회 지도 사항 >
  - 참여를 북돋우며 활동 중 어려움을 겪고 있는 학생을 파악한다.
  - Low-level : <자료 2> 뒤편의 <Vocabulary list>를 제시한다.

- [전체] 학생과의 상호작용을 통해 글의 주제를 교실 전체에 공유하고 판서한다.
  - Main idea : Adam saved the old person
- [전체] 글의 주제와 제목과의 연관성을 강조한다.

전개2 (25분)

√ <자료 2>에서 세부 정보를 찾아 <자료 3>을 완성할 것
√ <자료 3> 활동 시 어려움을 겪는 학생에게 적절한 도움을 제공할 것

● **Detail information**
- [개별, 10분] <자료 3>를 학생에게 나누어주고 상호작용을 통해 5W1H에 대하여 안내한다.

  < 예시 발화 >
  교사 : What are the '5W1H'?
  학생 : 'Who', 'What', 'When', 'Where', 'Why' and 'How'
  교사 : Yes, they are the most important things when asking questions.

- Scanning 전략을 지도하여 <자료 3>을 완성하도록 한다.
  - 글 전체가 아니라 필요한 부분만 선별하여 읽도록 한다.
- 아래 지도 사항에 따라 순회 지도를 실시한다.

  < 순회 지도 사항 >
  - 참여를 북돋우며 활동 중 어려움을 겪고 있는 학생을 파악한다.
  - High-level : 활동 참여에 대한 긍정적 피드백을 제공하고, Student teacher 역할을 부여하여 다른 학생을 도울 수 있도록 한다.
  - Low-level : 동료 학습자로부터 도움을 받을 수 있도록 Peer-scaffolding을 유도한다.

- [전체] 학생과의 상호작용을 통해 <자료 3>의 내용을 공유하고 판서한다.

● **Transition**
- 글이 기사 형식으로 쓰였다는 사실을 언급하며 다음 활동과의 연관성을 강조한다.

	응시자 작성 내용 3
	✓ <자료 4> 활동을 위한 교사의 예시를 제공하고 인터뷰를 진행할 것
전개3 (40분)	● **Teacher's demonstration** • [전체] Screen을 활용하여 <자료 4>에 대한 교사의 예시를 학생에게 제시한다. • [전체] Interview를 위한 질문 표현을 안내한다. 　• (예시) What did you do yesterday?, Why did you do that? 등 ● **Interview (Mingling activity)** • [전체, 3분] 교실을 돌아다니며 Interview를 하고 싶은 짝을 찾도록 한다. 　• 짝을 찾지 못하는 학생은 교사가 적극적으로 개입하여 짝을 만들어 준다. 　• 모두 짝이 있는지 확인하고 자리에 앉도록 지도한다. • [짝, 10분] 짝과 함께 서로 질문을 주고받으며 <자료 4>를 완성하도록 한다. 　• 인터뷰를 진행할 때 질문을 정확하게 하고, 눈을 맞출 것을 강조한다. ● **Transition** • [전체] 완성된 <자료 4>에 대해 학생과 상호작용하며 다음 활동에 대한 연관성을 강조한다. 　　　　　　　　<예시 발화> 　교사 : So far, we just finished interviewing our friends. Then, are you ready to become a reporter? 　학생 : Yes, teacher! 　교사 : Great! Then, let's write an article! ✓ <자료 4>를 바탕으로 <자료 5>를 완성할 것 ● **Write an article** • 학생에게 개인 Tablet PC를 꺼내어 Online Classroom에 접속하게 한다. • [개별, 20분] 자신이 작성한 <자료 4>를 바탕으로 <자료 5>를 완성하도록 한다. • <자료 5>에 대한 글쓰기 기준을 제시한다. 　　　　　　　　<글쓰기 기준> 　1. Content : Headline, Photo, 5W1H 　2. Length : 6 sentences or more • Authentic purpose : 우수 작품은 학교 신문에 게시된다는 사실을 언급하며 학생의 동기를 부여한다. • 아래 지도 사항에 따라 순회 지도를 실시한다. 　　　　　　　　<순회 지도 사항> 　• 참여를 북돋우며 활동 중 어려움을 겪고 있는 학생을 파악한다. 　• Low-level : 번역 프로그램이나 문법 확인 프로그램을 소개하며 적극적으로 활용할 수 있도록 격려한다. 　• High-level : 활동 참여에 대한 긍정적 피드백을 제공하고, 기사 내용을 조금 더 써 볼 수 있도록 유도한다.

✓ <자료 5>에 대한 발표 평가 기준 3가지를 제시하고 발표를 진행할 것

● Teacher's demonstration
- [전체] 자신이 작성한 기사를 기자가 되어 직접 발표해보는 활동을 소개하며 이전 활동과의 연계성을 강조한다.

<예시 발화>

교사 : So far, we just wrote the article. Then, why don't you become an actual news reporter? … Does it sound great? Awesome. Let's begin a presentation!

● Presentation
- 학생들에게 발표 평가 기준이 포함된 <Checklist>를 제공한다.

<Checklist>

1. Content	Headline	
	Photo	
	5W1H	
2. Language	6 + sentences	
3. Attitude	Clarity	
	Confidence	

- <Checklist>의 1과 2는 이전 활동의 <글쓰기 기준>과 연결됨을 보여주며 교수 내용과 평가가 일치함을 강조한다.
- 발표를 진행하고 <Checklist>를 작성하도록 한다.

마무리 (5분)
*활동 마무리, 다음 차시 안내
*주변 정리 지도, 인사

(3) 스크립트

> 응시자 작성 내용 1

✓ 〈자료 1〉의 그림을 활용하여 짝 활동을 진행할 것

    Okay, students! So far, we've checked the unit title and the lesson objectives. Then, are you guys ready to start the English class? Great! So, I'm going to give you this worksheet. Take one and pass them to the back. 수민 at the back, did you get the worksheet? Great! So, what do you see on the worksheet? Yes, there are pictures. However, 동우, in the third part, what do you see? Yes, there is a question mark, right?

    So, from now on, with your partner, 종민, 민종, you two, 수현, 현수, you two. Does everyone have their own partner? Great! So, with your partners, we are going to talk about the pictures and guess what would happen next. Okay? So 민재, what are we going to do? Yes, we are going to talk about the pictures with your partner and make a guess about what would happen next. Okay? I'm going to give you three minutes. 3 minutes, go!

✓ 짝 활동 결과를 교실 전체에 공유하며 학생과 상호작용 할 것

    Okay, time's up, students! Let's share what you talked about with your partners about what would happen next, okay? So, is there anyone who wants to share your ideas with your partners? Yes, 희원? Did everyone hear what 희원 just said? She said she's expecting some kind of sad ending. That's a great guess. Who else? 지환! Oh, 지환 and his partner said the man is going to jump into the fire. Yes, that's a great guess! Jump into the fire! And what else? Yes, 우현! Oh, 우현 and his partner said they think the man will save many people. That's a great guess. So, like this, after we saw two pictures, we can make a guess about what will happen next.

    Someone said there will be a sad ending, or he will jump into the fire, and he will save many people. Then, don't you want to know the real story? Do you want to know what actually happened next? Great! So, let's move on to the next part.

응시자 작성 내용 2

✓ 〈자료 2〉의 주제를 파악하도록 할 것

From now on, we are going to read a text. Okay, it's time to read! So everyone look at the second worksheet. 상우, what do you see on the second worksheet? Yes, there is a paragraph, right? So, from now on, we are going to find the main idea. Okay? But to find the main idea, do you have to read slowly or quickly? Yes, we have to read quickly. So, you don't have to understand every single word. Just read quickly and find the main idea. I'm going to give you three minutes. 3 minutes! Find the main idea. Go!

Oh, 민수, do you need help? Oh, the words in this paragraph are too difficult. Then, why don't you look at the back of the worksheet? What do you see? Yes, there is a vocabulary list, right? So, with this vocabulary list, can you find the main idea by yourself? Great! One minute left, students. Okay, time's up! So, let's find the main idea together. Main idea! So, is there anyone who wants to share your main idea? Yes, 민수! Oh, did everyone hear what 민수 said? He said the main idea is... Yes, Adam! Adam did what? Yes, Adam saved... Saved who? Adam saved the old person. Great job, 민수! So, like this, we can find the main idea.

However, let's look at the title, then. 현정, can you read the title for us? Yes, thank you. So, who's the teenager in the title? Yes, it was Adam. And who is the neighbor in the title? Yes, it was the old person, right? So, like this, we can see that the title and the main idea have a very close relationship to each other. Great? Good!

✓ 〈자료 2〉에서 세부 정보를 찾아 〈자료 3〉을 완성할 것

✓ 〈자료 3〉 활동 시 어려움을 겪는 학생에게 적절한 도움을 제공할 것

So far, we just found the main idea. Then, are you guys ready to read the text a little bit more closely? Great! So, everyone look at the third worksheet. 지환, what do you see on the third worksheet? Yes, there are six questions, right? However, in each question, there is a keyword. What kind of keywords can you see? Yes, 동우! We have what, and yes, who, where, how. Great! So, things like this, we call what? Yes, 종민! We call these kinds of keywords the 5 Ws and 1 H. So, remember, these keywords are very important when asking questions.

So, from now on, we are going to read the paragraph again to answer those 5W1H questions. However, to find those answers, do you have to read the whole sentence or just read the necessary part? Yes, 수민! We don't need to read every single word, just read the necessary part. Okay? So, 상민, what are we going to do? Yes, we are going to read the text again, read only the necessary part, and find the answers to those 5W1H questions, okay? I'm going to give you 10 minutes. 10 minutes. Go! Oh, 수현, you already finished? Wow, what a quick reader! Great job! Then, why don't you help your partner, 현수? I heard 현수 needs some help. Great! So, like this, friends can be better teachers. Good job!

One minute left, students. Okay, time's up! So, let's check the answers all together. So, what was the answer to number one? Yes, it was Adam, right? And what was the answer to the second question? What did he do? Yes, he saved his neighbor, right? And what was the last question? Yes, that's right. So, we just finished finding the main idea and answering those 5W1H questions. However, we've already seen this kind of reading text. Where did you see this kind of reading text? Yes, 희원! Great! Did everyone hear what 희원 just said? She said this text is like a newspaper article, right? Then, why don't you become actual news reporters? Sounds great?

<응시자 작성 내용 3>

✓ 〈자료 4〉 활동을 위한 교사의 예시를 제공하고 인터뷰를 진행할 것

Okay, so from now on, we are going to write an article. We are going to write an article and present our own article in front of the class. Sounds great? Cool!

However, before we write an article, what do we have to do first? Yes, we have to do an interview, right? So, from now on, we are going to interview our friends. Okay? So everyone look at the screen here. 상민 at the back, do you see the screen? So, what do you see on the screen? Yes, it's a video clip, right? So, in this video, I'm going to interview another teacher. Okay, let's watch the video first. All right! Okay, so we just finished watching the video clip. What was the video about? Yes, 민수! Yes, it was an interview. Then, did everyone hear some kind of useful expressions there? What kind of questions did I use? Yes, 민수! Yes, "What did you do yesterday?" And, yes, 종민! "Why did you do that?" Yes, that's a great expression to ask the reason. So, using these kinds of expressions, you are going to do an interview with your friends. Okay? So from now on, we are going to find our partners. So, everyone stand up, walk around the classroom, and find your partner. I'm going to give you three minutes. 3 minutes. Go!

Oh, 동우, do you need any help? Oh, you can't find your partner? Then, why don't you interview 종민 over there? I think he needs a partner too. Yes, you two can be great partners. Great job! One minute left, students. Okay, time's up! Take the desk in front of you and have a seat there. So, does everyone have their own partners? Okay, you two, you two … Great! So, everyone look at the fourth worksheet. What do you see? Yes, 수민 and 민수! Yes, you can see there are six questions, right? Six questions with the keywords of … Yes! Those 5W1H questions. So, with your partners, I'm going to give you 10 minutes, 10 minutes to do an interview and complete the fourth worksheet, okay? Great! However, when you do an interview, what's the most important thing? Yes, 종민! When you are doing an interview, it is very important to make eye contact. So, don't forget to make eye contact. And what else? Yes, 수현! Yes, when you are doing an interview, it is very important to ask questions clearly. So, make sure you're asking questions clearly. All right? So use the expressions that I used in the video, okay? All right, I'm going to give you 10 minutes. 10 minutes to do what, 종민? Yes, we are going to do an interview. 10 minutes. Go!

✓ 〈자료 4〉를 바탕으로 〈자료 5〉를 완성할 것

Time's up, students! So, everyone finished the interview? Can you share? Yes, 희원, what did your partner do yesterday? 원희 helped her grandmother! That's great! And what else? Yes, that was also a great interview. So, like this, we just finished the interview. Then, what do we have to do next? Yes, it's time to write an article, right? So, let's move on to the next part. Everyone, open up your tablet PCs and come to the online classroom. So, 민재, are you in the classroom? Okay, so what do you see in the classroom? Yes, there is an assignment, right? What else can you find? 민수! Yes, there is a sample writing. So, like this, based on the interview, we will write an actual article. Sounds exciting? Great! Then, 수현, can you read the first sentence of the sample writing for us? Yes, great! So, like this, your sample writing should include a headline. Like this, there are some points you should remember. So, I'm going to tell you one by one.

Remember... Like 수현 just said, your article should include a headline. So first, the headline. And ... Can you read the second part, 희원? Yes, your article should also have photos. Headline and the photos. And what was the last thing? It's the most important thing. Yes, 종민! Yes, your article should include all those 5W1H information. Okay? Great! And lastly, your article should have more than, Yes, six sentences. Okay? So when you're writing an article, remember these points. Okay? Great! And make sure the best article will be published in the school newspaper. How does it sound? Sounds exciting? Yes, great! So, I'm going to give you 20 minutes! 20 minutes to do what, 동우? Yes, we are going to write an article based on the interview. Okay? So don't forget these points. I'm going to give you 20 minutes! 20 minutes! Go!

Oh, 지환, do you need any help? Oh, you don't know how to write an article? Then, why don't you use the translation program or the grammar-checking program? There are many kinds of applications or programs you can use in this online classroom. Yes, so with these programs, can you do this work by yourself? Great! And 민재, you already finished? Wow, you're such a quick writer! Then, why don't you write a little bit more about it? You know, the more information you have, the better your article will be. Sounds great? Awesome!

✓ 〈자료 5〉에 대한 발표 평가 기준 3가지를 제시하고 발표를 진행할 것

One minute left, students. Is there anyone who needs more time? Okay, time's up! Everyone finished? Great! So, we just finished writing an article. Then, why don't we become real reporters? Sounds great? Okay, good! So, it's time to report our news article. Great! So, it's time to report. It's time to be actual reporters. Actual news reporters! Sounds exciting? Great!

However, before we begin a presentation, what do we have to do first? Yes, the checklist, right? So, I'm going to give you the checklist. Take one and pass them to the back. Take one and pass them to the back. Okay, 재민 at the back, did you get the checklist? Yes. So, what do you see on the checklist? Yes, there are three parts. So, what is the first part, 재민? Yes, it's content, right? It says content. And what's the second one, 수현? Yes, it's length, right? So, the second part is about the length. And what's the third one, 동우? Yes, it's the attitude. So, the third part is the attitude. And let's see the checklist a little more closely.

So, what does content mean? Yes, it means the headline, photos, and 5W1H. So, you should check about the headline and the photos and if the article has 5W1H information. And how about the second one? What's the meaning of length here? Yes, 희원! Yes, it means the six sentences. So, you should check if your friend's article includes more than six sentences. Okay? And the last part, the attitude. What does it mean by attitude? Yes, 지환! Yes, it means the presentation should be, yes, clear! So, the first part is clarity, right? And how about the second one? Yes, 다원? Yes, the presentation should be confident. So, the last part is confidence. So, with this checklist, you are going to listen to your friend's report. Your friend's news report, okay? Perfect! So, let's have our first presenter to the front.

수업 실연 Q&A

01. 깔끔하고 힘 있는 목소리를 내는 것이 어려워서 너무 고민인데 좋은 방법이 있을까요?

깔끔하고 힘 있는 목소리를 내는 것은 시험뿐 아니라 현직이 되어서도 중요한 부분입니다. 왜냐하면 목소리에 자신감이 차 있어야 학생들이 듣기에도 집중이 잘 되고 교사가 전달하는 내용에 신뢰가 생기기 때문입니다.

성량 자체는 타고난 부분이 있을 수 있겠지만 발성과 발음은 충분히 연습을 통해서 개선할 수 있습니다. 저의 팁을 알려드리자면 다음과 같습니다.

(1) 문장 끝 흐리지 않기

의외로 문장 끝을 흐리는 습관이 있는 분들이 많이 계십니다. 성격이 급하거나 긴장을 많이 하다 보면 말하는 도중에 다음 문장을 생각하게 되어서 앞 문장이 제대로 끝마쳐지지 않는 경우가 가장 흔한 경우입니다. 그러나 이러한 습관은 채점관에게 내용 전달이 제대로 이루어지지 않을 뿐 아니라 자신감도 떨어져 보입니다. 수업 장악력이 부족해 보일 수밖에 없죠.

(2) 천천히 말하기

빨리 말하는 습관이 있으면 발음이 뭉개지고 문법 실수를 할 확률이 높아집니다. 자연스럽게 수업 전달력에 문제가 생기죠. T-talk를 의도적으로 천천히 말하는 것도 발음의 정확도를 높여 전달력을 개선하는 좋은 방법입니다.

(3) 키워드 강조하기

모든 T-talk를 100% 출력으로 할 필요는 없습니다. 평소에는 70%의 성량을 유지하다가 중요한 부분에서만 100%를 보여주어도 순간적인 대조 효과로 아주 인상적인 수업 실연을 보여줄 수 있습니다. 중요한 부분 직전에 공백을 주고 정확한 발음과 평소보다 높은 성량으로 T-talk를 구사하는 연습이 필요합니다.

(4) 학생이 멀리 앉아있다고 생각하기

아무래도 혼자만 있는 공간에서 수업 실연을 한다는 것 자체가 아주 쑥스럽습니다. 아무도 없는 넓은 공간에서 크게 목소리를 낸다는 게 참 어색하죠. 그래서 수업 실연을 연습할 때는 항상 학생이 저기 멀리 앉아있다고 생각하는 것이 중요합니다. 스스로 머릿속에 상황을 그려서 자연스럽게 교실 전체를 장악할 수 있는 T-talk 연습을 해보시기를 바랍니다.

하루에 수업을 평균 3~4시간씩 해야 하는 교사로서는 수업 전달력 때문만이 아니라, 건강상의 이유로도 목 관리가 아주 중요합니다. 신규 발령을 받고 1~2주가 지나면 대부분 목이 쉬어있고, 심지어는 누적된 피로에 결국 허스키(?)한 목소리를 갖게 되신 고경력 선생님들도 많이 계십니다. 여러분은 꼭 목에 무리를 주지 않는 범위 내에서 전달력을 높일 수 있는 연습을 이 기회에 꾸준히 해보시기를 바랍니다!

02. 수업 실연을 할 때마다 제한 시간을 자꾸 넘습니다. 무엇이 문제일까요?

제한 시간을 초과하는 이유는 크게 두 가지로 볼 수 있습니다.

(1) 자동화 부족

반복되는 시나리오에 대하여 T-talk가 충분한 연습이 되어 있지 않기 때문에 말을 느리게 하는 경우가 있습니다. 또는, 머릿속으로 다음 대사를 생각하는 동안 비게 되는 오디오를 채우기 위해 불필요한 문장이 삽입되다 보니 시간이 길어질 수도 있습니다.

위와 같은 원인에 의한 시간 부족은 꾸준한 연습이 정답입니다. 보통 2차 준비 초반부에 이러한 고민이 있는 경우가 많습니다. 그러나, 기출 문제를 연도별로 살펴보면 반복되는 시나리오에 대한 감을 잡을 수 있고, 그 부분을 꾸준히 연습하다 보면 시간이 많이 단축되는 효과를 볼 수 있을 것입니다.

> **Tip**
>
> 수업 실연에서 반복되는 시나리오는 아래와 같습니다. 만약 시간 단축이 필요한 상황이라면 아래와 같은 부분에 대하여 T-talk를 미리 깔끔하게 정리하여 두고 자동화하는 연습이 중요합니다.
>
> 1. Main idea, Detail information 찾기 (Skimming, Scanning 지도하기)
> 2. Group 만들기, 개인별 역할 부여하기
> 3. 동료/자기 평가 실시하기, 체크리스트 소개하기, 평가 기준 안내하기

(2) 지나친 욕심

한편, 시간이 부족한 두 번째 원인은 배점과 관련 없는 부분을 생략하는 기술이 부족하기 때문입니다. 이러한 경우는 연습이 부족했던 첫 번째 원인과 달리, 오히려 연습이 충분히 이루어졌을 경우 생기는 문제입니다. 보여줄 것이 너무 많아 욕심이 생겨 시간이 부족해지는 상황인 거죠.

이럴 때는 오히려 지시 사항을 다시 한번 살펴보고 큰 틀에서 문제를 바라보는 관점이 필요합니다. 즉, 직접적으로 지시 사항에 해당하는 내용만 정확하게 보여주고 불필요한 부분은 과감하게 생략하는 판단력이 요구되는 것이죠.

이러한 판단력은 해당 문제에 대하여 '핵심 역량'이 무엇일지 생각하는 것이 아주 큰 도움이 됩니다. 따라서, 여러분이 만약 이러한 원인으로 시간 부족 문제를 겪고 있다면, 수업 실연의 흐름을 '핵심 역량'의 관점에서 생각하고 불필요한 부분을 생략하는 연습을 해보시기를 바랍니다.

03. 수업 실연할 때 지시 사항을 모두 다 외우고 들어가야 하나요? 짧은 시간에 어떻게 그것이 가능한지 너무 걱정됩니다.

수업 실연 지시 사항이 적게는 8개에서 많게는 10개까지 되다 보니, 이것을 외우는 것에 대하여 두려움을 가지는 경우가 많이 있습니다. 그러나, 수업 실연의 흐름을 '구조적'으로 파악하여 꾸준히 연습하다 보면 어느샌가 지시 사항이 머릿속에 자연스레 들어오는 경험을 하실 수 있게 됩니다.

수업 실연의 큰 틀을 Main activity와 Build-up activity의 관점에서 살펴보면 다음과 같습니다.

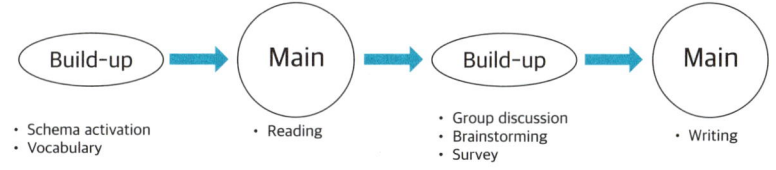

위와 같이 'Build-up → Main'의 두 세트로 수업 실연을 파악한 다음, 각 단계에 어떤 시나리오가 자주 등장하는지 알아둘 필요가 있습니다. 이렇게 머릿속에 틀을 먼저 그려놓은 다음, 해당 지시 사항이 어디에 들어가는지 생각하는 연습을 꾸준히 하다 보면 세부적인 부분은 약간씩 다를지 몰라도 전체적인 큰 틀은 같다는 사실을 깨닫게 됩니다.

 **04.** 활동 간 연계 부분이 너무 어렵습니다. 어디서 아이디어를 얻어야 할지, 연습하면 과연 실력이 늘 수 있을지, 어떤 관점으로 구상하여야 할지 궁금합니다.

 활동 간 연계 부분은 마지막까지 어렵게 느껴지는 것 중 하나입니다. 그러나 연습을 꾸준히 하다 보면 교실 환경이 머릿속에 그려지고 인사이트가 조금씩 쌓이게 됩니다. 포기하지 말고 꾸준히 고민하고 연습하는 것이 필요합니다.

'Check point #66'에서부터 언급되듯이 활동 간 연계를 자연스럽게 하기 위해서는 수업 실연의 전체적인 흐름을 큰 틀에서 바라볼 줄 아는 안목이 필요합니다. 모든 활동은 독립적인 것이 아니라, 서로 유기적으로 연결되어 있다는 사실을 잊어서는 안 되는 것이죠.

아래 표를 참고하여 수업 실연의 각 단계에 어떤 목적이 있는지 다시 살펴볼 필요가 있습니다. 그리고 Build-up에서 Main으로, General에서 Personalization으로 어떻게 활동이 구성되어 있는지 고민하여 이를 수업 실연에 적절히 T-talk로 녹여내는 연습을 해보시기를 바랍니다!

단계	예시 활동	목적
Schema activation	• 짝과 대화 나누기 • 마인드맵	• 오늘 수업 주제에 관심과 흥미 유발
⇩	⇩	⇩
Receptive Skills	• 읽고 이해하기	• 해당 주제 관련 지식 습득
⇩	⇩	⇩
Productive skills	• 글쓰기 • 영어를 활용한 결과물 만들기	• 배운 내용을 실생활에 적용 • 영어 활용 및 핵심 표현 연습
⇩	⇩	⇩
Evaluation	• 체크리스트 평가 • 발표 • 교사/동료 피드백	• 자신의 결과물을 공유 • 평가 활동에 참여하며 메타인지 향상

(자세한 내용은 체크리스트의 '라. Logical Development' 부분을 참고 해주세요.)

05. 꼭 수업 실연을 아기자기하고 활기차게 해야 할까요? 너무 오글거려서 못 하겠어요.

제가 처음 수업 실연을 준비할 때 참고할 수 있는 자료가 초등 임용 영어 수업 실연밖에 없었습니다. 아기자기한 수업 진행과 텐션 넘치는 교사의 태도, 심지어 챈트까지 … '나를 버려야 하는구나'라는 것을 깨닫고 좌절했죠. 이 질문을 하신 분도 아마 비슷한 감정일 것으로 생각합니다.

물론 성별에 따라 여자 선생님이 잘 소화할 수 있는 부분이 있고 남자 선생님이 잘 소화할 수 있는 부분이 있을 것입니다. 그러나 성별을 떠나 '내가 아닌 나의 모습'을 보여주기 시작하면 수업 실연을 할 때마다 아주 고통스러울 수밖에 없습니다. 심지어 그런 모습을 스스로 촬영해서 살펴봐야 하고, 남에게 보여주어야 한다고 생각하면 자괴감이 절로 들죠.

저는 영상 속 그 선생님처럼 발랄하게 수업을 진행할 자신도 없고, 능력도 없었습니다. 오히려 차분하고 논리적인 것이 저의 강점이었죠. 그래서 저는 그 때 당시 전형적인 수업 실연의 모습 대신, 안정적이고 교육적 배경이 튼튼한 수업 실연을 구성하려고 노력하였습니다. 그 결과는 지금 여러분이 보고 계시는 이 책이죠!

수업 실연을 연극으로 생각하라는 말이 많지만, 사실 본질은 연기가 아니라 교육이라는 사실을 유념할 필요가 있습니다. 즉, 자기 모습과 정반대되는 캐릭터를 꺼내어 수업 실연 연습을 한다는 것은 '수업' 연습이 아니라 '연기' 연습에 가깝다고 생각합니다.

따라서 맞지 않는 옷을 입어야 한다는 부담감을 떨쳐버릴 용기가 필요합니다. 나에게 어울리지 않는 것은 과감히 버리고 자신의 강점을 잘 나타내고 잘 소화할 수 있는 방식으로 약간의 창의성을 더해 보시기 바랍니다. 분명 좋은 결과가 따라올 것입니다!

06. Main idea를 찾는 활동에서 제목과 연결 짓는 부분이 인상 깊었습니다. 이때 혹시 자료에 제목이 이미 주어져 있다면, 제목 짓기 활동을 하지 않고 그냥 넘어가시나요? 수업 실연할 때 교사 재량으로 제목을 지웠다고 가정하고 제목 짓기를 할 수는 없을까요?

물론 여러분이 교사가 되어서 실제 수업을 준비하다 보면 주어진 자료를 교사의 의도에 맞게 수정할 일이 많습니다. 그러나 수업 실연의 관점에서 위 질문과 같이 '문제로 제시된 자료를 교사 재량으로 수정하는 것'은 시험 상황에서 추천하지 않습니다. 아래 세 가지 질문에 대해 한번 고민해 보시기 바랍니다.

(1) 과연 출제 의도에 맞는 방향일까?

여러분이 만약 제시된 자료를 임의로 수정한다면 그것은 출제 의도를 올바르게 파악하고 있는 것이 아닙니다. 제목이 주어져 있다면 왜 제목을 주었을지, 제목으로 무엇을 할 수 있을지를 고민하는 것이 적합한 구상 방향입니다.

(2) 과연 효율적일까?

여러분의 수업 실연을 바라보는 채점관은 당연히 해당 자료에 제목이 주어져 있다고 생각할 것입니다. 그러나 만약 여러분이 제목을 지운 상태로 학생들에게 제목 짓기 활동을 진행한다고 했을 때, 그 의도를 채점관이 이해하도록 유도하면서 수업 실연을 진행하기란 현실적으로 어렵습니다.

(3) 필요할까?

제목 짓기 활동은 지시 사항에 나와 있는 부분이 아닙니다. 이 뜻은, 직접적인 채점 요소가 아니라는 의미이기도 합니다. 따라서 만약 제목 짓기 활동을 진행한다면 운이 좋다면 좋은 인상을 보여줄 수는 있으나, 이와 정반대로 득점과 큰 관련이 없는 부분에 소중한 시간을 낭비하게 될 수도 있습니다.

저는 위와 같은 이유로 멀쩡한 제목을 지우는 무모한 결단을 내리지는 않았습니다. 그러나 제목이 버젓이 있는데 언급도 하지 않고 지나가기란 너무 아쉽죠!

따라서 저는 다음과 같은 활동을 진행하였습니다.

구상 단계에서 미리 Main idea의 단어를 제목과 몇 개 정도 겹치게 설정해 놓습니다. 그 후, Main idea를 찾아보는 활동을 진행한 다음 제목을 보게 하는 것입니다. 이후 T-talk에서 제목과 Main idea가 서로 긴밀한 관계가 있음을 공통된 단어를 통해 언급하고 활동을 마무리하였습니다.

O7. 블랜디드 수업에 관하여 준비해야 할 부분이 있을까요?

코로나 이후로 원격 수업 환경이 구축되어 모든 학생이 개인 전자기기를 학교에서 활용할 수 있게 되었습니다. 따라서 교실에서는 온라인 교육 플랫폼을 이용하거나 공유 문서 작업 과제, AI 활용 등 다양한 형태의 수업이 가능해졌습니다. 따라서 수업 실연에서도 이러한 상황을 가정한 문항이 얼마든지 출제될 수 있습니다.

(1) 새로운 교실 환경에 대한 T-talk 준비

아래와 같은 교실 속 전자기기 활용과 관련한 다양한 상황에 관하여 T-talk를 준비할 필요가 있습니다.

1. 학생들에게 Tablet PC를 꺼내어 Online classroom에 접속하기
ex) Turn on your tablet PC and come to the online classroom!

2. 공유 문서를 모둠원과 함께 작업하기
ex) Let's begin working on this online document with your group members.

3. 자료의 출처를 정확하게 표기하기
ex) Make sure you leave the right source.

4. 영상이나 사진 등을 검색해서 삽입하기
ex) Search for the photos and put them here.

5. 친구의 작품을 공유하거나 댓글 달기
ex) Share your writing in the online classroom and leave comments.

위 상황과 관련한 지시 사항이 출제된다면 어떻게 T-talk를 구성할 것인지 미리 고민을 해보는 것도 블랜디드 수업을 준비하는 좋은 방법입니다!

(2) 수업 차시 간 연계에 관한 준비

코로나 상황이 진정됨에 따라 출제 가능성이 크게 낮아졌다고 생각되지만, 온-오프라인 수업 환경이 차시 간 연계될 상황에 대하여도 가볍게 알아둘 필요가 있습니다.

(2-1) 온라인(이전) → 오프라인(수업 실연)

이전 수업이 온라인으로 진행되었을 때 수업 실연 상황으로 오프라인 수업이 제시된다면 가장 중요한 것은 이해점검입니다. 현실적으로 온라인 수업을 진행하면 학생들의 집중도도 많이 떨어지고, 교사로서도 학생의 이해도를 파악하기 어렵습니다. 따라서 온라인에서 오프라인으로 넘어오는 수업의 흐름이라면 반드시 본 수업 내용이 소개되기 전에 지난 차시에 대한 복습이 충분히 이루어져야 합니다. 그 이후, 거꾸로 수업의 틀에 따라 온라인 수업에서 배운 개념을 실제 상황에 적용하는 활동 중심 수업으로 해당 차시를 구성하는 것이 가장 이상적입니다.

(2-2) 오프라인(수업 실연) → 온라인(이후)

출제 가능성은 더 낮아 보이지만, 만약 현재 수업이 오프라인으로 진행되고 이후 수업을 온라인으로 진행한다고 가정할 경우, 가장 중요한 것은 '수업 내용의 일관성'입니다. 이상적인 방법으로는 오늘 배운 내용과 일관되면서 온라인 환경에서 수행할 수 있는 과제를 제시하는 것입니다. 대표적인 예로는 완성된 결과물을 Online classroom에 올리기, 친구의 작품에 댓글 남기기 등이 있습니다.

08. 학생 답변을 지도안에 작성해도 괜찮을까요?

교사의 수업 지도안에는 학생의 답변이 들어가면 안 된다고 이야기를 듣는 분들이 간혹 계십니다. 이 이야기의 맥락은 '수업은 활발한 상호작용이므로 예측할 수 없다. 따라서 학생의 반응을 미리 정해놓는 수업 지도안은 학생 중심 수업과 맞지 않는다.'라는 것입니다.

물론 위 말에 동의하지만, 학생 중심 수업이라고 할지라도 학생의 반응을 교사가 어느 정도 예측하고 준비하는 것은 필요합니다. 만약 이마저도 '학생 중심 수업'과 맞지 않는다고 한다면, 수업 지도안 자체가 의미가 없게 되겠죠.

따라서 저는 수업 실연 지도안에서 학생의 답변도 함께 포함하였습니다. 다만, 'Expected response(예시 발화)'라는 단어를 추가하여 교사가 단정적으로 학생의 대답을 정하는 느낌이 아니라, 교사가 의도한 질문에 대한 대답을 '수업을 계획하는 단계에서 예측'하는 의미를 포함하였죠. 답변의 개방성을 조금 더 높이는 것입니다.

09. 지도안에 이미 쓰인 부분은 수업 실연할 때 생략해도 괜찮은가요?

생략해도 괜찮습니다. 왜냐하면, 수업 실연 지시사항에 해당 부분을 실연하라고 언급되어있지 않았기 때문입니다. 수업 실연도 엄연히 시험이기 때문에 배점과 채점의 관점에서 접근해야 합니다. 요구하지 않은 것은 보여주지 않는 것이 좋습니다.

그리고 수업 실연 시험 자체가 '추상적인 지시사항을 어떻게 구체화할 것인가'를 묻는 것입니다. 그 구체화의 내용이 지도안에 나타나야 하고, 여기에서 변별력이 생깁니다. 따라서 모든 수험자에게 공통으로 제시된 부분은 수업 실연에서 중요하지 않다고 생각합니다.

따라서 지도안에 이미 쓰여있는 부분은 과감히 생략하고 본인이 쓴 부분에만 집중해서 수업 실연을 하는 것이 좋습니다. 괜히 요구하지도 않은 부분을 고민하면 시간을 낭비할 수도 있고, 다른 부분에서 보여줘야 할 부분이 충분히 드러나지 않을 수도 있기 때문입니다.

10. 수업 실연도 시험이니만큼 출제자의 의도가 있으리라 생각합니다. 그러면 혹시 특정 활동을 결정하는 데에 있어서 힌트가 되는 표현이 지시사항이나 자료에 있을까요?

저는 수업 실연 출제 단계에서 당연히 일정 부분 의도한 것은 있다고 생각합니다. 그러나 꼭 그것만이 정답이 되는 것은 아닙니다. 실제로도 전혀 다른 스타일의 수업을 진행하더라도 만점이 나오기 때문입니다.

이러한 모습을 보면 수업 실연 출제자가 던지는 지시사항은 마치 작곡가가 가수에게 가이드 녹음을 들려주는 것처럼, 여러 가능성 중 하나를 방향성으로서만 제시할 뿐, 꼭 그대로 따를 필요는 없다는 느낌이 듭니다.

따라서 '출제자가 의도한 그 활동을 반드시 맞춰야겠다'라는 '정답을 찾는 생각'보다는 조건을 충족시키면서 학생 중심 교육에 맞게 '자유롭게 활동을 구성'하는 것이 올바른 수업 실연 연습의 접근법이 아닐까 생각합니다.

곰쌤 영어과 수업 실연 체크리스트

1. 구상형 1번 번역 문항
    가. 기출 문제 번역 문항

    나. 실전 연습 문제 번역 문항

2. 번역 문항 예시 답변
    가. 기출 문제 번역 문항 예시 답변

    나. 실전 연습 문제 번역 문항 예시 답변

3. 주제별 아이디어 및 예시 답변
    Topic 01 ~ 24

영어과 심층면접 부록

'현직교사 곰쌤이 알려주는 심층면접 다진고기'에 수록된 내용을 영어과 면접 준비용으로 번역한 자료로, '다진고기'와 함께 활용하시면 더욱 효과적입니다!

Chapter 01

구상형 1번 번역 문항

 기출 문제 번역 문항

(1) 2025 기출문제

구상형 1.

Identify <u>one</u> problem of Minsu and <u>one</u> problem of the whole class, and suggest a solution for each problem.

> Minsoo is often late to school. Whenever he doesn't feel like going to school, he arrives later and later, even at 6th period. He even knows that whether he arrives in the second period or the sixth period, the tardiness is the same. Initially, Minsoo was the only one who was late, but over time, other students in the whole class began arriving late as well. As the number of students being tardy increases, the classroom teacher is seriously concerned about classroom management.

(2) 2024 기출문제

구상형 1.

Identify one problem that appears in Teacher Kim's class and suggest a solution from the perspective of lesson design.

> Teacher Kim has been facing many concerns lately. In the past, students were able to understand well enough with simple materials in text form, the blackboard, and verbal explanations, but that's no longer the case. Students now say things like, "The content we learn in class doesn't seem to be related to our lives," "The materials that are just in text form are quite boring," and "The class is so difficult to understand that it's hard for me to participate."

(3) 2023 기출문제

구상형 1.

The following are students' opinions after a metaverse class. Identify one problem from each student's opinion and suggest a solution for each.

> Student A : I wasn't able to connect to the metaverse several times, and I'm not familiar with how to do it. It takes a long time to log in for class, and I keep getting logged out, which is frustrating.
> Student B : The metaverse interface is complicated, so it's hard to focus during class.
> Student C : The metaverse-based lessons are fun, but it's disappointing that the assessments are still done in the traditional way, like quizzes.

(4) 2022 기출문제

구상형 1.

Based on the student cases below, explain each student's motivation style and suggest one appropriate task for each.

> Student A : I want to study hard to improve my grades and gain confidence in my academic abilities.
> Student B : When I work on assignments, I prefer to choose how to complete the task and decide on the content myself, rather than having the teacher directly assign it.
> Student C : I prefer working on group projects with friends in a comfortable environment rather than studying alone.

(5) 2021 기출문제

구상형 1.

Based on the student cases below, identify the cause of each student's problem and suggest one solution for each.

> Student A : I'm interested in subject A, but I'm hesitant to choose it because I don't think I'll get a high score.
> Student B : I think subject B might help with my future career, but I'm not confident in my memorization skills and I'm worried the class might be boring, so I'm unsure if I should choose it.

(6) 2020 기출문제

> 구상형 1.

In the following situation, identify three problems the teacher is facing and suggest a solution for each.

> The feedback the teacher received from students is as follows:
> - "There are too many performance assessments, and it's exhausting."
> - "Other teachers also assign performance assessments around the same time, and it's overwhelming."
> - "I don't understand why performance assessments are so important. I would prefer written exams instead."

(7) 2019 기출문제

> 구상형 1.

Identify two causes and two solutions for the following situation.

> Teacher Kim has repeatedly cautioned a student who is causing disruption by talking and making noise during class. However, a student who usually pays attention in class said, "Teacher, it's interrupting the flow of the lesson and slowing down our progress, so let's just ignore it and continue."

(8) 2018 기출문제

> 구상형 1.

Identify two causes and two solutions that Teacher Park can take for the following situation.

> Minsu, a student in Teacher Park's homeroom, comes from a multicultural family. He usually has a shy personality, but lately, he has been struggling to socialize with his friends and always appears gloomy. Recently, Teacher Park has noticed that Minsu seems to be avoiding other teachers as well, so as the homeroom teacher, Park decided to have a counseling session with him. During the session, Minsu said, "I can't get along well with my friends because our cultures are so different," and "I'm worried that my friends will make fun of my poor Korean."

(9) 2017 기출문제

구상형 1.

Identify two causes and two solutions that the homeroom teacher can take for the following situation.

> Student A tends to sleep a lot. She often oversleeps and arrives late to school, and during class, she has been caught sleeping and scolded by other teachers multiple times. The homeroom teacher conducted a counseling session regarding this problematic behavior, and Student A responded, "I have no intention of going to college. I don't know why I should go, and I just want to get my high school diploma." She also said, "I don't understand why I need to attend class. Actually, Teacher Kim is very supportive and teaches a subject I enjoy, so I try to listen in that class, but I really don't want to listen to or participate in other subjects."

실전 연습 문제 번역 문항

(1) 실전 연습 문제 1회

구상형 1.

Identify two causes and two solutions for the following problematic situation.

> Student A used to be a student who frequently arrived late but actively participated in class. Fortunately, she showed a tendency to improve her grades gradually. However, when the classes suddenly switched to online learning, her attitude changed dramatically. She began to come in late to first-period class almost every day, often requiring a phone call to wake her up. In the classroom, she used to raise her hand to present, but during online classes, she has become quiet and often does not respond when called.

(2) 실전 연습 문제 2회

구상형 1.

Below is a survey received from students before the class. Describe the learning styles of the three students and suggest one appropriate activity for each.

> Student A: I understand better when explanations are given through pictures rather than just text.
> Student B: I find it boring to sit in class every day. I wish the lessons were more active.
> Student C: I like memorizing things through rap lyrics. I want classes that are enjoyable to listen to.

(3) 실전 연습 문제 3회

구상형 1.

Identify two causes and two solutions for the following situation.

> Student A tends to express his actions or emotions excessively. Some classmates intentionally provoke Student A during class to disrupt or interrupt the flow of the lesson. This kind of incident has happened repeatedly, so the homeroom teacher asked the students to write down reasons for bullying Student A in the form of a note counseling session, but all of them submitted blank papers.

(4) 실전 연습 문제 4회

구상형 1.

Describe the motivational styles of each of the three students below and suggest one way to implement each motivational activity in your class.

> Student A: "I feel like my concentration drops a bit because the lessons are always taught with just text."
> Student B: "I'm not sure if what we learn in class is practical."
> Student C: "The exercises my teacher gave me are too hard and I don't feel confident."

(5) 실전 연습 문제 5회

구상형 1.

Present the evaluation methods desired by the three students below and suggest one way to implement each of them in class.

> Student A: "I want to take exams in a competitive way against my classmates."
> Student B: "I want to be evaluated based on how much I have improved compared to my past self."
> Student C: "I want to receive scores based on the effort I put in, regardless of the results."

(6) 실전 연습 문제 6회

구상형 1.

Identify two causes and two solutions for the following situation.

> In Teacher Park's class, seating is assigned by drawing lots every month. However, a student named Min-su approached Teacher Park and said, "Teacher, I have poor eyesight, so I can't study well if I sit in the back. I would appreciate it if you could seat me in the front." Teacher Park, noticing Min-su's good attitude in class and his strong willingness to learn, agreed to the request and assigned Min-su a seat in the front before drawing lots for the other students. However, afterwards, many students in Teacher Park's class began to dislike Min-su.

(7) 실전 연습 문제 7회

구상형 1.

Identify two causes in the following situation and suggest two ways to prevent such situations.

> Teacher Kim enjoys communicating with students through social media. However, one day, a student named Chan-seok captured a screenshot of Teacher Kim during an online class and posted it on his social media account. After seeing the photo, other students began to leave playful comments on Chan-seok's post featuring Teacher Kim. Teacher Kim told Chan-seok, "That photo makes me look unattractive, so please delete it." Chan-seok responded, "I think that photo looks fine! You enjoy communicating with us on social media, don't you?"

(8) 실전 연습 문제 8회

구상형 1.

Identify two causes of the problem presented in the situation and provide one solution for each.

> Teacher Park received the following complaint from the parent of his student, Min-hee: "Teacher, simply passing the home newsletters to the student isn't enough. I checked my child's bag, and it's full of home newsletters. There are many important notices there, but my child hasn't shown them to me, so we've missed a lot of information, and it's quite frustrating." Afterward, when Teacher Park asked Min-hee why she hadn't shared the home newsletters with her parents, Min-hee replied that she didn't want to talk to them.

(9) 실전 연습 문제 9회

구상형 1.

Identify two causes of the problem presented in the situation below, and suggest two solutions from Teacher A's perspective.

> Cheolsu, a third-year middle school student, is well-known for his high test scores. In fact, no one has ever scored higher than Cheolsu on exams. He knows that he studies better than others and believes that the third-year middle school material is too easy for him. Therefore, during class, Cheolsu said, "Since I already know what you're teaching, I'll just work on this," and began taking out a high school workbook to solve problems during the lesson. Teacher A felt uncomfortable with Cheolsu's attitude but ultimately allowed him to work on it during class.

(10) 실전 연습 문제 10회

> **구상형 1.**

Identify two causes of the problem in the following situation and suggest two solutions to address it.

> Student A is teased every day by classmates B, C, and D. Sometimes, B, C, and D even make harsh jokes that include insults directed at A. After noticing this, the homeroom teacher consulted with student A and asked how things were going with B, C, and D. Student A replied, "Honestly, I do feel bad, but friends usually joke around like that. I think if I show that I'm upset, it will make things awkward between us, so I'll just put up with it."

(11) 실전 연습 문제 11회

> **구상형 1.**

Identify two possible causes of the problem represented in the situation below and suggest two solutions for each.

> In Teacher Kim's homeroom class, student Young-cheol maintains a good attitude in subjects related to the college entrance exam but switches seats with a friend sitting in the back during other subjects and works on problems from the college entrance exam workbook during class. Teacher Kim decided to address Young-cheol's selective attitude toward subjects and asked, "Why do you behave this way?" Young-cheol replied, "Studying for the entrance exam during that time is more efficient. Besides, those subjects are not even related to my career path anyway."

Chapter 02

번역 문항 예시 답변

기출 문제 번역 문항 예시 답변

(1) 2025 기출문제

구상형 1.

Response Start	This is my answer to the question number one.
Topic Sentence 1	The reason for Minsu's frequent tardiness is his lack of a sense of responsibility and awareness of the importance of following rules.
Ideal Situation	A responsible student understands the significance of adhering to rules and recognizes that arriving at school on time is a fundamental duty.
Cause-Problem Situation Link	However, Minsu lacks awareness of the consequences of being late and perceives attendance as a personal choice, leading to a worsening pattern of arriving later and later.
Topic Sentence (Solution)	To address this issue, I will implement individual counseling and a reward system to encourage Minsu to be punctual.
Specific Description	For example, I will use the "I-message" communication method to empathize with Minsu's perspective while explaining how his tardiness negatively affects both his academic performance and the classroom environment. Additionally, I will introduce a positive reinforcement system, where he receives rewards for arriving on time over a certain period, helping him stay motivated to follow the attendance rules.
Positive Effect	Through this approach, Minsu will develop a habit of punctuality with a greater sense of responsibility and recognize how his actions influence the entire class. Furthermore, the reward system will help reinforce positive behavior, naturally encouraging him to be punctual.

Topic Sentence 2	Secondly, the main cause of the increased tardiness among the entire class is the lack of educational intervention and appropriate rule-setting by the teacher.
Ideal Situation	In a classroom with effective intervention and well-defined rules, the importance of rule adherence ensures stability and fairness.
Cause-Problem Situation Link	However, in the current classroom, the lack of clear attendance policies and consistent enforcement has led students to believe that arriving late carries no significant consequences.

Topic Sentence (Solution)	To resolve this issue, I will implement a "Tardiness Reduction Campaign" with a collaborative rule-setting activity.
Specific Description	For example, I will hold class meetings to establish clear attendance rules together with the students. After that, I will introduce a "Punctuality Challenge", where the entire class will receive a collective reward if all students arrive on time for a month.
Positive Effect	Through these efforts, students will gain a deeper awareness of the importance of following rules and naturally take more responsibility for their actions.

End of Response	That was my answer to the question number one. Thank you for listening.

(2) 2024 기출문제

구상형 1.

Response Start	This is my answer to the question number one.

Topic Sentence	In the situation described, the problem with Teacher Kim is that he didn't use effective strategies to motivate his students in class.
Ideal Situation	As a teacher, it's important to think about how to motivate students when planning lessons, just as much as it is to teach the material clearly.
Cause-Problem Situation Link	However, Teacher Kim didn't consider factors that help motivate students, like 'attention', 'relevance', and 'self-confidence'. Because of this, students had trouble understanding the lessons and participating.

Topic Sentence (Solution)	To address this issue, the teacher should identify what motivates his students and design lessons that fit those needs.
Specific Description	For example, he could use Keller's ARCS theory in his lessons. This means using videos and pictures to capture students' attention, creating activities that connect lesson content to their own lives, and providing different levels of quizzes to help all students succeed.
Positive Effect	By doing this, students will engage more with the lessons and feel more motivated because they can connect with the material in a way that suits their level.
End of Response	That was my answer to the question number one. Thank you for listening.

(3) 2023 기출문제

구상형 1.

Response Start	This is my answer to the question number one.
Topic Sentence (Problem 1)	The issue in Student A's opinion is the technical problems with using the metaverse for lessons and students not being familiar with it.
Ideal Situation	*(전체적인 답변 분량을 고려하여 생략)*
Cause-Problem Situation Link	*(전체적인 답변 분량을 고려하여 생략)*
Topic Sentence (Solution)	To fix this problem, the teacher can hold practice sessions ahead of time.
Specific Description	For example, before the actual class, the teacher can log into the metaverse platform with students and let them try out different features to get ready.
Positive Effect	This way, the teacher can identify technical issues, like problems accessing the metaverse and frequent logouts, and address them in advance. Also, practicing will help students feel more comfortable with using the platform.
Topic Sentence (Problem 2)	Next, Student B's opinion highlights that the layout of the metaverse is not user-friendly for learning.
Ideal Situation	*(전체적인 답변 분량을 고려하여 생략)*
Cause-Problem Situation Link	*(전체적인 답변 분량을 고려하여 생략)*

Topic Sentence (Solution 2)	To solve this, the teacher should choose a metaverse platform that allows for more user customization to create a better learning interface.
Specific Description	For instance, the teacher can learn about different platforms through training and select one that offers high customization options. Then, they can focus on the important features and avoid adding anything that might confuse students.
Positive Effect	This approach allows the teacher to create a learning environment that suits their teaching style. Students will find the simplified layout easier to engage with during lessons.
Topic Sentence (Problem 3)	Finally, Student C's opinion points out that students' needs were not understood, and traditional evaluation methods were still being used.
Ideal Situation	(전체적인 답변 분량을 고려하여 생략)
Cause-Problem Situation Link	(전체적인 답변 분량을 고려하여 생략)
Topic Sentence (Solution 3)	To address this issue, the teacher should analyze students' needs to better use the metaverse.
Specific Description	For example, the teacher can survey students before class to find out what they expect from metaverse lessons. Based on the results, the teacher can adjust how the metaverse is used for both lessons and assessments.
Positive Effect	This way, the teacher can develop new assessment methods instead of relying solely on traditional ones. Students will feel more involved since their needs are considered, leading to a more engaging and active classroom atmosphere.
End of Response	That was my answer to the question number one. Thank you for listening.

(4) 2022 기출문제

구상형 1.

Response Start	This is my answer to the question number one.
Topic Sentence (Motivation Methods)	Based on self-determination theory, students A, B, and C can be analyzed according to their needs for competence, autonomy, and relatedness.
Topic Sentence	First, for Student A, who is motivated by the fulfillment of competence needs, challenging tasks are appropriate.
Specific Description	Possible examples are conducting an advanced exploration activity on a related topic based on what they learned, solving real-life problems, or engaging in higher-level concept learning would be suitable.
Positive Effect	This will help Student A feel more challenged and motivated to learn. Also, as they work on these advanced activities, they will see their problem-solving skills get better, which will satisfy their need to feel competent.
Conclusion	Therefore, presenting challenging tasks like advanced exploration activities is appropriate for Student A.
Topic Sentence	Second, for Student B, who is motivated by the fulfillment of autonomy needs, tasks that allow for subject selection are appropriate.
Specific Description	Possible examples are allowing Student B to choose a topic they are interested in, conduct research and present a report in an appropriate format.
Positive Effect	This way, Student B will feel more engaged since they are performing a task they chose themselves rather than one assigned by the teacher, thus fulfilling their autonomy needs.
Conclusion	Therefore, a topic selection task is suitable for Student B.

Topic Sentence	Finally, for Student C, who is motivated by the fulfillment of relatedness needs, collaborative group tasks are appropriate.
Specific Description	Possible examples are presenting tasks that require cooperation to achieve the goals, such as jigsaw activities, pair activities or group learning.
Positive Effect	Through this, Student C will not study alone but will learn by cooperating with friends, fulfilling their relatedness needs.
Conclusion	Therefore, group collaborative tasks like jigsaw activities are suitable for Student C.

End of Response	That was my answer to the question number one. Thank you for listening.

(5) 2021 기출문제

구상형 1.

Response Start	This is my answer to the question number one.
Topic Sentence (Cause 1)	First, the reason Student A is struggling is the pressure to get good grades.
Ideal Situation	Learning about a subject that interests them can be a valuable experience, regardless of grades.
Cause-Problem Situation Link	However, due to the pressure to achieve high scores, Student A hesitates to choose Subject A, even though he or she is interested in it.
Topic Sentence (Cause 2)	On the other hand, the reason for Student B's problem is a lack of memorization strategies, which makes him or her feel less attracted to the subject.
Ideal Situation	In the learning process, having the right study methods is necessary. The more confidence he or she has in their learning strategies, the more appealing the subject becomes.
Cause-Problem Situation Link	However, Student B doesn't know effective memorization strategies, so he or she finds Subject B boring.
Topic Sentence (Solution 1)	To help Student A, I will conduct individual counseling.
Specific Description	For example, I will suggest that learning in areas he or she likes can be meaningful, regardless of scores. I will also emphasize that enjoying what he or she studies can lead to better results. If Student A focuses on what he or she enjoys, good grades will likely follow.
Positive Effect	Through this, Student A will feel less pressure about scores. He or she will focus more on genuine interest and curiosity about the subject, leading to a better learning experience.
Conclusion	So, I will do individual counseling with Student A to help reduce score pressure.

Topic Sentence (Solution 2)	For Student B, I will provide coaching on study methods.
Specific Description	For example, I will teach Student B different memorization techniques. These will include understanding-based memorization, organizing ideas or making diagrams.
Positive Effect	By trying different study methods, Student B will gain confidence in Subject B. He or she will also engage more in class because of the increased confidence.
Conclusion	Therefore, I will give study method coaching to Student B.

End of Response	That was my answer to the question number one. Thank you for listening.

(6) 2020 기출문제

구상형 1.

Response Start	This is my answer to the question number one.
Topic Sentence (Problem 1)	The first problem in the given situation is that Teacher A has prepared too many evaluations.
Ideal Situation	As a teacher, it is important to plan a reasonable number of evaluations so that students do not feel too much pressure.
Cause-Problem Situation Link	(전체적인 답변 분량을 고려하여 생략)
Topic Sentence (Problem 2)	The second problem is that the evaluation timing of Teacher A overlaps with that of other teachers.
Ideal Situation	If the evaluation timings overlap, students may have to prepare for several subjects at once. This can be confusing, so it is important to coordinate the evaluation times.
Cause-Problem Situation Link	(전체적인 답변 분량을 고려하여 생략)
Topic Sentence (Problem 3)	The third problem is that there has not been enough explanation about the importance of the evaluations for the students.
Ideal Situation	If students understand the purpose of the evaluations, they will participate more actively.
Cause-Problem Situation Link	(전체적인 답변 분량을 고려하여 생략)
Topic Sentence (Solution 1)	The first solution is to adjust the content and amount of the evaluations that students must take.
Specific Description	For example, I can simplify the evaluations. Instead of having students create results on their own, I can use formative assessments during class, observation assessments, or peer evaluations in group activities. This can help reduce the burden of evaluations on students.
Positive Effect	(전체적인 답변 분량을 고려하여 생략)

Topic Sentence (Solution 2)	The second solution is to discuss and coordinate the evaluation schedule with fellow teachers.
Specific Description	For example, I can check the evaluation plans for other subjects in advance. If the evaluation timings are too close, I will hold a meeting with teachers who teach the same grade to adjust the schedule.
Positive Effect	*(전체적인 답변 분량을 고려하여 생략)*
Topic Sentence (Solution 3)	The third solution is to have a pre-briefing session to explain the importance of the evaluations before they are conducted.
Specific Description	For example, the teacher can use this session to explain that evaluations are not just about choosing the correct answers from multiple choices. Instead, the goal is to see how well students can apply what they have learned to real-life problems.
Positive Effect	*(전체적인 답변 분량을 고려하여 생략)*
End of Response	That was my answer to the question number one. Thank you for listening.

(7) 2019 기출문제

구상형 1.

Response Start	This is my answer to the question number one.
Topic Sentence (Cause 1)	The first cause of the problem is that there is no atmosphere of mutual respect during class time.
Ideal Situation	It is necessary for both teachers and students, as well as for students to respect each other.
Cause-Problem Situation Link	However, because there is no atmosphere of mutual respect in the classroom, some students continue to disturb the teacher during class. There are even students who suggest ignoring that student.
Topic Sentence (Cause 2)	Meanwhile, the second cause is that Teacher Kim is not skilled in classroom management.
Ideal Situation	Classroom management skills include the ability to guide students during class, organizing content so that students can engage naturally, and distributing the lesson material appropriately across class periods.
Cause-Problem Situation Link	In the given situation, Teacher Kim's lack of classroom management skills caused students to be unable to focus and make noise, and some students began to worry about the lesson progress.
Topic Sentence (Solution 1)	The first solution to address these causes is to set classroom rules.
Specific Description	For example, the teacher can first mention the importance of having mutual respect during class time. The teacher can explain that to create a respectful atmosphere, rules need to be established. After that, the teacher can have students think of rules for the classroom together and make a promise by signing them.
Positive Effect	Through this, students will learn the importance of rules and how to respect each other. If mutual respect is created in the classroom, behaviors like ignoring the teacher or other classmates will disappear.

Topic Sentence (Solution 2)	The second solution is for the teacher to focus on self-development.
Specific Description	For example, the teacher can attend training on classroom management, record and review classroom problems, observe colleagues' classes, or seek advice from experienced teachers. These actions help the teacher improve their overall teaching abilities.
Positive Effect	Through this, the teacher can enhance the classroom management skills. With this expertise, students will naturally engage with the teacher's explanations, leading to smooth lesson progress and preventing problems like those in the given situation.

End of Response	That was my answer to the question number one. Thank you for listening.

(8) 2018 기출문제

구상형 1.

Response Start	This is my answer to the question number one.
Topic Sentence (Cause 1)	The first cause of the problem is that cultural differences are not accepted in the classroom.
Ideal Situation	Different cultures should be respected.
Cause-Problem Situation Link	However, the classroom does not have a good atmosphere for accepting different cultures. Because of this, Minsu has doubts about his own culture. This leads him to have a negative attitude.
Topic Sentence (Cause 2)	The second cause is that Minsu's poor Korean lowers his confidence.
Ideal Situation	Language is a way to express oneself and is important for self-esteem.
Cause-Problem Situation Link	Minsu thinks he is not good at Korean. Because of this, he has limits in expressing himself. This leads to low self-esteem and a lack of confidence.
Topic Sentence (Solution 1)	The first solution to these problems is to hold a cultural exchange event.
Specific Description	For example, I will have a time to recognize cultural differences in areas like food, relationships, and clothing.
Positive Effect	Through this, students will realize that different cultures exist. They will learn that there is no right or wrong between cultures. This will help create a classroom culture that recognizes and respects differences.
Topic Sentence (Solution 2)	The second solution is to offer a language support program.
Specific Description	For example, I will provide opportunities for students to learn Korean through after-school classes or partnerships with local multicultural centers.
Positive Effect	Through this, Minsu can improve his Korean skills. He will be able to express himself better. This will increase his self-esteem and lead to a more active school life.
End of Response	That was my answer to the question number one. Thank you for listening.

(9) 2017 기출문제

구상형 1.

Response Start	This is my answer to the question number one.
Topic Sentence (Cause 1)	The first cause of the problem is that Student A does not have a goal for her learning.
Ideal Situation	A strong desire to achieve her future goals can motivate her to learn.
Cause-Problem Situation Link	However, Student A has not found her goals yet. She thinks, "I don't know why I should attend class," and "I just want to graduate high school." This has made her lose motivation for learning.
Topic Sentence (Cause 2)	The second cause is the lack of emotional connection with her teachers.
Ideal Situation	Students often become more interested in subjects taught by teachers they feel close to.
Cause-Problem Situation Link	But, Student A has not formed emotional connections with any teacher except Ms. Kim. She expresses strong dislike for other subjects by saying, "I really don't want to listen or participate."
Topic Sentence (Solution 1)	The first solution to these problems is to have an activity called "Imagine Your Desired Future."
Specific Description	For example, I will have Student A imagine her life in 10, 20, or 30 years. She will explore what goals she needs to achieve at each time and what current goals she should set.
Positive Effect	Through this, Student A will understand what attitude she needs to show now to reach her future goals. This process will help her gain control and manage her behavior, leading to more motivation in school.

Topic Sentence (Solution 2)	The second solution is to ask for help from fellow teachers.
Specific Description	For example, I will get advice from Ms. Kim about activities that will interest Student A. I will also ask how Student A wants to relate to her teachers. Then, I will seriously share Student A's situation with the teachers who teach her and request their help.
Positive Effect	Through this, Student A will feel more emotional support from teachers who care about her. This relationship will help her gradually become more interested in her subjects and participate actively.

End of Response	That was my answer to the question number one. Thank you for listening.

실전 연습 문제 번역 문항 예시 답변

(1) 실전 연습 문제 1회

구상형 1.

Response Start	This is my answer to the question number one.
Topic Sentence (Cause 1)	The first cause of the problem is the lack of self-management skills in Student A.
Ideal Situation	To grow as a self-directed person, it is important to control one's own needs.
Cause-Problem Situation Link	However, online classes require more self-management than in-person classes. This has made Student A, who often arrives late, behave worse.
Topic Sentence (Cause 2)	The second cause is the lack of peer pressure, which leads to a decrease in motivation to learn.
Ideal Situation	Students often get motivated by wanting to follow their peers.
Cause-Problem Situation Link	But in online classes, there are no students around. Unlike in a classroom, this absence of peer pressure caused her to lose motivation to participate in class.
Topic Sentence (Solution 1)	The first solution is to suggest that she keep a time management diary.
Specific Description	For example, she should record when she wakes up, how long she concentrates, and when she takes breaks.
Positive Effect	Through this, Student A will be able to reflect on her behavior objectively. By developing this recording habit, she can improve her self-management skills.
Topic Sentence (Solution 2)	The second solution is to create an online portfolio.
Specific Description	For example, I will use Google Classroom for students to summarize what they learned each day. They will upload and share it with friends to comment on each other's work.
Positive Effect	Through this, Student A will see her friends' activities. This will motivate her to participate actively in online classes, just like in-person classes.
End of Response	That was my answer to the question number one. Thank you for listening.

(2) 실전 연습 문제 2회

구상형 1.

Response Start	This is my answer to the question number one.
Topic Sentence (Learning Styles)	Student A prefers pictures over words, so she is a visual learner. Student B likes being active instead of sitting still, so she is a kinesthetic learner. Student C enjoys fun classes, making her an auditory learner.
Topic Sentence	Each student benefits from different teaching methods. First, for Student A, who prefers pictures, using visual materials like charts is a good idea.
Specific Description	For example, if we're comparing things, we can use charts. To understand a story's flow, we could use comics. Using these visual tools will help her understand the class better.
Positive Effect	This way, Student A's understanding of the lessons will improve.
Conclusion	So, visual materials like charts, or comics will be great for Student A.
Topic Sentence	Next, for Student B, who prefers being active, we should use physical activities.
Specific Description	For example, we can do Total Physical Response (TPR) activities or have a fun cocktail party style class. These activities will get all the students moving and interacting.
Positive Effect	This approach will help Student B participate more actively in class. She'll have a lively and enjoyable learning experience.
Conclusion	Thus, activities like TPR or a cocktail party will suit Student B well.
Topic Sentence	Finally, for Student C, who wants fun classes, music-based lessons are perfect.
Specific Description	For instance, we can change the lyrics of songs or use chants. These activities will help her memorize vocabulary related to the topics. We can create sentences with key phrases and add a rhythm for singing and listening.
Positive Effect	With these music-based lessons, Student C will be more engaged and her focus during class will increase. Also, the rhythmic repetition will help her memorize more effectively.
Conclusion	So, using music, like changing song lyrics or chants, will be great for Student C.
End of Response	That was my answer to the question number one. Thank you for listening.

(3) 실전 연습 문제 3회

구상형 1.

Response Start	This is my answer to the question number one.
Topic Sentence (Cause 1)	The first reason for the problem is that Student A struggles with self-control over his actions and emotions.
Ideal Situation	To build good relationships, one needs to manage their emotions well. This ability can be learned through interactions with different people at school.
Cause-Problem Situation Link	However, Student A struggles to control his actions and emotions. He reacts sensitively to classmates' actions, leading to excessive behavior and emotional expression.
Topic Sentence (Cause 2)	The second reason is the classroom atmosphere, where students do not recognize the seriousness of teasing Student A and remain passive.
Ideal Situation	Many students being passive about teasing one student can lead to serious bullying issues. It is important to be aware of this.
Cause-Problem Situation Link	In this classroom, the students follow the crowd and don't see how serious their actions are. Because of this, they ended up handing in blank papers during the session.
Topic Sentence (Solution 1)	The first solution is to provide social skills coaching for Student A.
Specific Description	For example, I will ask Student A to think about his situation. He will consider which responses led to certain results. Then, we will talk about what could have happened if he had reacted differently. Finally, I will help him find better ways to respond.
Positive Effect	Through this, Student A will learn how to build social relationships. He will gain confidence and restore his friendships.
Topic Sentence (Solution 2)	The second solution is to conduct a media-based discussion class.
Specific Description	I will show videos about school violence or bullying. We will discuss the actions of the bully and the feelings of the victim.
Positive Effect	Through this, the students will reflect on their behavior from an outsider's perspective. They will gain a chance to think critically.
End of Response	That was my answer to the question number one. Thank you for listening.

(4) 실전 연습 문제 4회

구상형 1.

Response Start	This is my answer to the question number one.
Topic Sentence (Learning Styles)	Based on Keller's ARCS theory, Student A is motivated by attention, Student B is motivated by relevance, and Student C is motivated by confidence.
Topic Sentence	First, Student A is motivated by attention, so using varied presentation methods in class would be effective.
Specific Description	For example, I would use pictures, charts, or videos from YouTube or Instagram.
Positive Effect	This will help Student A stay interested and focused by seeing the content in a new way, different from the usual text-based methods.
Conclusion	Therefore, using pictures, charts, or videos like YouTube and Instagram is effective for Student A.
Topic Sentence	Second, Student B is motivated by relevance, so problem-solving tasks based on real-life situations would work well.
Specific Description	Possible examples are calculating the height of the tallest building in the neighborhood using math or creating a restaurant map using English phrases.
Positive Effect	Through this, Student B will realize the content learned in class can be applied in real situations, which will increase interest and motivation to learn.
Conclusion	Thus, problem-solving tasks based on real-life situations are effective for Student B.
Topic Sentence	Lastly, Student C is motivated by confidence, so it is best to provide learning experiences that offer success and choices.
Specific Description	Possible examples are offering tasks with levels of difficulty that match the student's abilities or allowing the student to choose assignments, which gives a sense of control.
Positive Effect	This will build Student C's self-efficacy and confidence, motivating them to learn more.
Conclusion	Therefore, a teaching method that provides success experiences and choices is suitable for Student C.
End of Response	That was my answer to the question number one. Thank you for listening.

(5) 실전 연습 문제 5회

구상형 1.

Response Start	This is my answer to the question number one.
Topic Sentence (Evaluation)	Student A prefers relative evaluation, Student B prefers growth-oriented evaluation, and Student C prefers effort-oriented evaluation.
Topic Sentence (Solution 1)	To meet these preferences, for Student A, team competition activities are suitable.
Specific Description	For example, teachers can divide students into teams to cooperate within the group but compete with other teams, and reflect this in the evaluation.
Positive Effect	Through these activities that encourage both teamwork and competition, Student A will participate actively in class.
Topic Sentence (Solution 2)	For Student B, we can include progress improvement in the evaluation.
Specific Description	For example, teachers can conduct regular formative assessments, and reward students who show a certain level of improvement compared to their previous test.
Positive Effect	This will allow Student B to feel a sense of accomplishment by competing with his or her past self and seeing personal growth.
Topic Sentence (Solution 3)	Lastly, for Student C, we can implement step-by-step project activities.
Specific Description	For example, teachers can break down the evaluation into stages, assessing participation, engagement, and task completion at each stage to measure effort.
Positive Effect	This will reduce the pressure on final results, allowing Student C to focus on consistent effort and show a strong willingness to participate in every class.
End of Response	That was my answer to the question number one. Thank you for listening.

(6) 실전 연습 문제 6회

구상형 1.

Response Start	This is my answer to the question number one.
Topic Sentence (Cause 1)	The first reason for the problem is that Teacher Park made a one-sided decision.
Ideal Situation	When making decisions that affect all students, like seating arrangements, it's important to gather everyone's opinion.
Cause-Problem Situation Link	However, Teacher Park decided the seating without asking other students, choosing the seat for a student with poor eyesight.
Topic Sentence (Cause 2)	The second reason is that students feel Teacher Park favors Minsu.
Ideal Situation	As a homeroom teacher, it's important to treat all students equally and fairly.
Cause-Problem Situation Link	Even though Minsu is well-behaved, showing special consideration for him could make other students think Teacher Park is favoring him.
Topic Sentence (Solution 1)	The first solution is to respect students' autonomy and give them a chance to make decisions.
Specific Description	For example, when making decisions about the class, teachers should give students time to share their opinions and consider different views.
Positive Effect	This way, students will feel respected, learn to participate in decision-making, and accept the rules they created. Minsu will also learn how to adjust to the result.
Topic Sentence (Solution 2)	The second solution is for the teacher to sincerely apologize to the students.
Premise	Teachers are human too, and can make mistakes.
Specific Description	So, when such issues arise, a teacher should admit mistakes, and even if the student is young, sincerely apologize for anything that may seem like favoritism.
Positive Effect	This will help students see the teacher as a person they can relate to, allowing for mutual understanding and the building of stronger relationships.
End of Response	That was my answer to the question number one. Thank you for listening.

(7) 실전 연습 문제 7회

구상형 1.

Response Start	This is my answer to the question number one.
Topic Sentence (Cause 1)	The first reason for the problem is that students do not fully understand privacy rights.
Ideal Situation	Sharing pictures or videos of someone without their permission on social media is a violation of their privacy.
Cause-Problem Situation Link	However, Chanseok did not understand this and captured an image of Teacher Kim during an online class. Other students also joined in without realizing it was wrong and posted playful comments.
Topic Sentence (Cause 2)	The second reason is Teacher Kim's light-hearted attitude toward the issue.
Ideal Situation	It is important to clearly explain why an action is wrong to correct behavior.
Cause-Problem Situation Link	Despite Chanseok's action clearly being a violation of privacy, Teacher Kim responded jokingly by saying, "Delete it because I look bad in the photo."
Topic Sentence (Solution 1)	The first solution is to provide online ethics education.
Specific Description	For example, lessons could include video materials or discussions on privacy rights, cyberbullying, comment etiquette, and personal data protection to teach students the proper behavior online.
Positive Effect	Through this, students will learn the ethics they need to follow in an online environment. They will also reflect on their behavior and become more aware of issues like privacy violations and cybercrimes.
Topic Sentence (Solution 2)	The second solution is for teachers to be strict when correcting students' wrong actions.
Specific Description	For example, while maintaining a friendly relationship with students online, teachers must clearly point out and guide students when they engage in actions like cyberbullying or privacy violations.
Positive Effect	This will help build trust between teachers and students. Students will respect teachers who correct their mistakes and guide them on the right path.
End of Response	That was my answer to the question number one. Thank you for listening.

(8) 실전 연습 문제 8회

구상형 1.

Response Start	This is my answer to the question number one.
Topic Sentence (Cause 1)	The first reason for the problem is the lack of communication between the homeroom teacher and the parents.
Ideal Situation	Indirect communication methods like sending newsletters are good, but sometimes direct communication is necessary.
Cause-Problem Situation Link	However, because Teacher Park lacked a direct communication channel with the parents, Minhee's parents did not receive important information, as they missed the newsletter.
Topic Sentence (Cause 2)	The second reason is Minhee's closed attitude toward her parents.
Ideal Situation	How a student interacts with his or her parents can affect their ability to adjust to school life.
Cause-Problem Situation Link	Minhee has a closed relationship with her parents, saying, "I don't want to talk to them," which is why she didn't give any of the school newsletters to her parents.
Topic Sentence (Solution 1)	The first solution is to create a social media group for parents.
Specific Description	For example, teachers could use Naver Band or a parent café to post small class events, students' activities, important newsletters, and announcements.
Positive Effect	Through this, a direct communication channel between teachers and parents would be opened, allowing parents to stay updated on important information and build trust in the teacher.
Topic Sentence (Solution 2)	The second solution is to conduct individual counseling sessions.
Specific Description	For example, teachers could have lunch counseling, walking counseling, or one-on-one meetings to understand how students feel about their relationship with their parents and provide appropriate advice. If needed, the teacher could work with a school counselor to ensure the student receives professional help.
Positive Effect	Through this, Minhee's reasons for her closed attitude toward her parents can be identified, and counseling can help improve her relationship with them.
End of Response	That was my answer to the question number one. Thank you for listening.

(9) 실전 연습 문제 9회

구상형 1.

Response Start	This is my answer to the question number one.

Topic Sentence (Cause 1)	The first reason for the problem is Chulsoo's lack of respect for others.
Ideal Situation	It's good to always be confident, but it is also important to develop an attitude that respects and considers others.
Cause-Problem Situation Link	However, because Chulsoo lacked this respect, he ended up saying things like, "I already know everything the teacher is teaching" and "I'll just work on my high school workbook during class."

Topic Sentence (Cause 2)	The second reason is that the lesson did not include activities for high-achieving students like Chulsoo.
Ideal Situation	In a classroom, students have different levels of achievement, so there should be activities that match each student's ability.
Cause-Problem Situation Link	In Teacher A's class, there were no activities designed for high-achieving students like Chulsoo, which made him feel that he didn't need to participate in the class.

Topic Sentence (Solution 1)	The first solution for Teacher A is to have a one-on-one meeting with Chulsoo.
Specific Description	For example, using "I" statements, the teacher can express how Chulsoo's behavior made him or her feel and have an open conversation with Chulsoo. Afterward, they can talk about the importance of respect for others, humility, and proper behavior.
Positive Effect	Through this, Chulsoo will learn to be more humble and show respect for the teacher and his classmates during lessons, participating more in class.

Topic Sentence (Solution 2)	The second solution is to assign Chulsoo a "class helper" role during lessons.
Specific Description	For example, students with high achievement levels, like Chulsoo, can be given the role of "class helper," where they can act as peer mentors to help students who are struggling.
Positive Effect	Through this, students who take on the "class helper" role can also improve their understanding in areas they might have overlooked. Meanwhile, the students receiving help will benefit from easier explanations, improving their understanding of the lesson.

End of Response	That was my answer to the question number one. Thank you for listening.

(10) 실전 연습 문제 10회

구상형 1.

Response Start	This is my answer to the question number one.
Topic Sentence (Cause 1)	The first reason for the problem is the way friends play by excluding others.
Ideal Situation	It's normal for friends to joke or tease each other, but if it goes too far or doesn't think about others' feelings, it can lead to bullying.
Cause-Problem Situation Link	In this case, excluding others became a usual part of playing among friends. This is why B, C, and D kept teasing and playing rough jokes on A, not realizing it was serious.
Topic Sentence (Cause 2)	The second reason is that Student A isn't honest about his or her feelings.
Ideal Situation	It's important to notice your own feelings and express them openly.
Cause-Problem Situation Link	However, Student A isn't good at controlling his or her emotions, so even when Student A feels bad, he or she couldn't express it in a healthy way.
Topic Sentence (Solution 1)	To fix the problem of excluding others, having discussions or lessons on how to build good friendships can help.
Specific Description	For example, students could talk about caring and respecting each other as friends. They could reflect on their past behavior and make promises to change.
Positive Effect	Through this, students will learn that teasing or playing rough jokes on one person isn't a good friendship and could be seen as bullying and this could gradually end the habit of excluding others.
Topic Sentence (Solution 2)	For Student A, emotional coaching could be a good solution.
Specific Description	For example, Student A could write a journal about his or her feelings or use emotion cards to express them.
Positive Effect	Through this, Student A will learn how to express feelings honestly. This will also help build friendships where students respect and understand each other's feelings.
End of Response	That was my answer to the question number one. Thank you for listening.

(11) 실전 연습 문제 11회

구상형 1.

Response Start	This is my answer to the question number one.
Topic Sentence (Cause 1)	The first reason for the problem is that Youngchul sees some school subjects as more important than others.
Ideal Situation	All school subjects are carefully chosen, so each one has its own value. It's important to respect this and treat all subjects with care.
Cause-Problem Situation Link	However, Youngchul thinks some subjects are more important than others, which is why he only pays attention in classes that are tested on the college entrance exam.
Topic Sentence (Cause 2)	The second reason is that Youngchul isn't motivated in these subjects because he doesn't see how they relate to his future career.
Ideal Situation	Students are more motivated when they understand how each subject connects to their future careers.
Cause-Problem Situation Link	However, Youngchul doesn't know how those subjects are connected to his future, so he assumes they aren't important and shows a poor attitude in those classes.
Topic Sentence (Solution 1)	The first solution is to have a one-on-one meeting with Youngchul.
Specific Description	For example, the teacher can explain how each subject was chosen to be taught in school and help Youngchul see that all subjects are valuable in their own way. The teacher could also talk about the importance of respecting all teachers, even if they are teaching the subjects he doesn't prioritize.
Positive Effect	Through this, Youngchul will realize that every subject in school was chosen for a reason and has value. He will stop ranking the subjects by importance, and his attitude toward learning and teachers will improve.

Topic Sentence (Solution 2)	The second solution is to connect these subjects with career-related lessons through an integrated curriculum.
Specific Description	For example, the career counselor could work together with the subject teachers to show how these subjects apply to future careers and how they are related to different jobs.
Positive Effect	Through this, students as well as Youngchul will realize that even though the subject isn't part of the college entrance exam, it is still related to their future jobs. This will motivate them to participate more actively in class.

End of Response	That was my answer to the question number one. Thank you for listening.

Chapter 03

주제별 아이디어 및 예시 답변

TOPIC 1.	Preventing School Violence

1	Keep a close eye on students
Topic Sentence	I'm going to keep a close eye on my students.
Premise	Many issues can be prevented by casually observing students.
Specific Description	For example, I will use class social media, lunch time or break time to keep a close eye on my students and provide immediate guidance whenever necessary.
Positive Effect	By doing so, the teacher can prevent small issues from turning into big ones, and the students can be more aware of minor acts of teasing.
Conclusion	Therefore, I will try to keep a close eye on my students to prevent bullying.

2	Motivation Monday
Topic Sentence	I will hold a class event called 'Motivation Monday' once a week.
Premise	If a classroom has a harmonious atmosphere where active conversation is encouraged, it is likely that there will be significantly less bullying in the classroom.
Specific Description	To give you a concrete example, I'm going to organize a Monday morning activity in which I'll present students with a motivational quote, ask them to share what it means to them, and share their own experiences.
Positive Effect	By doing so, students will be able to stay positively motivated in their schoolwork, and it will create a more interactive and harmonious classroom atmosphere.
Conclusion	Therefore, I will hold a class event called 'Motivation Monday' once a week.

3	Thirsty Thursday
Topic Sentence	I will hold a class event called 'Thirsty Thursday' once a week.
Premise	To prevent bullying, students need to feel comfortable with teachers and have good friendships.
Specific Description	For example, on every Thursday morning, I'm going to have a classroom greeting with drinks and casual conversation, like a café.
Positive Effect	By doing so, students will feel more comfortable approaching their teachers, and friendships will naturally develop as they talk to their friends face-to-face instead of staring at their smart phones.
Conclusion	Therefore, I will hold a class event called 'Thirsty Thursday' once a week.

4	Class unity event
Topic Sentence	I'm going to promote a 'Class unity event.'
Premise	Students feel closer to each other through the challenges they have to solve together as a team.
Specific Description	Therefore, I will organize a class sports or board game competition to give students a chance to work together as a team and bond as a group.
Positive Effect	By doing so, students will learn to manage conflict during the activity by cooperating, communicating and respecting each other. In addition, this sense of accomplishment will have a greater positive educational impact.
Conclusion	Therefore, I'm going to promote a class unity event.

5	Emotion coaching
Topic Sentence	For students who have difficulty with controlling their emotions, I will use 'emotion coaching', which is about accepting and expressing their feelings without hiding them.
Premise	Students' suppressed emotions often lead to problematic behaviors, so it's important to help them recognize and release them in a healthy way.
Specific Description	For example, the students can role-play or act out those emotions after they draw cards with different emotions such as "happy," "sad," "angry," and so on.
Positive Effect	By doing so, students will have an experience that allows them to release their suppressed emotions. Furthermore, by recognizing that "sad" is harder to express than they think, they will become better able to handle their own emotions.
Conclusion	Therefore, I will provide 'emotion coaching' to help students better control their emotions.

6	Media-based discussion
Topic Sentence	I'll provide a 'Media-based discussion' to prevent school bullying.
Premise	Students can better identify problems when they see their behavior through the eyes of a third party.
Specific Description	For example, the students will be shown a video clip of a bullying situation and discuss the behavior of the bullies and the feelings of the victims.
Positive Effect	By doing so, students will have the opportunity to look at their behavior from a third-party perspective and reflect on it.
Conclusion	Therefore, I'll provide a 'Media-based discussion' to prevent school bullying.

7	Bystander education
Topic Sentence	To prevent school bullying, I'll do a 'Bystander education program.'
Premise	The most important part of preventing school violence is educating bystanders about their role in it.
Specific Description	For example, after watching and discussing the video on Genovis Syndrome, I'm going to help them recognize the importance of the role of the bystander.
Positive Effect	This will make students feel more responsible as class members and encourage them to speak up when they see violence rather than remain silent.
Conclusion	Therefore, I'll do a 'Bystander education program' to prevent school bullying.

8	My angel activity
Topic Sentence	To prevent school bullying, I'll do a 'My angel activity.'
Premise	Creating a supportive environment is key to preventing school violence.
Specific Description	For example, the teacher could use a class meeting to gather ideas from students and then pair them with someone they can rely on either academically, like a mentor-mentee, or socially, like a lunch buddy.
Positive Effect	This will create a classroom atmosphere that is friendly and collaborative, building a sense of community and promoting a sense of peer support.
Conclusion	Therefore, I'll do a 'My angel activity' to prevent school bullying.

TOPIC 2. Addressing School Violence

1	Restorative justice program
Topic Sentence	To address school violence, I'll implement a 'Restorative justice program.'
Premise	Retributive justice education has been criticized for giving bullies a free pass and leaving scars on victims that never fully recover.
Specific Description	For example, I would use peer counseling, friendship circles, restorative conferences, etc. to restore relationships rather than focus on punishing the bullies.
Positive Effect	By doing so, students will learn the value of responsibility, forgiveness, and reconciliation, and they will be able to recover from the hurt and return to normal school life.
Conclusion	Therefore, I would implement a 'Restorative justice program.' that focuses on restoring relationships, not punishment.

2	Talk a walk with the student
Topic Sentence	I'll take a walk with the student to address the issue.
Premise	It is important to create a psychologically comfortable and relaxed atmosphere to get to know students better.
Specific Description	For example, I will take a walk around the school during lunch or after school to create a comfortable and relaxed atmosphere, in order to get a better understanding of the student's current state of mind and how he/she is feeling about school.
Positive Effect	By doing so, students will understand that their teacher cares about their situation, which builds trust. In addition, the teacher will have a better understanding of how they are doing and be able to provide what they need immediately.
Conclusion	Therefore, I'll take a walk with the student to address the issue.

3	Out-of-school counseling
Topic Sentence	I will spend time talking with the student outside of school to address the issue.
Premise	Since students tend to feel a little more free outside of school than inside, meeting them outside of school will give the teacher a better chance to hear what's on their minds.
Specific Description	Specifically, I'll take them to a store they might like, and we'll continue our discussion over a small meal.
Positive Effect	By doing so, students can talk in a more relaxed atmosphere than they would in school, and teachers can learn more about their students with more honest stories.
Conclusion	Therefore, I will spend time talking with the student outside of school to address the issue.

4	Work with parents
Topic Sentence	I will work with parents to address the school violence.
Premise	It is essential for schools and families to collaborate to successfully address the school violence.
Specific Description	To be specific, I will objectively communicate the facts to the parents of the victim and the bully, help them understand the situation for both students, and ask for their cooperation to make sure there is sufficient support at home.
Positive Effect	By doing so, students will be better able to overcome challenges because they will have support both at school and at home.
Conclusion	Therefore, I will work with parents to address the school violence.

5	Work with teachers
Topic Sentence	I will work with teachers to address the school violence.
Premise	Both victims and bullies may be dealing with significant mental and physical issues, and these issues can be better addressed by working with experts in school rather than alone.
Specific Description	For example, I will carefully observe the student's school life as a classroom teacher and communicate the results to the counselor or school nurse for advice.
Positive Effect	This will help teachers avoid making rash judgments that could hurt students. Moreover, it will allow them to be more knowledgeable and ensure that students are provided with the support they need.
Conclusion	Therefore, I will work with teachers to address the school violence.

6	Local community program
Topic Sentence	I will work with the local community to address the issue of school violence and encourage students to participate in various programs.
Premise	When students are emotionally unstable, it can sometimes be helpful for them to focus on something else rather than solely thinking about the problem.
Specific Description	For example, teachers could recommend and encourage students to participate in a variety of out-of-school activities, such as community volunteering, career exploration, or maker projects like woodworking classes.
Positive Effect	By doing so, students will not only gain information related to their career path, but also experience it and immerse themselves in new situations, allowing them to forget about school challenges and psychologically recharge through new relationships.
Conclusion	Therefore, I will encourage students to participate in the various programs offered by the local community.

TOPIC 3.   At-Risk Students

1	Individual counseling
Topic Sentence	I will provide an individualized counseling session with empathy and careful listening for at-risk students.
Premise	Even students you thought you had a good understanding based on observation may reveal things you didn't know during individual counseling.
Specific Description	To be specific, I will ask students about their school life over a casual meal outside of school, or I will take them for a walk around the school during their lunch break.
Positive Effect	This will help students know that they are receiving attention from the teacher, which will create a sense of self-regulation. Plus, the teacher will have a better understanding of the student based on their 1:1 conversations with them.
Conclusion	Therefore, I will provide an individualized counseling session with empathy and careful listening for at-risk students.

2	Emotional support
Topic Sentence	I'll support them emotionally after listening and empathizing with their situation.
Premise	Given that students who are at risk are likely to have low self-esteem and self-confidence, it is in the emotional dimension that they need to be supported first.
Specific Description	For example, I'll focus on the positive, praise the little things, and emphasize that failure is natural.
Positive Effect	Through these methods, teachers will be able to help students rebuild their self-esteem and self-confidence.
Conclusion	Therefore, I'll support them emotionally after listening and empathizing with their situation.

3		Praise even small actions
Topic Sentence		It is important for teachers to praise even the small actions especially for those students who are at risk.
Premise		Self-efficacy, which is the belief that you can do things on your own, is built through teacher's praise.
Specific Description		To achieve this, teachers could give praise for small behaviors, imbuing it with meaning, such as 'You're really paying attention in class today!' or 'You're smiling and getting along with your friends!'
Positive Effect		This kind of praise will help students gain emotional confidence, which in turn will lead to a more energetic school experience.
Conclusion		Therefore, I think it is important for teachers to praise no matter how small especially for those students who are at risk.

4		Provide a successful experience
Topic Sentence		I will provide students with a successful experience.
Premise		Students gain confidence and a sense of accomplishment as they accumulate small successes.
Specific Description		To achieve this, I will give them assignments that are at their level of difficulty in terms of learning, as well as assignments that they can succeed at with effort outside of learning, such as 'being punctual' and 'bringing their supplies.
Positive Effect		Through this, the student will begin to feel a small sense of accomplishment, which will increase their "self-efficacy" and give them the courage to gradually set bigger goals.
Conclusion		Therefore, I will provide students with a successful experience.

5		Socialization coaching
Topic Sentence		I'll provide socialization coaching to students who are at risk.
Premise		Social skills are often learned naturally, but some coaching can help if needed.
Specific Description		For example, I'll give students small tasks that are easy for them to accomplish, even if they don't talk to their friends, such as 'borrow an eraser from a friend' or 'say thank you.'
Positive Effect		This will help students learn how to socially engage, and their confidence will increase as they experience success. Furthermore, their friendships will be restored.
Conclusion		Therefore, I'll provide socialization coaching to students who are at risk.

6	Work with parents
Topic Sentence	It is essential to work with parents to help students who are at risk.
Premise	In order to understand the student in a more multidimensional way, it is important to not only observe the student from the teacher's perspective, but also from the parent's perspective.
Specific Description	For example, I will provide parents with a clear description of the student's situation and gather information from their perspective, such as how the student is behaving at home, what recent events have happened to the student, and what may have caused the student's behavior.
Positive Effect	By doing so, teachers will be better able to use the collective information to understand exactly what is behind and provide appropriate help to address it.
Conclusion	Therefore, I think it is essential to work with parents to help students who are at risk.

7	Work with teachers
Topic Sentence	It is essential to work with teachers to help students who are at risk.
Premise	Since the causes of at-risk students are complex and varied, classroom teachers may be able to provide better support if they work with experts rather than trying to do it alone.
Specific Description	For example, I will carefully observe the student's schoolwork and share what I found with school counselor or other senior teacher for advice.
Positive Effect	By doing so, students will be able to get the help they need with more specialized knowledge and the experience of more senior teachers.
Conclusion	Therefore, I think it is essential to work with teachers to help students who are at risk.

8	Local community program
Topic Sentence	Encouraging students to participate in various local community program can be one of the great solutions for at-risk students.
Premise	It's often the case that students may not be excited about school, but they are very interested in real-world experiences outside of school.
Specific Description	For example, I would encourage them to participate in volunteer work, barista workshops, baking classes, and other out-of-school activities.
Positive Effect	By doing so, students will not only gain information relevant to their career path, but also develop a goal-oriented attitude to set their own goals, which can be a turning point in re-energizing their school experience.
Conclusion	Therefore, I think encouraging students to participate in various local community program can be one of the great solutions for at-risk students.

TOPIC 4. Teaching Morality

1 — Reading literature

Topic Sentence	I think reading literature is important in teaching morality.
Premise	Through reading, we can learn how to empathize with and respect the feelings and actions of characters.
Specific Description	For example, I will select English literature from fairy tales to novels, focusing on the characters' situations and feelings. After that, I will encourage students to freely express their feelings through drawings and writing.
Positive Effect	By doing so, students will be able to develop the ability to understand and respect human emotions. Furthermore, this will build the empathy needed to address issues such as conflict with parents, cultural differences, and generational differences.
Conclusion	Therefore, I think reading literature is important in teaching morality.

2 — Gardening

Topic Sentence	Gardening can be a great activity for teaching morality.
Premise	Students can develop a sense of responsibility by growing plants.
Specific Description	As an example of this, students will be assigned each zone in the school garden where they will plant seeds to grow vegetables and then share them with their classmates at lunch.
Positive Effect	By doing so, students will develop a sense of responsibility for the crops they grow and realize the value of life. They will also learn the value of caring by sharing the fruits of their labor with their peers, which will create strong friendships.
Conclusion	Therefore, I think gardening can be a great activity for teaching morality.

3	Class unity event
Topic Sentence	Promoting class unity events can be a great way to incorporate morality education.
Premise	To develop morality, it's important to have experience interacting effectively with the people around you.
Specific Description	For example, teachers can organize sports club competitions, choir competitions, musical activities, etc.
Positive Effect	Through this, students will learn to manage conflicts, cooperate as a team, and respect each other. Not only that, but the sense of accomplishment of working together will have a greater educational effect of building great personality.
Conclusion	Therefore, promoting class unity events can be a great way to incorporate morality education.

4	Classroom angel
Topic Sentence	I'll suggest the activity called 'Classroom angel.'
Premise	Students can build morality by helping others.
Specific Description	For example, after gathering student opinions in a class meeting, I will set up pairs that students can rely on for academic aspects, such as mentor-mentee and homework helpers, or for social aspects of school, such as lunch buddies and walking buddies.
Positive Effect	By doing so, students will develop a sense of community and respect for others within a supportive culture.
Conclusion	Therefore, I'll suggest the activity called 'Classroom angel.'

5	Role play
Topic Sentence	I will plan a role-play activity for teaching morality.
Premise	Being able to understand, care for, and respect others is a fundamental part of building morality.
Specific Description	For example, I would hand out cards with characters on them and have students act out about what they would do if they were the character on the card.
Positive Effect	By doing so, students will be able to understand the situation of other characters and learn to respect and care for others based on that understanding.
Conclusion	Therefore, I will plan a role-play activity for teaching morality.

6	Jigsaw volunteer work
Topic Sentence	To teach morality, I will encourage students to participate in a 'Jigsaw volunteer work.'
Premise	Students can build morality through meaningful volunteer work.
Specific Description	For example, I'll do a jigsaw activity where each member goes to different places to volunteer and then shares their experience with the group.
Positive Effect	This will make students more responsible because they will need to tell their friends about their volunteer work. Additionally, by sharing their experiences with different volunteer programs, each member of the group will be more likely to want to participate where their friends have been. This will also help ensure that volunteering becomes an ongoing activity rather than a one-time event.
Conclusion	With these reasons, I think the 'Jigsaw volunteer work' is a great idea to teach morality.

7	Media-based discussion
Topic Sentence	I will introduce a 'media-based discussion' as part of the morality education program.
Premise	Building morality starts with being respectful to each other.
Specific Description	For example, I might show a story of a student who is left out and ignored, or a story of a happy class where everyone gets along, and then ask the students to share their thoughts on which class is better and why.
Positive Effect	By doing so, students will be able to reflect on their own behavior and realize the importance of creating a respectful classroom climate.
Conclusion	Therefore, I will introduce a 'media-based discussion' as part of the morality education program.

8	Caring Champion
Topic Sentence	I will award the title of 'Caring champion' to my students.
Premise	Students build great morality through activities that encourage consideration.
Specific Description	For example, I will use a class meeting to encourage students to help their peers and after a period of time, I will award the title of 'Caring champion' to my students.
Positive Effect	By doing so, students will be able to develop a sense of caring and a sense of accomplishment as they help other friends.
Conclusion	Therefore, I will award the title of 'Caring champion' to my students.

TOPIC 5. Self-management Competencies

1	Learning journals
Topic Sentence	I would recommend students keep a learning journal to help them develop self-management competencies.
Premise	Self-management starts with the habit of planning and writing things down.
Specific Description	To do this, I would encourage students to maintain a learning journal. This way, they can set a timeframe for themselves, establish goals to achieve within that timeframe, devise and execute strategies to reach their goals, and evaluate their progress at the end.
Positive Effect	This will help them build self-efficacy and gain confidence as it involves working on their own throughout the process of achieving their goals. Additionally, it will give them a sense of self-management and control.
Conclusion	Therefore, I would recommend students keep a learning journal to help them develop self-management competencies.

2	Learning style assessment
Topic Sentence	I'll encourage students to take a learning style assessment to develop self-management competencies.
Premise	In order to develop self-management skills, students must first know about themselves well.
Specific Description	For example, I will recommend various tests to assess students' learning style, personality, and career path. After interpreting the results, I will discuss them with the students.
Positive Effect	Through this process, students will gain a better understanding of themselves, and with this information about themselves, they will be able to develop strategies and habits to manage themselves effectively.
Conclusion	Therefore, I'll encourage students to take a learning style assessment to develop self-management competencies.

3	66-Day Habit Challenge
Topic Sentence	I will be running a '66-Day Habit Challenge' activity to help students build self-management competencies.
Premise	It is said that it takes 66 days for a person's behavior to become a habit.
Specific Description	To do this, I will design a habit-building challenge activity in which students set a habit they want to create, such as "solve 10 math problems every day," "memorize 10 English words," or "exercise for 30 minutes every day," and follow through for 66 days.
Positive Effect	This will give students the experience of working consistently to achieve the goals they have set for themselves. Furthermore, these activities will help them form good habits and develop the ability to control and manage themselves.
Conclusion	In these reasons, I will be running a '66-Day Habit Challenge' activity to help students build self-management competencies.

4	Reflective journals
Topic Sentence	To improve self-management skills, I would suggest that students keep a reflective journal.
Premise	Self-reflection is essential for self-management and steering yourself in the direction you want to go.
Specific Description	To be specific, I'm going to do some self-reflective activities, such as 'Identify bad habits', 'Write down what you regret doing today', and 'Identify what you need to change'.
Positive Effect	Through this, students will be able to recognize bad habits that they do unconsciously or habits that they need to change. By working to improve them, they will develop the ability to manage themselves and develop in a desirable way.
Conclusion	Therefore, I would suggest that students keep a reflective journal to improve self-management competencies,

5	Write an autobiography
Topic Sentence	To improve self-management competencies, I would introduce an activity to write an autobiography.
Premise	Developing self-management competencies requires deep exploration and reflection.
Specific Description	For example, I would introduce an activity where students reflect on their past experiences over one-year or six-month periods and write about who they are today.
Positive Effect	This will allow students to reflect and look back on themselves, which will inform their future plans. Not only that, but it will also give them a better understanding of themselves based on deep reflection and exploration.
Conclusion	Therefore, I would introduce an activity to write an autobiography to improve self-management competencies.

6	Imagine future self
Topic Sentence	To help students develop self-management skills, I will ask them to imagine what they want to be in the future.
Premise	Students develop self-management skills as they envision what they want to be and figure out what attitudes they need to have to achieve it.
Specific Description	To be specific, I will ask students to picture themselves 10 years from now, 20 years from now, 30 years from now, etc. and to explore what specific goals they need to accomplish over time to achieve their desired future. Additionally, I will encourage them to identify goals to set in the present.
Positive Effect	By doing so, students will be able to understand what attitudes they need to have now in order to achieve their future goals. As a result of this, they will feel more self-sufficient and motivated to manage their own behavior.
Conclusion	Therefore, I think the activity 'Imagine future self' is a great way to develop self-management skills.

TOPIC 6. Knowledge Information Processing Competencies

1	Resource-based learning
Topic Sentence	I will use resource-based learning to develop students' knowledge information processing skills.
Premise	Students can develop knowledge information processing skills by identifying which resources they need to utilize to solve a given problem.
Specific Description	To achieve this, I will design an activity that presents a contextualized problem and asks students to share their opinions and solutions using printed materials, electronic devices, and various statistics.
Positive Effect	By doing so, students will develop their knowledge information processing skills as they identify, select, and organize the resources needed to solve a given situation.
Conclusion	Therefore, I will use resource-based learning to develop students' knowledge information processing skills.

2	Research project
Topic Sentence	I will design a research project to improve students' knowledge information processing skills.
Premise	Students can improve their knowledge information processing skills as they research and explore what they are interested in.
Specific Description	Specifically, I would design a project lesson where students select an area of interest, decide on several subcategories, and research each subcategory using a variety of resources and verified information.
Positive Effect	By doing so, students will have the opportunity to explore their interests in greater depth. In this process, they will naturally improve their ability to find, verify, and utilize information.
Conclusion	Therefore, I will design a research project to improve students' knowledge information processing skills.

3	Utilize the 'Big6 Skills model'
Topic Sentence	To develop students' knowledge information processing skills, I will utilize the Big6 Skills model in the classroom.
Premise	Students can improve their knowledge information processing skills by understanding how and why they selected the information.
Specific Description	To achieve this, I will use the Big6 Skills model to design an activity where students write a report on their information processing process. They will identify the information they need, select the best resources, locate the information, put it to practical use, synthesize the information, and evaluate the effectiveness of the resources.
Positive Effect	By doing so, students will be able to examine how and why they chose the information, which will help them process and utilize the information.
Conclusion	Therefore, I will utilize the Big6 Skills model in the classroom to develop students' knowledge information processing skills,

4	Resource sharing public storage
Topic Sentence	I will create a public storage to share my teaching materials and share them with my students to improve students' knowledge information processing skills,
Premise	In the digital age, it is necessary to put all of teachers' materials in the public storage and allow students to access them, so that they can learn individually without the constraints of time and space.
Specific Description	To be specific, I will share all of my videos, lecture notes, and worksheets on the storage and make them available to students. Additionally, if the class is project-based and involves using various materials to create a final product, I will upload resources and information for students to browse freely.
Positive Effect	By doing so, students will be able to freely find the content they need in the public storage provided by their teachers, enabling self-directed, level-appropriate learning. They will also improve their knowledge and information processing skills as they locate and utilize the content for their projects.
Conclusion	Therefore, I will create a public storage to share my teaching materials and share them with my students to improve students' knowledge information processing skills.

TOPIC 7. Creative Thinking Competencies

1	Learner-centered lessons
Topic Sentence	I will apply learner-centered lessons to develop student's creativity.
Premise	Creativity is the ability to create something original that hasn't existed before. It can be developed through the process of self-learning, rather than through a teacher imparting knowledge.
Specific Description	For example, I will use student-driven lessons that incorporate project-based learning, problem-solving, discovery learning, etc.
Positive Effect	By doing so, students will have the opportunity to self-direct their learning and think from new perspectives, rather than receiving one-size-fits-all knowledge from a teacher in a traditional, teacher-centered classroom.
Conclusion	Therefore, I will apply learner-centered lessons to develop student's creativity.

2	Unstructured assignments
Topic Sentence	To develop student's creativity, I will present unstructured assignments.
Premise	When students are given unstructured assignments, they can approach the problem from a different perspective than they're used to thinking about it.
Specific Description	For example, I'll give students a specific, real-world problem situation, but I'll give them a task that allows for multiple correct answers rather than requiring them to find only one.
Positive Effect	This will allow students to think about different alternatives as part of the process of solving a problem rather than focusing solely on finding the right answer.
Conclusion	Therefore, I will present unstructured assignments, to develop student's creativity,

3	Incorporate various techniques into the class
Topic Sentence	I will incorporate PMI, SCAMPER, and Synectis techniques into my classes to foster creativity.
Premise	By applying teaching methods designed to foster creativity, teachers will be able to effectively guide their students.
Specific Description	For example, I'll use PMI for discussion/debate lessons, or incorporate activities that ask students to think of new uses for given objects.
Positive Effect	By doing so, teachers can encourage students to think creatively by exploring different alternatives.
Conclusion	Therefore, I will incorporate various techniques into my class to develop student's creativity.

4	Mastery learning
Topic Sentence	I will pursue mastery learning to develop creativity.
Premise	In order to create new knowledge, you must first master the basics.
Specific Description	As an example, I will regularly check for student understanding by formative assessments or use a variety of questioning techniques in the classroom.
Positive Effect	By doing so, students will have a complete understanding of the fundamental knowledge that supports creative thinking, enabling them to expand their thinking in new ways.
Conclusion	Therefore, I will pursue mastery learning to develop student creativity.

5	Classroom discussion/debate
Topic Sentence	I will facilitate a discussion/debate-style lesson to build creativity.
Premise	Students become more creative when they understand how others think and see new perspectives.
Specific Description	To accomplish this, I will actively utilize the discussion and debate method in my classroom. I will encourage multiple student opinions on a topic and help students develop open-mindedness and diverse perspectives.
Positive Effect	By doing so, students will hear from other students and understand the topic from a new perspective, which is a meaningful learning experience that stimulates expanded thinking.
Conclusion	Therefore, I will facilitate a discussion/debate-style lesson to build creativity.

6	Makerspace project
Topic Sentence	To develop students' creativity, I will introduce a 'Makerspace project.'
Premise	Students are encouraged to be creative when creating new things.
Specific Description	For example, teachers can give students a topic for their creations, let them design what they imagine, and then plan an activity where they use the makerspace to bring their designs to life.
Positive Effect	This process of giving students the freedom to design and build what they want will naturally stimulate their creativity.
Conclusion	Therefore, To develop students' creativity, I will introduce a 'Makerspace project.'

7	Open-ended questions
Topic Sentence	I will increase my use of open-ended questions in conversations to promote student creativity.
Premise	Whether students need to recall what they know or come up with something new depends on whether the teacher's questions are closed or open-ended.
Specific Description	For example, I will increase the use of open-ended questions in class, such as 'What would you do in this situation? Let's discuss it freely.' This approach encourages a range of possible answers and promotes open thinking, as opposed to closed-ended questions like 'Do you remember what this was?', which only require students to recall known information.
Positive Effect	By doing so, students will have to go beyond simply recalling what they know and think of new solutions for new situations. This will help promote open-mindedness in students, which in turn will help promote creativity.
Conclusion	Therefore, I will increase my use of open-ended questions in conversations to promote student creativity.

TOPIC 8. Aesthetic Sensitivity Competencies

1	Collaborative and comprehensive art activities
Topic Sentence	I will promote collaborative and comprehensive art activities to develop students' aesthetic sensitivity competencies.
Premise	Students' aesthetic sensitivity is greatly developed by not only appreciating works of art, but also participating in their creation and performing them.
Specific Description	To be specific, I would actively support a class to create a semester-long artistic activity, such as a play, musical, or choral performance, from planning to presentation, with all students participating.
Positive Effect	Through this, students will not only learn how to collaborate with others, but also develop aesthetic sensitivity through artistic engagement.
Conclusion	Therefore, I will promote collaborative and comprehensive art activities to develop students' aesthetic sensitivity competencies.

2	Humanities reading portfolio
Topic Sentence	I will design a humanities reading portfolio activity to enhance students' aesthetic sensitivity.
Premise	Students can develop empathetic understanding of humanity and cultural sensitivity through humanities reading.
Specific Description	For example, I will select books on various topics such as world cultures, literature, music, art, and philosophy for students to read at their own level. Then, I will design an activity where they will write a portfolio of their reflections on the book.
Positive Effect	Through this, students will not only be able to gain knowledge about various topics through books, but also gradually develop their aesthetic sensitivity by accumulating reading experience.
Conclusion	Therefore, I will design a humanities reading portfolio activity to enhance students' aesthetic sensitivity.

3	Participate in local arts activities
Topic Sentence	To develop students' aesthetic sensitivity, I will encourage students to participate in local arts activities.
Premise	Many communities have cultural activities for students, such as plays, musicals, museum visits, and orchestra performances, that are often associated with school district programs.
Specific Description	For example, I will encourage students to engage in diverse cultural and artistic experiences within our community by researching cultural and artistic programs offered by the district.
Positive Effect	By doing so, students will realize that the arts are close at hand by experiencing cultural arts experiences in their own neighborhoods. These experiences will also naturally develop their aesthetic sensitivity.
Conclusion	Therefore, I will encourage students to participate in local arts activities to develop students' aesthetic sensitivity.

TOPIC 9. Cooperative Communicative Competencies

1	Information gap activity
Topic Sentence	I'll introduce an information gap activity to develop students' cooperative communicative competencies.
Premise	Students can improve their communication skills as they share information and understand each other to achieve a common goal.
Specific Description	For example, the teacher can give 'Find the Difference' worksheets to students, so that each student can describe their picture and find the differences compared to their partner's picture.
Positive Effect	This will help students develop their communication skills as they explain their pictures to each other and check each other's understanding.
Conclusion	Therefore, I'll introduce an information gap activity to develop students' cooperative communicative competencies.

2	Classroom discussion/debate
Topic Sentence	I will use a discussion/debate style lesson to improve students' cooperative communicative skills.
Premise	Students can develop their communication skills as they explain their opinions and persuade others.
Specific Description	For example, I will design activities that allow students to discuss and debate a variety of topics in groups, listen to each other's ideas and respect them even if they do not agree, and provide logical arguments when necessary.
Positive Effect	By doing so, students will gain experience in explaining and persuading others of their ideas, and their communication skills will be enhanced by exchanging ideas from different perspectives.
Conclusion	Therefore, I will use a discussion/debate style lesson to improve students' cooperative communicative skills.

3	Role play
Topic Sentence	I'll design a role play activity to improve students' cooperative communicative competencies.
Premise	Communication skills are not only about being able to express your thoughts logically, but also about understanding and empathizing with others' feelings.
Specific Description	To achieve this, I will design an activity that asks students to understand and empathize with the emotions of the characters and then express those emotions through role-playing.
Positive Effect	By doing so, students will learn to truly understand and empathize with the emotions of their characters by acting them out, and this experience will help them develop communication skills.
Conclusion	Therefore, I'll design a role play activity to improve students' cooperative communicative competencies.

4	Peer counseling
Topic Sentence	To improve students' cooperative communicative competencies, I'll suggest a peer counseling activity to students.
Premise	Students can develop cooperative communication skills by explaining their situation to a friend or by empathizing with a friend's concerns.
Specific Description	For example, I will pair up students and introduce peer counseling methods, such as through notes, anonymous counseling, or in-person counseling.
Positive Effect	By doing so, students will develop an atmosphere of mutual respect by understanding and empathizing with the feelings of their friends in different situations. Additionally, they will also be able to improve communication skills through this counseling.
Conclusion	Therefore, to improve students' cooperative communicative competencies, I'll suggest a peer counseling activity to students.

TOPIC 10. Community Competencies

1	Collaborative assignments
Topic Sentence	I will provide collaborative assignments to help students build community competencies.
Premise	A sense of community comes from working together to come up with answers and address common goals.
Specific Description	To illustrate, I'll use a lesson that is designed to require students to work together to complete tasks, such as jigsaws and information gap activities.
Positive Effect	By doing so, students will develop the ability to work together to achieve their goals, and their sense of community will be enhanced through collaboration on the task.
Conclusion	Therefore, I will provide collaborative assignments to help students build community competencies.

2	Local community volunteering opportunities
Topic Sentence	I'll promote local community volunteering opportunities to help students develop their community competencies.
Premise	By helping others, students can develop a sense of community that builds society.
Specific Description	Thus, I will plan local volunteer activities for multicultural family support centers, local children's centers, children with disabilities, welfare centers, etc.
Positive Effect	By doing so, students will learn to care for and respect the people in need and develop an awareness of the communities that make up our society.
Conclusion	With these reasons, I'll promote local community volunteering opportunities to help students develop their community competencies.

3	Unified sports activities
Topic Sentence	I'll encourage students to engage in unified sports activities to build community competencies.
Premise	Students can build internal cohesion and a sense of community through unified sports activities.
Specific Description	Therefore, I would actively support a team-cooperative sports competition where the inclusive students can also participate.
Positive Effect	By doing so, students will realize that they need to work together to achieve a common goal. Plus, they will develop a sense of community as they learn to manage conflicts and be considerate during the activities.
Conclusion	With these reasons, I'll encourage students to engage in unified sports activities to build community competencies.

4	Individual role
Topic Sentence	Assigning an individual role to each student would be a great idea to help them build community competencies.
Premise	In order to build community competencies, it will be important to understand that the individual's role is an important factor in the harmony of the community.
Specific Description	Therefore, I'm going to assign individualized roles for classroom cleanup and provide feedback time so they understand how their roles contribute to the whole class.
Positive Effect	By doing so, students will experience how they contribute to the classroom. Not only that, but they will also understand the proper attitudes that they need to have as individuals in order to work together as a community.
Conclusion	Given these reasons, I believe assigning an individual role to each student would be a great idea to help them build community competencies.

5	Change makers
Topic Sentence	I will organize a Change Makers activity to build community competencies in my students.
Premise	A sense of community comes from students identifying what they want to improve in their own community and working to make it happen.
Specific Description	For example, I will select a specific area, such as my school, town, or city, identify what needs to be improved, and then design a project activity that will make a difference for the community.
Positive Effect	By doing so, students will recognize that they can make a real difference, and they will feel a sense of community as they feel proud that they have contributed to our society by participating in this activity.
Conclusion	Therefore, I will organize a Change Makers activity to build community competencies in my students.

6	Global issues discussion
Topic Sentence	I will include a classroom activity where students can have a discussion on global issues.
Premise	In an age of globalization, where barriers between countries are getting lower, the sense of community that students perceive will need to be broader.
Specific Description	To illustrate this idea, I'll have students share their thoughts and come up with solutions to various global problems, such as conflicts between countries, political and economic issues, racism, environmental challenges, and the gap between rich and poor.
Positive Effect	This will allow students to expand the range of communities they are aware of and will give them the opportunity to realize what it means to be a global citizen.
Conclusion	Therefore, I will include a classroom activity where students can have a discussion on global issues.

TOPIC 11.   Providing Career Guidance

1	Aptitude tests
Topic Sentence	I'll use various aptitude tests to provide career guidance to students.
Premise	Knowing your aptitudes can be the first step to finding a career path.
Specific Description	Therefore, I'll encourage students to take the MBTI or Holland Personality Test to discover their strengths and career preferences.
Positive Effect	By doing so, students will learn about jobs that are relevant to their personality types and discover what interests them.
Conclusion	Given this point, I'll use various aptitude tests to provide career guidance to students.

2	Career education support center
Topic Sentence	I'll recommend students to participate in various programs offered by a career education support center.
Premise	Taking advantage of off-campus career education programs can provide students with real-world, diverse experiences that they can't get in school.
Specific Description	For example, I will work with the Career Education Support Center, which offers a variety of activities for students, such as theater and film programs, woodworking programs, and makeup artist experiences.
Positive Effect	By doing so, students will be able to overcome the limitations of human and material resources for career activities that only take place in schools.
Conclusion	Therefore, I'll recommend students to participate in various programs offered by a career education support center.

3	Local experiential activities
Topic Sentence	To provide career guidance, I would encourage students to take part in local experiential activities.
Premise	Finding out what different careers are available in your neighborhood can help students find their path.
Specific Description	For example, I would recommend participating in activities organized by the local education community, such as visiting government offices, organizing bazaars, making calendars, and exploring various jobs.
Positive Effect	By doing so, the locals will feel more responsible for the students' education, and the students will be able to meet the different professions that make up the community and see them up close, which will spark their interest in the field.
Conclusion	Therefore, I would encourage students to take part in local experiential activities.

4	Parent guest speaker
Topic Sentence	I will organize a parent guest speaker event to provide students with real-world career insights.
Premise	Schools have a wide range of parents from different professions, so partnering with them can make career lessons more relevant to students.
Specific Description	For example, I'll organize for parents to give in-class talks about their jobs, or for students to visit their workplaces for hands-on activities.
Positive Effect	This will allow students to experience careers from a more intimate perspective since the speakers are their friends' parents. This approach will not only increase parents' interest in education but will also have a more direct impact on students' future career choices.
Conclusion	Therefore, I will organize a parent guest speaker event to provide students with real-world career insights.

TOPIC 12.	Basic Academic Skills Improvement

1	Discovering students' aptitudes
Topic Sentence	I would first help students discover their aptitudes to improve their basic academic skills.
Premise	If students identify their interests first, the academic work to achieve those goals will naturally follow.
Specific Description	For example, students can take MBTI or Holland personality tests, participate in work experience projects in local communities, or attend lectures given by parents from various professions to help them discover their interests.
Positive Effect	By doing so, students will be able to identify what they are interested in and what they are good at. This will also motivate them to cshoose the career they want to pursue in the future, increasing their own motivation to learn.
Conclusion	Therefore, I believe the first thing to improve basic academic skills is to discover their aptitudes.

2	Keep a learning journal
Topic Sentence	To help students improve their basic academic skills, I would encourage them to keep a learning journal.
Premise	To improve students' meta-cognitive skills, it's important to make a habit of recording one's learning on a daily basis.
Specific Description	For example, I will encourage students to keep a learning journal so that they can analyze what they planned, what they actually did, and what they couldn't do, helping them become aware of their capabilities.
Positive Effect	By doing so, students will be able to develop meta-cognition, modify their study habits, and become intrinsically motivated to study by seeing themselves making progress every day. Additionally, this will help them not only improve their academic performance, but also develop the self-management skills.
Conclusion	Therefore, I would encourage them to keep a learning journal to help students improve their basic academic skills,

	3	School district-funded initiatives
Topic Sentence		I will find various kinds of school district-funded programs and recommend them to students to help improve their academic skills.
Premise		The Department of Education offers a variety of programs to help students improve their academic skills.
Specific Description		For example, I'll encourage them to sign up for a mentoring club with university students, apply for one-to-one tutoring, or find out about an after-school study program with a prospective teacher, and then recommend their participation.
Positive Effect		This will allow teachers to provide a much higher quality program with the resources they need to improve their teaching. Not only that, students will be more motivated to learn because they will be in a new environment, and they will have access to experts who will be able to provide more personalized support.
Conclusion		Therefore, I will find various kinds of school district-funded programs and recommend them to students to help improve their academic skills.

	4	Mentoring program
Topic Sentence		I will organize an in-school mentoring program to improve basic academic skills of students.
Premise		Students often learn better from their friends than from their teachers.
Specific Description		For example, teachers can pair students who want to be mentors with those who want to be mentees. This allows them to share learning strategies, ask questions about topics they don't understand, and discuss self-management techniques for exams.
Positive Effect		By doing so, a mentor will be able to better organize and deepen their understanding of what they know, and a mentee will benefit from the support of a peer, which will not only help them build a stronger friendship, but will also help them improve academically.
Conclusion		Therefore, I will organize an in-school mentoring program to improve basic academic skills of students.

5	Talent exchange club
Topic Sentence	I will organize an in-school talent exchange club to improve basic academic skills of students.
Premise	If students are encouraged to teach their friends what they're good at, they can naturally generate excitement and enjoyment for learning.
Specific Description	As an example of talent exchange club, a student who is good at studying but not at soccer and a student who is good at soccer but not at studying can exchange their talents.
Positive Effect	In this way, students' need for competence will be fulfilled and their self-esteem will be boosted as their strengths are respected and recognized. In addition, collaboration and friendships will be fostered, as well as a natural interest in learning, which will lead to academic progress.
Conclusion	Therefore, I will organize an in-school talent exchange club to improve basic academic skills of students.

6	Self-directed study challenge
Topic Sentence	To develop students' basic academic skills, I'll begin a classroom activity called 'Self-directed study challenge.'
Premise	In order for students to advance their academic skills, they must first be willing and able to do so on their own.
Specific Description	For example, students will be given 10 days to record themselves studying during the exam period and post them in the class chat room to meet the 20-hour goal.
Positive Effect	By doing so, students will not only develop the habit of self-directed study but also be internally motivated by the sense of accomplishment that comes from reaching their goals. Additionally, as they witness their classmates studying, extrinsic motivation will naturally develop, creating a synergistic effect. This challenge cultivates a supportive and stimulating classroom atmosphere where students work hard towards their goals and support each other.
Conclusion	Therefore, to develop students' basic academic skills, I'll begin a classroom activity called 'Self-directed study challenge.'

TOPIC 13.   Health & Ecological Transformation Education

1	Cross-curricular project learning
Topic Sentence	I'll introduce cross-curricular project learning to help students learn about the relevant knowledge on the environment.
Premise	It would be more effective for students to actually take the initiative to carry out a project rather than just sit through a class.
Specific Description	For example, I'll introduce a student-led activity focused on topics such as fine dust and healthcare. Students will plan through discussion and debate, read relevant materials on the topic, and then collaborate to create a presentation. Finally, they will watch and evaluate their peers' presentations of their project results.
Positive Effect	This will provide students with a broader understanding of the issue, enabling them to recognize its seriousness firsthand.
Conclusion	Therefore, I'll introduce cross-curricular project learning to help students learn about the relevant knowledge on the environment.

2	Jigsaw campaign
Topic Sentence	I'll organize a Jigsaw campaign for an ecological transformation education.
Premise	The jigsaw activity will allow all students to actively participate, and the campaign will help spread awareness about the dangers of the issue.
Specific Description	For example, I will divide the students into groups and assign them research tasks on the causes, dangers, and solutions to fine dust pollution. Each group will then compile their findings and collaborate to create picket signs or social media cards for promoting awareness campaigns.
Positive Effect	By doing so, students will gain a deep and broad knowledge of environmental issues and develop a sense of responsibility and collaboration while organizing the campaign. It also builds community competencies that are fundamental to environmental awareness.
Conclusion	Therefore, I'll organize a Jigsaw campaign for an ecological transformation education.

3	Game activity
Topic Sentence	I'll introduce a health-themed game activity to raise students' awareness of the importance of their health.
Premise	Teachers will be able to better engage students in educational activities with games.
Specific Description	To illustrate, teachers can design a game activity where each student is given a character card with their health status and asked to find items to improve that character's condition.
Positive Effect	This will enable students to relate the character's situation to their own health conditions, helping them recognize the importance of healthcare more realistically. Additionally, it will motivate their interest in health, making the activity more educational than a simple informational lesson.
Conclusion	Therefore, I'll introduce a health-themed game activity to raise students' awareness of the importance of their health.

4	Book discussion
Topic Sentence	I will be leading a book discussion class to teach ecological transformation issues.
Premise	Since books contain a wide range of knowledge, reading can help students expand and deepen their understanding of relevant topics.
Specific Description	Therefore, I will read books with my students on various environmental topics, share thoughts, and engage in discussion activities on topics that divide the class.
Positive Effect	By doing so, students will develop a deeper understanding of relevant topics through reading and will have the opportunity to expand their thinking by sharing their thoughts with their peers.
Conclusion	In this reason, I will be leading a book discussion class to teach ecological transformation issues.

5	Documentary talk
Topic Sentence	I'll organize a documentary talk activity to engage students in ecological transformation education.
Premise	There are already many environmental documentaries available for educational purposes, and they often feature interviews with experts, natural landscapes, and other footage that is not easily available or accessible in everyday life.
Specific Description	To give an example, students can watch documentaries on the environment from various stations such as EBS or KBS and fill out a worksheet on related topics, or they can discuss and debate in groups.
Positive Effect	Through this, students will be able to appreciate aspects of nature that they would not normally have the opportunity to see and realize that they have a responsibility to preserve them. They will also be gaining more specialized knowledge through interviews with experts in their respective fields.
Conclusion	With these reasons, I'll organize a documentary talk activity to engage students in ecological transformation education.

6	Make posters or UCCs
Topic Sentence	I would encourage students to create content such as posters or UCCs focusing on Earth's problems.
Premise	During the process of creating posters or UCCs, a lot of learning about the related topics takes place. Additionally, by sharing this with others, students can make a positive influence.
Specific Description	To be specific, I will conduct student-participatory content creation activities such as creating UCCs for response manuals for each concentration of fine dust, making posters to reduce fine dust, and organizing interviews with experts. The completed works will be posted on the school website so that all students can be aware of related issues.
Positive Effect	By doing so, students will gain in-depth, relevant knowledge while creating a UCC or poster. Not only that, but they will make a positive influence by sharing their work with others.
Conclusion	Therefore, I would encourage students to create content such as posters or UCCs focusing on Earth's problems.

TOPIC 14. Multicultural Students

1	Media-based discussion
Topic Sentence	To create a respectful atmosphere in the classroom, I would organize a media-based discussion.
Premise	The most important thing in multicultural classroom environment is to develop an respectful mindset.
Specific Description	In a multicultural classroom environment, developing a respectful mindset is crucial.
Positive Effect	To be specific, I will share a story depicting a student isolated by indifference, as well as a story illustrating a happy classroom where everyone gets along. We will then discuss which classroom environment is preferable and why.
Conclusion	Therefore, to create a respectful atmosphere in the classroom, I would organize a media-based discussion.

2	Multicultural support program
Topic Sentence	To help students learn language more efficiently, I would recommend them to sign up for the multicultural support program in the local community.
Premise	Multicultural students often have difficulty with Korean culture or language.
Specific Description	Therefore, I will partner with the local multicultural family support center to provide Korean language and cultural adaptation education programs.
Positive Effect	By doing so, students will be able to have language exchanges with Korean volunteers matched by the Multicultural Family Support Center and will be able to adapt to Korean culture more quickly.
Conclusion	With these reasons, I would recommend them to sign up for the multicultural support program in the local community.

3	Theme-based classroom
Topic Sentence	I will conduct theme-based lessons that encourage students to take center stage.
Premise	Applying theme-based lessons can be an effective way to introduce other cultures, and it can even make multicultural students feel proud of their own culture.
Specific Description	For example, I'd like to introduce students to the traditional culture, food, and clothing of their country of origin.
Positive Effect	As a result, classmates may show interest in multicultural students by asking questions like, 'How does that food taste?' or 'Have you been there, what's it like?' This interest from peers can boost the confidence of multicultural students and foster stronger friendships.
Conclusion	Therefore, I will conduct theme-based lessons that encourage students to take center stage.

TOPIC 15.   Motivating Students

1	Challenging tasks
Topic Sentence	I would give challenging tasks to motivate students in my classroom.
Premise	High-achieving students are less likely to be interested in what they already know, and they have a lot of experience with success, so sometimes providing failure can help stimulate their motivation to learn.
Specific Description	Therefore, I'll utilize in-depth inquiry/experimentation activities, real-world problem-solving activities, project learning, and conceptual learning at a higher level.
Positive Effect	This will help students challenge themselves, revitalizing their motivation to learn. The sense of accomplishment that comes with solving the task will further motivate them to continue learning.
Conclusion	In this reason, I would give challenging tasks to motivate students in my classroom.

2	Student teacher
Topic Sentence	I'll assign a role called 'Student teacher' to those who become demotivated due to excessive preparatory study.
Premise	Even when you think you know something, the things you didn't understand are often revealed by explaining it to someone else.
Specific Description	To be specific, we'll assign them the task of helping other students with difficult material in class, like a 'Student teacher.'
Positive Effect	This will help them find their role in the class and motivate them to participate. They may also discover something they didn't know or gain a deeper understanding by teaching other students.
Conclusion	Therefore, I'll assign a role called 'Student teacher' to those who become demotivated due to excessive preparatory study.

3	Flipped learning
Topic Sentence	If the academic level of students is high enough, I believe utilizing flipped learning methods can be a great idea to motivate them.
Premise	Students get bored and disengaged in classes if the content is below their level.
Specific Description	Therefore, I will assign students to study the basic concepts of the lesson at home. Then, in class, I will provide a real-world, case-based application lesson where they can apply what they have learned to solve practical problems.
Positive Effect	By doing so, students will realize that what they know can be applied to real-world situations, which will increase their interest and motivation in the subject.
Conclusion	Therefore, I believe utilizing flipped learning methods can be a great idea to motivate students.

4	Emotional support
Topic Sentence	I would first try to provide emotional support to a student who is slumped over in class due to learned helplessness.
Premise	Students with learning disabilities often experience lower self-esteem, achievement, and self-confidence. Therefore, they require emotional support rather than solely academic assistance.
Specific Description	For example, I would start by listening to and empathizing with the student's situation. Then, I would help them overcome their learned helplessness by discussing strategies such as 'emphasizing the positive,' 'celebrating small achievements,' and 'normalizing failure.'
Positive Effect	This will help restore their low self-esteem, confidence, and self-efficacy. Moreover, this experience of accomplishment will stimulate their desire for self-improvement in the academic area.
Conclusion	In this reason, I would first try to provide emotional support to a student who is slumped over in class.

5	Provide a successful experience
Topic Sentence	Providing a successful experience to students with learned helplessness is an essential way to motivate students.
Premise	Learned helplessness is the result of repeated experiences of failure, so providing students with appropriate successful experiences can be a direct solution.
Specific Description	For example, I will adjust the level of difficulty to match the student's level, or I will give them assignments that are non-academic, such as "not being late," "coming prepared," etc.
Positive Effect	By doing so, the student will begin to feel a sense of accomplishment in small steps, which will boost their motivation and help them to gradually set bigger goals.
Conclusion	Therefore, I believe providing a successful experience to students is an essential way to motivate them.

6	Help students improve basic academic skills
Topic Sentence	I will recommend a variety of basic academic improvement programs for students experiencing learned helplessness.
Premise	To motivate students, it is important to provide individualized instruction at the student's level.
Specific Description	Therefore, I would recommend a variety of academic enhancement programs for the student, including after-school tutoring, community-based basic skills programs, and peer or college mentoring to help the student build confidence in the course content.
Positive Effect	This will allow students to master the basics of the subject matter and gradually build self-efficacy, confidence, and a positive self-perception of learning.
Conclusion	In this reason, I will recommend a variety of basic academic improvement programs for students experiencing learned helplessness.

7		Utilize physical activities
Topic Sentence		I will utilize physical activities to make the classroom more active.
Premise		Students are more likely to understand what they're learning when they are exposed to multiple stimuli, such as visual, auditory, and tactile.
Specific Description		To be specific, I will diversify my lessons with activities involving physical movements, such as Total Physical Response (TPR) exercises, or interactive activities where everyone gets up, walks around, and interacts with each other, like cocktail parties.
Positive Effect		For the teacher, this will prevent students from falling down because the lesson itself requires students to be physically active. For the student, it will allow them to be more active and engaged in the lesson, making it a fun and active learning experience.
Conclusion		Therefore, I will utilize physical activities to make the classroom more active.

8		Group work
Topic Sentence		I will utilize group activities that emphasize individual responsibility to prevent students from falling down in class.
Premise		By participating in group activities, students will be able to work together to encourage and motivate each other, fostering a collaborative relationship.
Specific Description		To achieve this, teachers can present a group activity with clearly separated roles within the group, but pursuing the same goal, like a Jigsaw.
Positive Effect		By doing so, students will be motivated by the class activity itself as they will have to do their individual roles for their group performance. It will also create a collaborative learning atmosphere as they encourage and help each other.
Conclusion		Therefore, I will utilize group activities that emphasize individual responsibility to prevent students from falling down in class.

9	Blended learning
Topic Sentence	I'll incorporate blended learning methods to motivate students, using a variety of online platforms.
Premise	Students get bored with the same type of lesson every time.
Specific Description	To prevent this, I will utilize a variety of online learning platforms to facilitate real-time quiz games, team competitions, online collaborative learning, etc. that combine in-person and online classes.
Positive Effect	This will allow teachers to revitalize their in-person classes, which are often limited to textbooks and lectures. Students will also be excited about this new way of learning and will be more engaged in class.
Conclusion	Therefore, I'll incorporate blended learning methods to motivate students, using a variety of online platforms.

10	Topic-based teaching
Topic Sentence	I'll use topic-based teaching methods in my lessons to motivate students.
Premise	Students are more motivated to learn when they are given the autonomy to explore their interests.
Specific Description	To be specific, I will let students choose a topic, research it over a period of time, and then write a report or create something to present.
Positive Effect	By doing so, students will be motivated to learn by fulfilling their need for autonomy through self-directed work.
Conclusion	Therefore, I'll use topic-based teaching methods in my lessons to motivate students.

11	Use edutech
Topic Sentence	I will actively use edutech in my classroom to motivate students to learn.
Premise	As technology advances and online platforms diversify, there are many edutech solutions that can effectively motivate students to learn.
Specific Description	To illustrate, I will familiarize myself with various teaching and learning models by using digital devices, and I will organize student engagement lessons with edutech tools, such as online learning platforms and metaverses.
Positive Effect	By doing so, students will be engaged by the new teaching methods, and the use of edutech tools that require active participation will enhance student engagement and make lessons more effective.
Conclusion	Therefore, I will actively use edutech in my classroom to motivate students to learn.

TOPIC 16.	Inclusive Classroom

1	Needs analysis
Topic Sentence	I would ask the student and parent if they need help, and if so, I would do a needs analysis to see what kind of help they need.
Premise	No matter how thoughtful you are, helping out in unnecessary situations can make someone feel left out.
Specific Description	To illustrate, I'll begin with individualized interviews with students and parents to determine if they need help and, if so, in which areas.
Positive Effect	In doing so, the student will develop independence by avoiding unnecessary assistance, and the teacher can prevent complaints of reverse discrimination, allowing for a more natural integration into the classroom.
Conclusion	Therefore, before I provide immediate assistance, I will first ask them if they need help and if so, I will conduct a needs analysis to determine what kind of help they need.

2	Caring Champion
Topic Sentence	I will award the title of 'Caring Champion' to students who show great respect to their peers in integrated education.
Premise	Getting support from your classmates can help you build strong relationships and make sure you feel like you're part of the class.
Specific Description	To be specific, I will use a class meeting to encourage students to volunteer to help a friend and award the student with a title of 'Caring Champion.'
Positive Effect	This will help students develop a sense of caring and accomplishment in helping others, and it will foster better friendships and a sense of community among the students being helped.
Conclusion	Therefore, I will award the title of 'Caring Champion' to students who show great respect to their peers in integrated education.

3	Modify assignment or test formats
Topic Sentence	I will modify assignments and tests to ensure that inclusive students are not disadvantaged in assignments or other assessment activities.
Premise	It would also be unfair to treat students the same regardless of their difficulties.
Specific Description	For example, I'll provide enlarged test papers for students with visual difficulties and repeated listening or reading scripts for students with hearing difficulties. Additionally, I'll make any necessary modifications to the test, such as extending the test time or using a different presentation format.
Positive Effect	This will ensure that the student is respected and given appropriate learning and assessment opportunities despite their challenges.
Conclusion	Therefore, I will modify assignments and tests to ensure that inclusive students are not disadvantaged in assignments or other assessment activities.

TOPIC 17.	Students in Need

1	Afterschool class
Topic Sentence	I'll create an afterschool class for students in need.
Premise	Students in need often lack access to private tutoring, so if they don't understand the content at school, they won't be able to address it elsewhere.
Specific Description	To be specific, I will organize an afterschool program focused on regular school subjects, providing an extra opportunity for students to study the topic in more depth.
Positive Effect	In doing so, the student will be able to build a trusting relationship with the teacher and fill in the gaps in their regular classroom.
Conclusion	Therefore, I'll create an afterschool program for students in need.

2	Local community program
Topic Sentence	I will encourage students in needs to sign up for the local community program.
Premise	Local community provides a variety of programs for students in needs.
Specific Description	For example, I would recommend local field trips, college student mentoring, or free tutoring programs for the students.
Positive Effect	In doing so, teachers can not only address the challenge of limited human and material resources, but also provide more direct and practical help to those students.
Conclusion	Therefore, I will encourage students in needs to sign up for the local community program.

3	Provide scholarship
Topic Sentence	For students in need, I will look for scholarship programs to recommend.
Premise	There are various scholarship programs in society for students who are struggling.
Specific Description	To be specific, I would first consult with the student and their parents, then search for various scholarships to recommend.
Positive Effect	This will not only allow the student to trust social institutions, but will also give them the courage to overcome their own environmental challenges.
Conclusion	Therefore, I will look for scholarship programs to recommend for students in need,

4	Treat them like any other students
Topic Sentence	For students in need, I believe it is essential to treat them like any other students.
Premise	Being overly caring or sympathetic to a student's struggles can actually hurt them even more.
Specific Description	To be specific, I will demonstrate respect in my vocabulary and language choices when interacting with students in need, avoiding any actions that may unintentionally hurt them by being overly sympathetic.
Positive Effect	In doing so, the teacher can ensure that the student doesn't feel ashamed of their struggles and will be encouraged to overcome the obstacles they are facing and move forward.
Conclusion	Therefore, I believe it is essential to treat them like any other students.

TOPIC 18.　Relationship with Parents

1	Emphasize common goals
Topic Sentence	I think it is important to emphasize the the goals of the parents and the school are the same.
Premise	When you identify common goals, a mutual collaborative relationship develops naturally.
Specific Description	For example, the teacher can emphasize that parents want their children to be happy and schools want their students to be happy, establishing a common goal.
Positive Effect	This will allow schools and parents to work together in a trusting and collaborative manner to achieve a common goal.
Conclusion	Therefore, I think it is important to emphasize the common the goals of the parents and the school.

2	Parent conferences
Topic Sentence	I will hold regular parent-teacher conferences to establish collaborative relationship with parents.
Premise	Parents are part of the community that makes up the school, so they have a right to know what's going on in the school.
Specific Description	For example, I'll invite parents to meet on a monthly or quarterly basis to discuss what we've been doing and our plans for the future, and to engage in conversation about it.
Positive Effect	In doing so, parents will be better informed about school activities, increasing their trust in the school. Additionally, teachers will face fewer unreasonable or personal demands and will gain a clearer understanding of the majority of parents' opinions.
Conclusion	Therefore, I will hold regular parent-teacher conferences to establish collaborative relationship with parents.

3	Online platform
Topic Sentence	I'll use online platforms, such as internet communities and social media, to keep parents updated on how students are doing at school.
Premise	As a parent, it's natural to want to know how your child is doing at school, and this information provides topics for meaningful conversations at home.
Specific Description	As an example, I will use Naver Band to allow parents to check their children's school life through photos of field trips, school events, and classroom activities.
Positive Effect	In doing so, parents will be better informed about their students' school experiences and will have the opportunity to discuss school with their children at home, increasing their satisfaction and trust in the school.
Conclusion	Therefore, I'll use online platforms to keep parents updated on how students are doing at school.

4	Active communication between the classroom and home
Topic Sentence	I believe that active communication between the classroom and home is essential for building a collaborative relationship with parents.
Premise	If communication between home and classroom is poor, students may struggle due to missing important information, and unnecessary misunderstandings could arise, leading to a loss of trust in teachers and schools.
Specific Description	For example, I will actively use KakaoTalk, Naver Band, and parent group texts to quickly share information about school events, class activities, and schedules.
Positive Effect	This will enable parents to quickly stay informed about what's happening at school and help teachers ensure that educational activities run smoothly without disruption. It will also foster a collaborative relationship between teachers and parents, increasing trust in the school.
Conclusion	Therefore, I believe that active communication between the classroom and home is essential for building a collaborative relationship with parents.

5	Exchange information about students
Topic Sentence	To build a collaborative relationship with parents, I believe it's essential to exchange information about students effectively.
Premise	Students often behave differently when they are in school and in home.
Specific Description	For example, I'll talk with parents about how students are doing in school, and I'll ask them about their routine after school, how they behave at home, and what they talk about with their parents.
Positive Effect	By doing so, teachers and parents will have a better understanding of their students by integrating information about their school and home lives. This will also help foster a trusting and collaborative teacher-parent relationship.
Conclusion	Therefore, I believe it's essential to exchange information about students to build a collaborative relationship with parents,

TOPIC 19.   Relationship with other Teachers

1	Mutual respect
Topic Sentence	I believe that mutual respect is important for good relationships with fellow teachers.
Premise	In a hierarchical culture, it's difficult to build meaningful connections when interactions are passive.
Specific Description	Therefore, I will respect the rich experience and professional knowledge of senior teachers, as well as the passion and proactive spirit of junior teachers.
Positive Effect	In doing so, I'll be able to learn from the experience of senior teachers and be inspired by the enthusiasm of junior teachers, fostering a school culture of mutual respect.
Conclusion	In this reason, I believe that mutual respect is important for good relationships with fellow teachers.

2	Collaborative attitude
Topic Sentence	I believe that maintaining a collaborative attitude among fellow teachers is important.
Premise	What happens at school is often not something you can solve alone.
Specific Description	So, I will be a teacher who actively reaches out to my grade level leader, counselor, school nurse, assistant principal, and principal whenever I need help with a particular issue.
Positive Effect	This will create a collaborative atmosphere where colleagues support one another, leading to better communication and mutual trust within the school. Additionally, when faced with a difficult problem, I'll be able to draw on their collective intelligence to find a more effective solution.
Conclusion	Therefore, I believe that maintaining a collaborative attitude among fellow teachers is important.

3		Consideration and compromise
Topic Sentence		I believe that consideration and compromise are necessary to create good peer-teacher relationships.
Premise		There are many times when people are working on a task and it doesn't end up in a way that everyone is happy with.
Specific Description		Therefore, I will be as considerate as possible of my fellow teachers when handling my work, and if I need to make compromises, I will view it as an opportunity to learn from a different perspective rather than as a loss.
Positive Effect		In doing so, a harmonious culture of mutual compromise and consideration will be created, making it easier for me to ask for help the next time I need it.
Conclusion		In this reason, I believe that consideration and compromise are necessary to create good peer-teacher relationships.

4		Demonstrate competence
Topic Sentence		I believe that demonstrating relevant competence is essential to building a trusting relationship.
Premise		In the workplace, it's important to be able to take responsibility for your work and do it well.
Specific Description		For example, I will work to improve my skills by reading the manual or getting a detailed handover from a senior colleague, ensuring I understand my responsibilities and perform them well.
Positive Effect		By doing so, I will not only feel more fulfilled in my own work but also integrate more smoothly into the workplace, earning respect and recognition from my coworkers. Additionally, this will build their trust in my ability to perform effectively.
Conclusion		Therefore, I believe that demonstrating relevant competence is essential to building a trusting relationship.

5	Mature treatment
Topic Sentence	To build a collaborative relationship, I believe it's important to treat others with maturity.
Premise	According to Argyris's Maturity–Immaturity Theory, people will behave maturely toward those who treat them maturely and immaturely toward those who treat them immaturely, even if they are the same person.
Specific Description	Therefore, I will always try to treat others in the workplace with dignity and maturity, which includes listening to and respecting their opinions and avoiding emotionally charged interactions.
Positive Effect	By doing so, it will encourage them to reflect on their own behavior and change their attitudes to be more in line with the mature treatment they deserve, which will ultimately contribute to creating a mature culture.
Conclusion	In this reason, I believe it's important to treat others with maturity to build a collaborative relationship.

6	Reflective attitude
Topic Sentence	I believe it's important to have an reflective attitude in order to build positive relationships.
Premise	In a conflict situation, it's rare for only one person to be entirely at fault and even then, it is often helpful for both sides to work together to resolve the conflict.
Specific Description	Therefore, I will be cautious of assuming I am always right and will review my actions with an open mind. I will also listen to others and remain reflective and receptive to their opinions.
Positive Effect	By recognizing one's own faults, one can more effectively resolve situations and, in the long run, improve oneself. Additionally, maintaining a reflective attitude will build trust among colleagues and contribute to a healthy workplace culture.
Conclusion	Therefore, I believe it's important to have an reflective attitude in order to build positive relationships.

7	Humble attitude
Topic Sentence	I believe that having a humble attitude is essential for forming collaborative relationships with teachers.
Premise	The nature of teaching is such that there is never one right answer, so everyone's beliefs and philosophies should be respected.
Specific Description	To be specific, I'll do my best to teach, but I'll also try to be humble enough to accept that my ideas and methods won't always be perfect, and I'll be open to advice and conversation.
Positive Effect	This will lead to constructive and productive conversations between teachers, where they can offer and accept advice to improve their own professional development.
Conclusion	Therefore, I believe that having a humble attitude is essential for forming collaborative relationships with teachers.

8	Be consistent with one's attitude
Topic Sentence	I believe it is important to be consistent in the relationships between teachers.
Premise	Personal relationships and emotions should not be allowed to get in the way of official school work.
Specific Description	For example, teachers need to be careful not to take advantage of other teachers simply because they're personally close, or to become emotional about their personal issues.
Positive Effect	By doing so, teachers will be able to avoid unnecessary misunderstandings that can lead to conflict with other teachers, and by always being consistent in their approach to their work, they will develop good working relationships with teachers who trust their expertise.
Conclusion	Therefore, I believe it is important to be consistent in the relationships between teachers.

TOPIC 20.   Relationship with Students

1	Treat them with respect, not control
Topic Sentence	I will treat students with respect, not control, in order to develop a healthy relationship with them.
Premise	If students are told what to do, it can only lead to resentment and rebellion. On the other hand, treating students with respect encourages them to think for themselves about why rules are necessary, fostering mature behavior.
Specific Description	Therefore, before I make a decision, I will always involve students in the decision-making process, treating them with respect.
Positive Effect	This will allow students to develop a sense of trust with their teachers and help them grow into democratic adults who can confidently express their opinions and respect the opinions of others.
Conclusion	Therefore, I will treat students with respect, not control, in order to develop a healthy relationship.

2	Look for the positive in students
Topic Sentence	I will try to find something positive about every student to build a positive teacher-student relationship
Premise	Every student has their own personality and strengths.
Specific Description	Therefore, I will keep an open mind and try to get to know my students through various activities and settings, rather than solely judging them based on what I see in my classroom.
Positive Effect	By doing so, teachers will be able to build a bond with their students by recognizing and praising their strengths. Students will feel empowered as they discover strengths they didn't know they had, leading to a much more positive school experience.
Conclusion	Therefore, I will try to find something positive about every student to build a positive teacher-student relationship

3	Distinguish between personal feelings and the role expectation
Topic Sentence	I believe it's important to distinguish between personal feelings and the role expectation when interacting with students.
Premise	Getzels and Guba's social regime theory suggests that the alignment between an individual's desire and role expectations is crucial for appropriate social behavior.
Specific Description	Therefore, I will try to determine what is appropriate between my personal feelings and the role expectations as a teacher and I'll try to make a balance between them.
Positive Effect	By doing so, teachers can show a great example of emotional stability, which is expected of them as educators. Moreover, students will develop trust based on teacher's consistent and stable behavior.
Conclusion	Therefore, I believe it's important to distinguish between personal feelings and the role expectation when interacting with students.

4	Reflect on their feelings
Topic Sentence	I believe that teachers should be able to reflect on their feelings to maintain a trusting relationship with students.
Premise	It is often the case that students who have nothing to do with the problem can be harmed by a teacher's emotional state.
Specific Description	Therefore, I will always take the time to examine my emotions and calmly reflect on their source when I feel sad or angry. I will also ensure that my behavior does not make students who are not involved feel uncomfortable.
Positive Effect	By doing so, teachers can prevent students from becoming targets of their own anger. Moreover, students will also perceive teachers as trustworthy individual who can demonstrate emotional stability.
Conclusion	Therefore, I believe that teachers should be able to reflect on their feelings to maintain a trusting relationship with students.

5	Ability to manage students
Topic Sentence	I believe that teachers should have a proper ability to manage students to build a healthy teacher−student relationship.
Premise	Teachers need to effectively guide students in the right direction at the right time.
Specific Description	Therefore, I will become a teacher who can employ different types of leadership, such as delegative, democratic, and transformational, based on the specific needs of each situation.
Positive Effect	This will allow teachers to guide students in an educationally desirable direction. Additionally, students will develop a strong relationship with teachers based on respect and trust.
Conclusion	Therefore, I believe that teachers should have a proper ability to manage students to build a healthy teacher−student relationship.

6	Offer a sincere apology
Topic Sentence	I believe that teachers should be able to offer a sincere apology when it is necessary to build a healthy teacher−student relationship.
Premise	Teachers are human before they are teachers, so they are imperfect and sometimes make mistakes.
Specific Description	Therefore, teachers should be willing to acknowledge their imperfections and apologize sincerely without letting their ego get in the way, even if it means apologizing to a student.
Positive Effect	By doing so, students will recognize teachers as human beings and empathize with their feelings, fostering a stronger human connection.
Conclusion	Therefore, I believe that teachers should be able to offer a sincere apology when it is necessary to build a healthy teacher−student relationship.

7	Avoid judging students by their scores
Topic Sentence	I believe that teachers should avoid judging students by their test scores to build a healthy teacher-student relationship.
Premise	Since different people have different talents, it is impossible to discover and assess all of a student's talents in a limited number of subject tests taken in school.
Specific Description	Therefore, I will treat students without prejudice based on their scores, viewing their scores only as a measure of their achievement in the subject, trying to understand them in diverse ways to discover their hidden talents and strengths.
Positive Effect	By doing so, students will develop a trusting relationship with a teacher who believes in their potential. With the teacher's support, they will discover their talents and strengths, which will enhance their self-esteem and foster a positive self-perception.
Conclusion	Therefore, I believe that it's essential for teachers to avoid judging students by their test scores to build a healthy teacher-student relationship.

8	Separate students' feelings from their behaviors
Topic Sentence	To build an effective teacher-student relationship, it is important to for teachers to be able to separate students' feelings from their behaviors.
Premise	As a teacher, maintaining clear and consistent expectations on student's behavior is essential.
Specific Description	Therefore, instead of blindly empathizing with a student's feelings and unconditionally approving their behavior, I will try to set clear limits on inappropriate behavior while maintaining a deep understanding and empathy for the emotional reasons behind their actions.
Positive Effect	This will allow the student to see a teacher not only empathizing with their feelings like a friend, but also offering advice for them like an adult, which will build a sense of trust that they can lean on.
Conclusion	In this reason, to build an effective teacher-student relationship, it is important for teachers to be able to separate students' feelings from their behaviors.

9	Be mindful of non-verbal communication
Topic Sentence	I believe that in order to build trusting relationships with students, teachers need to be mindful of their non-verbal communication.
Premise	Since adolescent students are often sensitive to facial expressions and behaviors, it is crucial to recognize the importance of non-verbal communication.
Specific Description	For example, I will focus not only on verbal elements like words but also on non-verbal elements such as behavior and facial expressions when communicating with students. Moreover, I will make sure that my words, facial expressions, and behavior are consistent and harmonious, rather than reacting without expression.
Positive Effect	By doing so, the student will feel secure in their teacher's response and will be able to make a deeper emotional connection with them.
Conclusion	Therefore, I believe that in order to build trusting relationships with students, teachers need to be mindful of their non-verbal communication.

TOPIC 21. Homeroom Management

1	Sense of integrity
Topic Sentence	I believe that in order to have good homeroom management, teachers need to cultivate a sense of integrity.
Premise	Because teachers have a lot of power over their students, they have a greater responsibility and need to remain impartial.
Specific Description	Specifically, I will search for various resources and lectures related to integrity and make myself familiar with the response manual for handling relevant situations.
Positive Effect	By doing so, teachers can avoid being linked to undesirable events like bribery and favoritism. Moreover, students will perceive their teachers as more trustworthy, with an image of integrity and fairness.
Conclusion	In this reason, I believe that in order to have good homeroom management, teachers need to cultivate a sense of integrity.

2	Provide literary, artistic, and physical learning experiences
Topic Sentence	I will provide literary, artistic, and physical learning experiences for my homeroom students.
Premise	For students to feel happy as human beings, being able to appreciate literature, art, and physical activities will help them lead fulfilling lives.
Specific Description	Specifically, for literature and the arts, I will designate a morning literature day and a musical appreciation day to provide students with opportunities to experience literary works and musical performances. Additionally, for physical education, I will promote class sports days to help students appreciate the value of playing sports.
Positive Effect	By doing so, students will develop as holistic individuals with rich experiences in literature, the arts, and physical education, rather than just accumulating academic knowledge. In addition, these activities will create a unified classroom atmosphere.
Conclusion	In these reasons, I will provide literary, artistic, and physical learning experiences for my homeroom students.

3	Maker activities
Topic Sentence	As a homeroom teacher, I will promote classroom maker activities.
Premise	In the context of the Fourth Industrial Revolution, there is increasing interest and importance in maker education to stimulate creativity.
Specific Description	For example, I'll have a class meeting to discuss and decide what to create, then use the makerspace to create the actual artwork, and lastly present each group's work to evaluate the others.
Positive Effect	By doing so, students will not only engage in Maker education but also learn the importance of collaboration and unity within the classroom, helping them to become creative individuals for the Fourth Industrial Revolution.
Conclusion	In this reason, I will promote classroom maker activities as a homeroom teacher.

4	Respect autonomy
Topic Sentence	I will be a homeroom teacher who respects students' autonomy.
Premise	It's important for teachers to respect students' autonomy in order for them to grow into adults who can understand democratic values.
Specific Description	Specifically, I will ensure that when making decisions about my classroom, no matter how small, I take the time to listen to my students and consider their opinions in the process.
Positive Effect	By doing so, students will learn to participate in the decision-making process. Additionally, setting classroom rules in this manner will create an environment where students understand the importance of rules and choose to follow them voluntarily, rather than feeling compelled to obey.
Conclusion	Therefore, I will be a homeroom teacher who respects students' autonomy rather than overpowering them.

5		Develop self-efficacy
Topic Sentence		I believe that it is important for homeroom teachers to be able to effectively develop their students' self-efficacy.
Premise		Satisfying the need for competence is essential for positive self-perception and high self-esteem.
Specific Description		To be specific, teachers can encourage talent exchange activities to discover students' strengths. Additionally, the teachers can regularly organize activities where students recognize and praise each other's strengths to help build their self-efficacy.
Positive Effect		By doing so, students will recognize their unique talents and build self-efficacy through the process of teaching and learning from each other.
Conclusion		Therefore, I believe that it is important for homeroom teachers to be able to effectively develop their students' self-efficacy.

6		Develop social skills
Topic Sentence		I believe that it is important for homeroom teachers to be able to effectively develop their students' social skills.
Premise		One of the biggest needs of adolescent students is the need for relatedness, which means the desire to form meaningful relationships.
Specific Description		To achieve this, teachers can create a café-like homeroom environment with drinks, music, and time for small talk with classmates.
Positive Effect		By doing so, students will learn how to build relationships with others, fulfilling their need for relatedness. Additionally, they will develop friendships where they can share their lives openly, naturally creating a harmonious and welcoming homeroom atmosphere.
Conclusion		Therefore, I believe that it is important for homeroom teachers to be able to effectively develop their students' social skills.

7		Use social media
Topic Sentence		To create a lively homeroom atmosphere, using popular social media platforms can be an effective strategy for teachers.
Premise		Since social media is already a big part of teen culture, it's a great way to better understand and connect with the students.
Specific Description		Therefore, I will utilize the social media platforms that my students frequently use, such as Facebook and Instagram, and actively engage with them online.
Positive Effect		By doing so, students will be able to feel closer to their teachers, and teachers will be able to better understand their students' relationships with each other, which will help with homeroom management. Furthermore, it will help prevent cyberbullying and teach internet etiquette.
Conclusion		In these reasons, using popular social media platforms can be an effective strategy for teachers to create a lively homeroom atmosphere.

8		Homeroom band
Topic Sentence		As a homeroom teacher, it would be a great idea to utilize the Naver Band.
Premise		If teachers share photos and videos of various activities at school with parents, it will create a more connected homeroom atmosphere.
Specific Description		To achieve this, I'll open a Naver Band exclusively for the parents of my homeroom class and use to share photos and videos of school activities and class events.
Positive Effect		By doing so, parents will be able to get a better sense of their child's school life. In addition, for teachers and students, the Naver Band will serve as a class portfolio and a space to record and cherish memories.
Conclusion		As a homeroom teacher, it would be a great idea to utilize the Naver Band.

TOPIC 22. Expertise on Teaching

1   Class consulting

Topic Sentence	I would like to sign up for class consulting to improve my expertise on teaching.
Premise	School boards offer various forms of support to help teachers enhance their expertise, including mentor-mentee programs and instructional consulting for new teachers.
Specific Description	To be specific, as a new teacher, I will actively search for various teaching consulting support provided by the school district to improve my teaching expertise, and apply to various consulting programs such as lead teacher consulting and mentor-mentee programs.
Positive Effect	This will allow me to learn from experienced teachers and enhance my skills in facilitating student-centered classroom activities.
Conclusion	Therefore, I would like to sign up for class consulting to improve my expertise on teaching.

2   Rehearse lessons

Topic Sentence	I believe that rehearsing a lesson can be a great way to make the lesson run smoothly.
Premise	Through rehearsal, teachers can learn to manage unexpected situations and enhance their classroom facilitation skills, contributing to their overall teaching expertise.
Specific Description	For example, teachers can rehearse their lessons before introducing a new teaching style by testing the devices they'll use in class to avoid technical issues and trying out new activities in advance.
Positive Effect	By doing so, teachers will be better equipped to handle unexpected situations in the classroom and will enhance their teaching expertise by developing a keen eye for detail.
Conclusion	Therefore, I believe that rehearsing a lesson can be a great way to make the lesson run smoothly.

3	Self-directed training
Topic Sentence	I would like to start self-directed training to enhance my teaching expertise.
Premise	One of the most important qualities of a teacher is being self-directed and proactive in seeking ways to improve their teaching.
Specific Description	To achieve this, teachers can watch and analyze videos of effective teaching practices or enroll in various courses offered by lead teachers and training institutes, allowing them to independently address and fill in any gaps in their skills.
Positive Effect	By doing so, teachers will not only identify their weaknesses but they will also enhance their teaching expertise, which will increase their sense of accomplishment and teaching efficacy, as they witness their professional growth.
Conclusion	Therefore, I would like to start self-directed training to enhance my teaching expertise.

4	Professional learning communities
Topic Sentence	Organizing professional learning communities can be a great way for teachers to enhance their expertise in teaching.
Premise	Interacting with others can be more effective than studying alone to improve one's expertise.
Specific Description	For example, teachers can create professional learning communities based on subjects within the same grade level or in senior-junior study groups. Afterward, they can then share their lessons publicly within these communities and receive feedback from other teachers to enhance their teaching practices.
Positive Effect	By doing so, teachers can foster a collaborative culture and benefit from the synergistic professional growth that comes from receiving advice and insights from diverse perspectives.
Conclusion	In this reason, organizing professional learning communities can be a great way for teachers to enhance their expertise in teaching.

5	Get feedback from students
Topic Sentence	I will regularly get feedback from students to improve my expertise on teaching.
Premise	It is the students who take your classes that can best identify improvements to your teaching.
Specific Description	Therefore, I'll give my students a survey at the end of the unit to ask them what they liked about the lesson and what needs to be improved. I'll then use the survey comments to better prepare for future lessons so that I can make them even more satisfied.
Positive Effect	In this way, I'll be able to provide better lessons based on my students' honest feedback, and my students will have more trust in my lessons because they know their opinions are valued.
Conclusion	In this reason, I will regularly get feedback from students to improve my expertise on teaching.

6	A class rule-setting activity
Topic Sentence	I believe that a class rule-setting activity is necessary to keep the class running smoothly.
Premise	Since class time involves teacher-student interaction, it's crucial to establish appropriate rules.
Specific Description	Specifically, teachers can use the first hour of class to engage students in an activity to establish classroom rules. This can include setting boundaries and making agreements about behaviors such as playing with friends, slumping over, and making noise.
Positive Effect	This will help students develop a respectful attitude toward others by following the rules they've set, and it will also help the class run more smoothly if teachers mention the reasons for following the rules, rather than improvising.
Conclusion	Therefore, I believe that a class rule-setting activity is necessary to keep the class running smoothly.

7	Include different learning styles
Topic Sentence	I will plan activities that include a variety of learning styles for effective lessons.
Premise	Learners can be categorized into different learning styles based on their preferred way of receiving and processing information, such as visual, kinesthetic, and auditory.
Specific Description	Therefore, I will design activities to satisfy the different learning styles of my students, such as using cartoons for visual learners, cocktail parties or TPR for kinesthetic learners, and chants or song lyrics for auditory learners.
Positive Effect	By doing so, I will be able to make lessons more engaging and effective by reflecting the different learning styles of the students. Moreover, students will be more motivated to participate in class with a variety of activities.
Conclusion	Therefore, I will plan activities that include a variety of learning styles for effective lessons.

8	Utilize a veriety of motivational methods
Topic Sentence	I will utilize a variety of motivational methods to keep the class engaged.
Premise	According to Keller's ARCS theory, learners are motivated when their needs for attention, relevance, confidence, and satisfaction are met.
Specific Description	To achieve this, I will use pictures, diagrams, YouTube, Instagram, and other visuals to capture attention and real-life problem-solving tasks to establish relevance. Moreover, I will provide success experiences through appropriately challenging tasks to build confidence, and a sense of accomplishment or a reward system to fulfill the needs for satisfaction.
Positive Effect	In this way, I'll be able to motivate students to engage actively, making the lesson more interactive.
Conclusion	Therefore, I will utilize a variety of motivational methods to keep the class engaged.

9	Create a class schedule
Topic Sentence	I believe it's important to create a step-by-step class schedule to ensure a smooth classroom operation.
Premise	When organizing lessons, it's important to plan by semester, quarter, and unit to ensure the activities run smoothly.
Specific Description	To be specific, teachers can create a detailed, step-by-step lesson plan that aligns with the grade level, semester, or midterm/final exams. This involves organizing activities, content, and progression for each step in a cohesive manner to ensure a structured and effective learning experience.
Positive Effect	By doing so, teachers will be able to maintain a stable course curriculum, making a balance between teacher-centered and student-centered lessons.
Conclusion	Therefore, I believe it's important to create a step-by-step class schedule to ensure a smooth classroom operation.

TOPIC 23. Expertise on Assessment

1	Appropriate amount of evaluation
Topic Sentence	In terms of the assessment expertise, I believe it's crucial to plan for the appropriate amount of evaluation.
Premise	It's important to keep a close eye on how much teachers can do and how much students can handle.
Specific Description	For example, teachers can refer to how it had been done in the past, what the steps were, and how long it took before planning for the evaluation.
Positive Effect	By doing so, teachers will be able to carry out the assessment plans they've prepared and students will be able to maintain their motivation by ensuring that the workload is manageable, giving them confidence to prepare thoroughly for the assessment.
Conclusion	Therefore, I believe it's crucial to plan for the appropriate amount of evaluation in terms of the assessment expertise.

2	Coordinate the evaluation periods
Topic Sentence	I believe it is important to coordinate the evaluation periods between fellow teachers in order for students to maximize their abilities.
Premise	For each subject, students should be given sufficient time to prepare for the assessment.
Specific Description	To achieve this, teachers can hold meetings with colleagues from other subjects to coordinate their schedules, ensuring that assessments are not too closely overlapping.
Positive Effect	By doing so, teachers will be able to reduce the amount of pressure on students who have to prepare for multiple subjects at the same time. In addition, spreading out the assessment schedule will give students enough time to prepare so that they can maximize their abilities.
Conclusion	Therefore, I believe it is important to coordinate the evaluation periods between fellow teachers in order for students to maximize their abilities.

	3	Mention the purpose
Topic Sentence		I believe it's important to mention the purpose and need for assessment to students.
Premise		To increase motivation to participate, it's important to give students a good prior explanation of the purpose.
Specific Description		To be specific, teachers can use the preview time before performance assessments to ensure that students understand the upcoming test is not solely about memorizing information and achieving a score. Instead, it's about applying what they've learned to solve real-world problems.
Positive Effect		By doing so, students will understand the purpose and necessity of the assessments they take, prepare diligently, and be more motivated to learn.
Conclusion		Therefore, I believe it's important to mention the purpose and need for assessment to students.

	4	Be fair with accurate criteria
Topic Sentence		In terms of the assessment expertise, I believe it's crucial to be fair with accurate criteria when evaluating.
Premise		To increase the reliability, it's important to remove subjective feelings and give scores based on objective criteria.
Specific Description		To achieve this, the first step is to carefully write out the rubric and have it reviewed by fellow teachers for clarity and comprehensiveness. The second step is to have multiple teachers score a single response using the rubric, which helps to improve the reliability and consistency of the assessment.
Positive Effect		By doing so, students will be able to understand and accept their results more easily, as they see the clear and fair criteria used in their evaluation. Additionally, teachers will enhance their assessment expertise by ensuring reliability and fairness in their grading, providing accurate and consistent standards.
Conclusion		Therefore, in terms of the assessment expertise, I believe it's crucial to be fair with accurate criteria when evaluating.

5	Utilize various methods of evaluation
Topic Sentence	In terms of the assessment expertise, I believe it's important to utilize various methods of evaluation.
Premise	Utilizing different kinds of assessments can have different pedagogical effects.
Specific Description	For example, teachers can utilize different types of evaluations, such as comparative assessments through team competition activities, growth-oriented assessments that compare a student's own growth, effort-oriented assessments using step-by-step project tasks, formative assessments, and absolute assessments based on achievement levels.
Positive Effect	By doing so, students will have the opportunity to engage in a variety of educational activities utilizing different assessment methods, and teachers will be able to reduce the burden of comparative assessment on students and stimulate a sense of achievement and intrinsic motivation.
Conclusion	Therefore, in terms of the assessment expertise, I believe it's important to utilize various methods of evaluation.

6	Ensure alignment between instruction and assessment
Topic Sentence	For effective evaluation, it is crucial to ensure alignment between instruction and assessment.
Premise	To establish assessment validity, each question must closely align with the activities and content covered in class.
Specific Description	In order to align teaching and assessment, teachers can utilize process-oriented assessments, recording the progress of each student. In addition, teachers can present evaluation tasks that ask students to apply what they have learned in class, making the entire lesson and assessment connected.
Positive Effect	By doing so, students will be more motivated to learn because their learning and classroom activities will be directly reflected in their assessments. Furthermore, the validity of the assessments will be ensured by the alignment of the teaching and assessment content.
Conclusion	Therefore, for effective evaluation, it is crucial to ensure alignment between instruction and assessment.

7	Consider students' diverse strengths and talents
Topic Sentence	As a teacher, I believe it's important to consider students' diverse strengths and talents when conducting assessments.
Premise	A student who is good at singing will be more motivated to learn if they have the opportunity to be assessed through singing activities, while a student who is good at sports will be more motivated if their assessments include athletic performances.
Specific Description	For example, I can plan an activity called "Create a Pop Song Reels," where students take on different roles that require various talents such as lyric translation, singing, dancing, and operating cameras or audio equipment.
Positive Effect	By doing so, students will be more motivated to participate in assessment activities because their diverse interests and talents will be respected, and as teachers, we will be able to make assessment more student-centered by incorporating their diverse talents into our assessments.
Conclusion	Therefore, I believe it's important to tailor assessments to students' diverse strengths and interests.

8	Test discrimination
Topic Sentence	For effective evaluation, it is crucial to ensure appropriate test discrimination.
Premise	The essence of assessment is to accurately identify students' achievement levels and differentiate between varying degrees of understanding and performance.
Specific Description	To be specific, when designing assessments, teachers can use the six stages of Bloom's Taxonomy of Complexity: Knowing, Understanding, Applying, Analyzing, Synthesizing, and Evaluating to present different levels of difficulty.
Positive Effect	By doing so, teachers will be able to accurately identify student performance as they present evaluation tasks that require different levels of understanding.
Conclusion	Therefore, for effective evaluation, I believe it is crucial to ensure appropriate test discrimination.

9		Provide future direction after an assessment
Topic Sentence		In terms of the assessment expertise, I believe it's important to provide future direction after an assessment.
Premise		Since scores are merely a quantification of current academic achievement, a student's future can be shaped significantly by their ongoing efforts and dedication.
Specific Description		Therefore, when I share assessment results with students, I won't just provide their scores. I will also offer guidance on future direction by mentioning what they should focus on in the future and what they need to work on.
Positive Effect		By doing so, students will develop a positive, goal-oriented attitude towards their potential for improvement, focusing on future growth rather than dwelling on past scores.
Conclusion		In this reason, I believe it's important to provide future direction after an assessment.

TOPIC 24. Educational Perspective

1	Prioritize a student's happiness
Topic Sentence	In my perspective, a teacher's priority should be to help students feel happy and engaged in school, providing positive and supportive environment.
Premise	Because the school is where students spend as much time as home, their happiness at school is the most important factor in their lives.
Specific Description	To be specific, I will ensure that students' needs for autonomy, competence, and relatedness are met in school. For autonomy, I will guide students to create their own rules based on sense of responsibility, rather than imposing rules on them. To support competence, I will facilitate class talent exchange activities actively. Lastly, to foster relatedness among my students, I will organize a weekly morning activity called "Talk It Out Day."
Positive Effect	By doing so, students will feel more empowered to express their opinions, discover their talents within the school community, and develop relationships with teachers and peers that contribute to their overall happiness.
Anticipated Opposition	Of course, meeting autonomy, competence, and relationship needs alone may not be sufficient to enhance student well-being.
Defense	However, I believe that these three elements are fundamental aspects of school life and they should be prioritized before addressing other needs for happiness.
Conclusion	Therefore, as teachers, we should be able to prioritize a student's happiness in school.

2	Learn from students
Topic Sentence	I believe that a teacher's role extends beyond teaching students, which means they should also be open to learning from them.
Premise	In an ever-changing society, it's important to recognize that teachers need to constantly change and grow.
Specific Description	To realize this, I will not only perceive my students as beings to be taught, but also observe them closely with an open mind to learn from them. For example, in terms of school life, I'll look for what I can learn from a student who is good at listening to their friends' problems and think, "Oh, that's a great way to get them to open up and have a good conversation!" or in terms of academics, I'll look for a student who effectively explains concepts to their friends and think, "Oh, that's a great way to teach them."
Positive Effect	This can lead to a stronger teacher-student relationship where the student is recognized for their talents. In addition, teachers can use their interactions with students as opportunities for growth, and this sense of accomplishment will make their teaching career more rewarding.
Anticipated Opposition	It is true, of course, that a teacher must have a firm philosophy and a strong conviction to lead a student to the right path.
Defense	However, as our society undergoes rapid change, the core values and competencies are also evolving. So, as a teacher, I believe it's crucial to adapt and respond effectively to these trends and changes in order to lead students effectively.
Conclusion	Therefore, I believe that teachers should have open minds and be willing to learn from students.

3	Embrace students with respect
Topic Sentence	In my perspective on education, I believe that teachers should be able to embrace students with respect.
Premise	Students learn how to respect others through their own experiences of being respected by others.
Specific Description	To make this happen, I will regularly listen to my students' stories and spend time in the classroom during breaks and lunch to build rapport with them. In addition, I will also try to understand their perspectives without imposing adult judgments.
Positive Effect	This will help students realize that they are respected as individuals, and this experience of being respected will help them develop into human beings who are able to respect others.
Anticipated Opposition	Some people might think it's important to be strict with students when they show bad behavior.
Defense	However, as a teacher, I believe it's important to differentiate between a student's emotions and their behavior. When a student misbehaves, it's essential to empathize with the emotional reasons behind their actions while maintaining firm boundaries on behavior. This will help students feel accepted while also guiding them effectively.
Conclusion	Therefore, I believe that teachers should be able to embrace students with respect.

4	Help students develop essential competencies
Topic Sentence	I believe that teachers should play a crucial role in helping students develop the essential skills and competencies they will need to prepare for the future.
Premise	Since our society is changing faster than ever before, as educators, we need to recognize that the stage on which our students will perform in the future is not the same as it is today.
Specific Description	To realize this, I will research and apply teaching methods focused on the Fourth Industrial Revolution to my classes. Specifically, instead of delivering fragmented knowledge, such as memorizing a list of words, I will present the lesson content with context to develop contextual understanding and problem-solving skills. I will also incorporate various teaching models into the classroom to develop empathy, communication and community skills, self-direction, and creativity, which are skills that will be increasingly important in the future.
Positive Effect	By focusing on these essential competencies, I will be able to enhance students' motivation and engagement in class. Moreover, this will contribute to cultivating a future generation that is better prepared to navigate the challenges and opportunities of the 4th Industrial Revolution and other societal changes.
Anticipated Opposition	Someone might say that teacher's role is not only about imparting knowledge, but also about teaching the social skills.
Defense	However, I believe that academic and social skills can be seamlessly integrated into teaching. There are countless opportunities to blend the two. For instance, introducing a foreign culture in a lesson can teach students to respect cultural diversity. Similarly, reading a novel about a marginalized character and then engaging in a theater activity can help students deeply empathize with different perspectives and emotions.
Conclusion	In these reasons, I believe that teachers should play a crucial role in helping students develop the essential skills and competencies they will need to prepare for the future.

5	Help students become autonomous democratic citizens
Topic Sentence	I believe that a teacher should be someone who can create a horizontal atmosphere to help students become responsible and autonomous democratic citizens.
Premise	Creativity, which is increasingly being valued as a key competency, is more likely to be nurtured in a free, horizontal environment that respects individual personalities, rather than in an oppressive atmosphere. Similarly, in today's society, where unverified information is easily accessible, critical thinking skills are better cultivated in an autonomous and democratic environment.
Specific Description	To achieve this, I will actively encourage student participation in the decision-making process within the class. I will ensure that the class president and vice president clearly understand their roles as representatives of the students and foster an open environment where students feel comfortable sharing their opinions. Additionally, regarding class rules, rather than imposing rules and expecting compliance, I will gather students' idea and make final decisions through voting.
Positive Effect	Through this, students will come to realize the necessity of rules and grow into individuals who autonomously and responsibly act. Moreover, fostering critical thinking and creativity in a free and horizontal atmosphere will cultivate democratic citizens prepared for future society.
Anticipated Opposition	Of course, in the position of a teacher who often needs to manage dozens of students alone, creating a hierarchical atmosphere can be one effective method for efficient classroom management.
Defense	However, I believe that creating a horizontal atmosphere is also an effective approach in the long run. This is because if we establish an autonomous atmosphere early on, the need for teacher intervention decreases as we progress through the later stages.
Conclusion	Therefore, I believe that a teacher should be someone who can create a horizontal atmosphere to help students become responsible and autonomous democratic citizens.

6		**Humble attitude open to learning**
Topic Sentence		I will always be aware that my thoughts may not always be correct and try to be a humble teacher open to learning.
Premise		In the future, what was once considered correct in the past may no longer be applicable due to societal changes and advancements. Therefore, teachers should always be open-minded and able to respond to changing demands from students, parents, and society.
Specific Description		Therefore I will be a teacher who maintains a humble attitude, always open to learning, in order to adapt to evolving demands and changes. Furthermore, I will pursue continuous self-development through ongoing development courses or professional learning communities,
Positive Effect		Through this, I can become a confident teacher who feels self-efficacious, evolving with diverse thoughts and constructive opinions. Moreover, by aligning with the changing demands of society, I can provide appropriate lessons, not only impacting students positively but also preparing them for the future society effectively.
Anticipated Opposition		It is true, of course, that teachers should be confident in what they are teaching.
Defense		However, I believe that maintaining a confident attitude and a willingness to constantly learn are not mutually exclusive. While maintaining confidence in what they are teaching, it's also important to approach new learning with a humble and open mindset.
Conclusion		For this reason, I will become a teacher who has a humble and open mindset, ready to learn something new for the rapidly changing future.

7	Encourage students to go beyond their limits
Topic Sentence	In my perspective on education, I believe that teachers should be able to encourage students to go beyond their limits, just like a sports coach.
Premise	According to the Zone of Proximal Development (ZPD) theory, students have a gap between their current abilities and their potential capabilities that can be bridged with appropriate assistance from teachers to maximize their potential.
Specific Description	To achieve this, I will carefully observe students to identify their strengths and potential. Then, I will provide appropriate motivation tailored to their needs by praising their achievements and consistently discovering areas where they show potential. This will help them build self-efficacy and a sense of accomplishment, fostering intrinsic motivation. Additionally, when students doubt their abilities or encounter obstacles, I will support them by encouraging perseverance and guiding them forward.
Positive Effect	Through this, the student will actively find solutions without becoming discouraged by the challenges, having a growth-oriented attitude. Furthermore, the teacher can perform the role of a supportive coach, much like a dependable coach beside an athlete, ensuring that the student's potential is maximized to the fullest extent.
Anticipated Opposition	Of course, it is true that methods focused solely on improving athletic abilities may not be perfect for developing students' personal growth.
Defense	However, just as overcoming physical limits leads to growth, I believe that personality traits such as self-efficacy, achievement, and self-esteem also develop through mental resilience, increasing the capacity for oneself.
Conclusion	Therefore, I believe teachers should be just like a sports coach who can encourage students to go beyound their limits.

8	Help students to have positive self-perception
Topic Sentence	I believe that teachers should be able to help students to have positive self-perception, developing their self-respect and self-love.
Premise	Forming a strong sense of self-esteem is important not only for physical health but also for mental well-being.
Specific Description	To achieve this, teachers can help students take time to focus solely on themselves, rather than how they compare to others, such as their grades. Moreover, teachers can set up activities to help them figure out who they are as a person, what they like, what they're good at, and who they want to be.
Positive Effect	Through this, the student will cultivate self-esteem through experiences focused on themselves rather than comparing with others. Furthermore, this high self-esteem will provide them with a healthy mindset and resilience to navigate challenges wisely and recover effectively when faced with difficulties in the future.
Anticipated Opposition	Of course, it is true that we cannot ignore the positive effects that can be gained through comparisons with others, such as competition.
Defense	However, if the students are too sensitive and exposed to an overly competitive environment, there is a risk of developing a negative self-perception, unable to respect other's achievements.
Conclusion	Therefore, I believe that teachers should be able to help students to have positive self-perception, developing their self-respect and self-love.